SPACE LAW

AND

GOVERNMENT

SPACE LAW

AND

GOVERNMENT

ANDREW G. HALEY

New York

APPLETON-CENTURY-CROFTS
Division of Meredith Publishing Company

To Delphine

FOREWORD

IN THIS FOREWORD I intend to indicate that the great new problems confronting civilization in the Age of Space require the close and devoted attention of the social scientists as well as of the natural scientists, and that principles of justice and order should be established in these early days of man's exploration of space. *Space Law and Government* is a penetrating examination and analysis of such principles and, as such, merits the careful attention of thoughtful people in all walks of life. By this, of course, I do not mean to indicate that I agree or disagree with the statements or conclusions of the author or of the authorities relied upon.

Our Earth is only one planet in our entire solar system. Our sun is only one of millions of stars in a single galaxy. Our galaxy is only one of many galaxies in the universe. Man and life as we know it on this earth exist only within a minute portion of the whole range of conditions within the Cosmos.

Man's vexing problems thus take their proper place when observed from afar. It is therefore fitting and proper that we urge every avenue be explored to set aside the manmade problems that plague this world and join others to explore jointly what lies outside this small world of ours. I note that a major portion of *Space Law and Government* is devoted to discussing international cooperation in space exploration on official and nongovernmental levels. This is indeed useful.

The United States already is pursuing an active program of cooperation with many other countries of the world. I would repeat here again what we have so often said before: our program is open to all nations. We hope that improved international relations as among all peoples will be furthered by man's move into outer space.

It is my earnest hope and the hope of all Americans that such international cooperation programs can be expanded to the fullest and that we, together with all the nations of the world acting jointly and cooperatively, can explore what lies beyond us. From such cooperation will be derived practical experience in fairness and justice both in outer space and on the earth itself.

From the beginning of time until about five centuries ago, men lived out their lives on earth without hope of rising above the station of their birth. They had no expectation of freedom—no expectation of justice—no thought of individual rights—no conception of a voice in governing themselves. Then came the discovery of the New World—the world of the Americas. Since that day, man has climbed steadily to his noblest heights. His status—economically and socially—has risen through every century. Most importantly, the spirit of freedom and justice has proven its viability.

Discovery, exploration, and a floodtide of invention for five centuries have brought the liberation of the human spirit and the elevation of human dignity and worth. Freedom as we know it would not have come into existence—and certainly would not have survived—without the opening of this great new frontier on earth. Today the unlimited reaches of space constitute the New World of freedom.

The distinguished background of the author and the painstaking research which has gone into this book point up the value of *Space Law and Government*.

> Lyndon B. Johnson
> *Vice President of the United States*

I have known Mr. Haley for many years, having served with him in the military during the Second World War. He is an author, scientist, and lawyer. He is outstanding in the field of communications law and possesses the finest of credentials to offer what is to my knowledge the first comprehensive study on space law and government.

Space Law and Government examines the role of intergovernmental and nongovernmental agencies in focusing attention on scientific and legal aspects of space exploration, and proposes guides for their future contribution. In the accurate words of his publisher, Mr. Haley's scientific and legal points are "deftly made, thoroughly authenticated and represent a panoramic synthesis of the clearest thinking on space law, government, and the relationship that should exist between the two."

I am confident that *Space Law and Government* will be a major contribution to our emerging Space Age. Mr. Haley has devoted to the preparation of this work a matchless integrity and years of research and exhaustive study of the legal and sociological aspects of space flight. I commend this work to my colleagues with confidence.

The Honorable Carl Albert
*Majority Leader, United States
House of Representatives*

Space technology has progressed with astonishing speed in the eight years since we opened our eyes to the vista of the cosmos by inaugurating the earth-satellite program in connection with the International Geophysical Year. We have made great technical progress, and we must now examine the rule of law to govern man when he penetrates the regions of the moon and stars. Andrew G. Haley's new book, *Space Law and Government,* has been published at a most appropriate time.

For those of us who will not live to realize the ultimate penetration of time and distance barriers by future astronauts, there is reassurance and comfort in the publication of Mr. Haley's plea for world cooperation and restraint in space exploration. We and our descendants must not simply be launched into other environments with no thought of the rules of conduct which much be observed. This book will serve as a primer for lawyers who must ask themselves what we intended when we embarked on the first spatial voyages. I know they will find fundamental strength and logic in the rules and concepts advanced in this book.

Mr. Haley embodies the benefit of his knowledge and experience in his penetrating book. It is a major contribution to the world's understanding of the nature of man's activities in space and in the legal consequences flowing from such activities. It deserves an honored place among the great and epoch-making legal studies in the libraries of the world.

My colleagues in the legislative field are well served by the publication of this work. Prior to this time we have had nothing more than a compendium of disparate views of our own and foreign authors for reference in the drafting of national space laws and the consideration of compacts with other nations. Now, however, we are privileged to possess a scholarly, authoritative, and encyclopaedic treatise on the law of space. I value the work highly.

I express appreciation for Mr. Haley's dedicated and timely exposition of the law of space. His views will be evaluated in the light of a distinguished and comprehensive career of two decades in all aspects of the space endeavor. He has combined his skills in law, the sciences, and commerce in this brilliant articulation of space jurisprudence. The work will occupy a distinguished position in my library and in the collections of all who labor in the causes of peace and ultimate success in space flight.

No man has a more comprehensive understanding of the complex problems associated with the space effort than has Andrew G. Haley. It has been his avocation. He has generously given of his time, energy and money in solving them. His work in the important area of space law has been outstanding. He has been a sterling leader in urging the nations of the world to recognize the international importance of writing laws pertaining to space, to avoid the vacuum that can embarrass them in the near future. Andrew G. Haley has earned our wholesome respect and our gratitude.

The Honorable George P. Miller
Chairman, House Committee on
Science and Astronautics

PREFACE

EXPLORATION OF THE UNIVERSE has been a dream of man since he first emerged on earth, and this yearning of the human spirit appears to dwell in all of us. I vividly recall a spontaneous and indeed dramatic outpouring of this deep instinctive desire.

The incident was brought about in the following manner. At an early date, before World War II, General H. H. Arnold, commander of the United States Army Air Corps, envisioned the inevitability of a global war and, perhaps, the necessity in the continental United States or in areas in the periphery of Europe to mount military operations on the European continent. He anticipated the use of heavy aircraft requiring auxiliary power to take off from short and hastily constructed airfields. The task of developing these jet-assisted take-off (Jato) motors was assigned to a small rocket group working under Dr. Theodore von Kármán in the California Institute of Technology.

The eminent President of Cal Tech, Dr. Robert A. Millikan, became highly concerned over the involvement of the University in production scale manufacturing, and Dr. von Kármán was assigned the task of determining whether an existing company would assume the burden of development and production of Jato units and, if not, what solutions were available. The Cal Tech "rocket group" thoroughly surveyed the companies in the Los Angeles area and other areas. None was interested in this highly experimental and "frenetic" wartime enterprise so Dr. von Kármán called upon me to seek solutions with the Cal Tech "rocket group."

And now we come to the point of this anecdote, namely, in the spring of 1941 I met at the California Institute of Technology with Dr. Theodore von Kármán, Dr. Frank J. Malina, Dr. Martin Summerfield, John W. Parsons, and E. S. Forman, and we decided that the only recourse was to create a rocket manufacturing facility of our own. We knew the task would be extremely difficult and perhaps unrewarding, and we could expect help from no "normal" source. We would be looked at askance and talked of as men from Mars—and the financial road might well be impassable.

At this meeting the incident occurred which has always loomed most importantly in our minds over the years—the spontaneous declaration by all of us that our real and abiding purpose in embarking on this harrowing and even dangerous business was actually to satisfy our interior inspiration that whatever we did would be in furtherance of man's exploration of the universe. Each of us voluntarily gave voice to the inspiration we felt, and I shall never forget the ever-present humor of Dr. von Kármán as he turned to me and said, "Now, Andy, we will make the rockets—you must make the corporation and obtain the money. Later on you will have to see that we all behave well in outer space." With a twinkle in his eye, he added, "After all, we are the scientists but you are the lawyer, and you must tell us how to behave ourselves according to law and to safeguard our innocence."

This was the beginning of the rocket research, development, and manufacturing company which our little group named Aerojet, and our effort would never have been initiated if we had lacked the bond between each of us which resides in the soul of man—the yearning to explore the universe.

A student of Dr. von Kármán, Dr. Simon Ramo, before a Senate Committee, asked this question: "How can we justify a large national space research program whose true objective is scientific discovery across all the spectrum of science if we are going to leave out the life sciences?" And he said, "An analogy would be a 'pretended' university that taught physics but not biology. A narrow program could be limited to instruments and be a quicker program. A broad program must add man; it will be slower but fuller."

Von Kármán's great friend, Dr. Harold C. Urey, also told the Senate: "... the real reason for undertaking the space program is an innate characteristic of human beings; namely, some curious drive to try to do what might be thought to be the impossible—to try to excel in one way or another—to try to do what has never been done before. The whole written history of men of all countries attests to this characteristic of human beings. Many examples of this can be drawn. Homer's poems record the interest of the ancient Greeks in things of this sort. We have the continuing interest in exploration of all kinds. How the ancients dared to take fragile boats across what were dangerous seas. How the Portuguese under Henry the Navigator dared to go around Africa to India. The enormous daring of Christopher Columbus crossing the Atlantic in boats which we would not think of using today. There are many other illustrations of a similar kind. In my own lifetime I have followed the exploration of the poles by Peary, Scott, and Amundsen, the flight of Lindbergh across the Atlantic,

Byrd's flight to the South Pole, and more recently the climbing of Everest, which has been in the newspapers just in the last few days. Now we have the spectacular flights of the astronauts from the USSR and the United States about the earth. These drives of people are akin to other activities such as building the Parthenon and the temples of the ancient world, the building of St. Peter's with its marvelous decorations at a time when it represented great effort and sacrifice on the part of the people of these countries. We might also mention literature, art, and music which were supported in previous times by the church and nobility at very considerable cost and sacrifice."

The eminent Dr. Colin S. Pittendrigh, Department of Biology, Princeton University, advised the United States Senate:

I am, however, just as certain that this whole category of effort in the space biology program, environmental physiology, is fully subsidiary in importance, as a scientific goal, to the search for life outside the earth. Biologists have come to refer to that part of their subject concerned with extraterrestrial life as exobiology. It must be emphasized that in this search for extraterrestrial life we can be even less certain as to the dividends which the cost in money and manpower will return. It may well be, and there are some who will say this is an understatement, that Mars—the only serious candidate for another home of life in our solar system—will prove barren when we get there. But I believe that there cannot be the slightest hesitation, while facing fully our responsibilities as citizens as well as scientists, in urging strongly that the venture be undertaken. More than that, unless I wholly mistake the nature of man and science, we are not really free to pass up the challenge and the opportunity to pursue this goal that rocketry has made available to us.

Specifically with respect to the question of extraterrestrial life, one of the issues which is confronting us is the practical difficulty of what kind of instruments should be sent on a soft landing to Mars. That question cannot be answered in any systematic sense, because the biologists to this day cannot really systematically answer what life is anyway. A great deal of theoretical work is needed in the pursuit of this apparently simple question: Is there life on Mars?

The question at stake in exobiology is in the opinion of many of us the most exciting, challenging, and profound issue not only of the whole space program, not only of this century, but of the whole naturalistic movement that has been a dominant aspect of the growth of science from its foundation. What is really at stake in space biology is the chance to get a new perspective on what Thomas Huxley called man's place in nature. It is possible that exobiology will bring us a new level of discussion on the meaning and nature of life, in general. I would like to amplify on that very strong statement, if I may, for just a moment.

This view has inevitably led us to question the uniqueness and centrality of man in the universe—and, therefore, his whole meaning—in an even profounder way than we were forced to when the Copernican and Darwinian insights were made known to us.

If there is life on Mars, in fact, if we can demonstrate its independent origin, as we might, in principle, from its chemical basis, then we shall have an enlightening answer to our question of improbability and uniqueness in the origin of life as a whole. Arising twice in a single planetary system it must surely occur abundantly elsewhere in the staggering number of comparable planetary systems.

A great American scientist, Dr. Lloyd V. Berkner, told the United States Senate:

Certainly, the prospect of critically examining life on Mars is potentially the most exciting and potentially profitable scientific and philosophic vista of space exploration. But looking beyond, can we visualize visiting other planets? Certainly Mercury is far too hot and must be limited to unmanned exploration. The crushing force of gravity on Jupiter is unthinkable to manned landing. But a satellite of Jupiter such as Europa, not much different from our Moon, might be within our ultimate reach. Certainly the exploration of Jupiter or even Saturn may thus, through their satellites, ultimately come within the reach of later centuries.

What about the stars? Here, within the limits of our scientific knowledge we can be quite positive. No known source of energy can carry us much beyond the limits of our planetary system, more especially within the lifespan of a man. Certainly, this lifespan, relative to a terrestrial frame of reference, can theoretically be enhanced indefinitely, as the space vehicle closely approaches the velocity of light. But we just don't have any source of energy even distantly available to do this. So our study of the universe by space methods at least for the next few centuries, or at least until some entirely unanticipated scientific discovery, is forbidden by science and must depend on the powerful new methods of space astronomy, probably ultimately based on the moon.

In the achievement of these scientific objectives, there are a wide variety of opportunities for international collaboration. In tracking, readout of data, exchange experiments, and many other areas, space offers opportunities for durable international threads of personal and national communication that binds nations together and creates new systems of law and order.

When we reach the stage of Martian landing, one can devoutly hope for an international venture that can bring the scientists of the world together in solving the most challenging and difficult scientific problems ever to be undertaken.

But, the great bulk of the peoples of the world have not yet acquired this particular brand of sophistication. They appreciate and share our aspirations to reach to the stars, and find a satisfying excitement, now that this seems almost within reach. This is the primitive instinct that has made man great. I cannot forget a night in the Mideastern desert, when a native grasped my sleeve and pointed excitedly to the sky, exclaiming: "Look, mister, look— American sputnik." You may argue that an American Peace Corpsman might do more for this man as an individual; yet, lurking in the background, is the realization that the Peace Corpsman may have no opportunity to function at all, if our privilege to lead is eroded. Here lies an irreversible value judgment that only history can test.

Because of this very primitive and deep-seated instinct to conquer the unconquered, the space race between the U.S. and the USSR is inevitable. Men everywhere see, in the conquest of space, the peaceful demonstration of the superiority of one of the two competing systems of economic organization—capitalism versus communism. The conquest of space has become a symbol of the challenge to each system to demonstrate its superiority—to "put up" or shut up. Now, some may deplore this situation as foolish, or un-gentlemanly, or costly, or unintellectual—but that's the way it is, and we had better accept it if we want to retain our free system. The Russians recognize it with: first sputnik; first hit on the Moon; first man in space; first photo-graphs of the back side of the Moon; first try (failed) to reach planets; first shot at Mars; and the heaviest payloads—all spectaculars. (I would add, parenthetically, moreover, that it may be better for both sides to shoot some dollars into space than to shoot them at each other.)

Ever since Dr. von Kármán made his kindly and humorous remark about space law, I have most seriously considered the formulation of the rule of law for outer space. And this brings me to another anecdote.

Together with the Prince of Hanover, I conducted a lecture tour of a score of American universities in November 1957; and we ended up at a meeting sponsored by the International Law Group of Harvard University. The event was organized by Robert D. Crane who was at that time obtain-ing his law degree at Harvard. After the meeting the Prince of Hanover and I had dinner with Mr. Crane's delightful family, and we discussed at length principles of international law as related to space law problems. In April 1961, I learned that Mr. Crane was in Washington and I immedi-ately offered him legal association. This book probably would never have been written except for the remarkable analytical capacity of Mr. Crane and his unexcelled ability to quickly assemble source material. He gath-ered into six large volumes (which have now multiplied, see Appendix V, pp. 529-539) all of my papers, speeches, comments, and so on. He also made a highly informed and precise study of all the literature on space law, and he recommended to me that I codify my original contributions and comments into a book. Unfortunately, Mr. Crane could not help me in this task because he was appointed Director of the Space Research Institute of Duke University.

Fortunately, Stephen E. Doyle, of Duke University Law School, with Crane's volumes of my collected prior writings covering a twelve-year period, compiled and annotated material which resulted in a manuscript comprising a good deal of the first draft of the present book. In this editing he was assisted by Peter B. Maggs, Michael J. Henry, both of Harvard Law School, and Robert B. Flint, of Georgetown University Law School. The work done by this group was most useful and exact. Without this compilation I am afraid that I would not have had the courage to proceed with the writing of the book as it is now presented.

I am particularly indebted to Messrs. Doyle, Maggs, Henry, and Flint for their meticulous editing of my writings which are embodied in Chap-ters 1, 2, 3, 5, 10, and 11. I shall never forget the very proper concern Stephen Doyle felt about the constant use of my name in Chapter 11. We ardently desired to maintain the best traditions of "good taste" by eliminating my name, and this could easily have been achieved if Chapter 11 had been written as a simple autobiography—in which event I could simply narrate the facts in the first person. There seemed to be no precise cure because it happened that during the period commencing in 1950 (and, indeed, until the present time) I was very active throughout the world in carrying on missions in connection with and on behalf of astronautics nongovernmental international organizations. There was no way to erase the personal allusions and still maintain a coherent commentary and I could not convert this chapter into an autobiography—so Doyle performed a stalwart job in minimizing my name. Later, Messrs. Swezey, Habetz, and Washburn did their best to eliminate my name from textual footnotes and from the Index.

The editors of my publications also admirably assisted in contributing to my anonymity in this manner: after each chapter I had listed my speeches, papers, and (I thought) properly labeled these original writings, "source material"—but the publisher has changed the label to "additional references." I suppose the editors are technically correct in that I have brought a good deal of the original source material "up to date," but the fact remains that the writings actually constitute the entire substance of the book.

With respect to liability for personal and property damages in space activities, I had written an article, "Space Vehicle Torts," for the *University of Detroit Law Journal*, which was reprinted in the *Insurance Law Journal* (see Appendix V), which I determined must be brought up to date and more thoroughly annotated. In this task I was ably assisted by Ibrahim F. I. Shihata of Harvard University.

The Index is solely the work of a group composed of Robert D. Swezey, Jr., of Harvard University, Stephen A. Habetz, of Georgetown University Law School, and Alan V. Washburn, of the University of Chicago Law School.

Basically, my approach in this book was to give a sufficient history and analysis of the technical developments in order to afford any type of reader an insight into the matrix of the "physical" problems being discussed. Necessarily, any technical discussion in a book of this nature must be of a basic character and must deal with primary principles and objectives only. An example of what I mean is clearly evident from my comment on page 192 concerning the synchronous orbit or "stationary" communications satellite and the difficulty of establishing an equatorial orbit. This comment was written by me in June, 1963; but despite my misgivings Syncom achieved a synchronous orbit on August 15, 1963! Dynamic results are being attained week by week on both sides of the Atlantic, and no book can be written which would embody the record or projection of achievement even for the next one or two years. I therefore necessarily have furnished the reader with the fundamental "building blocks" only by setting forth the main sources of historial and current information and knowledge.

It will be quite obvious to the least sophisticated reader that I have made no attempt to narrate the latest scientific achievements, but I have, in my opinion, related the fundamental "background" information. I have also devoted considerable space to the activities and achievements of the rocket pioneers and indeed some of the contributions of contemporary workers and leaders. Here again, a "pioneer" is most often someone who has worked in the field during the past ten years or even during the past quinquennium. I believe, however, the narration contains sufficient introductory material to support the points at issue.

Andrew G. Haley

Washington, D.C.
Sept. 5, 1963

CONTENTS

The promise and challenge of space endeavor

Presenting a brief statement of the many and varied benefits man may anticipate receiving from his efforts in space exploration, this chapter sets out the
fundamental problems to which this entire work is addressed—the need for regulation of man's activities as he enters into the new realm of space. The conclusion
is reached that unless a clearly defined, internationally organized, legal regime
is established in the early stages of space exploration, the crystallization of unilateral practices infringing upon the rights of the several nations of the world—
and other similar problems—may have gone too far for a solution to be found
through peaceful means. The underlying principles of all man's activities in space
should be (a) all benefits derived are in behalf of all mankind, and (b) the free
use of outer space is assured to every nation for all peaceful and scientific
purposes.

1–1   The actual and potential benefits

In the brief span of years since the first satellite was launched, a tremendous investment of time, money, and effort has gone into space
industries and related fields. Many governmental, quasi-governmental, and
private research organizations have made concerted attempts to survey
the existing benefits and to suggest other potential benefits which mankind
as a whole can derive from this investment; and they have succeeded in
compiling some rather impressive lists.[1] In general terms—and putting

[1] One elaborate and inclusive survey of the practical values of space exploration
was compiled by Philip B. Yeager, a member of the professional staff of the Committee
on Science and Astronautics of the U.S. House of Representatives (HOUSE COMMITTEE

aside for a time the question of the military value of space activities—it can readily be said that present space activities have already produced new jobs and new categories of work, new consumer goods, increased emphasis on educational programs and facilities, and in fact a host of economic and other values.

The greatest benefits to come from space activities, however, are probably still unseen and unpredictable—just as on many previous occasions the vision of society has been inadequate to appreciate the full consequences of great developments at the time they occurred. When Columbus sailed from Spain nearly 500 years ago, he was seeking a shortcut to the Indies, an objective that he signally failed to achieve. His expedition was nevertheless justified in the eyes of his Spanish masters because it led to the discovery of Aztec and Inca gold; and even this wholly unforeseen dividend was quite miniscule compared to his discovery of an entire New World. Yet in Columbus' time, and for some 200 or more years thereafter, the supreme importance of his explorations was consistently undervalued. There is a lesson in this for us today who stand on the threshold of explorations that seem breathtaking and almost, but not quite, beyond human achievement.

Similarly, there were learned scientists even after the creation of the atom bomb [2] who questioned the practical utility, for purposes other than destruction, of the development of fissionable materials and atomic energy techniques. Yet today we find radioactive isotopes in widespread use in industry, agriculture, and medicine; food irradiation, nuclear power reactors, and reactors for shipboard use are all accomplished facts, and this is hardly the beginning. Experience has shown time and again that developments in one area of interest can provide benefits in other areas, and this same process is already evident in the case of space exploration. The converse, naturally, is also true, for knowledge gained in activities entirely divorced from outer space can provide genuinely valuable contributions to the space effort.

Such factors as these were clearly taken into account when the United States Government, during the year that followed the launching of *Sputnik I*, first embarked upon a space program on a priority basis. Its position was stated then by the President's Science Advisory Committee:

> Scientific research, of course, has never been amenable to rigorous cost accounting in advance. Nor, for that matter, has exploration of any sort. But if

ON SCIENCE AND ASTRONAUTICS, 87TH CONG., 1ST SESS., THE PRACTICAL VALUES OF SPACE EXPLORATION, Comm. Print, 1961). Another exhaustive survey was produced at the Brookings Institution by Donald N. Michael, *et al.* (H.R. Doc. No. 242, 87th Cong., 1st Sess., 1961). A summary of Michael's findings, along with other reports on the economic and technological consequences of space activities, is contained in BLOOMFIELD, ed., OUTER SPACE: PROSPECTS FOR MAN AND SOCIETY (1962).

2 Cf. PRACTICAL VALUES OF SPACE EXPLORATION, *op. cit. supra* note 1 at 4-5.

we have learned one lesson, it is that research and exploration have a remarkable way of paying off—quite apart from the fact that they demonstrate that man is alive and insatiably curious. And we all feel richer for knowing what explorers and scientists have learned about the universe in which we live.[3]

It thus appears safe to predict that space activities will make far-reaching practical contributions to the welfare of mankind. But space flight is a long-term process which will unfold over many generations, and it would not be realistic for us today to try to predict its ultimate impact in any detail. From our present position of historical knowledge we can see that it would have been futile for Columbus to have attempted to ascertain the long-range utility of his voyages beyond their application to 15th-century civilization. This would have been asking too much of the human mind. It would be equally futile today to try to ascertain the precise long-range utility of space flight far beyond our present civilization and its needs. Nevertheless, there are many immediate, short- and medium-range benefits—more, in fact, than most persons have yet imagined—which hold incalculable promise for mankind.

The economic utility of extended space operations is not at all obvious in the same sense in which the discovery of America proved economically "useful" to the Crown of Spain. Even if mines of gold or silver should be developed on the moon or Mars, it is at present hard to imagine circumstances that would warrant bringing those metals back to Earth by rocket vehicle. This does not mean that man may not ultimately exploit the natural resources found on other heavenly bodies, but for at least an indefinite period the material benefits of space will consist not so much of what we *find there* as of the scientific and economic side-effects of the vast technological efforts required to *get there* in the first place. As Dr. Hugh L. Dryden, pioneer space scientist and co-founder of NASA, has pointed out,

> . . . perhaps the greatest economic treasure [of the present Space Age] is the advanced technology required for more and more difficult space missions. This new technology is advancing at a meteoric rate. Its benefits are spreading throughout our whole industrial and economic system.[4]

The economic ramifications of space developments are attested to most obviously, day by day, in the growth of the space industry itself. In leading newspapers and stock reports an even greater amount of space and attention is devoted to "space issues," which with truly remarkable speed have blossomed into a major financial category. Likewise thousands of space-oriented companies across the United States, from

[3] THE PRESIDENT'S SCIENCE ADVISORY COMMITTEE, INTRODUCTION TO OUTER SPACE 6 (1958).

[4] *Penrose Lecture*, presented by Hugh L. Dryden before the American Philosophical Society, Philadelphia, April 21, 1960.

giant airframe manufacturers to small electronic specialty plants producing such items as magnetic memory drums for missile/space guidance systems, are working full shifts. The economic boom in the Cape Canaveral, Florida, area is by now a rather hackneyed example of regional impact, but there are many others. One of the most striking is the way in which electronics manufacturing for advanced missile and space systems has contributed to the industrial rebirth of New England that began gathering momentum in the latter part of the 1950's.

Not all geographic areas and manufacturing specialties have benefited to the same extent; and there has been political as well as strictly economic concern, for example, over the failure of Middle Western firms to obtain a proportionate share of government space contracts. However, in a competitive economy there is no intrinsic reason why space benefits should flow equally and automatically to all companies and all sectors of industry. This economic upsurge is thus requiring flabby muscles to flex and complacent minds to revitalize and function productively once again —or else remain indefinitely on the sidelines. The aircraft industry, in particular, has been undergoing a corporate and technological revolution because of the shift in government purchases from manned aircraft to missile and space systems. These changes have caused profound readjustments for any companies that did not attempt soon enough to develop the necessary "know how" for the new technology.

Yet the over-all picture is one of definite promise. At a time when the effects of industrial automation upon employment are becoming a lively issue, it is noteworthy that the actual development of the space industry has rendered false various earlier predictions that it would be a low user of manpower. It has been pointed out that the space industry, as an employer, gives its greatest benefits to those who least need help—the scientists and engineers—but they are not the only ones who have found new job opportunities. A Labor Department survey as of fiscal year 1959 showed that in the missile industry (fairly comparable to the space industry *per se*) there was a ratio of one worker to slightly under $11,000 in sales, which was twice as many men employed in relation to sales as in the production of, say, heavy construction equipment. It is small wonder, then, that the Mercury man-in-space project alone by the end of 1961 was involving over 200,000 individuals, working in around 4,000 different companies. By no means all of these individuals were employed full-time on Project Mercury, but it is still safe to say that that one project created tens of thousands of jobs in American industry. Nor will it be much longer, at the present rate, before the space program is giving direct employment to a larger working force than even the automobile industry.[5]

---

[5] BLOOMFIELD, *op. cit. supra* note 1 at 74-75. The Labor Department survey to which reference is made was published under the title *Manpower in Missiles and Aircraft Production* (Industry Manpower Survey No. 93, August 1959).

The space industry, of course, is not a single, clearly recognizable entity such as the automobile industry. It is really a complex of related industries, all of which devote a major portion of their efforts to work on space projects (and usually missile projects simultaneously). In fact, it is hard to think of a single major scientific or engineering field that is not, or will not be, somehow involved in the technology of space flight. Even so, some will obviously be involved much more heavily than others. The boost given to the computer field, for example, and especially high-speed light-weight computer development, is immeasurable. Another obvious case study is offered by the propulsion industry. In July of 1957, just before the first satellite was launched, the Executive Vice President of the Olin-Mathieson Corporation predicted—quite boldly, it then seemed—that high-energy fuels to power supersonic aircraft and rocket vehicles would become a billion-dollar business within the next ten years. That prophecy has already proved overly conservative.

The creation of new firms and expansion of old ones to handle space contracts is only one aspect of the economic impact of space developments. There is also the "fall out" of technical and scientific innovations that were first devised in answer to space requirements but have found further application in purely earth-bound activities. To be sure, the average citizen has little use for huge rocket engines or high-speed computers. It has even been argued that the new gadgets and techniques spawned by space activities are too complex or too specialized to find as widespread use in industry as those that resulted from previous technological revolutions. Possibly this is true; it is still much too early to see just how the conquest of space will compare with the development of the automobile or the airplane in terms of useful by-products for society at large per billion dollars expended. But useful by-products from space endeavor are already accumulating at a steady pace.

A favorite example among popular writers on space and related topics is the use of temperature-resistant ceramics, originally developed for missile re-entry nose cones, in the manufacture of pots and pans. Similarly, tools which were designed for easy operation under zero-gravity (weightless) conditions during flight through space are now being hailed as simplifying all kinds of home repairs. Medicinal uses have been found for liquid rocket fuel ingredients—and so on. Perhaps even the development of model satellite kits and other such "space toys" should be listed as an example of the indirect technological "fall out" from space activities.

As suggested by the medicinal side-effects of rocket-fuel developments, there will be practical benefits in the area of the life sciences as well as in the creation of new industrial and consumer goods. Indeed, man-in-space programs are bringing a vast concentration of talent to bear upon the problems involved in protecting space crews against radiation hazards, against all kinds of physiological stress, and against such psychological hazards as sheer boredom. The findings from these efforts cannot help but be of value in coping with similar problems elsewhere. And at a more speculative—perhaps even fanciful—level, it has been suggested that weightlessness and other space environmental conditions might prove decidedly beneficial in the treatment of heart disease and other organic disturbances. Apparently, though, not enough thought has been given so far to the possibilities of satellite therapy to make a reliable appraisal of its potential merits.

Meteorological and communications satellites cannot properly be classed among the indirect benefits of space exploration, since they are space vehicles themselves. They are, however, two categories of space vehicle that offer very direct practical advantages for terrestrial activities, and their development has been greatly accelerated, furthermore, by the transfer of technical innovations from other types of space activity—military, man-in-space, etc. In any event, instrumented satellites are already serving as communication links for intercontinental radio and television transmission. And as we increase our proficiency in the use of satellites for meteorological observations and analysis, we can expect more accurate long- and short-range weather forecasting, on both a continental and a local basis. Organized, satellite-based weather service will result in obvious benefits to agriculture and other weather-dependent activities, and therefore to the well-being of all nations.

Basic scientific research is still another field in which space developments hold out the prospect of major advances. The spectacular research achievements of instrumented earth satellites—geophysical, geodetic, and astrophysical—are today well known. More advanced satellite-borne sensors and transmission equipment will provide astronomical observations of a sort that cannot possibly be equalled at the earth's surface. In addition, lunar and planetary probes are already extending research on cosmic radiation, meteoritic dust, and magnetic fields far out into space. The combined earth-moon mass, the moon's distance, and the earth's orbit are just a few of the features that are not yet known exactly but are of fundamental scientific (and astronautical) significance. Many more research programs might of course be added to this list, including investigations of the surface environment of the moon and neighboring planets. The practical worthwhileness of operations on these other bodies can be determined only when the necessary facts are known—and it is important to gain this knowledge so that appropriate decisions as to future action can be made. The very lack of such knowledge is in itself an important reason for undertaking space flight.

From the research standpoint it is also worth noting that space offers four outstanding features that are extremely difficult and in some respects impossible to create, for experimental purposes, in a terrestrial laboratory. These are, first, near-absolute vacuum; second, extreme low temperatures and large temperature differences; third, intense radiation ranging from infrared to X-rays; and fourth, weightlessness. There is reason to hope that experimentation under these conditions will some day have definite value for industry (and perhaps for medicine), but in addition there will be much that can be learned in terms of basic, "unapplied" scientific knowledge. Moreover, whenever we encounter forms of life on other planets, it is wholly probable that these will both constitute fascinating topics of study in themselves and suggest, by way of comparison, invaluable new insights into the nature of life as it has been known on earth.

And yet the benefits from the conquest of space that are most easily grasped by the average man are probably the political benefits. The achievement by any nation of such high levels of technical excellence as the space field requires is a remarkable accomplishment, and a nation's international reputation and prestige can only be enhanced by such a development—assuming that the art is not abused by the artist, and that the effort made is one aimed at benefiting and not destroying mankind. The prestige to be derived from space activities is thus an important and sought-after reward.[6] This factor is particularly evident during periods such as the present Cold War, when prestige is frequently more important than force in international leadership.

There are two major aspects to the prestige rewards of space activity. One is the reward of notoriety for the first-in-time achievement. Many such rewards have already been obtained by Soviet scientists; these achievements have in large measure been the result of superior Soviet thrust power. The other aspect involves the intrinsic value of the contribution made by a particular space accomplishment. The prestige gained from a valuable contribution to man's welfare is an important and lasting reward, and many such rewards have been earned by American space scientists. Putting the first satellite into orbit was a spectacular achievement; giving the world an operative meteorological or communications satellite system may in the long run be the more rewarded contribution in terms of prestige. The spectacle fades in the mind's eye; but the practical daily contribution to the benefit of humanity continually feeds a sense of appreciation.

A less talked-about but nonetheless real political benefit of space flight is the fact that it encourages closer ties among nations. Some specific examples of cooperation in space research and related pursuits will be cited in later chapters of this volume. However, space does more than provide new opportunities for international cooperation. More fundamentally, perhaps, it cannot help but make more apparent than ever the impracticality of war. The technical and scientific standards required for coping with the problems of interplanetary operations are so high that if

---

[6] PRACTICAL VALUES OF SPACE EXPLORATION, *op. cit. supra* note 1 at 17.

these capabilities were applied with hostile intentions, to the narrow confinements of one planet, the prospect of mutual annihilation would become even more likely than it is already. Thus, by no realistic standard of reasoning can space flight have any other effect than that of urging saner alternatives to the classical last resort of international politics.

Indeed, some of the leading social scientists and historians have held that space activities may in time divert the urge or drive of men to wage war. As a kind of substitute outlet for the material and psychological needs which have in the past led to war, the conquest of space may absorb the energies, resources, imagination, and aggressiveness which have historically nurtured conflict among nations. Although the theory is perhaps highly speculative, in a world of nuclear powers and ethnicidal possibilities, this may yet become one of the great practical values of space exploration—the displacement of war. The same prospect has been stated with unusual eloquence, and on slightly different grounds, by Arthur C. Clarke, science writer and originator of the communication satellite concept:

> We all know the narrow, limited type of mind which is interested in nothing beyond its town or village, and bases its judgments on these parochial standards. We are slowly—perhaps too slowly—evolving from that mentality towards a world outlook. Few things will do more to accelerate that evolution than the conquest of space. It is not easy to see how the more extreme forms of nationalism can long survive when men begin to see the Earth in its true perspective as a single small globe among the stars.[7]

As this statement suggests, space flight will tend to stress the fundamentally unifying characteristics of man over local customs, history, and the place in which he is born. When regional differences have lost their devastating capability to arouse misunderstanding and hatred among peoples, without losing their ability to contribute to the local color and individuality of human culture, then freedom and richness of life will have been increased immeasurably.

Needless to say, this condition will not come about overnight, however much it may be "accelerated," as Clarke predicts, by the conquest of space. Hence, in the meantime, the leading powers can ill afford to neglect the military potential of space operations. Even without indulging in futuristic speculation about the military value of lunar or Martian bases, it is easy to distinguish such concrete military applications of space technology as hypersonic gliders for bombing and reconnaissance; the capability of operating satelloids and satellites for reconnaissance purposes; and, in fact, free space operations up to altitudes of several thousand miles by which terrestrial areas can be kept under constant surveillance. Of course, it is not strictly accurate in this connection to speak of

---

[7] CLARKE, THE CHALLENGE OF THE SPACESHIP 7-8 (New York: Harper & Row, Publishers, Inc., 1959).

space technology as finding military applications, when so much of that technology was originally an offshoot of military developments, in particular long-range missilery. Advanced military and space technology overlap at so many points that they are to be distinguished mainly in terms of their objectives, not their scientific basis or engineering characteristics. The same electronic brain could guide a missile or a satellite— or for that matter run an automated factory, to cite once more an example of the broader economic impact of these activities.

There is still another motivating factor that is common to both short- and long-term aspects of space flight and is frankly not subject to rational justification. Because of human curiosity and zest for adventure, people simply want to explore the new space frontier. This is a fundamental urge, as elemental as the desire for material comfort or bodily security. For the individual who does not personally travel to the moon or work in a space industry, one of the largest benefits of space flight will be a sense of vicarious participation in a great human endeavor, and a new breadth of understanding of the universe around him. Arthur C. Clarke has given apt expression to this aspect of space exploration, too. As he puts it:

> ...our civilization is no more than the sum of all the dreams that earlier ages have brought to fulfillment. And so it must always be, for if men cease to dream, if they turn their backs upon the wonder of the universe, the story of our race will be coming to an end.[8]

In sum, space flight is likely to contribute more material and spiritual improvements to life on this planet than any other single economic or social measure. It is capable of bringing this about not only by virtue of the specific benefits already indicated but also by gradually creating a more intense feeling of belonging to the same planetary community. This feeling will provide a necessary condition for greater effectiveness of all actions aimed at raising the dignity, as well as the responsibility, of man. And such improvements, in turn, will both increase the utility of space flight itself and unlock creative forces in all facets of human civilization. These cascading consequences, whose potential exceeds our imagination —just as the ultimate consequences of Columbus' discovery far exceeded his expectations—may be among the most important contributions of space flight to the future of mankind.

1-2 Space flight and the rule of law

The legal implications of all the factors which have been discussed so far in this chapter could easily be expanded into a multi-volume treatise, occupying a score of researchers for a whole decade in its compilation. The present work will attempt instead merely to outline some of the needs

[8] *Id.* at 15.

of law for the space age, and to present some of the thinking of those who have considered the problem to date. Nevertheless, it can be stated at the outset that the legal implications of astronautics are merely one aspect of a broader theme—that of the social and behavioral framework within which man's scientific and engineering space exploits are taking place. And it is regrettable but true that the social and behavioral sciences, of which jurisprudence is one, have lagged behind the accelerating advances of the physical and natural sciences into the space environment. The physicists and engineers have made possible the expansion into space of a social-political structure which is simply not yet prepared to cope with the problems and challenges of this new realm.

International agreements to bring about peaceful regulation and encouragement of astronautics must therefore be achieved in the very near future, or this unprecedented boon to human welfare may well become a most efficient means to the degradation and self-destruction of mankind. Whatever the ultimate products of space exploration and occupation may prove to be, man in his present state of civilization will in large measure determine whether they will be beneficial or nefarious. He will do so by the development of or the failure to develop a body of law which will govern his activities in space. As there exists today no body of statutory or case law appropriate for space travel, and as all problems in connection therewith are international in nature, clearly an international formulation of space law must evolve.

The noted scholar and pioneer in the field of space law, Dr. Welf Heinrich Prince of Hanover, author of the first doctoral thesis on space law (Göttingen University), emphasized one of the difficulties facing the lawyer who attempts to formulate these rules when he pointed out that lawyers "have a constitutional inclination to judge new problems according to the principles they have applied to old," and therefore naturally seek first of all "to see whether the legal maxims hitherto accepted on and above the earth cannot be employed in judging happenings outside the atmosphere." [9] As a matter of fact, both the lawyer and the statesman will have to realize that the legal problems involved in space travel and exploration are different in kind from those involved in maritime navigation and air navigation, so that only limited analogies may be derived from the corpus of maritime and air law.[10] Moreover, the development of a body of law for space activities will necessarily be a gradual process.

[9] Address by Welf Heinrich Prince of Hanover before the American Rocket Society, Washington, D.C., November 1957.
[10] Ribo Durán, *El derecho en los umbrales de la era espacial*, Revista de Aeronáutica, Feb. 1961 (Spain). Señor Ribo Durán points out that Alex Meyer, at the Congress of International Astronautical Federation, which took place in 1952 at Stuttgart, presented his theory, "Astronautical law can never be based on the law of aerial navigation, because of the distinction in nature between airspace and interplanetary space."

The American Bar Association has already recommended the writing of codes for space by nongovernmental, international federations such as the International Astronautical Federation, and also by intergovernmental agencies such as the special commissions of UNESCO. But is it apparent that the world is not going to develop a code for outer space in a few days, or a few months, or even a few years; and it will be necessary for the groups mentioned and others like them to provide the competent officials of the United Nations and of the separate national governments with information and viewpoints, if the world is to reach a state of understanding and agreement on this highly contentious matter.

One of the basic doctrines to be established now upon which the law of space must be built is that any natural object in space is not subject to any earthly jurisdiction or sovereignty. No single nation may justifiably assert a paramount claim to any other heavenly body or portion of outer space. Thus, as far as space is concerned, we must promulgate the principle of *res communis*—the property of all. At the other end of the spectrum, from broad principles such as this, there is a great need for detailed regulatory provisions dealing with current technical problems. One of the latter is the use of radio frequencies; the difficulties and complexities of this problem alone occupy an entire chapter in the present volume.

Then, too, the Soviet Union and the United States have already sent into outer space many vehicles which are not controllable. A collision in which two orbital bodies would hit and exfoliate, but continue in some irregular orbit for many more hundreds of years, would constitute a threat to life and property in outer space—and many similar threats are possible. Objects have been placed in orbit—both satellite vehicles and spent rocket stages—that could come back to earth at almost any place. Such objects might land on the Kremlin, on the Vatican, or on Buckingham Palace; as far as the dispersion factor is concerned, we still do not know enough. We do know that satellites do not come back as small particles or completely exfoliated, because they would burn up; but objects in space may come back as great chunks if they were large enough to start with and if they are not brought down in a controlled re-entry. Finding answers to these problems, naturally, is not easy. Ideally, however, no objects should be allowed to go into outer space without a code of law requiring that they be controllable; they should be earth-returnable, or capable of being projected into orbits around the sun or into some other area where they could not be injurious to life, property, and near-terrestrial navigation.

Legal questions have also been raised by certain types of military experiments carried out in space. On July 9, 1962, the United States in Project Starfish fired the second nuclear test device known to have been detonated in space. This experiment created an artificial radiation belt, which some observers at home and abroad promptly decried as capable of inflicting untold bodily harm and destruction of property (e.g., deterioration of satellite-borne solar-cell power supplies). Statements were advanced in the British press that this hydrogen blast, and the Argus and Westford projects that preceded it, were actually tortious acts in space. According to this thesis, if space is free for scientific and peaceful purposes, the creation of potentially lethal and damage-causing conditions by any state in an area where it has no power of sovereignty must bring upon that state liability for its action. But where is an alleged injured party to go? What are the standards of the measure of damages? The mere raising of such questions based on the tangible and existing problems which the physical sciences have created underscores the need for positive action by the jurists and statesmen of the world. In all probability the Starfish, Argus, and Westford projects were ultimately beneficial to mankind because of the scientific knowledge gained from them, but a proper forum is still desirable, if only to dispel conjecture and criticism.

Enough has now been said to give some idea of the potential legal difficulties; subsequent chapters will document them in more detail. What remains to be mentioned here is the heartening fact that heads of state on both sides of the Iron Curtain have publicly recognized the need for cooperative action in obtaining solutions. Most noteworthy of all in this respect is the record established by President Eisenhower during his term of office in the United States. The courage he displayed in authorizing the conduct of earth satellite activities in connection with the International Geophysical Year was followed by numerous statements of principle concerning the uses of outer space—statements so fundamental in character that their wisdom has not been superseded by the subsequent declarations of other statesmen.

The thesis of President Eisenhower was based upon the proposition that the space age is actually a new era in human civilization, and that the emergence of this new era poses vital issues. Will outer space be preserved for peaceful use and developed for the benefit of all mankind? Or will it become another focus for the arms race—and thus an area of dangerous and sterile competition? President Eisenhower raised his voice time after time warning that the opportunity to preserve peace in outer space is fleeting, and he expressed his fear that before long, civilization would have passed the point of no return. In his farewell address to the United Nations in 1960, Eisenhower proposed:

1. We agree that celestial bodies are not subject to national appropriation by any claims of sovereignty. 2. We agree that the nations of the world shall not engage in warlike activities on these bodies. 3. We agree, subject to appropriate verification, that no nation will send into orbit or station in outer space weapons of mass destruction. All launchings of spacecraft should be verified in advance by the United Nations. 4. We press forward with a program of

international cooperation for constructive peaceful uses of outer space under the United Nations. Better weather forecasting, improved world-wide communications and more effective exploration not only of outer space but of our own earth—these are but a few of the benefits of such cooperation.

This Eisenhower Doctrine was fully adopted by President Kennedy and by Premier Khrushchev of the Soviet Union in their March 1962 exchange of letters on the subject of space cooperation. President Kennedy stated that perhaps we could render no greater service to mankind through our space programs than by the joint establishment of an early operational weather satellite system, designed to provide global weather data for prompt use by any nation. To initiate the service, he proposed that "the United States and the Soviet Union each launch a satellite to photograph cloud covers and provide other agreed meteorological services for all nations." In his response, Premier Khrushchev agreed with the areas of action outlined by President Kennedy, stating that these areas have become ripe already and demand immediate cooperation between the United States and the USSR:

In the future international cooperation in space exploration, if we can now lay a firm basis for it, will doubtless spread to ever new and new fields of space research. We hope that the scientists of the Union of Soviet Socialist Republics and the United States of America will be able, hand in hand with the scientists of other countries, to take up the elaboration and implementation of many projects for space exploration.

The voice of Vice President Lyndon B. Johnson was also heard in March 1962, when, at the meeting of the International Telecommunication Union in Washington, he observed that during the past few years there had been a great deal of discussion of the dazzling prospects open to all mankind through the realization of space flight. "But," he added, "the talk has not been accompanied by enough action. We must not only desire cooperation; we must take positive steps to achieve it." In effect, while the heads of state—the political macrocosm—were discussing the eternal verities of space cooperation, the bureaucrats of the microcosmic world have all too often been playing defensive games of chess to "contain" all aspects of international legal barter relating to space endeavor. The International Telecommunication Union, following the March 1962 meeting and pursuant to United Nations directive, issued an immense volume, containing much useful material on possible programs and areas of discussion. But the report contained only one decisional statement of agreement, namely, that an Extraordinary Administrative Radio Conference would be held in Geneva in October 1963! Similarly, after weeks of plenary sessions in New York and special sessions in Geneva, the Legal Subcommittee of the United Nations Committee on the Peaceful Uses of

Outer Space adjourned in June 1962 and asserted in terse language that there was a lack of agreement on any point under consideration. The following year, it had scarcely more success.

Fortunately, these examples of futility are not the whole story even at the microcosmic level. As subsequent chapters will make clear, numerous national and international bodies, both governmental and otherwise, have been devoting earnest consideration to the legal aspects of space activity. Such organizations as the International Astronautical Federation, with its International Institute of Space Law, have provided an important forum for study of the issues by legal scholars and others from all major countries. With each passing day, in fact, the international community of jurists and social scientists becomes more aware of the need for action in this field, and more intent on closing the gap that now exists between the social and the physical sciences in all matters relating to space exploration.

The gap between the social and physical sciences was also one of the topics discussed by Chief Justice Earl Warren in an address delivered in February 1963, at the Georgia Institute of Technology. "The simple fact is," declared the Chief Justice, "that law has not kept abreast of science." [11] The answer, however, is not to put a restraining hand on science. The real danger does not lie in the fact that science is setting too fast a pace for the other disciplines: "The real danger lies in the lack of a lawful world. . . ." [12] A world ordered under the law will contain and resist the pressures to employ scientific knowledge for destructive purposes. "If science is to serve the peaceful purposes of mankind," the Chief Justice went on, "it must be given a peaceful setting in both domestic and world law." [13]

Warren admits that the law has been slow to move in the past. Changing conditions have rarely been anticipated. Instead, the law has waited idly by for problems to develop, "and then belatedly sought to make rules for solving them." [14] For example, our own immediate forefathers scarcely anticipated the forces and the problems that were turned loose during the post Civil War period by the new industrialization—by the rapid transformation of an agricultural society into an industrial society. And the social and political dislocation that followed, as manifested by the protest movements at the turn of the century, bore witness to this fact. The key question is this: Can we today afford a similar dislocation? Will there be time enough, when crisis stirs him to action, for man to reconstruct his affairs according to the rule of law? Warren does not give a direct answer, but the implication is, given the awful destructive power of modern science, that there will not be time enough.

[11] Warren, Address at the Georgia Institute of Technology 3, February 13, 1963.
[12] *Ibid.*
[13] *Id.* at 1-2.
[14] *Id.* at 4.

The way out, according to the Chief Justice, is for the law to keep pace with science. His words are in keeping with great publicists, such as John Cobb Cooper, who have spoken in a similar vein. "There is no reason," Warren states, "why we cannot make legal research accomplish the same function as scientific research." [15] This means that the law should no longer wait to be stirred by crises. The law should anticipate changing conditions. It should anticipate impending crises. It should, in other words, look to the future. And as the future beckons man into outer space, man must look there too for the rule of law ("We know that there must be a law of space if men are to fly to the moon and the planets"). If he does not, the consequences may be fatal: "A world without law is hell-bent for destruction with or without scientific discoveries." [16]

There have been, however, a few—if only a few—encouraging signs that man will not wait for catastrophe to strike before applying the rule of law to outer space. The resolution of the United Nations General Assembly of December 1961, which declared that international law applies to outer space, is one of these encouraging signs. But as John Cobb Cooper pointed out in February 1963, the legal status of outer space is still far from settled. Moreover, grave disputes exist between members of the United Nations. "There is no understanding," Cooper asserts, "as to what constitutes authorized activities in outer space 'in conformity with international law.'" [17]

The areas of disagreement are both grave and deep, and as the *Washington Post* pointed out editorially in April, 1963, the outlook for an early agreement is not propitious.[18] According to Cooper, the most pressing questions are these: (1) Should space vehicles or satellites be permitted to gather intelligence data? (2) Should private corporations be permitted to explore outer space? (3) What is meant by the term, "peaceful uses of outer space"? But the problem that probably contains the most potential dangers is that concerned with determining the line of demarcation between a nation's "airspace" and "outer space." This question, Cooper believes, could cause grave international complications unless dealt with immediately and successfully: "As a jurist I feel that outer space law must determine and state the rights of States to use the area which we call 'outer space,' and must, at the same time, fix the area in which such international rights exist." [19]

From England, a similar plea for the rule of law in outer space comes from C. Wilfred Jenks, an associate of the Institute of International Law.

[15] *Ibid.*
[16] *Id.* at 2, 5.
[17] Cooper, *Current Developments in Space Law* (paper presented at the 1963 Southeastern Regional Meeting of the American Society of International Law, February 1-2, 1963).
[18] Washington Post, April 20, 1963.
[19] Cooper, *op. cit. supra* note 17.

The moment for asserting the principle that outer space is not for national appropriation, states Jenks, is now; and the assertion should come with "the full authority of the international community"—preferably, from the United Nations.[20] Should such a declaration be delayed, individual nations will ultimately lay claim to outer space, and a satisfactory international agreement might then be impossible.[21]

Jenks proposes, among other things, a "Monroe Doctrine for the Moon," which would exclude all unilateral claims to sovereignty. This, too, should be openly declared by the United Nations. Space exploration in general, moreover, should be organized "as a world service." But if this chance is lost, then, at the very least, a "space for peace pool" should be organized, which would represent a complete pooling among nations of all activities in outer space. But whether pooled or operated independently, space activities should be subject "to the direct regulatory authority of the United Nations. . . ." On this point, Jenks is emphatic. For now, however, he feels only the principle need be established. Time will take care of the details.[22]

In agreement with Jenks that time is of the essence in applying the rule of law to outer space are two former Columbia University law professors, Philip C. Jessup and Howard J. Taubenfeld. "Major international problems that linger," Jessup and Taubenfeld warn, "do not always disappear." [23] Such problems will become "less soluble as positions become inflexible and entrenched—vested interests grow and national pride is involved, even where 'security' is only a fig leap for rapacity." [24] This has been the lesson of history. With this warning, they go on to emphasize that "space problems are essentially earth-bound." And the motivation for dealing with these "earth-bound" problems is none other than survival itself.[25]

For Jessup and Taubenfeld, the basic rule that must be contained in any international agreement on outer space is that expressed by Dag Hammarskjold in May 1958, that "outer space, and the celestial bodies therein, are not considered as capable of appropriation by any state. . . ." [26] Jessup and Taubenfeld would not stop merely with one of the many suggested international organizations which would leave the actual execution of the international will in national hands. Such an organization would be unworkable. What is needed is an international organization that can take part in "direct international decision-making." They suggest that perhaps

[20] JENKS, THE COMMON LAW OF MANKIND 405 (London: Stevens and Sons, Limited, 1958).
[21] Ibid.
[22] Id. at 405-07.
[23] JESSUP & TAUBENFELD, CONTROLS FOR OUTER SPACE AND THE ANTARCTIC ANALOGY 274 (New York: Columbia University Press, 1959; London: Oxford University Press, 1959).
[24] Ibid.
[25] Id. at 272.
[26] Id. at 275.

some totally new organization might be needed for the job. "The occasion for a fresh approach," they emphasize, "has arrived." [27]

But it is not merely the men and women in the law schools that speak with a sense of urgency. In 1958, Sir Winston Churchill told a meeting of the American Bar Association, "Justice knows no frontiers. . . . We have now reached the point where nations much contrive a system and practice to resolve their disputes and settle them peaceably." [28] On this side of the Atlantic, Senator Kenneth Keating of New York told the Congress, in 1959, that "civilization has now reached a point at which a gap between our moral and technical tools could be fatal." "The rule of law in the age of space," Keating continued, "is not a matter of philosophy, but a matter of survival." [29] Nor have such pleas been coming solely from people in civilian life. "Our plans should envisage," writes Colonel Martin Menter, United States Air Force, "a world where eventually the rule of law shall resolve differences among nations." The Space Age, Menter states, carries with it the portent of extending terrestrial disputes into outer space. It is thus necessary that the rule of law be adopted "as the means of settlement of national differences." [30] Charles S. Rhyne, a former president of the American Bar Association, has aptly spelled out the alternatives facing us today: [31]

> We must recognize that the tremendous developments in the field of nuclear science compels us toward a pragmatic choice between two alternatives: either we must learn to live with the expanding forces for the atom, or we must die, and our civilization with us, as the victim of those forces.

In another address, Rhyne made some specific suggestions for meeting the needs of the day. He called for the establishment of a "National Law Center" in Washington, D.C. Here men and women both from the law and from science—both teachers and students—would gather for a continuing program of research, teaching, and discussion in such fields as nuclear energy law and the law of outer space. In this way, the forces and problems released by science and technology might be immediately seized and tempered by the law.[32] It is an answer, in a sense, to Earl Warren's plea for legal research to keep pace with the problems posed by man's expanding scientific horizons.

Among the numerous Soviet spokesmen who have affirmed their belief in the rule of law for outer space—while at the same time accusing the

[27] *Id.* at 280-81.

[28] Churchill, Address to Meeting of the American Bar Association, London, England, 1958, in *American Bar Association—Meeting in London,* pp. 43-44.

[29] Congressional Record, March 10, 1959, p. A1975.

[30] Menter, *Astronautical Law,* pp. 62-63 (Thesis No. 86, Industrial College of the Armed Forces, May 1959).

[31] 82 REPORTS OF AMERICAN BAR ASSOCIATION 199 (1957).

[32] Rhyne, *The Space Era and George Washington University* (Address before the General Alumni Association of George Washington University, April 26, 1958).

United States of various actions directly contrary to that goal—is the legal scholar E. A. Korovin. Taking as his point of departure the statements of both Soviet and United States political leaders to the effect that outer space must be reserved for peaceful purposes, Korovin insists that the full attainment of this objective is inseparable from the attainment of complete and general disarmament, "... for there can be no peace in space without pacification on earth." However, he implicitly recognizes that world disarmament is unlikely to be accomplished overnight. In the meantime, he calls for international cooperation in the solution of "individual legal problems that become topical as man continues the conquest of outer space"—meaning such things as assistance and liability in the case of space accidents, as well as prevention of contamination of the cosmos either by radiation effects or by "the foul atmosphere of the 'cold war.'" [33]

Another Soviet legal expert concerned with the problems of outer space, G. P. Zhukov, spoke in a very similar vein at the recent Fifth Colloquium on the Law of Outer Space, held in Varna, Bulgaria, in September 1962. He, too, emphasized the matter of disarmament, not only as a means of assuring the peaceful use of outer space but also on the assumption (which may or may not be well founded) that funds released by disarmament would be devoted to the cause of space exploration. He likewise called for an international agreement that would specifically define the term "peaceful uses" as applied to outer space and would exclude such practices as the launching of reconnaissance satellites—even though the launching state may insist that its purposes are wholly non-aggressive. The repeated discussion of reconnaissance satellites by Zhukov and other Soviet legal writers is, of course, uniformly directed against the conduct of the United States, and there are still other instances of disagreement between the two nations with regard to specific details of the rule of law in space acivities; but in many of these instances the disagreement appears relatively easy to bridge. Moreover, it is at least a step in the right direction that official and unofficial spokesmen of both nations have explicitly recognized the need for law in outer space. "Until recently," as Zhukov observes, "the question of legal regulation of activities of States in space seemed to be something farfetched and fantastic. Today, in view of the huge successes in exploring space, in the first place by the USSR and also by the United States, this question acquires not only theoretical but also practical interest." [34]

There are some, to be sure, who see no need or at least no practical possibility of reaching agreement at this time on the law of outer space.

[33] Korovin, *Urgent Tasks of Space Law*, 5th Colloq. (Haley ed., Washington, D.C., 1963).

[34] Zhukov, *Problems of Space Law at the Present Stage*, 5th Colloq. (Haley ed., Washington, D.C., 1963).

One argument frequently given is that the astronautical experience of the various nations is still too limited to permit the construction of a comprehensive space legal code. However, the distinguished American lawyer William A. Hyman has observed that a useful, concise statement of legal principles for space could be adopted by the nations of the world even without first reaching agreement upon a detailed codification of space jurisprudence. Hyman cites the example of the Ten Commandments, which served as the *basis* for "millions of laws subsequently made by men" rather than being drawn up only *after* a general codification of human laws had been made. Moreover, he emphasizes the present urgency of an agreement on space legal principles:

> The vacuum in Space is law. It must be remedied, and immediately! . . . The stake in Space is not mere scientific supremacy. It is not an olympic contest. It is not the advance of empire, nor the extension of sovereignty of any nation into the celestial world. It is survival—the survival of mankind.[35]

Fittingly, it was Hyman who submitted to the Inter-American Bar Association, meeting in Bogota, Colombia, in February 1961, a statement of guiding principles which he labeled the "Magna Carta of Space." Hyman believed that these principles, if adopted by the nations of the world, would at least go a long way toward meeting the *immediate* requirement for legal norms to govern space exploration. Among the more important provisions was one stating that outer space and all uninhabited celestial bodies should be deemed *res communis* (common to all) and not simply *res nullius* (belonging to no one, but subject to appropriation under the traditional international law of discovery and settlement). This "Magna Carta of Space" provided further that space should be used solely for peaceful purposes; that there should be a recognized neutral zone between airspace and outer space in which all craft should have the right of innocent passage; and that procedures should be established for identification and registration of all space vehicles and for the allocation and control of radio frequencies in space. There were several further provisions along these same lines. The entire declaration of principles was approved by the Inter-American Bar Association, although one of the specific provisions included by Hyman—that there should be no nuclear experiments conducted in space—was only barely adopted.[36]

The foregoing example is just one of various attempts that have been made by nongovernmental groups to draw up statements of legal principles for the regulation of space activities. Another recent contribution is the "code" of space law prepared by a study group under the sponsorship of the David Davies Memorial Institute of International Studies in

[35] Hyman, *The Magna Carta of Space,* 5th Colloq. (Haley ed., Washington, D.C., 1963).
[36] *Ibid.*

London. Professor R. Y. Jennings of Cambridge University was chairman of the group, which had a distinguished membership made up of public officials, academic scholars, and others. The final draft of the code was prepared in the form of suggested clauses for an international treaty on space law and was presented at the Varna colloquium, as well as being submitted to the United Nations. It resembled other such statements in affirming that the use of outer space is free to all for peaceful purposes and that no claims of sovereignty can be permitted over other celestial bodies. The document calls for international agreement on a specific, even though admittedly arbitrary, demarcation line between airspace and outer space at 50 miles or 80,000 meters; recommends compulsory jurisdiction of the International Court of Justice when parties to a dispute involving the use of outer space cannot reach an amicable settlement by other means; and clearly recognizes the need for international action on such matters as registration and identification of space vehicles and the fixing of liability for damages incurred through space operations.[37]

It is perhaps well to close this introductory discussion by taking note of the fact that the world's spiritual as well as political and scientific leaders have repeatedly called for the extension of the rule of law to outer space. In 1956, even before the launching of the first artificial satellite, Pope Pius XII addressed the delegates to the Seventh Congress of the International Astronautical Federation, assuring them that God had not intended to limit man's efforts to this one planet but had placed "the whole creation" at his command. At the same time, Pius emphasized that the technical and scientific achievement of mankind in the conquest of space must go hand in hand with a true spirit of cooperation among nations:

> The common effort of mankind to attain the peaceful conquest of the universe should more greatly impress in the conscience of men the meaning of society and solidarity so that all men have the feeling of being part of the great family of God, of being the children of the same Father. But to fathom this truth, there is need of no less respect for truth, for submission to reality, for courage, than for scientific research. The most advanced explorations into space will only serve to bring a new reason for disunion if they are not effected along with a deeper moral intention and a more conscious attitude of devotion in the higher interests of mankind.[38]

Similarly, Pope John XXIII, in offering prayers for the Soviet cosmonaut Andrian Nikolayev, while the latter was in orbital flight about the earth, observed that today's astronauts are "carrying on that exploration of creation encouraged by Sacred Scripture in its earliest pages: 'Ingredimini super terram et replete eam' [Go upon the earth, and fill it]." [39] Comment-

---

[37] Horsford, A British Code of Space Law, 5 SPACEFLIGHT 52-53 (1963).
[38] Pope Pius XII, Allocution to Delegates of the International Astronautical Federation on the Subjects of Science and Astronautics (September 1956).
[39] On Exploring Outer Space, 8 THE POPE SPEAKS 228 (1963).

ing further on "these wonderful flights and trips through space," the Pope stated:

> ... Oh, how We wish that these undertakings would take on a meaning of homage rendered to God, creator and supreme lawmaker.
> Just as these historic events will take their place in the annals of the scientific knowledge of the cosmos, may they also become an expression of true and peaceful progress, contributing toward the sound foundation of human brotherhood.[40]

In view of the above statements by Pope John, it is clear that his many eloquent pronouncements on the need for a peaceful world order—as expressed in the encyclical *Pacem in Terris* and in his memorable Easter message of April 1963—are not purely earth-bound in their implications. A rule of law that extended only to the top of the atmosphere (however that limit might be defined) would be not only politically unrealistic but also incomplete from the standpoint of the moral and ethical principles on which any lasting world order must be based.

[40] *Id.* at 229.

Additional References

Andrew G. Haley, *Rule of Law in Outer Space: Letter to the Editor,* New York Times, Feb. 18, 1961, p. 18; _____, *Commercial Aspects of Our National Space Law,* The Commercial and Financial Chronicle, Jan. 5, 1961, p. 1; _____, *Space Exploration—The Problems of Today, Tomorrow and in the Future,* in SECOND COLLOQUIUM ON THE LAW OF OUTER SPACE 44 (1960); _____, *Law of Outer Space—Practical Legal Rules for Human Conduct* 16 FED. COM. B.J. 163 (1959); _____, *Space Age Presents Immediate Legal Problems,* in FIRST COLLOQUIUM ON THE LAW OF OUTER SPACE 5 (1959); _____, *Space Flight: A Look Ahead,* Astronautics, Nov. 1958, p. 28; _____, *The Commercial Implications of Missiles—Satellite—Space Age,* The Commercial and Financial Chronicle, Mar. 13, 1958, p. 1; _____, *The Law of Space—Scientific and Technical Considerations,* 4 N.Y.L.F. 262 (1958); _____, *Law Must Precede Man Into Space,* Missiles & Rockets, Nov. 1957, p. 67; _____ & Rosen, *On the Utility of an Artificial Unmanned Earth Satellite,* 25 JET PROPULSION 1 (1955); *Law and Economics of the Space Age:* Lecture by _____ & Dr. Welf Heinrich Prince of Hanover, Princeton University, Physicians Scientific Society, Detroit Law School, University of Michigan Law School, University of Chicago Law School, Northwestern University Law School, University of Wisconsin Law School, University of Minnesota Law School, Civic Group of Butte, Mont., University of Montana, Gonzaga University Law School, University of Washington Law School, University of California Law School, Salt Lake City Chamber of Society, University of Utah College of Law, UCLA Law School, Denver Chamber of Commerce, University of Colorado Law School, St. Louis University and Washington University Law Schools, Harvard University International Law Club, Institute of Military Law, Chicago Section of the American Rocket Society, Twin Cities Section of the American Rocket Society,

Spokane Bar Association, Pacific-Northwest Section of the American Rocket Society, Northern California Section of the American Rocket Society, Southern California Section of the American Rocket Society, Holloman and New Mexico and West Texas Sections of the American Rocket Society at Holloman Air Force Base, Central Colorado Section of the American Rocket Society, St. Louis Section of the American Rocket Society, New England Section of the American Rocket Society, National Capital Section of the American Rocket Society, Georgetown Law School, American University Law School, Catholic University Law School, Maryland University Law School, November 1957.

2

The traditional bases of
international law

This discussion considers the fundamental nature of human law, explaining its anthropocentric character. With this in mind, two traditional schools of international law, the positivist orientation and the natural law theory, are analyzed and their fundamental conflict examined. The writings of a leading positivist are discussed, and the general theory of the positivist position explained. The philosophy of natural law is then discussed as a more desirable basis for the emergence of a new international law of space. Natural law is shown to be based upon unchanging fundamental moral principles arising out of the nature of man, and its role as a guide to change of specific rules of law in accord with changing circumstances is examined. The problem of the need for change in the law is discussed in light of the counter-balancing need for stability which is an essential character of the law. A brief historical review indicates that the philosophy of natural law was first suggested as a basis for international law at a time when a revolutionary new problem similar to that of our own time had just arisen—the discovery of the new world. The unfortunate consequences of the failure to adopt such a basis at that time are also noted. Consent of the nations, i.e., the process of tacit expression of consent through custom and usage, is introduced as a basic step in the international law-making process.

2–1 The anthropocentric nature of law

In the first approach to space jurisprudence we will consider some basic principles of anthropocentric law. It is simply the law of human beings. *Corpus Juris Secundum* states that the term "law" is frequently employed as referring to a science of principles; and, specifically:

... a science or system of principles or rules of human conduct; a system of rules and principles, in which the rights of parties are protected and enforced; a system of rules conformable to the standards of justice and on an enlarged view of the relations of persons and things as they practically exist; a mass of principles classified, reduced to order, and put in the shape of rules, agreed on by ascertaining the common consent of mankind; rules promulgated by government as a means to an ordered society; the enforcement of justice among men.[1]

It is also said that the very definition of law is *sancto sancti jubens honesta et prohibens contraria.*

The outstanding philosophers and the great works of history have defined the naked essence of anthropocentric law in one simple concept, the Golden Rule. "We should behave to friends," said Aristotle, "as we would wish friends to behave to us." The New Testament was even more encompassing: "Therefore all things whatsoever ye would that men should do to you, do ye even so to them: for this is the law and the prophets"; and Mohammed was merely expounding on the same theme when he said, "Do good unto others as God has done unto thee." In the Torah, the Babylonian Talmud, Epictetus, Seneca, Ahikar, Abdullah Ansari, Bidpai, Sadi, Confucius, Mahabharata, and Sutra Kritanga—indeed, wherever man has set down the essence of law—this one simple concept emerges.

This essence of anthropocentric law is the attempt to create a system of rules governing relations among human beings based on the principle that each person should be obliged to treat others as he would have himself treated. This principle logically requires equal treatment of all according to an impartial standard. In order to achieve such impartial treatment, it is necessary that the law be relatively constant. Indeed, it is necessary that it be based on fundamental principles such as those contemplated in the structure of natural law.

2–2 Conflicting philosophies of international law

Recognizing that the law must change in accordance with changing circumstances, we must not be misled into thinking of the law as something so mutable that it can be changed arbitrarily so as to lose its essential character. The stability of law through time and the constancy of its application are basic attributes which are necessary to the functioning of organized human society. Impairment of its stability, therefore, should not be undertaken lightly. The problem, then, is that some change in law is necessary, but not just arbitrary change. The change must be guided and restrained by fundamental principles which will serve as an anchor to keep the law within the channel of its essential character. There

---

[1] 52 C. J. S. *Law* (Footnotes omitted) (Brooklyn: American Law Book Company, 1947).

are certain fundamental moral principles arising from the nature of man which are unchanging and which underlie, or should underlie, every body of law in every human community. Because of the differing circumstances in different times and places, the specific rules which embody the fundamental principles and achieve the result we call "justice" may vary —but only as guided and restrained by the fundamental principles.

Another significant and essential realization in this discussion is that however much political wisdom goes into the determination of what the law is, there remains outside of the law the political question: Should the law be respected?

Professor Myres S. McDougal of Yale University has commenced work, along with associates, on a series of studies which will present a general theory of law and apply it to problems of international order. *Studies in World Public Order* (1960) is the first in this series. Professor Roger Fisher, of the faculty of Harvard University, in reviewing this work,[2] attempts to explain the dichotomy that exists in present international legal theory. "At a time," he says, "when the single most important problem facing the world is to preserve and improve the international order, somebody besides the international lawyer should understand wherein we international lawyers disagree."

As Fisher observes, "most fundamentally, McDougal is opposed to the notion that rules should dictate decisions," holding instead that:

> . . . both relevant policies and technical rules are commonly and necessarily formulated in pairs of opposites and . . . the appropriate function of such formulations is not to dictate decisions but to guide decision-makers to all the factors in a context which should be taken into account in making rational decisions (page 333).

The positivistic school, of which McDougal is a leading exponent, recognizes the flexibility in the rules, i.e., the specific content of existing laws, and urges that they be used consciously and explicitly to serve the proper ends of a democratic society. As McDougal states: "What law 'is' . . . depends primarily . . . upon the ends preferred." [3] Professor Fisher reacts to this position by stating: ". . . for this country and others to accept [McDougal's] analysis and recommendations as the basis for future action would, in my view, be little short of disastrous."

Professor Fisher points out that on the international scene today "the application of archaic rules" has not frustrated national action. On the contrary, international rules have been construed by nations in the light of their national policies. Indeed, nations have felt free to ignore that portion of traditional law which seemed to conflict with their policies. And

---

[2] Fisher, Review of McDOUGAL *et al.*, STUDIES IN WORLD PUBLIC ORDER (1960), 135 SCIENCE 658 (1962).

[3] McDOUGAL *et al.*, STUDIES IN WORLD PUBLIC ORDER 93 (New Haven: Yale University Press, 1960).

now, Fisher goes on, McDougal has appeared on the scene "with his cure-all remedy of domestic vintage, urging 'more policy, less rules.'" "Is it a wonder," Fisher asks, "that some of us, seeking to strengthen the rules and to persuade countries to pay more attention of them, regard Mc-Dougal as spreading the contagion rather than the cure?"

Fundamental principles cannot be overthrown in the interest of political expedience. Our systems of national and international law in their independent and interdependent context cannot serve humanity to insure justice if national interests dominate in the considerations of what law should be. As Fisher has pointed out with logic once again, how can people and countries respect a system of law based on the premise that there are no rules and that everyone decides for himself what is reasonable under the circumstances? Obviously, a system based on such self-judging criteria offers little hope for international order. Nations and national leaders recognize quite readily that their survival depends upon avoiding internal anarchy. "They respect the legal rules that give them power," Fisher points out. But avoiding internal anarchy is not enough. Today survival is also contingent upon avoiding international anarchy. "We need not only an understanding of the political foundations of international law," Fisher concludes, "we also need to understand the legal foundations of international politics." [4]

In considering the anthropocentric law as applied to space we may well examine the function of the surveyor's transit. We must have a means of looking back to get our bearing, or we will be unable to set a straight course in the future. Because such pursuit seems more useful, we will look more on the modicum of good thinking, and neglect the plethora of the bad. By searching the record of the past, we may find that no useful purpose was served by burning Socinus and Servetus for their alleged derelictions, so why burn Heisenberg or Yukawa for their doctrine of the principles of uncertainty to satisfy the cult of mechanical positivism? Or, more in point, we should take a look again at what happened to the Indians to forfend against galacticide; we must consider colonialism to make certain that such practices are never permitted in space; and so on. We must climb to a realistic and veracious plateau of evaluation.

Hugo Grotius, the great seventeenth-century Dutch jurist, was one of the first to attempt to codify international law. He wrote a treatise on the law of war which contains much of the basic material for modern international law. Endeavoring to establish an immutable distinction between right and wrong, Grotius surveyed those general principles of morals that seemed to him sufficient to illustrate the nature of law. He then proceeded, in the words of Dugald Stewart, "to inculcate the general adoption of the best usage introduced on these subjects in times then recent and to per-

---

[4] Fisher, *op. cit. supra* note 2, at 660.

suade all nations to pursue it by reasons of justice, by considerations of interest...." [5] The views of Grotius are carried over into present-day international law, and he is widely regarded as one of its founders.

Let us look now at the law as it has grown up since Grotius' day. Green Haywood Hackworth saw international law as "a body of rules" or system of jurisprudence, governing the relations between states, which had evolved out of experiences and necessities—developing as it were with the march of civilization. It was the increasing realization, among nations, as Hackworth points out, that "their relations *inter se,* if not their existence, must be governed by and depend upon rules of law," that gave birth to international law. And as Hackworth states further, customary— as distinct from conventional—international law is based on "the common consent of nations." Moreover, when there is doubt of the existence or application of a particular rule of international law, resort can usually be had to treaties, official pronouncements, the writings of publicists, or the decisions of national and international tribunals that express the law of nations.[6]

The term "body of rules" is somewhat misleading, for there is no codification or clear understanding of the precise content of international law. Hackworth himself makes this clear. He states that international law is based on an "indefinite number of factors." The authorities cited by Hackworth make an effort to enumerate these factors. Thus, in *Galban & Co. v. United States,* the United States Court of Claims held:

> International law is a system of rules founded upon long-established customs and acts of states and international agreements, not inconsistent with the principles of natural justice, which Christian and civilized states recognize as obligatory in their relations and dealings with each other, as well as with the citizens and subjects of each.[7]

A 1916 Congressional report noted that international law is:

> ... a complex system, composed of various ingredients. It consists of general principles of right and justice, equally suitable to the government or individuals in a state of natural equality and to the relations and conduct of

---

[5] Mackintosh, *Review of Dugald Stewart's "General View of the Progress of Metaphysical, Ethical, and Political Philosophy, Since the Revival of Letters in Europe,"* 27 EDINBURGH REV., or CRITICAL J. 230, 234 (1816).

[6] HACKWORTH, DIGEST OF INTERNATIONAL LAW 1 (1940); Many leading publicists have provided definitions of international law, e.g. MILAN BARTOS, 1 MEZHDUNARDNO JAVNO PRAVO 9 (Yugoslavia 1954); PAUL GUGGENHEIM, 1 TRAITÉ DE DROIT INTERNATIONAL PUBLIC 1 (Switzerland 1953); LASSA FRANCIS LAURANCE OPPENHEIM, 2 INTERNATIONAL LAW (Lauterpacht ed. 8th ed. 1955); RADHABINOL PAL, CRIMES IN INTERNATIONAL RELATIONS 19 (India 1955); GEORGES SCELLE, COURS DE DROIT INTERNATIONAL PUBLIC 4 (1948); MANUEL SIERRA SIERRA, DERECHO INTERNACIONAL PUBLICO 15 (3rd ed., Mexico 1959); G. I. TUNKIN, *Co-existence and International Law* 95 RECUEIL DE COURS DE L'ACADÉMIE DU DROIT INTERNATIONAL 1, 6 (1958).

[7] 40 Ct. Cl. 495, 504 (1905); note also the discussion in Case of the S. S. "Lotus," P.C.I.J., Ser. A, No. 10 (1927).

nations; of a collection of usages, customs, and opinion, the growth of civilizations and commerce, and of a code of conventional or positive law.[8]

Hall, in his treatise on international law which is also cited by Hackworth, readily admits "the weakness and the indeterminateness of the
sanction of international law." But this in itself cannot be an absolute bar
to the admission of international law as law. In practice, he says, "international rules are cast in a legal mould, and are invariably treated ... as
being legal in character," i.e., as somehow comparable to the positive law
of "organized communities." Hall does not deny that international rules
lie on the extreme frontier of law; but he concludes that ". . . on the whole
it would seem to be more correct, as it certainly is more convenient, to
treat them as being a branch of law, than to include them within the
sphere of morals." [9] Hackworth, too, holds that international law possesses
the characteristics "common to municipal law." [10]

During the first two decades of the twentieth century, there was a
tendency for legal writers to regard international law as nothing more
than positive law, law enacted by a government for the regulation of a
society. This concept of international law recognized only those rules of
law which were accepted by the judges of courts of justice, which were
applied by them in decisions of cases, and which entered into judgments
and were executed.

Since 1920 there has been a tendency to challenge this approach,
typified by the work of such writers as Max Huber,[11] Nicolas Politis,[12]
Georges Scelle,[13] J. L. Brierly,[14] Hersch Lauterpacht,[15] Philip Jessup,[16]
and C. Wilfred Jenks.[17] While their views continue to be questioned, they
are symptomatic of a shift in the weight of opinion. This shift reflects
both the impact on international law of the work of contemporary writers
on jurisprudence, including Holmes, Cardozo, Pound, Duguit, and Gény,
which has made a revaluation of the Austinian outlook necessary, and

[8] H.R. Rep. 69th. Cong. 2d Sess. 2 (1916), cited in 1 HACKWORTH, DIGEST OF
INTERNATIONAL LAW 2-3 (1940).

[9] Quoted in 1 HACKWORTH, DIGEST OF INTERNATIONAL LAW 5-6 (1940).

[10] 1 HACKWORTH, DIGEST OF INTERNATIONAL LAW 1 (1940); contra, TRIEPEL,
VÖLKERRECHT UND LANDESRECHT (1899).

[11] DIE SOZIOLOGISCHEN GRUNDLAGEN DES VÖLKERRECHTS, 1928.

[12] LA JUSTICE INTERNATIONALE, 1924; LES NOUVELLES TENDANCES DU DROIT INTER
NATIONAL, 1927; LA MORALE INTERNATIONALE, 1944.

[13] PRÉCIS DU DROIT DES GENS, 1932.

[14] THE LAW OF NATIONS, 5th ed., 1955; THE OUTLOOK FOR INTERNATIONAL LAW,
1944; THE BASIS OF OBLIGATION IN INTERNATIONAL LAW, 1958.

[15] PRIVATE LAW SOURCES AND ANALOGIES OF INTERNATIONAL LAW, 1927; THE
FUNCTION OF LAW IN THE INTERNATIONAL COMMUNITY, 1933; THE DEVELOPMENT
OF INTERNATIONAL LAW BY THE INTERNATIONAL COURT, 1958.

[16] A MODERN LAW OF NATIONS, 1948; TRANSNATIONAL LAW, 1956; THE USE OF
INTERNATIONAL LAW, 1959.

[17] THE COMMON LAW OF MANKIND, 1958; LAW, FREEDOM AND WELFARE, 1963;
THE PROSPECTS OF INTERNATIONAL ADJUDICATION, 1963.

a conscious attempt to adapt the law to the changed and growing needs of international society.

All of these writers are preoccupied with the relationship of stability and change in the development of the law. Wilfred Jenks, for instance, places great store on the potential contribution to the growth of the law of custom, general legal principles, equity, and public policy, and emphasizes the inhibiting influence on legal development of the inductive approach of the positivist school.[18]

2–3 The need for sound concepts

The positivist conception of international law as a body of law with characteristics "common to municipal law" has implications which are repugnant to the actual experience of space flight, since it heavily emphasizes existing specific rules of law and recognizes only those consented to by governments. The law governing the airspace of the earth is based solely on the absolute right of sovereignty of each nation to the space above its territory. And it is pointed out in detail in Chapter 5, below, that if the existing international law relevant to the discovery of new territory were extended to outer space, it would create the possibility of claims of sovereignty by individual nations over celestial bodies.

It is surprising, therefore, to find the Sixteenth Session of the General Assembly of the United Nations adopting a resolution to the effect that (1) "International law, including the Charter of the United Nations applies to outer space and celestial bodies"; (2) all states are free to use and explore outer space and celestial bodies in conformity with international law; and (3) outer space and celestial bodies "are not subject to national appropriation." (See Appendix I-F(1).)

If one examines the matter logically, there is an attempt made here by the General Assembly to modify existing international law. The Assembly recommended that international law be extended to outer space, but it also recommended that outer space should not be subject to national appropriation. Since the existing specific rules of international law, if simply extended to cover outer space, might not favor such a result, the existing rules are modified in one respect. By such a blanket extension of the totality of "international law, including the Charter of the United Nations," the General Assembly has created a situation in which many such modifications as the one here indicated will be necessary.

On a number of past occasions, treaty makers and judicial bodies have had to bring about the solution of legal problems in connection with new developments in civilization and to modify the existing law in so doing. We will discuss this point very briefly and refer only to a few American authorities.

[18] Cf. THE PROSPECTS OF INTERNATIONAL ADJUDICATION, 1963.

As Justice Louis Brandeis stated, in *Jaybird Mining Co. v. Weir*, "It is a peculiar virtue of our system of law . . . that an expression in an opinion yields later to the impacts of facts unseen." [19]

Likewise Justice Benjamin N. Cardozo pointed out, in *Paradoxes of Legal Science*, "The impact may come from a new fact. It may come from a changing estimate of policy or justice . . . [W]hat was ruled or next to ruled was well enough often according to the wisdom of its day. The light of a new day has set it forth as folly." [20] Indeed, it has been argued that the principle of stare decisis—meaning to stand by previous decisions —"perpetuates error, prevents courts from adopting the law of the changed needs and desires to society, . . . it is the abdication of reasoning power, judgment and responsibility of the present generation of lawyers." [21] And as Justice Brandeis has said, "In differentiation, not in uniformity lies the path of progress." [22]

Chief Judge John T. Loughran, of the Court of Appeals, State of New York, stated the case succinctly:

> I cannot go along with those who insist upon a rigid and mechanical adherence to the decisions of the past, without regard to the impact of later day social, economical and political changes that have been wrought in the world about us. Indeed if we were to be limited to slavish adherence to precedents and were not free to apply the decisions and their underlying principles to changing conditions and situations which did not exist and were not contemplated when the decisions were made, our decisional law would in great measure be no more advanced today than it was many generations ago.[23]

The danger in paying deference to the past, Judge Loughran continued, is that it may lead to approaching current issues "with minds attuned only to the spirit and attitudes of a by-gone day. . . ." With such an approach, one cannot be responsive to the needs and interests of the present.[24] And once again we come to Justice Brandeis, who, in reviewing the Supreme Court's history in breaking with previous decisions, stated that the Court had bowed "to the lessons of experience and the force of better reasoning, recognizing that the process of trial and error so fruitful in the physical sciences is appropriate also to the judicial form." [25] Justice Oliver Wendell Holmes summed up the same idea in this manner. "It is revolting," he

[19] 271 U.S. 609, 619 (1926).

[20] CARDOZO, THE PARADOXES OF LEGAL SCIENCE 63 (1928); CARDOZO, THE NATURE OF THE JUDICIAL PROCESS 150 (1921) quoted in *Decisions in The Court: Stare Decisis or "Flexible Logic"?*, 34 A.B.A.J. 887, 888 (1949).

[21] *Decisions in The Court: Stare Decisis or "Flexible Logic"?*, 34 A.B.A.J. 887 (1948).

[22] SOLOMON GOLDMAN, THE WORDS OF JUSTICE BRANDEIS 63 (1953).

[23] Loughran, *Some Reflections on the Role of Judicial Precedent*, 22 FORDHAM L. REV. 1 (1953).

[24] *Id.* at 2.

[25] 285 U.S. 393, 406-10 (Footnotes omitted) (dissenting opinion).

said in *The Path of the Law,* "to have no better reason for a rule of law than that so it was laid down in the time of Henry IV." [26]

In a more philosophical tenor, John Dewey wrote that the great evil underlying the doctrine of immutable antecedent rules is that it sanctifies the old and "constantly widens the gap between the current social conditions and the principles used by the courts. . . ." To Dewey, the sanctification of the ready-made and the antecedent was the chief obstacle to intelligent social reform. "If this be so," he concluded, the "infiltration into law" of a more experimental type of logic "is a social as well as an intellectual need." [27] Also apt is Justice Felix Frankfurter's dissent in *Braniff Airways v. Nebraska Bd.,* where he said, "One of the most treacherous tendencies in legal reasoning is the transfer of generalizations developed for one set of situations to seemingly analogous, yet essentially very different, situations." [28] The Supreme Court of the United States authoritatively handled both the folklore and the philosophy of the law in *Chicago and So. Air Lines v. Waterman S.S. Corp.* In words that could easily be extended to reflect the present space age situation, the Court admitted the contention that there was a certain kinship between air, water, rail, and motor transportation, and that similar regulations might often be suitable for public carriers of all four categories; but it still warned that "these resemblances must not blind us to the fact that legally, as well as literally, air commerce, whether at home or abroad, soared into a different realm than any that had gone before." [29]

Whether intentionally or otherwise, the foregoing comments all underscore the weakness of the basic positivist position which lacks a body of principle more fundamental than existing specific rules of law. And, since we cannot adopt the narrow positivist position that the presently existing specific rules of international law as recognized by governments should simply be extended to outer space, we must delve more deeply into the general nature of law and of international law, and attempt to return to fundamental principles in order to lay a solid foundation upon which to build a new structure of international law for the space age. [30]

2–4 *Vitoria and the natural law school*

In searching for a philosophy of law to govern space travel we may look to the writings of certain publicists of the 15th and 16th centuries. Their theories are especially pertinent here when we consider that they gave the

---

[26] Holmes, *The Path of the Law,* 10 HARV. L. REV. 457, 469 (1897).
[27] John Dewey, *Logical Method and Law,* 10 CORNELL L. Q. 17, 26-27 (1924).
[28] 347 U.S. 590, 603 (1953) (dissenting opinion).
[29] 333 U.S. 103, 107 (1948).
[30] Note the use of this analysis by the Indian diplomat S. S. Lall in *Space Exploration—Some Legal and Political Aspects,* 2d Colloq. 75, 79-81 (Vienna: Springer-Verlag, 1960).

"natural theory" of international law its most searching examination at precisely the time when man was last faced with a major expansion in the effective size of his universe and with the resulting need to devise new systems of law—following the discovery of the new world. We are on a similar threshold today.[31]

The school of international law which maintains that natural law should be the basis for international law is said to have been founded by Francisco de Vitoria. By his definition, the law of nations is "the law which natural reason has established among all nations." [32] Natural law, the keynote of Vitoria's philosophy, is a

> ... system of rules and principles for the guidance of human conduct which, independently of enacted law or of the systems peculiar to any one people, might be discovered by the rational intelligence of man, and would be found to grow out of and conform to his nature, meaning by that word his whole mental, moral and physical constitution.[33]

St. Thomas Aquinas also attributed immutable features to natural law when he said that "the natural law contains certain universal precepts which are everlasting, whereas human law contains certain particular precepts, according to various circumstances." [34]

Natural law is not intangible and non-existent as followers of the positive school of law insist. Natural law is not imposed by the sovereign, because it grew up before a sovereign existed, nor is it imposed by a sovereign's legislature. It does not exist as a written code and in fact has never existed in statutory form. Rather, it is "a state of mind, which is however a fact, that certain rights and certain duties [are] necessary in any and every society composed of human beings." [35]

Vitoria extended the principles of natural law and applied them to international law as a basis of cooperation in the world community. He was motivated to a great degree by a reaction to the conduct of the explorers in the new world, and the treatment accorded those who had been found in newly discovered territory. The Indians were being deprived of land and liberty by adventurers interested only in gain; and Vitoria was not alone in championing the rights of the original inhabitants of the Americas.[36]

The conflict revolved around two opposing factions—those set on per-

[31] As Col. Martin Menter states, "The natural law has been the guide for much of our past and present laws and should be looked to in determining future provisions of astronautical law." Col. Menter is one of the leading modern exponents of the natural law school, and the conclusions of his outstanding thesis develop the position exceptionally well. See Menter, *Astronautical Law*, Symp. 349, 392-393.

[32] In JAMES BROWN SCOTT, THE SPANISH ORIGIN OF INTERNATIONAL LAW 33 (Washington, D.C.: Georgetown University, 1928).

[33] BLACK, LAW DICTIONARY 1177 (4th ed. 1951).

[34] 1 ST. THOMAS AQUINAS, SUMMA THEOLOGICA, Part II, Ques. 97, art. 1.

[35] SCOTT, *op. cit. supra* note 24 at 101.

[36] *Id.* at 23-24.

sonal advantage and those interested in missionary work. The success of the first class would have meant annihilation of the Indians. With this need, then, for a law to govern a nation's actions in new territory and in relation to other nations, Vitoria set forth his principles of international law.

There was no doubt, Vitoria said, that "the rule of law of nations is that what belongs to nobody is granted to the first occupant." [37] This rule, he claims, cannot be applied to America, for the land was held in lawful possession by the Indians. He states further that "the Spaniards have a right to travel into the lands in question and to sojourn there, provided they do no harm to the natives, and the natives may not prevent them." According to Vitoria, the law of nations, which is either natural law or derived from natural law, constitutes the basis for this rule. No state, then, could prevent a citizen of one state from traveling or living in another state, "provided this in no way enured to their hurt and the visitors did no injury." [38]

Vitoria's system of international law is based upon the association of a community of interdependent states each possessing rights and reciprocal duties—a natural society in a world bound together by mutual intercourse. "Nature has established," Vitoria adds, "a bond of relationship between all men." [39]

Vitoria recognized that the Indians were divided into states and peoples who owned the land in their respective jurisdictions and had an organized system of government. They were "States of the New World to which he would attribute the rights of States in the Old World." [40] Hence, the Spanish conquerors could not lawfully assume the leadership of the New World without the assent of the populace. Irrespective of size, form of government, or religion, all states are equal and independent in the system of law that Vitoria professed. Each state, then, possesses the rights of others, and all are under a duty to conform their actions to the rights of all. Moreover, Vitoria explicitly discarded the method in vogue among the Romans of extending their own Empire in "the cause of allies and friends." He found no lawful basis for granting Spain any territorial rights in America under the pretext of going into that region as the powerful outsider offering aid to some weaker state. He expressly states that there did not seem to be any other "juridic title whereby the Romans came into possession of the world save in right of war, and the most especial cause of their wars was the defense and protection of their friends." [41] Such a rule of conduct Vitoria could not accept as being capable of governing an international community framed upon the law of nature.

[37] VITORIA, DE INDIS ET DE IURE BELLI RELECTIONES 139 (Nys, ed. 1917).
[38] *Id.* at 151.
[39] *Id.* at 153.
[40] SCOTT, *op. cit. supra* note 24 at 25.
[41] *Id.* at 38.

In governing the relations between individual states, a wrong received is a "single and only just cause for commencing war," says Vitoria.[42] Natural law principles permit this, for the basic premise of that principle has been abrogated by the state which initially inflicts the wrong. But, as Vitoria points out, extension of an empire is no cause for a war. Neither could Spain exclude other states from communicating or trading with the New World, nor exclude persons from other states who wished to settle there. "The whole world is in a certain sense a single community [and] possesses the right to prescribe equitable and appropriate laws for its members." [43]

As the Brazilian international lawyer, H. Valladão, recently pointed out, the European colonizers were applying to the possession of new territories overseas the same rules evolved in Roman Law relative to the possession of wild animals, which became effective by virtue of their capture wherever it occurred. Valladão then describes as "unanswerable" Vitoria's attack on this procedure in which he argued that the Spaniards could no more justify the possession of territories in the Americas than could the American Indians have justified the possession of territory in Spain—had they discovered Spain as Spain had discovered America.[44]

Vitoria's international law principles were further extended by another Spaniard, Francisco Suarez, who accepted the basic tenets of Vitoria's work and proceeded to make clear distinctions between natural law and law of nations. Writing after the death of Vitoria, he advocated the necessity of an association of states and the necessity for laws to govern the association. The law of these states, Suarez said, comes about "in great part by natural reason, nevertheless not sufficiently and immediately for all matters; and therefore certain special laws could be introduced by the usage of these same nations. . . ." [45]

The basis of these laws, however, is natural law founded on reason, "the law everywhere existing among human beings in society toward its members and itself." [46] Such law was to be distinguished from law of nations, however, for natural law is immutable and common to all universally, while the law of nations is common to some, not all. Natural law has as its origin natural evidence, while the law of nations is positive and human in its origin and susceptible of change. The law of nations, applicable as it may be to the world community, is still founded on "probability" and the "common judgment of men." [47]

The great distinction made by Suarez is that natural law arises of

---

[42] *Id.* at 46.
[43] *Id.* at 62.
[44] Valladão, *The Law of Interplanetary Space*, 2d Colloq. 156, 163 (Vienna: Springer-Verlag, 1960).
[45] 2 Suarez, De Legibus xix. 9.
[46] Scott, *op. cit. supra* note 24 at 92.
[47] *Id.* at 97.

"necessity from the nature of things by an evident and logical deduction from natural principles." The obligatory character of natural law is due to its natural source, prohibiting that which is evil *per se*, while the law of nations defines the evil which is prohibited. Regardless of the distinctions in the two legal systems, they have certain points in common. They are both "in a certain sense common to all people, ... they apply only to human beings and they both include precepts, prohibitions, and also certain privileges and permissions." [48]

The basis of both Vitoria and Suarez's principles of international law is the law of nature. It is the law of reason "not agreed upon by the few nor the many, but by all," and providing the fundamental precepts with which the world has always been acquainted.[49] It is the law of individuals governing their ordered existence, and it is applicable to states as well when applied by the citizens comprising the state.

Suarez envisioned, as did Vitoria, an international community composed of independent, perfect states bound by "a certain unity," with each "a member in a certain fashion of this universe, so far as it concerns the human race." [50] Such an international community was an outgrowth of government as found in territorial states, based upon the natural impulse of men toward social relationships, urging them to unite.

While the "natural law" theory of international law was regarded a generation ago as discredited, there has been during the last forty years a marked revival of "natural law" thinking. Professor James Brown Scott in his work, *The Spanish Origins of International Law*, recalls the story of President Wilson who "warned one of the belligerents of the World War against the commission of an 'overt' act in violation of the law of nations or of the neutral rights of the United States. When asked what he meant by an overt act, he replied that he could not tell, but that he was sure he would recognize it when he saw it. He did, and the United States declared itself to be in a state of war with the Imperial German Government." Scott adds further:

> The Constitution of the United States is itself a tribute to the law of nature. The Constitution is a supreme law; it is not to be changed by the legislature, as an ordinary statute. It can be amended, indeed, and in that sense is not immutable; but it can only be amended by an express vote of three-fourths of the States of the American Union. Every written constitution made by its framers superior to a statute of the legislature is a recognition, unconscious perhaps, of the law of nature—that is to say of a law of general effect, beyond the power of the ordinary law-making body to modify.[51]

Universal rules of natural law governing the outward acts of mankind "furnished a political ideal for individuals, laying the foundation for the

---

[48] 2 SUAREZ, DE LEGIBUS xix. 1.
[49] 1 RICHARD HOOKER, ECCLESIASTICAL POLITY VIII 10.
[50] 2 SUAREZ, DE LEGIBUS xix. 9.
[51] SCOTT, *op. cit. supra* note 24 at 107.

United States sovereignty," observes Professor Jesse S. Reeves. He also said that "the principles of the law of nature assisted in giving to the founders of the Republic an idealistic conception of its rights as a nation and of its duties toward other States." [52]

Hackworth admits that "phrases of the so-called 'law of nature,' doctrines of equity and morality, as well as certain principles common to local law, etc., have become infused in and made a part of international law." [53]

The law of England was influenced by the principles of natural law, Scott says, and the latter is, therefore, regarded as an integral portion of the legal theory, thought, and practice of England. "Nowhere is this more strikingly obvious than in the appeal to reason in the system of equity administered by the Lord High Chancellor in Courts of Chancery...." Here, the Courts have administered justice in cases which were not covered by written law in the same way as the praetors of Rome displaced the narrow and highly technical law of the Roman citizens by natural law. "The rule of reason," Scott concludes, "is declared applicable in the English-speaking world as in the tribunals of Continental Europe, whenever, in the opinion of judges, it should be applied in the absence of a definite law governing the transactions in question." [54]

Professor F. W. von Rauchhaupt began teaching international law at Heidelberg University in 1922. In a paper presented during the First Colloquium on the Law of Outer Space in 1958, he pointed out the similarity between the situation that faced the world in 1492 as a result of the discoveries of Columbus and the problems of the new space age. Professor von Rauchhaupt surveys the works of Vitoria and Suarez and finds in them guidance for dealing with these problems. He points out that Hugo Grotius is generally regarded as the direct successor of the Spanish internationalists and frequently quoted them in his works. He then goes on to say:

> With Grotius, too, the emphasis remains on the law of war, but serving only as a means of obtaining the more pleasant condition of a final peace, which in turn would provide conditions under which an international and lawful community could be developed without hindrance.[55]

Professor von Rauchhaupt concludes his discussion with the remarks: "The final solution [for developing a law of space] will probably be based on the law of nature or even divine law, and will inevitably be guided by legal logic." [56]

[52] Reeves, *The Influence of the Law of Nations Upon International Law in the United States*, 3 AM. J. INT'L L. 547.

[53] 1 HACKWORTH, DIGEST OF INTERNATIONAL LAW 1 (1940).

[54] SCOTT, *op. cit. supra* note 24 at 105-06.

[55] Von Rauchhaupt, *A Light From the Past to Show Up the Legal Problems of Our Age of Space*, 1st Colloq. 2 (Vienna: Springer-Verlag, 1959).

[56] *Id.* at 3.

Unfortunately, there is no doubt that the strongest trend in international law today is only a self-serving, axiomatic law which is nothing more than positivist municipal law. Wars, colonialism, and strong nationalism throughout the world have thus overwhelmed the sound basis of international law for which Vitoria and others argued.

Such treatment as positivist jurists accord the foundation upon which international law is based—that is, regarding it as based on a mere system of mutable, man-made laws—is completely antithetical to the idea of law itself. Certainly, to disregard the law of nature and place wholly in its stead man's positive law is not a sound way for the world community to build its rules of conduct in opening the new frontier in space. It means accepting the structure and throwing out the foundation. Worse still, it means placing us in a position similar to that in which the Old World found itself on the discovery of the New World.

These views are also concurred in by the Brazilian scholar Valladão. "Will the planets and satellites which will be reached by man remain subject to the same juridical regime as the great European discoveries of the XVth and XVIth centuries?" he asks. The objective of discovery in that day, he reminds us, was merely to conquer, occupy, and subdue. And for centuries "International Law has been paying for this original sin." [57]

In this discussion we have been concerned primarily with the question of what gives law validity, and we have contrasted the basic positivist position, which maintains that validity originates from promulgation by governments, with the essential and elemental natural law position, which maintains that validity derives from accordance with fundamental moral principles arising from the nature of man. These positions are philosophically opposed. In practice, however, many specific rules of law may pass the tests of validity of both positions. Both positions also recognize one basic law-making process, although the natural law proponent recognizes the possibility of an invalid law resulting from such a process, and the positivist does not.

2–5 The process of formulation of law

The essence of the law-making process (at least for people in nations which are heirs to the Western constitutional democratic tradition) is that rules for proper conduct become obligatory, and therefore assume the character of law, when they are consented to by the people of the community which the rules are to govern. In the world in which we live, we are used to thinking of this as a conscious and formalized process, involving periodic elections, meetings of designated representatives, etc. But there is no *world government* to whose legislative and judicial branches

[57] Valladão, *The Law of Interplanetary Space*, 2d Colloq. 156, 163 (Vienna: Springer-Verlag, 1960).

we may look for pronouncements which constitute international law. The international procedure most similar to the national or municipal law-making process appears to be the treaty-making procedure, which does involve explicit, formal consent as expressed by governments. This procedure, however, is only the final step in the actual chronology of the formation of what we know as formal international law today. The tacit expression of consent through custom is a primary law-making process, developing rules which are regarded as binding by the community and which perform the functions of law in regulating human and national relationships.

It is acknowledged by all competent authorities on international law that the doctrine of custom or usage creating principles of international law is an ancient one. As Nys has pointed out, in every area of jurisprudence, custom or usage is the earliest form in which the positive law makes itself felt. Thus, to a very large extent, the art of legislation may be described as the codification of customs that already exist—and that tend to become stereotyped through legislative treatment. "No single treaty," Nys observes, "can have the value of a well-established custom as a guide to our knowledge of the law of nations either in itself or as interpreted by the international consciousness of a particular epoch." [58]

The role of the doctrine of custom and usage, coupled with the equally important doctrine of consent, is no less significant today than it was in the formative periods of the law of the sea or the law of the air. We shall examine in detail the development of new elements of international law—basic principles in the law of space—which were conceived and developed in an atmosphere of international consent and practiced as a customary usage in the recent expansion of space activity. In the following chapter, the doctrine of consent is discussed in detail. The fundamental principles we have been discussing here are identified as underlying the formation of the new law of the space age, and the history of the growth and development of a new space legal principle is traced in detail.

[58] Nys, *Development and Formation of International Law* (pts I & II), 6 Am. J. Int'l L. 1, 279 (1912).

Additional References

Andrew G. Haley, *Sovereignty in Space*, Review of Contemporary Law, Dec. 1960, p. 3; ——, *Space Exploration—The Problems of Today, Tomorrow and in the Future*, in Second Colloquium on the Law of Outer Space 44 (1960); ——, *The Law of Space and Outer Space*, 33 So. Cal. L. Rev. 370 (1960); reprinted in part, 10 L. Rev. Digest 77 (1960); ——, *Law of Outer Space—Practical Legal Rules for Human Conduct*, 16 Fed. Com. B.J. 163 (1959); ——, *Law and the Space Age*, 5 St. Louis U.L.J. 1 (1958); ——, *Law of Outer Space—A Problem for International Agreement*, 7 Am. U.L. Rev. 70 (1958); ——, *The Law of Outer Space: Scientific and Anthropocentric*

Considerations, 7 Avia/Vliegwereld 478 (1958); ——, *Space Law and Metalaw—Jurisdiction Defined,* 24 J. AIR L. & COM. 286 (1957); ——, *Space Law and Metalaw—A Synoptic View,* Harvard L. Record, Nov. 8, 1956, p. 1; ——, *The Present Day Developments in Space Law and the Beginnings of Metalaw,* Canadian Oil Journal, March, April, May 1957; ——, *Basic Concepts of Space Law,* 26 JET PROPULSION 951 (1956); *Metalaw—The Science of Universal Jurisprudence: The Third Essay:* Paper by ——, Before the Fourth Colloquium on the Law of Outer Space, International Institute of Space Law, XIIth International Astronautical Congress in Washington, D.C., Oct. 3, 1961; *Legal Problems of Outer Space Occupancy:* Address by ——, Forum of the International Society of Aviation Writers in United Nations, New York, April 23, 1958; *Jurisdiction Beyond the Earth:* Address by ——, Rotary Club of Charlotte in Charlotte, N.C., June 7, 1955; ——, *Comuniçôes na era espacial,* Astronáutica (Brazil), Maio-Junho, 1962, p. 2; ——, *El Derecho Interplanetario: Soberanía sobre el espacio extraterrestre,* Ingeniería Aeronáutica y Astronáutica (Spain), Mayo-Junio, 1959, p. 1.

National consent to overflight

Historically the control of air above the land has passed from the individual man, to his overlord, to the municipal government, and today it is vested in the state by municipal and international law alike. Passage through the superjacent air has become a privilege to be gained by treaty or denied by right. The development of international treaties on air passage, which has been confined to the twentieth century, is examined in detail in this chapter, and the growth of municipal and international law on the topic of control of airspace is traced. International custom and the doctrine of consent have long existed as basic principles upon which law is built. The doctrine of consent is traced as it developed in custom and usage during the International Geophysical Year. Through application of accepted practices, the nations of the earth have developed a new principle of international law—i.e., by common consent to an evolutionary step they have acknowledged that *outer space may be used for peaceful and scientific purposes without regard to the national sovereignty of subjacent territory.* An extension of this principle is found in recent developments directed toward the creation of satellite systems in the communications, meteorological, and radiation fields.

AIRSPACE SOVEREIGNTY: A BRIEF HISTORICAL SURVEY

3–1   The "ad coelum" doctrine

In an earlier discussion [1] of the international law relating to rights in airspace, we have seen that this law is not international—it is a hodge-podge of laws of individual nations which assert absolute sovereignty over

[1] Chapter 2 §2–4.

airspace. There have been a few pious declarations of international organizations hinting at the need for some sort of freedom of the air;[2] but there is really no such freedom. This matter needs to be discussed in detail because it has a direct bearing on space flight and the unmanned satellites of the earth.

Historically, the sovereign has always asserted exclusive, absolute dominion over the land and everything incident to the land, including the space above it. This has been the traditional civil law, as well as the private and public international law on the subject, and it is the law today. In England, for example, landowners were traditionally held to have extensive private rights of ownership of the air and subsurface areas; but these private rights were *granted* by the sovereign. They were based on a fundamental maxim[3] of English Common Law which provided generally that private ownership of land extended from the earth indefinitely up to the sky and indefinitely down into the earth.[4] In any event, these private rights could be asserted only against other private citizens, and the sovereign power in no sense parted with its paramount right to control the space above its territory. Today, moreover, the sovereign powers have withdrawn such private rights in most of the instances where they originally existed.

In effect, the maxim *cujus est solum ejus est usque ad coelum* ("whose is the soil, his it is up to the sky") applied satisfactorily as long as the activities of society remained as they were when the rule developed; but once lighter-than-air vehicles and aircraft came into use, it was soon realized that the doctrine was too restrictive. Large exceptions were then cut out of the rule, until an entirely distinct body of air law was developed. It is interesting to note, however, that while the individual property owner's right to exclude flights over his land has been severely limited,

[2] E.g., the Paris Convention of 1906, §3–2 (this chapter).

[3] "*Cujus est solum ejus est usque ad coelum.* Whose is the soil, his it is up to the sky. Co. Litt. 4a. He who owns the soil, or surface of the ground, owns, or has an exclusive right to, everything which is upon or above it to an indefinite height. 9 Coke 54; Shep. Touch. 90; 2 Bl. Comm. 18; 3 Bl. Comm. 217; Broom. Max. 395." "*Cujus est solum, ejus est usque ad coelum et ad inferos.* To whomsoever the soil belongs, he owns also the sky and to the depths. The owner of a piece of land owns everything above and below it to an indefinite extent. Co. Litt. 4." BLACK, LAW DICTIONARY 453 (4th ed. 1951). For a discussion of the Roman origins of this Common Law maxim see SCHICK, WHO RULES THE SKIES: SOME POLITICAL AND LEGAL PROBLEMS OF THE SPACE AGE, 4ff. (1961). Also see Cooper, *Roman Law and the Maxim Cujus est Solum in International Air Law,* 1 McGILL L.J. 23 (1955); VERPLAETSE, INTERNATIONAL LAW IN VERTICAL SPACE 95-99 (1960).

[4] Also see, however, the dictum in Pickering v. Rudd, 4 Camp. 219, 221; 171 Eng. Rep. 70 (N.P. 1815), by Lord Ellenborough that the flight of balloons over the property of others did not make the owners of the balloons liable to an action in trespass *quare clausum fregit* (wherefore he broke the close). Blackburn, as Judge, reacted by stating that he understood the good sense of Lord Ellenborough's doubt (in Pickering) "though not the legal reason for it." Kenyon v. Hart, S. 249, 252; 122 Eng. Rep. 1189 (K.B. 1865).

almost all nations lay claim to some power to exclude flights by foreigners over their territory.[5] This power is expressed in their statutory law, or is reserved by them in treaties.

The principle of *cujus solum* has been discarded for private property rights versus public interest in the airspace, i.e., aircraft transportation. Similar results will have to follow with respect to national sovereignty over outer space, where the doctrine of *cujus solum* must be abolished as unworkable and impractical.[6]

3–2   Early twentieth-century and World War I developments

International concern over the rights of governments in airspace became significant at the beginning of the twentieth century—approximately the time of the Wright brothers' first flight. In 1902 the Institute of International Law, meeting in Brussels, considered a proposed convention on the regulation of aerial navigation.[7] The proposal was drafted by Paul Fauchille, who presented it again in modified form to the 1906 meeting of the Institute. On that occasion he summarized his central thesis in the following terms: "The air is free, subject to the right of security and defense of the subjacent state." [8]

Fauchille would have made the air free to commerce and travel, just as is the sea. The provision for national security measures, while vague and indeterminate, was a reasonable reservation of sovereign rights to protect against civil negligence or hostile action through the air, but it was not intended that any nation should usurp the air completely. To be sure, the Fauchille proposal was never implemented in an international convention. It is significant, however, as being the first attempt at codification of the subject. It is also significant because it is one of the few times that the publicists have seriously considered "freedom of the air."

Certain provisions carrying out detailed aspects of the 1906 proposal were adopted when the Institute met again in 1911. Fauchille and L. von Bar prepared the basic document which required the marking of aircraft, and which attached the nationality of the country of registration to the aircraft.[9] Similar provisions have appeared in later international agreements on the use of airspace. The Paris Convention of 1919, for example, adopted the provisions suggested at the 1911 meeting of the Institute of International Law as to aircraft registry and nationality.

---

[5] Over 100 nations have claimed sovereignty over the superjacent airspace in their constitutions or statutes. See Chapter 4 §4–2.

[6] L & K Rep. 104, §613; Guldimann, *Cujus est solum eius est usque ad coelum,* 1 Zeitschrift für Luftrecht 213 (1952).

[7] 19 ANNUAIRE DE L'INSTITUT DE DROIT INTERNATIONAL 19-114, 335-37 (1902).

[8] 21 ANNUAIRE DE L'INSTITUT DE DROIT INTERNATIONAL 293, 295 (1906) (translation).

[9] ANNUAIRE DE L'INSTITUT DE DROIT INTERNATIONAL 23 (1911); *id.* at 303.

Fauchille's proposal was brushed aside by all nations during World War I, when each nation asserted its absolute dominion of space above its land. For most countries the maintenance of neutrality required such action. The Kingdom of The Netherlands was especially vocal in warning belligerent foreign aircraft away from the air over its territory, and in doing so it described on a number of occasions the legal nature of its sovereignty over its airspace. This nation was directly on the air route between Great Britain and Germany, over which the airplanes and zeppelins of the two nations traveled in bombing raids. The Netherlands coast was also close to the areas of naval warfare in the North Sea.

In August 1914, The Netherlands interned a German hydroplane which had been forced down in waters near its coast. The German government took the position that the aircraft was like a warship because (a) it was attached to a warship, and (b) it was in itself a war vessel while in the water. Germany argued that as a warship the hydroplane should be permitted by neutral Netherlands to be repaired within a certain time and then to leave the Netherlands area pursuant to international law of the sea. The Netherlands Minister of Foreign Affairs rejected these contentions and addressed a note to the German Government on September 11, 1914, which insisted that "airplanes, including hydroairplanes," were "things *sui generis* which do not fall within the application of the articles of the Proclamation of Neutrality dealing with the treatment of warships." The Minister then went on to argue that, since airplanes were not specifically granted the same status as warships in the Proclamation of Neutrality, they would have to be treated in accordance with "the general rule by virtue of which any part of the armed force of the belligerent is to be interned when it is found on the territory of the Netherlands." And he claimed that his position conformed strictly "to international law, *especially since no special treaty provision exists with respect to the treatment of belligerent aeroplanes on the territory of a neutral power.*" [10] (Emphasis supplied.)

The same rule was applied when the flight was not on a war mission. In 1915, The Netherlands interned a German aviator who had not been engaged in any aggressive operation, but had been on a training flight. The Netherlands denied a request of Germany for release of the pilot and airplane on the following grounds, which are worth quoting in full:

The great liberty of action of an airplane, the facility with which it reconnoiters and escapes all control, have necessitated in its respect a special and severe treatment. If an airplane is found above Netherlands territory it is immediately fired upon, the only means to force it to respect the neutrality

[10] Netherlands, Ministry of Foreign Affairs, Recueil de diverses communications du Ministre des Affaires Etrangères aux Etats-Généraux par rapport a la neutralité des Pays-Bas et au respect du droit des gens 144-45 (1916) (translation).

of the territory. If the aviator lands on territory of the Kingdom, whether of his own volition or in consequence of the firing or for any other reason, he is interned with his airplane.

The fact that the apparatus has flown over Netherlands territory or even that it has only landed there is sufficient cause for this measure.

Indeed the case where an aviator crosses the aerial frontier by mistake differs essentially from that of the soldier who crosses it by mistake on the ground. The circumstances in which the latter enters Netherlands territory permit the authorities guarding the frontier to find out whether or not his presence within the territory of the Kingdom is due to a mistake unconnected with military operations.

On the other hand the circumstances which have caused a belligerent aviator to land on Netherlands territory or to fly over it are not subject to ascertainment by Netherlands authorities. *That is why the Government cannot admit with respect to aviators any exception to the rule which prescribes their internment.* [Emphasis supplied.] [11]

In line with the position it had taken, The Netherlands government protested a flight of German zeppelins over The Netherlands on September 8, 1915, which arose because of navigational errors in foggy weather. The Netherlands note stated that the two zeppelins had apparently crossed the western frontier of the kingdom coming from the North Sea, and that they should immediately have sought to "regain that same maritime frontier"—despite the fact that in so doing they would have been going farther away from either German or German-occupied territory. The fact that they were clearly attempting to reach German-held territory by passing through Netherlands airspace was construed as a willful violation not only of the neutrality but also of the national sovereignty of The Netherlands. As the note observed: *"Flying over the territory of a state without its consent is incompatible with respect for its sovereignty."* [12] (Emphasis supplied.)

The next time this happened (February 1, 1916) The Netherlands, without previous warning, fired on the German zeppelin. Germany protested that by the airship's erratic actions The Netherlands should have known that the zeppelin was operating off course under *force majeure*. The Netherlands government replied to the effect that German airships should simply "keep themselves always far enough away" from Netherlands territory to avoid the possibility of passing over that territory either by navigational error or because of adverse weather conditions. The Netherlands claimed that a neutral power was in no way obligated to find out for itself precisely why "belligerent aerial forces" happened to be above its territory. And it continued:

In the interest of the defense of the state no less than in view of the maintenance of a strict neutrality a neutral power therefore has the right to oppose

11 *Id.* at 139-40 (translation).
12 *Id.* at 136-37 (translation).

forcibly all passage of its frontiers by belligerent airships unless they should indicate by a signal—white flag or other distinctive sign—their intention to land. Considerations of humanity may lead the authorities to resort to force only after having tried to warn the aviator that he is above neutral territory, but in view of the foregoing such notice is not obligatory. . . .[13]

As a result of this exchange, in December 1916 the two nations adopted a system of distress signals. The German government also agreed that in case of distress it would not object to the internment of the airship and its crew for the duration of the war, after landing in Netherlands territory.

The Netherlands also interned some United States aircraft and airmen during the war. Other neutral nations did likewise—notably Switzerland, Denmark, and Norway. The maritime nations, however, usually released aircraft personnel when they were rescued on the high seas and transported to neutral ports.[14]

As for the belligerent nations, there was no doubt during the war that the sovereign at war assumed absolute dominion over the airspace above its ground. This was usually asserted in a formal declaration. The United States, for example, was governed by the proclamation of President Wilson regulating civilian flying during World War I.[15]

3–3   From World War I to World War II

After World War I the law of absolute sovereignty over airspace was formalized in the Paris Convention for the Regulation of Air Navigation (1919),[16] which provided that ". . . every Power has complete and exclusive sovereignty over the air space above its territory."[17] The Convention defined "territory" as national land area, colonies, and adjacent territorial waters.

The Paris Convention of 1919 also established other significant provisions which pertain to the rights of nations to airspace. While granting "complete and exclusive sovereignty" to the individual nations, it required them to observe the following conduct:

1. Aircraft of foreign nations have freedom of "innocent passage" over national territory subject to certain regulations.
2. Regulations made by the sovereign as to flights over its territory shall apply without distinction among nations.
3. A sovereign may set up "prohibited zones," and foreign aircraft must

[13] Id. at 142-43 (translation).
[14] 1926 UNITED STATES NAVAL WAR COLLEGE INT'L L. SITUATIONS 100-01; 1 GARNER, INTERNATIONAL LAW AND THE WORLD WAR 471-83 (1920); 2 MERIGNHAC & LEMMONON, DROIT DES GENS ET LA GUERRE DE 1914-1918 409ff. (1921).
[15] Proclamation of Feb. 28, 1918 appended to §1042a, U.S. Comp. Stat. 1918 ed., embodying Title I, §1, Chapter 30 of the Espionage Act of June 15, 1917.
[16] 11 L.N.T.S. 173.
[17] Art. 1, 11 L.N.T.S. 190.

not fly over such zones. In case of violation of such prohibitions, foreign aircraft must give the international distress signal and land promptly.

4. No contracting state might, except by a special and temporary authorization, point the flight above its territory of an aircraft which does not possess the nationality of a contracting state.
5. The provisions of the 1911 meeting of the Institute of International Law as to aircraft registry and nationality were adopted in the Convention.
6. Military flights may not cross foreign airspace without the permission of the sovereign.
7. Transportation of munitions and explosives over foreign airspace is prohibited.[18]

The Paris Convention was an outgrowth of World War I and, in the opinion of some, it was an undesirable and unwise agreement because it reflected wartime philosophy. Albert Roper, for example, condemned "this brutal suppression of the freedom of the sky, so dear to eminent jurists in the early years of the century." Roper lamented the fact that while some governments had been "more liberal than others in the exercise of their right of sovereignty . . . not one has thought of renouncing it." Even those that had not signed the Convention had embodied the same spirit in their internal legislation—a situation that he attributed both to the effect of the world crisis in intensifying "the national spirit" and (to an even greater degree) "the terrible lessons of the war," which had brought home "the importance of the danger from the air. . . ."[19] In any event, the Paris Convention became binding on most of the nations of the world; and its philosophy is practically unchanged today.

The United States representative signed the Convention in 1920 with reservations permitting United States private aircraft to fly over "forbidden zones" in the United States, where foreign aircraft could not fly, and further allowing the United States to make agreements with Canada and any non-signing nations in the Western Hemisphere.[20] The latter provision was designed to reserve the United States' right to negotiate with other American nations if they did not ratify the Convention. The Convention was not ratified by the United States Senate, because of the provision which placed the administrative body, the International Commission for Air Navigation, under the League of Nations, to which the United States did not belong; nevertheless, United States observation of the terms of the Convention was effective on an unofficial basis.

As soon as the Paris Convention was signed, the prohibitions against flight of aircraft of non-signing nations over territory of the signers became burdensome. A protocol providing for exceptions to this provision

[18] 1 L.N.T.S. 173.
[19] Roper, *Recent Developments in International Aeronautical Law*, 1 J. AIR L. & COM. 395, 405-06 (1930).
[20] Telegram from Secretary of State Colby to U.S. Ambassador Wallace in Paris, No. 772, April 9, 1920 MS. Dep't of State file 579. 6D 1/486.

was ratified, and an amendment was made effective on October 27, 1922, which provided:

> No contracting State shall, except by a special and temporary authorization, permit the flight above its territory of an aircraft which does not possess the nationality of a contracting State, unless it has concluded a special convention with the State in which the aircraft is registered.[21]

In late 1922 and early 1923, the Commission of Jurists, appointed pursuant to a resolution adopted by the 1922 Washington Disarmament Conference, met at The Hague to prepare Rules of Aerial Warfare.[22] The Rules adopted at The Hague were not formalized as a treaty, but they are still of some interest. They provided, among other things, that belligerent military aircraft must not "enter the jurisdiction of a neutral State" (art. 40); and that a neutral government must first seek to prevent the entry of such aircraft and then use any means at its disposal "to compel them to alight if they have entered," after which the aircraft together with all the occupants should be interned (art. 42). The General Report of the Commission of Jurists explained that these provisions were limited to military aircraft because only in their case was the prohibiton of entry "absolute"—the entry of "private or public non-military aircraft" being left to the discretion of the neutral state. Only in two cases was any provision made for exceptions to the internment of belligerent military aircraft. One of these concerned flying ambulances. The other had to do with "aircraft on board a warship," which were deemed a part of the warship and were therefore to "follow the fate of that warship" on entering neutral ports or waters; if the warship entered under circumstances that made it immune to internment, the aircraft would likewise escape.[23]

In the Convention Relating to the Regime of the Straits signed at Lausanne, July 24, 1923, a special temporary provision setting forth the rights and duties of Turkey as a neutral power in time of war was agreed upon by the Balkan and Middle East nations which joined in the Convention. It read as follows:

> Military aircraft will receive in the Straits similar treatment to that accorded under the Thirteenth Hague Convention of 1907 to warships, pending the conclusion of an international convention establishing the rules of neutrality for aircraft.[24]

[21] 78 L.N.T.S. 439.

[22] COMMISSION OF JURISTS TO CONSIDER AND REPORT UPON THE REVISION OF THE RULES OF WARFARE, REPORT (1923); 1 HACKWORTH, DIGEST OF INTERNATIONAL LAW 45-46 (1940); MOORE, INTERNATIONAL LAW AND SOME CURRENT ILLUSIONS, AND OTHER ESSAYS 182 (1924).

[23] COMMISSION OF JURISTS TO CONSIDER AND REPORT UPON THE REVISION OF THE RULES OF WARFARE, REPORT 260-62 (1923). To like effect is Harvard Research in International Law, *Rights and Duties of Neutral States in Naval and Aerial War*, arts 95-97, in 83 AM. J. INT'L L. SPEC. SUPP. 764-69 (1939).

[24] 28 L.N.T.S. 115, 125.

The first major conference of private air law authorities after the end of World War I took place at Paris in 1925, when the International Technical Committee for Aerial Legal Experts (known as CITEJA from its French initials) was created. The work of the CITEJA dealt mostly with such matters as liability for damages caused by aircraft, and insurance coverage for passengers and property. Its work was not connected with international rights to aerial navigation, nor with sovereignty over air space; but the matters of private rights decided by the CITEJA applied only in nations where foreign air transportation had been authorized by the sovereign authority.

Although the United States, as already mentioned, was not an official participant in the Paris Convention of 1919, it adopted a national statute setting forth its claim of sovereignty over the airspace above its territory which was similar to the provisions of the Paris Convention. This was done in 1926 in the Air Commerce Act,[25] whose language is still retained in large part. The present statute is the Federal Aviation Act of 1958 and reads as follows:

> The United States of America is declared to possess and exercise complete and exclusive national sovereignty in the airspace of the United States, including the airspace above all inland waters and the airspace above those portions of the adjacent marginal high seas, bays and lakes, over which by international law or treaty or convention the United States exercises national jurisdiction. Aircraft of the armed forces of any foreign national shall not be navigated in the United States, including the Canal Zone, except in accordance with an authorization granted by the Secretary of State.[26]

An agreement similar to the Paris Convention of 1919, the Spanish-American Convention on Aerial Navigation, was signed by Spain and certain Latin American nations at Madrid on November 1, 1926.[27] This agreement followed substantially the provisions of the Paris Convention. It was not signed by the United States.

During this period the United States was also giving some consideration to questions of airspace sovereignty in time of war. Its attitude with regard to the role of neutrals was expressed in a message of September 1927 addressed by the Department of State to Commander Richard E. Byrd, which cited the then purely hypothetical case of the United States acting as a belligerent with Portugal as a neutral. The State Department asserted that under such conditions, "the mere landing" of a United States military plane in the Azores to refuel or make repairs would neither violate Portuguese neutrality nor warrant internment of the plane. The State Department message saw no reason, in fact, why "an airship of a belligerent Power on a long-range cruise would be entitled to less favora-

25 52 Stat. 1028 (1926).
26 72 Stat. 798 (1958) 49 U.S.C. §1508 (1958).
27 3 HUDSON, INTERNATIONAL LEGISLATION 2019 (1931).

ble treatment in a neutral port than would a man-of-war which ... is allowed to enter for a limited time for the purpose of refueling or making necessary repairs." On the other hand, the Department spokesman carefully refrained from expressing any opinion as to whether a military aircraft should be frankly "treated as a warship." [28]

The following year the republics of the Western Hemisphere (plus Spain) drew up a general agreement which was known as the Habana Convention.[29] This Convention served the purpose of uniting the nations of the Western Hemisphere which had abstained from ratifying the Paris Convention. The Habana Convention was ratified by the United States Senate, and it remained the supreme law of the Western Hemisphere on this subject until World War II.

The terms of the Habana Convention relating to national ownership and dominion over airspace provided for each contracting state in time of peace to accord freedom of innocent passage to the private aircraft of other contracting states—subject to certain conditions set forth in the Convention—and stipulated that the regulations adopted by any contracting state with regard to admission of aircraft of other contracting states over its territory should be "applied without distinction of nationality." [30] The American nations thus followed closely the terms of the Paris Convention. Both conventions limited flying rights to other contracting States and both left each of the contracting States with full power to deny the right of entry to aircraft of any non-contracting State. Still other terms of the Habana Convention recognized the right of sovereigns to set up restricted zones (provided that such zones were barred without discrimination among foreign nations) and the right of any two nations to conclude bilateral agreements.

The first bilateral agreement on air navigation entered into by the United States was with Canada in 1929.[31] This agreement dealt with the regulation of flights between the United States and Canada and certain other matters relative to flying personnel and equipment. The agreement was amended in 1938.[32]

In 1929 the Universal Postal Convention was signed at London. The Provisions Concerning the Transport of Postal Letters by Air were intended to permit unrestricted transportation by air of mail among nations. The United States assented to the provisions of this part of the Convention.[33]

[28] The Assistant Secretary of State (Castle) to Commander Richard E. Byrd, Sept. 30, 1927, MS., Dep't of State File 700.00111/-.

[29] Feb. 20, 1928, 47 Stat. 1901, T.S. No. 840.

[30] Id. art. 4.

[31] Agreement With Canada, Oct. 22, 1929, 47 Stat. 2575, E.A.S. No. 2.

[32] Air Navigation, Arrangement With Canada, July 28, 1938, 53 Stat. 1925, E.A.S. No. 129.

[33] Universal Postal Union, June 28, 1929, 46 Stat. 2523.

In 1929, at the insistence of Germany, all States which had joined in the Paris Convention of 1919 invited all non-member States to an extraordinary session to consider extensive amendments to the 1919 and 1922 conventions. The United States attended but did not enter into the Convention. Nevertheless, all of the original signatory nations except Persia agreed to the amendments, and the Convention was thus renewed.

The international conferences on aerial law which had been instituted by Fauchille and others in 1902 among private participants were revived with representatives of governments in attendance in the late 1920s and early 1930s. The Second International Diplomatic Conference on Private Air Law was held in 1929 at Warsaw, Poland. The conference dealt with the liability of air carriers for death or injury to passengers or damage or destruction of property. The United States agreed to the Warsaw Convention,[34] with certain modifications and reservations, and it thus became binding on United States aircraft owners and operators.

A Sanitary Convention for Aerial Navigation was concluded at The Hague in 1933. The Convention prescribed the actions which must be taken by aircraft if various diseases are detected in international flight. The United States Senate ratified this treaty in 1935.[35]

Participants in the Third International Conference on Private Air Law (Rome, 1933) agreed to two more conventions. The first was the Convention for the Unification of Certain Rules Relating to the Precautionary Attachment of Aircraft. Previously, aircraft in international flight might be attached as security for an alleged debt before a judgment was entered —a practice which frequently resulted in serious delay and other interruptions to international air transportation. The Convention did away with this type of inconvenience. The Rome meeting also adopted a Convention for Unification of Certain Rules Related to Damages Caused by Aircraft to Third Parties on the Surface, which limited the liability of the owner or operator of an aircraft but provided for reasonable compensation to the injured party. The Convention required the owner or operator of the aircraft to provide surety before invoking its provisions.

The United States Senate did not ratify the Rome Conventions. The question of defenses which could be asserted by insurers against claims for payment was the principal matter disputed by the United States. At the Fourth International Conference on Private Air Law held at Brussels in 1938 the United States objections were studied, and a protocol on this matter was produced at the Conference. However, the protocol was not satisfactory to the United States, which again failed to ratify the Convention.

In 1938 the United States enacted the Civil Aeronautics Act, which in

[34] Oct. 12, 1929, 49 Stat. 3000, T.S. No. 876.
[35] Aug. 12, 1933, 49 Stat. 3279, T.S. No. 901.

addition to regulating domestic aviation provided for the flight of commercial aircraft of foreign nations over the United States in accordance with authorizations issued by the Civil Aeronautics Board (then the Civil Aeronautics Authority).[36]

The United States concluded bilateral agreements with Canada and France in 1939 which governed the extensive international flying between the two North American neighbor nations and also the newly established trans-Atlantic commercial service.[37] The agreements provided for air routes and restrictions which would be mutual between the respective nations, so that carriers of one nation would not suffer unfair competitive disadvantages because of privileges granted to its own carriers by the other nation.

In 1939 the President of the United States issued an Executive Order regulating the flight of foreign and domestic aircraft in the Canal Zone. This was evidence of the United States' assertion of jurisdiction over airspace in the Canal Zone area. In the same year, however, a Panamanian court challenged the sovereignty of the United States in this area, claiming in reply, that the Republic of Panama had sovereignty over the airspace. The Department of State instructed the United States Ambassador to the Republic of Panama to call to the attention of that nation the fact that the United States had traditionally assumed jurisdiction over the airspace in the Canal Zone area pursuant to well-established international law.[38] The United States' sovereignty over Canal Zone airspace has not been challenged since that time.

Also in 1939 Great Britain called a conference at which a convention was adopted for exemption of liquid fuels and lubricants used in air commerce from taxation by foreign nations. The United States had not provided such exemption in the Revenue Act of 1932 [39] and desired four additions to be made to the text of the convention before it could be accepted. None of the four suggested changes was made, and the United States did not agree to the convention.

The outbreak of the Second World War in 1939 and the vital role played by aircraft in that conflict gave renewed significance to the legal rights of nations to the airspace above their territories. As in the previous conflict, this question was particularly important to the neutral countries. The general rule was that belligerent nations' aircraft could not enter the domain of a neutral country—and that domain included the airspace both above the land itself and above the adjacent territorial water of the neutral country. When the republics of the Western Hemisphere adopted

36 These provisions are now found in 72 Stat. 798 (1958), 49 U.S.C. §1508 (1958).
37 Agreement With Canada, Aug. 18, 1939, 54 Stat. 1805, E.A.S. No. 159; Agreement With France, July 15, 1939, 53 Stat. 2422, E.A.S. No. 153.
38 4 HACKWORTH, DIGEST OF INTERNATIONAL LAW 389-91 (1942).
39 47 Stat. 169, 266, §617.

a general declaration of neutrality at Panama on October 3, 1939, it thus
provided that they would:

> ... regard as a contravention of their neutrality any flight by the military
> aircraft of a belligerent state over their own territory. With respect to non-
> military aircraft, they shall adopt the following measures: such aircraft shall
> fly only with the permission of the competent authority; all aircraft, regardless
> of nationality, shall follow routes determined by the said authorities; their
> commands or pilots shall declare the place of departure, the stops to be
> made and their destination; they shall be allowed to use radiotelegraphy only
> to determine their route and flying conditions, utilizing for this purpose the
> national language, without code, only the standard abbreviations being al-
> lowed; the competent authorities may require aircraft to carry a co-pilot or a
> radio operator for purposes of control. Belligerent military aircraft transported
> on board warships shall not leave these vessels while in the waters of the
> American republics; belligerent military aircraft landing in the territory of
> an American republic shall be interned with their crews until the cessation
> of hostilities, except in cases in which the landing is made because of proven
> distress. There shall be exempted from the application of these rules cases in
> which there exist conventions to the contrary.[40]

There were press reports at this time to the effect that Germany was
claiming the right to fly over territory of The Netherlands and Belgium
at a height in excess of three miles, acting on the theory that national
sovereignty over the airspace is limited to a distance equal to the maritime
territorial belt.[41] The Netherlands firmly rejected this proposition and advised in 1939 that it considered "the air column over the Netherlands ...
an integral part of its territory up to an unlimited altitude." It announced
that "the flying, *at any altitude,* over Netherlands territory by belligerent
aircraft" would be regarded as a violation of its neutral status, and that
The Netherlands government would "employ all possible means for the
maintenance of its neutrality in the air." [42] (Emphasis supplied.)

There were a number of incidents during the war involving the various
neutrality rules and declarations. The United States permitted a Canadian
aircraft and crew to leave the United States following a forced landing on
its soil on March 9, 1940. The plane had been on a training flight when
it mistakenly entered the United States airspace.[43] Turkey interned four
American military planes with their crews, after forced landings in Turkey
in June 1942.[44] And France, having left the war, interned an American

---

[40] *Report of the Delegate of the United States of America to the Meeting of the
Foreign Ministers of the American Republics, Held at Panama, Sept. 23-Oct. 3, 1939,*
44 Dep't of State Conference Ser. 55-56 (1940).

[41] Kuhn, *Aerial Flights Above a Three-Mile or Other Vertical Limit By Belligerents
Over Neutral Territory,* 34 Am. J. Int'l L. 104 (1940).

[42] The Minister of The Netherlands (Loudon) to the Under Secretary of State
(Welles), Sept. 5, 1939, MS. Dep't of State File 740.00111 European War 1939/600.

[43] Att'y Gen'l Jackson to Sec'y Hull, March 11, 1940. MS Dep't of State File
842.248/83.

[44] MS. Dep't of State File 811.248.

Army plane which made a forced landing in French Guinea in May 1942.[45]

Canada enacted in 1939 and 1940 a number of wartime measures governing foreign air traffic over its territory. These included the Defence Air Regulations [46] which the United States treated as a suspension of prior agreements between the nations. As a result of such suspension, the United States ordered that Canadian aircraft must obtain advance entry permits before they could enter the United States. In the 1940 amendments to Canada's Defence Air Regulations [47] the objectionable provisions were eliminated, and the United States then rescinded its order requiring Canadian aircraft to obtain entry permits.

Toward the end of the Second World War in 1944, a Convention on International Civil Aviation was concluded in Chicago, Illinois. With respect to sovereignty over airspace the Convention explicitly recognized that "every state has complete and absolute sovereignty over the airspace above its territory." [48] The term "territory," under the Convention, was defined as "the land areas and territorial waters adjacent thereto under the sovereignty, suzerainty, protection or mandate of such state." [49]

As is evident from its title, the Chicago Convention pertains only to civil aircraft. However, it further declared in Article 8 that "no aircraft capable of being flown without a pilot shall be flown without a pilot over the territory of a contracting state without special authorization by that state and in accordance with the terms of such authorization." [50] This would clearly apply to pilotless aircraft, if such were operated as civil aircraft within the airspace, but it does not apply to guided missiles or satellites in trajectory or orbiting beyond the airspace. The latter do not meet the definition of "aircraft" as set out in Annex 7 of the Chicago Convention and, therefore, would not fall within the limitations of Article 8. This Convention—the most recent major international agreement concerning civil aviation—has been ratified by sixty-seven nations,[51] and it is in force today. Among the nations which have not ratified the

---

[45] MS. Dep't of State File 811.2351 T.

[46] 1939 P.C. 2483 (Can.).

[47] 1943 P.C. 1890 (Can.).

[48] 61 Stat. 1180 (1947), T.I.A.S. No. 1591 (1947).

[49] *Id.*, art. 2.

[50] See generally Machowski, *The Legal Status of Unmanned Space Vehicles*, 2d Colloq. 110-11 (Vienna: Springer-Verlag, 1960).

[51] The states which have ratified the Convention are: Afghanistan, Argentina, Australia, Austria, Belgium, Bolivia, Brazil, Burma, Ceylon, Canada, Chile, China (Taiwan), Colombia, Cuba, Czechoslovakia, Denmark, Dominican Republic, Ecuador, El Salvador, Ethiopia, Finland, France, Greece, Guatemala, Haiti, Honduras, Iceland, India, Indonesia, Iran, Iraq, Italy, Ireland, Israel, Japan, Jordan, Korea, Laos, Lebanon, Libya, Liberia, Luxembourg, Mexico, Morocco, Netherlands, New Zealand, Nicaragua, Norway, Pakistan, Paraguay, Peru, Philippines, Poland, Portugal, Spain, Sweden, Switzerland, Syria, Thailand, Turkey, Union of South Africa, United Arab Republic. United Kingdom, USA, Uruguay, Venezuela, and Viet Nam. Air Laws 1402-07.

Convention are the U.S.S.R., China (Mainland), Hungary, and Bulgaria.

Simultaneously with the Chicago Convention in 1944, the International Air Services Transit Agreement was drawn up and signed.[52] The Transit Agreement was not signed nor ratified as a treaty. It was never submitted to the United States Senate for ratification and its status is certainly that of an "executive" agreement. The Transit Agreement, therefore, could not affect State sovereignty, as formally recognized in Article 1 of the Chicago Convention, and in the Air Commerce Act of 1926 and the Civil Aeronautics Act, insofar as the United States is concerned. Under this agreement each of the contracting states grants to the other contracting states, in respect to scheduled international air service by civil aircraft, the privilege to fly across its territory without landing and also the privilege to land for non-traffic purposes, subject to the payment of reasonable fees for the use of airports and other facilities.[53] No clause of the agreement restricts the sovereignty of the states over airspace as established in the Chicago Convention. Fifty-six states are now parties to this agreement.[54]

Commenting on the Convention on International Civil Aviation, several writers have observed that the doctrine of absolute sovereignty over airspace is now firmly imbedded in international law.[55] Indeed, "it may certainly be now accepted as the primary rule of the international law of the air, and must be considered by any world organization." [56]

3–4 Post-war developments

Since the signing of the Chicago Convention no similar international agreements of its scope and general nature have been executed, although in the field of space activities, several significant international agreements have been entered into by a number of nations.

In 1948 the Convention on the International Recognition of Rights in Aircraft was completed and signed on June 19, at Geneva.[57] Known as the "Mortgage Convention," this agreement concerned only aircraft and in no way affected any thinking on the problems of sovereignty or consent with respect to upper national limits.

During the 1950s the international scene was often brightened by new vistas of international scientific cooperation. The International Geophysi-

[52] Dec. 7, 1944, 84 U.N.T.S. 389, 50 Stat. 1693, E.A.S. No. 487.
[53] *Id.*, art. 1.
[54] TREATY AFFAIRS STAFF, OFFICE OF THE LEGAL ADVISOR, DEP'T OF STATE, TREATIES IN FORCE 210 (1962).
[55] Cooper, *Air Transport and World Organization*, 55 YALE L. J. 1190, 1195 (1946); Rhyne, *International Law and Air Transportation* 47 MICH. L. REV. 41, 43 (1948).
[56] Cooper, *op. cit. supra* note 55 at 1195.
[57] [1953] 1 U.S.T. & O.I.A. 830, T.I.A.S. No. 2847.

cal Year (IGY) was the principal highlight of this type of activity. Other significant events were the establishment of a Committee on the Peaceful Uses of Outer Space in the United Nations and the formation by the International Council of Scientific Unions (ICSU) of the Committee on Space Research (COSPAR). Similarly, in the decade of the fifties the International Astronautical Federation was born and grew rapidly to keep pace with the swift developments in astronautics.

On December 1, 1959, an important international agreement, the Antarctic Treaty, was signed in Washington, D.C. by representatives of twelve nations.[58] Providing as it does for international scientific cooperation in exploring the continent, while carefully skirting the problem of conflicting territorial claims, it has since been the subject of much writing by legal experts. To some, the Antarctic Treaty holds great promise as a source of inspiration for international cooperation in space. Seen in proper perspective, however, this document would appear to have much the same value for the development of a space legal structure as the law of the sea and the law of the air. Attempting a carry-over of these anthropocentric, earth-bound, and largely joint-municipal laws into a situation of entirely new and largely unrelated parameters is not the way to establish a legal structure in space. Neither the blanket extension of "international law" nor a labored extension of analogies to existing laws will do.[59] New and extensive structures must and will emerge and then, hopefully, the fundamental principles of the space legal order will not be the same self-serving municipal enactments intended to regulate men on earth.

An important first step toward this necessary objective was the achievement of the International Geophysical Year, with the resulting principle of free use of outer space for peaceful and scientific purposes. However, before discussing in detail the IGY program and its potential significance for the development of space law, it will be helpful to review briefly the history of the doctrine of consent in international law.

[58] See Appendix I-A.
[59] "All points of similarity . . . revealed between space danger and air danger do not, however, afford sufficient ground for applying the rules of air law to the Cosmos. Application of the latter would mean little less than recognition of each country's 'complete and exclusive' sovereignty over the cosmic sector above it. In the practical sense this would mean that the entire programme of scientific space exploration could be thwarted by the protests of just a single country over which the earth satellite might fly. . . . Therefore, one is bound to agree with A. Haley who says that the problems facing mankind in conquering the Cosmos 'are by their very nature different from those which concern maritime and air navigation, and possess little analogy to maritime or air law.'" Korovin, *International Status of Cosmic Space*, Symp. 1062, 1964.

THE ROLE OF CONSENT
IN THE INTERNATIONAL LAW-MAKING PROCESS

3–5   *Consent as expressed through custom*

The frequent use of the words "custom" and "usage" interchangeably in international law has sometimes led to a need for definition. J. L. Kunz clarifies matters by pointing out that customary international law is comprised of two elements, usage and *opinio juris,* the latter representing the conviction of the nation taking the action that it is doing so legally.[60] Usage, says Kunz, consists of a practice, whether of positive acts or omissions, continued and repeated without interruption and applied by the overwhelming majority of states which hitherto had an opportunity of applying it.[61] Still another legal writer refers to customary law as law developed by the repetition of acts.[62]

The leading publicists have discussed the effect on international law of both usage and consent.[63] Grotius taught that natural law existed without a law-giving authority and contrasted this with the positive law which proceeded from varied external sources. Positive law he divided into divine law, whose source was the church; civil law, whose source was the legislatures; and *jus gentium* (the law of nations), whose source was the will of all nations or of the many, expressed in the wide and persistent usage or the consent of such nations.[64] Gaius also contrasted *jus civile,* the civil law, which he taught was the dictate of enlightened reason, with *jus gentium,* the product of common consent.[65]

In 1758 the Italian publicist, Emeriche de Vattel, expounded his belief that a substantial portion of international law was based on the consent of nations, whether presumed, expressed, or tacit. As an illustration of international law founded on tacit consent de Vattel pointed out that

[60] Kunz, *The Nature of Customary International Law,* 47 Am. J. Int'l L. 662 (1953). These two elements are also distinguished in Case of the SS Lotus, P.C.I.J. ser. A. No. 10 at 18 (1927); Accioly, Manual de Dereito Internacional Publico 20 (4th ed. Brazil 1958); Hudson, The Permanent Court of International Justice 1920-1942 20 (1943); Korovin, in Mezhdunarodnoe Pravo (International Law) 8 (Kozhevnikov ed. USSR 1957); Verdross, Völkerrecht 84 (4th rev. & enl. ed. Austria 1959).

[61] Kunz, *op. cit. supra* note 60 at 666.

[62] Kopelmanas, *Custom as a Means of Creation of International Law,* 18 Brit. Yb. Int'l. 127 (1937).

[63] See, for example, Oppenheim, 1 International Law 15 (New York: Longmans, Green & Co., Lauterpacht ed., 8th ed., 1955; Courtesy of David McKay Company, Inc.). Here the writer states that "common consent is the basis of all law," and explains that it can "only mean the express or tacit consent of such an overwhelming majority of the members that those who dissent are of no importance."

[64] Lawrence, The Principles of International Law 33 (7th ed., rev. by Winfield, 1923).

[65] *Ibid.*

since devastation of territory and slaughter of peaceful inhabitants had occurred rarely in recent years it had become established in international law that such conduct was forbidden.[66]

The 17th and 18th centuries produced certain legal scholars, among the most prominent of whom are Samuel Rachel, Johann Wolfgang Textor, C. von Bynkershock, Frederick Carl von Moser, and G. F. van Martens, commonly referred to as belonging to the school of "positivism." [67] This school taught that international law is the sum of the rules by which states have *consented to be bound* and that such consent could be given expressly, as in a treaty, or by implication. S. Pufendorf, Rachel, and Heinrich Triepel all regarded custom as a means of expressing tacit consent.[68]

The courts have also recognized that a principle of international law could be established by the common consent of nations. A judicial decision of 1871, in a case involving a collision of a British and an American ship,[69] held that the pertinent rules of navigation having been accepted as obligatory by more than thirty of the principal commercial states of the world, these rules became the law of the sea. The court, taking notice that by common consent these rules had been acquiesced in as a general obligation, stated:

> Undoubtedly, no single nation can change the law of the sea. . . . Like all the laws of nations, it rests upon the common consent of civilized communities. It is of force, not because it was prescribed by any superior power, but because it has been generally accepted as a rule of conduct. . . . And it is evident that unless general assent is efficacious to give sanction to international law, there never can be that growth and development of maritime rules which the constant changes in the instruments and necessities of navigation require.[70]

In a much earlier case, the Supreme Court of the United States held that the slave trade had become legal in international law through the general assent of a large portion of the world. Chief Justice John Marshall noted in this decision that "that which has received the assent of all, must be the law of all," and while each nation might renounce the principle for its own people, it could not do so for people in other nations.[71]

The effect of consent and usage was discussed again at the turn of the century in the case of the *Paquete Habana*,[72] involving the action of the United States in capturing Spanish fishing vessels off Cuba, during the war with Spain. The decision handed down in this case held that by the

---

[66] *Id.* at 37.
[67] Borchard, *International Law*, 7 ENCYC. SOC. SCI. 169 (1944).
[68] NUSSBAUM, A CONCISE HISTORY OF THE LAW OF NATIONS 232 (Revised ed. 1954).
[69] *The Scotia*, 81 U.S. (14 Wall.) 170 (1871).
[70] *Id.* at 187-88.
[71] *The Antelope*, 23 U.S. (10 Wheat.) 66, 121-22 (1825).
[72] 175 U.S. 677 (1899).

general consent of the civilized nations of the world, and independently of any express treaty or other public act, it was an established rule of international law that coastal fishing vessels, unarmed and honestly pursuing their peaceful calling, were exempt from capture as prizes of war. Such a rule, said the court, was founded "by an ancient usage among civilized nations . . . gradually ripening into a rule of international law." [73] Then, in words which might someday be used in regard to satellites, it added:

> By the practice of all civilized nations, vessels employed only for the purpose of discovery or science are considered as exempt from the contingencies of war, and therefore not subject to such capture. It has been usual for the government sending out such an expedition to give notice to other powers; but it is not essential.[74]

In the majority of these cases it can be seen that the consent of which the courts speak is the tacit consent expressed by usage. Adherence to international awards of arbitral tribunals and to the judicial rulings of international courts is a further example of the expression of tacit consent. While there is usually no express treaty provision to the effect that such decisions are binding upon the parties, they are considered declaratory of an existing rule of positive law developed through custom.[75] Custom is in fact the source of most of our existing international law. As Charles G. Fenwick has pointed out, the "great body of international law" is the result not of "legislative enactment" but of "informal agreement," by which he means "the slow process of common usage." He observes that from both a legal and a political standpoint the various nations "are no more than a group of independent units voluntarily agreeing to observe certain rules to which they have given their implied or express consent." These rules, furthermore, rest on "a purely contractual basis" that Fenwick believes is chiefly to be found in "the practices of nations which have been followed with sufficient regularity and consistency as to take the form of fixed custom." [76]

Customary law is as much a positive, man-made law as is treaty law.[77] Treaty and custom are merely two different ways of showing the consent of a nation to a particular action. Often treaties and conventions merely go to show "the existence of general usage which the parties wished to

---

[73] *Id.* at 686.

[74] *Id.* at 709.

[75] Hudson, International Tribunals 124 (1944).

[76] Fenwick, *The Sources of International Law,* 16 Mich. L. Rev. 393, 394-395 (1918).

[77] Kunz, *The Nature of Customary International Law,* 47 Am. J. Int'l L. 662, 665 (1953); *but see* Korovin in Mezhdoravodnoe Pravo (International Law) 8-9 (Kozhevnikov ed., USSR 1957); Minjasian, Istochniki Sovremenh 090 Mezhdunarodnogo Prava (Sources of Contemporary International Law) (USSR 1960).

record for convenience . . . or the dissatisfaction of the parties with existing usage and their desire to improve on it. . . ." [78]

When the agreement of several nations is embodied in a treaty, it is
needless to look elsewhere for an expression of their consent. When the
consent is not formally expressed, one may then look for it in the "usage"
of customary law. As one court has said, "With respect . . . to customary
law, *in so far as it should arise without any agreement at all,* an actual
practice is presupposed, which must be continued and permanent. . . ." [79]

There is nothing about a formal treaty which makes it sacrosanct—
which makes it even an essential source of international law.[80] A treaty is
merely a formal expression of the will of the contracting states—a formal
method by which the nations involved show their consent to some act or
agreement or series of acts and agreements. In many instances the principle set forth in the treaty itself may have been established in international law long before the signing of the formal document itself.[81]
Indeed, there are principles of international law which have never been
embodied in treaty form but are nonetheless valid; and, by the same token,
the mere fact that some purported rule of international law has been
enacted in a treaty does not automatically give it validity.[82]

3–6   Time required to establish consent

In most instances the consent of nations to a principle of international
law is not formally expressed but is shown by a period of usage, normally
extending over a long period of time. However, as Kunz has stated, "International law contains no rules as to how many times or for how long a
time . . . [a] practice must have been repeated." [83] In this connection,
Kunz argues that the now generally accepted rule of customary international law concerning the sovereignty of subjacent states over the airspace actually developed, "contrary to the preceding proposals of the
science of international law, during the First World War." [84]

A closely related question is that posed by another author who asks,
"What is the legal nature of the first act which by repetition accompanied

[78] Pollock, *The Sources of International Law,* 2 COLUM. L. REV. 511 (1902).
[79] Lubeck v. Mecklenburg-Schwerin, Staatsgerichtshof (Ger.) reported and translated in 1 HACKWORTH, DIGEST OF INTERNATIONAL LAW 15 (1940).
[80] See Kunz, *op. cit. supra* note 77. The author there points out that many international lawyers have concentrated their studies since 1920 nearly exclusively on the
particular international law of the League of Nations, and today the United Nations,
ignoring the transformation of customary general law which is taking place.
[81] Pollock, *op. cit. supra* note 78 at 511.
[82] Morgenthau, *Positivism, Functionalism, and International Law,* 34 AM. J. INT'L L.
260, 276 (1940). Note also the adoption of our position by Lall in *Space Exploration
—Some Legal and Political Aspects,* 2d Colloq. 75, 79-81.
[83] Kunz, *op. cit. supra* note 77 at 666.
[84] *Ibid.*

by the required *opinion* may in the course of time develop into custom?" [85]
The same writer concludes that "in most instances it is a waiver of a
right," but notes that "the space of time required for the formation of
custom is dependent upon the length of time during which the conditions
giving rise to such a custom are in existence." [86]

As to the period of usage needed to establish a principle of law, still
another writer first points out that for one nation to revoke without
cause privileges that it has granted to a second nation "by tacit consent"
may be just as injurious as the breaking of a treaty. He then cites the
example of transit privileges given to the troops of another nation. Such
privileges may be granted by treaty, in which case they at once become
a right or they may be granted by tacit consent—that is, by continuing
permission of the practice without protest—in which case they again become a right that cannot be altered unilaterally. And he proceeds to the
heart of the problem:

> It may, however, be difficult to say when such obligations begin, for in-
> stance, when transit, silently suffered, becomes a kind of servitude on the soil.
> There is a difference, also, in usages. Mere forms of intercourse may have
> little binding force, but principles admitted in common in a silent way, and
> giving birth to common habits, as well as mutual privileges conceded without
> treaty, appeal to the moral sense of nations. [87]

In a similar vein, Fenwick, after first calling attention to the difficulty
of deciding how numerous or how frequent a series of acts must be in
order to show "general acceptance" of some rule of international law, goes
on to emphasize that there has been no "central court of the nations" to
settle the question. "What adds to the difficulty," he suggests, "is that the
number of nations being relatively small there have been too few cases . . .
to make it possible to deduce a common rule. . . ." [88]

There is in any event, no rule in international law which would require
that consent, clearly shown, must be fortified by prolonged usage. Long
ago Triepel recognized that under certain conditions one single act of
international practice based on usage might suffice for a rule of international law. [89] Normally a long period of usage has been required before
a principle could become established as a part of international law, but
this is so only because in most cases the consent of nations could not be

[85] Silving, *"Customary Law": Continuity in Municipal and International Law*, 31
Iowa L. Rev. 614, 624 (1946).

[86] *Id.* at 625. Here the writer referred to Dixon, Irmaos & Cia v. Chase Nat'l Bank,
144 Fed. 2d 759 (1944), where the court found a custom of sending a bill of lading
by air to exist. He pointed out that obviously the custom had to be fairly new since air
mail service itself was fairly new.

[87] T. D. Woolsey, International Law 26-27 (T. S. Woolsey ed., 6th ed. 1901).

[88] Fenwick, *op. cit. supra* note 76 at 395.

[89] This view is mentioned in the case cited, *supra* note 79.

ascertained by other nations except over a long period of years. It has been pointed out that during the Middle Ages, for example, the sovereign states that existed "were so widely separated geographically, and engaged in so little intercourse of any sort, that there was no need of rules governing their relations" [90]—nor was there much need to ascertain the manner in which other sovereigns were conducting their affairs.

Poor communications long made it difficult for one nation to learn of the activity of another, and so there was little opportunity to express either consent or non-consent to such conduct. Indeed, it required several years before a large number of nations were faced with, or affected by, the same problem. The present situation, however, is entirely different. An earth satellite will pass over numerous countries in a period of hours and these nations are immediately aware of the launching. Knowledge of the impending launching may even have been available for a considerable time prior to the actual event. In view of this, the nations could be expected to express their consent—or non-consent—in a timely manner.

It must be noted here, in conclusion, that the doctrine of consent as discussed in the last two sections of this chapter has met with criticism by some legal writers. Several authors have criticized the doctrine by arguing that a newly created nation is bound by established international law from the date of such a nation's establishment, in spite of the fact that it does not give its consent. This is true. But this is merely confusing the *origin* or *establishment* of international law with the *obligatory* force of international law. There is no inconsistency in holding that international law may be *established* by the consent of the many nations and then holding that nations established later should be *bound* by it irrespective of their consent. The international law, therefore, is binding upon all civilized states irrespective of their individual consent, and no one state can by its own act release itself from the obligation. In other words, consent is the legislative process of international law, though it is not the source of legal obligation. A rule once established by consent (which need not be universal) is binding because it has become a part of the general law, and it can then no longer be repudiated by the action of individual states.[91]

With this discussion of the role of consent and its accepted binding effect, we are now in a position to examine the contribution made by the International Geophysical Year to the development of the law of space. As this writer first pointed out, in a paper delivered in November 1955,

[90] 30 Am. Jur. *International Law* §8 (Rochester: Lawyers Co-operative Publishing Company, 1958).

[91] 1 Hackworth, International Law 5 (1940), quoting Smith, Great Britain and the Law of Nations 12 (1932). For a clarifying discussion of the confusion that has arisen over the use of various terms such as "consent" in international law see Corbett, *The Consent of States and the Sources of the Law of Nations*, 6 Brit. Yb. Int'l L. 20 (1925).

the nations of the earth merely by their acceptance of the IGY satellite
program had set in motion the international law-making process.[92] The
historical development of the IGY, and the manner in which a new principle was established through consent, must now be set forth in detail.

THE INTERNATIONAL GEOPHYSICAL YEAR
AND THE DEVELOPMENT OF THE LAW OF SPACE

3-7   The IGY: organization—purpose—scope

In the light of the untrammeled nationalist sovereignty now prevalent,
the inauguration of the unmanned earth satellite activities stands out as
perhaps the most felicitous incident of the present generation. The entire
program could have been stopped by the protest of a solitary sovereign
nation over which a satellite might pass. The program could have been
endlessly delayed by making it the subject of detailed international negotiation and final understanding. Its inauguration in a peaceful and un-
complicated manner is thus a great achievement of scientists throughout
the world, and the background of this epochal event deserves extended
commentary.

International cooperation in the study of our physical environment was
not, of course, an entirely new phenomenon. The importance of geophysical data gathered over relatively remote areas of the earth was recognized
in the last century in the conduct of the First International Polar Year, in

---

[92] Cooper, in *Legal Problems of Upper Space*, Symp. 66, 70, referred to the up-
coming earth satellite flight during the IGY, saying:

> Two authorities have already dealt with the legal problems of this flight. Mr.
> Andrew G. Haley, General Counsel of the American Rocket Society, presented a
> paper at the annual meeting of that Society in November, 1955, in which he seemed
> to suggest that the areas of space above the atmosphere to be used by the satellite
> might be subject to some sovereign control of the subjacent states, but that failure
> of any state to object to the International Geophysical Year satellite program at
> the time of its announcement was all that was required in order to make the
> completion of the program possible.

Yeager and Stark, in *Decatur's Doctrine—A Code for Outer Space?*, Symp. 156, 162,
survey "what some of the other leading thinkers in the field are saying" about the
rules that are most likely to develop for the utilization of outer space. In this discussion they state:

> Andrew G. Haley, General Counsel for the American Rocket Society, former
> counsel for the Federal Communications Commission and legal advisor to the
> International Telecommunications Conference, takes the position that the failure of
> any nation to object to the satellite program of the International Geophysical Year
> amounts to a tacit world agreement to treat space at the announced satellite distance
> as "free." He suggests that this agreement has had actual legal impact and will
> make difficult any future attempts to assert rights in space above the atmosphere.

These authors find an almost complete unity of view among public officials and
lawyers in favor of freedom of outer space, and they endorse this view themselves.

1882-83, when meteorological, magnetic, and auroral stations were first established in Arctic regions. A Second International Polar Year was held in 1932-33, fifty years later; and these two international endeavors contributed greatly to our knowledge of the earth's magnetism and of the ionosphere. The IGY, however, was in every sense a much larger undertaking. Its directing body, the Special Committee for the International Geophysical Year—known as CSAGI from its French initials—had a membership composed of representatives of the International Council of Scientific Unions, the International Astronomical Union, the International Union of Geodesy and Geophysics, the International Scientific Radio Union, the International Union of Pure and Applied Physics, the International Union of Geography, and the World Meteorological Organization. Through these other organizations, the Joint Commission of the Ionosphere and the Joint Commission on Solar and Terrestrial Relationships were also represented.

The CSAGI held a provisional meeting in October 1952, when it asked all countries to form national committees for the IGY and to submit recommendations as to the program that should be carried out. The first plenary sessions of the CSAGI took place at Brussels, Belgium, in July 1953. At this meeting the program proposals of 26 collaborating nations were taken under consideration, resulting in the establishment of a tentative outline for the basic IGY program. The various national committees then set to work on detailed planning of the activities that were to make up those parts of the over-all IGY program for which they would be responsible. In late September and early October of 1954, some 38 nations that had already prepared detailed programs were represented at a CSAGI meeting held in Rome to discuss these separate programs and integrate them with one another. The Rome meeting produced a basic plan for IGY activities which was adopted by all the delegations present.[93]

The scientific mission of the IGY, as evolved through these and other international gatherings, was well expressed in a report issued in August 1955 by the United States National Committee for the International Geophysical Year (USNC–IGY):

> The principal fields of study during the IGY will be solar activity, longitude and latitude, glaciology, oceanography, meteorology, geomagnetism, aurora and airglow, ionospheric physics, seismology and gravity, cosmic rays and upper atmosphere rocket studies, including the use of instrumented satellite vehicles. Inherently, these fields are characterized by their global nature. The chemist or the physicist can perform experiments in his laboratory, establishing the conditions of these experiments. The laboratory of the geophysicist is the Earth itself and the experiments are performed by nature; his task must be to observe these natural phenomena on a global basis if he is to secure solutions and to develop adequate theoretical explanations. This is one of the compelling reasons for the world-wide scope of the IGY in 1957-58:

[93] United States National Committee for the International Geophysical Year, *United States Program for the International Geophysical Year 1957-1958* (1955) at vii-viii.

to observe geophysical phenomena and to secure data from all parts of the world; to conduct this effort on a coordinated basis by field and in space and time so that the results secured not only by American observers, but by participants of other nations, can be assembled together in a meaningful manner. Only through such an enterprise as the IGY can synoptic data be satisfactorily and economically acquired.[94]

Ultimately, at least 64 nations undertook to assist in the IGY program, namely:

Argentina, Australia, Austria, Belgium, Bolivia, Brazil, Bulgaria, Burma, Canada, Ceylon, Chile, China (Taiwan), Colombia, Cuba, Czechoslovakia, Denmark, Dominican Rep., E. Africa, Ecuador, Egypt, Ethiopia, Finland, France, all of Germany, Ghana, Greece, Guatemala, Hungary, Iceland, India, Indonesia, Iran, Ireland, Israel, Italy, Japan, Dem. Rep. Korea, Malaya, Mexico, Mongolian People's Rep., Netherlands, New Zealand, Norway, Pakistan, Panama, Peru, Philippines, Poland, Portugal, S. Rhodesia, Romania, Spain, Sweden, Switzerland, Tunisia, U. of S. Africa, USSR, UK, US, Uruguay, Venezuela, Vietnam Dem. Rep., Rep. of Vietnam, Yugoslavia.[95]

The People's Republic of China (Mainland), originally listed as a participant, withdrew from formal collaboration when the Nationalist Chinese Government was recognized as a participating member. However, activities on the mainland continued to be associated with the IGY program on an informal basis.

The other nations remained as formal participants; and their contributions, though naturally varying in magnitude, involved wide use of both governmental and nongovernmental resources. Active participation in the program was required of each nation, of its army, navy, air force, and coast guard personnel and facilities; of such governmental agencies as those concerned with standards, radar, radio, meteorology, coast and geodectic surveys, geological surveys, and all types of official scientific and research organizations. In addition, parallel, non-official institutions were involved, including universities and observatories in those few countries where such institutions are not controlled by the state, and, by agreeing to support actively the satellite program, the various nations also agreed to the legal validity of that project.

Initially the CSAGI did not provide for a special Rocket Group, much less a satellite program. However, the importance of upper atmosphere investigations was emphasized at the XIth General Assembly of URSI (i.e., International Scientific Radio Union, one of the participating members of CSAGI) which was held at The Hague, August 23 to September 3, 1954.[96]

[94] *Id.* at viii.
[95] United States National Committee for the International Geophysical Year, National Academy of Sciences, Release, Sept. 2, 1955.
[96] Report to the National Research Council, USA National Committee of the URSI on the XIth General Assembly of the URSI at The Hague, Aug. 23-Sept. 3, 1954, Submitted to Dr. William W. Rubey, Chairman, National Research Council, Oct. 18, 1954, by A. H. Waynick, Chairman, USA National Committee of URSI.

A highly significant report on investigations of the ionosphere was submitted to this assembly on August 28, 1954, by Prof. S. Fred Singer of the United States, who was also a strong advocate of satellite experimentation. Moreover, the General Assembly of URSI adopted a series of resolutions which included the following item:

14. *Study of solar radiation in the upper atmosphere.* URSI recognizes the extreme importance of continuous observations, from above the E region, of extraterrestrial radiations, especially during the forthcoming [International Geophysical Year].

URSI therefore draws attention to the fact that an extension of present isolated rocket observations by means of instrumented earth satellite vehicles would allow the continuous monitoring of the solar ultraviolet and X radiation intensity and its effects on the ionosphere, particularly during solar flares, thereby greatly enhancing our scientific knowledge of the outer atmosphere.[97]

Following the URSI meeting at The Hague in August 1954, a meeting of CSAGI was held in Rome, September 30 to October 4, 1954. At this meeting a Rocket Group (Working Group XI) was formed, consisting of H. E. Newell, Jr. (USA), Chairman; J. Debrach (Morocco); N. C. Gerson (USA); T. Gold (Great Britain); R. Montalbetti (Canada); M. Nicolet (CSAGI); D. R. Ramanathan (India); S. F. Singer (USA); and K. Rawer, observer. This group proceeded to outline a Rocket Program for the IGY, and in its minutes there appeared an entry giving explicit support to the conduct of satellite experiments in connection with the IGY. Having cited "the great importance of observations during extended periods of time of extraterrestrial radiations and geophysical phenomena in the upper atmosphere" as well as "the advanced state of present rocket techniques," the official minutes of the Rocket Group placed on record, "CSAGI recommends that thought be given to the launching of small satellite vehicles, to their scientific instrumentation, and to the new problems associated with satellite experiments, such as power supply, telemetering, and orientation of the vehicle."

Meanwhile, ever since 1952 the American Rocket Society had been advocating that the National Science Foundation of the United States undertake studies of a satellite program. In most respects its recommendations were parallel to those of URSI and CSAGI.[98] Still other significant national and international scientific bodies had likewise endorsed an earth satellite program. Thus the world was gratified to receive the news on Friday, July 29, 1955, that such a program would be launched under the auspices of USNC–IGY. A memorable announcement, in simple language and direct terms, stated:

Plans for the construction of a small, unmanned, earth-circling satellite vehicle to be used for basic scientific observations during the forthcoming

[97] Int'l Scientific Radio Union Information Bull., Nov.-Dec. 1954, p. 6.
[98] 25 JET PROPULSION 631 (1955).

International Geophysical Year were announced today by Detlev W. Bronk, President of the National Academy of Sciences, and Alan T. Waterman, Director of the National Science Foundation. The project, which is entirely scientific in nature, will be sponsored by these two organizations as part of the United States program of participation in the International Geophysical Year. Technical advice and assistance will be provided by the scientists of the Department of Defense who have long been engaged in research on the upper atmosphere. The Department of Defense will provide the required equipment and facilities for launching the satellite.

The program for such a vehicle was stimulated by a resolution passed by the Special Committee for the International Geophysical Year (French abbreviation CSAGI) at its Rome Meeting in October, 1954. It is planned that the developmental work be completed in time for a successful launching during the International Geophysical Year, which is a period set aside during 1957 and 1958 for world-wide observations in the fields of the earth sciences by some 40 nations. The planning for this period of intensive research on an international basis is under the sponsorship of the International Council of Scientific Unions (ICSU) which established CSAGI to plan, organize, and direct the cooperative effort. Each participating country is planning and developing its own program for this period, and the results obtained will be made available to the scientists of the world.[99]

The world received this announcement with acclaim. The International Astronautical Federation (IAF) convened in Copenhagen two days after the announcement and cabled President Eisenhower that it regarded the undertaking "as one of the highest importance and an assured step in the evolution from aeronautics to astronautics." The IAF message went on to express particular pleasure concerning "the announcement that the scientific data obtained will be available to all nations as testimony of the peaceful application of rocket technology for the benefit of all mankind." [100] This cable was signed on behalf of the member societies of the IAF, namely: Sociedad Argentina Interplanetaria of Argentina; Oesterreichische Gesellschaft für Weltraumforschung of Austria; Sociedade Interplanetaria Brasileira of Brazil; Sociedad Interplanetaria Chilena of Chile; Dansk Selskab for Rumfarts Forskning of Denmark; Association Egyptienne Astronautique of Egypt; Gesellschaft für Weltraumforschung of Germany; British Interplanetary Society of Great Britain; Associazione Italiana Razzi of Italy; Japanese Astronautical Society of Japan; Vazduhoplovni Savez Jugoslavije of Yugoslavia; Nederlandse Verenigung voor Ruimtevaart of Holland; Norsk Astronautisk Forening of Norway; Agrupación Astronáutica Española of Spain; Svensk Interplanetarisk Selskap of Sweden; Schweizerische Astronautische Arbeitsgemeinschaft of Switzerland; South African Interplanetary Society of Union of South Africa;

99 National Academy of Sciences, Release, July 29, 1955.

100 Minutes of the Sixth International Astronautical Congress, Copenhagen, Aug. 1-6, 1955.

American Rocket Society and American Astronautical Society of the United States.[101]

Officials of nations throughout the world expressed their friendly and even enthusiastic approval of the project. A news dispatch from Moscow quoted Premier Nikita S. Khrushchev as stating, on the subject of the American satellite announcement, that "if it is in the interests of humanity, the Soviet Union is always prepared to support it." [102] It is worth noting that just four months earlier, in April 1955, the Russians themselves had announced the organization, under the directorship of the noted physicist P. Kapitsa, of an "International Commission for Interplanetary Communications."

3–8 The free flight principle for earth satellites

As we have seen, July 29, 1955 was a momentous day in history. Under the principles of existing international law, any sovereign state could have declared that no man-made earth satellite might pursue an orbit over its territorial domain and that if such a satellite were launched, having such an orbit, the consequent violations of its territory would constitute an act of war. A state might have claimed that the very inception of such a program required preliminary international agreement, or else the mere planning of it would be the subject of justifiable suspicion and would lead to the involving of international sanctions of some kind. Quite to the contrary, none complained, none protested, and the program proceeded. The scientists had benefited mankind as a whole in a field where the lawyers might well have failed.

The principle of free flight for earth satellites was thus established by the general consent of the nations.[103] Those that did not express their active encouragement, at least accorded tacit consent by refraining from any type of protest. To be sure, in spite of strong support for this principle among major international organs, including the U.N. Committee on Peaceful Uses of Outer Space and many leading publicists and scholars,[104] some writers would still deny that it has been established.[105]

[101] Signatures by Frederick Durant, President, IAF; Professor Teófilo Tabanera, Vice President, IAF; Ing. Buch Andersen, Vice President, IAF.

[102] N.Y. Times, Aug. 2, 1955, p. 8.

[103] This section dealing with tacit consent was offered as part of a paper presented by the author in Nov. 1956. Pépin, *The Legal Status of the Airspace in the Light of Progress in Aviation and Astronautics*, Symp. 188, 193, cites the author as authority for the statement that no protests having been made against the United States IGY satellite project, the United States "appear to consider that they have received the tacit consent of the other States." The "doctrine of consent" was also featured in an issue of the HARVARD LAW REVIEW appearing in 1960 and received wide approval as a result. (*National Sovereignty of Outer Space*, 74 HARV. L. REV. 1154, 1167.)

[104] U.N. Doc. A/4141; CHAUMONT, LE DROIT DE L'ESPACE 37 (1960) L & K Rep. 9.

[105] Becker, *The Control of Space*, 39 DEP'T OF STATE BULL. 416 (1958); Gorove,

For example, Richard T. Murphy, Jr., expressed certain reservations in an article written in 1958, in which he first cited this writer as authority for the fact that other international scientific efforts similar to the IGY had occurred previously, particularly the International Polar Years. "Mr. Haley," he then continued, "is encouraged enough by this universal acceptance to conclude that, within the very narrow framework of the fact situation presented by the satellite launch (i.e., a scientific and cooperative venture), the very universality of the acceptance lends to it the weight of international custom and, because of the nature of the event, the single instance is effective to that end without need of further repetition." Murphy himself, however, proceeded to argue that it would be "clearly improper" to conclude from "this international taciturnity . . . that the nations of the world are now willing to accept a limit to the doctrine of air sovereignty in a general and unqualified manner."

In support of his thesis, Murphy noted further that Haley had called for United Nations action to assure the freedom of space and had admitted that in the meantime satellite activities were "at the sufferance of the nations of the world." [106] In effect, Murphy cites the admitted ability of the nations to have delayed or even halted the satellite program as evidence that they have not really diminished their claims of sovereignty. Yet, in the last analysis, their ability to impede the program if they wished merely makes their failure to do so all the more significant.

In an earlier section of this chapter, it was pointed out that the Chicago Convention of 1944—whose general tendency was to strengthen the doctrine of national sovereignty over airspace—made reference to unmanned aircraft in its Article 8, requiring that they not be flown over the territory of a contracting state without its consent. In so far as this provision may be said to refer to the flight of earth satellites such as those launched in the IGY, the requirements of the article have been satisfied, since more than sixty of the signatory nations, as well as other nonsignatory nations, assented to the satellite program.[107] However, the consent of so large a number of nations, taken collectively, goes even farther than to authorize the passage of certain specific satellites through particular sectors of near-terrestrial space. In practice, it established in international law the general principle of free flight for scientific satellites.

On the Threshold of Space: Toward Cosmic Law, 4 N.Y.L.F. 305 (1958); e.g., Schick, Who Rules the Skies: Some Political and Legal Problems of the Space Age 19 (1961); Osnitskaya, *Mezhdunarodno-Pravovye Voprosi Osvoenija Vozdushnogo Prostranstrva* (International Law Problems of the Conquest of Cosmic Space) 1959 Sovetskij Ezhegodnik Mezhdunarodnogo Prava (Soviet Yearbook of International Law) 51, 56.

[106] Murphy, *Air Sovereignty Considerations in Terms of Outer Space,* Symp. 198, 207-09.

[107] See generally Machowski, *The Legal Status of Unmanned Space Vehicles,* 2d Colloq. 110-11 (Vienna: Springer-Verlag, 1960).

It is true that no single formal treaty emerged from the myriad agreements involved in the IGY; nevertheless, a valid and binding world pact emerged from these acts of agreement and cooperation, by operation of traditional principles of international law. This international pact may be abstracted in written form from the thousands of documents and exchanges from which the IGY evolved, for there is nothing about a formal treaty which makes it sacrosanct or makes it even an essential source of international law. As noted in an earlier context, in many instances the principles set forth in the treaty itself may have been established in international law long prior to the signing of the formal document itself; although it should be remembered, there are rules of international law which are not valid, even though enacted in such instruments.

The rule of free satellite flight is really not unlike several propositions that have long been recognized by international law. Thus, while the sovereignty of a nation extends into its territorial waters, this right is subject to a right of innocent passage for ships of other nations, because of the importance of freedom of navigation to all states.[108] It has been held that even vessels of war, although serving no commercial purpose, are not necessarily deprived of the right of passage under peaceful conditions, and still less other public ships devoted to scientific purposes. In the words of Charles C. Hyde, "So long as the conduct of a vessel of any kind is not essentially injurious to the safety and welfare of the littoral State there would appear to be no reason to exclude it from the use of the marginal sea." [109]

The Second Commission appointed by the Hague Conference for the Codification of International Law in 1930, created especially to study the subject of territorial waters, provisionally approved certain articles that sought to define the right of innocent passage. The Commission construed the passage of a vessel to be innocent unless it made use of a nation's territorial waters for some act that was harmful to the security, the "public policy," or the "fiscal interests" of the nation in question. Another article then stated flatly, with regard to all foreign vessels other than warships, that it was contrary to international law for a coastal nation to raise any obstacles against their innocent passage through the territorial sea.[110]

Some years earlier, Convention X signed at the Second Hague Peace Conference of 1907 had provided that military hospital ships, "the names of which have been communicated to the belligerent powers at the commencement or during the course of hostilities," should be respected and be immune to capture. This convention gave similar protection to hospital

[108] 1 HACKWORTH, DIGEST OF INTERNATIONAL LAW 624 (1940).

[109] 1 HYDE, INTERNATIONAL LAW CHIEFLY AS INTERPRETED AND APPLIED BY THE UNITED STATES 517 (Boston: Little, Brown and Company, 2d rev. ed. 1951).

[110] CONFERENCE FOR THE CODIFICATION OF INTERNATIONAL LAW (The Hague, March-April 1930), REPORT OF THE SECOND COMMISSION (TERRITORIAL SEA), L. N. Pub. No. C.230 M. 117, 1930 V. at 7-9.

ships equipped by private individuals or recognized relief societies of belligerent or neutral countries.[111] Convention XI, adopted at the same conference and ratified by the United States, also gave exemption from capture to vessels charged with religious, scientific, or philanthropic missions.[112] In all these examples, a type of permissive spirit seems to be evident that recognizes and allows peaceful passages. It is this same spirit, when acknowledged and abided by for a reasonable period of time, that will be the basis for the emerging principle of freedom of outer space for peaceful uses.

As law comes into being by consent, one problem that arises is the problem of administration. Although the free passage of artificial earth satellites over the territory of the sovereign nations of the earth is legal, and no nation may now deny that passage unless such denial is based upon grounds of self-defense, the need for international regulation of space activities that was touched upon in the first chapter still exists. Fortunately, at the present time there are available several official, semi-official, and nongovernmental organizations, which with some adjustments could meet the needs of administration of space controls and apply sanctions for violations. Such matters naturally require time for solution —time to accomplish the many steps of international negotiation and agreement.

In the meantime, the United Nations could study the legal aspects of the problem, and especially endeavor to achieve an understanding among all nations on the question of space jurisdiction. Either through the processes of the United Nations or by multilateral treaty-making, the principle should be established, at least as an interim proposition, that whereas jurisdiction will repose in a state with respect to defenses against warlike or unfriendly high-altitude rockets and satellite vehicles, surely scientific investigations by means of such vehicles will not be circumscribed because of passage over national domain—but that such passage must conform to rules of safety adopted by the nations of the world as a working entity. The term "interim proposition" is used advisedly because no compromise can be made with the basic proposition that the area beyond the aeropause may be claimed by no nation. Indeed, areas in space may be claimed by mankind as a whole only to the extent that any specific use will be for the benefit of all mankind and to the detriment of no other intelligent creature.

3–9 Increasing cooperation—the free flight principle at work

The thesis presented in this chapter with respect to the establishment in international law of the principle of free use of space for peaceful pur-

---

111 6 HACKWORTH, DIGEST OF INTERNATIONAL LAW 458 (1943).
112 Oct. 18, 1907, 36 Stat. 2396, T. S. No. 544.

poses has so far been principally based on the approval, whether tacit or express, that the nations of the world accorded to the original announcement that the United States would conduct a satellite program as part of the IGY, and to the subsequent steps taken by the United States to implement such a program. However, the first scientific satellite actually launched was the Soviet Union's *Sputnik I*, in October 1957. The reception accorded to this achievement by the leaders of the free world, among others, further strengthened the principle of free use.[113] Even though the non-Communist nations felt more than a little uneasy about the Soviet technological prowess that was so strikingly demonstrated by the *Sputnik* launching, their only serious criticisms of the experiment concerned the Soviets' failure to divulge all relevant information about the satellite—not the mere fact that it was flying over their territories. Equally significant have been the increasingly numerous instances of active cooperation among nations in satellite activities, whether this cooperation took the form of jointly-operated tracking stations, the actual sharing of satellite vehicles by the scientists and engineers of different countries, or some other form of collaborative endeavor.

An early call for active international cooperation in space activities was contained in the report *International Cooperation in the Exploration of Space*, issued in 1958 by the Select Committee on Astronautics and Space Exploration of the United States House of Representatives. This report observed that the national effort in space and in astronautical activities generally had "thus far been largely a matter of fulfilling urgent demands or meeting immediate needs in carrying out specific military programs as well as those from the International Geophysical Year." [114] However, the report emphasized the need for long-range planning, and in particular it proposed a five-point plan for "a series of studies covering basic problems involved in getting a sound, long-term policy under way." One such study was to be concerned with the prospect for international cooperation in space efforts, and another, significantly, with the "legal problems bound to evolve as the Space Age advances." Then, with regard to the former topic, the report stated:

> This first study, on international cooperation in the space effort, seems more pressing than the others. The opportunities for realizing international cooperation on the free world's terms are immediately available. But some im-

[113] "During most of the history of international law the principal source of law has been international custom. This will of course continue to be an important factor. For example, the basis was laid for one of the most important principles of space law—that of the freedom of space—when the first Russian satellite passed over the territories of all the nations of the world without protest." LARSON, WHEN NATIONS DISAGREE 23 (1962).

[114] STAFF OF THE SELECT COMMITTEE ON ASTRONAUTICS AND SPACE EXPLORATION, 85TH CONG., 2D SESS., INTERNATIONAL COOPERATION IN THE EXPLORATION OF SPACE 1 (Comm. Print. 1958).

minent decisions lie ahead of us if we are to take advantage of these opportunities. The building cement for all future policy in this field is being set now, and it must be set firmly and well. Scientific ideas can be revised when new discoveries are made, but popular and national attitudes are harder to change, once established. In a matter like scientific cooperation, these attitudes play a critical part and must be reckoned with.[115]

Although the comments on USSR and affiliated national attitudes can hardly be termed favorable, as presented in this report, it was pointed out that the "demonstrated professional ability" of the Soviet scientists naturally gave rise to the hope that mankind in general might "share in the results of their work." The report cited both the "openly avowed" Communist goal of world domination and the Soviet Union's "totalitarian approach to life" as reasons why Soviet cooperation could not be taken for granted "in a broad space program of the kind the free world is coming to regard as essential." And, it said further, "The burden of proof rests on the Soviet Government." [116]

That burden seems to have been recognized by the government of the USSR. Immediate steps are now being taken by the governments of both the United States and the USSR to create a sound cooperative program in the area of space meteorological activities, and this precedent, once established, could lead to immeasurable benefits to all mankind through the program in question and the myriad other cooperative agreements that could eventually follow. There is no question as to whether the Russian leaders believe in the utility of such a joint effort. As General Georgii I. Pokrovskiy has stated:

> If the benefits mankind could gain from improved weather forecasts were to be measured in terms of money, it would run to an annual saving of thousands of millions of rubles. This sum is so large that it could more than compensate for all the money spent on space research.[117]

The primary problem that cooperative efforts will be concerned with will be effective control of the mechanics of any program. The details as to who will make a rocket or satellite payload, where it will be launched, how and by whom it is to be monitored will all become issues in the negotiations that must follow the initial agreements. Making proposals for laudable and obvious efforts for "the benefit of mankind" is only the preliminary to long drawn-out technical discussions, in which political considerations will play an unfortunate, scientifically unnecessary, but still effective role.

Be that as it may, in the March 1962 exchange of letters already described in the first chapter of this volume, President John F. Kennedy and

---

115 *Id.* at 2.
116 *Id.* at 8.
117 Pokrovskiy, *Space Exploration and International Relations, a Discussion*, International Affairs, June 1961, p. 62. See generally Crane, *Developing Space Legal Strategy*, 6 ORBIS 281 (1962).

Premier Nikita S. Khrushchev agreed to commence talks on a US–USSR joint meteorological satellite venture for the forecasting of world weather that would inevitably be for the benefit of all mankind. If one bears in mind the analysis of the results of IGY cooperation which has been presented above, it becomes obvious that a further extension of the consent doctrine has resulted from the agreement of the two leading satellite-producing countries to enter into this joint effort. In the March 1962 exchange of letters between the state leaders, concrete proposals were set forth. (The text of these letters is contained in Appendix I-D.) None of the proposals was rejected; and plans were made to agree on the further steps necessary to attain cooperative use of earth-circling *photo-capacity* satellites for meteorological research.

Some Soviet scholars have objected to the United States' present *Tiros* weather satellite program on the ground that *Tiros* photographs foreign territory and provides weather information that could be militarily useful.[118] However, obviously neither nation will be in a position, once this proposed joint program commences, to complain of passage over its territory of a scientific photo-capacity satellite. Being intended for surely peaceful purposes, i.e., meteorological investigations, not even the incidental fact that the satellites might under optimum conditions photograph the terrain as well as clouds will be subject to challenge. In this joint effort then, there is again a reinforcement of and conformity to the emerging principle we have been discussing: *outer space may be used for peaceful and scientific purposes without regard to subjacent sovereignty.*

The primary limitation on this principle, as it has grown, has been that *whatever benefits are derived from these space activities are benefits procured on behalf of and for the betterment of all mankind.* An entirely different problem may still exist with respect to the legality of *ex parte* activities, secretly conducted, even if for alleged scientific and peaceful purposes. However, disclosure of the information procured as the property of all nations has been the U.S. practice with respect to its meteorological findings; and such practice was never restricted to meteorological data. Thus the announced intention of the United States in connection with the IGY satellite program to make known not only the wavelength of the radio instruments carried but also all scientific data whatsoever to be gathered from the experimentation certainly contributed to the worldwide approval that program received.[119] Moreover, the pri-

---

[118] Korovin, *Borba za Kosmosi Mezhdunarodnoe Pravo* (The Fight for the Cosmos and International Law) in KOSMOS I MEZHDUNARODNOE PRAVO (The Cosmos and International Law) 5, 7-9 (Korovin ed. USSR 1962); Petrov, *Sputniki-shpiony i Mezhdunarodnoe Pravo* in *id.* at 171, 176-77; Zadorozhniji, *Oshovnye Problemy Nauki Kosmicheskogo Prava* (Basic Problems of Cosmic Law) in *id.* at 23, 51.

[119] Bin Cheng, *International Law and High Altitude Flight: Balloons, Rockets and Man-made Satellites*, 10 INT'L & COMP. L. Q. 487 (1957), Symp. 141, citing agreement of this writer, connects the openness of U.S. activities with the assent received by the IGY satellite program.

mary goal identified by President Kennedy for the proposed joint Soviet–
United States meteorological satellite effort is also the general dissemination, through the World Meteorological Organization, of all information
received. This is the same as the present United States practice with
respect to the *Tiros* program, and it meets the full requirements of the
emerging international law of space. Secret intelligence-gathering by
satellite vehicles is, of course, a somewhat different matter. It may well
appear essential from a security standpoint, but the maintenance of a
high secrecy level in many of the operations and the lack of disclosure of
results could leave a country in an embarrassing position before the critical legal scholars of the world.

Additional References

Space Communications and Exobiological Problems: Address by Andrew
G. Haley, Before the Medical Society of the State of New York Convention in
Rochester, May 9, 1961; _____, *Rule of Law in Outer Space: Letter to the
Editor,* New York Times, Feb. 18, 1961, p. 18; _____, *Medical Jurisprudence in
Outer Space,* 3 ARCHIVES OF ENVIRONMENTAL HEALTH 315 (1961); _____,
Sovereignty in Space, Review of Contemporary Law, Dec. 1960, p. 3; _____,
*A Basic Program for the 1963 Extraordinary Administrative Radio Conference
on Space Communications* in PROCEEDINGS OF THE IXTH INTERNATIONAL ASTRO-
NAUTICAL CONGRESS, STOCKHOLM 1960; _____, *Law of Outer Space—Practical
Legal Rules for Human Conduct,* 16 FED. COM. B.J. 163 (1959); _____, *Inter-
national Scene,* Astronautics, Feb. 1958, p. 70; _____, *The Law of Space—
Scientific and Technical Considerations,* 4 N.Y.L.F. 262 (1958); *Legal Prob-
lems of Space 1960-1970:* Paper by _____, Before the Conference on Space
Technology in Los Angeles, Oct. 1, 1960, and in Norman, Okla., Oct. 4, 1960;
Survey of Legal Opinion on Extraterrestrial Jurisdiction: Paper by _____, Before
the Space Law Colloquium of the IXth Congress of the International Aeronautical Federation in Stockholm, Aug. 16, 1960; *The Law of Space and Outer
Space:* Address by _____, Pacific Southwest Conference on International Law
at the University of Southern California, March 5, 1960; *Space Exploration—
The Problems of Today, Tomorrow and in the Future:* Paper by _____, Before
the Second Colloquium on the Law of Outer Space in London, Sept. 4, 1959;
Law of Space—Space Sovereignty: Address by _____, Before the Universities
and Scientific Groups in Vienna, Warsaw, Moscow, Prague, Belgrade, Athens,
Cairo, Johannesburg, Rome, Barcelona, Madrid, Lisbon, Amsterdam and Paris,
May-June 1959; *Scientific and Social Developments of Outer Space:* Lectures
by _____, National Capital Section of the American Rocket Society and Army
Corps of Engineers' Course on "Science and Rocketry" in Ft. Belvoir, Va.,
Nov. 8, 1958; *Legal and Economic Aspects of Astronautics:* Address by _____,
Dansk Interplanetarisk Selskab in Copenhagen, March 14, 1958.

The limits of national sovereignty

With respect to the question of the upper limits of national sovereignty, great confusion is found to exist in the writings of commentators because of the mingling of authentic legal postulates and scientific data with speculative political considerations. In order to arrive at a considered opinion, it is necessary first to examine the references to and definitions of "airspace" in existing municipal law, but these provisions throw little light on the basic problem. On the other hand, numerous writers and scholars have examined the issues involved, and the weight of authority clearly favors the adoption of some sort of demarcation between the airspace or atmosphere and "outer" space, based on scientific criteria. It is shown that one proposed solution, the "von Kármán line," should serve as the terminal point for civil and criminal venue, and in general for the exercise of national sovereignty, because the scientific and jurisprudential considerations determining the line are entirely realistic, identifiable, and sufficient. The development of the X-15 rocket ship and its successors (often mistakenly called "planes"), with their ability to travel in air and space, has been taken by some writers as making meaningless if not impossible the clear delineation of a national upper limit. This argument and other principal objections to the von Kármán line are examined and discussed in detail. In conclusion, several alternative approaches to the upper limits problem are examined.

HOW HIGH DOES NATIONAL SOVEREIGNTY EXTEND?

4–1 An introduction to the problem

Within the world community of jurists, lawyers, and sociologists, many have been devoting close attention in recent years to the problems of the rule of law in outer space. One such problem is that of defining space jurisdiction, and not only is it a legal and scientific question but also, through the many additional ramifications involved, it may well develop into a first-class problem in international relations. It must be treated soberly and objectively, for as Arthur Dean, distinguished United States lawyer and ambassador at many of the Geneva disarmament conference sessions, has pointed out, "We must not let the future of space law be determined by *ex parte* statements which are not carefully examined by an impartial body of scholars." [1]

Actually, the space law community, national and international, believed that Mr. Dean's remark concerning "*ex parte* statements" was obviously inadvertent. As early as 1952 the American Rocket Society (ARS) organized a space flight committee, composed of distinguished American scientists, which considered the entire ambit of space law problems.[2] At the initial meeting of the committee, the level and content of the discussions reflected clearly the extensive thought and preparation that went into the organization of the program. Beginning with a broad discussion of the appropriate scope of investigation and terms of reference, the day-long meeting included discussion of unmanned sounding rockets, long-range missiles, the "earth-bound" manned rocket, earth satellites both unmanned and manned, orbital space stations, one-way lunar rockets, exploratory and scheduled space flight, aero and space medicine, telemetering, the technical problems involved in achieving all of the above, the utility of these activities for human civilization, the extent and manner of possible international cooperation, and, finally, the position of the American Rocket Society. This was one of the most significant contributions to the organization of space activities. Subsequent meetings of the committee produced considerably more detailed and valuable information, which was extremely useful in future ARS activities. Gradually, however, the work of the original committee was taken over by a large number of new ARS technical committees, including the Space Law and Sociology Committee.

The International Astronautical Federation, composed of learned societies from thirty nations,[3] including most of the East European countries, has held colloquiums on the law of outer space at The Hague (1958), London (1959), Stockholm (1960), Washington (1961), Varna, Bulgaria (1962), and Paris (1963). For its part, the American Bar Association, under the leadership of its former president, David F. Maxwell, has established a committee on the law of outer space within the framework of the section on international and comparative law. These activities are only a few of many, and they are not easily classifiable as "*ex parte*" when they are so obviously extensive in composition.

[1] Letter to the Editor, New York Times, Jan. 16, 1961, p. 26, col. 4.

[2] The following were present at the first meeting of the Committee on May 17, 1952: A. G. Haley (Chairman), R. W. Porter, M. W. Rosen, K. R. Sterling, F. C. Durant III, J. R. Youngquist.

[3] See Appendix III-A.

The failure of many lawyers to do the "bread-and-butter job" of examining international law, international treaties, and the statutory laws of the nations of the world with respect to the jurisdictional aspects of airspace is the prime cause of confusion in this area. More than a hundred nations, speaking individually through their constitutions or statutes, have asserted their sovereignty over the airspace above them. The International Civil Aviation Convention adopted at Chicago in 1944 (discussed in the previous chapter) is the most recent multilateral expression on this subject, and it is only one of many existing international agreements that touch in one way or another upon the matter of airspace sovereignty.

Yet where, exactly, is that point which separates airspace from what is variously called outer space or cosmic space—and, more important, which separates the realm of national sovereignties from a domain of international space law in the making? [4]

Even the simplest and perhaps the earliest of solutions to the upper-limit problem was one fraught with complications. Marek Zylicz,[5] in an article dealing with "Some Problems of Astronautical Law," [6] has pointed out that Grotius "recognized freedom of space at an altitude beyond the range of a hunter's weapons." But which weapons? How big a hunter? Standing where when he fired—on the highest mountain? It is obvious from this simple illustration that no solutions will be easy. The most reasonable, generally acceptable solution will prove the best.

We know that in all pertinent fields of science one must deal with median curves based upon an immense family of related curves. As a practical guide for the space age, the weight of authority favors a measure of a similar kind, now termed the von Kármán primary jurisdictional line. This line was suggested by Dr. Theodore von Kármán [7] and adapted by the author on the basis of a diagram by Masson and Gazley of the Rand Corporation. It will be treated in detail in Section 4-4 of this

[4] Discussing the position that national sovereignty extends upward indefinitely, and that the Paris and Chicago Conventions were drafted in this belief and therefore do not limit sovereignty in any way, see Hildred and Tymms, *The Case Against National Sovereignty in Space*, 1958 THE AEROPLANE 712; Hingorani, *La Souveraineté sur l'espace . . . atmosphérique*, 20 REVUE GÉNÉRALE DE L'AIR 248 (1958); Peng, *Le Vol à haute altitude et l'article 1 de la Convention de Chicago, 1944*, La Revue du Barreau de la Province de Québec, June 1952, p. 277; de la Pradelle, *Les Frontières de l'Air*, RECUEIL DES COURS DE L'ACADÉMIE DE DROIT INTERNATIONAL (1956). *Contra*, Cooper, *Flight-Space and the Satellites*, 7 INT'L. & COMP. L. Q. 82 (1958); Hogan, *Legal Terminology for the Upper Regions of Atmosphere and for the Space Beyond the Atmosphere*, 51 AM. J. INT'L. L. 362 (1957). Delbert M. Draper writes that the upper limit should be the ionosphere, since this will allow each nation privacy but will not interfere with scientific experimentation. Draper, *Satellites and Sovereignty*, JAG J. Sept.-Oct. 1956, p. 23.

[5] Asst. Prof., Warsaw Faculty of Law, Poland.

[6] Symp. 1157, 1160 n. 20.

[7] At the time of his death in May 1963, Dr. von Kármán was chairman, Advisory Group for Aeronautical Research and Development (AGARD) for the NATO; Chief Consultant, Aerojet-General Corp.

chapter, but it must be defined at least briefly at the outset since much of the following discussion will make reference to it, directly or indirectly. Simply stated, the von Kármán line is intended to represent the line of demarcation between the aeronautic and astronautic regions. The line is located at *approximately* 275,000 feet, which may well be changed somewhat as physicists and lawyers hammer out agreements as to where an aeronautical vehicle no longer may perform and where molecular oxygen dissociates and airspace no longer exists. But after all the data have been reduced, the boundary probably will not differ materially from the von Kármán line as now conceived.

In essence, the line represents a mean or "median" measurement. It is comparable to such measures used in the law as "mean sea level," "meander line," "tide line"; but it is more complex than these. In arriving at the von Kármán jurisdictional line, myriad factors must be considered —other than the factor of aerodynamic lift. These factors have been dis-

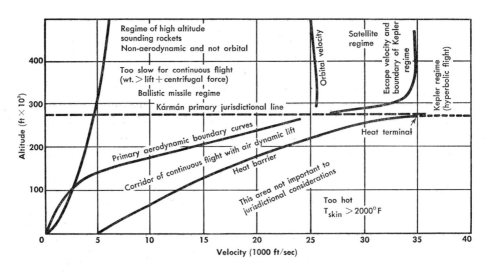

Figure 1 Diagram showing regimes of atmospheric and extra-atmospheric flight, and depicting the jurisdictional boundary lines. The von Kármán primary jurisdictional line: (1) aerodynamic lift is completely dissipated; (2) no more viable air; (3) "air" as used in international treaties and in thousands of national statutes no longer exists; (4) the aeronautical regime ends under the "record establishing" practices of the Federation Aeronautique Internationale; (5) the regime of exobiology commences; (6) atoms dissociate and molecular construction ends; (7) the Kepler regime has "taken over"; (8) although there will be fluctuations in the von Kármán line, a median jurisdictional curve will be established through measurements—just as in the case of radio regulation of interference which has the full force of law and treaty protection.

cussed in a very large body of literature and by a score or more of commentators. They include the physical constitution of the air; the biological and physiological viability; and still other factors which logically join to establish a point at which air no longer exists and at which airspace ends.

4-2 Basic research on the upper limits question

Many factors have contributed to the raising of discussion on this problem. The launching of the first artificial satellite was not only one of the world's most impressive scientific events, it was also the advent of a new epoch involving basic extensions of man's concepts of the social sciences. For example, one very important question immediately posed was, "What actually is the legal status of *Sputnik?*"

At first, idle curiosity led the author to wonder whether the statutory law of any nation might be violated, or whether any legislature, by prophetic foresight, had enacted laws making claim to sovereignty in outer space. While an immense amount of study and examination of statutes yet remains, at the time of the launching of *Sputnik I* the author began a program of research on the statutory law of all the nations of the world in the field of airspace jurisdiction. Resulting extensive discussions of this field have been printed in eleven languages—English, French, Spanish, Swedish, Arabic, German, Russian, Czech, Serbo-Croatian, Polish and Japanese.[8]

For weeks after the launching of *Sputnik I,* a concerted study of the statutory laws of many nations continued. However, the study was limited by language barriers. A search was made through every available compendium, but no complete answer was found. Finally the aid of Senator Warren G. Magnuson (Chairman of the Senate Committee on Interstate and Foreign Commerce) was sought. Through the diligent efforts of governmental staff members, a wealth of materials was soon produced for study.[9] From this study the stark fact emerged that in this field there are literally hundreds of statutes and thousands of regulations of all the nations of the earth which directly affect nation qua nation and the individual as such. They are backed in each case by the strong arms of the police and the courts of the nations of the world, as well as by the ability of international bodies to invoke sanctions of all kinds.

---

[8] These discussions took the form of speeches and addresses on the author's 1958 European tour; see Appendix V-B, 135-144.

[9] Reports were received on the statutory language covering jurisdiction over airspace of the following nations: Afghanistan, Argentina, Australia, Belgium, Brazil, Bulgaria, Canada, France, Germany, Great Britain, India, Iran, Ireland, Israel, Japan, Lebanon, Mexico, Netherlands, New Zealand, Republic of the Philippines, Republic of China (Taiwan), Romania, Saudi Arabia, Switzerland, Thailand, Union of South Africa, USSR, USA, and Yugoslavia. Modern usage employs the word "airspace" in most statutes, but in older contexts the use of "air space" is still found.

It is interesting to note that statutes of more than 100 nations make direct reference to "airspace" and that approximately a score of treaties among the nations of the world also make reference to that term. "Airspace" and "atmosphere" are the only terms employed in these statutes and treaties, and they are treated as synonymous. In the statutes of the United States, the term "airspace" is employed in several instances: 72 Stat. 798 (1958), 49 U.S.C. §176 (1958), declares the "complete and exclusive national sovereignty" of the United States "in the *airspace* of the United States." Similarly, in 2 *Canal Zone Code* §14, 50 Stat. 486 (1937), the United States asserted "to the exclusion of all foreign nations, sovereign rights, power, and authority over the *airspace* above the lands and waters of the Canal Zone." And in the so-called security provisions which were added to the Civil Aeronautics Act, 72 Stat. 800 (1958), 49 U.S.C. §1522 (1958), the United States provided for the establishment by the Secretary of Commerce of security zones in "the *airspace* of the United States." Finally, in the Federal Airport Act, 60 Stat. 179 (1946), 49 U.S.C. §1115 (1958), the Administrator of Civil Aeronautics was granted authority to cause the conveyance of Federal lands "or any easement through or other interest in *airspace*" to the appropriate public agency controlling the airport project. (Emphasis added in the foregoing quotations.)

Nowhere in any of the statutes or treaties of any of the nations is the term "airspace" defined. It is also interesting to note that, in the exhaustive studies completed to date, no statute has been found which expressly purports to extend sovereignty above "airspace." Air, as used in this context, does not include the atmosphere of other planets or meteoric dust; it is "air" as that word is normally understood.

In *Adams Aeronautical Dictionary* (1959), published by the United States Government Printing Office, "air" is carefully defined as follows:

air, *noun*. 1. The gaseous substance surrounding the earth, being principally a mixture of gases (although often considered a single gas), and consisting mainly of nitrogen and oxygen, in the ratio of about four parts of the former to one of the latter, but containing also varying amounts of water vapor, and relatively small quantities of the gases argon, carbon dioxide, hydrogen, neon, helium, krypton, and xenon. Particles of dust and smoke, bacteria, spores, etc. suspended in the air are not usually considered a part of it. Air extends upward with decreasing density from the surface of the earth, having a normal pressure of about 14.7 pounds per square inch at sea level. Air is both compressible and elastic, and its principal importance in aeronautics is its character as a fluid, thus affording a medium or means of support for aircraft. . . . 3. A gas—in this sense esp. in some combinations and attributive uses. . . . 4a. The air (in sense 1) regarded as the realm or medium in which aircraft travel or operate. b. This air conceived of as a medium for commerce, warfare, etc. by the use of aircraft—disting. from the land and sea, as, transport by *air*, or, the conquest of the air. . . .

Additional definitions are given in Appendix IV-A.

Under all rules of statutory construction, we must consider air and airspace as such, not as something else. In high altitudes air may be extremely rarefied, but it is still air until the atoms of which it consists dissociate. The precise identification of this point, i.e., the upper limit of "airspace" and hence the possible upper limit of national sovereignty,[10] is a problem that some writers have regarded as perhaps insoluble.[11] Some say it is a pointless differentiation, essentially academic and useless at this time.[12] Still others, however, including the great bulk of reputable scholars, insist that this question is of prime importance and that it demands an answer.[13]

During the fall of 1957, Welf Heinrich Prince of Hanover, and the author lectured at twenty-six American universities and at numerous European universities on "The Law of Outer Space." Following these lectures, in 1958, the American Bar Association (ABA) organized its Committee on the Law of Outer Space with David F. Maxwell (then retiring president of the ABA) as chairman and the author as vice-chairman. The Committee has been quite active since that time. (See the detailed discussion of its creation in Chapter 11 *infra*.)

In 1958 the American Bar Foundation received a grant from NASA for the purpose of supporting research by this Committee and the compilation of a report. The task was assigned to Nicholas Katzenbach of the University of Chicago and Leon Lipson of Yale University, and the preliminary report, which perforce dealt with the upper limits problem, was submitted and approved at the August 1959 meeting of the ABA in Miami.[14]

The report was somewhat more satisfactory than the attenuated UN committee work to that date; but, as pointed out by the dean of commentators on space law, John Cobb Cooper, the report seemed to imply that the problem of airspace and outer space boundaries was a purely theoretical question which was neither in need of solution now nor, perhaps, in the future. With this point Cooper vigorously disagreed. Believing it a "most practical and urgent question," Cooper asked that there be early international agreement defining the boundaries of air-

[10] Ikeda, *Who Owns Outer Space?*, Bungei Shunju (Japan) (extra issue) November 1957, p. 4; Katz, *Who Owns Space?*, Maclean's Canada's Magazine, Jan. 18, 1958, p. 13.

[11] L & K Rep. 15; Gál, *Some Legal Aspects of the Use of Reconnaissance Satellites*, 5th Colloq.

[12] E.g., Beresford, *The Future of National Sovereignty*, 2d Colloq. 5, 8 (Vienna: Springer-Verlag, 1960). "Sovereignty is neither necessary nor sufficient for solving the problems created by the space age."

[13] E.g., *Air Law and Space Law—An Analysis*, paper by William Strauss presented at McGill University, March 1962. In this paper fourteen different proposed boundaries are listed. On upper limits problems see generally Helfer, *Who Owns Outer Space*, Family Weekly Magazine, March 30, 1958, p. 12; Hildred and Tymms, *The Case Against National Sovereignty in Space*, 1958 The Aeroplace 712.

[14] L & K Rep., Symp. 779.

space—an area where sovereign states would have complete, absolute, and unilateral rights—and outer space—an area where a certain degree of freedom should exist for all states. "If discussion of the limits of airspace and outer space is too long delayed," Cooper argued, "the problem will rapidly became almost insoluble." [15] The author officially concurred with the viewpoint of Professor Cooper.[16] It is also interesting to compare the position taken in the report with the statement by G. P. Zhukov, Academic Secretary of the Commission on Cosmic Law of the USSR Academy of Sciences, that "with a favorable solution of the problem of the use of outer space for military purposes, the problems of the extent of the sovereignty of states 'upwards' would be considerably simplified." [17]

On page 9 the ABA report states, "While no writer has as yet examined definitively all national statutes regulating flight, those that have been cited employ jurisdictional language closely parallel to that of international conventions." Two months prior to the publication of the final version of this report the author presented a paper in Stockholm, Sweden, at the XIth Congress of the International Astronautical Federation, in which air laws of more than sixty major nations were discussed in detail.[18] At that time no similarly detailed study had been done, nor to our knowledge has there been one of comparable scope since.

One particularly distressing aspect of the Lipson and Katzenbach effort was that the report did not adequately state the concept of the von Kármán jurisdictional line. The diagram given above as Figure 1 portrays the corridor of continuous flight with aerodynamic lift which ends at the von Kármán line. This diagram is not intended to portray the flight possibilities of rocket craft, but *only* the limitations on the potentialities of aircraft flight; the corridor has nothing to do with the flight of rocket-powered vehicles. Nor has the diagram anything to do with the completely different problem of *guidance*. Strangely enough, the ABA report considers the use of air for guidance purposes as somehow affecting the legal nature of the vehicle. However, while the content of a vehicle and the nature of its mission may affect its legal status, the presence of wings or a stabilizer certainly does not. (More will be said on this topic in another section *infra*.)

4–3   A survey of major writers' views

In order to state as accurately as possible a scientific definition of the area where the jurisdiction of terrestrial law ends and the jurisdiction of space law begins, it is desirable, and indeed necessary, to review the opin-

[15] See these comments as set out in the minutes, 1959 PROCEEDINGS, AMERICAN BAR ASSOCIATION SECTION OF INTERNATIONAL AND COMPARATIVE LAW 215-33 (1960).
[16] *Ibid.*
[17] Zhukov, Remarks, Symp. 1072, 1083.
[18] 3rd Colloq. 37 (Stockholm: Swedish Astronautical Society, 1961).

ions of the authorities on the subject. Unfortunately, because of the failure of some publicists to furnish the Library of Congress with their writings —and the consequent lack of indexing thereof in the United States—it has been impossible to consult all writings of all the authorities who have dealt with space law.

For this review, reference has been made particularly, but not exclusively, to the works of John Cobb Cooper, Professor of Law and formerly Director of the Institute of International Air Law, at McGill University, Montreal, and also formerly a member of the Institute for Advanced Study at Princeton University. In the author's opinion, Dr. Cooper is one of the most competent world legal authorities. He is undoubtedly the dean of American air law experts, and he is a past president of the International Institute of Space Law.

Dr. Welf Heinrich Prince of Hanover has the unique distinction of being the first formal student of space law. As a graduate student at Göttingen in 1953, he had the imagination and courage to choose as his doctoral dissertation, *Air Law and Space,* and his work has already earned the standing of a classic in the field of space law. Dr. Alex Meyer, of the University of Cologne, another of the world's foremost authorities on air law, read the first paper in Europe on space law at Stuttgart during the Third Congress of the International Astronautical Federation held in September 1952. Dr. C. Wilfred Jenks, of the International Labor Office in Geneva, has contributed one of the truly great discussions on the problems of space travel and space law, and his works are dealt with extensively in this text. Mr. Oscar Schachter, Director of the General Legal Division of the United Nations, has made several contributions in the field of space law, each of which is characterized by great clarity of thought and expression. Similarly, Mr. P. K. Roy, Director of the Legal Bureau of the International Civil Aviation Organization (ICAO), has shown acute awareness of the evolving problems concerned with space navigation and has kept ICAO alerted to these problems. And the views of other scholars, lawyers, and public officials will be cited in the following survey.

"Certain jurists have insisted that the territory of a State is limited by the ability of that State to make its laws effective," Professor Cooper wrote in 1951. This he considers to be a harsh rule when applied to sovereignty in space. It would mean that the more powerful states, with their high altitude rockets, would be able to control the "airspace" over their surface territories. The weaker states, however, would be unable to exercise such control. "Can we be said to live in such a world," Cooper asks, "where the physical power at any one time of any particular state determines its international right to consider the region above its surface territories as part of its national territory?" If the "rule of effectiveness" is to be applied to the determination of the rights of states in space, Cooper believes that every state—no matter how weak and no matter how small—should have territorial rights that extend "as high as the rights of every other State, no matter how powerful." He suggests, then, that in the absence of international agreement the territory of every nation should extend "upward as far into space as it is physically and scientifically possible for any one State to control the regions directly above it." [19]

He cautions, however, that there are limitations to this rule, especially when the enormous distances involved are taken into account, and he admits quite frankly that the rule is not offered as a final solution. For example, it leaves open such vital questions as the "extent of control" that is contemplated and the means to be employed in determining "the ability of the most powerful State" to exercise control above its territory. But in defense of the rule, Cooper maintains that "it provides the basis for a fairly liveable world in which the weak State is not at the mercy of the strong." [20]

On April 26, 1956, in an address before the American Society of International Law in Washington, D.C., Professor Cooper proposed a three-zone concept of sovereignty. One zone, which he designated "territorial space," would extend from the ground to a height where aircraft, as now defined, can operate. This zone would constitute an area where the subjacent state has full sovereignty exactly as provided by Article I of the Chicago Convention. The second zone, or "contiguous space," would extend on up to 300 miles above the earth's surface. The subjacent state would still have sovereignty throughout this area, but there would exist within it a right of transit for all non-military flights. The third and last zone, which would cover all space above the "contiguous zone," would be "free for the passage of all instrumentalities." He suggested further that any such definitions should be worked out under the aegis of the United Nations and that the pertinent regulations should be promulgated by the International Civil Aviation Organization.[21]

Dr. Meyer expressed full accord with Cooper's thesis that an international agreement was necessary to cope with the legal status of outer space. He also stated that the solution to the question lay in considering outer space as "a free area like the open sea." From mere practical considerations, Dr. Meyer observed, it would be impossible to fix an area in outer space which would correspond with the area of a subjacent state. ("The enormous distances between the surface of the earth and the outer

19 Cooper, *High Altitude Flight and National Sovereignty*, 4 Int'l. L.Q. 411, 417-418 (1951).

20 *Id.* at 418.

21 Cooper, *Legal Problems of Upper Space*, PROCEEDINGS OF THE AMERICAN SOCIETY OF INTERNATIONAL LAW AT ITS FIFTIETH ANNUAL MEETING HELD AT WASHINGTON, D.C., APRIL 25-28, 1956, 85 (1956). For additional remarks by another scholar in favor of Cooper's position see Knauth, *Remarks on International Air Law* at 102 in the PROCEEDINGS.

space make it impossible to state whether an event occurring in the outer space has occurred just above a certain state of the earth.") Meyer, however, did have some doubts about the usefulness of Cooper's "contiguous zone," which he took to be an extension of the concept of territorial waters. Meyer protested that little similarity exists between the situation on earth and the situation in outer space; since air becomes just gradually "thinner and thinner," there is "no determined shore" between airspace and outer space. Even so, he recognized the need to fix limits between the one and the other by international agreement, and he was content to say that the exact height of the demarcation "will be a question to be decided by the experts." [22]

One of Cooper's later surveys of proposed solutions gives qualified approval to the von Kármán line, noting that it "is capable of physical and mathematical demonstration at a reasonably stable height" but citing criticism to the effect that the line will vary with changes in climatic conditions. (Similar criticism, of course, could be made against the hundreds of millions of radio measurements which have established a master curve establishing a median interference factor.) Cooper, himself, declared that the airspace over which states have sovereignty "includes only areas where sufficient gaseous atmosphere exists to provide aerodynamic lift for such flight instrumentalities as balloons and aircraft." In the same connection he refers to outer space as "beyond the territorial sphere of any state," but cites the lack of agreement on the boundary between territorial airspace and outer space, or on the legal status of the "intermediate area" in which there may be insufficient gaseous atmosphere to support strictly aeronautical flight vehicles but enough to retard and "cause the fall" of space-flight instrumentalities such as satellites, "thus endangering the state below." [23]

G. P. Zadorozhnij, on his part, would set the limit to national sovereignty below the zone in which satellites orbit.[24] A Formosan scholar, Dr. Ming-Min Peng, takes a contrasting position. He maintains that at least until interplanetary travel becomes a reality, the sovereignty of nations over the space above them should be considered to extend to the limits of all flight. He points out that the operative scope of the Chicago Convention of 1944, which embraced the national sovereignty principle, extends to the outermost part of the atmosphere, and he justifies its use despite all practical difficulties on the ground of the immense danger to

[22] Meyer, Comments in Proceedings of the American Society of International Law at its Fiftieth Annual Meeting Held at Washington, D.C., April 25-28, 1956, 96, 97-98 (1956).

[23] Cooper, Missiles and Satellites: The Law and Our National Policy, 44 A.B.A.J. 317, 321 (1958).

[24] Zadorozhnij, Osnovnye Problemy Nauki Kosmicheskogo Prava (Basic Problems of Cosmic Law) in Kosmos i Mezhdunarodnoe Pravo (The Cosmos and International Law) 23, 46 (Korovin ed. USSR 1962).

subjacent states which otherwise must exist. Dr. Ming-Min Peng argues that nations have always considered themselves supreme in the whole area above their territory, and that the sovereignty statements in the Conventions of this century were never considered by the contracting parties to be limitative in nature but went to the limits of space thought to be usable by man.[25]

Jenks takes the position that the national sovereignty concept cannot be applied beyond the earth's atmosphere because the realities of interstellar space make such a concept "a meaningless and dangerous abstraction." He cites the general approval of the IGY satellite launching plans as an example of the acceptance of his thesis in international practice.[26]

Jenks further draws a useful analogy between space beyond the atmosphere of the earth and the high seas; indeed, he believes this to be a more valid comparison than one between outer space and airspace. Even assuming that the difficulties posed by such basic astronomical facts as the precession of the earth on its axis (facts which continually alter the relationship of particular sovereignties on earth to space beyond the atmosphere) could be successfully overcome, Jenks would still oppose projecting the sovereignty of a state into outer space. Such an approach "would be so wholly out of relation to the scale of the universe as to be ridiculous. . . ." It would be "like the Island of St. Helena claiming jurisdiction over the Atlantic."[27] Thus Jenks proposes that outer space be a *res extra commercium*, which will be incapable of appropriation by any particular state. He also makes three more proposals: (1) the United Nations should have jurisdiction over space activities; (2) failing this, common international rules and standards should be adopted which would cover a wide range of problems likely to arise; (3) rules must be adopted governing "the extent to which, and manner in which" nations may protect themselves against interference from outer space with matters lying within their territorial jurisdiction.[28]

Mr. Oscar Schachter pointed out as far back as 1952 the importance of knowing precisely what is meant by airspace. "Does the term 'air' extend only to the upper atmospheric regions?" he asks. "Should it be defined in terms of the composition and/or density of the gases?" Mr. Schachter suggests that, since the word appears in aviation treaties and apparently is intended to refer to such areas in the atmosphere as will support flight by aircraft (including balloons), the reasonable approach would be to

25 Ming-Min Peng, *Le Vol à haute altitude et l'article 1 de la Convention de Chicago, 1944,* Revue de Barreau de la Province de Québec.
26 Jenks, *International Law and Activities in Space,* 5 INT'L & COMP. L.Q. 99 (1956), reproduced in THE COMMON LAW OF MANKIND at 382-407 (1958).
27 *Id.* at 103-104, reproduced in THE COMMON LAW OF MANKIND at 388-389 (1958).
28 *Id.* at 113-114, reproduced in THE COMMON LAW OF MANKIND at 390-393 (1958).

establish a definition in these terms. He then points out that "whatever may be the precise boundary of the airspace, it is clear that when we go beyond it we are legally in a no man's world." After a brief discussion of the idea that jurists had held of indefinite extension of sovereignty upward for reasons of safety and protection of the underlying state, Mr. Schachter says that "although this approach might have seemed plausible to international lawyers years ago, it can hardly be justified when we consider its possible application [to space flight]." To concern oneself with the possibility of falling objects and the pull of gravity in considering the upward extent of national sovereignty "is not only unsound scientifically but quite useless from the standpoint of legal rules."

A brief survey of the Cooper theory of effective control only convinces Schachter that it creates more problems than it solves. As he states:

> There certainly does not appear to be any compelling reason in law or principle to carry national sovereignty this far. Indeed, any attempt to extend national territory higher than the airspace is bound to involve difficulties. Why not, then, fix the limit at the upper boundary of the airspace and no higher? [29]

Beyond the airspace, Schachter (like Jenks) points out that the development of law could well follow the example of the freedom we enjoy on the high seas. Such a development would, he says, "dramatically emphasize the common heritage of humanity and serve, perhaps significantly, to strengthen the sense of international community which is so vital to the development of a peaceful and secure world order." [30]

Mr. John A. Johnson, General Counsel of NASA, delivered a cogent statement that apparently reflected governmental opinion [31] on this problem, during the 1962 annual meeting of the ABA in San Francisco.[32] Beginning with fundamental considerations and building upon them, Johnson pointed out that "national territory is three dimensional." Then, he indicated that there is now no agreed legal definition of the exact upward extent of territorial "airspace." The power of a nation to exclude from its airspace any undesired activity is cited next, and the existence of present bilateral and multilateral treaties based on this rule is discussed.

---

[29] Schachter, *Who Owns the Universe?* in STAFF OF SENATE SPECIAL COMMITTEE ON SPACE AND ASTRONAUTICS, 85TH CONG., 2D SESS., SPACE LAW, A SYMPOSIUM 9, 15-17 (Comm. Print 1958). This article originally appeared in ACROSS THE SPACE FRONTIER (Ryan ed. 1952).

[30] *Id.* at 17.

[31] This assumption is based on two facts: (1) the absence of the usual reservations of personal opinion, and (2) the fact that the text of this statement was distributed by NASA on NASA News Sheet letterhead.

[32] *The Future of Manned Space Flight, and the "Freedom" of Outer Space,* Address by John A. Johnson, Before SICL, ABA, San Francisco, August 4, 1962.

By tying together discussion of superjacent air and contiguous sea, the topic of national security is raised. But, Johnson points out, "the disturbing or threatening nature of an activity in outer space does not depend upon its being directly over the territory of the nations affected." He therefore concludes, in the light of these facts, that the interests of subjacent states would not be served by the extension of their sovereignty to extremely high altitudes. What is required, he insists, is a form of international control over specific space activities.

The NASA official goes on to point out that, with the circling of many satellites over all nations without permission or protest, "the only conclusion that may reasonably be drawn . . . is that the nations have not regarded territorial sovereignty as extending as high as the point at which the orbiting of these satellites has occurred." He then states that this is the basis for the proclamation by the U.N. Committee on Peaceful Uses of Outer Space (UNCOPUOS) that outer space is "free for exploration and use by all States in conformity with international law."

Johnson's chief original contribution was his statement that the "primary question is not where outer space begins but where the upward reach of the exclusive power of the underlying State ends." The boundaries may or may not turn out to be the same. "In any event," he continued, "I feel that the emphasis is somewhat misplaced when the problem is stated in terms of drawing the boundary line of outer space."

Going on to discuss the problems of trajectory length of escape and re-entry activities of space vehicles, Johnson points out that, in his estimation, these problems are political in nature but their solution will be couched in legal terms. He then cites the view of one scientist to the effect that the X-15 type vehicle defeats the establishment of a clear-cut airspace-outer space distinction, and he identifies this view as that of "the scientist and engineer working in this field." The "Quigg fallacy" (see Section 4-6 of this chapter) is then followed through to its logical conclusion, with the discussion touching upon *Mercury, Dyna-Soar,* and other such vehicles. "I think it is evident," Johnson concluded, "that if this problem [i.e., defining the limits of national sovereignty] is to be solved it will be done on the basis of an accommodation of the political interests of the States concerned, and not on the basis of scientific or technological criteria."

If Johnson's conclusion is correct, the determination of an upper limit based on some physical or scientific standards—as encouraged by other writers—can no longer be hoped for. But is the question really one that can be left to the politicians to settle? This author does not accept such an outcome as inevitable, nor does he regard it as a desirable solution, since a political demarcation arbitrarily worked out on the basis of political expedience would at best be a tenuous settlement of doubtful permanence.

Dr. Welf Heinrich Prince of Hanover argued in the doctoral thesis already mentioned, in relation to the problem of sovereignty and jurisdiction, that

> . . . all those facts which make the close affinity of the air space with the earth appear to accord with the laws of nature, in no way apply to the vacuum beyond the atmosphere, for only the air-filled regions are so automatically connected with life on the surface of the earth that they may be considered part of it. This "correlation determined by considerations of space and sovereignty," however, does not exist between the area beyond the atmosphere and the lands and waters underneath it.

In his opinion, two conditions must be fulfilled before any area can be considered an integral part of a nation's territory: "There must be an area with frontiers which, although invisible, will be capable of being determined. On the other hand there must be a possibility of exercising 'effective control.' " And neither of these two conditions, he points out, can apply in the case of regions beyond the atmosphere.

Hanover continues his discussion by listing several telling arguments against the indefinite upward extension of national sovereignty. The constant motion of the solar system, and of the earth and sun within it, is one irrefutable argument that he gives. On all these grounds, he concludes that the area beyond the atmosphere, just like the airspace above the high seas and above any regions that lie outside the territorial jurisdiction of any state, "must be deemed free territory." [33]

More recently, Hanover has tended to support the von Kármán line as placing a workable upper limit upon the earth's atmosphere, for purposes of developing a space legal structure. "I am now inclined," he has said,

> . . . to the more practical suggestion of Mr. Th. von Kármán and Mr. A. G. Haley, who point out that it is possible to measure scientifically the altitude at which aerial devices are no longer able to support themselves by their own lifting power but by the centrifugal force of the earth—as in the case of the satellites. This seems to be a reasonable height at which to fix the boundary of sovereignty from earth.[34]

He has commented also that "only an international convention could settle" the upper limits question, and that "such a convention could perhaps best be reached within the framework of a wider [United Nations] agreement leading to a controlled reduction in armaments of all sorts." [35]

Dr. Eugene Pépin is another scholar who would limit national sovereignty to the atmosphere; although he does not define the boundary in quantitative terms, his thesis is compatible with the von Kármán line.

[33] Hanover, *Air Law and Space,* Thesis submitted to the Faculty of Law and Political Science at the Georg August University of Göttingen, 59-60 (1953) (Footnotes omitted) (translation). Substantially the same material appears in Symp. 271, 317-19.

[34] Hanover, *Problems in Establishing a Legal Boundary Between Air Space and Space,* 1st Colloq. 28, 29 (Vienna: Springer-Verlag, 1959).

[35] Hanover, *Circle of Thoughts,* 2d Colloq. 59 (Vienna: Springer-Verlag, 1960).

According to Pépin, "it should be taken for granted that over and around the surface of the earth (land or sea areas) there is what the scientists call 'atmosphere,' over certain parts of which national sovereignty is extended; and above the atmosphere there is 'space'.... Therefore, from a legal point of view, there are only two zones: one, the air or atmosphere, which has a legal status already defined in an international instrument, and the other, the space of a still undefined status." [36]

Similarly, C. E. S. Horsford regards the airspace sovereignty concept underlying the Chicago Convention as "inadequate" and "largely inapplicable" to the medium of space. "All operations in space," he points out, "will be conducted so far above what is now accepted as the airspace above a nation's territory, and so impossible will it be to observe any limitations of a territorial nature such as frontiers demand, that it is in the law of the sea that the answer would seem to lie." [37] Turning to maritime analogies, Horsford reasons that "in the light of modern international theory, outer space itself is likely to be considered a free navigable area as are the high seas...." [38]

Bin Cheng, a member of the Faculty of Law at University College, London, also feels that national sovereignty at extreme heights would be almost impossible to define, even for "States of continental dimensions." What will eventually happen, he concludes, is that nations will be forced to "subject the whole of outer space to the same regime as the high seas," although he does not rule out the possibility of establishing a contiguous zone, of presumably intermediate status, on the outer fringes of the atmosphere.[39] These observations may be construed as placing Cheng in the above company of those who oppose extension of national sovereignty to outer space and would allow its free use above a certain line—perhaps the von Kármán line.

The importance of reaching some common ground in this matter is underlined by many authorities, including Professor Cooper, as we have seen in his comments on the ABA report. Nevertheless, the positions expressed by official or quasi-official spokesmen of the powers which lead in space exploration have been on the cautious side.

Loftus Becker, while Legal Adviser of the U.S. State Department, wrote as follows: "Although the United States has plainly asserted its complete and exclusive sovereignty over the airspace above its territory, at no time

---

[36] Pépin, *Space Penetration*, PROCEEDINGS OF THE AMERICAN SOCIETY OF INTERNATIONAL LAW AT ITS FIFTY-SECOND ANNUAL MEETING HELD AT WASHINGTON, D.C., APRIL 24-26, 1958, 229 (1958).

[37] Horsford, *The Law of Space*, J. OF THE BRITISH INTERPLANETARY SOC., May-June 1955, 144-145.

[38] *Id.* at 146.

[39] Bin Cheng, *International Law and High Altitude Flights: Balloons, Rockets and Man-made Satellites*, 10 INT'L. & COMP. L.Q. 487, 493 (1957).

have we conceded that we have no rights in the higher regions of space." [40] Here he is speaking as a statesman and diplomat, invoking the political article of the United Nations covenant; he is not, of course, speaking as a lawyer. Similarly, a Soviet spokesman has stated that "the outer altitude of space sovereignty must be established in such a manner as to protect the state against encroachments on its territorial sovereignty." [41] However, G. P. Zhukov has stated, "It seems to me that from the standpoint of the security of states the height to which sovereignty extends above is not of decisive importance." [42] And a Polish jurist, while adhering to the criterion of security, still suggests that an upper limit to sovereignty might be set by an international convention. [43]

Dr. Alex Meyer, as indicated previously, lines up with the spokesmen who oppose the extension of national sovereignty concepts into outer space. Taking issue with both Becker of the USA and A. Galina of the USSR, as an air law specialist from the German Federal Republic, he highlights the impossibility of establishing in outer space a defined territory which would correspond to the boundaries of a particular state on earth. Even if the laws of nature could be amended to achieve this dubious end, Meyer joins Prof. Oliver Lissitzyn in the belief that it is also impossible to establish effective control over an area thus defined in outer space. The rights of sovereignty, he concludes, cannot be realized in outer space. He offers solace to those concerned about national security, however, by granting that states may engage in outer space activities on the basis of rights other than sovereignty, e.g., the right of self-defense. [44]

It should be noted, too, in this connection that even when such terms are used as "airspace," "air," "atmosphere," and so on, each and every sovereign nation quite clearly seems to claim that no man-made object or vehicle may pass over it at any height if such passage is for the purpose of acquiring military intelligence or constitutes a threat in some manner to the subjacent state. This claim is not easy to make effective, and has already been ignored in practice; but it must probably be regarded as the accepted international law relating to sovereignty.

On the other hand, it is encouraging to note that the satellites launched by the USSR and the USA during and following the International Geophysical Year (IGY) orbited the earth above the von Kármán jurisdictional line without evoking claims that "national airspace" had been

---

[40] Becker, *Major Aspects of the Problem of Outer Space*, 1958 DEP'T STATE BULL. 962 (1958).

[41] A. Galina, *K Voprosu o Mezhplanetnom Prave*, Sovetskoe Gosudarstvo i Pravo, July 1958, 52, 57.

[42] Zhukov, Remarks, Symp. 1072, 1082.

[43] Sztucki, *Security of Nations and Cosmic Space*, Symp. 1164.

[44] Meyer, *Some Problems Relating to Space Law*, 2d Colloq. 120 (Vienna: Springer-Verlag, 1960).

violated. It is encouraging also that the great powers, while cautiously disinclined to make formal renunciation of any rights in space which they may have, are not asserting definitive claims which would freeze them in cold war postures of opposition and thus preclude future agreement. A similar forbearance has led to the conclusion of the Antarctic Treaty. Instead, national views appear to be going through a process of development and maturation, influenced both by progress in the space art and by the growing realization that no nation can hope to achieve dominance in the vast realm of space.

What is the viewpoint of one who approaches this question from a supranational background? Mr. Oscar Schachter was Deputy Director of the United Nations Legal Department in 1952 when he took the position which we have seen above and which in general may be bracketed with those of Cheng, Hanover, Jenks, Meyer, Pépin, and the author. On that occasion, after calling for a limit to national sovereignty at the upper boundary of the airspace, Schachter went on to urge that "outer space and celestial bodies" be considered the common property of all mankind, over which no nation would be permitted to exercise domination. "A legal order," he said, "should be developed on the principle of free and equal use, with the object of furthering scientific research and investigation." [45]

This is, of course, an individual opinion. The United Nations officially has taken no position on a legal distinction between airspace and outer space. A report made in June 1959 by the U.N. *ad hoc* Committee on Peaceful Uses of Outer Space (UNCOPUOS) deemed any attempts at such official definitions premature at that time. It did suggest, however, that one approach to the problem would be to establish the limits of airspace and outer space within some practicable range, and that the type of activity conducted in space could also be explored as a basis for legal control.[46] (Later U.N. actions are discussed in detail in Chapter 10.)

George J. Feldman, a participant in the work of the Committee, took issue with its omission of the delimitation problem from the list of priority problems. He commented:

> It may be true, as the committee says, that an international agreement based on current knowledge and experience would be premature. Again, however, the important thing is to begin now—conduct research, make studies and investigations, and work out the principles on which an agreement may ultimately be based (subject to change in the light of later knowledge).

Feldman also suggested that, by changes it made in a draft report, the Committee gave implicit approval to treating outer space as *res communis*

[45] Schachter, *supra* note 29 at 15-17.

[46] Galloway, *The United Nations Ad Hoc Committee on the Peaceful Uses of Outer Space, Accomplishments and Implications for Legal Problems*, 2d Colloq. 30 (Vienna: Springer-Verlag, 1960).

omnium—the common possession of all.[47] Indeed, the Committee was explicit in expressing its belief that with the unchallenged launching of space vehicles during and after the IGY "there may have been initiated the recognition or establishment of a generally accepted rule to the effect that, in principle, outer space is, on conditions of equality, freely available for exploration and use by all in accordance with existing or future international law or agreements." [48]

On the question of whether the study of the legal problems of space is premature, Pépin offered an interesting historical sidelight in a lecture delivered in April, 1959, at the Institute of Air and Space Law, McGill University, Montreal. He pointed out that in 1900, three years before the first flight of the Wright brothers, the Institute of International Law discussed a draft convention on the legal status of aircraft. And he observed further that "if we want to reach agreement on questions affecting all states in the world, we cannot wait until situations become crystallized, in fact, nor until rules of custom—which are often difficult to modify—have been established."

It is also interesting to note the treatment of this subject in the 1959 Staff Report of the Select Committee on Astronautics and Space Exploration, established by the 85th Congress of the United States, with George J. Feldman as Director and Chief Counsel. The report first considers the position of experts in the United States and elsewhere who champion a case-by-case approach. For example, Rear Admiral Chester Ward declared in 1957, as Judge Advocate General of the U.S. Navy, that "we are being distinctly premature if we attempt to set up or to propose specific rules of space law at this early stage." [49]

The Staff Report then examines the opposing view of those who hold with Pépin, Jenks, and others that "the possibility of developing the law on sound principles depends *primarily* on an initiative being taken in the matter before *de facto* situations have crystallized too far." Weighing the contrasting stands, the report finds various reasons why the latter position is more convincing.[50]

In surveying the many comments on national upper limits the Staff Report also noted:

[47] Feldman, *The Report of the United Nations Legal Committee on the Peaceful Uses of Outer Space: A Provisional Appraisal,* 2d Colloq. 19, 22 (Vienna: Springer-Verlag, 1960).

[48] U.N. Doc. No. A/4141, at 6-170 (1959).

[49] Ward, *Projecting the Law of the Sea into the Law of Space,* JAG J., March 1957, 3-8. A more detailed exposition of this point of view is given by McDougal and Lipson, *Perspectives for a Law of Outer Space,* 52 AM. J. INT'L. L. 407 (1958). Lipson and Katzenbach, REPORT ON THE LAW OF OUTER SPACE (1960) also falls in the "wait and see" category.

[50] SURVEY OF SPACE LAW, STAFF REPORT OF THE SELECT COMMITTEE ON ASTRONAUTICS AND SPACE EXPLORATION, H.R. Doc. No. 89, 86th Cong. 1st Sess. 1-8 (1958).

Some of the leading writers on space law have interpreted the lack of objection to the satellite flights as setting a precedent in international law
[citing the author and Oscar Schachter at this point]. According to this
interpretation, outer space is now free by general practice and agreement
of nations, at least for scientific and peaceful flight, no matter what its status
was before the satellites were launched, and even though the satellite flights
were originally sanctioned by tacit consent alone. Consequently the legal
situation would remain unchanged when the IGY satellite program ends.

The Staff Report criticized this view on two points. In the first place, the
report contended that it lacked "the practical advantage of forcing an
early attempt to reach international agreement on the uses of outer space,"
Secondly, it was dismissed as representing "a rather extreme minority
view." [51]

Yet in the presentation by this author that is cited in the Staff Report
as embodying a viewpoint which is likely to inhibit early international
agreement, several specific proposals and requests were made. One of
these was that the President of the International Astronautical Federation
be empowered to name a committee which would draft a definition of
"airspace" and recommend a rule delimiting airspace jurisdiction. In the
same presentation, the von Kármán line and the Sänger regimes (on the
latter, see Section 4-8 of this chapter) were clearly offered as possible
starting points for research on the upper limits problem. To state that the
legal analysis of the results of the IGY cooperation did not imply the need
for an attempt to reach international agreement was to take the analysis
completely out of context. This author readily agrees that the legal analysis of the giving of express and tacit consent may be termed "begging"
the question of the upper limits of national sovereignty, in that the conclusions of such analysis hold true regardless of the altitude of the activity; but there is no valid reason to imply that the question had not been
approached. (See Chapter 3.)

Stephen Gorove takes cognizance of wide agreement that the "elonga-
tion of national sovereignty into the limitless spheres of the universe is
... untenable" and that sovereignty "should not reach beyond the airspace." He sees the future development of space law, however, as hinging
less on resolution of the disputed extent of the airspace than on the
decision-making factors of world power politics. To Gorove, therefore, the
establishment of an acceptable international inspection system is the most
urgent problem.[52]

A clue to the direction of development for international space law may
be found in the development of domestic air law. The very doctrine of

[51] *Id.* at 12.
[52] Gorove, *On the Threshold of Space: Toward a Cosmic Law* (Pt. I), N.Y.L.F.
305 (1958).

national sovereignty over the airspace which a handful of commentators would expand to all outer space is the relatively recent expression of the rights of a larger group, the nation, over the once supreme individual property owner. The necessities of modern air transportation have caused the courts to declare those superior rights. Thus the Supreme Court of the United States in *United States v. Causby*, a 1946 case which is a landmark in U.S. air law, held: "It is ancient doctrine that a common law ownership of the land extended to the periphery of the universe—*Cujus est solum ejus est usque ad coelum*. But that doctrine has no place in the modern world." [53] May it not eventuate that a still larger group, the family of nations, will one day declare its dominance in the realm of space law?

One more recent survey of the upper limits question was contained in an article by Captain George D. Schrader of the U.S. Air Force legal department, adapted from his thesis presented to the War College of Air University. In this article Schrader reviews both the legal terminology and the historical background of the question at issue. He considers several of the proposed solutions, and he leaves no doubt that in his mind the von Kármán line is best. Having cited this author extensively concerning its technical aspects and legal implications, he summarizes his discussion of the von Kármán line as follows:

> Therefore, Haley, by a very logical approach, establishes two basic needs— first, a definition of airspace which has as a point of departure a feasible area susceptible to both concurrent legal and physical determination, and secondly, an area in which subjacent states can exercise their sovereign rights within limits presently accepted by international law.[54]

A notable feature of Captain Schrader's discussion of the upper-limits question is that it forms part of a broadly integrated treatment of the entire problem of national sovereignty in outer space. While proposing that the von Kármán line be adopted by both Russia and the United States, he also proposes that both these countries grant to the International Astronautical Federation (IAF) the task of formulating ground rules for conducting space activities and that the International Institute of Space Law should work in conjunction with the IAF in identifying the various legal problems that are likely to affect space activities. In making this suggestion, he is careful to point out that he is by no means suggesting the adoption of a comprehensive space code which he believes to be premature at the present time. However, once the IAF has completed its task and the USSR and the United States have reached agreement on specific proposals, Schrader feels that these agreements and proposals should be submitted to the United Nations for formal adoption. He feels, too, that

[53] 328 U.S. 256, 260-61. (Footnote omitted.)
[54] Schrader, *National Sovereignty in Space*, MILITARY L. REV., July 1962, p. 53.

the United States and Russia should transfer to the United Nations all their sovereign interests above airspace—as defined under the terms of the von Kármán line—and that other nations should follow this example. Lastly, in his view, the International Court of Justice should be made the final arbiter of all legal matters pertaining to outer space.[55]

Despite the support given by Schrader and various other authors to the proposed von Kármán line, we must examine the pronouncements of William Strauss, Assistant to the General Counsel, Library of Congress, that the "multiplicity of proposals for fixed boundary lines between airspace and outer space make it quite apparent that there is little agreement on the scientific facts." [56] He says the top of the "atmosphere" has been estimated at anywhere from 10 to 650 miles above the earth's surface, depending upon the particular viewpoint and research interests of the scientist discoursing. He forgets that the facts themselves are well known or ascertainable, but the principal difficulty lies in deciding which ones are relevant, and how they should be weighted, in resolving the jurisdictional question. In any event, it is hard to accept Strauss' further conclusion that we may "have to forego any legal distinction between airspace and outer space and, instead, determine national jurisdiction (or the lack thereof) in terms of types of vehicles, i.e., those depending on support by aerodynamic lift and those propelled by rocket power and centrifugal force." [57] This commentator would require a space carrier from Mars to stop just short of Earth's airspace—which would indeed be a difficult and somewhat worthless feat!

SCIENTIFIC CONSIDERATION OF THE VON KÁRMÁN LINE

4–4 Essential features of the concept

Never before in the history of mankind has the necessity arisen so quickly to state legal parameters in connection with a vast new area of social change. The legal problems presented by the advent of space flight have been climacteric, and technology has far outstripped the formulation of the legal rules. The gap has widened to the point that even the peace of the world may be threatened.

In arriving at a level-headed statement of the jurisdiction of space law, the lawyer must obtain help from the physicist to determine just where "airspace" ends. We must ascertain this outer boundary because hundreds

[55] Id. at 73.
[56] Strauss, op. cit. supra note 13 at 25.
[57] Id. at 25.

of local laws of more than a hundred nations, and the restrictions of a score of international treaties, are bound tightly to the physical concept of airspace. And, as C. Wilfred Jenks has stated, "no lawyer should indulge in abstract speculation on the subject without first familiarizing himself with the scientific background and outlook. . . ." [58]

Ironically enough, the lawyer finds the main crackpots and nuisances among engineers and sociologists who assume the role of amateur lawyers and give vent to rather silly if harmless rhapsodies in a field wholly unfamiliar to them. To them the very real task of delimiting airspace is wholly unnecessary. The sound scientist, on the other hand, avoids legal interpretation while at the same time making an essential contribution by staying within his technical expertise and keeping the lawyer well advised on appropriate physical phenomena. Such was the most helpful role of Dr. Theodore von Kármán.

As was pointed out in a preceding section, Dr. von Kármán suggested practical methods of formulating the jurisdiction of airspace. Figure 1 [59] is intended to indicate what is known as the von Kármán primary jurisdictional line. The data which are contained in the diagram, and which will be explained below, are based on a paper delivered by Dr. von Kármán at the University of California in the spring of 1957 [60] and on a diagram made by Masson and Gazley of the Rand Corporation showing the possible ranges for continuous flight in the velocity-altitude coordinate system.

Jean Rivoire, in an article in 1958, commented that the formulae for an international agreement on outer space have been many; they have contained "several attractive aspects, but they have proved to be difficult to put into practice when subjected to detailed examination." In Rivoire's opinion the best solution would be one which met four necessary demands. First of all, the solution should not present an obstacle to progress; rather, it should guarantee the utilization of astronautics for peaceful purposes. Furthermore, the solution—whatever it might be—should be in accordance with both the fundamental principles of law and the latest

---

[58] Jenks, *The International Control of Outer Space*, 3rd Colloq. 3, 7 (Stockholm: Swedish Astronautical Society, 1961).

[59] An earlier version of this diagram was included in a paper presented at the VIIIth Annual Congress of the International Astronautical Federation in October 1957 at Barcelona, Spain. Quoting that paper as a source, E. Foncesca, in his paper *Dynamical Limitation of the Freedom of Space*, 2d Colloq. 24, interpreted the "Haley thesis" as placing the primary jurisdiction line at 800 kilometers. This was clearly erroneous. Eighty-four kilometers would have been more accurate. Another misinterpretation appears in the same colloquium in Valladão, *The Law of Interplanetary Space*, 2d Colloq. 57. There Mr. Valladão states: "Luis Tapia, supported by Andrew G. Haley, mentions the limit between the two spaces as the 'Kármán' line, after the American scientist who established the separation between the two spaces at 300 miles from the earth." Fifty-two miles would be more accurate.

[60] Von Kármán, *Aerodynamic Heating—The Temperature Barrier in Aeronautics*.

scientific data. Moreover, it should be clear, simple, and elastic, so as to meet changing technical conditions. Lastly, there should be harmony between it and agreements, conventions, and the like, that are now in force.[61] Examining these criteria closely and applying them to the von Kármán line, as it is explained here, one can readily see that every element is satisfied.

To establish sound bases for the demarcation of atmospheric and space jurisdiction it is necessary to consider that the conditions for accomplishing aerial flight, that is, to circle at constant altitude, may be expressed by the equation, Weight = Aerodynamic Lift + Centrifugal Force. The aerodynamic lift decreases with altitude because of the decreasing density of the air, and in order to maintain continuous flight after the air lift has been reduced to zero, centrifugal force must take over.

Consider the flight of Captain Ivan C. Kincheloe in which he took the X-2 rocket ship to 126,000 feet altitude. At this height aerodynamic lift carries 98% of the weight and only 2% is sustained by centrifugal or Kepler force. Thus it can be seen that the flight of the X-2 was strictly an aeronautical adventure and did not partake of space flight. Later flights of the X-15 have, however, by official announcement, penetrated the Kepler regime at the von Kármán line.

The limits of aeronautical flight are clearly drawn on the Masson and Gazley diagram, where airborne flight is shown to be a function of altitude and velocity. The velocity is limited by the altitude so that the maximum speed at sea level would be about five thousand feet per second. Beyond this point the friction of the atmosphere produces skin temperatures of more than 2,000°F. Similarly, altitude is limited by velocity. At a speed of five thousand feet per second the maximum altitude attainable by a pilot-driven aircraft is approximately 150,000 feet. This velocity is not sufficient to attain greater altitude. Therefore, there are two borderlines for continuous flight with aerodynamic lift—the heat barrier, which determines the maximum velocity, and the altitude barrier, which is a ratio between lift and Kepler force. Between these two barriers there is a corridor of continuous flight which terminates when at an approximate speed of 25,000 feet per second and an altitude of about 275,000 feet the Kepler force takes over and aerodynamic lift is gone. This is a critical jurisdictional line, marking the *theoretical limit of air flight*, which is here termed the von Kármán line. It must be noted with care that the exact location of this line of primary jurisdiction is not presented as an apodictic solution of the problem.

The von Kármán primary jurisdictional line may eventually remain as presented above or, as a result of such developments as improved tech-

[61] Rivoire, *Design for a Law of Space*, 1st Colloq. 97, 98-99 (Vienna: Springer-Verlag, 1960).

niques of cooling and more heat-resistant materials, it may be significantly changed. But these changes will be only in the exact location of the von Kármán line, for the existence of the line is certain, and wherever it is finally drawn will be the place where "airspace" terminates.

It would be senseless to build a surface trans-Atlantic steamer to perform the undersea function of a submarine. The functions of the spacecraft and the aircraft are essentially even more disparate. In arriving at a reasonable von Kármán line, physicists and lawyers inevitably will reach agreement as to the point where the aeronautical vehicle no longer may perform efficiently and within reasonable physical and engineering parameters.

4–5 Additional factors

The limitations on airspace are not solely determined by considerations of velocity and altitude. A. M. Mayo [62] has pointed out that control of the pilot's immediate environment from the standpoint of pressure and atmospheric composition becomes increasingly difficult as a function of both flight duration and altitude. He goes on to state that at altitudes below approximately 70,000 feet the problem of pressurization and composition can be taken care of relatively easily by pressurizing outside air. At higher altitudes, pressurization of the outside air becomes increasingly difficult both from the standpoint of the power required and from that of handling the very high temperatures resulting from extreme ratios. He also states that, as outside pressures become negligible with respect to cockpit pressure, the problem of explosive decompression or even gradual loss of pressure becomes so acute that until pressurized cockpits are as highly reliable as the wings and basic structure of present-day aircraft we will need to provide some pressurization safety equipment.

Mayo states that data as to the intensity and scope of cosmic radiation, together with data regarding its effect on human beings, are needed by the engineer. Questions relating to the existence of dangerous levels of other space radiations, such as X-rays from the sun, must also be surveyed. No completely practical approach to the protection of aircraft occupants against high-energy radiations has yet been outlined. It is possible that relatively simple solutions could be found both to the problem of pressurization safety equipment and to that of protection against harmful radiations, were it not for the fact that weight is such a primary consideration in all matters of aircraft design. Until solutions are found which

[62] The statements by Mayo are taken from Physics and Medicine of the Upper Atmosphere. A Study of the Aeropause (Albuquerque, 1952). (Report of a symposium sponsored by the USAF School of Aviation Medicine and the Lovelace Foundation for Medical Education and Research.)

do not overburden the aircraft, pressure and radiation present a barrier to high-altitude air flight as real as any.

The limitations placed on propulsion by the realities of high-speed, high-altitude atmospheric flight have been discussed by R. M. Salter.[63] In order for airborne vehicles (those using forward motion to derive lift from the atmosphere as opposed to lighter-than-air vehicles) employing air-breathing power plants such as jet engines to fly at very high altitudes, it is necessary for such vehicles to operate at supersonic speeds not only to provide sufficient lift but also for adequate thrust. At an altitude of 20 miles, for example, the required Mach number for a ramjet is over 5 (i.e., five times the speed of sound), and the resultant incoming air has a stagnation temperature of the order of 2,000°F. Since energy must be imparted to this air at higher temperatures, it may be seen that a present engineering limitation on suitable fuels and materials is approached. This is particularly true with the use of nuclear heating.

All these considerations will enter into the final determination of the von Kármán line. So will the danger of material collisions with the airframe, escape problems, the numerous problems posed by combined stresses and, indeed, many fundamental questions of the construction of aircraft as such.

There are, of course, some writers who remain unconvinced and even confused by the von Kármán line because it fails to lay down an absolutely rigid line between airspace and outer space. These writers fail to understand that there are many situations in science where one must deal not with rigid definitions but with an approximate median, based on an immense family of curves. Moreover, as Spencer M. Beresford has pointed out, a purely static spatial solution to the problem of jurisdiction and sovereignty in outer space seems hardly relevant to the major political, military, and economic policy factors involved.[64] Those factors, in effect, are the very opposite of static.

A close parallel to the concept of the von Kármán line is probably quite readily recognizable in the multi-variable determinations which are employed in the work of the Federal Communications Commission. Many of the "legal" aspects of Commission work are based on mean curves. Perhaps the most basic of these is the "primary service contour" of a broadcasting station. Another example is the definition of the "service area of a base station" in the Domestic Public Land Mobile Radio Service. The limits of this service area for stations engaged in two-way communication service are defined as being described by a field strength contour

[63] Salter, in id. at 480-87.

[64] L & K Rep. 104, §615; *The National Aeronautics and Space Act of 1958*, an Address by S. M. Beresford, Before the Aircraft Club of Washington, Wash., D.C., June 10, 1958. Beresford is also opposed to extending the laws of the air and sea into space. Beresford, *Sovereignty in Outer Space*, Address at the Law School, University of Virginia, Charlottesville, Virginia, Nov. 13, 1958.

of 37 decibles above one microvolt per meter. For stations engaged in one-way signal service the limits are described by a field strength contour of 43 decibles above one microvolt per meter. Within the area there is an expected service reliability of not less than ninety per cent.[65] As this last provision makes quite clear, exact and immutable lines are neither expected nor demanded in all areas of the law. So it is with the von Kármán line.

Professor Stephen Gorove of New York University Law School is one of the few writers who understood this concept as it was first presented. In a paper delivered in 1958, he referred to this author as claiming, in accord with the von Kármán thesis, that "airspace terminates at the jurisdictional boundary line which, on the basis of our *present* scientific knowledge, may be *provisionally* set at the height of approximately 275,000 feet." [66] (Emphasis added.)

Even those skeptics who deny much, if not all, usefulness in present attempts to define the limits of national sovereignty have a healthy and justifiable respect for legitimate efforts such as this to reach a realistic determination. Messrs. Lipson and McDougal of Yale, for example, after decrying the waste of time and effort on the problem by some scholars, go on to declare: "Other efforts to arrive at boundary definitions as functions of altitude, mass, velocity, heat resistance, and other physical variables combined, seem more technically sophisticated and might survive a little longer in the progress of scientific knowledge and engineering technology." [67] A citation of the author's work following this statement gives evidence that at least some thought is being given to these ideas even in unexpected places.

Whether the von Kármán line will be officially adopted naturally remains to be seen. Even if not embodied in any formal international convention on airspace sovereignty, it is perfectly possible that the von Kármán line may become a recognized principle of international law by virtue of usage in statutes, regulations, and purely informal agreements. For example, in a recent interim change in Air Force Manual 25-13, the U.S. Air Force has established as the official demarcation of the required height to qualify as an astronaut a line fifty miles above the surface of the earth (264,000 feet). This official Air Force standard is, of course, reasonably close to the altitude at which the proposed von Kármán line would be located.

Another interesting development along this same line was the tentative agreement reached in 1960 between the United States and the USSR on

[65] FCC Reg. §21.504, 47 C.F.R. 21.504.
[66] Gorove, *On the Threshold of Space: Toward a Cosmic Law. Problems of the Upward Extent of Sovereignty*, 1st Colloq. 69, 72 (Vienna: Springer-Verlag, 1959).
[67] McDougal and Lipson, *Perspectives for a Law of Outer Space*, 52 Am. J. Int'l. L. 407, 425 (1958).

standards for judging the records set by manned rocket-vehicle flights. In the proposed rules, which were to be submitted to the Fédération Aéronautique Internationale for adoption, space flight was defined as flight to or above 62 miles altitude (100 kilometers). In commenting on the accord, the journal *Aviation Week & Space Technology* recalled that there was as yet no international legal definition of the dividing line between the atmosphere and space and pointed to the warning of some space law specialists that "if such definitions are not agreed upon soon, custom is likely to become accepted as law." [68] It was noteworthy that representatives of the United States and the Soviet Union here agreed upon joint sponsorship of a point adjacent to that which the median curve of the von Kármán jurisdictional line would indicate as the end of airspace and the beginning of outer space. It was also encouraging to observe a first-class engineering journal raising the question of customary law!

4–6　The "rocket plane": an alleged problem

There is one particular objection raised with respect to the von Kármán line which holds that the existence of such rocket-powered craft as the *X-15* will inevitably detract from or even destroy whatever useful delineation it might provide. This objection, which is seriously regarded by many persons, was given its "classic" formulation by Mr. Philip Quigg in 1958.

Quigg commented that "a definition of space which permits sovereignty to extend to the extreme limits of the atmosphere will be largely meaningless." [69] After noting the widespread agreement that "outer space must not only be declared free but its frontiers defined," Quigg examined—and found wanting—the author's attempt to establish a clearly definable boundary in terms of the von Kármán line. His criticism is worth quoting at some length:

> The clarity of Haley's [more appropriately, Dr. von Kármán's] proposed boundary has been muddled considerably by the announcement that the Air Force plans to fly an experimental aircraft to more than twice the altitude at which aerodynamic lift is gone. The *X-15* will thus soar well above the perigee of *Explorer III* (110 miles) and may reach that of the first three sputniks (145 to 150 miles). It will accomplish this, however, much as an old car gets over a hill—by gaining maximum speed on the straight-away and counting on its weight and speed to carry it up the grade. So the *X-15* is expected to achieve a speed of some 5,000 miles an hour in level flight with most of its weight supported by aerodynamic lift; then turning upward, and with a final booster from its rocket motor, it will coast into the realm of satellites, gliding back to earth immediately, its energy exhausted.

[68] Aviation Week & Space Technology, Oct. 10, 1960, p. 33.
[69] Quigg, *Open Skies and Open Space*, 37 Foreign Affairs 95, 99 (1958). Symp. 463, 466.

The significance of this vehicle is that it blurs the distinction between air-craft and spacecraft and may indeed be the prototype of future spaceships. The first human to be placed in orbit is likely to be borne in a winged craft, not a pure rocket. The wings will give him greater stability and control in take-off and ease his glide back to earth. And before space stations are avail-able to be used as transfer points from aircraft to spacecraft, the descendants of the X-15 may be so highly perfected that flight will be an unbroken spec-trum from atmosphere to space. While this does not invalidate the dis-tinction between zones of aeronautical and astronautical flight (even Under Secretary of Defense Quarles has supported the concept as a way of dis-tinguishing between airspace and outer space), it becomes somewhat more doubtful that the boundary proposed by Haley will be accepted as the limit of national sovereignty.[70]

Quigg's prediction concerning the first human to be placed in orbit has already been proved inaccurate, unless one accepts a somewhat tortured definition of "winged craft, not a pure rocket." For the rest, certain of his observations are plausible, at first glance, but they are really no more pertinent with regard to the legal usefulness of the von Kármán line than the fact that all the rockets and satellites which rise above that line must first pass through the airspace below it. The question of maneuvering in airspace has never had the slightest reference to airspace jurisdiction; and the X-15 itself is a rocket vehicle, *not* an aircraft, no matter how it is considered.

Much to the annoyance of those who have knowledge of the scientific facts, the above-quoted message has been referred to time after time and has even achieved the dignity of an illustrative reference parameter in some articles.[71] If the statement is examined with any care, one is baffled in attempting to explain it, since it is so unrelated to facts—any facts—let alone the von Kármán jurisdictional line.

Mr. Quigg's analysis reflects substantial confusion as to the true nature of aircraft and space vehicles. An aircraft, properly considered, is a vehicle which must subsist on air because it "breathes" or at least requires the support of air, and which is not designed or intended for flight into outer space. Space vehicles, by contrast, may well use the air as a frictional

---

[70] *Id.* at 99, Symp. 466-67. In Murphy, *Air Sovereignty Considerations in Terms of Outer Space,* Symp. 198, 210-11, Mr. Murphy notes that there have been many sug-gestions based on aerodynamic properties of vehicles and the physical properties of air. He concludes:

This, too, would seem to be an unsatisfactory test, although it brings us into a field of discussion where some limitation is accepted as a basic premise and where it is possible to sift out elements which contribute to a workable proposal. It is unsatis-factory in that aeronautical engineers are constantly producing aircraft of a design capable of flight both in air-supplying-lift and in the very thin air where thrust alone maintains flight. . . . Hence we are again faced with the kind of flexible standard under which the law can work only under the greatest handicap. In the last analy-sis, there can be no defensible correlation between the political and economic legal theories of national sovereignty and the purely physical laws of the forces of lift.

[71] Symp. 790; 1st Colloq. 40 (Vienna: Springer-Verlag, 1959).

guidance aid on entry or departure; and they might well use air-breathing assistant take-off devices, such as enormous airplanes for launch platforms or ramjet or athodyd motors for initial assistance during their momentary flight through the air. But these circumstances will not change their essential nature as rocket-powered space vehicles which are at most only incidentally dependent on air. Nor do such factors in any way affect the validity of the von Kármán line.

The reference to "winged craft, not a pure rocket" is notably lacking in precision. Presumably, however, Mr. Quigg meant here to denote something comparable to the X-15; and in reality the whole excerpt becomes more inexplicable in view of the use made of the X-15 as an illustration. The X-15 has wings, but nevertheless it *is* a pure rocket, having no air-breathing devices and depending for its own propulsive capacity on rocket power only. The mere fact that it has the configuration, surfaces, and controls which enable it to make temporary use of air for guidance does not convert it into an *aircraft* in the normal sense of that term. Once this vehicle leaves the earth's air, it must depend upon the trajectory already established or upon some other method of guidance.

In all justice to Mr. Quigg, it must be pointed out that even some NASA officials do not seem to understand the basic principles involved in this matter.[72] Under the assumptions of the Quigg approach, however, any vehicles—vehicles designed for earth orbiting or for voyages to the moon, the planets, and even the stars—would not be considered space vehicles if they used air guidance surfaces during the brief seconds of their departure from or return to the earth. Indeed, if they utilize the earth's air in any fashion at all, it seems, they would not be space vehicles. Thus, by a logical extension of the Quigg thesis, the use of a parachute or any form of air-drag brakes would mysteriously transform an earth-orbiting satellite into an aircraft and thereby subject it to the airspace jurisdiction of the nations of the earth. Along with the X-15, the *Dyna-Soar* would also become an aircraft, because this vehicle, which is a boost-glide orbital space craft, depends on air glide both at departure and upon return and is to be fitted with large stabilizer fins on the booster. The *Mercury* capsule, designed as a manned satellite, would likewise be a mere airship, as the two-stage *Mercury* landing package employs a parachute landing system (air brakes, of course!) with maximum reliability.[73]

It is, in short, both surprising and somewhat discouraging that so inadequately thought-out a criticism as the "Quigg fallacy" should have

[72] Address by Robert E. Horner, Associate Administrator, NASA, to the Second Annual Industry Missile and Space Conference, Detroit, Michigan, NASA Release, June 16, 1959.

[73] Statement by Dr. H. L. Dryden, NASA Release, May 19, 1960.

obtained a significant place in the literature. It was particularly surprising to see John A. Johnson of NASA following in Quigg's footsteps, as mentioned earlier in this chapter.

Ingo V. Munch, in a review of the 1st and 2d Colloquia on Space Law, welcomes the fact that some of the papers presented were written by scientists and physicians, believing that "work on space law without a real understanding of the technical questions connected with space flight can hardly be worthwhile." [74] This point is particularly significant, and in fact it cannot be overemphasized.

4–7 A Soviet criticism

Feliks Nikolayevich Kovalev and Ivan Ivanovich Cheprov, both members of the Legal Office of the Soviet Ministry of Foreign Affairs, dealt in some detail with aspects of the von Kármán line when they wrote the first full-scale Russian treatise on space law, *Na Puti k Kosmicheskomu Pravu* (Toward Cosmic Law), published in June 1962.[75] In Chapter 1 of this volume, the authors describe seven basic approaches to the delimitation of airspace from cosmic space. The first two approaches discussed are the "identification of the sphere of action of state sovereignty with the terrestrial atmosphere" and "the delimitation of the sphere of action of state sovereignty by the altitude which aircraft can reach." The third approach, which they describe on pages 42-43, is the "determination of the sphere of action of state sovereignty by means of coordinates of altitude and velocity"—i.e., the von Kármán concept, which they introduce as the approach "proposed by the American lawyer, A. Haley, with reference to the ideas of the rocket specialist, von Kármán." Because they make many apparently trenchant criticisms of the von Kármán line as a primary jurisdictional boundary, it seems advisable to reproduce their arguments at some length.

After first presenting a brief descriptive summary of the von Kármán line—illustrated with a reproduction of the original 1957 version of the Masson-Gazley diagram—the Soviet writers go on to say:

> The "demarcation of air and cosmic jurisdiction," in Haley's opinion, can be accomplished by means of a curve which he calls the "primary jurisdictional boundary." Evidently, it is envisioned that all flights "below" this line are in airspace, whereas all "above" are in cosmic space.
>
> This proposal suffers from the same defects, though perhaps not in as pronounced a manner, as the preceding proposals. The "primary jurisdictional

[74] Munch, Review of 1st Colloq. and 2d Colloq., 10 ARCHIV DES VÖLKERRECHTS 120 (1962).

[75] Earlier in 1962, a collection of essays entitled KOSMOS I MEZHDUNARODNOE PRAVO (The Cosmos and International Law) was published, under the editorship of Ye. Korovin.

boundary" will be altered by further alloys, and in the event that a convertible airspace vehicle is created this boundary would be transformed into the most intricate and artful curve with knots and loops. According to the diagram, instrumentalities located over one and the same geographic point and at the same altitude will in one case be in "airspace" (e.g., at an altitude of 250,000 feet they move at a velocity of about 30,000 feet per second), and in another case will be in "cosmic space" (if their velocity is less and they are in "noncontinuous" flight, as in the case of ballistic rockets). As a result, if foreign aerodynamic instrumentalities and intercontinental ballistic rockets would fly over a neutral state at approximately the same altitude, this state could protest against the former, but not against the latter—which is an obviously absurd state of affairs.

Apart from this, the Haley diagram does not correspond even in its present form with the actual flight possibilities. By his own admission at the Colloquium on the Law of Outer Space in London in 1959, the configuration of the "primary jurisdictional boundary" is determined not only by altitude and velocity, but by many structural peculiarities of flight instrumentalities, by the degree of cosmic radiation, and by a series of other factors. These reservations in essence connotate a further deviation toward the theory of limiting the sphere of action of state sovereignty to an altitude which air instrumentalities can reach.

Haley was also obliged to make the reservation that the spheres of aeronautics and astronautics are interconnected, as he put it, "by a very small corridor." (A. G. Haley, "Space Exploration—The Problems of Today, Tomorrow and in the Future," Proceedings, Second Colloquium on the Law of Outer Space, London, 1959, pages 51-52). However, according to the determination of Haley himself, this corridor is not at all so small—it extends spatially from 37.3 miles to 3,728 miles above the earth's surface, and, of even greater importance, it is precisely this "corridor regime" which contains such a category of flight instrumentalities as ballistic missiles. What about their status? To declare that they are simply "transitional," without even revealing what this transition means juridically, is completely insufficient. However, Haley does not offer in this regard anything more explicit.

A curious feature of this discussion is that it is largely based on a resurrection of the 1957 Masson-Gazley diagram, which has been considerably revised since that time. To be sure, on page 98 of this book the Soviet authors cite "First Colloquium on the Law of Outer Space, The Hague, 1958" in which a revised version of the diagram they criticize appeared; yet they make no reference to the later diagram. In fact, since 1957 later versions of the diagram have appeared in more than a dozen publications, with textual revisions taking into account both early criticisms and current advances in technology. Nevertheless, Messrs. Kovalev and Cheprov insist on attacking the 1957 version, when any well-equipped library might have provided them with several that are both later and more advanced. The use of such dated materials suggests that adequate and up-to-date library facilities simply are not available in Russia for research in the social and juridical sciences, because the authors themselves are outstanding Soviet legal scholars, and their volume, generally speaking, is of unquestionable quality and dependability.

Specifically these critics have claimed:

1) That the primary jurisdictional boundary is represented by a curve. This has not been the case since early 1958. (See Figure 1 *supra*.) The proposed von Kármán line is a fixed horizontal boundary which is located at an altitude established by examining the physical, thermodynamic, aerodynamic, exobiological, physiological and mechanical problems involved in air and space flight.

2) That the boundary will be altered by further progress of technology. This point has been fully discussed above.

3) That instrumentalities located over one and the same geographic point and at the same altitude will in one case be in "airspace", . . . and in another case will be in "cosmic" space. This is physically impossible.

4) That the diagram "even in its present form" (could this mean that later diagrams were consulted and ignored?) does not correspond with actual flight possibilities. No further discussion is offered here, and there does not seem to be any particular point made.

5) That multiple factors are considered in determining the von Kármán line and that, therefore, this author is apparently in favor of "limiting the sphere of action of state sovereignty to an altitude which air instrumentalities can reach." If this is intended as a criticism of the von Kármán line, it fails to disturb the theory of the line, i.e., that activities normally contemplated as within the "airspace" should be within the control of the underlying sovereign, while activities above the "airspace" are free to all nations for peaceful purposes.

6) That "Haley was obliged to make the reservation that spheres of aeronautics and astronautics are interconnected, as he put it, 'by a very small corridor.'" Citing the 2d Colloquium, the writers continue by claiming that Haley determined this corridor to extend "from 37.3 miles to 3,728 miles above the earth's surface." However, the figures quoted here have been taken entirely out of context. At the Colloquium, they were used merely to represent the approximate dimensions of the "escape regime" defined by Dr. Eugen Sänger, on which more will be said in the next section of this chapter. Nor was the von Kármán line even mentioned anywhere in the same passage.

4–8 *Some alternative approaches*

It is clear that the satellites now in orbit have passed through the von Kármán primary jurisdictional line. The velocity of each of the satellites is approximately 17,500 miles per hour, and even at perigee they are normally over 100 miles high. The regime of these vehicles in relation to that of aeronautical flight is shown by a schematic drawing (Figures 2 and 3) by Dr. Eugen Sänger of the Forschungsinstitut f. Physik d. Strahlantriebe, Stuttgart. Dr. Sänger places the limits of aeronautics proper at about 60

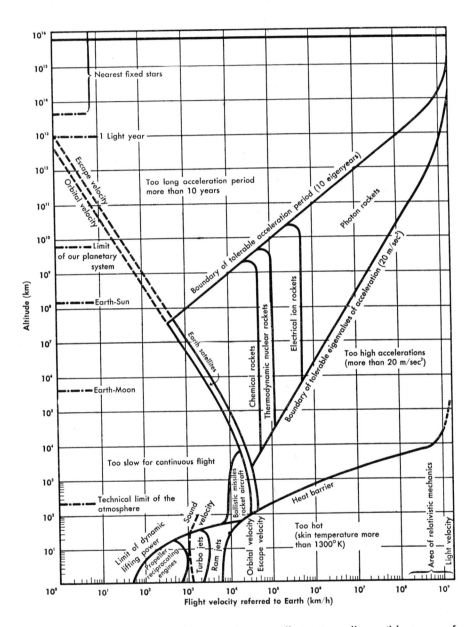

Figure 2 The E. Sänger schematic diagram illustrating all possible types of flight regimes (altitude versus velocity).

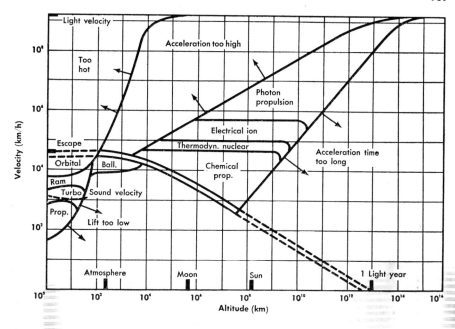

Figure 3 The S. F. Singer adaptation of the Sänger schematic diagram illustrating all possible types of flight regimes (velocity versus altitude).

kilometers (37.3 miles). Though aerodynamic lifting power is gradually replaced by centrifugal force from the trajectory curvature beyond a velocity of 10,000 kilometers (6,214 miles) per hour, the intersection of the curves of limit of aerodynamic lifting power and heat barrier is nevertheless physically real. As the utmost limit of the ramjet, it is also the definite limit of aeronautics. Ballistic rockets and rocket-powered space craft, on the other hand, are not limited by this barrier of aerodynamic lifting support, so that their possible flight altitudes increase to several thousand kilometers and their flight velocities approach orbital velocity, where the aerodynamic lifting power is completely replaced by the inertial forces of the circular orbit about the earth. Thus, the ballistic missiles which placed the satellites themselves into orbit entered the domain of pure astronautics upon reaching orbital velocity. It can therefore be seen that only a very small corridor connects aeronautics with astronautics, i.e., the altitudes and velocities between the final limits of aerodynamic lift and orbital velocity.

Beyond this corridor there open the immense vistas of interplanetary, interstellar, and intergalactic flight which, surprisingly enough, are also limited in much the same way as the aeronautic flight regime is limited. This domain of pure astronautics, as indicated on Dr. Sänger's diagram, is bounded by two limiting curves both of which are biological in nature. The lower limits are set by the maximum capacity of the human body to withstand the forces of acceleration. The upper boundary results from the consideration that for tolerable values of uniform acceleration, the duration of the acceleration necessary to achieve certain distances becomes too great with respect to the natural lifetime of humans. Dr. Sänger estimates the maximum altitude obtainable to be farther than the moon, but not as far as the sun if current means of propulsion (i.e., chemical rockets) are used. With the use of nuclear rockets, electrical ion rockets and the ultimate, the photon rocket, this maximum altitude may, of course, be greatly increased.

In scientific terms there are, then, three distinct regimes of flight, each possible within certain ascertainable, but by no means ascertained, limits: (1) the aeronautical regime; (2) the corridor of atmospheric escape; (3) the astronautic regime. The aeronautical regime is well regulated by law, and the jurisdictional problems it presents have been solved by treaty. The third, the astronautic regime, has been described as a legal "no-man's world" [76] over which the nations of the earth have no jurisdiction. This leaves the question of the escape corridor, which in Dr. Sänger's diagram extends from 37.3 to about 3,728 miles. Is it to be free for all to use, or are there reasons for extending terrestrial jurisdiction to encompass it?

Sänger himself, it must be noted,[77] is of the opinion that national jurisdiction should end at the upper limit of flying altitude for aerodynamic vehicles—i.e., just this side of the "escape regime." On the other hand, the latter concept naturally brings to mind once again the proposal of John Cobb Cooper that a zone of "contiguous space" be recognized, sandwiched between "territorial space" and outer space, in which subjacent states would retain sovereignty but all non-military flights would enjoy an automatic right of passage. The upper limit of Cooper's "contiguous" zone was set at 300 miles, so that it would include only a small portion of the "escape regime," and in fact they are quite clearly not the same thing. Nevertheless, they are alike in that each occupies the middle or intermediate position in a three-part scheme.

Because of political problems of international negotiation, Cooper's "contiguous space" idea is not readily susceptible to implementation. On the other hand, under certain conditions national jurisdiction will be quite indirectly but effectively maintained over what might be called "contiguous space." For example, the recovery of full-scale nose cones of the *Jupiter* and other rockets has hastened the day when the nations of the earth can be offered point-to-point rocket communications involving many services. Professor Cooper believes that the first commercial use of rocket

76 Schachter *op. cit. supra* note 29.
77 Astronautics, March 1960, p. 18.

vehicles will be for mail transportation between New York and London. This service and other services will gradually be extended to the four corners of the world—Melbourne to London, Moscow to Los Angeles, Buenos Aires to Chicago, Los Angeles to New York. The trajectories of each of these routes will naturally be different, and will involve different altitudes. Some of these rockets will describe a trajectory requiring heights of 300 miles or less, and others will probably require heights in excess of 1,000 miles—extending well into the "escape regime." In either case, national jurisdiction will be effectively maintained by the granting of launching and landing rights, and thus there will be indirect national control with respect to point-to-point earth rockets over contiguous space.[78] With the advent of manned rocket ships, this control undoubtedly will become more severe because of vastly increased considerations of safety and other problems.

More study will certainly be necessary before any final decision can be made as to whether, as some have urged, territorial sovereignty should cease at the aeronautical frontier—the von Kármán line—or whether some measure of direct control above this region be provided, perhaps along the lines suggested by Professor Cooper.

Still another approach to this problem is outlined by Eurico Fonseca in a paper delivered in 1959 which de-emphasizes the lineal boundary and would make the velocity of a given vehicle the decisive factor in determining it to be either aeronautical, and thus subject to national sovereignty, or astronautical, thus enjoying the same freedom as a ship on the high seas. The critical velocity in his scheme would be escape velocity:

> All manned space ships or even unmanned space vehicles whose speed is superior to the escape velocity for a given planet are to be considered free as are ships on the high seas and therefore they will be subject only to the general or special laws of the launching country and thus subject to the international agreements signed by it.[79]

A further proposed solution is that of G. Vernon Leopold and A. L. Scafuri of the Special Committee on Space Law of the State Bar of Michigan, who hold that the key distinction should be one between suborbital flight, on the one hand, and orbital or super-orbital flight on the other. At the request of the author for a concise expression of their views,

---

[78] In Milankovic, *The Legal Problem of Outer Space*, Symp. 1213, 1216, the writer points out that:

> It does not appear very logical to divide that single trajectory of a rocket into two phases each with a different legal regime. All the rocket did was to connect two points on the earth. There can hardly be any doubt that from the legal point of view it should be considered that every flying instrumentality connecting two points on the earth—regardless of its means of propulsion or trajectory—has never left the zone of state sovereignty.

[79] Fonseca, *Dynamical Limitations of the Freedom of Space*, 2d Colloq. 24, 25-26 (Vienna: Springer-Verlag, 1960).

Leopold and Scafuri provided the following abstract for inclusion in this work:

Historically the theories of vertical ownership and airspace sovereignty were developed to protect inhabitants on the surface against elevated objects which, according to everyday human experience, are prone, gravitationally, to drop from above and cause damage and injury. However, unlike aircraft or even ballistic missiles, craft engaging in true cosmic missions are obliged to operate at angular momenta and eccentricities such as to preclude their unpowered and unguided return to earth. Therefore, why should the law of the sovereign airspace have application to vehicles which without additional application of power, will remain aloft indefinitely? Any accommodation circumscribing territorial sovereignty at a particular altitude might work a gratuitous limitation upon subsequent state countermeasures in a technologically more advanced era. It would therefore be far more preferable to consider vehicles exempt from the territorial sovereignty of underlying states regardless of the altitude attained by them, during that interval of time during which their angular momenta and eccentricity exceed the minimum required by them for unpowered orbiting. Conversely, whenever they reduce their momentum or eccentricity below this minimum, they become once more subject to the regulatory jurisdiction of overflown states.

The suggested dynamic parameter is far superior to any static altitude boundary under which jurisdictional characterization of a particular craft would depend solely upon its spatial position at the instant of observation, or, to put it differently, through whose column of territorial airspace it happens to be flying when observed. Moreover, Drs. Berger and Ricupito of the Lockheed Division have estimated that even at this primitive stage of the art, tracking of a given craft over five seconds of its flight path, followed by one hundred seconds of computing time, would suffice for a ruling as to whether the craft was moving suborbitally and therefore subject to the sovereign jurisdiction of surface states, or whether the momentum and eccentricity of its flight satisfied the minimum criteria for exemption therefrom. In view of the almost universal need among nations for developing foolproof and all-seeing missile warning systems, it seems reasonable to project that within the very near future global facilities for detecting, tracking, classifying, and perhaps even disciplining all objects moving within detection range of our planet will become available.

. . . Prominent scientists repeatedly point out that, while suborbital flight is primarily ground-oriented and therefore of concern mainly to the security and other vital interests of surface states, cosmic flight, as defined above, is not. By way of example, orbital push-button bombs, while possible, are far more cumbersome, expensive, and vulnerable to defensive countermeasures than anti-surface ballistic missiles launched from concealed surface bases. If the yardstick proposed by some writers, that of the predominating pattern of use, were applied, suborbital flight uses, as a category, ought to remain primarily excludable by unilateral state action, whereas orbital and superorbital uses by and large could be considered as shareable among all states. Vertical territorial sovereignty would not suffice in any event against offensive application of cosmic missions. Orbital spying, for instance, could be conducted from a wide angle. If sufficiently objectionable it could be dealt with by offended states only through assertion of the right of self-defense. Acceptance of the theory here proposed would simply mean that disciplinary measures against offending spacecraft engaging in cosmic flight would no longer be predicated upon the theory of airspace sovereignty.

Hopefully, such unilateral state exclusionary measures will become unnecessary as specific accommodations will be reached, preferably within the legislative and enforcement framework of an international cosmic surveillance authority to be hereafter established. Since the institutional framework of such an organization would lend itself equally well to achievement of accommodations relative to cosmic uses which are unrelated to flight, i.e., signal transmission, rights to non-terrestrial resources, etc., the suggested proposal goes far beyond answering merely the drop threat. A jurisdictional dichotomization of this nature, it is submitted, would establish a pattern for cosmic order.[80]

In connection with this same proposal, Leopold and Scafuri asked Dr. Eugen Sänger for a concrete opinion whether the "dichotomization of space flight into two broad categories, suborbital and orbital" would in effect constitute a division into two clearly distinguishable classes—of which (a) the first (suborbital) would "overwhelmingly" include uses that "bear a direct relation to the security and other vital interests" of subjacent states and should thus remain under their exclusive regulatory authority, and (b) the second (orbital) would include for the most part only uses which "indirectly or casually affect the security and other vital interests" of subjacent states and could thus be readily placed under the control of an international authority. To this question Sänger responded, "In the present, technically primeval, initial state of astronautic development, I think such a distinction is possible, although it would rather soon be made obsolete, the future technical goal of aeronautical and astronautical engineering being the complete spatial independence of their vehicles." As one specific weakness of the Leopold-Scafuri system, he stated that "with the appearance of continuous rocket propulsion engines" it would be necessary to add a third category of control to cover "vehicles usable as aircraft and as spacecraft alike, and which do not follow present trajectories."

Sänger also observed that he personally considered "a limitation in altitude of the national sovereign airspace, analogously to the offshore limitations of maritime law, to be more efficient [in the long run] than a limitation of national sovereignty to certain categories of vehicles." More specifically, after reviewing the history of jurisdiction relating to airspace, Sänger stated that nothing had caused him to change his opinion that for physical reasons the flying altitudes of aerodynamic and aerostatic vehicles cannot exceed roughly 35 to 50 miles, and that he still adhered to his "opinion rendered in Hearing Report 1433 of the U.S. House Committee on Science and Astronautics to the effect that national airspace should be limited to that altitude."

[80] An abstract prepared for the author.

In an article appearing in January 1962, Drs. Hubertus Strughold and Oskar Ritter, two leading space scientists, outlined in general form still another series of fundamental physical data upon which the "legislation" of space law may depend. In particular, they placed what could be termed the finishing touches on a recently developed classification of strata:

0-72	miles	Nitrogen and Oxygen (now dissociated and no longer "air")
72-600	miles	Oxygen (now dissociated and no longer "air")
600-1,500	miles	Helium (now dissociated and no longer "air")
1,500-6,000	miles	Hydrogen (now dissociated and no longer "air")
6,000-60,000	miles	Magnetosphere
60,000-1,000,000	miles	Gravisphere [81]

The 60,000 to 1,000,000 mile range indicated for the gravisphere is not as exclusive as might appear from the chart, because the authors also describe it in an independent setting, as stretching from the earth itself to considerably beyond the 1,000,000-mile limit. To be exact, they define gravisphere as a sphere of predominant gravitational influence, i.e., as that region of the general gravitational field where the force exerted by a given celestial body prevails over those issuing from other celestial bodies. Strughold and Ritter distinguish further between an inner gravisphere and an outer gravisphere. The former is the region within which a satellite can be held in orbit by the gravitational attraction of a planet. Hence the authors call it the "potential satellite sphere." The latter represents the region beyond the inner gravisphere where the gravitational force of a planet is still strong enough to have an appreciable effect on the trajectory of a space vehicle. For this outer sphere or region the authors also use the term "gravipause." The inner gravisphere, however, is the more important for astronautics, and the authors consider it in considerable detail.

The earth's inner gravisphere, or potential satellite sphere, reaches out one million miles from the earth's center. This means that a satellite can orbit the earth from a distance four times as great as the distance between the earth and the moon. Beyond this sphere, the gravitational field of the sun is predominant, and a space vehicle becomes a satellite of sun, but for several million kilometers it still remains within the earth's outer gravisphere, or gravipause.

The radius of the potential satellite sphere of any planet in the solar system depends upon two factors: the planet's mass and its distance from the sun. The radii (in millions of kilometers) of potential satellite spheres of bodies in our solar system are as follows: Mercury, 0.22; Venus, 1.0; Earth, 1.5; Mars, 0.5; Jupiter, 53; Saturn, 65; Uranus, 70; Neptune, 116; Pluto, 57; Moon, 0.060.[82]

[81] The measurements from 0 to 60,000 miles are based on a report by Dr. Robert Jastrow of NASA. N.Y. Times, Dec. 25, 1961.

[82] Strughold and Ritter, *Planetary Gravispheres*, Astronautics, Jan. 1962, pp. 26-27.

The scientists point out that these measurements, when considered on a proper scale, represent very small gravitational domains in the vastness of interplanetary space. Nevertheless, they state that for purposes of "practical subdivision of space relevant to navigation and those aspects of space law concerning space vehicles" the earth's inner gravisphere can properly be considered the "gravitational territory" of the earth. In the same way, the other planets can be said to have their gravitational territories. "Traveling outward from the terrestrial or any other planetary space," they continue, "a space vehicle enters *interplanetary space*, part of the solar gravitational sphere, which, far out in interstellar space, blends with the gravitational spaces of the neighboring stars." [83]

The usefulness of these observations in terms of limitations on sovereignty or jurisdiction is amplified clearly in this passage:

> In the early phases of astronautics, we are of course mainly interested in the gravitational domains of the earth and neighboring bodies, such as the moon, Mars, and Venus. Knowledge of their extension informs us when a rocket or space vehicle has left the gravitational territory of the earth and has become a planetoid or a satellite of the moon.
>
> Another astronautical significance is this: As a spacecraft, coming from one celestial body, may go into a parking orbit anywhere within the potential satellite sphere of another body, this sphere assumes in space navigation an importance analogous to that of a harbor in maritime operations or, at least, to that part of the coastal waters where a ship can lie at anchor.
>
> Thus, the gravispheres represent the substrate for a new dynamographic subdivision of space, and as such are an important part in a "geography" of space, or *spatiography*, useful in astronautical navigation, bioastronautical considerations, and space law.[84]

But the entire proposal has really nothing to do with space jurisdiction or air law.

A final demarcation line that may be mentioned here is one that was featured in news reports concerning the three-orbit flight of Scott Carpenter. During the flight, Carpenter took 60 photographs of the earth's horizon for M.I.T. scientists, to help in the development of a guidance system. In each instance, half the picture frame was covered with a blue filter, and half with a red filter. And, as one article explained:

> In the blue half of each photo, the earth was dark and hazy. But the outer edge of the atmosphere was clearly visible and distinct, appearing as a sharp blue band. This is due to the "Rayleigh scattering" effect: The outer atmosphere reflects, or "scatters," most of the blue portion of the sun's light—the reason why the sky appears blue. The scattering ends abruptly at an altitude of 30 miles, providing a much sharper horizon line. Thanks to Carpenter's blue ring, space pilots will have a reliable road marker on the way home.[85]

[83] *Id.* at 27, 38.
[84] *Id.* at 38.
[85] Newsweek, July 16, 1962, p. 74.

The ending of blue sky at the thirty-mile level is just another example of the many possible solutions scientists will discuss. However, in establishing the most reasonable limit of national sovereignty, few proposals have the multiple advantages that we have seen in the von Kármán line.

With characteristic decision, the British made a landmark contribution to the space jurisdictional question through studies sponsored by a private foundation, which were later adopted as a working understanding by the British Foreign Office. (See further discussion on page 20.)

The British Code of Space Law was the result of eminent British lawyers and scientists working under the aegis of the David Davies Memorial Institute, London. The first provision thereof reads:

> An attempt has been made to define airspace and outer space in terms of sovereignty, and to fix a level at 50 miles (80,000 meters). The altitude of airspace has never been authoritatively defined, either in the Paris Convention of 1919, or in the Chicago Convention of 1944. It was therefore thought desirable to fix a height, albeit an arbitrary one, and this height was finally selected as being a mean between powered aircraft flight and minimum satellite orbit. The X-15 can now exceed this height, but in view of the United States government's intention to evolve a craft capable of both orbital and atmospheric flight, any boundary will one day be crossed, and so an arbitrary height seems essential for any legal regime. It is suggested that a hybrid craft should be subject to the regime in which it is at any one time operating.[86]

The jurisdictional level fixed by the British—if considered as a median curve—is precisely the same as the von Kármán Line.

[86] Horsford, *A British Code of Space Law*, 5 SPACEFLIGHT 52-53 (London: B.I.S. 1963).

Additional References

Andrew G. Haley, *Space Exploration—The Problems of Today, Tomorrow and in the Future,* in SECOND COLLOQUIUM ON THE LAW OF OUTER SPACE 44 (1960); ——, *The Law of Space and Outer Space,* 33 So. CAL. L. REV. 370 (1960) reprinted in part, 10 L. REV. DIGEST 77 (1960); ——, *Law of Outer Space—Practical Legal Rules for Human Conduct,* 16 FED. COM. B.J. 163 (1959); ——, *Space Age Presents Immediate Legal Problems,* in FIRST COLLOQUIUM ON THE LAW OF OUTER SPACE 5 (1959); ——, *International Cooperation in Astronautics,* Foreign Service Journal, April 1958, p. 1; ——, *Law of Outer Space—A Problem for International Agreement,* 7 AM. U.L. REV. 70 (1958); ——, *The Law of Outer Space—Scientific and Technical Considerations,* 4 N.Y.L.F. 262 (1958); ——, *Space and Metalaw: Jurisdiction Defined,* 16 J. OF THE BRITISH INTERPLANETARY SOCIETY 472 (1958); ——, *Recent Developments in Space Law and Metalaw,* Harvard L. Record, Feb. 7, 1957, special supplement; ——, *Basic Concepts of Space Law,* 26 JET PROPULSION 951 (1956); ——, *Space Law and Metalaw,* PROCEEDINGS OF THE VIITH INTER-

NATIONAL ASTRONAUTICAL CONGRESS, ROME 1956 435; *Summation of Questions Involved in the Technical and Legal Regulations of Space Exploration:* Lecture by _____, Seminar Course on Space Science and Technology of the Instituto Nacional de Técnica Aeronáutica, "Estéban Terradas" in Madrid, March 29, 1960; *The Law of Space and Outer Space:* Address by _____, Pacific Southwest Conference on International Law at the University of Southern California, March 5, 1960; *The Law of Outer Space—Scientific and Economic Considerations:* Address by _____, Nederlandse Vereniging voor Ruimtevaart and Koninklijke and Nederlandse Vereniging voor Luchtvaart at The Hague, March 4, 1958; *Space Law—The Development of Jurisdictional Concepts:* Paper by _____, Before the VIIIth Annual Congress of the International Astronautical Federation in Barcelona, Oct. 6-12, 1957.

5

Sovereignty over celestial bodies

In the past history of mankind, nations have laid claim to newly discovered territories in a variety of ways and on a variety of legal grounds, but all these traditional practices appear singularly inapplicable to the situation man will face as he ventures onto other celestial bodies. Moreover, the need for a prompt solution to the problem of sovereignty over celestial bodies is clearly emphasized by the epochal technological achievements in the conquest of space. Six "peaks" of technical achievement are identifiable and four of the first five have been realized—in each instance by the USSR. Of the six peaks, three have definite reference to jurisdiction and sovereignty in outer space, i.e., the ownership of natural objects in the cosmos. If one nation were to perform all the historically accepted rituals and duties of an exploring state seeking dominion on the moon, such nation, under classical legal theory, might claim jurisdiction over the moon. Without regard to nation *qua* nation, however, the interests of humanity demand that limits of terrestrial jurisdiction be defined, and that beyond this point the rule of *res communes* must prevail in cosmic space. The same attitude is reflected in the reports of the national legal societies of the USA and the USSR, and those of the Committee on the Peaceful Uses of Outer Space of the United Nations. A highly significant body of legal comment and analysis is available; but, if it is to be of any use, it appears that this great fund of thinking must be converted by international nongovernmental organizations into reality. The hope of humanity reposes in the imperishable words of Eisenhower, Kennedy, and Johnson, and it is hoped that official bureaucracy will implement the words of the Chiefs of State.

NEW LANDS AND CLAIMS OF SOVEREIGNTY

5–1 Terrestrial precedents

The existing practices of nations are the primary indicia of international law. To solve a problem such as "Who shall own the moon?" let us look first to the criterion of these "existing practices."[1] And let us go back into history to the days of exploration and conquest when new worlds were found and claimed in the name of royal sovereigns. With the discovery of these regions, referred to by the scholars of the day as *terra nullius*—land which belonged to no one—many legal issues arose. For instance, was it sufficient for the navigators to make the initial discovery, plant the royal emblem, and then once more embark? Or was it necessary that there be an occupation in order to acquire dominion over the new-found region? An initial effort was made by the Pope to settle these questions. Almost immediately after Columbus' discovery, the famous Papal Bull of 1493 was issued dividing the world between Spain and Portugal by a meridian running one hundred leagues west of the Azores through both Poles. Probably the most significant aspect of this document is that it introduced the notion of law to the problem of new territories and recognized the tenuousness of the "right of grab." This Papal Bull, however, settled nothing. Neither England nor France ever consented to abide by it, and Spain and Portugal promptly altered the demarcation line themselves by the Treaty of Tordesillas of 1494.

Both Spain and Portugal also sought to justify their claims on other legal grounds. The nations of Europe were coming to recognize that the mere discovery of new territory did not carry with it the indicia of ownership. Accordingly, in an effort to put teeth into their claims of dominion over the *terra nullius*, they carried out formal ceremonies of taking possession—ceremonies whose exact details often varied quite markedly, but which were still alike in their supposed legal effect.

Thus, lawyers point out, the Portuguese and French were usually content with the performance of ceremonies very simple in nature, such as the erection of a cross, or other monuments, bearing the royal arms.[2] The Dutch also adhered to the simplicities and usually erected no religious symbols whatever.[3] The Russians buried copper plates bearing their coat

---

[1] See Schachter, *Who Owns the Universe?* in STAFF OF SENATE SPECIAL COMMITTEE ON SPACE AND ASTRONAUTICS, 85TH CONG., 2D SESS., SPACE LAW, A SYMPOSIUM 8, 15-16 (Comm. Print 1958). This article originally appeared in ACROSS THE SPACE FRONTIER (Ryan ed. 1952).

[2] KELLER, LISSITZYN & MANN, CREATION OF RIGHTS OF SOVEREIGNTY THROUGH SYMBOLIC ACTS 1400-1800 23, 101 (1938).

[3] *Id.* at 132.

of arms,[4] and the English carried away with them a piece of "turf and twig" to establish their sovereignty.[5] The Spaniards, on the other hand, were accustomed to observe a highly elaborate ritual.[6]

In America the statement has frequently been made by international experts that, at the time of the European explorations in the Western Hemisphere, discovery was a sufficient basis for a claim to sovereignty over the newly discovered lands.[7] It is not always clear whether writers use the term "discovery" to mean discovery alone, or whether they mean to include within that term the formal taking of possession in the name of the sovereign which has usually accompanied the discovery. In this connection, an interesting case arose some years after the U.S. acquisition by conquest of the Philippines. The Island of Palmas, which is close to certain Philippine islands, was claimed by both Holland and the United States. The claims were submitted to arbitration, and Holland won on grounds unimportant to this discussion.[8] The United States contended, however, "that discovery as such, i.e., the mere fact of seeing land, without any act, even symbolical, of taking possession, involved *ipso jure* territorial sovereignty and not merely an 'inchoate title,' a *jus ad rem*, to be completed eventually by an actual and durable taking of possession within a reasonable time." The United States contended, then, that discovery alone conferred real legal sovereignty and not a simple claim to ownership.[9]

A slightly less extreme position is that of the experts who have asserted that the formal ceremony of taking possession—the symbolic act—is generally regarded as being sufficient to establish immediately a right of sovereignty over, or a valid title to, the areas so claimed and need not be supplemented by the performance of other acts, such as "effective occupation." A right or title so acquired and established has been considered good against all subsequent claims set up in opposition thereto unless, perhaps, transferred by conquest or treaty, relinquished, abandoned, or successfully opposed by continued occupation on the part of some other state.[10]

Whether or not actual occupation and settlement of new territory are considered legally necessary for laying claim to it, there has never been much doubt that, in practice, effective occupation gives strong backing to the other forms of claim. It is thus significant that Columbus provided further legal justification for Spanish claims by leaving part of his crew

---

[4] *Id.* at 142.

[5] *Id.* at 49.

[6] *Id.* at 43.

[7] 1 HACKWORTH, DIGEST OF INTERNATIONAL LAW, 398 (1940).

[8] Island of Palmas (United States v. the Netherlands), SCOTT, HAGUE COURT REPORTS 2d. 83, 6 U.N. Rep. Int'l Arb. Awards 829 (1928).

[9] SCOTT, HAGUE COURT REP. 100, 6 U.N. Rep. Int'l Arb. Awards 850 (1928).

[10] 1 HACKWORTH, DIGEST OF INTERNATIONAL LAW 398 (1940).

on the Island of Haiti before he returned home from his first voyage.[11] In recent years, however, the Permanent Court of International Justice at The Hague has ruled that settlement alone is not sufficient either—that a nation must assert its sovereignty over new lands through political power or jurisdiction.[12] Under the rules set down at The Hague, some kind of permanent and formally organized settlement would normally be required, and it would be very difficult for these rules to apply in the case of the moon, which (as the scientists tell us) is basically inhospitable and unsuitable for permanent settlement because of the extreme scarcity if not outright lack of air and water. This is perhaps fortunate, since the first nation to claim the moon would acquire a unique military advantage. Only common control among all nations would eliminate the possibility of using the moon as a base for aggressive war.

Even without actual settlement, the development and working of resources on the moon or other celestial bodies could perhaps be handled in a manner similar to the working of an oyster bed or a bed of pearls. In the Persian Gulf, for example, there are certain pearl beds that have been worked by Arab tribes for centuries. Although this land has never been owned by the Arabs, their rights thereto have been consistently respected by international custom.[13] In this same manner, the nations which first develop resources on the moon could obtain exclusive rights over those resources which no other nation could legally challenge. It must be emphasized, however, that they would not "own" the land on which the resources exploited are located.

One obvious place to look for precedents for the handling of sovereignty over other celestial bodies is Antarctica, which appears largely unsuited for conventional settlement even though its outer fringes, at least, are considerably more hospitable than the moon. Unfortunately, the lessons to be drawn from Antarctica are still far from clear. A great number of conflicting, overlapping, and ill-defined claims have accumulated; and while at present no nations are inclined to come to blows over Antarctic territory, neither is any true settlement in sight.

In 1929, for example, Norway made it clear by note that it was not at this time claiming sovereignty over the polar region. The Norwegian government was merely making the point that Amundsen's exploration constituted a valid basis for "a claim of priority to acquire such territories whenever the requirements of international law as to effective occupation of a new territory shall have been fulfilled." [14] Before Amundsen made his polar flights of 1925 and 1926, he was authorized to claim a similar right

[11] Schachter, *op. cit. supra* note 1 at 9.
[12] *Id.* at 10.
[13] *Id.* at 12.
[14] Minister Bache to Sec'y Simpson, April 15, 1929, MS. Dep't of State, File 857.014163; 1 HACKWORTH, DIGEST OF INTERNATIONAL LAW 453-54 (1940).

of priority on behalf of Norway even over the land that he might discover by aerial reconnaissance, without actually landing.[15]

In 1929, the same year as the Norwegian note mentioned above, the British government reminded the United States that "a British title already exists by virtue of discovery" over Coats Land, Enderby Land, Kemp Land, Queen Mary Land, Wilkes Land, King George V Land, and Oates Land.[16] The height of stuffiness was exemplified in the note from the British Ambassador, Sir Ronald Lindsay, to Secretary Hull in 1934, in which Lindsay scolded the United States Government and Lincoln Ellsworth for establishing a new mission at Admiral Byrd's former base on the Ross Barrier without first obtaining airplane landing privileges, radio license, and postal permits from the New Zealand Government.[17]

None of these claims has even been withdrawn by any of the nations involved, but they have been suspended, in a manner of speaking, by the recent Antarctic Treaty. In the course of presentation made at the Fourth Colloquium in Washington in October 1961, David F. Maxwell, Chairman of the American Bar Association Committee on the Law of Outer Space, made the following statement:

> The [Antarctic] treaty itself fulfills the highest hopes of mankind. Forged on the anvil of long and tedius negotiation, it epitomizes the ultimate in diplomatic achievement. Its terms embody all of the guideposts necessary to insure the exploitation of Antarctica for the benefit of all mankind—limiting specifically its use for peaceful purposes, prohibiting any measures of a military nature, establishing freedom of scientific investigation, facilitating the exchange of information among participating countries, and providing for an inspection system to insure compliance.[18]

Mr. Maxwell does not mention, however, that Article IV of the Antarctic Treaty includes some rather large reservations. Thus, under this article, it is made clear that no claims of territorial rights or sovereignty are renounced by any of the various contracting states; nor are any "acts or activities taking place while the present Treaty is in force" to be construed as "a basis for asserting, supporting or denying" such claims in future.[19]

Seen in proper perspective, this treaty, the supposed archetype for the problems of space law, is no more than the grandest internationally agreed upon "question-begging" that diplomacy has devised. To allay and mini-

[15] Ambassador Bryn to Sec'y Hughes, Nov. 12, 1924, MS. Dep't of State, File 857.014/16; 1 HACKWORTH, DIGEST OF INTERNATIONAL LAW 400 (1940).

[16] Ambassador Howard to Sec'y Kellogg, No. 526, Nov. 17, 1928, MS. Dep't of State, File 031 Byrd South Polar Expedition 138, enclosure; 1 HACKWORTH, DIGEST OF INTERNATIONAL LAW 455 (1940).

[17] Ambassador Lindsay to Sec'y Hull, No. 33, Jan. 29, 1934, MS. Dep't of State, File 031 Byrd South Polar Expedition/142; 1 HACKWORTH, DIGEST OF INTERNATIONAL LAW 455-57 (1940).

[18] Maxwell, *Outer Space—The Key to World Peace Under Law*, 4th Colloq. 15, 22 (Norman, Oklahoma: University of Oklahoma Research Institute, 1963).

[19] The Antarctic Treaty is printed in full in Appendix I-A.

mize the problems that did, *and still do,* exist in Antarctica, this treaty was drawn up. To ascribe to the treaty so high a place in the efforts of international diplomacy as Mr. Maxwell suggests would, in this author's opinion, encourage the taking of just such temporary and stop-gap measures in the area of our immediate space problems—prime among which is the problem of national sovereignty.

5–2 Proposed solutions for the moon and beyond

In context after context as problems are examined it must be kept in mind that as space science and technology move forward at hypersonic speed, the law cannot afford to remain earthbound. The mildest possible penalty for such a lag will be confusion. The maximum price we may pay is mutual destruction. As already discussed, exploration, settlement, and control of land have been sufficient in the past to establish a claim of ownership. In recent years, the emphasis has been placed less on the taking of physical possession and settlement than on displaying the authority of government through political control. The whole problem is presented sharply today, as we have also seen, in connection with claims to the Antarctic region. This area has been claimed by a number of nations, a variety of legal grounds, but so far none of these claims has been generally accepted, and the controversy remains essentially unresolved.

This situation foreshadows the conflict that may arise when the first manned rocket ships reach another celestial body. If past practices are followed, the first landing will involve all sorts of acts intended to support claims of sovereignty—a flag will be planted and appropriate names will more than likely be given to various sites. We may then read accounts of lunar "Washingtons" and "New Yorks," [20] and surface features of Mars may well be named after Khrushchev, De Gaulle, and Queen Elizabeth II. In place of some of the older ceremonials, scientific instruments will undoubtedly be left behind. Governments may even attempt to exercise control by issuing licenses to visit or reside on other celestial bodies, claiming the right to exclude all those who are unlicensed. Thus would be re-created the old story of land-area rivalry. This insanity has led to wars of conquest and made slaves out of Africans and Indians, in complete disregard of the rights of the people already living in new-found lands.

The great astronautics powers, the United States and the USSR, through their Chiefs of State, have declared that placing men on the moon is a feasible and immediate project. Both nations are committed to this objective and both nations will succeed in this exploit in the relatively near future. We cannot minimize the possibility of successful projects by the Western European community in the very near future. Only time will tell whether cooperative efforts among nations to establish permanent

[20] Schachter, *op. cit. supra* note 1 at 10.

bases on the moon will succeed. The successful effort by a single nation might well afford that nation an "ultimate weapon." The seriousness, and indeed, the immediacy of the moon exploit cannot be minimized. The juridical and political status of the moon must be established by international agreement at this time.

Already numerous spokesmen have expressed opposition to any establishment of convention claims of sovereignty over other celestial bodies. At the VIII International Astronautical Congress at Barcelona in 1957, this author made a proposal that the moon be declared a free and autonomous land. Aldo Armando Cocca of Argentina, in discussing this proposal, declared that the moon did not "constitute either a territory or a zone in space," that it be declared "autonomous," "sovereign," or "independent," and that there exist no "rights of ownership on or over the moon." Cocca then proposed a draft declaration stating that the moon should be proclaimed free for use by all states, that regulations governing the exploration of lunar resources should be created, and that a right of way for all the states of the earth should be established on the moon.[21] Dr. Cocca has appropriately pointed out that, when talking of the moon or Mars we are naturally constrained to use the word *territory* when, he says, in the case of the moon we should use the word *lunarity*.

Mr. Michael Aaronson, in an article discussing the discovery of celestial bodies, makes the point that precedents and principles should not be sought from law that prevailed during the time of Columbus, Magellan, da Gama, and Cabot. He develops this point further in a very interesting analysis which points out the twentieth-century tendency away from reliance on ancient practice. He concludes by emphasizing that new concepts will be required in formulating "the comprehensive law of space" —concepts which obviously would not include the traditional law of discovery.[22]

At a special meeting sponsored by the Committee on Space Law and Sociology of the American Rocket Society in New York in April 1962, Colonel Martin Menter also commented on some of the problems man will encounter in exploring and settling upon other planets. He pointed out that the process of exploration will be quite different in several respects from the experience of most former exploration on earth. Instead of working inland from a shoreline, space travelers will probably be able to disembark at spots of their own choosing "on the land masses concerned"; but he added that merely touching upon another celestial body will not necessarily lead to effective occupation of that body. Such matters as lack of food, water, and oxygen, radiation hazards, variations in tem-

---

[21] Cocca, *Principles for a Declaration With Reference to the Legal Nature of the Moon*, 1st Colloq., 34, 34-36 (Vienna, Springer-Verlag, 1959).

[22] Aaronson, *Space Law*, Symp. 221, 229-31; Aaronson, *The Legal Control of Space*, 1957 THE LISTENER 1018.

perature, and other dangers will intrude. Hence, even if past "earth-law" did apply to outer space, initial visits would create at most inchoate rights. But man will eventually extend his activities to other celestial bodies, and it may be assumed that he will attempt to carry his laws with him, just as he did in moving from one place to another on earth. "Remember," Menter says, "the earth itself is but a land mass in space." It is perfectly possible, therefore, that claims of sovereignty will ultimately be made to land masses in outer space.

For this reason, Menter argues that an appropriate international agreement concerning sovereignty over celestial land areas should be reached in good time. If this is not done before man reaches another celestial body, he fears, then nations which have established inchoate sovereignty rights may be reluctant in the end to give up those rights. "The time to resolve this problem, therefore, is before such a factual situation may develop." Colonel Menter believes that the United Nations resolution of December 20, 1961, which declared celestial bodies "not subject to national appropriation," is a step in the right direction; and he urges that the resolution's guiding principles be embodied in a formal international agreement.[23] (For further discussion of this aspect of the U.N. resolution, see Section 5-3, *infra.*)

One rather unusual approach to these problems is evident in an excellent treatise completed in 1959 by Philip C. Jessup and Howard J. Taubenfeld.[24] The two writers studied in minute detail the possibility of drawing upon the experiences of the nations involved in the Antarctic Treaty and other past efforts at multinational administrations, in order to develop a legal system applicable to the administration of space activities both within and outside the present United Nations structure; and, in conclusion, they propose the formation of a Cosmic Development Corporation (CODEC) which would reflect "the interests and contributions of all nations in its composition." They even suggest that "in the early period where no large populations were involved" such a corporation might well "provide governmental services in outlying areas, as did the great trading companies of the age of discovery on Earth." [25]

During the Fourth Colloquium on the Law of Outer Space, held in Washington, D.C., in October of 1961, Dr. Welf Heinrich Prince of Hanover commented on this topic in a manner that was keenly analytical but perhaps overly cautious in approach. He observed that while the concepts known to our terrestrial jurisprudence (such as *res nullius, res communis,* "sovereignty," and "occupation") are "scarcely applicable in

[23] Menter, *Jurisdiction Over Land Masses in Space*, PROCEEDINGS OF CONFERENCE ON SPACE LAW, SPONSORED BY THE AMERICAN ROCKET SOCIETY, NEW YORK CITY, APRIL 24, 1962. (To be published.)

[24] JESSUP & TAUBENFELD, CONTROLS FOR OUTER SPACE AND THE ANTARCTIC ANALOGY (New York: Columbia University Press, 1959).

[25] *Id.* at 282.

space," there is a natural temptation to make use of them in considering space problems. He said further that the landing of a Russian missile on the moon in 1959 had nothing to do with the "establishment of a national sovereignty" there, because "the presuppositions to fulfill the concept of establishing sovereignty were not yet in existence." Hanover proceeded to state that it was at least possible ("it may well be . . . perhaps in a few years") that in due course the presuppositions or conditions for "establishing a nation's sovereignty" will be satisfied on other celestial bodies. He thus declared himself "opposed to making definite plans at the outset," either one way or the other, regarding the legal status of celestial bodies.

What Hanover proposed instead was the establishment of some institution within the framework of the United Nations which would act originally as an information center concerning activities in space but would grow into a kind of supervisory body. Such an institution, in due course, might exercise "arbitrational functions" with respect to the rights of different nations in their undertakings on other celestial bodies. At the same time, Hanover emphasized that we are still too ignorant concerning the nature of these other bodies and "their meaning to mankind" to attempt to classify them on the basis of existing legal principles. He was even careful to point out that we may sooner or later come across "intelligent and sapient beings" who "will look upon us as prehistoric." For all these and other reasons, he concluded,

> Our conduct should be so that we enter this new realm in space without prejudice or preconceptions, for this would only produce destruction before our conceptions have ripened from theory to knowledge. . . .
>   Should not our zeal for research, which always has to cope with new, revolutionary experiences in the technical-scientific field, also remain open-minded to new solutions in the juridical field. The unfathomable universe offers us—providing we succeed in entering it—vast potential. Let us not transfer into space the worst abuse on our earth, of which Mephistopheles says in Goethe's *Faust:*
>   All laws and statutes
>   are transmitted like
>   chronic ills from race
>   to race.[26]

In his writings, Oscar Schachter has pointed to the body of custom which has grown up internationally and states that in space a similar evolution of custom—and of customary law—will undoubtedly take place.[27] It would seem preferable, however, for jurisdiction beyond the earth to

---

[26] Hanover, *Sovereignty in Outer Space,* 4th Colloq., 119, 126-27 (Norman, Oklahoma: University of Oklahoma Research Institute, 1963).

[27] Schachter, *op. cit. supra* note 1.

be settled in a more definitive fashion. The world has had enough of anarchy. Strict rules must be laid down for nations to follow while out in space, and the rules should be both formulated and enforced by an international commission. Space and its conquest pose problems that are unique: they require unique legislation.

Nor is jurisdiction beyond the earth a nebulous and distant problem. Flight into space is already an actuality, and interplanetary voyages by manned spaceships have been predicted to take place before the end of the sixth decade of the twentieth century. Will people be interested in transplanting their roots to the new world of space? Indicative of public sentiment is the story told of the member of the British Interplanetary Society who issued to a few friends and colleagues a "British Stellar Passport." A London tabloid splashed a picture of the "passport" across its front page. Hundreds of persons immediately made application therefor, announcing their readiness to trade this world for another. Plaintively, the scientists were forced to announce that they were not yet prepared to sell tickets from Liverpool Airport to Mars. Not yet, but soon.[28]

In any case, it cannot be emphasized too often that technology has forged ahead more rapidly into the realm of space than have the social sciences, including the science of jurisprudence. We find countless illustrations in history of the seriousness of such a situation. The successful voyages of Columbus to the New World were indeed momentous from the standpoint of the natural sciences, but they opened the way for the destruction of the Indian civilizations and for the spread of Negro slavery through both Americas. In the same way, the white man violated the Polynesian Islands and decimated the population principally by introducing tuberculosis and other diseases. The effective enforcement of principles of law and justice should have prevented these catastrophes.

THE PROBLEM BEFORE US

5–3 The chronology of the problem

Since before the advent of *Sputnik I*, the author has expressed the belief that the starkly important initial phases of the space epoch (the basic achievements which could be accomplished in the foreseeable future) were sixfold and in order of chronology would consist of:

1) the first earth-orbital unmanned space vehicle;
2) the first probe into space reaching beyond the gravitational control of earth;

[28] Time, Dec. 10, 1951, p. 83.

3) the first landing on the moon of an unmanned space vehicle;
4) the first lunar-orbiting unmanned space vehicle;
5) the first earth-orbiting manned vehicle;
6) the first landing of man on the moon.[29]

It is obvious that in the anticline and syncline of these peaks of achievement there are immense contributory and subsidiary achievements, such as the development of efficient propulsion systems, life-support systems, guidance systems, communication systems and power sources, and the overcoming of the technical problems posed by departure from and re-entry to bodies in space, notably the earth and moon. Then there was a horde of other special achievements connected with such projects as Martian and Venusian probes and the photographing of the far side of the moon. Nevertheless, so long as the achievement of these great peaks was a matter of speculation in the realm of the natural sciences, many felt that the duty of the lawyer did not go beyond parallel speculation in the scope of the social sciences. Times have now changed.

On October 4, 1957, to be exact, the USSR successfully launched *Sputnik I*—a one hundred and sixty pound orbital vehicle instrumented to measure internal temperatures and pressures and which circled the earth about every ninety-six minutes for a period of three months.[30] Here was the achievement of the first peak.

On January 2, 1959, the USSR launched *Mechta* (*Lunik I*), a vehicle of about one and one-half tons, carrying about eight hundred pounds of instrumentation designed to measure temperature and pressure inside the vehicle and to study gas components of interplanetary matter, corpuscular radiation of the sun magnetic fields in space, meteoritic particles, and primary cosmic radiation.[31]

In giving the accolade to *Mechta* one must not forget the achievement by the United States of *Pioneer I*, which climbed more than seventy thousand miles into space and returned to earth on October 11-12, 1958. Accomplishing many firsts, *Pioneer I* measured earth's magnetic field, observed that the trapped radiation surrounding the earth is in the form of a band, and determined micrometeor density in space.[32] Nor, indeed, should we forget *Pioneer III*, launched by the United States to a height in excess of sixty-three thousand miles and returning to earth—a cycle which occurred on December 6-7, 1958, and resulted in the major discovery that there are two radiation belts around the earth.[33]

The third peak listed above was achieved by *Lunik II*. Launched by the USSR on September 12, 1959, it landed on the moon near the Sea

[29] See Appendix V-B. Originally outlined in Item 76. Developed in later papers.
[30] Space Technology Laboratories, SPACE LOG 2 (Herrick ed. April 1960).
[31] *Id.* at 5.
[32] *Id.* at 4.
[33] *Id.* at 5.

of Tranquility after traveling about two hundred and thirty-seven thousand miles. The USSR informs us that *Lunik II* was instrumented to obtain information concerning internal temperature and pressure, earth-moon magnetic fields, meteorites, and radiation.[34]

One might well argue that the achievement of *Lunik III*—launched by the USSR on October 3, 1959—in circling the moon and returning to earth orbit [35] should also be considered a peak in view of the fact that the far side of the moon was photographed by instrumentation carried in this vehicle and the photographic data successfully transmitted to earth. Indeed this achievement, in combination with the earlier success of *Lunik II* in planting a Russian flag on the moon, might easily suggest the possibility of some claim of sovereignty based on traditional concepts of international law.

Under traditional legal concepts the planting of a symbol of possession and sovereignty, such as the flag of a nation, would give an incipient, or, as an international lawyer would say, inchoate right to the surface claimed. (In spite of the later landing of a U.S. spacecraft on the moon, the priority in time of the USSR makes discussion of its rights the proper subject of our attention.) Immediately after the landing of *Lunik II*, however, Academician L. I. Sedov, President of the International Astronautical Federation and Chairman of the Commission on Astronautics of the USSR Academy of Sciences, said that the USSR claimed no ownership of the moon by virtue of the flag-symbol.[36] Premier Khrushchev confirmed this statement during his tour of the United States.[37] Nor has any official of the USSR, to the author's knowledge, commented on the claim of ownership by virtue of discovery and mapping which could reasonably arise from the achievement of *Lunik III*.

Which nation will first achieve peak number 4—inauguration of the moon-orbiting satellite—and which nation will first achieve peak number 6 and proceed beyond the mere landing of human beings on the moon to actually colonizing the moon? If all these peaks were to be achieved by the USSR, that nation could well claim, under the applicable tests of classical and extant international law, that its right to complete jurisdiction over the moon was indisputable because of (*a*) the first planting of its flag, (*b*) the first discovery and mapping, (*c*) the first effective and constant reconnaissance, and (*d*) the first effective control achieved through the presence on the moon of USSR citizens and armaments. In this con-

[34] *Id.* at 6. The landing on the moon engendered a number of discussions of the legal problems involved. E.g., Bauza Araujo, Derecho Astronáutico, 261-67 (Uruguay 1961). Rodríguez Rincón, Aspecto Jurídico de la Conquista del Espacio Extraterrestre 100 (Mexico 1961). Szadeczky-Kardoss, *Bekes egyutteles a vilagurben* (Peaceful Coexistence in Outer Space) Egyetemi Lapok, Oct. 14, 1959.

[35] Space Technology Laboratories, Space Log 7 (Herrick ed. April 1960).

[36] N.Y. Times, Sept. 15, 1959, p. 1, col. 5.

[37] N.Y. Times, Sept. 17, 1959, p. 18, col. 3.

nection, however, the Soviet lawyer Korovin has made the rather ambiguous statement that "there is no doubt . . . that the criterion of effective earthly occupation, which is not always applicable even to the whole of the Earth (for example in the Arctic or Antarctic), is even less suitable for application to outer space, to the planets or stars." [38]

These prospects certainly do not seem to alarm the American government lawyers, and in fact the attitude of the official lawyers of the USSR with respect to clarifying the legal status of the moon and of objects in outer space appears to be about the same as the official United States attitude.[39] From a legal standpoint it is obvious that, the closer the two great astronautical powers approach the moon, the more distant they become from efforts to clarify and enunciate a solution for the problems of lunar sovereignty and the rule of law in outer space.

Some American lawyers, on the other hand, have strongly supported the viewpoint that land jurisdiction should be clarified through international agreement, and that a rule of law should be established without further delay for outer space.[40] The thinking of this group of lawyers, including the author, is most admirably stated in an editorial which appeared in *Life* magazine in 1959, and which stated among other things:

> We can't agree, and neither does the staff report of the House Committee on Astronautics and Space Exploration. Why wait for the conflicts already foreseeable to become real cases? We are then in what Senator Keating calls "the giddy cycle of law chasing power and never quite catching up." It is preposterous that there should be no general international consensus on whether a nation can claim rights on the moon or not. Although various groups have done much good work in this field and the technical bibliography is already huge, "the only attitude which all the governments appear to share is: Caution."
>
> Our State Department is at least as cautious as the rest. We refuse to make or concede any precise national claims in outer space, or to forfeit the right to make or deny any in the future. We reserve the right to act like a dog in the manger—if we ever get in the manger. The only law of space we feel sure about is that the right of self-defense applies there as elsewhere. But since this is generally agreed upon, surely we can be a lot more constructive about rules for peaceful behavior in space.
>
> There is something offensive to common sense about the extension of earthbound national sovereignties to other planets. The least we can ask of our international lawyers is that they make space as free as the high seas. The Russian moonshot is just one more reminder of the growing urgency. The U.S., whose traditions and interest is [*sic*] to promote international law everywhere, has the clear duty of taking the initiative.[41]

[38] Korovin, Remarks, Symp. 1072, 1073.

[39] Osnitskaya, *Doktrina Mezhdunarodnogo Aava; Osvoenie Kosmos* (International Law Theory and the Conquest of the Cosmos), in KOSMOS: MEZHDUNARODNOE PRAVO (The Cosmos and International Law) 88, 109 (Korovin ed. USSR 1962).

[40] SURVEY OF SPACE LAW, STAFF REPORT OF THE SELECT COMMITTEE ON ASTRONAUTICS AND SPACE EXPLORATION, H.R. Doc. No. 89, 86th Cong. 1st Sess. 4 (1958).

[41] From an Editorial in Life Magazine, Oct. 5, 1959, p. 50.

It is unfortunate too, that the work of the United Nations Legal Committee, the Committee on the Law of Outer Space of the American Bar Association, and the USSR Juridical Committee on Cosmic Law, should thus far be encyclopedic in nature—with the result that these great forums are failing to contribute in an effective manner to the wealth of thinking on the law of outer space.[42]

Indeed, it appears now that to avoid the slowing process of political haggling this urgent and even critical task must be undertaken by non-governmental international organizations such as the International Institute of Space Law of the International Astronautical Federation. It is a pity that purely national committees and official international bodies have so far been incapable of synoptic thinking!

The United Nations, having taken a look at the issues presented and the solutions offered, has commenced the piecemeal and stop-gap solution which the author predicted, several years ago, would be adopted.[43] The advocates of the U.N. and U.S. Government "wait and see" policy will undoubtedly point to the General Assembly Resolution of December 20, 1961 [44] and ask, "What more do you want?" However, as we have pointed out earlier, what is needed is not the broad meaningless language that "international law ... applies to outer space" and "celestial bodies are free for exploration and use by all states in conformity with international law and are not subject to national appropriation." The invitation which immediately follows these quoted statements is what was needed in 1955, *not* in 1961: "The General Assembly ... Invites the Committee on Peaceful Uses of Outer Space to study and report on the legal problems which may arise from the exploration and use of outer space."

Negatively phrased sweeping generalizations are not contributing to the solution of the immediate problems. We now need agreement on what men *may* do, what effect their actions *will* have, where they *may* go and how they *may* travel. Listing in vague terms what outer space is, or is not, will not serve the purpose; and to say that outer space and its celestial bodies "are not subject to national appropriation" is only the temporary means of putting off the question of what may be done. This single limitation does not prevent the use of other means to secure control. Processes and practices other than "national appropriation" still exist unrestrained, and we have not even yet agreed upon what constitutes "national appropriation" here on earth. As a matter of fact, this is the very crux of the Antarctic problem. Hence a number of scholars have emphasized in their

---

[42] Bibliographies of works on space law include: UNIVERSITY OF OKLAHOMA, BIBLIOGRAPHY OF THE SPACE LAW COLLECTION (1959); HOGAN, A GUIDE TO THE STUDY OF SPACE LAW; Symp.; U.N. LIBRARY, A BIBLIOGRAPHY OF THE LAW OF OUTER SPACE; U.S. AIR FORCE, SPACE LAW BIBLIOGRAPHY, AFP 110-1-4 (July 1961). See Appendix V-A.

[43] See Appendix V-B, Item 70.

[44] This resolution is reproduced in full in Appendix I-F(1).

writings that neither the U.N. Resolution nor the pattern set by the Antarctic Treaty is a cure-all.[45]

5-4 Contrasts in earth-bound and space sovereignty

We have progressed in our development of space vehicles to the point where we must reflect upon certain crucial political and legal problems. At present, our *Tiros* satellites photograph the cloud cover over Russia without the permission of Mr. Khrushchev, and a reconnaissance satellite in the near future will expose to the naked eye any point on our globe. Reconnaissance by photo or television equipment is not conducive to the creation of trust and good will among sovereign powers: to some nations it could well be offensive, and it is conceivable that retaliatory measures will be taken. It may be expected that the United States in line with its declared "open skies" policy will advocate the employment of spacecraft for international inspection purposes. Well-established doctrines of international law deem it permissible to photograph one state from the territory of another. Some commentators therefore urge that the law of space should recognize complete freedom of photography from any point in the earth's atmosphere as a natural extension of this principle.

Here we must again remember to distinguish national airspace from outer space. There does not appear to be much doubt that outer space— defined as that region in which the earth's atmosphere in no way affects the operation or flight of space vehicles—must be free, like the seas, from exclusive appropriation by any nation. While security considerations demand that national sovereignty be preserved in airspace, no relevant reasons exist to foreclose from any nation the lanes of outer space. To grant an exclusive license or monopoly of outer space to any sovereign power could only slow man's conquests, for in this field, as in others, competition is perhaps the most effective catalyst.

Planetary conquest raises somewhat different considerations, although it has been urged that planets, like outer space, should not be subject to the jurisdiction or administration of any sovereign power. When we have finally realized manned space flight to our neighboring planets, we will face a situation not unlike that confronting the explorers of the "new world" in the 15th and 16th centuries,[46] but there will be new aspects to the problems in space which terrestrial claims will not have involved in the past.[47]

Initially, space vehicles will be owned by nations or groups of nations, and the extension of international regulation will be fought jealously. But

[45] E.g., Herczeg, *The Exploration of Outer Space and the Safety of States,* 5th Colloq. (Haley ed., Washington, D.C., 1963).

[46] ARMANDO COCCA, REFLEXIONES SOBRE DERECHO INTERPLANETARIO 13 (1958).

[47] Excellent discussions of these problems appear in CHAUMONT, LE DROIT DE L'ESPACE 104-21 (Paris: Les Presses Universitaires de France, 1960).

gradually and inexorably, traffic will increase, new propulsive systems will be found which will reduce the cost of construction and operation; emigration will commence; meteorite mining will become an industrial objective; and all the ancient problems of law will be reasserted under vastly more complicated circumstances. Again there will arise—in a new frame of reference—problems of neutrality and belligerency, of nationality, domicile, statelessness, internment, asylum, sequestration, blockade, hovering, extraterritoriality, embargo, reprisal, boycotts, expropriation, piracy, contraband, customs, prize proceedings, emigration, immigration, mandates, colonies, tortious violations, civil claims, venue, jurisdiction, and so on.

It may be too much to hope that civilization will hold these matters in check—a view which is cynical in an ultimate sense, because lack of containment would project our destructive forces and philosophies throughout the universe. We do not share this view, however, as we believe that space exploration and settlement will dignify and enrich mankind, erase devastating economic problems forever, afford vistas of the mysteries of creation immeasurably more challenging and interesting than we now conceive of, and engender a measure of tolerance and compassion so that man will rise above his past.

We are experiencing now some of the errors brought about by the improper planning of our forefathers. The colonial system has proved unworkable, and experience, therefore, teaches us to have more vision in our new conquests. (This, of course, assumes Earth will be the conqueror and not the conquered.) An international treaty would be one way of coping with these problems. A better solution appears to be control by the United Nations or some other world body. In any event, it could never make good sense for each country to announce an individual policy for dealing with its conquests.

Planning and the enunciation of a uniform policy must be done at a higher level. One matter of particular concern to any program of space exploration and settlement is the immigration policy to be followed. Should there be a quota system predicated upon selection from all nations? On what basis will we select the talented men and women required to establish and sustain human civilization on the planets of our conquest? If resistance is met by our explorers, how should it be met; if a policy of force is adopted, how will a planetary expeditionary force be selected? By a "higher level" is meant definitive agreement in principle among Chiefs of State.

The age of regular manned space flight is not far off. We must commence our planning and programming *now*. The problems are international in scope and require the pooling of every available talent. Perhaps if we engage successfully in international cooperation in outer space, our earth-bound perspectives will be altered. A common international goal of such magnitude and importance might bring about termination of the cold war and might, as a consequence, release for space exploration and development and other beneficial objectives that part of the world's resources heretofore dedicated to military uses.

This would be an economic revolution dwarfing the introduction of agriculture or the development of mechanized production, and lifting mankind to new levels of self-realization. A dream? Yes, but not so much more fantastic than the starry-eyed dreams of our greatest scientists who talked in times past of the possibility of flight or the harnessing of atomic power. Technological advances have made possible a considerable measure of reality in the "dream" world of our ancestors, and there is no reason to believe such progress will not continue. Advancement in technology could well be the necessity that will mother the invention of a one-world mentality.

Additional References

Andrew G. Haley, *Sovereignty in Space,* Review of Contemporary Law, Dec. 1960, p. 3; ——, *Space Exploration—The Problems of Today, Tomorrow and in the Future, in* SECOND COLLOQUIUM ON THE LAW OF OUTER SPACE 44 (1960); ——, *The Law of Space and Outer Space,* 33 SO. CAL. L. REV. 370 (1960) reprinted in part, 10 L. Rev. Digest 77 (1960); ——, *Law of Outer Space— Practical Legal Rules for Human Conduct,* 16 FED. COM. B.J. 163 (1959): ——, *Space Age Presents Immediate Legal Problems, in* FIRST COLLOQUIUM ON THE LAW OF OUTER SPACE 5 (1959); ——, *Can Russia Claim the Moon?,* The American Weekly, Jan. 19, 1958, p. 2; ——, *Law and the Space Age,* 5 ST. LOUIS U.L.J. 1 (1958); ——, *Law of Outer Space—A Problem for International Agreement,* 7 AM. U.L. REV. 70 (1958); ——, *Law Must Precede Man Into Space,* Missiles & Rockets, Nov. 1957, p. 67; ——, *Space Law and Metalaw—Jurisdiction Defined,* 24 J. AIR L. & COM. 286 (1957); ——,*Outposts in the Sky,* The American Weekly, Feb. 20, 1955, pp. 10; *Metalaw—The Science of Universal Jurisprudence: The Third Essay:* Paper by ——, Before the Fourth Colloquium on the Law of Outer Space, International Institute of Space Law, XIIth International Astronautical Congress in Washington, D.C., Oct. 3, 1961; *Medical Jurisprudence in Outer Space:* Paper by ——, Before the Medical Society of the State of New York Convention in Rochester, May 9, 1961; *The Moon—Its Stark Importance to Humanity:* Remarks of ——, National Missile Space Conference Panel Discussion on "The Space Challenge—Philosophy" in Washington, D.C., Feb. 16, 1960; *Sociological Transition—Space Law and Metalaw:* Paper by ——, Before the First Inter-American Symposium on Astronautics in São Paulo, July 15, 1959; *Law of Space—Space Sovereignty;* Address by ——, Before the Universities and Scientific Groups in Vienna, Warsaw, Moscow, Prague, Belgrade, Athens, Cairo, Johannesburg, Rome, Barcelona, Madrid, Lisbon, Amsterdam and Paris, May-June 1959; *The Peaceful Uses of Outer Space:* Address by ——, Ninth Annual Conference of National Organizations in Washington, D.C., March 9, 1959; *The Law of Outer Space:* Address by ——, Delta Theta Phi Law Fraternity in Washington, D.C., Oct. 17, 1958; *Space Flight as World Economic Solution:* Address by ——, Member Society of the International Astronautical Federation in Dublin, Feb. 23, 1958; *Space Law:* Address by ____, JAGD Reserves at the Pentagon, Jan. 14, 1958; *Space Law and Metalaw—Jurisdiction Defined:* Paper by ____, Before the American Rocket Society in Washington, D.C., April 3-6, 1957; *Basic Concepts of Space Law—The Unmanned Earth Satellite:* Paper by ____, Before the Twenty-Fifth Anniversary Meeting of the American Rocket Society in Chicago, Nov. 14-18, 1955; *Jurisdiction Beyond the Earth:* Address by ____, Rotary Club of Charlotte in Charlotte, N.C., June 7, 1955.

Space vehicle regulations

In this discussion of specific matters—the specific content of the regulatory scheme—the individual and necessary elements which will constitute the new law of the space age are considered. Allowing countless man-made objects with lethal potential to hurtle unrestrained through space is to invite international discord, harsh retaliatory measures, and unending complaints of avoidable damage and destruction. To determine the extent of responsibility, liability for damages, and all other forms of civil and criminal violations of the rights of others, some indication of what is expected, allowed, demanded, and prohibited must be promulgated. Whether in the form of a code, a treaty, or the charter of some administrative agency, regulations for the policing of space activities must be established. Action in this area is already overdue. The specific content and final form of the regulatory scheme must obviously be the result of an evolutionary process, but that evolution must begin now. And though there is no point in attempting immediately to set out a universal code, among many areas to be investigated there are several which *must* be considered at this time.

BASIC REGISTRATION AND SAFETY LAWS

6–1 National and international registration

In the early days of the automotive industry, for all practical purposes, a state of lawlessness existed with respect to operation of motor vehicles on the public highway. A driver needed no license; his car was not necessarily registered; he did not worry about vehicle safety inspection; and if he so desired he could take his life into his hands and tear down the highway at thirty to thirty-five miles an hour, completely unrestrained except by road conditions. Then, with expansion in industry, population and the general economy, autos were put in many more garages. Accidents, reckless driving, and public hazards soon made the public authorities realize that it was necessary to regulate this means of transportation that was so potentially dangerous in unregulated use.

Colonel Martin Menter stated the case well when he wrote that today man is affected by written rules or laws from "before he arrives in his cradle at birth until long after he withers in his grave." For each new activity that man devises, there must be a new set of legal principles for its regulation and protection; otherwise man would be faced with "chaos, lawlessness, and the arresting of further progress." And as Menter observes, space flight can be no exception: "The rule of law must be applied in future aerospace activities." [1]

Today, the USA and USSR have sent dozens of vehicles onto the unpaved, unrestricted highways of outer space, and again a system of lawless anarchy is developing. Abuses in radio usage; unreported vehicles performing undisclosed functions at undisclosed distances from earth; unrecorded launchings; secret payloads; and many other space practices are completely unrestrained to date. Somewhere the nations of the earth must begin a common system of regulation, identification, registration, and licensing. Leopold and Scafuri, two outstanding contributors to the literature on space law, have suggested that "all craft [while engaged in space flight] be subjected to the exclusive regulatory jurisdiction of an international space authority with whose flag and agency they should be deemed invested." [2] However, since national security is so inexorably tied in with activities in space, no nation with astronautic ability will readily agree to international controls internationally imposed. The only alternative system immediately available—although it is not a really satisfactory alternative—is, of course, a national system. And in the nations involved in space activities today, we may rest assured that a "national" or "governmental" system of controls is strictly followed—with launch and prelaunch registrations taking place, and with every detail of success or failure in every aspect of the work being meticulously recorded for future reference.

In the immediate future other nations will advance into the arena of space activities. To consider first the matter of registration, what are their systems to be? Should they, too, develop an *ex parte* system, unique in every respect in relation to those existing? If this practice is followed by each astronautically maturing nation, we will come, once again, down

---

[1] Menter, *Legal Problems of Space Exploration and Travel*, 33 JAG J. 4 (1962).

[2] Leopold and Scafuri, *Orbital and Super-Orbital Space Flight Trajectories—Jurisprudential Touchstones for a United Nations Space Authority*, Symp. 520, 535.

the long road of parallel developments (on a national level) of a system of regulation which admittedly should be internationally administered. Registration of vehicles—their weight, payload, trajectory, function, expected life, and all other pertinent data—could obviously involve matters of national security. But there is apparently no reason why all those facts that are relevant but not necessarily crucial in nature could not be disclosed, e.g., the time of a launch, the trajectory or expected orbital path, the vehicle weight, and matters of similar import, which are frequently released to the press for publication.

If an international commission were functioning, this material could be carefully logged and efficiently kept in readily accessible sources. A uniform system of reporting activities would slowly come into being, and smaller, later-arriving astronautical powers would come into an existing framework of registration, with precedent to act as guide and a centralized office to be notified. As the numbers of vehicles increase, the work of this office would grow in importance.

Many relevant facts will be made available through a system of registration. The source of damage-causing vehicles, for example, will be internationally identifiable. Indeed, the sources of all existing vehicles will be on permanent record. Vehicles violating communications or other regulations will be identifiable, together with the country that launched them, and measures can then be taken to prevent further abuses. As long as only two or three nations are actively involved in space activities these may seem naive observations, but when there are eight or ten different nations continually launching vehicles into space, the problem of numbers alone will be acute.

Whatever the systems of recordation hitherto employed by American and Soviet space scientists and officials, a uniform system should be agreed upon for the future. An international agency, preferably within the U.N., should be established to localize and formalize the registration activity. The longer we wait to tackle this problem, the greater its dimensions become and the more difficult of solution. The General Assembly resolution of December 20, 1961 is a positive step in the right direction, although it certainly creates no binding obligation upon any nation to comply with the proposed system. In Part B of this resolution, the General Assembly declares as a guiding principle that the United Nations "should provide a focal point for international cooperation in the peaceful exploration and use of outer space." It then calls upon all nations launching vehicles into space to supply prompt information to the U.N. Committee on the Peaceful Uses of Outer Space (UNCOPUOS), so that the registrations of launchings can be accomplished; requests the Secretary-General to keep a "public registry" of the information so provided; and requests the Committee in cooperation with the Secretary-General to maintain close contact with both governmental and nongovernmental space organizations, promote the exchange of information relating to space activities, and, in general, encourage the study of all measures tending to enhance international cooperation in these matters.[3]

Although the United Nations has in fact established an open registry of space vehicles, this has not yet become the definitive and comprehensive listing that is clearly desired by the General Assembly. The United States and the USSR have each challenged the completeness of satellite data submitted by the other to the United Nations registry.[4] Nor do the U.N. and COSPAR listings agree in every respect either with each other or with the listings published by the U.S. National Aeronautics and Space Administration. In other ways, too, the implementation of the General Assembly's resolution still leaves much to be desired. Nevertheless, perhaps the example set by that resolution, plus whatever experience is gained in attempts to implement it, may ultimately lead to the formulation of a uniform code that is acceptable to all concerned and is subscribed to by all astronautical nations.

Since in the eyes of some nations of the world no unsubscribed agreement is binding, the need to obtain express written agreement may be important. If, however, all but one or two of the leading space powers subscribe, after a reasonable time of general concurrence, even nonsignatory powers could be held to be under the regulations. In the cold war struggle today, it is to be seriously questioned whether any of the leading nations can afford to ignore an internationally sponsored effort to obtain a uniform registration system.

6–2 Licensing

Although the listing of space vehicles in some kind of international registry as they are launched is obviously desirable and even essential, it is not sufficient by itself. The actual licensing of vehicles to leave the earth's atmosphere is also necessary, and in fact it should have begun long ago. It is one of the measures that this author had in mind when, as early as 1958, he encouraged the adoption of formal legislation on both the national and the international level in order to prevent the development of some of the problems of unregulated space activity that we are faced with today.[5] At present, the role of the International Telecommunication Union, discussed *infra,* Chapter 10, is essentially that of a licensing commission, but it is very limited in its competence to control.

The question of greatest concern to any licensing body with respect to space activity must be the evaluation of the function of each proposed vehicle. Is it to carry an electronically-sensitive payload into deep space,

[3] See Appendix I-F(1).
[4] N. Y. Times, October 10, 1962, p. 24.
[5] Haley, *Space Age Presents Immediate Legal Problems,* 1st Colloq. 5 (1959).

to report back to earth certain physical facts for an expected period of eighteen months and then plunge into the sun; or is it to rise to a height of three hundred miles and explode a nuclear device for purposes of scientific analysis? The contrast is clearly and factually important.

The actual functions to be performed by space vehicles should be closely watched by an internationally comprised body of competent experts. The uses and abuses of space are potentially many and varied; but many of the abuses could be eliminated by the establishment of a competent agency to regulate activities through licensing, and the agency, acting as an information clearing house, could disseminate all data legitimately obtained by licensed activities.

6–3 Pre-flight inspection

Of all the proposed regulations that one can imagine perhaps the most unpalatable, to all nations, would be one requiring inspection by an international agency. We have seen in recent years that merely suggesting the presence of observers has been enough to cause the termination of talks on nuclear test ban treaties. This is an extremely delicate matter but is of primary importance in the regulatory scheme of space activities.

For the nations to agree on a pre-flight listing of time, place, trajectory and purpose of a launching, and then to allow an international team to inspect the vehicle, its size, content, nature of components and safety features, we will have to reach a much more sophisticated level in our diplomatic cooperation. Perhaps no one will openly admit at this time that such a system is not as heinous as we have been led to believe; and perhaps no one is now ready to acknowledge the need for stringent policing of space activities; but everyone informed in the art is well aware that unless international agreements can be reached and effective measures taken soon, the hope for eventual success in this area will slowly fade.

To establish a system of registration and licensing coupled with inspection by an independent international team of scientists, if the groundwork were begun today, would take years. To put off such an undertaking for later years will make even more difficult the reaching of international agreement. To create such a system will necessitate compromises and sacrifices on the part of all parties concerned; each nation obviously will have to lessen its rigidity somewhat in matters of security. Nevertheless, a working system of internationally controlled inspection of space vehicles would be a major accomplishment not only in the realm of space flight, as such, but also in the larger struggle to attain an age of peaceful development for all mankind.

6–4   *Dangerous instrumentalities*

A problem closely associated with inspection is the determination of what can be allowed in a space vehicle as payload or cargo. With the continual advances in thrust power permitting ever larger dimensions of space vehicles, the mere size of these vehicles tends unavoidably to increase their potential as hazardous instrumentalities. In the early stages of space flight the orbiting of payloads of sixty or one hundred pounds was not uncommon, and their relative potential as harmful or dangerous instruments was correspondingly slight. As these small vehicles would fall back into the atmosphere in response to the pull of gravity, air friction would cause them to burn like meteors and be consumed. However, as sizes increase, so does the ability to survive penetration of the atmosphere, and huge chunks of metal, melted and twisted but intact, can then reach to the surface of the earth. The problem of possible liability for such occurrences is carefully and fully discussed in Chapter 8.

Accompanying this potential of harm due to size of the space vehicles is the problem of dangerous cargo. What will happen if a nuclear-powered spacecraft explodes for some technical reason beyond human control in space? What of the liability for the radioactive debris? Particularly if such an explosion took place during launch within the atmosphere, the consequences could be immediate, far-reaching, and lethal.

In most of the air codes in existence today the national governments have restricted the flight of aircraft carrying explosives, weapons, ammunition and similar instrumentalities, so that the problems of air safety are not compounded. A pertinent section of the Canadian Air Regulations, for example, states:

> Explosives and other dangerous articles or substances shall not be carried on board any aircraft except as authorized by the Minister.[6]

In Germany, the corresponding section of the law states:

> Weapons, ammunition, explosives, poison gases, nuclear fuels, or other radioactive materials and other articles that have been declared dangerous by a legal provision . . . may be transported only with the permission of the authorities.[7]

These instances are typical of many in which special rules have been promulgated to restrict unlimited carriage of dangerous articles in the air. With respect to space, however, the law remains unwritten long after the uses of space have begun. No international agreements of any binding effect exist; and there are no immediate prospects that this lack will be remedied.

---

[6] Air Regulations §800 (1) (Can.).

[7] Law Concerning Air Navigation, Jan. 10, 1959, §27, [1959] 1 Bundesgesetzblatt 9.

To be sure, the resolution of the U.N. General Assembly of Dec. 20, 1961, cited in part above, points out that many of the international problems existing with respect to controls are in need of immediate attention. Also the Legal Subcommittee of UNCOPUOS, during May and June of 1962, listed a series of "other legal problems suggested for future study," all of which touch in one way or another upon the need for regulation of space activities. To quote from the report that it submitted to UNCOPUOS:

> These problems include: (1) demarcation between outer space and atmospheric space; (2) jurisdiction and law applicable to men in outer space and manned stations on celestial bodies; (3) measures to prevent interference with space projects due to scientific experiments or other space activities; (4) prevention of contamination of or from outer space and celestial bodies; (5) *controls over the launching and orbits of spacecraft and artificial satellites;* (6) United Nations control of radio and television programs through outer space instrumentalities. [Emphasis supplied.] [8]

The mere recognition of such problems is certainly a major step, but mankind cannot afford to be continually suggesting topics "for future study," when there is a clear need to give them immediate attention.

The regulation of vehicles to control their content is not something that will accommodate itself to a simple solution. The strategic and scientific knowledge to be gained by unrestrained experimentation with explosive and nuclear-type detonations in space is—so we are told by scientists —potentially great. Yet the counterbalancing considerations of safety, including the avoidance of radioactive contamination of large areas of space and even possible damage within the atmosphere and on the earth's surface, cannot be ignored. In many instances laws are promulgated through a system of weighing and balancing—evaluating the potential service to be rendered by a specific act as opposed to the actual or potential damage that may result from it; the general good to be derived as contrasted with the private deprivation. Thus, even though no clear and readily obtainable answer exists with respect to the problem of dangerous instrumentalities in space activity, some action must be taken now to examine possible solutions. Again the need for an international agency or commission arises. And again the problems of the cold war, national interests, and the worldwide ideological struggle cloud the issues that are in such dire need of resolution.

6–5 The case for regulation—a growing consensus

Although the lack of positive action to date concerning the regulation of space activities is perhaps discouraging, there has been a steadily growing body of opinion in favor of such regulation. Some of the most in-

[8] See Appendix I-F(8).

teresting early observations on the subject were made by Vladimir Mandl in *Das Weltraumrecht: Ein Problem der Raumfahrt* (The Law of Space: A Problem of Space Travel) which was published as far back as 1932. In his comprehensive survey of the potential space-legal problems, Mandl discussed even aspects of the financial risks that might be incurred. He pointed out that the great public interest and the many benefits of space endeavor would justify the use of public funds; but he assumed that private capital would also participate, and he admonished that financial regulations should be promulgated to provide for accurate accounting in these ventures and to prevent unhealthy and unwanted speculation.[9]

Even in 1932, Mandl could see that the launching and landing of space vehicles should be put under close scrutiny and regulation. Vehicle safety rules, registration of launch time and trajectory were all recommended by Mandl. Once a craft was in space, Mandl believed that it should be governed by the law of its launching nation; and since he foresaw the possibility of private ownership, he suggested the nationality be that of the owner or majority of owners of the craft. He would also give to the captain of a spacecraft the powers of a ship's captain at sea.[10]

Mandl stated in 1932 that "airspace" was the vertical limit of national sovereignty, but he did not attempt to define that term beyond stating that it ended where aircraft could no longer sustain flight. Another important fact realized by Mandl was that the existing law of the air and sea provided only very limited analogies to outer space, and that the law of space was essentially a law *sui generis*. He did feel, however, that the rules on presumption of death and insurance claims would be closely tied to those of maritime law. Mandl was very strongly in favor of absolute liability for damages caused by spacecraft to third parties, but he felt that liability to passengers should be based on either fault, negligence, or contractual breach. Mandl even foresaw the need for special provisions safeguarding the patent and author rights of space vehicle owners, to protect them from attachment.[11]

Over twenty years later, A. Shternfel'd in his book *To Whom Does Outer Space Belong?*, published in Moscow in 1956, outlined certain preliminary international norms which he felt necessary for the development of astronautics. These included the creation of a U.N. commission for coordination of scientific space research; exchange of information by scientists and technicians; freedom of international projects and limitation of private initiative in the field of astronautics; control and coordination of tests, including trajectories, launch times, velocities, etc.; the adoption of measures to reduce the number of possible accidents in connection with take-off, flight, and descent of space vehicles; prohibition against, or at

[9] MANDL, DAS WELTRAUMRECHT: EIN PROBLEM DER RAUMFAHRT (Germany, 1932).
[10] *Ibid.*
[11] *Ibid.*

least limitation upon, the use of astronautical objects for military purposes; and the imposition of sanctions against states which violate agreements on the peaceful application of astronautics. Among the possible measures mentioned by Shternfel'd for prevention of accidents were the taking of special precautions against radioactive infections and the adjustment of trajectories in certain cases so that a test flight would go principally over water rather than land areas. And he concluded:

> It is quite clear that all these questions, in spite of their complexity, can be solved if there is a positive approach by the negotiating parties and if artificial satellites are utilized only for peaceful scientific purposes.

In a paper presented at the First Colloquium on the Law of Outer Space at The Hague (1958), Senator Kenneth B. Keating offered a broad, detailed and analytical survey of the problems involved in the formal development of a space legal structure. His primary argument was in favor of a shift of emphasis from problems of sovereignty to the more immediate and pragmatic problems of civil uses of outer space, licensing, agency regulations, and effective coordination of space activities. He indicated the need for attention to the filing of rocket flight plans, interchange of scientific information, the regulation of radio usage, the development of space navigation aids, and discussion concerning the free uses of space for scientific purposes.

Senator Keating emphasized the role that could be played by the International Astronautical Federation (IAF) in efforts of this type, making the point that the U.N. had a reputation for ineffectiveness in such areas and was therefore a poor agent to do the initial work. He also discouraged recourse to the International Civil Aviation Organization (ICAO), citing as his reasons the already burdensome workload and the specialized manner of thinking of the ICAO. Although other writers and publicists have expressed satisfaction with the absence of a space legal code or—like M. Mellor in his 1955 address to the French Society of Air Law—have asserted that it would be a singular error to prefabricate the law of outer space,[12] Keating stated his conviction that the positive approach in favor of a space code is the proper and realistic attitude. While Senator Keating may go too far in his own belief that the issue of national sovereignty in space can be put aside in order to concentrate on issues involved in the practical civil uses of space, his support for the immediate development of a space legal structure is naturally encouraging.

C. E. S. Horsford's remarks are also fairly comprehensive on this topic. In different articles he has pointed out that an international organization —perhaps modeled on the ICAO—should be created to establish regulations for landing procedures, navigational aids, and communications

---

[12] L'Astronautique et le droit, 18 REVUE GÉNÉRALE DE L'AIR 356 (1955).

for space vehicles. The international agency, says Horsford, should be analogous to the International Trusteeship Council and should control and regulate all interplanetary operations. Spacecraft should all be identified with their launching nation, he feels, and that state could then be subject to regulation by the proposed international agency. A reasonable altitude for the ending of national sovereignty in Horsford's scheme is 500 miles: beyond that point space is free, and below it nations maintain sovereignty.[13] Immediate action is necessary, moreover, since the international rules controlling national air sovereignty rights developed by the Paris and Chicago Conventions are wholly inadequate to deal with the unique problems of space flight.[14]

R. Becker likewise called attention to the need for action when, speaking before the Inter-American Bar Association at Miami in April 1959, he encouraged the immediate establishment of a comprehensive code for the control of outer space. He argued that the growing technical and military powers of Soviet Russia would tend to hamper such a development, and that establishing a code might even become impossible unless negotiations were completed before Russia achieved a position of consolidated strength. Robert Bendiner, on his part, has pointed out that the lack of official action toward establishing a space code is in marked contrast both with the obvious need for such action and with the consensus of experts who have studied the problem.[15] Of course, the lack of action would be explained by some writers, including E. A. Conway, on the ground that international cooperation for the regulation of space activities especially in so far as the limitation of armament may be involved is unlikely to be attained as long as the USA and USSR are at varying levels in

[13] Horsford, *The Law of Space*, 14 J. OF THE BRITISH INTERPLANETARY SOC. 144 (1955); Horsford, *Principle of International Law in Space Flight*, 5 ST. LOUIS U. L. J. (1958). A. N. Holcombe believed that ultimately all spacecraft should be owned and operated by an international agency. He points out that the *ad coelum* doctrine cannot reasonably or practically be extended into space. Due to the limitations on national sovereignty the international agency is the appropriate operator in space. Until this agency can be organized and become operative, states launching and operating vehicles in space should all register with this proposed agency. Holcombe, *Relationship of the United Nations to Outer Space: Strengthening the United Nations*, A REPORT OF THE COMMISSION TO STUDY THE ORGANIZATION OF PEACE 216 (1957).

[14] Margo, *Legal Status of the Airspace in the Light of Progress in Aviation and Astronautics*, 75 SOUTH AFRICAN L. J. 106 (1958); Mellor, *L'Astronautique et le droit*, 18 REVUE GÉNÉRALE DE L'AIR 399 (1955); Monro, *Law for the Heav'n's Pathless Way*, N.Y. Times Magazine, Feb. 16, 1958; *Nécessité d'un accord sur la souveraineté de l'espace extra-atmosphérique*, 19 REVUE GÉNÉRALE DE L'AIR 159 (1956); *Outer Space Sovereignty Agreement Needed*, 23 J. OF AIR L. & COM. 81 (1956). In support of the immediate need for work toward a competent international space authority, see also Kroell, *Eléments créateurs d'un droit astronautique*, 16 REVUE GÉNÉRALE DE L'AIR 222 (1953); Lindley, *Cooperation in Space*, Newsweek, Jan. 20, 1958, p. 28.

[15] Bendiner, *Who Owns Outer Space*, 18 The Reporter Magazine 17 (1958).

the arms race.[16] Neither nation, Conway reasons, will do anything that might tend to freeze an adverse imbalance of power—a conclusion that would render illusory the argument for prompt action advanced by Becker.

There are certain moderates or limited-attempt spokesmen who see little if any hope for agreement on a general space code, yet feel that there is a real possibility of progress in clearly defined areas. One of these spokesmen is Professor A. B. Rosevear of McGill University, past director of the Institute of Air and Space Law. Rosevear concludes that international technical agreements relating to such matters as telecommunications are much more likely to be successfully concluded than is a general agreement on the rule of law in outer space. Therefore, he states, maximum effort should be directed toward the adoption of actual working agreements in these limited areas.[17] Another of the writers selecting specific areas for attention is Marek Zylicz, who observes that certain questions "demand an immediate solution." Among these he lists the determination of the upper limit of national air sovereignty, the establishment of rules and regulations governing the travel of spacecraft, international recognition of the right of recovery of spacecraft, agreement concerning responsibility for damages caused by spacecraft—and other questions along much the same lines.[18]

After discussing the establishment and apparent acceptance of the principle of the free use of outer space for peaceful and scientific purposes, Arthur Larson, in his book *When Nations Disagree*, continues:

> The Legal Committee of the United Nations *ad hoc* Committee on Peaceful Uses of Outer Space recently made a report concluding that a space code is not yet feasible. But the questions that loom in the distance will not be as easy or as free from tension as the first one. It is submitted that, to the extent that we can clearly see unavoidable legal questions coming, we should get to work on anticipating and solving them by agreement as soon as possible. If we wait until someone lands on the moon before starting to discuss what rights are thereby acquired, it may be too late to expect an amicable solution.[19]

This same attitude of awareness of the immediate need for some positive action is widely held, as we have seen, by responsible and perceptive scholars and jurists. As Michel Smirnoff has pointed out, the inherent dangers to all mankind from a failure to reach international agreement for control of space flight are so obvious that the need for action "was

[16] Conway, *Outer Space and Peace*, Commonwealth, January 10, 1958, p. 374. See also Gorove, *On the Threshold of Space: Toward Cosmic Law*, 4 N. Y. L. F. 305 (1958).

[17] See Rosevear, *The Search for Agreement on the Rule of Law in Outer Space*, 4th Colloq. (Norman, Oklahoma: University of Oklahoma Research Institute, 1963).

[18] Zylicz, *Some Problems of Astronautical Law*, Symp. 1157, 1162.

[19] LARSON, WHEN NATIONS DISAGREE 61 (1962).

immediately recognized by men of many countries." "Those men," he continues, "were politicians, technicians, but especially they were jurists." Smirnoff even affirms optimistically that "at a time when it is so difficult to reach agreement in other fields, ... space activity is one field where agreement has a good chance of being reached." He then calls upon jurists all over the world to "work out a system which will be acceptable to all the nations." [20]

There are opponents of this view; some radically oppose any attempts to formulate space law at the present time, while others take a moderate or limited position. Nevertheless, this brief survey of the attitudes of responsible writers in the space field clearly brings out the consensus of opinion that exists in favor of immediate action, working toward the formulation and formalization of regulatory, safety, and liability law to govern space activities.

ADMINISTRATIVE PROBLEMS

6–6 An international administration—nature and composition

In formulating any regulatory scheme for space, the most fundamental considerations are those of its administration. No body of law or set of rules is of any value without its enforcement and administration. To administer the needs of the world in its space ventures, an unprecedented organization will be required. The staff will be tremendous, and much of its work highly technical. The policing of space and of the various national activities in space will require widespread communication facilities, as well as trained specialists who can evaluate and act in essentially unique situations. The basic composition of this organization will challenge the ingenuity of the diplomats, government officials, and political scientists. All the nations will demand representation, and none will be willing to suffer control. The benefits of an ordered society will be expected, but the necessary sacrifices to obtain them will be made grudgingly, if at all.

To what extent existing organizations, governmental or nongovernmental, can be adapted or expanded to meet the needs of space regulation is the question to which Chapters 10 and 11 are addressed. Here we shall discuss only the problems inherent in an organization or organizations of the necessary size and scope, once they are created. Where and by whom will the police force of the administration be trained? How will it be organized? Where will the men and women who comprise the rank and file of such an organization be found?

[20] Smirnoff, *Space Law as an Element of Understanding Among Peoples of the Earth*, 4th Colloq., 220, 225-26 (Norman, Oklahoma: University of Oklahoma Research Institute, 1963).

In formulating the controls to be exerted on space activities, the international lawyers, economists, scientists, diplomats, and many others will be able to overcome these problems only very slowly in the beginning. It is not realistic to assume that a code or treaty will suddenly come into being and an organizational structure along with it for enforcement. Existing facilities will be used at first. Just as the Secretariat of the U.N. has been assigned certain expanded areas of responsibility by the General Assembly,[21] the International Telecommunication Union (ITU), World Meteorological Organization (WMO), International Council of Scientific Unions (ICSU), Committee on Space Research (COSPAR), and others, will assume expanding responsibility for certain areas of space activity.

With the expansion of existing facilities, existing practices in securing personnel will probably continue in force. The growth could follow closely the patterns set in previous expansions of U.N. agencies. Whether this is good or bad, desirable or lamentable, it seems inevitable. What is not inevitable is the end result of this expansion. The final form of the organizational structure for administrative control of man's space activities is as far from our eyes and minds as the present-day structure of the Federal Government of the United States is from the original expectation of the founders of that government. But this should be no deterrent. What is needed now is the foresight and planning with respect to space that those original drafters demonstrated in creating the Union of the Thirteen States.

With a planned, long-range program soundly drafted, each nation of the world could concretely provide for the measure of cooperation and support appropriate to its own place in the effort to conquer space. Creating the administration will be only the first step, but a necessary one, and its rudiments may well be available already within the structure of the United Nations and other international organizations.

6–7 Jurisdiction, inquiry, and settlement of disputes

The administration of the rules and regulations for space could follow many paths. For example, national and exclusive controls could be employed. An attempt to formalize such a position was made in Geneva in June of 1962 when the representative of the USSR to the Legal Subcommittee of UNCOPUOS submitted a proposal entitled "Declaration of the Basic Principles Governing the Activities of States Pertaining to the Exploration and Use of Outer Space." This proposal read in part: "All activities of any kind pertaining to the exploration and use of outer space shall be carried out solely and exclusively by States; the sovereign rights

---

[21] See §6–1 of this chapter.

of States to the objects they launch into space shall be retained by them." [22] Under a system of national exclusive control, jurisdiction over an astronaut would be clearly fixed as long as he was within a vehicle or station, in space or on a celestial body. He would be subject to his national law and regulations and responsible to his country of origin for his actions.

An alternative method would be to put the vehicle in space or the manned station under the jurisdiction of an international commission. This commission could promulgate regulations for behavior and hold full responsibility for enforcement. A judicial branch of the commission, international in composition and under no national controls, could serve as the primary court for violations. An appeal from such a court could then be taken to a counterpart of the International Court of Justice, created to review cases involving individuals' claims and individual defendants. (The International Court of Justice is itself a forum for state litigations, and individuals have no standing before it.)

In any event, some form of jurisdiction will have to emerge. Especially when colonies or manned stations are established on other celestial bodies, the activities of men on these bodies cannot be left completely free and unrestrained. This is true for many of the same reasons why we must regulate men on earth, but in space there are even more considerations. Oxygen and food supply will be vital to the life of all persons in a manned station. Abuse of these life-giving materials might well become a felony or even a capital crime.

Naturally, with the creation of an international agency, commission, or treaty organization, more problems will be amenable to solution than those we have discussed above. One function of such an organ could be the conduct of investigatory or inquiry proceedings on alleged breaches of any regulations that may be promulgated on the subject of space activity. The evaluation of a given practice in the light of existing law will necessarily have to be performed by a non-participant in the activity in question, and an international commission might well serve as the required objective observer of the practices of nations and their agents.

In instances involving disputes between two or more nations, the possibility of arbitration by a specially appointed group within the commission or agency should also be carefully examined. Whether arbitration decisions or findings in such cases would be appealable to a higher level would be dictated by the fundamental agreements or treaties upon which the organization of the commission or agency is built. However, assuming the growth of acceptance of the jurisdiction of the International Court of Justice at The Hague, these matters might well be appealable to it.

[22] See Appendix I-F(2).

6–8 Specialized agencies

Within an international regulatory organization for space activities, specialized agencies for controls in limited areas of special practice will inevitably arise. Violations of traffic controls and frequency allocations, organized flight paths, and mining and prospecting regulations are all potential sources of dispute. So are the health problems of contamination and inspections, quarantines and isolation. And no one agency or commission could hope to contain a staff competent to evaluate all the possible problems with the necessary expertise. Thus specialized agencies, probably subsidiaries of existing international bodies, must eventually play a very prominent role in space administration and regulations.

Yet merely to create a series of specialized agencies is not enough. In communications, for example, the International Telecommunication Union, affiliated with the U.N., is now the primary source of determination of frequency allocations. When these allocations are violated, as they have been in the past, some agency within the international structure will have to have authority to apply sanctions to such violations. At present, no such sanctioning body exists, and there is no more effective sanction available than irate expressions of disdain for the violator. Situations of this kind will multiply in space activity as regulations are developed, and unless the specialists can support their regulations by the application of sanctions, the violations of rules will go on.

6–9 Police power: the problem of enforcement

The foregoing discussion in this chapter has been offered, in many instances, in contemplation of the existence of a police power in some international agency. If, in this time of extreme nationalistic tendencies and ideological struggles, it is difficult even to discuss the question of an international police power, actually creating one would be a far greater struggle. Eventually, however, some recognized police power must come into being in order to enforce the regulations of the many international and interplanetary activities which the space age surely will bring upon us. If no effort is made to cope with and resolve this problem today, the only justifiable expectation is that it will be much more onerous tomorrow. Some writers are extremely optimistic regarding the potential role of the U.N. in enforcing controls of space activity. Donald W. Cox, for example, has written that one of the prime shortcomings in all the literature on the establishment of an upper limit to national sovereignty is the absence of any clear realization that a U.N. police force is needed for purposes of enforcement.[23] In any event, the problem of police power

[23] Cox, *International Control of Outer Space*, Missiles and Rockets, June 1957, p. 68.

and enforcement—assuming a body of law for space can be promulgated —is one of the questions to which leading figures on both national and international levels must devote a major amount of time and effort.

6–10 Trespass and nuisance

Although the doctrine of nuisance is to be examined in detail in Chapter 8, it may be useful to consider at this point some problems in enforcement of the rights of individuals, business enterprises, and nations in space activities. With the great number of new and unusual ventures man will indulge in as he enters space, many new legal problems may arise in the area of the law of torts, and specifically with respect to trespass and nuisance.

What is to be private property in space? If all or almost all space vehicles are government owned and sponsored, at least for the early years, space vehicles will be public property—but only in the sense of governmental ownership. Passage between vehicles when not invited, and for other than emergency reasons, may be as much a violation of private property as intrusion onto the private property of one's neighbor on earth.

Through activities engaged in by scientists and explorers in space, nuisances of unexpected nature may well be created. The use of explosives in prospecting, for example, may have far more wide-reaching effects on the moon, where the gravity force is only one-sixth as great as on earth. Debris from mining exhausts and chemical smoke from the new machines of space activity may also prove nuisances which must be curbed.

Derek H. Hene has pointed out that there is very little extant law applicable to the use of the atmosphere for experiments on the control of weather. This is another matter of public international concern, and it is apparent that immediate national and international regulations should be promulgated to control such uses of the atmosphere.[24] Obviously, too, the same or similar regulations would have to apply not only to low-altitude cloud-seeding experiments but also to more sophisticated experiments conducted in the upper atmosphere and at satellite altitudes.

With the development of situations of this kind, the entire ambit of problems we have discussed will again be raised. Decisions will be required as to: the applicable law; the proper forum before which relief may be sought; the element of government or agency of administration which is to handle and settle the problem; the method of enforcement of

[24] Hene, *The Legal Aspects of Rainmaking*, 19 THE MODERN LAW REVIEW 285 (1956).

laws or regulations; apprehension of criminals or of violators of the personal rights of others; and many more problems which at present lie in the hiatus so many leading scholars have deplored as existing with respect to the law of space.[25]

6–11 Liability in general

In launching and employing space vehicles in its activities, each nation active in space must certainly stand responsible for injury and damages to person or property. When enterprises with a high level of hazard potential are undertaken in the future, an international commission or agency could require the posting of an indemnity bond to cover the possible liabilities to be incurred. The issuance of such bonds may develop into an entirely new branch of high finance. Whatever arrangements are eventually provided, it is clear that, with the unprecedented hazardous activities space flight will usher in, some parallel development must follow to provide a framework wherein the liabilities of states and corporations can be realistically met.

6–12 Statute of limitations

Another area of law in which adjustments must be made to meet the needs of space concerns tolling and running of applicable statutes of limitations on certain claims. A three-, five-, or six-year limit on the time within which one must commence the prosecution of a claim may no longer be a realistic limitation, for reasons of time consumed in space travel. The underlying reasons for the statute, i.e., the avoidance of stale claims and the intention to encourage suit, if there must be a suit, within time limits insuring a minimal level of recall in the minds of witnesses and parties, may need to be reappraised in the light of time elapsed in space travel. The benefits normally derived from the prompt pursuit of a claim may be more than offset by the consideration that a man should at least be allowed to return to earth to initiate his claim.

This problem will be another to which any international regulatory organ attempting to administer the laws of space will need to devote some attention at the outset. Indeed, failure to draft provisions that would allow a "reasonable time" to make a claim of injury, damage, or lawlessness, may encourage the performance of just such acts as are least desirable in space. Considerations of enforcement, jurisdiction, standing to sue, and many other technicalities will all have to be examined, in arriving at the final determination of what statutes of limitations shall apply.

25 E.g., Cooper, *The Law of Space and the Chicago Convention*, PROCEEDINGS, CONFERENCE ON SPACE LAW SPONSORED BY THE AMERICAN ROCKET SOCIETY, NEW YORK CITY, APRIL 24, 1962. (To be published.)

6–13 *Allowance of egress*

Who may leave the earth to travel in space? The analogies derived from present law are of little assistance. Any discussion of the legality of restricting the freedom of human beings to leave their countries necessitates an understanding of the nature of the individual's "right" to depart from such confines. Hugo Grotius (1583-1645), the father of international law, taught that in the absence of an express prohibition, or a custom to the contrary having the force of a convention, the right to emigrate could be fully and freely exercised. He asserted that whoever submits to a government does so solely for his own good, and based the rule of freedom of emigration on the natural obligation of preserving oneself.[26] Samuel Freiherr von Pufendorf (1632-94), another of the founders of international law, held that members of a society ought to be permitted to go anywhere they wished if by doing so they could improve their lives.[27]

While authorities on law are divided on the question of a king's right in the earliest days of common law to restrain a subject from leaving the realm, the fact remains that travel abroad was one of the activities carefully supervised in order to prevent subjects from becoming "infected" with foreign, new, and hence presumably dangerous, ideas. This policy was implemented by resort to the writ of *ne exeat regno* by which the king commanded a subject not to go out of the realm. The same writ, under one name or another, is used in many countries at this time, but is generally restricted to cases of equitable debts and claims. One early English law proscribed the sending of children out of the country for the purpose of attending Catholic seminaries. This law was subsequently broadened to prohibit Catholics from leaving for any purpose.[28]

The doctrine of free egress was brought to the United States by the colonists, who from the first acted on the principle later expounded by Sir William Blackstone (1732-80) that English subjects had the right to come and go as they pleased unless a royal injunction had been issued against them.[29] While the Constitution of the United States says nothing explicit about the right of United States citizens to leave the country, the Supreme Court, in a recent decision, held that in the absence of statutory authorization the government could not deny a citizen his right to a passport.[30]

Who, then, should be denied egress to space? If we are to avoid sub-

[26] GROTIUS, DE JURE BELLI ET PACIS LIBRI TRES 253-54 (Scott ed. 1925).
[27] 2 PUFENDORF, DE JURE NATURAE ET GENTIUM LIBRI OCTO 1348-49 (Scott ed. 1934).
[28] 4 BLACKSTONE, COMMENTARIES ON THE LAWS OF ENGLAND *55.
[29] Chitty, Note in BLACKSTONE, COMMENTARIES ON THE LAWS OF ENGLAND 369 n. 3 (Chitty ed.).
[30] Kent v. Dulles, 357 U.S. 116 (1958).

jecting each man's right to enter space to the municipal law of his nation or to some form of "international" rule which merely incorporates these municipal rules, we must devise norms which take into consideration the needs of man and the realities of space flight. If an individual is to be denied entrance to space, the justification of the denial should be based on some fact or facts relating to the nature of space travel and the character and identity of the individual. Municipal considerations of a state's internal policy should not govern, for it must be understood that the right of an individual to leave his community or nation is not identical with his right to enter space. A man may be completely free to leave the confines of his state and at the same time not free to leave the earth.

Paradoxically, the first to be excluded should be those who would exclude others for any political reason, because their moral make-up obviously would be inimical to the concepts of fundamental justice on which space law must be founded. We should also exclude the "nefarious," or impiously wicked, according to the original Roman law meaning of the word. As the welfare and happiness of all crew members or passengers must be of paramount importance, the ultimate decision as to who might be included in the complement of any particular voyage should undoubtedly rest with the travelers as a body.

Another basis for restricting those who may explore space, at least in the beginning, might well be the purpose of the emigration. Thus permission might initially be granted only to space technicians, much in the same manner as permission to travel to areas of war or civil unrest is currently restricted to specified categories of persons such as reporters, nurses, and so on. Also, travel in Europe immediately after World War II was restricted because of the shortage of food and overtaxing of transportation facilities. For a while it may be necessary to limit travel to other planets for similar reasons—that is, shortages of transport, oxygen, and food.

6–14　Military uses of outer space

We are concerned in this work with one principal idea, the establishment of the rule of law in outer space. In addition to fixing the terminal point of terrestrial jurisdiction, we must cope with many other legal problems peculiar to the space age. For example, if we succeed in delimiting outer space and seek to confine its use to peaceful purposes, how do we define "peaceful"? Does it mean "non-military," or as Feldman suggests, "non-aggressive"? [31] Soviet writers, on their part, tend to use

[31] Feldman, *The Report of the United Nations Legal Committee on the Peaceful Uses of Outer Space: A Provisional Appraisal*, 2d Colloq. 19, 23; *contra*, Gal, *Some Legal Aspects of the Uses of Reconnaissance Satellites*, 5th Colloq. (Haley ed., Washington, D.C. 1963).

the word "peaceful" as a blanket term to describe the activities of the Soviet state. Thus Yevgeniy Korovin states:

> There are two opposing political courses on the issue of the international status of space, just as in all contemporary international politics. One course— that of the Soviet Union and all other countries of the Socialistic camp—is the path of peace, equality of rights and friendly cooperation among nations and countries, opening broad vistas of learning about our world environment and subordinating the powerful forces of Nature to man's mind and will. The other course—that of the imperialists—is the path of international terror and violence, stockpiling and perfecting all possible means of destruction. They consider the study of cosmic space as a process of saturating the outer space surrounding the globe with military weapons.[32]

In a similar vein, G. P. Zhukov asserts that all U.S. military uses of outer space are inherently aggressive.[33]

Mrs. Eilene Galloway has discussed this problem in a manner which clearly underscores the great amount of valuable time and effort that can be consumed in mere definition of terms. As she points out, there has been discussion of a possible "distinction between military and civilian uses of outer space" on the basis of differentiation between "aggressive" and "non-aggressive" vehicles. However, she emphasizes that these terms would have to be satisfactorily defined, especially if embodied in treaty form, and that the task of definition is far from easy. A satellite capable of launching nuclear bombs could obviously be termed "aggressive," but certain other types of space vehicle could be described as either "aggressive" or "non-aggressive," depending on the viewpoint of the observers. One example that she cites is that of a communications satellite used for purposes of psychological warfare on a global scale: this might be considered "non-aggressive" by the launching nation, but might be regarded as "aggressive" by the governments against which it was aimed, even if used in a cold war situation rather than a time of open hostilities. Similarly, a reconnaissance satellite would appear "non-aggressive" to the nation that launched it for the sake of obtaining advance warning of a surprise attack, but it might well be considered "aggressive" by other nations over which it passed. She thus concludes, "To equate 'aggressive' with 'military' and 'non-aggressive' with 'civilian' would not clarify the situation sufficiently

---

[32] Korovin, *International Status of Cosmic Space,* Symp. 1062, 1071-72. However, Korovin also suggests (*id.* at 1066):

> Two groups of acts should be differentiated from the standpoint of world relations and international law: acts in the Cosmos that are acts of war, and those that are not acts of war but serve in international relations as expressions of mistrust, ill-will and similar cold war consequences.

[33] Zhukov, *Mezhdunarodnoe Sotrudnichestvo v Mirnom Ispol'zovanii Kosmosa* (International Cooperation in the Peaceful Use of the Cosmos), in *Kosmos i Mezhdunarodnoe Pravo* (The Cosmos and International Law) 114, 124 (Korovin ed. USSR 1962).

at the international level to prevent the use of outer space for purposes other than the benefit of all mankind." [34]

In this same connection, one of the most unfortunate episodes for the orderly development of space law was its involvement in the 1957 proceedings of the United Nations Subcommittee on Disarmament in London. This involvement was inevitable, because the question of control of objects entering outer space could not be kept wholly separate from the larger problem of world disarmament. However, it meant that the issues of space law found their first and in some respects most critical official examination in the intense political atmosphere of the London Conference —whereas the statement of these issues and the formulation of jurisdictional concepts and regulatory rules should ideally have been undertaken long before by appropriate juridical bodies of the United Nations and of such agencies as the International Civil Aviation Organization.

Loftus Becker has correctly observed that there are two countervailing factors in the formulation and application of international law. The first of these is pure legal theory; the second is the political capability of the states involved. The interjection of political factors into the formulation of international law is thus regrettable, but unavoidable.[35] And if political factors cannot be ignored—however much this author has sought to avoid them in past writings—neither can one ignore the classical *ultima ratio* of international politics, warfare. War is the last resort, the ultimate decision; and that stark decision is not within the science of jurisprudence but is the final consideration of politics.

No lawyer could deny the right of the United States, or any other sovereign nation, to protect itself, and it is unthinkable that a nation would relinquish one iota of its sovereignty in this respect in outer space or anywhere else. Thus if any nation in the world should project a military missile over the United States without its permission, whether at an altitude of 1,000 feet or 1,000 miles, the author would hold that this is wholly outside the law and is an act of war.

The most effective weapon for the nonaggressor state is simply to have exclusive control of the "invincible weapon"; the next best protective measure is the ability to take unpreventable retaliatory measures against

[34] Galloway, *Peaceful Uses of Outer Space and the Military Role*, PROCEEDINGS, CONFERENCE ON SPACE LAW SPONSORED BY THE AMERICAN ROCKET SOCIETY, NEW YORK CITY, APRIL 24, 1962 (To be published); also appearing in *Hearings On H.R. 101000 (Superseded by H.R. 11737) Before the Subcommittee on Manned Space Flight of the House Committee on Science and Astronautics, 1963 NASA Authorization*, 87th Cong., 2d Sess., No. 2, pt. 2 at 1065 (1962).

[35] PROCEEDINGS OF THE AMERICAN SOCIETY OF INTERNATIONAL LAW AT ITS FIFTY-SECOND ANNUAL MEETING (Wash., D.C. April 24-26, 1958) 266 (1958). See also Berkner, *Earth Satellites and Foreign Policy*, 36 FOREIGN AFFAIRS 221 (1958); Lissitzin, *Comments on Recent Technological Developments: Political and Legal Implications for the International Community*, PROCEEDINGS OF THE AMERICAN SOCIETY OF INTERNATIONAL LAW, as above, this footnote, 243.

the aggressor. The legal principle involved here flows from the *lex talionis*, which requires the infliction upon a wrongdoer of the same injury which he has caused to another. The principle is expressed in the Mosaic Law by the formula, "An eye for an eye; a tooth for a tooth." In modern international law the term describes the rule by which one state may inflict upon the citizens and property of another state effective injuries. In a real sense, the responsible officials of a nation who fail to provide the means for retaliation are guilty of what might be termed the crime of *ethnocidal negligence*.

Although some lawyers have reasoned that the reaches beyond "airspace" are still devoid of any rule of law,[36] we have seen in Chapter 3, *supra*, that the consent of the nations of the world to the program of the International Geophysical Year established the principle of law that nations may place in earth-orbit space vehicles designed for peaceful scientific uses. But clearly there is a second principle which must be added to the rule of law in outer space, namely, the basic right of national self-preservation, as embodied in Article 51 of the Charter of the United Nations.[37] In brief, a nation is justified in protecting itself from attack no matter where the staging area of the attack may be, including on the high seas or in outer space, and a nation may carry its defensive forces to such areas. The great unresolved problem, so far as defensive measures in space are concerned, is to translate the general recognition of this right of self-defense into some workable criteria for distinguishing between the defensive and offensive uses of space.

In addition to the two mentioned, the rule of law in outer space also includes a third principle, namely, the norm of orderliness. This norm has received more recognition than is generally known. It embraces the orderly use of the radio spectrum—which belongs to all mankind—including the development and use of devices which will turn off transmitters on space vehicles so that interfering signals may be eliminated; it also embraces the use of devices that will cause earth-orbiting vehicles to return to earth, so that they will not perpetually exist as a hazard to safety and property in outer space; and so on.

Thus, the inspired lawyer-politician has before him a broad set of alternatives that range from consideration of the *ultima ratio* to the drafting of practical regulations for the use of radio frequencies in outer space. For example, the strategic consequences of the control of the moon immediately invoke consideration both of the *ultima ratio* and of orderly

[36] See the discussion in Kovalev and Cheprov, ISKUSSTVENNYE SPUTNIKI ZEMLI I MEZHDUNARODNOE PRAVO (Artificial Satellites of the Earth and International Law), 1958 SOVETSKIJ EZHEGODNIK MEZHDUNARODNOGO PRAVA (Soviet Yearbook of International Law) 129; but see Kovalev and Cheprov (Solving the Problem of Outer Space), SOVETSKAE GOSUDARSTVO I PRAVO, July 1960, pp. 136-37.

[37] Compare the discussion in Osnitskaya, *International Law Problems of the Conquest of Space*, Symp. 1088, 1092.

solutions above and beyond resort to warfare. In any event, as already emphasized, military considerations cannot be completely ignored, and nations must evaluate carefully the positions they wish to take and the extent to which military policy is to be dovetailed with technological and scientific long-range planning.

Additional References

Andrew G. Haley, *Commercial Aspects of Our National Space Law*, The Commercial and Financial Chronicle, Jan. 5, 1961, p. 1; ____, *Medical Jurisprudence in Outer Space*, 3 ARCHIVES OF ENVIRONMENTAL HEALTH 315 (1961); ____, *Sovereignty in Space*, Review of Contemporary Law, Dec. 1960, p. 3; ____, *Space Exploration—The Problems of Today, Tomorrow and in the Future*, in SECOND COLLOQUIUM ON THE LAW OF OUTER SPACE 44 (1960); ____, *The Importance of Astronautical Radio in the Space Age*, Signal, May 1959, p. 82; ____, *Law of Outer Space—Practical Legal Rules for Human Conduct*, 16 FED. COM. B.J. 163 (1959); ____, *Space Age Presents Immediate Legal Problems*, in FIRST COLLOQUIUM ON THE LAW OF OUTER SPACE 5 (1959); ____, *Space Flight: A Look Ahead*, Astronautics, Nov. 1958, p. 28; ____, *International Cooperation in Astronautics*, Foreign Service Journal, April 1958, p. 1; ____, *Basic Concepts of Space Law*, 26 JET PROPULSION 951 (1956); *Summation of Questions Involved in the Technical and Legal Regulations of Space Exploration:* Lecture by ____, Seminar Course on Space Science and Technology of the Instituto Nacional de Técnica Aeronáutica, "Esteban Terrades" in Madrid, March 29, 1960; *The Law of Space and Outer Space:* Address by ____, Pacific Southwest Conference on International Law at the University of Southern California, March 5, 1960; *Legal and Economic Aspects of Astronautics:* Address by ____, Dansk Interplanetarisk Selskab in Copenhagen, March 14, 1958; *Jurisdiction Beyond the Earth:* Address by ____, Rotary Club of Charlotte in Charlotte, N.C., June 7, 1955.

7

Space communications

The area of space law most immediately involved in current space activities is communications regulation. Here a survey of radio fundamentals is offered to provide needed vocabulary and background essential to a clear understanding of the problems involved.

After summarizing some of the principal uses of telecommunications in space activities, this chapter considers in detail the complexity of the technique of determining frequency allocation needs and assignments. The limited achievement of the 1959 Geneva Conference where the first allocations were made specifically for space purposes, and the planning for the 1963 Extraordinary Administrative Radio Conference are discussed, leading to a consideration of projected future requirements in this field, with special reference to proposed world-wide satellite communications systems. After exhaustive study of other important technical considerations affecting the international regulation of space communications, the chapter concludes with a report of some technological advances which offer hope for future amelioration of crowding in the radio spectrum.

SOME BASIC ASPECTS OF RADIO USE

7-1   The elements of a radio system

In early 1960 Edward Wenk, Jr.[1] compiled the first of several detailed studies on radio frequency controls in space telecommunications. As part of the original study, Mr. Wenk reviewed in detail many of the basic facts of radio which should be understood by anyone who seeks to appreciate

[1] Senior Specialist in Science and Technology, Legislative Reference Service, Library of Congress.

the nature and complexity of space telecommunications problems.[2] Naturally, many outstanding texts exist in which much fuller coverage of these matters is available,[3] but in the following paragraphs we will incorporate portions of Mr. Wenk's writing (very slightly adapted), in order to provide a layman's introduction to the technical vocabulary and ideas that will be featured in this chapter.

> Radio communication involves a wireless electrical circuit utilizing the radiation of energy in the form of electromagnetic waves. A system for radio communication between two stations at any distance apart consists of three primary elements: (1) a controlled source of emission, or transmitter, including an antenna for radiation; (2) a receiver to intercept and convert the signals to intelligible form; and (3) the transfer mechanism by which the energy is propagated from the transmitter to the receiver. For a particular communication service, specifications may be made of the available electrical power for emission, the practicable antenna size, portability of equipment, the distance between stations, and the "density" of information to be conveyed or speed of message transfer. Within these boundary conditions, selection of necessary radio apparatus and of the frequency for transmission then depends critically on an intricate interrelationship between all three elements: i.e., transmitter, receiver, and medium of energy propagation. Of these, the matter of propagation characteristics is often the controlling factor.
>
> To begin with, light waves, X-rays, gamma rays, and radio waves are all familiar forms of electromagnetic energy, and all follow the same natural laws. All display essential properties of frequency, velocity, intensity, direction of travel, and plane of polarizations; the most significant characteristic distinguishing one from the other is *frequency*. The frequency of electromagnetic energy is the number of cycles per second that the intensity of signal varies when passing successively from what may be considered a positive to a negative phase, in the fashion of a geometric sine wave. The distance occupied by one complete cycle—i.e., the linear dimension in space from one positive peak to the next of a single electromagnetic wave in an entire wave train—is termed the *wavelength*. All radiation is considered to travel with the velocity of light, taken as roughly 186,000 miles per second in free space. A relationship is thus established between frequency and wavelength as:
>
> W equals V/f
> where
> $\quad W \quad$ is wavelength in metric or English system of length (i.e., meters or feet);
> $\quad V \quad$ is the velocity of light in compatible dimensions of length per second (i.e., meters per second, feet or miles per second [4]); and
> $\quad f \quad$ is cycles per second.
>
> When the frequency becomes quite large, the units employed are kilocycles (1000 cycles), megacycles (1 million cycles), and gigacycles [5] (1 billion cycles), all referred to the time interval of one second. . . .

---

[2] STAFF OF SENATE COMM. ON AERONAUTICAL AND SPACE SCIENCES, 86TH CONG., 2D SESS., RADIO FREQUENCY CONTROLS IN SPACE TELECOMMUNICATIONS 8-14 (Comm. Print 1960).

[3] E.g., TERMAN, ELECTRONIC AND RADIO ENGINEERING (4th ed. 1955).

[4] In practical applications the English system of units is seldom used.

[5] The term "gigacycle" was introduced at Geneva (in 1959) but is not yet in widespread use.

From the point of view of communications, the radio spectrum is presently considered to cover the continuum of frequencies in the range of 10 kilocycles per second ... (kc/s) to 40,000 megacycles per second (Mc/s). By international agreement, the spectrum has been subdivided into numerous bands, each identified with a particular service or group of services such as fixed, mobile, amateur, air or maritime navigation beacons, standard-frequency, broadcasting, etc. Each service has been assigned a number of nonadjacent bands throughout the spectrum. . . .

Dominating this situation is the bald fact that there is but one radio spectrum. As was pointed out in the treatise of "Radio Spectrum Conservation," a report of the Joint Technical Advisory Committee (JTAC) of the Institute of Radio Engineers—Radio-Television Manufacturers Association,[6] it has become increasingly clear that the spectrum is public domain which must be conserved as carefully as if it were farmland, forest preserves, water power, or mineral wealth. . . . This resource is extraordinary in that it is both uniformly distributed and widely prevalent, not just through the earth, but throughout the entire universe. However, unlike many other resources, it cannot be consumed; it can be neither publicly nor privately owned; it cannot be physically confined within jurisdictional boundaries. Yet for effective utilization, it must be skillfully managed, treasured, and delicately allocated as though it were a rare and limited mineral.

Service assignments within this finite span of radio spectrum are heavily governed by the fact that propagation characteristics at different parts of the spectrum are not alike. In addition to recognizing this frequency independence, the selection must take into account other technical factors such as transmitter power associated with a certain use (mobile stations almost always have lower power available than fixed stations); the limiting size of an antenna array (also small antennas are compatible with vehicles); the range desired; the estimate of interference, either man-made or natural; the erratic qualities of the upper atmosphere as a factor in propagation, considering the reliability of service desired; and the feasibility of channel sharing.

In consideration of all these factors, a prime criterion of frequency nomination is the development of a maximum ratio of signal strength to background noise—a sophisticated equivalent to seeking the best guarantee of successful reception.

The strength of a radio signal is measured in terms of the voltage induced in a conductor (antenna) one meter long when the magnetic flux of the radiation sweeps along the conductor with the velocity of light. This quantity is usually so feeble that it is in millionths of a volt (microvolt), or less.

Radio signals are usually generated by equipment utilizing vacuum tubes (or more recently semiconductors) which serve as oscillators. The circuits are tuned so that electromagnetic energy is generated on the desired wavelength and then radiated into space through an antenna. The size of antenna required for optimum performance is related to the wavelength employed, and in fact there is a direct proportion between wavelength and antenna length. High-frequency (short-wave) signals thus permit use of shorter or more compact antennas than low-frequency signals. Some antennas may be directional, and resemble optical systems in arrangement and appearance.

For a radio station to emit a steady signal of constant frequency, however, is insufficient for the transmission of intelligence. Further control of the signal is required. One method termed "amplitude modulation" involves

---

[6] JOINT TECHNICAL ADVISORY COMMITTEE, INSTITUTE OF RADIO ENGINEERS—RADIO-TELEVISION MANUFACTURERS ASSOCIATION, RADIO SPECTRUM CONSERVATION (1956).

varying the intensity of signal in accordance with the information (sound) to be transmitted, depending on the receiver to detect or "demodulate" the signal and reproduce it in its original form for comprehension. Alternately, the amplitude may be kept constant, and the frequency itself varied slightly from a base assignment in accordance with the intelligence to be transmitted. Such a process is termed "frequency modulation" and forms the core of most communication systems utilizing the higher register of the spectrum. Obviously, with such systems, individual transmissions are not made on discrete frequencies, but actually involve distinct and finite bandwidths; the width required is in turn a function of the number of "bits" of intelligence that are to be transferred in any given interval of time. In the case of television, for example, the number of dots necessary to be converted into a complex picture pattern without flicker requires a far broader band than does the transmission of audible sound.

At the receiving end of the communication circuit, the system requires an antenna to intercept energy from the radio waves continuously passing by the reception point. By proper tuning, the receiver must then separate the desired signal from the conglomerate of signals of all frequencies being abstracted, and demodulate or convert the signal back to a facsimile of the original transmission. Further amplification of signal may then be required to produce acceptable sound levels or TV picture brilliance.

Obviously, if two signals are being transmitted on the same frequency and develop equal field strength at the receiver location, the clarity of reception is lost. The receiver has no capability for discrimination between two such signals, and thus the only means for preventing such elementary sources of interference is to exert control over the transmitters themselves by licensing separate frequencies for emission. To reduce the hazard of accidental interference through overlap from poor techniques, transmitter tuning procedure, etc., "guard" bands are provided between active bands.

Thus, out of what may appear as an almost infinite spectrum—on which at first glance an exceedingly large number of stations could operate side by side—the number of individual noninterfering transmissions shrinks to such an extent that crowding of the airways is already present in most of the spectrum and is inevitable in those parts of the unallocated spectrum that are being cultivated through new techniques. Partial solution of the problem lies in the process of channel-sharing, but for this arrangement to be satisfactory in terms of freedom from interference (except for time-sharing) transmitters must be geographically separated, use low power, and employ frequencies wherein propagation is limited to short distances.

Radio waves may travel from transmitter to receiver antennas by several mechanisms. For convenience, these have been generally classified as skywaves, tropospheric waves, and ground and space waves.[7]

Skywaves refer to energy that is propagated in the upper atmosphere between 40 and 100 miles above the earth's surface under such conditions as to be affected by the ionosphere. This region contains various layers of rarefied gas which, in being ionized by solar radiation, display the property of reflecting and refracting radio waves back to the earth. Depending on the height of the particular layer, waves may be caromed between the ionosphere and earth several times in traveling through the sky. This phenomenon thus accounts for most long-distance communication making use of a "skip" mechanism. Because of the diurnal and seasonal fluctuations in the height of

[7] *Id.* at 19-125.

various ionized layers above the earth, considerable variation in signal intensity occurs between day and night, and between summer and winter.

Tropospheric waves are similar to skywaves except that they are affected by properties of the lower atmosphere in the 10-mile portion closest to the surface of the earth, where reflection and refraction also occur, influenced by (among other things) moisture content of the air and marked transition in air density.

When transmitting and receiving antennas are at the surface of the earth and oriented vertically, a groundwave exists that is supported at its lower edge by the presence of the earth's surface. This groundwave accounts for propagation of most standard broadcast signals in the daytime. When the antennas are elevated, similar waves may travel from transmitter to receiver along the earth, perhaps deflected by bouncing on an irregular surface. In one sense, these waves are analogous to visible light originating at the transmitter in that the propagation characteristic in terms of range and behavior may be thought of as corresponding to a "line of sight."

Still another mechanism of radio communication is that of scatter propagation. Techniques utilizing this medium constitute one of the most dramatic developments in radio communication in recent years. In certain frequency ranges, particularly 25–60 Mc/s, a certain amount of incident electromagnetic energy appears reflected in the ionosphere, and scattered forward, counter to the usual experience at that frequency wherein no reflection is observed. The phenomenon, analogous to the scatter of light from a searchlight illuminating a cloud, appears best explained by the ionizing influence of meteor trails which in the aggregate provide enough of a reflecting or scattering medium that directional signals of high power may be propagated by "skip" for far greater distances than is ordinarily expected in that range of frequencies.

These different modes of propagation are involved separately and collectively at different frequencies. Unfortunately, the salient facts of radio propagation cannot be summarized in a statement of a few judiciously chosen sentences. The details are exceedingly complex, and the state of the art is rapidly changing, particularly at the end of the spectrum most applicable to space communication. That the situation is so involved stems from the fact that the radio spectrum is spread over frequencies which, from one end to the other, are in the ratio of 10 million to 1; by contrast, the corresponding frequency spread in the optical spectrum is only 2 to 1.

The lowest radio frequencies, 10 to 200 kc/s, are characterized by the existence of a groundwave which is propagated at great distances, and by relatively stable ionospheric phenomena. Signals may thus be received over much of the earth, free of fading and diurnal or seasonal variability. On the other hand, the atmospheric noise is stronger, and greater power must be employed to override the background static.[8] Also, as noted earlier, larger antenna arrays are required at these longer wavelengths. As a consequence, frequencies at the low end of the radio spectrum are mainly suitable for commercial telegraphy or telephony, and for military application where the importance of communication traffic justifies the investment for high-power transmitters and huge antenna structures. The lower frequencies are also employed for long-distance navigation.

Between 200 and 2000 kc/s, there occurs a transition of propagation mode

[8] Static from thunderstorm activity is propagated much farther at low frequencies, whereas the upper reaches of the spectrum are almost static-free.

from a predominantly groundwave transmission to one of skywave. At the low end of this range, propagation in the daytime is by groundwave, and substantially stable communication is possible. Over paths of good conductivity such as sea water, the disparity of propagation between both ends of this frequency range is not so marked. However, nighttime propagation is characterized by skywave phenomena and thus, at any distance involving the participation of the ionosphere, is accompanied by serious fading. By and large, this band has been employed for commercial audio broadcasting. Particularly for this service, radio equipment has been highly engineered for frequency stability and freedom from drift that would cause interference.

Transmissions in the 2 to 30 Mc/s range (short-wave) propagate primarily via the ionosphere, which accounts for exceedingly long ranges of thousands of miles with but little power. The lower frequencies are most often used for long-distance nighttime service; the higher are utilized in the daytime. Because of the hazard of periodic interruptions in service due to cyclical and diurnal disturbances of the ionosphere, transmitters using these ranges usually reserve several alternative frequencies so that a selection can be made of the auxiliary one most suitable at the time communication is desired. Disturbances due to sunspot activity and solar flares cannot be similarly overcome; communication must then rely on transoceanic and continental cables.[9]

Propagation on 30 to 300 Mc/s (very high frequency, VHF) and 300 to 3000 Mc/s (ultra high frequency, UHF), is limited most of the time to line-of-sight distances, although substantially all of the mechanisms of reflection, refraction, scattering, and guided propagation occur here. Tropospheric and other irregularities greatly influence the distance of reception. As the frequency is raised, it becomes progressively easier to provide directivity, thus making possible systems confined to narrow paths in space. Such systems are both more secure from interception and freer from extraneous interference.

Even higher directivity can be obtained at frequencies above 3000 Mc/s (super high frequency, SHF, and extremely high frequency, EHF). This characteristic coupled with the small antenna needed, and thus low power, give radar (which utilizes an echo-ranging principle) its qualities of definition. The distance range, however, is little beyond the horizon for this frequency order, since apparently the ionosphere plays no important part in this propagation.

Longer-distance communication can be effected by use of relay stations, and is economically feasible up to 19,000 Mc/s. Beyond that, a limitation is introduced by the screening effect of raindrops during heavy precipitation. At even higher frequencies, such absorption occurs from atmospheric water vapor or oxygen molecules.

7–2   Uses of space telecommunications and the need for cooperation

The broad implications of space communications are playing an increasing role in several aspects of our country's foreign policy. In view of the international importance of a positive, well-informed American

---

[9] The 11-year cycle of sunspot activity reached its most recent peak in the summer of 1957.

policy on space communications, there is growing need to understand the policy alternatives that are available. First, however, it will be helpful to comment on the value of space telecommunications and on a number of technical factors which will affect the attainment of international agreement in this area.

The most obvious value of space telecommunications is its use as a basic component of any effort to explore outer space, specifically through its use in tracking, guidance, and information recovery. The integrity of radio communications is as necessary to the success of a mission as is the performance of the launch vehicle itself.

Potentially one of the most serious effects of radio interference is on the guidance control of the vehicle at launch, during flight, and at re-entry. Deflection at launch can be hazardous to both life and property. Interference during flight or on re-entry can also be hazardous [10] and, in addition, can cause the loss of vital data from costly and difficult experiments. Uncontrolled re-entry into the earth's atmosphere, in particular, will court the danger of destruction through frictional heating. To prevent this, radio tracking and command control, free of interference, must be maintained throughout the re-entry process until successful recovery has been effected, or else the vehicle and any occupants may burn up without even knowledge of what happened.

As Col. James D. Flashman, writing in *Signal*, the journal of the Armed Forces Communications and Electronics Association, points out, "as our efforts become increasingly ambitious and costly, the opportunity for a second chance becomes proportionately less. The first try must be a success, otherwise lives may be lost, millions of dollars may have been expended wastefully, to say nothing of the loss suffered by national prestige." This means that we must at all times "be able to track space vehicles accurately, observe their programming and record their data transmissions in the most minute detail and inject control and guidance instructions instantly at will." Col. Flashman emphasized that without positive international regulation "virtually all our activities in space communications and electronics will be conducted in an atmosphere of calculated risk, subject to the whim of the negligent, inexperienced, or inept co-user of the radio spectrum, within whose power it is to wreck completely an operation upon which the prestige of an entire nation may rest." [11]

A large but less well known field of space communications concerns the reception of radio signals which are not man-made. This field, known as radio astronomy, has for several years been pursued for strictly scientific purposes in an attempt to determine the age of the universe, ascer-

[10] See Chapter 8.

[11] Flashman, *Positive Control of the Electromagnetic Spectrum*, Signal, journal of the Armed Forces Communications and Electronics Association, May 1959, p. 46.

tain its dynamic processes, and gather other types of astronomical or astrophysical data. More recently radio astronomy has promised to be of great value as a navigational aid, by enabling space vehicles to be guided by invisible emanations of stars not subject to optical interference from clouds or to interference from the earth's magnetism near the poles. The tools of radio astronomy, and in particular the great new disk antennas measuring hundreds of feet across, are unparalleled tracking instruments, making possible communication with a 150-watt transmitter 150 million miles away in the outer reaches of the solar system.[12] Radio astronomy also plays a part in the advance prediction of solar disturbances, geomagnetic storms, and related phenomena, so that one can, for example, avoid certain types of dangerous radiation during manned space flights. This prediction function also permits advance planning for communications traffic during radio blackouts, which is vital to national security.

A newly developing field of space communications is the use of satellites for commercial purposes and as public information media. The commercial use of communications satellites has become almost a necessity to handle the 700 percent increase in transoceanic communications anticipated during the decade of the 1960's. Even the new transistorized cable planned for about 1970 would be inadequate by 1965, five years before it is to start operation. Space telecommunications must therefore become an integral element of the world's increasingly internationalized economy.

Of perhaps equal importance is the function of space communications in the current battle throughout the world for the minds of men. The impact of communications on underdeveloped peoples has changed the political map of the world during the past generation, and, with the spread of modern communication facilities by means of satellite relays to all parts of the world, this impact may be even more pronounced in the future.

As a critical consideration in the formulation of our nation's foreign policy, the importance of space telecommunications can hardly be overemphasized. Nevertheless, efforts to secure international protection for space communications have by no means been successful. The principal reason is the fact that radio frequencies are a scarce resource. Although in theory the number of radio frequencies is without limit, in actuality the number of frequencies available for space communications is restricted to a small percentage of those needed.

Almost the entire frequency spectrum is already allocated to other nonspace uses, and the problems of reallocation, including the cost of replacing equipment designed for specific frequencies, make provision for

12 STAFF OF THE SENATE COMMITTEE ON AERONAUTICAL AND SPACE SCIENCES, 86TH CONG., 2D SESS., RADIO CONTROL IN SPACE TELECOMMUNICATIONS (70 Comm. Print 1960).

the needs of space communications a highly contentious matter. The task of reserving frequencies for space communications is complicated by the necessity of attaining complete or nearly complete elimination of man-made interference, particularly for radio astronomy and for delicate tele-metering requirements. Furthermore, the Doppler effect makes it neces-sary to reserve bands for space communications that are considerably wider than would be necessary for the normal earth transmitter. Extra width for space communication bands is also required by the increasingly complicated messages, such as weather photos, which are being used in space communications, and by the use of frequency modulation for better reception. Of greatest importance is the fact that for technical reasons many of the unsaturated frequencies are not suitable for space communi-cations.

The principal technical factor controlling the allocation of frequencies for space use is the difficulty or unreliability with which certain fre-quencies propagate through the ionosphere or, above 10,000 megacycles, even through raindrops or water vapor. Other important factors are the decreasing directivity of signals possible, and the decreasing effective-ness of the small or compact antennas in space vehicles, as the frequency is reduced; the erratic effect on certain frequencies of the upper atmos-phere; and the variability from one frequency to another of interference, including background interference not caused by man.

The problem of frequency suitability is particularly acute in the field of radio astronomy, where reception of emissions from certain elements in space—specifically, deuterium, hydrogen, and hydroxyl—does not allow any choice among frequencies. If the signals are to be received at all they must be received on the specific frequencies of each element.

As a consequence of the limited spectrum suitable for space communica-tions and of the occupation of much of this spectrum by other users, inter-national agreement is all the more necessary to reserve certain frequencies for space use. Subsidiary problems calling for international agreement are the registration, identification, and automatic cut-off of satellite trans-mitters.

In addition, international machinery must be improved to establish an orderly process of review so that the spectrum crowding can be alleviated by the application of new technical developments. New techniques are constantly being developed to open up other portions of the spectrum, to provide better control of the quality of emissions so as to reduce the size of the necessary guard bands between operating frequencies, to decrease band width requirements, and to decrease background noise inherent in receiver components so as to increase the signal to noise ratio. Without effective international organization, however, the utilization of the new techniques in spectrum allocation may suffer a time lag of several years.

THE INTERNATIONAL PROBLEMS

7–3   The problems of frequency allocation

In all forms of astronautical communications, lawful use must be made of radio frequencies within the framework of pertinent international treaties and agreements. Unfortunately, this requirement has by no means been consistently observed; and if the nations of the world are to meet their international obligations in this matter, it will be necessary for the lawyer to intervene and make himself heard both in the United Nations and in the International Telecommunication Union (ITU).

What is "lawful" in this context is defined principally in the International Telecommunication Convention and in the Radio Regulations adopted pursuant thereto. Article 3 of the International Telecommunication Convention provides in paragraph 2(a) that the purposes of the Union created by the Convention (i.e., the ITU) shall be in particular to "effect allocation of the radio frequency spectrum and registration of radio frequency assignments in order to avoid harmful interference between radio stations of different countries." Article 44 of the same Convention provides that all stations, whatever may be the purpose of their establishment and operation, must be "operated in such a manner as not to result in harmful interference to the radio services or communications of other members or associate members or of recognized private operating agencies, or of other duly authorized operating agencies which carry on radio service." Furthermore, the article carefully enjoins all members and associate members to take "all practicable steps to prevent the operation of electrical apparatus and installations of all kinds from causing harmful interference to the radio services or communications mentioned. . . ."

This theme is emphasized again in the Radio Regulations annexed to the Convention, which state in Article 3 of Chapter III:

> 1. The countries, members of the Union, adhering to these Regulations, agree that in assigning frequencies to stations which, by their very nature, are capable of causing harmful interference to the services rendered by the stations of another country, they will make such assignments in accordance with the table of frequency allocations and other provisions of this chapter.

> 2. The frequencies so assigned shall be selected in such a manner as to avoid causing harmful interference with services carried on by stations using frequencies assigned to them in conformity with the provisions of this chapter and which are entitled to international protection from harmful interference as provided in Article 11.

In Article 2 of Chapter IV of the Radio Regulations it is provided that each country, to obtain international recognition of a frequency assignment which it has made "to a fixed, land, broadcasting, radionavigation land, or standard frequency station within its jurisdiction or control," or if it has made some change in an existing frequency assignment, shall notify the International Frequency Registration Board in Geneva "by any means of suitable record communication." The article states that any "frequency assignment which is in full conformity with all provisions of the Radio Regulations" is then to be "recorded in the *Registration Column.*" On the other hand, a frequency assignment which in some way "contravenes the provisions of the Radio Regulations, but on the use of which the notifying country insists, shall be recorded in the *Notification Column.*"

It must be mentioned at this point that not until December 21, 1959 (26 months after the launching of *Sputnik I*) was provision specifically made in the ITU Radio Regulations for radio allocations to the space and earth/space radio services.[13] Prior to that time the astronautical services were not officially defined in the Convention and Radio Regulations—or officially by any government. Thus, actual use of radio in astronautics antedated national and international agreement by more than two years; and during that period 43 vehicles were launched into orbit or on space probe missions by the USSR and the United States. More than 73 radio transmitters were included in these space vehicles. Some of the transmitters are expected to continue operating indefinitely: *Vanguard I's* small 108.03-megacycle transmitter, for example, is estimated to have an indefinite transmitter lifetime. It has been publicly announced that transmissions from these vehicles were made on frequencies ranging from the region of 20 megacycles to the region of 100 megacycles [14] and it is understood that the range of frequencies used on a classified basis was even more extensive. Radio transmissions from earth to the space vehicles, both during and after launching, involved large additional bands of the radio spectrum.

Even in the absence of formal international allocations of radio spectrum space to astronautical use, frequencies were sometimes "cleared" on an informal basis for use in space programs. This was the very least that accepted standards of international behavior appeared to demand. On other occasions, however, there was no attempt at "clearance"; and there were also definite instances of interference by space transmissions with other forms of radio use, in violation of a basic policy agreed to by all nations.

Before proceeding further, it is well to emphasize that this discussion is not primarily intended as a criticism of any one nation or administration. The views expressed here are those of a lawyer, not a politician, and this work simply embodies a plea for international cooperation in providing radio facilities for astronautical purposes—an objective which is essential to the orderly progress of civilization and peaceful relations

[13] ITU Radio Regulations, Dec. 21, 1959, ch. III, art. 5, T.I.A.S. No. 4893.
[14] STAFF OF THE SENATE COMMITTEE ON AERONAUTICAL AND SPACE SCIENCES, *supra* note 12 at 41-42.

among nations. Specifically, it is not the purpose here to condemn the USSR for the use by Soviet satellites of the standard frequency of 20 megacycles, or the frequency of 40.002 megacycles.[15] The author is fully aware that nations other than the USSR have come to the conclusions that frequencies in the range of the standard frequency must be used for study of the ionosphere and that no specific permission need be obtained from the ITU for use of the standard frequency. On the other hand, it has been customary for states throughout the world to report their operations on the standard frequency to the International Frequency Registration Board, and the USSR did not comply with this practice. Moreover, to use the frequency of 40.002 megacycles, permission of the ITU is definitely called for, and this was not obtained in connection with the Soviet satellite experiments.

The frequency 20.005 megacycles used by the *Sputniks* is in the center of the frequency band 19.990–20.010 megacycles which the ITU has assigned as the Standard Frequency Service.[16] Stations employing frequencies in this band conduct "a radio communication service for scientific, technical, and other purposes, providing the transmission of standard and specified frequencies of stated high precision, intended for general reception." [17] In fact, 20.005 megacycles is the exact frequency assigned to Station PEN in Kootwijk, The Netherlands.[18] Then, too, the experimental station of the United States National Bureau of Standards, Station WWV, has the assigned frequency of 20.0 megacycles. The ITU has assigned a guard band of 10 kilocycles on each side of this frequency to prevent interference with Station WWV's operations, and the signals of the Soviet satellites at 20.005 megacycles were 5 kilocycles within this zone of interdiction.

Station WWV transmits the official time signals of the National Bureau of Standards, and constant checks on these time signals are made at various points, such as the Bureau's radio reception center in Boulder, Colorado. This reception was actually interfered with by the *Sputniks*.[19] Furthermore, the Bureau of Standards maintains chains of recording stations for radio noise measurement in areas throughout the world, and these stations operate on the quiet part of the guard band of the standard channel or 20 megacycles. These stations also were interfered with by the *Sputniks*.[20] It is true that the period of interference was not great;

15 TASS dispatch, Oct. 4, 1957.

16 ITU Radio Regulations, Dec. 21, 1959, ch. III, art. 5, T.I.A.S. No. 4893.

17 *Id.*, ch. I, art. 1, §1.

18 BUREAU OF THE INTERNATIONAL TELECOMMUNICATION UNION, LISTE DES FRÉQUENCES (Switzerland 1947).

19 UNITED STATES NATIONAL BUREAU OF STANDARDS, CENTRAL RADIO PROPAGATION LABORATORY, REPORT (1958).

20 *Id.*

nevertheless, interference of this sort is something that could become very serious indeed. It must be remembered, too, that the standard frequency of 20 megacycles is allocated for world-wide use and that the experience of the United States is cited here only on an illustrative basis.

The signals on the frequency of 40.002 megacycles were likewise in an actively-used frequency band. In Region 1 (Europe, Soviet Asia, and Africa) and Region 2 (the Western Hemisphere) the frequency 40.002 megacycles is allocated to fixed and mobile radio communications services. In Region 3 (Asia and Oceania) aeronautical radio navigation services are assigned this frequency. The frequency 40.0 megacycles, just 2 kilocycles away from the frequency used by the Soviet satellites, is the assigned frequency of radio stations on the Isle of Guernsey and in Guanabacoa, Cuba. Similarly, the signal at 40.002 megacycles was less than one megacycle below the frequency assigned to a broadcasting station in Brocken, Germany, operating on an assigned frequency of 41.0 megacycles.

The International Telecommunication Convention and the Radio Regulations clearly show that the use by the USSR of 40.002 megacycles per second (wavelength of about 7.5 meters) was contrary to international law.[21] There can be no doubt as to the use of this frequency by the satellites *1957 Alpha, 1957 Beta*, and *1958 Delta,* as the actual frequencies were frankly designated in official publications of the USSR and literally thousands of readings on the frequencies were made at points throughout the world.[22] On no occasion did the USSR apply to the appropriate agencies of the ITU at Geneva for permission to use the frequency of 40.002 megacycles, and indeed the appropriate agencies of the ITU were not officially notified of the use of this frequency by the *Sputniks*. In this connection it must be kept in mind that the USSR is a signatory member of the ITU and has been one of the most active and helpful nations participating in its work.

It is important to note once again that until December 1959 the use of radio frequencies in space communications was not subject to any express or formal international agreement. Hence before that date, and in some respects even after it, one could technically argue that the dissemination of radio signals from vehicles in outer space was not covered by any form of binding international law—that existing arrangements applied only within the bounds of "airspace," and not in outer space where no nation or nations could properly claim jurisdiction.[23] However, these considerations could not apply in the case of transmissions from earth *to*

[21] ITU Radio Regulation, Dec. 21, 1959, ch. III, art. 5, T.I.A.S. No. 4893.
[22] Pravda, Oct. 9, 1957, p. 2 col. 5; *id.* Oct. 5, 1957, p. 1 col. 5-6; Radio, Aug. 1957, pp. 18-20; *id.,* July 1957, pp. 17-23 (USSR).
[23] See Symp. 65, 76; 271.

space; and transmissions *from* outer space were perfectly capable of interfering with radio uses in "airspace."

7–4 Efforts at international allocation for space purposes

In Chapter 3 and again in Chapter 8 we examine some of the dangers of uncontrolled spacecraft. In the context of communications, it cannot be emphasized too often that radio controls, guidance, tracking, and scanning are essential elements in the use and safety of space travel. Abuses of allocations leading to confusion of radio commands could result in extensive losses and irreparable damage. This fundamental tool of the space scientist must be kept in working condition, and the lawyers and diplomats at the council tables must be constantly aware that the burden is upon them to create and enforce workable laws and rules of the road for the use of radio in space travel.

One important requirement, to be discussed in detail in Section 7-7 *infra,* is the control of the radio transmitter on an earth-circling vehicle so that it will not continue to operate indefinitely. At present, radio engineers throughout the world are possessed of the unpleasant knowledge that for indeterminate periods certain frequencies are being in a sense usurped for satellite operation to the possible detriment of assigned frequency usage. The radio spectrum is limited, and the frequencies involved are extremely valuable; they may be quite essential to some other services. Accordingly, there must also exist a radio command or other device capable of silencing these earth-circling vehicle radio transmitters.

Years ago the author recognized these problems, and since then he has endeavored to alert the world to the need for constructive solutions.[24] In response to such efforts, the American Rocket Society, on its part,

[24] Col. Martin Menter of the U.S. Air Force prepared a thesis in May of 1959 dealing with astronautical law. In discussing the legal problems arising in conjunction with astronautical development, he wrote:

> Andrew G. Haley, who is currently the general counsel of the American Rocket Society, has been actively engaged for many years in the technical and legal aspects of missile developments. His views are public record in testimony, addresses, and writings that have been published in past years, varying from discussions of technical problems of rocketry to philosophical discussions of the law that should apply in our relations with planets on which life exists. He has frequently discussed the problem in communications arising out of the Soviet *Sputnik's* use of frequencies which, under the International Telecommunication Convention and the Radio Regulations thereunder, were previously assigned. This problem has been recognized and it is anticipated that states will amend their national legislation to embody new provisions relating to astronautical radio; further, that the international problems will be resolved through the International Telecommunication Union (in which both Soviet Russia and the United States are active participants) by the allocation of portions of the spectrum for astronautical radio.

Menter, *Astronautical Law,* Symp. 349, 374. This is the text of Thesis No. 86, May 1959, Industrial College of the Armed Forces, Washington, D.C. (1959). See also, on these and related efforts, Appendix I-J.

established committees on Space Communications and Guidance and Navigation. As General Counsel of the American Rocket Society, the author has made appearances, pleadings, reports, and comments in proceedings instituted by the Federal Communications Commission looking toward reallocations and new allocations of radio frequencies to the various services, including astronautical radio. He has served on various committees dealing with these problems; and he has worked—informally as early as 1952, subsequently in formal representations [25]—to convince the ITU of the necessity for special allocations of frequencies for space uses. Fortunately, the ITU is composed of more adhering nations than practically any other international organization. It has had an excellent record of achievement, and though its first formal action with regard to space allocations was not as prompt as might have been desired, it has certainly taken more action in connection with astronautical problems than has any comparable international body. Appendix I-J contains a brief discussion of United States and international action on space telecommunications in the ITU and the CCIR.

Also, efforts have been made to provide the technical groundwork upon which the needed allocations must be based. An agency of the ITU, the International Radio Consultative Committee (CCIR), has the task of studying the scientific and technical problems connected with the radio communications. The investigation of such phenomena as ionospheric and tropospheric effects on wave propagation is the special province of the CCIR. This committee does not allocate frequencies; rather, it has the duty "to study technical radio questions and operating questions the solution of which depends principally on considerations of a technical radio character and to issue recommendations on them." [26]

In view of the importance of the CCIR to the astronautics program, the author traveled to Warsaw to attend the CCIR conference in that city during August 1956. There he presented the views of the International Astronautical Federation, which were assembled from the scientists of several countries. He proposed that the CCIR undertake a review of the requirements of astronautical radio frequencies and promised the cooperation of the IAF in this endeavor. The result was that the IAF was advised to seek consultative membership in the ITU, and the hope was expressed that "collaboration with [the IAF] would give excellent results." [27] The CCIR did not agree to undertake studies at that time. However, in due course it did form a Study Group IV (Space Systems) "to study systems of telecommunications with and between locations in space." And upon

[25] Minutes of the Thirteenth Plenary Meeting of the CCIR, Warsaw (1956).
[26] International Telecommunication Convention, Dec. 22, 1952, [1955] 2 U.S.T. & O.I.A. No. 1213, T.I.A.S. No. 3266, art. 7, §1(3). For a breakdown of the Study Groups of CCIR see Appendix III-E.
[27] Op. cit. supra note 25.

application by the IAF, the ITU granted that organization full non-governmental consultative status, with the right to participate in Administrative Conferences of the Union and in the meetings of the CCIR. This cooperative approach resulted in some genuine progress in the efforts to bring order into astronautical radio.

These and other developments leading to the 1959 Geneva Conference, where the first space frequency allocations were made, are fully traced in Chapter 11, Section 11-8. At the Geneva Conference, in the aggregate 127 megacycles of the spectrum between 1,000 and 10,000 megacycles was set aside for space use, and the allocations in this portion of the spectrum (as well as all other allocations to space services) were made for research purposes. No frequencies were allocated for world-wide operational use, as in a satellite communications system.

The radio frequency allocations to the space and earth/space radio services adopted at Geneva are listed in Appendix I-B. The contents of this appendix may be compared with prior proposals and requests for radio spectrum space which were made by the IAF, the American Rocket Society, the Committee on Space Research of the International Council of Scientific Unions, and others. See, for example, the IAF proposals, which the author presented to the ITU at Geneva in August 1959 as Official Observer of the IAF, and which are listed also in Appendix I-C. It is apparent that the IAF requests were not fully met in the subsequent ITU allocations. The IAF fully documented the need for the allocations listed in Appendix I-C; nevertheless, no allocations were made in the ranges 320–328.6, 890–942, 4380–4400, and 10,000–10,100 megacycles, or in the spectrum reasonably near those bands.

The over-all radio frequency allocations adopted at Geneva in 1959 were thus far from adequate to meet the needs of existing, planned, and foreseeable astronautics programs. Many of the participants in the Geneva Conference were quite conscious of this fact. On the one hand, the USSR and Czechoslovakian delegations at Geneva espoused the view that inadequate data existed to justify making civilian and world-wide allocations in the spectrum above 200 megacycles. On the other hand, the delegations of France, the United Kingdom, and the United States urged that selected and definite radio frequencies throughout the spectrum from 2.5 to 31,800 megacycles be allocated to the space and earth/space radio services.[28]

Fortunately, before the end of the Conference there was one point of agreement. An *ad hoc* group representing the USSR, Czechoslovakia, France, the United Kingdom, and the United States, unanimously recommended that an Extraordinary Conference be held in 1963 on four major matters related to astronautical radio allocations. The program for the Extraordinary Conference recommended by the group was:

---

[28] Notes of the author, U.S. Delegate.

(i) to examine the technical progress in the use of telecommunication for space research and the results of technical studies by the CCIR and other interested organizations (including, presumably, the IAF);

(ii) to decide on the allocation of frequency bands for the various categories of space telecommunication which are considered essential on the basis of the results of space research so far and other technical studies;

(iii) to consider whether there is a continuing need to make frequency allocations for space research purposes, and if so to take appropriate action in this regard;

(iv) to adopt, if such action is considered desirable, certain new provisions in the Radio Regulations to provide for the identification and control of radio emissions from space vehicles, taking into account the possible recommendations of the CCIR.[29]

The preceding recommendation was unanimously adopted. By this action, the Conference "recognized that existing regulations did not correspond to reality." [30] Therefore, a new Conference was tentatively scheduled for 1963, and in fact over 80 nations reached agreement for an Extraordinary Administrative Radio Conference to be held in that year.[31]

The program outlined in Appendix I-H is roughly what was presented as a first approximation of the requirements of space communications.[32] As the task is a world-wide one requiring international cooperation, the author urged that the International Astronautical Federation serve as a central fact-finding body, and a special committee was established within the IAF for the preparation of recommendations to the CCIR. Meantime, the constituent societies of the IAF also worked with their national administrations in the preparation of basic data for the 1963 Conference. The American Rocket Society, for example, prepared extensive technical data in response to a formal Notice of Inquiry issued by the Federal Communications Commission (FCC) on May 19, 1960, "as to frequency needs for space communications on a longer-range basis, in view of the expected rapid developments in space communications." The FCC stated, "This technical information will assist the Commission in its preparatory work leading to a United States position for future international conferences on space communications needs." The FCC con-

---

[29] Third Report, *Ad Hoc* Group, Frequency Allocations for Space Research, ITU, Administrative Radio Conference, Geneva, 1959, Doc. No. 478-E, Oct. 28, 1959.

[30] Abstract of Busák, *Radio Communications and Cosmic Space Legal Problems,* Paper delivered at the First Czechoslovak Conference on Rocket Technique and Astronautics, Liblice, April 22-23, 1960.

[31] Held Oct. 7, 1963 in Geneva, Switzerland.

[32] The representatives of several United States government agencies, industrial groups, and scientific and educational organizations were consulted as to a preparatory program for the 1963 Extraordinary Administrative Radio Conference. They donated their time and effort on an individual basis to the review and criticism of the program. Their participation was entirely unofficial and in no way represents viewpoints based on their official or professional associations.

currently reopened its over-all inquiry into allocations in the microwave range (above 890 megacycles), in order to receive factual data as to frequency needs for space communication.[33]

The extreme importance of the 1963 Conference can be gauged from the tremendous need for spectrum space which has been created within the United States alone by governmental and nongovernmental organizations for use in their space communications projects. In early 1961, the Office of Civil and Defense Mobilization (now Office of Emergency Planning) conducted a survey of governmental agencies including the Department of Defense, Federal Aviation Agency, NASA, AEC, the Labor, Post Office and Treasury Departments, the National Academy of Sciences, and the U.S. Information Agency, requesting estimates of their radio needs for the decade 1960-1970. The survey concerned purely governmental operations, no consideration being given to the needs of nongovernmental users. Within one portion of the spectrum, from 1,000 to 10,000 megacycles, the total estimates indicated that the amount of spectrum space needed for governmental space communication activities was over twice what was likely to be available.

This survey (and naturally other data as well) provided a basis for the document "Preliminary Views of United States of America—Frequency Allocation for Space Radio Communication," which the Office of Emergency Planning produced, working together with the Federal Communications Commission. These preliminary views were approved by the State Department, and on October 16, 1961 they were circulated to the embassy staffs of the nations of the world for reactions and comments. (See Appendix I-G.)

7-5 Trends and requirements in space telecommunications

The overriding problem which must be considered in the formulation of a national policy for the 1963 Conference is the conflict between earth radio services and space radio services. Radio users in both fields contend for allocations of scarce frequency space throughout the spectrum, and if the present estimates of government agencies and nongovernmental bodies prove to be reasonable, there will not be enough spectrum space for both earth and space services.

The nations of the world have made enormous investments in telecommunication equipment to support space programs. Great Britain's Jodrell Bank radiotelescope, for example, is the largest in the world. It represents a major factor in the success of many different space programs and in tracking the space vehicles of all nations. The USSR has also made great expenditures for research and development in telecommunications

[33] Federal Communications Commission, Public Notice 88695, May 19, 1960.

related to the efficient use of the radio spectrum in space programs. In the United States, major fiscal expenditures are planned for the space program. The budget of NASA alone for fiscal year 1963 amounted to nearly four billion dollars.[34]

The scope of future requirements may also be seen in the numbers of vehicles scheduled for launching by the United States and other nations. As of 1960, some 260 major vehicles were planned for the coming decade by the NASA organization alone; and the total ultimately launched by all United States agencies, plus other astronautical nations, will turn out to be far in excess of this figure.[35] The scientists responsible for the planning of space programs are thus faced with critical problems as to the adequacy of present radio allocations for the space and earth/space services. It is essential to inquire whether the telecommunication requirements of the planned NASA vehicles as well as all the present space vehicles can be accommodated on the existing channels allocated to space and earth/ space radio services. And can the space programs of the USSR and other nations over the next decade be carried out using only the present radio allocations? These are fundamental questions which must be answered, and they are even more complex than would appear at first glance.

Pertinent details as to frequencies, power, and the like, of the telecommunication equipment carried by space vehicles launched by the USSR and the United States are published regularly by various governmental sources.[36] However, it must be borne in mind that these tabulations do not show the frequencies used in earth-to-vehicle transmissions. Also, the radio frequencies required for communications on earth incident to the original launching of the vehicles are not tabulated. An idea of the complexity of the telecommunication requirements for one vehicle is shown in Figure 1. Figure 1 describes the *Ranger-Tonto* moon vehicle complex which was originally scheduled by NASA for launching in 1961. A two-stage rocket vehicle (an *Atlas* and an *Agena-B*) was to be used to propel a vehicle (*Ranger*) to the vicinity of the moon, where the capsule (*Tonto*) would be detached and landed on the moon with the assistance of a retrorocket. The *Ranger* failed to respond to commands properly, when fired in early 1962, and its primary mission failed. However, a second *Ranger* shot did strike the moon, although technical malfunctions again prevented the receipt of some important data.

In the over-all *Ranger-Tonto* operation, practically every function of radio operation was involved: communications and telemetering on the earth before and during launching; tracking, command, guidance, teleme-

---

[34] This figure is taken from the Senate bill, S. 2848, 87th Cong., 2d Sess. (1962).

[35] *Hearings on a Review of the Space Program Before the House Committee on Science and Astronautics*, 86th Cong., 2d Sess. pt. 1 at 188 (1960).

[36] STAFF OF THE SENATE COMMITTEE ON AERONAUTICAL AND SPACE SCIENCES, *supra* note 12 at 41-42.

try, and navigation during the journey; and telemetry after the expected landing on the moon. Television was provided for scanning the moon from the *Ranger* vehicle until its impact with the moon; radiotelegraph, radiotelephone, and data transfer were to be employed throughout the operation.[37]

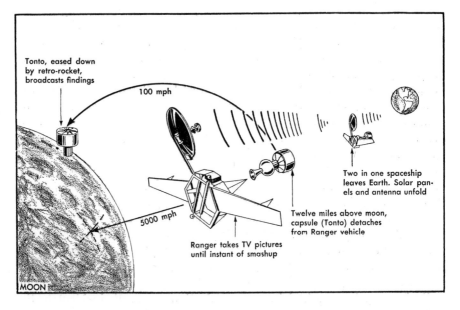

Figure 1   Ranger-Tonto moon vehicle—telecommunications requirements.

The uses of telecommunications required for *Ranger-Tonto* will be multiplied by a substantial factor when the first manned flight to the moon is made. Describing some of the basic problems affecting the selection and allocation of frequency space for lunar projects and deep-space communications, E. Rechtin of Jet Propulsion Laboratory stated in a report to the author (on behalf of Dr. W. H. Pickering and W. K. Victor) dated May 10, 1960:

> The preferred command frequency has not yet been selected. One of the most significant features of lunar and interplanetary communications is the use of directive antennas aboard stabilized spacecraft. Such antennas are required in order to obtain sufficient information from the moon and the planets to make the trip worthwhile. Under these conditions, deep space communications more nearly resemble a microwave relay link than any other conventional earth-communication system. Thus the frequency choice tends to be in the region of 1,000 to 10,000 Mc/s, the antennas tend to be of reasonable size (between 85′ and 250′ in diameter), and the radiated powers

[37] Newsweek, May 9, 1960, pp. 78-80.

of 10 watts to 10 kilowatts aboard the vehicle are supplied by highly efficient and stable triodes and klystron amplifiers. The exception to this situation in deep space communications is the case of transmitting from the earth to an omnidirectional receiving antenna aboard the vehicle; in this situation, one tends toward somewhat lower frequencies. However, in this exception the bandwidths are very narrow, the intention of the communication link is solely to direct the spacecraft to turn on equipment and to aim directive antennas at the earth, and the use is infrequent.

The principal difficulty with the present assignments is that there is insufficient bandwidth available between 2,000 and 6,000 Mc/s to accommodate the 24-hour communication satellites, lunar and interplanetary communications, precision ranging systems, and the like. This question quite possibly could be resolved by declaring that communication satellites would receive an allocation on strictly commercial grounds and that such communications are really not space communications for scientific purposes. The 24-hour communications satellite is a simpler way of building microwave links across continents and across oceans and has little or nothing to do with the exploration of space.

As already suggested, it is necessary to consider not only numbers of vehicles but also many other factors—the nature of assigned missions, length of transmission life, area of use, earth control of transmissions, and so forth. In almost every case, the trend is in the direction of more stringent and more complex requirements.

The *Sputnik I* transmissions were useful for tracking and making pioneer experiments on radio propagation in space. While of essential importance, the work of *Sputnik I* (and indeed of all succeeding space vehicles) must be increased in a truly geometrical ratio, and indeed beyond that to a final elan worthy of mankind. In a short period the state of the art has progressed to a great degree: considerable information on geodesy, propagation, meteorology, the solar ultraviolet spectrum, X-rays in the high atmosphere, auroral particles, space radiations, system performance, and the nature of other bodies in our solar system has been transmitted to earth from the Russian and American vehicles.[38] The USSR produced the first photographs of the reverse or "dark side" of the moon; the USA has determined the existence of the Van Allen radiation belts; and we have learned of the transmission capabilities of small transmitters operating deep in space from *Pioneer V*. Telecommunications is the essential link by which data concerning these matters was transmitted to earth.

With solar or nuclear-energy power supplies, the "life" of radio transmitters in space vehicles is practically unlimited. One of the *Vanguard I* transmitters may continue to operate for 200 to 1,000 years, according to NASA.[39] For many practical purposes, the future use of the frequency

[38] *Hearings on NASA Authorization for Fiscal Year 1961 Before the NASA Authorization Subcommittee of the Senate Committee on Aeronautical and Space Sciences,* 86th Cong., 2d Sess., pt. 1 (1960).

[39] STAFF OF THE SENATE COMMITTEE ON AERONAUTICAL AND SPACE SCIENCES, *supra* note 12.

involved is restricted. The experience with this vehicle thus indicates a compelling need for international agreement on means to control and terminate transmission from space vehicles. Control is technically possible. We can command the various telemetering and other components of space vehicles in use at present. And by means of data storage, information obtained at a given time can be recorded for transmission later on command from earth.

Fortunately, frequency-sharing is possible in many aspects of space telecommunication. NASA has learned, for example, that frequency-sharing is possible in many of its space programs. Except for high-power scatter operations, area protection, rather than clear channel protection, is sometimes adequate. And where a transmitter in space can be controlled from earth, the transmissions of several vehicles can be "phased in" so as to operate at different times on the same channel.[40]

Another area in which extensive study is needed relates to the limitations and characteristic parameters of space radio systems to be operated in the foreseeable future. Such matters as the equipment characteristics, range, interference, and the like, must be considered.

Wernher von Braun categorizes the limitations and required parameters of the major components of space vehicle telecommunication equipment as follows: [41]

		Limitations	Required Parameters
1.	Antennas	physical size beamwidth	high gain small size
2.	Power sources	capacity low efficiency large size	long life high efficiency small size
3.	Transmitters	low power output low efficiency low operating frequency for high power output	high power high efficiency small size narrow bandwidths
4.	Receivers	high noise factor poor sensitivity large size	high sensitivity low noise factor small size
5.	Modulation subsystems	——	small size

The ranges of transmissions from space vehicles have been shown to be much greater than anticipated. Attenuation of radio signals from transmitters in space vehicles is of a lesser order than expected. *Pioneer V*, for example, traveled to a distance of 8,000,000 miles before the efficiency of

[40] Personal interview with J. B. McElroy and D. G. Mazor (NASA), both speaking unofficially.

[41] Telegram from Dr. Wernher von Braun, ABMA, Huntsville, Ala., to the author, May 12, 1960.

its 5-watt transmitter became so low as to justify terminating its trans-missions. The 5-watt transmitter had been scheduled to operate only to the extreme distance of 5,000,000 miles. Out of that range it was expected to transmit first 32 bits of information per second, then 16, 8, and finally 1 bit per second. The minimum transmission speed was not reached until the vehicle had reached almost the 8,000,000 mile mark.[42] *Pioneer V's* more powerful 150-watt transmitter was then turned on and was also ex-pected to produce signals receivable on earth at a distance far in excess of what was estimated as its range prior to launching.[43]

Achievements in the field of miniaturization have permitted scientists to concentrate a greater amount of specialized equipment into restricted limits of space and weight. United States instrumentation specialists, for example, combined into one device, *Telebit*, three basic functions: telem-etry, tracking, and command.[44]

The designers of the Telebit system combined six major design objec-tives so that large amounts of information could be transmitted from space vehicles with only 10 pounds devoted to the transmission system in the vehicle. By increasing the weight of the system to 200 pounds, enough equipment could be carried so that a television picture could be transmitted from the moon. The relation of range to size and weight is shown in Figure 2, which was prepared by the Telebit system designers and represents knowledge based on actual experience with the *Explorer* and *Pioneer* series of space vehicles. It does not, however, represent the ultimate achievement that is possible through miniaturization techniques.

The attenuation of radio signals from space vehicles, the so-called "focusing effect" of the earth's atmosphere, and other factors governing the effective range of transmitters must be determined with accuracy.[45] One critical phenomenon is the "plasma effect," described by Darrell Romick and others, of the Goodyear Astronautics Department:

> Highest attenuation rates, caused by hypersonically generated plasma sur-rounding re-entering vehicles, occur over the 10 Mc/s to 10 Gc/s region. It appears that transmission may be effected by utilizing the VLF, micro-wave, or even the optical band. However, due to the disadvantages inherent with very low or extremely high frequencies, methods of communicating through the plasma over the VHF–UHF bands are being examined.[46]

It is known that in transmissions among earth, satellites, moon, Venus, Mars, and other planets, still other phenomena must be considered. For

[42] *Pioneer V 150 Watt Transmitter Turned on at 8 Million Miles,* NASA News Re-lease 60-194, May 8, 1960.

[43] *Op. cit. supra* note 38 at 620.

[44] Mueller, *Telebit–Integrated Space Navigation and Communication System,* As-tronautics, May 1960, p. 26.

[45] Personal interview with George P. Adair, Adair Engineering Co., Washington, D.C., speaking unofficially.

[46] Report by D. C. Romick, C. M. Kelley, J. Roth, T. D. Stonerook and C. J. McKeel, Goodyear Aircraft Corp., Akron, Ohio, to the author, May 12, 1960.

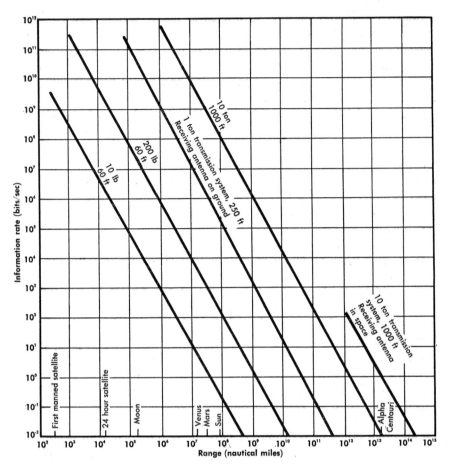

Figure 2 The Telebit system (information rate versus range for future systems).

example, the Doppler shift at all positions (on earth, on the vehicle, on the moon and planets) must be taken into account.[47] The Doppler effect in space flight is illustrated in Figure 3.

The axial rotation of the planets, Faraday rotation, and tracking and stabilization of the same are additional factors for study and consideration.[48]

Extraterrestrial noise—galactic noise, radio stars, solar radiation, planetary radiation, and so forth—affect the selection of frequencies. Noise

[47] Tischer, *Propagation—Doppler Effect in Space Communications,* 48 PROCEEDINGS OF THE IRE 589 (1960).

[48] Bond, Cahn, and Meyer, *Interference and Channel Allocation Problems Associated with Orbiting Satellite Communication Relays,* 48 PROCEEDINGS OF THE IRE 608 (1960).

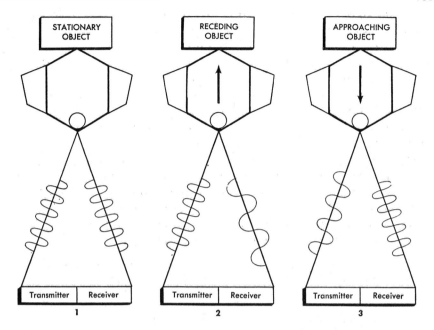

Figure 3 The Doppler shift in space telecommunications.

1. The received signal reflected from a stationary object has exactly the same frequency as that of the transmitted signal.

2. The received signal reflected from a receding object has a frequency of less cycles per second than that of the transmitted signal, the actual difference depending directly upon the speed of recession.

3. The received signal reflected from an approaching object has a frequency of more cycles per second than that of the transmitted signal, the actual difference depending directly upon the speed of approachment.

Measurement and comparison of the transmitted and received frequencies provide a means for determining whether the object is stationary, receding, or approaching; and if receding or approaching, the actual speed. The accuracy of the speed determination is exactly the same degree of accuracy as the measurement of the transmitted and received frequencies.

within the equipment itself is a factor affecting both receiver and transmitter performance.[49]

In commenting on the effects of extraterrestrial phenomena upon frequency selection, S. F. Singer has pointed out that "with our better knowledge of the emission of radiation from the sun, which produces an ionosphere, one can now start to make certain predictions concerning

[49] Smith, *Extraterrestrial Noise as a Factor in Space Communications,* 48 PROCEEDINGS OF THE IRE 593 (1960).

the likely electron density" of other planets. By this means, furthermore, one can derive "the radio frequencies which can be transmitted through such a planetary atmosphere to establish, for example, communication with a station on the surface of the planet." Singer notes that, in the case of the earth, the ionosphere limits communication to radio frequencies above 15 megacycles and preferably higher. "It would be important," he adds, "to establish even now the likely range frequencies which can be transmitted through the gaseous envelopes of other planets which are likely to be the target of space exploration. . . ." [50]

There have been described in technical journals various types of emission—AM, FM, FM/FM, PCM, and others.[51] The exact operating parameters of vehicle, antenna, power supply, and nature of intelligence to be transmitted will all enter into the determination of the emission requirements. In this regard J. R. Dempsey of General Dynamics Astronautics (formerly Convair Astronautics) points out:

> In general, multiple modulation systems such as FM/FM result in loss of power efficiency but make possible multiple data channels on a single carrier. It can be shown under certain signal-to-noise ratios that AM or single side-band AM is more efficient than FM for voice communications. Under strong signal conditions the converse can be shown to be true. Digital transmission methods will find much use in future space communications systems. Thus, we do not find it desirable to limit the transmission to a particular type of transmission on a general basis but rather to define the frequency spectrum to be made available.[52]

Finally, the needs of special projects such as satellite-borne weather observation instruments, communications relays, interplanetary navigation, and a new system of terrestrial navigation using radio signals from earth satellites, all must be studied.

The use of space vehicles in weather observation has already reached a meaningful stage of development, and extensive data are available as to the radio spectrum requirements of such programs. Photographs of cloud cover and other meteorological data have been gathered by the *Tiros* vehicles, developed by NASA, the United States Army and Radio Corporation of America.[53] These satellites are among the most elaborate electronics packages yet sent into orbit around the earth. They include miniature television cameras, video tape recorders, transmitters, solar-cell and rechargeable-battery power supplies, and an array of control and communications equipment. In the first four days of operation, *Tiros I* sent by television nearly 1200 pictures. The 2-watt transmitters operated in

[50] Report from S. F. Singer, University of Maryland, to the author, May 9, 1960.

[51] Sanders, *Communication Efficiency Comparison of Several Communication Systems*, 48 PROCEEDINGS OF THE IRE 575 (1960).

[52] Report from J. R. Dempsey, General Dynamics Astronautics, San Diego, Cal., to the author, May 11, 1960.

[53] *Weather Eye in the Sky*, Electronic Age, Spring 1960.

the 200-megacycle region of the spectrum. The tape recording facilities included 400 feet of specially developed tape which could be used repeatedly.

Similarly, substantial data are now available as to space communications relays. J. R. Pierce's original work published in 1955 on *Orbital Radio Relays* [54] contained one of the first scientific approaches to the matter of space communications satellites. Pierce foresaw situations where up to 10 megawatts power would be required for the transmission to a 1000-foot sphere of a 5-megacycle video signal. He calculated that greater power would be required for smaller spheres, and drastically reduced power for a system using several satellite repeaters.

The original work by Pierce was viewed with some skepticism, but we are now witnesses that satellite relays are within the realm of reality. One of the industrial giants of the United States long ago joined in a program of actual operation of a passive communications satellite, albeit an experimental one. [55] This was Project Echo, initiated by NASA in conjunction with Bell Telephone Laboratories. The gigantic sphere used for relay was launched into orbit, inflated in space, and operated on an experimental basis. The frequencies 960 megacycles and 2390 megacycles were used in this project. The subsequent success of the active communications satellite *Telstar* has removed all grounds of skepticism, but it has intensified the problem of frequency allocation. An active satellite can not only transmit television signals, it can handle many voice messages simultaneously. It has been estimated that a successful relay system could carry 900 voice messages simultaneously, whereas the present Atlantic cables can handle less than 160 calls simultaneously. [56]

Radio Corporation of America, which is also involved in transoceanic common carrier communications, has developed keen interest in space relays. RCA has under way extensive research into space relay systems, and an extremely wide frequency bandwidth for such communications has been mentioned informally. [57]

The military are interested in space communications relays, as a matter of course. Testimony of Dr. Herbert York of the Department of Defense before a subcommittee of the U.S. Senate in 1960 indicated that the armed forces could develop a system in one year on a crash basis, if desired. [58] The likelihood, however, is that the perfection of space techniques will be accomplished by civilian agencies and industry.

[54] Pierce, *Orbital Radio Relays*, 25 JET PROPULSION 153 (1955).

[55] Ryerson, *Passive Satellite Communication*, 48 PROCEEDINGS OF THE IRE 613 (1960); Vea, Day & Smith, *The Use of a Passive Spherical Satellite for Communication and Propagation Experiments*, 48 PROCEEDINGS OF THE IRE 620 (1960); *Hearings on the 1961 NASA Authorization Before the House Committee on Science and Astronautics*, 86th Cong., 2d Sess. pt. 2 at 669.

[56] Kinney, *Stay Tuned to Space*, The Airman, March 1960, 26, 28.

[57] Personal interview with P. B. Siling, RCA, speaking unofficially.

[58] *Op. cit. supra* note 38, pt. 1 at 505.

Navigation systems using radio transmissions in space form a large part of present research and development in the astronautical sciences. In many respects, position fixing in space involves techniques similar to those used on earth.[59] Nevertheless, substantial differences exist in the two fields, and telecommunications affords the essential servant to assist in the determination of positions in space. One very promising technique for this purpose, involving high-precision radio navigation, was discussed by J. W. Crooks, Jr. of Convair-Astronautics at the 1959 Ballistic Missile Symposium in Los Angeles. It featured communication at microwave frequencies between two or three ground stations and a space vehicle at ranges extending up to the distance from earth to Saturn. Since the system offered high precision, it was suggested that perturbation of the vehicle's orbit as it approached the target planet be used in determining the relative position of the spacecraft and the planet for purposes of terminal guidance.

As described by J. R. Dempsey, president of General Dynamics Astronautics, this navigational system

> ... would involve frequencies in the microwave region, optimum probably being between 1,000 and 10,000 Mc/s. The frequency transmitted from the ground transmitter and the frequency retransmitted from the space vehicle would be approximately related by a common multiple. For example, the frequency transmitted on the ground might be approximately 5050 Mc/s and the frequency returned by the space craft be 5000 Mc/s, where one is the 100th harmonic of 50 Mc/s and the other is the 101st harmonic. In addition, these signals would be modulated with sub-carriers possibly ranging as high as one megacycle. Data bandwidths involved in this system would be extremely narrow, much less than a cycle per second, even though the sidebands may extend out beyond a megacycle of either side of the carrier. This type of operation is typical for CW range systems employing correlation detection techniques. The emission would have the general characteristics of narrowband frequency modulation systems with discrete modulation frequencies up to one megacycle or higher. Frequency allocations should allow for Doppler shifts.[60]

Earth navigation systems using reflected transmissions from natural or artificial objects have been proposed also, and research in this field is underway. One proposal is to place three or four satellites in orbits at distances of from 1,000 to 12,000 miles from earth. Signals from such satellites would then be used in determining positions on earth.[61] The proponent of this method, Alton B. Moody, recognizes the possibility of

[59] Clemence, *Interplanetary Navigation,* 48 PROCEEDINGS OF THE IRE 497 (1960).
[60] Dempsey, report *supra* note 52.
[61] Moody, *Navigation Using Signals From High-Altitude Satellites,* 48 PROCEEDINGS OF THE IRE 500 (1960).

error, and the inability to obtain total coverage of the earth at any time, and he has portrayed the problem as visualized in Figure 4. Naturally, the extent of the radio frequency requirements for such systems must be a matter of concern to those participating in the 1963 conference.

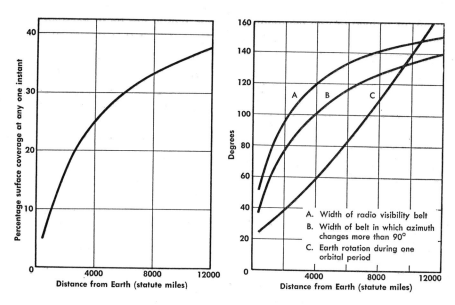

Figure 4 Inability to obtain total coverage of earth at any one time by earth navigation system.

7–6 World-wide satellite communications

As we know, American space technology has made it possible to establish immediately a world-wide satellite communications system. The importance of such a system consists in the fact that one of the principal values of man's space efforts to the peoples of the world, at least during the present generation, will be the use of satellites to facilitate international communications. The United States thus has an unprecedented opportunity to establish the leadership of free men in the peaceful use of outer space; it must formulate as soon as possible and send to all the nations of the world its proposals for an international satellite communications system.

Diligence is essential, since time and again superior planning and speed in implementation by the Soviet Government have left the United States in second place in the exploration of outer space. The United States Government has an obligation to the American people and to all the peoples of the world to develop and insure the freedom of space communications.

Inaction in this regard would constitute failure to use the talents of American scientists and engineers and would in fact be inexcusable.

In the process of establishing space communications with all possible speed, we have protected the interests of free enterprise, and we must continue to do so. Government ownership and operation of the system itself, or indeed of any component thereof, would not be in keeping with our free enterprise traditions. We must never forget that the position our young nation has achieved in the world over the past century is due in large part to the freedom which has been given private enterprise to excel in a competitive market, or, in the case of a public utility, to operate under government regulation on a fair, efficient, and profitable basis. A reversal of this traditional policy would be a confession to the world that the United States has lost some faith in its own social, political, and economic philosophy.

A number of suggestions were made leading up to the final form of the Communications Satellite Act of 1962 (in Appendix II-B). Among the principal suggestions were the following:

1. A joint venture participation by existing common carriers in one international satellite radio-communication system. Since the satellite system is merely another method of communication, which supplements existing means of radio and cable communication, and since the proper discharge of the carriers' obligation to provide services in the public interest cannot be effected if responsibility is shared by those in no way connected with the operation of the carriers, there is no need for including ownership participation by other than common carrier companies.[62]

2. A system whereby the space communications company would operate the satellites and lease frequency bands to all the common carriers. This one company would be owned jointly by the public and by the communications companies with only the publicly-held stock to have voting rights or pay regular dividends.[63]

3. A system proposed by the American Telephone and Telegraph Company providing for a joint venture of all common carrier interests, both American and foreign, which have the direct responsibility for rendering international telecommunication services, with participation by each carrier in accordance with its relative use of the satellite communications system. The precise type of interest might vary according to the wishes of the particular carrier, one carrier participating through some form of ownership most appropriate to its own domestic legal system, another carrier participating by means of leasing facilities.[64]

[62] S. 2650, 87th Cong., 2d Sess.
[63] S. 2814, 87th Cong., 2d Sess.
[64] Testimony of James E. Dingman, Exec. VP, AT&T, *Hearings on S. 2650 and S. 2814 Before the Senate Committee on Aeronautical and Space Sciences,* 87th Cong. 2d Sess. 307-32 (1962).

In any event, we must immediately work to resolve all the technical problems—even if the solutions we now accept must be modified at a later date. It is not realistic to commit ourselves now to use passive or active relay stations; or to say definitely whether these relays should orbit around the Equator or around the Poles, or whether they should perform their services in random orbits. The life of these artifacts will only be for two or three years, and we can improve our technology as we gain experience and provide service.

Several of the problems involved were underscored by Commissioner T. A. M. Craven of the Federal Communications Commission (FCC), speaking at the University of Washington in Seattle in June 1962. Indeed, referring specifically to proposals for international television broadcasting directly to the homes of the people of the world, Commissioner Craven argued that some problems were presently insurmountable. These include, he said, the language and time differences around the world, the technical difficulties posed by high-power transmitters capable of "living" in the environment of space, the rocket-thrust requirements for placing large weights in orbit at the desired altitude, "the all-important problem of how much and what part of the radio spectrum could be allocated to the new service," the working out of transmission standards, and, finally, "the cost of this method as compared to others." Commissioner Craven then indicated that "the scientific fraternity is confident that the technical problems are not too difficult of solution," but he added that "the cost of establishing such a satellite television broadcasting system could vary from several hundred million dollars to over one billion dollars." Asking if this system is necessary, Craven replied to his own question: "Personally I would say, no."

Craven went on to say that, to be fully utilized, "global television broadcasting direct to the homes of the people of all nations of the world" would require "social changes, economic sacrifices, and international cooperation of a degree unheard of in the past." However, he emphasized that "this apparent negative approach to one aspect of space communications" did not mean that he was lacking in optimism "about the potential of such systems for the improvement of existing point-to-point communication facilities." He expressed full agreement with the statement made by President Kennedy in one of his press conferences to the effect that space communication offers the United States the first major use of space technology for peaceful and "practical" purposes. Craven therefore urged "that we proceed now with the development of practical uses for space communications and leave the more unrealistic theoretical uses, such as global television, as a goal to be achieved in the future when and if it can be demonstrated that there is a need for such application."

The significant role to be played in communication satellite development by the private enterprise of the world was discussed by another member of the Federal Communications Commission, Rosel H. Hyde, in an address on space communications that was also delivered at Seattle in June 1962. Stressing the need for additional channels over which communications may flow, Commissioner Hyde stated that "when a communications satellite system is a working reality, it will be a joint accomplishment of private industry communications research and government research in rocketry." He pointed out that the United States had traditionally "placed the responsibility for both domestic and international communications in the hands of the common carriers" and that, in the final analysis, "it will be these carriers who will bear the responsibility to the public for services provided over the satellite system just as they are now responsible for service over cable or radio facilities." The FCC, in particular, had consistently held "that the carriers alone could do the job —and do it more promptly and efficiently than it could be done by any other means." However, he also warned that no matter who finally put up a space communications system or who owed it, the system would be government-regulated. "And our statute books don't allow regulated industries to make many new millionaires." In addition, foreign governments would necessarily have a share in the revenues, with the result that many people would be "getting pieces of what some people have viewed to be a pie-in-the-sky."

The legal problems arising from the great new scientific advances in the area of satellite intercommunications involve many aspects of national and international law. The immediate applications of such communications are for meteorological, navigational, and transmission-of-intelligence purposes. Ultimate uses will, of course, involve communications between satellite and satellite in space, manned satellite to earth and back, manned satellite to celestial objects in space (such as the moon), and for many other purposes, including direct communication. Nationally, the officers and directors of the Communications Satellite Corporation face intricate problems many of which are not susceptible of immediate solution and indeed some of which until this time defy solution.

Even the rudimentary problem of the initial financing of the daily business of the Corporation is difficult to solve. A credit of five million dollars has been obtained—and of this amount, five hundred thousand dollars have been appropriated—but what of the future? The Corporation is *not* exempt from the provisions of the Securities Exchange Act and the management of its affairs is directly involved with the Federal Communications Commission, the National Aeronautics and Space Administration, Presidential oversight, and, of course, all actions are subject to the scrutiny of the United States Congress.

It cannot be denied that the basic function of the satellite is simply that of a relay station. In its SEC-required prospectus for the investing public the Corporation will not only have to account for financial potentiality of its domestic operation but also for the international operation. Fortunately, on the domestic side, pursuant to Section 305(a) of the Act, the Corporation can own and operate satellite terminal stations when licensed by the (Federal Communications) Commission under Section 201(c)(7), so that at least in the United States, the operation itself is not purely "relayed" in nature but reception is also involved. This will not be true in foreign countries all of which will control their own terminal stations.

How much revenue may the investing public expect to receive from the domestic source? Each of the great foreign powers is looking to its share of the revenue from satellite relay operations.

The international legal involvements and problems almost defy analysis and most certainly the greatest expertise will be required to solve the multitude of legal problems which will soon arise.

The Corporation is not exempt from the obligation of the FCC to permit effective competition in the field of communications and, in particular, in the procurement of the necessary equipment and services for establishing and operating the satellite system itself and related ground stations. This provision of law may result in a fantastic burgeoning of "paper work" throughout American industry but there are indications that the FCC regulations designed to promote competition in procurement will be reasonable.

Furthermore, the European nations are indeed determined to take a significant part in supplying the "hardware" as well as the "know-how" in all aspects of satellite communications and the problems presented by such participation—in the light of the United States statutes—require reconciliation of national statutory systems.

What will the prospectus have to say about the final feasibility of the entire project? Certainly, if other nations place satellite relay stations in orbit, the competition may well be too severe to afford any rational basis for private investment. Then there is a scientific controversy as to which system should be adopted—the lower level satellite system, or the high level or synchronous orbit satellite.

The CEPT—states of Europe—have indicated generally that they will subscribe to and cooperate with the United States satellite program, but Great Britain has at least three caveats to this general understanding, the most important being communications with Commonwealth countries. A knowledgeable approach to the Western European complex would indicate that we may expect complete cooperation based upon the results of "hard-headed" negotiation. There is no indication at this time that the Communist countries will not cooperate in the program inaugurated by the United States—but here again a knowledgeable approach would indicate that the USSR is probably "sounding out" countries in both hemispheres with the thought of scoring an ideological victory in the field of communications.

We have already observed three successful demonstrations of the lower-level orbiting satellites—*Telstar I, Telstar II*, and *Relay*. The initial attempt to place in orbit a synchronous orbit satellite was unsuccessful. What will the SEC-required prospectus tell the investing public of these problems—as it is not beyond the realm of possibility that even if there are no foreign-operated satellites with which to compete, we may still have to expend here in the United States several hundred million dollars to achieve the synchronous orbit relay station. And we should also keep in mind that the capacity to transmit by cable all manner of communications including broad band services such as facsimile, teletypewrite data transmission, and television, although presently inadequate and difficult of achievement, is quite without theoretical limit. As a matter of fact, engineers in American industry and engineers in several other countries are working assiduously on transistorized cable systems. One trans-Atlantic carrier has announced transistorized cable development having ten times the present capacity of cable telephonic circuits. We may well expect very important developments indeed in the use of laser technology before the synchronous orbit relay station is finally in operation. This matter will be discussed in Section 7-9. And, moreover, do we not find great potentialities for global communications in the second and successful Westford experiment?

The successful launching and operation of a synchronous orbit satellite depends upon one of two solutions: (1) launching the vehicle from the United States using a "dog leg" technique to place the vehicle in approximately equatorial orbit; or (2) creating a launch-site and operational base in some true equatorial site (such as Brazil). The technical problem was almost, but not quite, overcome in the first "dog leg" launching, and it may be necessary eventually to utilize an equatorial site. The latter solution has been proposed by very knowledgeable communications carriers, such as General Telephone and Electronics Corporation —but, of course, such companies are willing to accept any reasonable solution. The astonishing success of *Syncom II* creates a positive basis for faith in the ultimate solution of all these questions.

As lawyers we must look to the problems; and as lawyers we must hope that we will make real contributions toward the solutions of the problems. These problems are receiving the massive consideration of the staffs at the White House, State Department, FCC, NASA, and of the Corporation itself; and, of course, the private carriers are performing services of equal import. Having briefly sounded the tocsin, the law will now be touched upon.

On August 31, 1962, the Congress approved and sent to President John F. Kennedy for signature, the Communications Satellite Act of 1962.[65] With the President's signature, the measure became law on the same day.

65 Public Law 87-624; 76 Stat. 419 (August 31, 1962).

The breadth of the Congress' vision is shown in Section 102 of the Act in which it was declared to be the policy of the United States

> ... to establish, in conjunction and in cooperation with other countries, as expeditiously as practicable, a commercial communications satellite system, as part of an improved global communications network, which will be responsive to public needs and national objectives, which will serve to communication needs of the United States and other countries, and which will contribute to world peace and understanding.[66]

To emphasize the truly global nature of its interests, the Congress declared in Section 102(b) of the Act that care and attention must be directed toward providing commercial communication satellite services to the economically less developed countries and areas as well as those which are more highly developed. Emphasis was also placed on the desire to provide for a more efficient and economical use of the frequency spectrum and, ultimately, to benefit the consumer through the better quality and potentially lower rates possible with satellite communications.[67]

The vehicle selected to achieve these national goals was the Communications Satellite Corporation, whose operation is required to conform to the following policies enumerated in Section 102(b) of the Act:

1. Nondiscriminatory access to the system for all authorized users.
2. Maintenance of the maximum competition in the provision of equipment and services utilized by the system.
3. Maintenance and strengthening of competition in the provision of communications services to the public.
4. Compliance with the Federal antitrust laws.[68]

Specifically, the Corporation is authorized by Section 305 of the Communications Satellite Act of 1962 to conduct and contract for research, to plan, initiate, construct, own, manage and operate a commercial satellite system, either by itself or in conjunction with foreign governments or business entities, and in short, to take all of the actions necessary to organize, develop, and operate a successful business venture, subject to close governmental regulation.[69]

The Corporation is in legal existence and is rapidly proceeding with its organization. The Articles of Incorporation of the Corporation, which by the terms of Section 302 of the Act have required the approval of the President of the United States, have been adopted and are in full force

---

[66] Sec. 102(a), 76 Stat. 419(1962).
[67] Sec. 102(b), 76 Stat. 419 (1962).
[68] *Ibid.*
[69] Sec. 305, 76 Stat. 419(1962).

and effect. In Article III of its Articles of Incorporation, the Corporation states its purposes as follows:

Section 3.01. The purposes for which the Corporation is organized are

(a) to further and carry out the purposes and achieve the objectives of the Satellite Act; and

(b) to do everything necessary, desirable, advisable, or convenient for the forbearance and accomplishment of such purposes and the achievement of such objectives, and to do all other things incidental thereto or connected therewith which are not forbidden by applicable law or these Articles, including without limitation to acquire, own, use, convey, and otherwise dispose of and deal in real property or any interest therein.[70]

The Corporation is a private entity organized also for the purposes of conducting a communications common carrier service for profit. It is, however, made subject to close governmental regulation by Section 201 of the Act under which specific tasks are assigned to the President, NASA, and the FCC.[71] The Corporation, as indicated above, is to operate in an international sphere and will be required to discover ways and means of working in conjunction with foreign governmental agencies and with foreign corporations.[72]

The problems which the Corporation is now facing are many and are unique in the experience of American private enterprise. In speaking of the difficulty of the task facing the Corporation, Leo D. Welch, the Chairman of the Corporation, said the following:

New companies face substantial business risks even when they start out in well known fields. This Corporation will venture into new areas full of great promise but also full of great unknowns, so that both our risks and our opportunities are, of course, correspondingly larger. At this stage, there are still many unknown factors important to our operations that can be defined only after further research and development.[73]

While Mr. Welch was speaking principally of technical and financial trail blazing, his remarks also well apply to some of the legal "great unknowns" which the Corporation faces as it attempts to act as a privately owned common carrier subject to Federal regulation and given tasks of an international character of great complexity. What legal problems may be faced in the future can best be appreciated by an analysis of each area of Federal regulation and a look to what international problems are on the horizon.

As indicated above, pursuant to Section 201(a) of the Communications

---

[70] Communications Satellite Corporation, Articles of Incorporation, Article III, Sec. 3. 01.

[71] Sec. 201, 76 Stat. 419 (1962).

[72] Sec. 402, 76 Stat. 419 (1962).

[73] Statement of Leo D. Welch, Chairman, Communications Satellite Corporation before the Subcommittee on Applications and Tracking and Data Acquisition of the Science and Astronautics Committee of the United States House of Representatives, April 30, 1963.

Satellite Act of 1962, the President of the United States is directed to play an active role in assisting and guiding the activities of the Corporation. The President's special responsibilities, as enumerated in the Act may be summarized as follows:

1. Aid in the planning and development of a national program for the establishment and operation of a commercial communications satellite system.
2. Continuously review all phases of the development and operation of such a system and of the Corporation.
3. Coordinate all governmental activities in the field of satellite communications.
4. Exercise such supervision as may be necessary or appropriate over the relationships of the Corporation with foreign governments or agencies.
5. Insure that timely arrangements are made for foreign participation in the establishment and use of the system.
6. Take steps to make sure that satellite communications facilities will be available to meet the needs of the government.
7. Use his authority to help attain efficiency in the use of the radio spectrum and technical compatibility with existing communications systems both foreign and domestic.[74]

As can be seen, the President's responsibilities under the Act are extremely broad. His powers to discharge those responsibilities are bound to be construed as being correspondingly broad. For example, in one draft of the bill when before the Congress,[75] the President was charged with exercising "general supervision" over the relationships between the Corporation and foreign governments and interests. The word "general" was deleted from the final revision of the Act because it suggested a limitation on the President's powers and responsibilities with respect to the formulation and execution of the foreign policies of the United States.[76]

The President did, of course, have a great and decisive role in the formation of the Corporation. This role was specified in Section 302 of the Act, under which the President was directed to appoint the initial incorporators of the Corporation and to pass upon the Corporation's Articles of Incorporation.[77] This phase of his responsibility has been passed. As indicated above, however, most of the President's powers are continuing in nature. Under Section 303 of the Act, which governs the formation of the Board of Directors of the Corporation, once the incorporators' tasks are completed, the President shall appoint three of the fifteen members of the Board of Directors.[78] Although the President's Directors are only one-fifth of the membership of the Board, they are appointed to three-year terms whereas the remaining twelve Directors, six of whom are to

[74] Sec. 201, 76 Stat. 419 (1962).
[75] H.R. 11040, 87th Congress, 2nd Session.
[76] See *Communications Satellite Act of 1962*, Report No. 1584, Committee on Commerce, United States Senate, 87th Congress, 2nd Session, at 15.
[77] Sec. 302, 76 Stat. 419 (1962).
[78] Sec. 303(a), 76 Stat. 419 (1962).

be elected by the common carrier stockholders and six by the public stockholders, serve one-year terms only. Therefore, in the event that there is any great degree of turnover on the Board, the President's Directors will represent a continuity which will certainly add to the weight of their views. These Directors will not represent the President, but will be responsible to the stockholders. Deputy Attorney General Katzenbach made this clear in his congressional testimony.

In addition to the President's powers and responsibilities, three Federal agencies are given specific tasks under the Act. From a legal standpoint, perhaps the most important role is that assigned to the FCC. The technical role assigned to NASA is of great practical importance but assuming that a workable satellite system may be designed and the launching of the satellites is no longer a problem, the basic regulatory task with regard to the Corporation falls to the FCC. The unique role of the Department of State will be discussed below.

Section 201(c) of the Act enumerates the responsibilities and powers of the FCC in considerable detail. In fact the complete outline of the regulatory function which the FCC has already begun to exercise is given. A summary of the requirements is as follows:

1. Insure effective competition in the procurement of apparatus, equipment and services and, in consultation with the Small Business Administration, provide an equitable opportunity to small business to supply the corporation.

2. Provide access to the Corporation's services by authorized carriers on a nondiscriminatory basis under just and equitable rates.

3. Upon advice from the State Department to proceed, institute proceedings to require an extension of service to a foreign point.

4. Require that the Corporation's technical facilities are compatible with ground systems and that proper interconnections are maintained.

5. Prescribe accounting procedures and engage in rate making so that the public consumer benefits from any economies realized.

6. Approve the technical characteristics of the satellite and ground terminal facilities.

7. Grant authorizations for the construction of ground terminal facilities to authorized carriers on the basis of the public interest, convenience and necessity.

8. Determine which carriers are authorized carriers for the purpose of receiving a portion of the initial stock issue and to use the services of the Corporation.

9. Authorize any issue of stock by the Corporation subsequent to the initial issue and authorize the Corporation to borrow money or assume any obligation.

10. Require additions and extensions in service in the public interest, convenience and necessity.

11. Formulate rules and regulations to implement these requirements.[79]

[79] Sec. 201(c), 76 Stat. 419 (1962).

The role of the FCC is basically designed to protect the public interest in the absence of competition among several commercial communications satellite common carriers and to serve as an alternative, in the American tradition, to outright governmental ownership and control.[80] The powers enumerated in the Communications Satellite Act of 1962 are in fact an extension of the broad regulatory jurisdiction which the FCC now exercises, under Titles II and III of the Communications Act of 1934, as amended, with regard to domestic and international common carriers.[81]

For example, under the present provisions of Section 214(d) of the Communications Act of 1934, as amended, the FCC has the power, on its own initiative and after a full opportunity for hearing, to require carriers subject to its jurisdiction to extend their lines and services where a need therefor has been determined to exist.[82] Section 201(c)(3) of the Communications Satellite Act adds nothing substantive to the powers of the FCC under Section 214(d). The principal effect of 201(c)(3) is to make it mandatory that the FCC institute proceedings under Section 214(d) upon advice by the Secretary of State that communication with a foreign point is in the national interest. It still remains for the FCC to determine in a Section 214(d) proceeding whether or not to order the extension of service based upon an application of the criteria of Section 214(d). Of course, those criteria will be applied within the policy frames of reference of both the Satellite Act and the Communications Act.[83] As a matter of law, the decisions made by these agencies, if considered arbitrary or capricious by the Corporation, could be challenged in the Courts.

While many of the regulatory functions assigned to the FCC with regard to the Corporation are based on functions now exercised over domestic and international wireline and radio common carriers, the specific tasks which the FCC must perform are nevertheless deeper and broader than those presently performed. With reference to the above stated example, the jurisdiction of the Secretary of State to require the FCC to institute extension proceedings and the advisory role of NASA before such a directive issues are matters new to the FCC's experience and will require a great amount of close coordination among the agencies of government involved.

It should be kept in mind, moreover, that although the statutes do not expressly so provide, the Findings, Orders and Directives of both the FCC

---

[80] See *Paper on Commercial Communications Satellite System*, Frederick Ford, Commissioner, Federal Communication Commission, presented at Inter-American Bar Association XIII Conference, Panama City, Republic of Panama, April 19-26, 1963 (FCC Mimeo 34493).

[81] 47 U.S.C. 151, 201 *et seq.*

[82] 47 U.S.C. 214(d).

[83] Sec. 201(c)(3), 76 Stat. 419 (1962).

and the State Department are enforceable only in so far as the requirements are technically and economically feasible. This basic proposition
appears fully developed in the legislative history of the Act.

In a number of ways, the FCC is venturing into regulatory *terra in-
cognita* to the same extent that the Corporation is exploring unknown
and, until the present, unknowable areas. For example, the Communications Satellite Act leaves open the question of the ownership and control
of the ground terminal facilities without which no communications satellite system is possible. Section 201(c)(7) of the Communications Satellite
Act of 1962 empowers the FCC to grant construction permits and licenses
for ground terminal facilities either to the Corporation itself or to one or
more of the authorized common carriers to be served by the Corporation.[84] In each case a separate determination must be made.[85] The statutory standard to be applied in these cases is the same as that which the
Commission has been applying since its creation, i.e., the public interest,
convenience and necessity, yet the factual elements on which the public
interest findings are to be made are largely new to the FCC's experience and will require a rapid broadening of its expertise.

In the area of selection of the licensee of ground terminal facilities
alone, the FCC will be required to balance technical and economic considerations against such matters as the clear mandate of the Congress to
foster competition among the carriers authorized to receive service from
the Corporation. In such a case, should a showing of clear technical superiority and efficiency by a carrier prevail over the FCC's possible reservations about the impact of a grant on competition? After all, it will only
be a few of the many authorized carriers which will have the technical
and financial resources to construct such ground terminal facilities as
those at Andover, Maine, and Holmdel, New Jersey. Therefore, the question may well become one of competition between selected carriers only,
since for the foreseeable future most carriers will be *hors de concours.*
Much of the theory of the Act, and indeed of this discussion, becomes
obviously moot when it is understood that the basic transmission and reception standards, and the "hardware" and the operational techniques
must be agreed upon globally—by all the nations of the world of which
the United States is the most important—but it does not stand alone. This
same consideration must have a profound bearing on the decisions made
by the other nations of the world as few satellite communications systems, at least in this stage of history, could exist without having access to
the North American market.

Congress wisely left the determination as to the ownership and operation of ground stations to the FCC since there is a wide range of technical, economic, and policy factors to be considered in such a determination and the underlying factual data is yet to be developed. Such a

---

[84] Sec. 201(c)(7), 76 Stat. 419 (1962).
[85] *Op. cit. supra,* note 76 at 18-19.

determination could be made either the subject of rule-making procedure by which the Commission could resolve, the questions involved in the number, location, and ownership of ground stations, or it could be the subject of a comparative licensing procedure. The effects of a grant to either the Corporation or to one or more carriers upon competition is of course one factor to be weighed along with many others.

The global problems in connection with patents have received no public notice—but in this field also many problems will arise.

The FCC has already embarked on its regulatory career in space. On December 17, 1962, it amended its Rules and Regulations to add the initial elements of a new Part 25 governing communications satellites.[86] Since the first task facing the Corporation is the initial issuance of its stock, the regulations thus far adopted under Part 25 have all dealt with the establishment of qualifications of common carrier stockholders and the issuance of stock. In addition, the FCC on February 26, 1963, authorized the Corporation to enter into a line of credit agreement not to exceed $5,000,000 with a syndicate of ten banks and, pursuant to the terms of such agreement, to borrow $500,000 to meet initial expenses. This was the first exercise by the FCC of its authority over the fiscal affairs of the Corporation conferred by Section 201(c)(8) of the Communications Satellite Act of 1962.[87]

The task of the FCC in its role as principal regulator of the Corporation has been well stated by Commissioner Frederick W. Ford in a paper presented to the XIIIth Conference of the Inter-American Bar Association. Commissioner Ford, after describing some of the provisions of the Communications Satellite Act of 1962, said the following:

> This is simply a bare outline of the regulatory responsibilities that will face the Communications Commission as the story of satellite communications unfolds. The problems will be novel and challenging. Public utility regulation in the United States, like most human endeavors, has had its short-comings as well as its benefits. It will be the task of the Communications Commission in the years to come to equal the boldness and originality of the scientists and engineers who have created this technology by creating a regulatory scheme that will adhere to fundamental time-tested concepts but will at the same time be flexible enough to accommodate such enlightened and original concepts in thought and procedure as may be necessary if the new system is to realize fully its potential.[88]

The FCC's action authorizing the Corporation to enter into a line of credit agreement and to borrow preliminary operating funds was specifically stated to be a temporary expedient to serve until the initial issue

[86] Report and Order of December 17, 1962, Docket No. 14865, FCC 62-1303 (Mimeo 28543).

[87] FCC Public Notice, Report No. 1156, February 27, 1963, Nonbroadcast and General Actions (Mimeo 31971).

[88] *Supra,* Note 80.

of its stock is completed.[89] Although the Communications Satellite Act of 1962 does not mention the SEC, that agency will play a vital role in the initial life of the Corporation and in the Corporation's continuing need for access to the capital market. An indication of the uncertainties regarding the Corporation's prospective needs for capital may be found from the following quotation from Leo W. Welch, Chairman of the Corporation:

> It is as yet too early to compute the cost of the [communications satellite] system in concrete figures. Others who have studied this question have made estimates that vary over a wide range between $100,000,000 and $1,000,000,000, but the assumptions on which these estimates are based include so many unknowns that we would not care to put forth any figure of our own as yet, even as a guesstimate.[90]

The Communications Satellite Act of 1962 is silent concerning the formalities to be observed in connection with the issuance of stock in the Corporation. During the hearings before the House Interstate and Foreign Commerce Committee, Dr. E. C. Welsh, Executive Secretary of the National Aeronautics and Space Council, who spoke as the major Administration proponent of H.R. 11040,[91] was questioned by Congressman Springer of Illinois concerning whether or not the Securities Act of 1933 would apply to the issuance of stock in the Corporation. Dr. Welsh testified that it was his belief that such issuance would have to meet all of the requirements of that Act and that no exemption from registration was contemplated.[92] A statement by the SEC published at page 358 of the Hearings before the House Committee indicates that the Act "... is not intended to have any effect on the application of the Federal securities laws to the Corporation or to the securities of which it is the issuer." The SEC statement goes on to state that the registration requirements of the 1933 Act and the reporting requirements of the 1934 Act would apply to the Corporation.[93]

The fact that any stock issued by the Corporation must comply with the requirements of the Securities Act of 1933, as amended,[94] will have a considerable effect on the Corporation's access to capital. While the Communications Satellite Act of 1962 places a duty on the President and a number of governmental agencies and instrumentalities to facilitate and hasten the creation of an effective commercial communications satellite system, the SEC remains charged with its obligations under Section 8 of the Securities Act of 1933 to require a full and complete disclosure to the

[89] *Supra,* Note 87.
[90] *Supra,* Note 73.
[91] *Supra,* Note 75.
[92] Report of Hearings before Committee on Interstate and Foreign Commerce, House of Representatives, on H.R. 10115 and H.R. 10138, March 13, 1962, at 370.
[93] *Ibid.,* at 358.
[94] 15 U.S.C. 77a *et seq.*

public of all material facts concerning the issue.[95] The need for the SEC to make its statutory determination will, of course, have a vital effect on the timing of the initial and subsequent issues. It will also have a profound effect on the effectiveness of the required prospectus as an aid in the sale of stock to the public. For example, what would be the effect if the SEC required that the words "Speculative Issue" be stamped across the face of the prospectus as is occasionally done in cases where the SEC considers a greater than normal risk to be involved.

There are many items of information required to be disclosed in a Federal prospectus which should present little or no special problem to the Corporation. Such required data as the amount of the underwriters' discounts or commissions, the plan of distribution, if there are to be sales for considerations other than cash, the capital structure, the general use to be made of the proceeds of the issue, pending legal proceedings, and identity, background and renumeration of officers and directors should fall in this group. With regard to other crucial elements in the required prospectus, the legal and international involvements and problems almost defy analysis and the preparation of a prospectus acceptable to the SEC will require the greatest legal and financial skills.

Section 10 of the Securities Act of 1933, as amended, requires that the Federal prospectus contain most of the information outlined in Registration Statement required by Section 7 of the Act.[96] Item 9 in the Registration Statement calls for a full disclosure of the nature of the business and the manner in which the business is to be conducted. This is the most important single item in the Registration Statement and, hence, in the prospectus. All facts of material importance to the business of the registrant must be accurately disclosed. In a field which the Chairman of the Corporation describes as "full of great unknowns" the problems of setting forth with accuracy, clarity, and completeness all material facts relating to the business to be conducted are indeed great.

The foregoing observations apply with equal force to Item 10 of the Registration Statement which requires a complete description of all material facts relating to the registrant's plant, equipment, and other property. Where the ultimate identity of such properties depends in such large measure on the outcome of proceedings before the FCC, the technical assistance of NASA and the success of State Department negotiations with foreign governments, the problem of giving a meaningful description in the prospectus on which the investor can rely is apparent. Again, in the case of Item 20 of the Registration Statement a full and complete disclosure must be made of the interests of the management and other "related" persons in any of the material transactions of the Corporation. This requirement looks forward to *proposed* transactions as well as past

[95] 15 U.S.S. 77h.
[96] 15 U.S.C. 77j; 15 U.S.C. 77h.

transactions. With the uncertainties surrounding the future transactions of the Corporation a full, accurate and complete disclosure in this regard will require nearly prophetic talents.

In addition to the SEC problems, there will also be problems which must be solved under the Blue Sky Laws of the many states in which the Corporation's stock may be expected to be offered for sale. An example of this impact of the differences between the requirements of state securities laws and the Federal requirements is the fact that the Articles of Incorporation of the Corporation provide for cumulative voting in all elections of Directors.[97] This provision, which is not required by the District of Columbia Business Corporation Act,[98] under which the Corporation is organized, has doubtlessly been added because of a requirement of the California Securities Commission which views the absence of such rights ". . . as a negative factor in determining whether or not the proposed issuance and sale is fair, just and equitable." [99] The requirements of other states will doubtless have their effect.

As has been stated above NASA has been assigned specific statutory tasks in connection with the mission of the corporation. These tasks may be summarized as follows:

1. Advise the FCC on technical matters.
2. Cooperate with the Corporation in research and development activities.
3. Furnish to the Corporation such satellite launching and associated services for research and for the operating system on a reimbursable basis.
4. Consult with the Corporation on the technical characteristics of the satellite system.
5. Furnish other necessary services to the Corporation on a reimbursable basis.[100]

In addition to the above enumerated duties, NASA is by implication assigned the task of advising the State Department on the technical feasibility of extending commercial communications satellite services to foreign users.[101] It is obvious that the purchase of NASA satellite launching and associated services will be among the major expenses involved in the Corporation's activities. In addition, the viewpoint of NASA will play an important role in determining what projects are undertaken. Therefore, while NASA is assigned no regulatory role with regard to the Corporation's activities, it will in other important ways exercise a major influence on the courses of action which the Corporation adopts or is required to adopt.

[97] *Supra,* Note 70, Article V, Section 5. 04.
[98] 29 D.C. Code, Chapter 9.
[99] California Administrative Code, Title 10, Chapter 3, Subchapter 2, Section 367. 1, effective November 9, 1959.
[100] Sec. 201(b), 76 Stat. 419 (1962).
[101] See Sec. 201(c)(3), 76 Stat. 419 (1962).

The Department of State is assigned two specific areas of responsibility under the Communications Satellite Act of 1962. Under Section 402 of the Act, the Corporation is required to notify the Department of State whenever it enters into business negotiations with respect to its activities with any international or foreign entity, either governmental or otherwise. Upon receipt of such notification, the State Department is required to advise the Corporation of "relevant foreign policy considerations." [102] At the request of the Corporation to do so, the Department is required to render assistance to the Corporation in the actual conduct of such negotiations.[103]

In addition, the terms of Section 201(c) of the Act provide that the Secretary of State, presumably on his own initiative, at the request of the President or at the request of a foreign government, may consult with NASA on technical matters and may direct the FCC to institute proceedings looking towards the extension of the Corporation's services to new foreign points of communication.[104]

In this context, also, it appears from the legislative history of the Act that any such directives must be based upon findings of technical and economic feasibility—and that the question of reasonableness is the subject of judicial review.

As was indicated at the outset, the major problems which the Corporation will face, and which are absolutely crucial if it is ever to begin to succeed in its undertaking, lie in the international field. The foreseeable problems are many. The very real problems which cannot yet be perceived may many times outnumber those which are now foreseen. Most of the acute legal problems involved which are now apparent have been referred to above. Some few examples should be enough to again stress their importance.

Section 402 permits the Corporation to engage in business negotiations abroad subject to notification to the Department. But Sections 201(a)(4) and (5) require the President to supervise the relationships of the Corporation with foreign countries to insure that such relationships are consistent with our national interests and foreign policies; and further to insure that timely arrangements are made for the participation by foreign entities in the establishment and use of the system. Accordingly, the President has a very comprehensive responsibility for participation in foreign negotiations. The practical effect is that the President will decide what negotiations involve merely "business" or "commercial" matters and what negotiations involve foreign policy.

Another problem in the international field may plague the Corporation in the future. Although the Corporation is a private corporation, it is also

[102] Sec. 402, 76 Stat. 419 (1962).
[103] *Ibid.*
[104] Sec. 201(c)(3), 76 Stat. 419 (1962).

a common carrier. Under Section 201 of the Act, the Department of State can require the FCC to institute proceedings looking toward the extension of service to new foreign points.[105] In determining which foreign countries should receive service from the Corporation, the State Department must be guided by the Declaration of Policy and Purpose contained in Section 102 of the Act wherein, as indicated previously, it is provided that "... care and attention will be directed toward providing such services to economically less developed countries and areas as well as those more highly developed." [106] Here again the mirage must be dispelled— only Congress can provide funds of the order of magnitude envisioned at this time. It is doubtful that the American investor can become involved.

The policy of requiring the Corporation to furnish service to less developed nations does not necessarily conflict with the basic premise of common carrier rate-making. All points served by a common carrier need not be profitable. Service may be required to be furnished to unprofitable or high cost points as part of the general undertaking of the utility, so long as the extensions of service to such marginal areas does not impair the over-all ability of the carrier to perform its general undertaking. It may be true that the discriminatory or preferential pricing based upon ability to pay is, under most circumstances, unacceptable rate-making. The policy of the Communications Satellite Act, however, to promote the establishment of services with less developed countries may permit such pricing as reasonable. This is a most difficult and complicated problem which cannot be adequately or meaningfully evaluated or resolved at this time.

On the basis of all of the complex factors involved and the many elements which remain unknown, the statements cited above by Commissioner Ford [107] and Chairman Welch [108] concerning the difficulties and risks which face the Corporation and its investors may very well prove to be the merest understatements. The tasks to be accomplished and the problems to be solved in achieving an effective system of satellite communications are overwhelming in their magnitude.

The problems of satellite communications have been frankly reviewed herein and little has been said concerning the hopes and prospects of this great new technology. Undoubtedly, the American most knowledgeable in the technology and the international involvements of radio communications is T. A. M. Craven. He was the first of the radio officers of the Navy, which included S. C. Hooper, John Cobb Cooper, W. G. H. Bullard, and E. K. Jett. He has observed the progress of radio communications techniques from the beginning. He has been an expert consultant in radio

[105] *Ibid.*
[106] Sec. 102, 76 Stat. 419 (1962).
[107] *Supra,* Note 80.
[108] *Supra,* Note 73.

engineering as a private citizen and as a senior adviser in many capacities to the United States Government. He has participated in the international radio conferences involving the United States Government since 1927. He has served two years as Chief Engineer and almost fourteen years as a Commissioner on the FCC; and he was Chairman of the United States Delegation to the International Administrative Radio Conference in Geneva in 1959, which authorized the first radio facilities for space use, and also provided for the 1963 Extraordinary Conference on space communications.

These facts are mentioned only to demonstrate the point that Commissioner Craven, while fully aware of all the obstacles facing the development of satellite communications, has maintained complete confidence that all problems will be solved and that mankind will immensely benefit from this technology. Commissioner Craven's great-grandfather, Captain T. A. M. Craven, commanded the USS *Tecumseh* under Admiral Farragut at the Battle of Mobile Bay. With gentle humor Commissioner Craven recalls that Admiral Farragut uttered the immortal words which have inspired courage in so many people—"Damn the torpedoes!...go ahead!...full speed!" Commissioner Craven points out that his great-grandfather still reposes in Mobile Bay in the destroyed wreckage of the *Tecumseh*—but Farragut won the battle. Commissioner Craven is firm in his belief that this satellite communications battle for humanity will be won although a few participants, like his great-grandfather, may perish along the way.

And, as a final antidote to many gloomy projections, recently a great American company has come forward with a proposal to build passive satellites which would reduce the cost of the satellites themselves, and the ground stations could be simple installations which any nation could afford to construct! [109] Several other systems are in process.

TECHNICAL CONSIDERATIONS

7–7 Problems of orbital radio commands

The remarkable progress which has been made in the development and use of solar batteries as a direct source of power in satellite vehicles and as a means for recharging more conventional batteries has created serious problems in space communications. If radio transmitters are assured of indefinite operational life through the employment of ever more efficient solar batteries and recharging cells, the possibilities become increasingly great that the very limited number of frequency bands available for space

[109] *Feasibility Study and Preliminary Design of Gravity-Gradient-Stabilized Lenticular Test Satellite*, Goodyear Aircraft Corporation, Akron 15, Ohio.

communications will become subject to technically "annoying" and even disruptive or destructive interference from transmitters on board satellites which are still in orbit even though their usefulness as experimental or intelligence devices has ended.[110]

As we must deal with the conservation and safety of life and property, a second and more serious long-range problem must also be considered, namely, the continued orbiting of man-made space vehicles for periods of undetermined length—extending even to centuries or millennia. This uncontrollable "space trash" will constitute a hazard to safety of life and property in outer space as long as it continues in orbit.

It is quite clear that the radio command problem is simple of solution, whereas the disposal of "space trash" is most difficult to solve, and the latter problem is really the most serious by far. Certainly, the "probabilities" of collision and all aspects of threats to safety over the next century should be the subject of a searching study under the supervision of NASA by such organizations as the Rand Corporation. But let us return to the first and more simple problem.

As a minimum, at least two things must be done in order to prevent the frequency bands from becoming "annoyed" or disrupted by signals from satellites which have outlived their usefulness. The first solution is to require the employment of command circuits on all transmitters, tele-metering transmitters and beacons as well, so that emissions may be termi-nated when the satellite has served its function. Since the possibility of malfunction is as great in regard to transmitter command circuits as it is with any other satellite component, we must expect that all useless trans-missions may not be terminated when desired by a signal from the earth. To guard against this eventuality it also appears necessary to install in the satellite vehicle itself some capability for the modification of orbit upon command from the earth so as to permit the destruction or retrieval of the vehicle. Through transmitter command and orbital command, those charged with responsibility for the conduct of space activities can exercise almost complete control over the operation of each vehicle's transmitters, thus making it possible to ensure the vacation of frequency space when more important uses are contemplated.

Fortunately, progress is being made in the area of transmitter control, at least, although this progress has not been uniform among the various agencies.

For a more thorough evaluation of the problem of transmitter control and frequency availability, it may be well at this point to analyze some transmitter frequencies that have been used and the provisions, if any, which were made to control the transmitters. For example, NASA indi-

110 Proceedings, XIth International Congress, *A Basic Program for the 1963 Extraordinary Administrative Radio Conference on Space Communications* at 175 *et seq.* (Vienna: Springer-Verlag, 1961).

cated as of November 1960 that ten satellite vehicles were in orbit with
their transmitters in operation.[111] These vehicles were:

Name/Country	Launch Date
Vanguard I (US)	March 17, 1958
Explorer VII (US)	October 13, 1959
Tiros I (US)	April 1, 1960
Midas II (US)	May 24, 1960
Transit II-A (US)	June 22, 1960
NRL Satellite (US)	June 22, 1960
Echo I (US)	August 12, 1960
Courier I-B (US)	October 4, 1960
Explorer VIII (US)	November 3, 1960
Tiros II (US)	November 23, 1960

The *Vanguard I* satellite has established a clear record for transmission
longevity. This satellite was equipped with two transmitters, operating
on 108 megacycles with 10 milliwatts and 108.03 megacycles with 5 milliwatts. The first transmitter was powered by mercury batteries. The second
to all appearances continues to be powered by six groups of solar converters. While the transmitter powered by the mercury batteries ceased
operation April 5, 1958, less than one month after launch, the solar-
powered transmitter will continue to operate indefinitely. In the planning
of the *Vanguard* satellite it appears that long life of the solar converters
was not taken into account. While the *Vanguard's* second transmitter has
a power output of only five milliwatts, the fact of interference on 108.03
megacycles to signals from more recently launched vehicles cannot be
dismissed as unimportant. It is interesting to note that all of the *Vanguard*
satellites launched subsequent to March 17, 1960, were equipped with
mercury or silver zinc batteries.[112] *Vanguard III*, which was successfully
launched September 18, 1959, was equipped with chemical batteries
powered for transmission life of only 85 days.[113] The curtailment of the life
span of chemical or other batteries represents a practical solution to our
problem. It appears, however, that where solar converters are used some
means of command operation is required.

This problem also exists with respect to the *Tiros* satellites which have
been placed in orbit and are continuing to transmit intelligence by means
of their transmitters. *Tiros I* was successfully launched by NASA on
April 1, 1960. Designed primarily as a weather observation satellite,
Tiros I carried two frequency modulation transmitters operating on 235
megacycles with power output of 2 watts. In addition, this satellite carried

[111] NASA, International Satellite and Space Probe Summary, NASA Release No.
60-295, Nov. 3, 1960. Since the date of that report, *Tiros II* was launched on Nov. 23,
1960.
[112] NASA Space Activities Summaries S-59-14, S-59-6, S-59-4 and S-50-1, Sept.,
1960.
[113] NASA Space Activities Summary S-59-14, Sept., 1960.

two tracking beacons operating on 108 and 108.03 megacycles with 30 milliwatts power.[114] The power for the transmitters was supplied by nickel-cadmium batteries charged by solar cells; the power output was expected to average about 19 watts. The importance of control over the *Tiros I* transmitters becomes readily apparent when it is realized that the bandwidth of the television transmissions from the satellite was 62.5 kilocycles.[115] This sophisticated satellite, which transmitted on three frequencies, one of which required a 62.5 kilocycle bandwidth, is clearly an illustration of the need for earth-to-satellite radio control circuits. Happily, not only was the main carrier channel at 235 megacycles equipped with control circuits, but also provision was made for the two low-power tracking beacons to be commanded off when the satellite's usefulness came to an end.[116]

The *Tiros II* satellite, which NASA successfully placed in orbit on November 23, 1960, incorporated all the protective features of *Tiros I* within a more versatile framework. *Tiros II* was equipped with two 235.0-megacycles transmitters operating with a power output of 2 watts, one 3-watt transmitter on 237.8 megacycles and two 30-milliwatt tracking beacons operating continuously on the frequencies 108.0 and 108.3 megacycles. The 235-megacycle and 237.8-megacycle transmitters were operated on and off by ground command.[117] Similarly, when the vehicle's useful life was ended, the tracking beacons could also be turned off by command.[118] The later *Tiros* vehicles were also equipped for transmission termination on command.

At the start of 1961 two satellites in the *Explorer* series were orbited by NASA. *Explorer VII* was successfully orbited by NASA on October 13, 1959 and is expected to continue in orbit for a period of from thirty to forty years.[119] Two transmitters were carried with the satellite, the first operating on 20 megacycles with an output power of 600 milliwatts. The second transmitter was the tracking beacon operating on 108 megacycles with 15 milliwatts. The transmitters were powered by solar cells and rechargeable nickel-cadmium batteries. The 20-megacycle transmitter was timed to cut off one year from launching date. The beacon was timed to operate for only two months and it has gone silent.[120]

Explorer VIII was successfully placed in orbit on November 3, 1960. On board was a single transmitter operating on 108 megacycles with 70 milliwatts power. The power was supplied by mercury batteries.[121] No

[114] NASA Space Activities Summary S-60-5A, July 6, 1960.
[115] *Tiros I* Satellite Payload, NASA Release No. 60-152, April 1, 1960, p. 3.
[116] *Id.* at 6.
[117] *Tiros* Satellite Payload, NASA Release No. 60-299, Nov. 23, 1960, p. 2.
[118] *Id.* at 8.
[119] Missiles & Rockets, July 30, 1962, p. 70.
[120] *Id.*; NASA Space Activities Summary S-59-15, Sept. 1960.
[121] NASA Space Activities Summary S-60-19, Nov. 3, 1960.

solar cells were used in this satellite, nor was there any command cir-
cuiting; thus when the batteries expired all transmission would cease.[122]
It appears that for the *Explorer* series, NASA has decided to solve the problem of frequency crowding by timing the life of the power supply rather
than by building command circuits into the satellites. This is to be contrasted with the practice followed in connection with *Tiros*, where, as
described above, even the tracking beacons can be commanded.

Full details concerning the *Midas* series of Air Force satellites have
not been released; however, from the nature of the task performed by this
satellite—the detection of missile launchings by infrared sensors [123]—informed opinion is that some degree of control over transmission is exercised either by radio command circuitry or by the use of timers. In the
case of *Midas II*, which was successfully launched by the Air Force on
May 24, 1960, data-link telemetry transmitting infrared scanner information ceased functioning two days after the launch.[124] The fact that NASA
continued to list *Midas II* as being in orbit with transmitter in operation
would appear to indicate that the tracking beacon was not controlled or
that, if it was controlled, a timer was used which was not yet programmed
to cut off the beacon or had failed to function properly. (*Midas II* had
an anticipated orbital life of 40 months.)

By their nature and function some satellites cannot be commanded on
and off. An example is the Navy's *Transit* series. Designed to demonstrate
the feasibility of all-weather global navigational information for ships and
aircraft, to provide accurate time standards and to obtain more accurate
geodetic measurements, *Transit II-A* consisted of two separate vehicles
and carried in the first vehicle two ultra-stable oscillators and transmitters
operating on the frequencies 54, 324, 162, and 216 megacycles. An additional transmitter was carried in the second vehicle operating on 108
megacycles and transmitting data on solar radiation for a Naval Research
Laboratory study.[125] The transmitters were completely powered by solar
energy employing nickel-cadmium batteries for power storage. *Transit
II-A* was estimated to have on orbital life of approximately fifty years;
transmitter life was estimated to be up to one year.[126]

Since it had as its main purpose the aiding of navigation, *Transit II-A*
was designed for continuous transmission. The importance of the service
afforded by the *Transit* series and other programs of similar purpose serves
to emphasize the importance of providing for the silencing of transmitters
aboard space vehicles which no longer serve any useful function. Such
a measure will simplify the problem of obtaining interference-free spec-

[122] Morton J. Stoller at *Explorer VIII* Press Conference, Nov. 3, 1960.
[123] NASA Space Activities Summary S-60-9, June 3, 1960.
[124] *Ibid.*
[125] NASA Space Activities Summary S-60-10, July 1, 1960.
[126] *Id.* But see Missiles & Rockets, July 30, 1962, at 70 which indicates *Transit II-A*
was still transmitting more than two years after launching.

trum space for such vital services as that provided by the *Transit* satellites.

As can be seen from the preceding discussion, some space satellites do not fall within the category of vehicles which should have transmitter command circuitry. However, there have also been some satellites which for no apparent reason were not equipped for transmitter command. The *Echo I* satellite may be taken as an example of a satellite in which command circuitry was desirable but in which no provision was made for it.

Echo I, which was successfully placed in orbit on August 12, 1960, carried two transmitters appended to its balloon-like body and a third attached to the third stage of the launching vehicle, which also achieved orbit.[127] The two transmitters on the balloon operated on 107.94 megacycles with 10 watts output while the third-stage transmitter operated on 108.06 megacycles with 60 milliwatts output.[128] All three transmitters were tracking beacons and served no other function.[129] No transmitter control was employed.

Each of the tracking beacons in operation of *Echo I* and its third stage was equipped with 70 solar cells and five nickel-cadmium storage batteries as its power supply.[130] Since no one knew precisely how long the balloon-like satellite would be in orbit or when the transmitters would go silent,[131] it appeared that two more frequencies in the critical 108-megacycle band were to be occupied for an indefinite period of time.

In terms of control over radio transmitters, the Army's *Courier* series of satellites presents an encouraging contrast to the now antiquated beacon system incorporated with *Echo I*. Both *Courier I-A* and *Courier I-B*, which were successfully launched on August 18, 1960, and October 4, 1960, were equipped with four frequency-modulation transmitters powered by 19,200 solar cells with power storage afforded by nickel-cadmium batteries.[132] The entire operation of the transmitters, as well as much of the other intricate instrumentation contained in the vehicles, could be controlled from ground stations by means of radio command. Thus when any *Courier* satellite has outlived its usefulness the transmitters can be silenced by the transmission of a command signal.

Most of the present series of satellite projects, and some projected series, are employing or will employ transmitter control through command circuitry or timing devices.[133] It appears definite that the *Tiros, Explorer,* and ionosphere beacon projects of NASA will continue to make use of control

---

[127] John W. Towsend, Ass't Director for Space Sciences, Goddard Space Flight Center, Press Conference Project *Echo I,* Aug. 12, 1960, at 6.

[128] NASA Space Activities Summary S-60-13, Aug. 15, 1960.

[129] William J. O'Sullivan, Head of Space Vehicles Group, Langley Research Center, Press Conference Project *Echo I,* Aug. 12, 1960, at 15.

[130] *Op. cit. supra* note 128.

[131] Interview cited above 129; *op. cit. supra* note 128.

[132] NASA Space Activities Summaries S-60-15, Aug. 26, 1960; and S-60-17, Oct. 6, 1960.

[133] See *Samos I,* NASA Space Activities Summary S-60-18, Oct. 19, 1960.

of some kind, probably in most instances command.[134] It is also clear that most of the military space vehicles will be equipped with command circuits.[135] Unfortunately, it is not known whether or not all future vehicles will be so equipped. This is particularly true of the use of tracking beacons where control circuits serve no other purpose than to silence the transmitter once the useful life of the satellite is ended.

Even if all future satellites are equipped with transmitter controls, there is no certainty that some circuits will not fail to function, thus causing unproductive uses of scarce space frequencies. In order to back up the electronic command devices, some measure of orbital command appears necessary, and this presents problems of much greater complexity. Various space experiments have employed retrorockets, spin controls, and other devices for the purpose of guiding the space vehicle into and out of orbit. If we are to exercise maximum control over space vehicle transmitters, we must regularly provide some such means of changing the orbit on command so as to cause the destruction of a useless vehicle or else retrieve it from space.

Orbital control is best exemplified by the techniques used for both Soviet and United States manned orbiting satellites. In manned flight, obviously, the orbit must be controlled in order to permit safe return of the inhabited space capsule to earth. In most other types of space experiment, orbital control is not so critical a consideration; indeed, for nonrecoverable satellites carrying only scientific instrumentation, there may be no requirement for it whatever in terms of the vehicle's mission *per se.* Nevertheless, an example of what might be done even with unmanned space vehicles is offered by the U.S. Air Force's recently abandoned *Saint* system, which envisaged an unmanned space satellite with some degree of capability to maneuver in space once orbit was achieved. The *Saint* (space inspection satellite) was planned to have restartable rocket engines for longitudinal and transverse thrust, to permit forward and lateral movement. Attitude-control jets were also required to insure the efficient use of the television apparatus that was to be included in the instrumentation. Only a small amount of maneuvering thrust was thought to be needed to permit the *Saint* to depart from its orbit and approach an unidentified space object.[136]

For various reasons, of which one was naturally the complexity of the system itself, the Air Force in late 1962 announced that it was abandoning the *Saint* effort.[137] However, it was pointed out that the knowledge and experience gained in the project would in many cases be transferable to

[134] Interview with Paul A. Price, NASA, Washington, D.C., Nov. 22, 1960.
[135] Interview with Colonel Paul Nadler, ARPA, Washington, D.C., Nov. 22, 1960.
[136] *USAF Launches Anti-Satellite Program,* Aviation Week & Space Technology, Nov. 14, 1960, pp. 26-27.
[137] *USAF Halts Saint Work; Shifts to Gemini,* Aviation Week & Space Technology, Dec. 10, 1962, p. 36.

other space endeavors. It is ardently to be hoped that the capability for ground-controlled maneuverability that was investigated in connection with the *Saint* project will ultimately prove compatible with all our satellite vehicles, so as to permit their removal from orbit upon completion of their useful lives. It may be found, however, that orbital command of the complexity envisaged in the *Saint* satellite is not necessary to accomplish this end. It is possible that some simpler method can be developed, possibly a combination of design elements similar to those now employed in the Air Force's *Discoverer* series which would permit the removal from orbit of the instrument package by means of ejection and retrorockets either at the direct command of ground stations or as the result of the operation of timing devices.

Since radio transmissions from positions in space have effects which go beyond the activities of any one nation, the requirement that transmitter and orbital commands be used must be applied to each nation which undertakes space activities. At present the Soviet Union is the only other world power which has an independent space capability. And it is well to note that the Russians have amply demonstrated their ability to control a vehicle's orbit, both in their manned orbital flights and in certain other experiments. For example, in the case of *Spacecraft II* (*1960 Lambda*) we may be sure that orbital control was exercised by Soviet technicians, since the satellite capsule containing a variety of instruments and animals was successfully recovered during the vehicle's 18th orbit on August 20, 1960.[138] Furthermore, *Lunik III* (*1959 Theta*), the vehicle that photographed the far side of the moon, indicated a capacity for a very high degree of control over the attitude of a vehicle after it is launched. Naturally, any nation that can accomplish a feat such as this can also easily arrange to turn off a space-vehicle transmitter. Thus, while the USSR has not released much detail concerning its ground-to-space vehicle-control activities, informed opinion concedes that it does possess the ability to exercise a high degree of both transmitter and orbital control.

It would appear, therefore, that both of the world's space powers have the needed present capability; and as evidenced by the *Saint* project, greater refinements in orbital control may be expected. The next step must be to seek to achieve international agreement on transmitter and orbital controls without further delay. The future appears to hold the prospect of many more satellites carrying active radio transmitters than the number now in orbit, and the need for providing mechanisms for vacating frequencies at the end of the useful life of a satellite will increase in urgency with each new transmitter placed in orbit.

[138] NASA Space Activities Summary F-60-2, Aug. 29, 1960.

7–8   Transmission identification procedures

This chapter would not be complete without a discussion of a monitoring of radio transmissions from space vehicles. The essential data used here are in part borrowed from the work of the CCIR, and in particular from a report by George S. Turner, Chairman of the Study Group of the CCIR on radio monitoring: "Monitoring At Fixed Monitoring Stations Of Radio Transmissions From Space Vehicles."

There are several factors influencing the choice of, or the necessity for, different techniques of observation and measurement of transmissions from vehicles in space as contrasted with observations and measurements of transmissions from fixed and mobile radio stations on or near the earth (including among the latter, transmitters in conventional aircraft or balloons moving at relatively much slower speeds than space vehicles). With reference to space vehicles, it is important to note: (1) the difference in received as against transmitted frequency, and the varying nature of the received frequency, caused by the Doppler effect, (2) the generally weaker field strength at the earth-receiving point due to distance and relatively low transmitter power, (3) the general necessity to "acquire" the signal and then to track the space vehicle with high-gain, highly directive receiving antennas, and (4) the relatively short time that a near-earth orbiting satellite is above the horizon for a given fixed monitoring point so that its radio transmissions are received well enough to permit good observations and measurements.

Agencies launching space vehicles will, of necessity, continue to provide for the required accurate tracking and telemetry reception to meet their special needs. Moreover, monitoring stations presently engaged in enforcement of domestic laws and regulations, and engaged in international monitoring pursuant to article 13 of the ITU Radio Regulations, will participate in space monitoring activities as a natural extension of their regular operations. For the present, such stations in the United States are developing special technical facilities, training personnel in space-monitoring techniques, and making observations or measurements at the specific request of space agencies, particularly with respect to interference problems and identification of interfering signals. The discussion in this section refers to such programs as these, rather than to the monitoring performed by the space agencies themselves.

Because of the Doppler effect, the apparent carrier frequency of an orbiting earth-satellite transmitter, as measured by a fixed monitoring station, is high with respect to its true frequency when the satellite is approaching the monitoring station and low when it recedes from the station. A measurement gives the true frequency only when the satellite is at the very point in its particular pass closest to the station. When this occurs, the rate of frequency change is maximum. An orbital path directly over the monitoring station will produce the maximum frequency shift and also the highest rate of change.

To determine the true frequency and the extent of Doppler shift, the basic requirement is a rapid frequency-measuring technique and a means of accurately timing each measurement. The latter may be accomplished by making use of Standard Time transmissions. A means of automatic recording of frequency and time will produce the best results. If measurements are taken every few seconds and plotted against time, a curve is obtained from which the center of the portion showing the greatest rate of change can be estimated with reasonably good accuracy, possibly to within ±0.1 kilocycle/second.

A plot of the frequency change with respect to time might be expected to produce a smooth curve if the measurement accuracy is high; but less than a smooth curve is sometimes obtained in practice, apparently due to the effects of propagation through the ionosphere as a function of the refractive index. There are also indications that ionization at the satellite when it is passing through the ionosphere disturbs the Doppler frequency shift and contributes to the causes of excursions from a smooth curve. These variations have been observed between 20 and a few hundred megacycles, with the effect becoming greater the lower the frequency. However, if a smooth curve is drawn, the true frequency can be estimated to an accuracy sufficient to serve the present needs of the monitoring service.

The apparent occupied bandwidth of satellite transmitter as measured at a fixed monitoring station varies because of the Doppler shift in the same manner as described for the carrier frequency. This effect is not of practical significance at present from an external interference standpoint, and in fact it is doubtful that the spectrum analyzers available at monitoring stations have sufficient resolution to detect it when the entire signal is being observed under operating conditions of weak signal and relatively high background noise. Nevertheless, it should be realized that the amount of frequency shift is slightly larger for portions of the signal near the upper edge of the occupied band than for signal components near the lower edge. This difference could amount to several hundred cycles per second, or more, for the wide bandwidths proposed for some of the future space transmissions on frequencies above 100 megacycles.

The extra spectrum occupied by a space signal because of the Doppler frequency shift is of importance in considering potential interference capabilities of the signal. Therefore, monitoring stations will be required to measure the total band occupied during the period of observation, as well as the apparent bandwidth at any instant. For a particular satellite, the total band will be maximum for an orbital path directly over the monitoring station. Automatic frequency tracking provisions in the receiver and a means of taking relatively fast photographs of the bandwidth displayed on a spectrum analyzer oscilloscope will facilitate this work. Otherwise, the techniques of measurement will not differ greatly from those for stationary earth transmitters. A series of photographs should be taken if possible, with the time of each photograph recorded, so that correlation can be made if desired with the time that the frequency *vs.* time curve shows, the apparent carrier frequency to be closest to the true frequency; and so that the total spectrum occupied during the time of observation can be noted. The most difficult problem is that of obtaining a strong signal over the noise level to allow for use of the maximum resolution of the spectrum analyzer.

In general, just as in more conventional monitoring surveillance, equipment for monitoring signals from space vehicles must have adequate flexibility to cover a wide range of frequencies. (Of course, the needs of a particular research or operating space agency may well be satisfied with spot frequency coverage, but as already pointed out this discussion is concerned with less specialized monitoring stations.) Also, the location of the monitoring station should be such that interference from man-made signals and noise is at a minimum. The receiving antennas should have high gain, with a provision for adjustment in both horizontal and vertical planes. Wideband antennas, such as the log periodic type, have an advantage for general monitoring in that greater frequency coverage with one antenna is possible. Antenna transmission line losses should be kept low. Consideration should be given to the use of converters at the antenna, to lower the frequency to reduce line loss. Low-noise amplifiers at the antenna are also suggested. Based on experience to date in receiving satellite signals below 1000 megacycles, the antenna and transmission line system should have an over-all gain of several decibels over a no-loss half-wave dipole system.

Automatic "sweeping" of a band of frequencies, by varying the receiver tuning, and automatic recording of intercepted signals on a chart-type ink-line field strength recorder will assist in "acquiring" space signals and in timing their duration.

An electronic frequency counter with timed print-out has been found best for taking high-speed measurements to follow the Doppler shift. A stable transfer oscillator is desirable to permit frequency measurements where it is not possible to make a direct count of the space transmitter signal, although manual adjustment of the transfer oscillator slows down the measurements and introduces an additional error due to difficulties in keeping it in exact zero-beat with the signal.

Good results have been obtained at United States monitoring stations in the tracking of satellite signals by manual adjustment of antenna azimuth and elevation, and by manual adjustment of the receiver tuning to follow the Doppler frequency shift. Nevertheless, antenna and receiver tracking is to be preferred if practicable, and will undoubtedly become more important for satisfactory monitoring as space frequencies above

1000 megacycles are required to be received and measured at international monitoring stations.

For economic reasons, and because a general-coverage receiver is required at monitoring stations, the latter cannot equal the extremely low noise figures that are possible for fixed-frequency receivers used by space agencies in monitoring of their own vehicle transmitters. However, the receiver should have a relatively low noise figure and be capable of receiving signals in the order of a few hundredths of a microvolt at the receiver input. It should also have a wide range of adjustable bandwidth, to permit reception of both wide and narrow-band space transmissions. Adjustments to 1 kilocycle/second or less will be needed for some signals on the lower space frequencies.

Because of the high cost and narrow frequency-band characteristics of the maser and parametric-type amplifiers, they have not yet been found practicable for use in general monitoring of space transmissions.

To facilitate "acquisition" of the signal from a space vehicle, it is desirable to be able to sweep a narrow band of frequencies automatically and to record the received signals both aurally and on a field-strength recorder. United States monitoring stations have developed a sweeping device for this purpose.

Considerable thought has been given in the United States, in the work of CCIR Study Groups IV and VIII, to the possible need of space agencies and monitoring stations for a call sign or other special identifier to facilitate identification of space transmissions. At the present time, the techniques employed by space agencies in satellite and other space vehicle tracking, as well as those foreseen for communications and other uses of space transmissions, are such that special identifiers are not essential. There being no requirement on the part of the tracker and user for use of identifiers, to require their use to facilitate monitoring observations could impose limitations adversely affecting reliability, weight, cost, and operation of the system involved.

It has been found possible at United States monitoring stations to identify the transmissions of particular satellites from signal characteristics and ephemeris data furnished by the space agency concerned. It would thus appear that the provisions of article 19, paragraph 737, International Radio Regulations (Geneva, 1959), relating to recognized means of identification other than call signs, will be met if agencies launching satellites and other space vehicles will continue to make such information currently available to monitoring services. The following information will assist in identification: (1) carrier frequencies, (2) orbit time, (3) angle of inclination of orbit to equator, (4) equator crossing time and longitude of crossing, (5) perigee and apogee distances, and (6) signal characteristics such as type of modulation and bandwidth for each frequency.

From the ephemeris data, United States monitoring stations have been able to calculate when a particular satellite will be above the horizon for a particular monitoring station and what are the distances involved, in order to predict reception and assist in identification.

Then, too, a graphical method has been found very useful for determining expected reception times for orbiting earth satellites on the basis of past reception data. Using the time of the beginning of reception on the various passes, one can plot time of reception against date, both on a linear scale. Straight lines drawn through points indicating past reception for successive days can be extended ahead a week at a time, and points added as obtained, to indicate whether future correction in the slope of the lines are needed. With this method, predicted beginning of reception of a satellite signal has been found accurate to within approximately 6 minutes.

A graphical method has also been found useful to determine the maximum line-of-sight distance to a satellite, in order to give an indication whether reception on a given pass should be possible. A curve is drawn from scaled line-of-sight distances plotted against elevation distances. Then from elevations at perigee and apogee furnished by the space agency, maximum line-of-sight distance can be read from the curve for any satellite.

Another aid that has been found helpful is a world globe pivoted to rotate on its north-south axis, with the satellite orbit represented to scale by a loop of wire marked off in minutes of the orbital period. With the loop positioned over the globe at the correct inclination angle which the orbit makes with the equator and synchronized at the equator crossing times and longitudes, the relative positions of the monitoring station and satellite can be determined for the time when reception is to be expected.

Simple slide-rule-type rotary disc computers have been constructed by United States monitoring stations to facilitate calculations of the positions of a satellite from the ephemeris data. One such computer that is particularly helpful consists of three discs and is used to determine all of the right ascensions of an orbit as the satellite crosses the equator for a 24-hour period, after the information for one crossing is obtained. The stationary outer disc indicates the longitude at the equator. The next disc rotates and is marked off in increments of the total time of one orbit to the same scale as the inner disc, which also rotates and is divided into 24 hourly segments. If one of the divisions of the orbit-segment disc is set to the known longitude of an equator crossing and the 24-hour inner disc set to the same point for the time of the crossing, all of the right ascension equator crossings for a 24-hour period can be read opposite the orbit-segment marks. (Note: if one of the orbit time segments comes out less than the time of one orbit in constructing the disc, it should be disregarded in using the computer.)

A graphical aid which has been found useful to monitoring stations in determining the position of a satellite in its orbit with respect to time, and in determining line-of-sight distances, is a scale drawing of the orbital plane and essential related distances from the center and surfaces of the earth, perigee and apogee positions and times, etc. Such a chart can be drawn from orbital information furnished by the space agency concerned.

Procedures have been discussed here for the identification of transmissions from space vehicles based on past experience involving the comparison of measured and observed signal characteristics with published information, and comparison of the time of closest approach to a monitoring station—as determined from the measured Doppler shift of the carrier frequency and from varying azimuth (bearing)—with ephemeris data. However, with the increased use of operational satellites, immediate positive identification by monitoring stations of all intercepted space-vehicle transmissions by these methods may become too time-consuming. Therefore, certain additional procedures may have to be adopted. A communications system involving either passive or active orbiting satellites could be identified by the call sign or other identifier of the ground station reflected from or relayed by the satellite, even if this did not immediately identify the particular satellite of a multi-satellite system. Furthermore, in enforcement-type monitoring of space vehicle transmissions—particularly where non-compliance with radio regulations or cases of interference are observed—monitoring stations could log all possible information concerning frequency and bandwidth measurements, direction of signal arrival, type of modulation, and other signal characteristics, and request identification, based on these data, from identification and tracking centers maintained by space agencies. The time that the satellite is closest to the monitoring location on a given pass, as determined from Doppler shift measurements, and the carrier frequency as measured for this time will be of utmost importance to the space center in effecting identification.

7–9   A glimpse of the future

During the next generation the achievements of science in the field of communications technology will surpass by a multiple factor all of man's past achievements in this field, including the remarkable inventions that we now call telegraphy and telephony, radio disseminations of all kinds, and even television and picture technology in general. The bright vistas of technical progress are indeed heartening. On the other hand, the prospects for concomitant sociological and legal progress on the face of the earth and on any planet which may be dominated by mankind are indeed disheartening, because the very purpose of communications is now distorted by dominant considerations of national interest, and the ability to receive communications is highly attenuated by language barriers and by "tribal" customs of humans.

We are all fundamentally concerned with the immense sociological and legal problems which confront mankind, but the prospects for technical achievement must first be understood, even if in a very general manner. By way of analogy, let us briefly consider the development of air and space travel.

During the first stage, the propeller airplane was developed, using what is basically the thrust developed by a screw in an ocean of air in the same manner that a blade propels a ship in an ocean of water. This stage, let us assume, ended with the "turboprop" airplane.

The second stage may be roughly described as the age of the "pure jet." Now we find the screw abandoned, and transportation is freed from the shackles of the surface wheel and a highly inefficient type of engine. Thrust is directly derived from the atmosphere in a "not so highly complicated" thermodynamic system. Enormous savings in engineering gear on the one hand, and in traveling time on the other hand, are achieved.

And so we come to the third stage, the age of the rocket power-plant which unshackles man from both the wheel and the atmosphere, and enables him to traverse the universe. The types of motors are so many in number and so varied that it would be quite inappropriate to discuss or even to outline roughly the alpha to omega of solid rockets to radiation propulsion devices.

We proceed with our analogy to communications. In reviewing modes of transportation we did not discuss the oxen and the drag harrow or the horse and buggy but at once considered the aircraft. In the case of communications, however, there is one primitive technique—light signaling—which, as we shall see below, will again become one of the most significant means of communication. With this important though rather peculiar reservation, we will characterize the first stage as the stage of electrical communications which resulted in the epochal advent of the telegraph and telephone.

The second stage is the "radio age"—the age of wireless, in which the radio spectrum is utilized for all forms of communications, including telegraphy, telephony, television, and so on. Radio has enabled man to communicate by signaling, by voice and by the transmission and reception of pictures; this he has done throughout the world and, to a significant extent, throughout the solar system. The most disheartening aspect of the radio age is not the abundance of inventions and possibilities of use, but the limitations of the spectrum itself. As an example of the extent of present-day use of the radio spectrum, in the United States there are more than 2.5 million radio transmitters in the safety and special services categories alone. These categories do not include broadcasting stations, common carrier systems, or the vast military and governmental radio systems. New techniques such as single side band transmissions have made possible additional radio assignments; even so, our constantly expanding use of the available radio frequencies is outpacing the development of new devices designed for frequency conservation and sharing.[139]

And so we come to the third stage in communications—a stage in which nature exposes to man possibilities that are so widespread and useful as to defy description and challenge the imagination. This third stage involves fundamental departures from the present-day use of radio frequencies. Just one example which has recently received much public attention is the use of coherent, message-bearing light waves. This technique, while today in an elementary state of development, has been employed experimentally, with the light waves focused and disciplined so that they move in phase as radio waves do. A far greater system capacity is inherent in coherent light-wave communication than is possible within the confines of the radio spectrum. Through the use of coherent light the number of communication paths may thus exceed by a factor of thousands of times those made available in the radio spectrum.[140]

The availability of new communications systems with vast capacity is of vital importance to the development of space communications during the next twenty-five years. At the 1959 Extraordinary Administrative Radio Conference in Geneva, for example, we were able to secure a total of only slightly more than 130 megacycles of the entire radio spectrum between 10 and 10,000 megacycles for use in space.[141] Even this small portion of the spectrum was restricted to "space research" functions, and the entire question of providing adequate space for operational use (communications, guidance, command, data transmission, navigation, and so on) was postponed until late in 1963. Meanwhile, a world-wide study group of the International Radio Consultative Committee went to work atttempting to "fit in" vast new demands for spectrum space, to coordinate all space allocations with the existing terrestrial allocations, and to arrive at recommendations for action by the 1963 conference. The task was one of the most staggering assignments which had ever faced the CCIR and the International Telecommunication Union.

To be sure, the radio spectrum cannot be wholly discarded as the principal medium for the development of space communications during the next generation. Too much research and development have gone into our present and proposed space communication systems, and too much "hardware" has been developed on the basis of radio capabilities even to consider such a wholesale change. Nevertheless, we must look to the areas of coherent light, maser and laser technologies, gamma ray transmissions, and other scientific breakthroughs, for relief from the stifling effects of the

[139] *Looking to Space for More, Faster Communications,* Business Week, Feb. 25, 1961, at 82.

[140] See generally *Laser Challenges Radar For Space Use,* Aviation Week & Space Technology, July 24, 1961, at 71-72.

[141] ITU Radio Regulations, Dec. 21, 1959, ch. III, art. 5, T.I.A.S. No. 4893.

crowding and other inadequacies which characterize the present radio spectrum.

At the Space Communications Roundtable held during the XIIth International Astronautical Congress in October 1961, unique communication possibilities using "unconventional techniques" were discussed by a panel consisting of Dr. Eberhardt Rechtin of the Jet Propulsion Laboratory (Chairman), Dr. George F. Smith of Hughes Research Laboratories, Mr. J. W. Ogland of Westinghouse Electric Corporation, Dr. Jozef W. Eerkens of Aerospace Corporation, Dr. J. P. C. Leiphart of the U.S. Naval Research Laboratory, Dr. J. P. Gordon of Bell Telephone Laboratories, and Dr. Huber Heffner of Stanford University. These techniques promise the "breakthrough" in space communications technology which we now seek. At this stage, they are purely experimental, but enough is known today to justify accelerated development and perfection of the new methods. Dr. Rechtin, in setting the theme of the roundtable, stated that "at the present time and with available techniques, conventional radio communications in the frequency band of 20 megacycles to 20 kilomegacycles is satisfactory for efficient space communications within the solar system." "The purpose of the roundtable," he then proceeded to make clear, "is to discuss possible communications techniques outside of the conventional communications band." [142]

The roundtable participants directed their attention to three principal systems of space communications which do not involve the use of the radio frequency spectrum. Drs. Smith and Gordon discussed the use of light frequencies for radar and communication purposes. Basically the use of light-frequency systems involves laser (optical maser) technology and forms of optical equipment. Mr. Ogland reported on the use of ultraviolet radiation. He reported on the status of presently successful techniques in power generation and the vast ranges which are possible for communication using the ultraviolet system. Dr. Eerkens considered the unique possibilities for communication in atmosphere-free space by means of gamma radiation emanating from nuclear reactors used in propelling spacecraft.

Dr. Smith discussed types of communications and radar tasks that appear to be reasonable in the next decade or two using laser and other optical equipment. The exact methods whereby laser systems can be implemented, he said, are "not easy to specify at this time partly because there are still some big unknowns in the area of modulation and receiving techniques." It is possible, however, according to the roundtable participants, to make probably meaningful order-of-magnitude calculations as to bandwidths which will be available at interplanetary distances.

The laser was developed by Hughes Aircraft Company and Bell Tele-

[142] Rechtin, in Abstract, Space Communications Roundtable, XIIth International Astronautical Congress, Washington, D.C., 1961.

phone Laboratories, and other firms have contributed significantly to the field. "Laser" is an acronym derived from "light amplification by stimulated emission of radiation." Basically, a laser produces strong oscillations by focusing radiation. Intense light is one product of the device, and the potential uses include optical radar and the destruction of selected living cells for surgery.[143]

At this point it is essential to differentiate between laser and maser technology and to comprehend the functions and capabilities of each system. Basically, masers perform the same function with respect to signals generated on very high radio frequencies as lasers do with light radiation, namely, they focus and intensify radiation and set up strong oscillations. Maser amplifiers and oscillators convert the internal energy of a molecular system into microwave energy by the interaction of electromagnetic radiation directly with the molecular system.[144] Thus, the form of energy produced by master action is an electromagnetic signal in the microwave frequencies region. Laser action, on the other hand, produces an emission of electromagnetic energy on frequencies in the range of light.

In the laser transmitter a suitable active material (solid, liquid, or gas) is placed between two parallel mirrors and excited from a special light source called a "pump" which usually surrounds the active material. Energy from the pumping light excites atoms in the active material, causing them to emit light which is reflected back and forth between the two mirrors. A process of further light stimulation produces significantly greater intensity, and ultimately an extremely narrow beam of great intensity is projected.

The unusual characteristics of the laser make it extremely useful for space vehicle navigation, according to the authors of a report prepared by General Precision, Inc., and presented at the 1961 meeting of the Institute of Navigation. A highly accurate radar capacity is inherent in this system, and it is estimated that an error of not more than one mile would be encountered when two vehicles are 100,000 miles apart. Furthermore, an extremely small power input would be required. In comparison with conventional radar systems using radio frequencies, the laser enjoys substantial advantages. The accuracy of velocity measurements is greater for the laser system. In the target acquisition phase, the position of a very small object may be determined through automatic scanning of a great volume of space. Where scanning is not required, the power advantage of the laser system enhances its value greatly in comparison with the conventional radar system.[145]

During the Space Communications Roundtable, Dr. Smith pointed out

[143] Supra note 140.

[144] Sarbacher, Encyclopedic Dictionary of Electronics and Nuclear Engineering (1959).

[145] Supra note 140.

that, in the past, communications at optical frequencies have been severely restricted by the low intensities of available incoherent light sources with black body temperatures limited to a few tens of thousands of degrees Kelvin. The laser, as a coherent light generator, provides an improvement of some six orders of magnitude in spectral brightness and makes possible optical communications at interplanetary, and perhaps even interstellar, distances. The coherent radiation from a laser can be focused into an extremely narrow beam with optics of modest size. This permits efficient transmission to large distances. Since the light is monochromatic, filters can be used to discriminate against sunlight or starlight.

In principle, Dr. Smith stated, it is possible to modulate a laser beam with a microwave signal, giving a very large channel capacity. New techniques for modulation and coherent detection will be required, and are being developed. He added that the intense narrow beam from a laser can be used for optical ranging in a Colidar (coherent light detection and ranging) system. In rudimentary experiments with a ruby laser, it has been possible to achieve seven-mile ranges in broad daylight. It should be possible, he said, to detect the surface of the moon with an improved ranging system using current laser and optical technology—as was in fact achieved not many months later.

From considerations of diffraction limitations and shot noise effects, Dr. Smith states, it is shown that the channel capacity of a given one-way communication system is theoretically proportional to frequency. At optical frequencies, however, the diffraction-limited beams involved become too narrow for reliable aiming. In terms of practical limitations, the channel capacity is inversely proportional to the operating frequency, the square of the ranging and the square of the transmitting antenna beamwidth. When fairly conservative numbers are used, this relation predicts an eight-kilocycle bandwidth for a one-way Mars-to-Earth laser system. Dr. Smith adds that Dr. C. H. Townes has suggested more optimistic assumptions which give $10''$ cycles of bandwidth. Townes' system would be visible to the naked eye at one-tenth light year and detectable at several tens of light years.[146]

The laser in its present state of development is severely limited by its inability to transmit such types of information as sound. It may be possible to develop some substitute for conventional sound transmission by recording, or some other form of breakdown of components. In this respect, it is significant that in August 1961 the first overtone of a beam of light was produced by physicists at the University of Michigan. The laser's intense beam of pure red light was focused into a quartz crystal. The second harmonic—a deep blue beam—was produced as a result of the extremely high intensity of the red light at this focus. The laser light

[146] Communication from Dr. George F. Smith to the author, Oct. 8, 1961.

has a focused intensity one billion times greater than sunlight on the Earth's surface, and this intensity produces blue light from the red in much the same way that overtones are produced in music. The physicists who observed the phenomenon suggested the analogy of a guitar, which produces certain musical sounds when strummed, and more intense overtones when vigorously "twanged." [147]

The principal implication of the successful overtone experiment in laser technology is that it may open the way for the practical use of electromagnetic waves in the frequency region of light for communication purposes. A second potential field of development relates to the investigation of the properties of materials which have been beyond study in the past, e.g., the non-linear optical properties of various materials.

Minneapolis-Honeywell Company has developed a communication system which uses what it terms "ray guns" to transmit voices secretly and silently. The system consists of sending and receiving units each shaped like a gun. The devices are aimed at each other, and a narrow beam of infrared radiation is transmitted. Words spoken into the device are converted by electronic means into infrared, transmitted between the sending and receiving units, and converted back into sound. This device has an extremely limited range of some twenty miles, which makes it of no practical significance for space communications.[148] Development and improvement of the system and adaptation to the laser technique, however, may well provide a highly useful device for space communications.

Mr. Ogland, in his presentation to the Space Communications Roundtable, as well as in an earlier paper,[149] has discussed the development of basic techniques operating in the ultraviolet spectrum. He points out that the rapidly advancing space technology of today, with vehicles being developed for missions to tremendous distances, demands an efficient means of communicating with maximum security and minimum power consumption. When communicating in space, no absorption, reflection, or scattering occurs. The main factors determining range, then, are antenna gain and receiver noise; and it is well known that with given dimensions the highest antenna gain is obtained with the shortest wavelengths. Optical frequencies, therefore, will give the narrowest beams and highest antenna gains. Infrared would suffice with regard to optical beaming ability, if it could be produced in a point source of sufficiently high power density. But no such source is known which can compete with sources emitting shorter wavelengths. Furthermore, Ogland declares, "noise considerations favor the shorter wavelengths, especially the ultraviolet." All the planets and other cold objects in space have a temperature high enough for gen-

[147] News Release, University of Michigan News Service, Physics Department, Aug. 11, 1961, made available by Science Service, Washington, D.C.

[148] Office Files, Science Service, Washington, D.C.

[149] Ogland, *Ultracom, Ultraviolet Communications* (1960) (unpublished).

erating noise in the infrared spectrum, but their temperature is not high enough for generating UV (ultraviolet). The sun radiates in UV and thus constitutes a large source of noise, but it also radiates on all the other wavelengths including radio, so that any high-sensitivity receiver will be noisy or blanketed if its antenna covers the sun. An optical receiver, because of its narrower beamwidth, can better avoid this situation. The noise of most importance in a UV sensor is the shot noise, which Ogland discussed in connection with range derivation.

Westinghouse Electric Corporation has been working on an ultraviolet communications system (Ultracom) which could provide narrow band communication over distances up to 20 million miles. At such ranges a radiated power of one watt is employed, and there is a power consumption of only a few watts. According to Westinghouse, in order to achieve the same ranges using radio frequencies, the radiated power would have to be 100 times greater and possibly more. The Westinghouse system employs a small and extremely intense spot-source of narrow band ultraviolet radiation which can be amplitude-modulated easily. The generator consists of a cathode ray tube coated with phosphor that produces ultraviolet radiation when excited by an electron beam.[150]

Ultraviolet communications systems appear to be restricted to use between positions or objects in space. Terrestrial communications would be prohibited because of absorption and attenuation of ultraviolet radiation in the earth's ozone layer and atmosphere. On the other hand, it was pointed out that the ultraviolet region of the electromagnetic spectrum offers frequencies at least one million times as great as those in the radio band normally used for space communications. Furthermore, far less power and much smaller antennas and receivers are required than at radio frequencies. The significance of these factors in space vehicle design is obvious.

The ultraviolet transmission system offers still another vital advantage, communication privacy—as well as a degree of security from man-made and natural interference.

In 1960, Westinghouse demonstrated an experimental ultraviolet communications system by which both television and voice were transmitted over a short distance. Amplitude modulation was achieved by varying the intensity of the electron beam.

At the Space Communications Roundtable, Mr. Ogland showed that the range for one watt of transmitted power at narrow bandwidth modulation, using non-coherent radiation, has been extended to millions of miles. These long ranges are attained by concentrating the radiation in a beam as narrow as two minutes of arc, which gives an antenna gain of about 77 decibels. The evident problems are to build point emitters of

[150] Klass, *Ultraviolet Tested for Communications*, Aviation Week & Space Technology, Dec. 19, 1960, at 75.

sufficiently high power density and to design detectors suitable for detecting a limited number of quanta. Ogland discussed some of the presently successful techniques in power generation, and derived a range equation similar to that of radio communication which shows the ranges possible for various parameters of values.[151]

An investigation has been made by Dr. Eerkens as to the use of reactor gammas for communications in space. Dr. Eerkens pointed out that nuclear power reactors employed in future space systems will produce large quantities of gammas as a by-product. Gamma-beam modulation methods were observed in the course of his investigation, and it was determined that this phenomenon would be limited to communication in outer space, since the gammas are heavily scattered and absorbed in the atmosphere. Gamma radiation would thus be dissipated or absorbed before receipt at an earth station.

Dr. Eerkens pointed out the advantages of the gamma communications system, particularly the relief of demands on the radio frequency spectrum which may be obtained by the use of the gamma frequency regime. Furthermore, the gamma-ray communications system permits the use of smaller antenna components and produces better focus and resolution at the higher frequencies.

This system converts what was heretofore regarded as a "nuisance," namely, the production of gamma rays in a nuclear reactor, into an asset of substantial value in a space exploration program. As Dr. Eerkens stated, "whereas the generation of microwaves or radio waves would require a special electric power source and wave generating equipment, the source of gammas is 'for free.'" [152]

Dr. Eerkens has proceeded beyond the study of transmission methods to a consideration of methods of carrying information on the gamma beam. He reports that a chopper placed in front of the conical opening, consisting of a rotating disc with equally spaced holes in it, could impart the required information on the gamma beam by modulation of the rotational speed of the disc. Other mechanical methods such as vibrators are also envisioned for the production of information to be transmitted by the gamma beam.

Dr. Eerkens' computations indicate that low-quality voice would be transmitted approximately 48 miles by a typical moon-based power plant. With an optimized over-all design, a 10- to 100-fold improvement in range is possible. Dr. Eerkens estimates that code could be transmitted 8,000 miles under assumptions which are required at this time, and there is a potential improvement to an 80,000- to 800,000-mile maximum range.

Since the Space Communications Roundtable, Dr. Huber Heffner of

[151] Ogland, *op. cit. supra* note 150.
[152] Eerkens, *Gamma Ray Communications*, in Abstract, Space Communications Roundtable, XIIth International Astronautical Congress, Washington, D.C., 1961.

Stanford University has had occasion to review the proceedings and to comment on them at the request of the author. Dr. Heffner's remarks [153] are summarized as follows:

The papers of the IAF Communications Roundtable session have largely been related to the question of optimum frequency for a communications system operating across vast distances. The answer to this question involves our capability in building a transmitter and its associated modulator, our knowledge of the transmission medium, its absorption and noise characteristics, and our capability of constructing a sensitive receiver. Except in the radio frequency range, our knowledge of all these factors is so slight and our rate of progress so great that it makes little sense to attempt at this time to predict the future course of space communications.

The basic problem which underlies all these system considerations, according to Dr. Heffner, is that of transmission of information. Before any choice of optimum frequency can be made, we need a theory of communications which is valid at optical and higher frequencies. Sheer bandwidth available does not necessarily imply greater channel capacity if we are forced to take quantum effect into account. We now desperately need a quantum theory of communications. Some steps have been made in this direction, and there is some evidence that a low-frequency quantum in some sense carries more information than one at high frequencies. If this is so, it will have a profound effect on our choice of frequency. Regardless of the solution to this problem, Dr. Heffner continues, there are a few things which we can say concerning the cost of communicating at optical frequencies or beyond. For example, it can be very generally shown that the best phase sensitive detector requires at least one photon per resolution time (reciprocal of the bandwidth) to equal the unavoidable quantum noise generated. Thus, since the high-frequency photon is more energetic, more power must be received at the detector for a given bandwidth if the carrier frequency is raised. Dr. Smith has shown that one can more than buy back this power cost by the increased gain of given system antennas as frequency increases, but only at the expense of increased aiming difficulties. If it turns out that the channel capacity also varies with frequency, these conclusions may have to be modified.

According to Dr. Heffner, this narrow beam width which goes along with high antenna gains limits the usefulness of the optical radar mentioned by Dr. Smith. Such a radar, he concludes, would certainly be impractical for search purposes, since the time required to scan an appreciable solid angle would be huge.

Dr. Heffner states that he is not as pessimistic as some others appear to be regarding the efficiency of the optical maser (laser). There are one or two schemes for d. c. pumping of optical masers which may provide high efficiency. One of these, still speculative, would involve the doping

[153] Communications From Dr. Huber Heffner to the author, Oct. 8, 1961.

of an appropriate semiconductor and the excitation of optical levels by injected electrons. This and other schemes might provide efficiencies as high as those now obtained in microwave generators. As an aside, Dr. Heffner notes that it is a curious fact that we are now able to generate kilowatts of optical power while we struggle greatly to generate one watt at a wavelength of one millimeter.

Regarding the ultraviolet system discussed at the roundtable, Dr. Heffner comments that Mr. Ogland spoke of a communication system at ultraviolet frequency which uses incoherent radiation. Dr. Heffner adds that here only amplitude modulation can be employed and none of the advantages taken of phase discrimination which are possible in a coherent system. Of course, we do not now have a coherent source in the ultraviolet, but this is a fast-moving field, and we might well anticipate the existence of coherent sources not only in the ultraviolet but also in the infrared in the next few years.

Dr. Heffner made some additional remarks concerning the incoherent system using gamma rays that was described by Dr. Eerkens. Dr. Eerkens implied that in a space vehicle the system would be "free" in the sense that the cost of the source, the reactor, could be charged to other budgets. Such a consideration may be misleading, Dr. Heffner contends, since the mass of a suitable modulating system might be inordinately great, and mass is perhaps most costly of all. Moreover, Dr. Heffner believes that Dr. Eerkens is incorrect in asserting his system is jamb-proof.

Dr. Heffner concluded, with respect to the over-all merits of the proposals made at the Space Communications Roundtable, that "a session of this sort five years from now might provide answers to the questions which at the moment we can only raise."

From our present plateau of civilization, there certainly is no clear or hopeful vista of man's utilization of these most promising technical developments in communications. In the first place, on earth there exists an almost hopeless "jungle" of languages. The customs and idols of the "tribe" tenaciously and almost fiercely grip large segments of the earth's peoples, and these customs and idols operate as extreme forces of divergence. On the one hand, there is no clear prospect of eliminating language barriers or tribal divergences from man's adventure in outer space; and, on the other hand, there is no clear indication of solutions on earth. There are, to be sure, some tiny "glimmerings" of enlightenment, such as uniform navigational codes and languages, the small progress of "universal languages" and, of course, automatic language translation systems, and so on.

During the course of the next generation, communications from outer space, and especially communications involving the mass dissemination of news and cultural and informational programs, will undoubtedly be tied down to relay transmission and redissemination on earth only by the respective governments on earth. And one may expect the same fate to await tribal groups which have been located on objects in outer space. This sorry situation is due to the bleak and devastating conflicts among the nations of earth, where there seems to be constant necessity to "slant" the news and even to censor most cultural and informational programs.

In reviewing the problems of radio orbital commands and transmission identification procedures, and in "taking a look" at the prospects for technical developments in the future, it has been necessary for commentary to be historical and rudimentary. The purpose has been to shed some light on the *beginnings* of developments. It will be quite impossible in this book to describe the almost unbelievable day-by-day progress being made in these technical fields and, in particular, in the areas of laser research, which result almost daily in new discoveries and improvements.

It may be unfortunate that the names of individual scientists and the contributions of commercial companies are mentioned, as it is a simple fact that by now there are a multitude of additional scientists and great industrial organizations making lasting and even profound contributions in the field of all types of communications. For example, recently, Sylvania Electronic Systems delivered to the Air Force a two-channel optical system using polarization modulation with a laser and delivering received signals of one order of magnitude over certain intensity systems.

In a survey report made by Barry Miller in *Aviation Week* (April 22, 1963), some of the areas of laser applications were considered: "Ranging from earth off both cooperative and non-cooperative space targets such as earth satellites; tracking and attitude determination of missile launch vehicles during powered phases of flight; re-entry communications; spaceborne altimetry; Doppler optical navigation; air, space, ground-based surveillance; air and spaceborne fire control; battlefield range finders, battlefield illuminators; optical data processing; underseas surveillance; radiation weapons; welding; secure communications; displays, data printers and recording."

It is quite evident that scientific investigations in the optical spectrum are but steps in the ever-ascending climb toward new plateaus of knowledge. Inexorably, each successive achievement also involves consideration of law and government. For example, the technique we now call the laser may well develop into the most deadly weapon contrived by man!

There is really no technical reason to prevent direct reception of transmission from point to point on earth through the means of space satellites, or from transmitting points in outer space to earth, or from earth to points in outer space. Eventually, in the case of mass disseminations, direct reception must be permitted; but this evolution may well take hundreds and maybe thousands of years.

In the author's paper, *Metalaw—The Science of Universal Jurisprudence*, which was delivered at the XIIth International Astronautical Congress and which discussed the possibility of sentient creatures on other planets, it was asserted that the universal sphericity of planets has an important bearing on the process of evolution. Thus, in examining our own world, it can be seen that the fact that man has lived on a confined surface has resulted in a concentration of "contacts." His psychosocial relationships commenced to form at the moment of his emergence as *Homo sapiens*, and day by day during the progress of civilization this confined surface has inexorably brought men closer together, until the very geography of man's "prison" has caused him to create artifacts enabling him to meet and merge and enhance his psychosocial nature on every part of the globe. Thus man emerges as a highly specialized psychosocial creature because of the confining sphere on which he has evolved.

Undoubtedly, the greatest of these artifacts is the communications system which provides a means of massive dissemination of all manner of news and informational and cultural programs to the most remote points on earth. Over the generations this artifact is bound to break down the barriers of the "tribe" and of nationalism. In the meantime, a world agency must be set up to hasten the process of human convergence. The community of nations fortunately created what is now the International Telecommunication Union in 1866, and this oldest-of-all governmental international organization is ideally equipped for the object in question. The first step is to make the ITU an operational agency which would initially coordinate and police point-to-point and mass communications from the moon, Mars, and other natural objects in outer space. In so doing the ITU would act as a kind of world communications commission to enforce order among the nations of the earth, pursuant to the individual laws of such nations.[154]

The next step will be for the ITU gradually to evolve a uniform set of regulations for all nations of the earth and to enforce these regulations. The completion of this task may take several generations or even hundreds of years. Finally, of course, national restrictions must be abrogated, and the ITU will emerge as an untrammeled world agency acting as a servant not only of the peoples of the earth but also of the human dwellers in outer space.

In a recent lecture, Sir Gerald Beadle, former head of the television network of the British Broadcasting Company, expressed his agreement with the statement of President Kennedy that to provide a mass means of dissemination of intelligence is a most critical objective of civilization. Indeed, this discussion may well be concluded with Sir Gerald's own words, in which he envisions a global network capable of breaking "through the

---

154 But see *A légitér és a kozmikus terseg nemzetkozi jogi helz zete* (The Status of Air Space and Outer Space with Respect to International Law), lecture by Dr. Imre Csabafi presented at Szeged University, March 28, 1960; and Iványi and Szadeczky-Kardoss, *Az Urkajózás a kozlekedés és a hirszogalat szemszogebol* (Space Flight From the Point of View of Transport and Telecommunications), Kozlekedési kolony, July 5, 1959 which suggest solution of these problems by international agreement.

language barrier and giving us all something of that sense of world citizenship, without which the human race is surely doomed." [155]

It is heartening to note that at the Extraordinary Administrative Radio Conference (EARC) convened in Geneva by the International Telecommunications Union on October 6, 1963, the United States proposals included: a total of 2725 Mc/s of spectrum space for the communication-satellite service, all but 100 Mc/s of which would be shared with line-of-sight radio-relay systems on the basis of sharing criteria developed by the International Radio Consultative Committee (CCIR) of the ITU; provisions for the use of satellite relay stations by the aeronautical mobile (R) service and satellite-borne aids to aeronautical radionavigation; exclusive frequency bands for the radionavigation-satellite service; frequency bands for both narrow-band and wide-band meteorological satellite systems; and a family of frequency bands throughout the spectrum for space research, all but one of which would be allocated exclusively to that service.

[155] Speech Before the New York Chapter of the Academy of Television Arts and Sciences, Oct. 5, 1961.

Additional References

Andrew G. Haley, *Space Communications and Cooperation With Iron Curtain Countries: Part II*, Signal, Dec. 1961, p. 12; _____, *Space Communications and Cooperation with Iron Curtain Countries: Part I*, Signal, Nov. 1961, p. 39; _____, *Developments Leading to and the Need for the 1963 Extraordinary Administrative Radio Conference on Space Communications*, 28 TELECOMMUNICATIONS J. 1 (1961); _____, *A Basic Program for the 1963 Extraordinary Administrative Radio Conference on Space Communications*, in PROCEEDINGS OF THE IXTH INTERNATIONAL ASTRONAUTICAL CONGRESS, STOCKHOLM 1960; _____, *Space Exploration—The Problems of Today, Tomorrow and in the Future*, in SECOND COLLOQUIUM ON THE LAW OF OUTER SPACE 44 (1960); _____, *International Scene—Preliminary Report on the Actions of the Geneva Meeting With Respect to Astronautical Radio*, Astronautics, Nov. 1959, p. 20; _____, *International Astronautical Federation and Space Communications: Remarks before the Delegates to the Administrative Radio Conference of the International Telecommunications Union, Geneva, Switzerland, Oct. 1959*, Reprinted in TELECOMMUNICATIONS JOURNAL, Nov. 1959; _____, *Space Communications*, Morning Electron (Bulletin of the International Telecommunications Conference), Sept. 25, 1959; _____, *The Importance of Astronautical Radio in the Space Age*, Signal, May 1959, p. 82; _____, *Space Age Presents Immediate Legal Problems*, in FIRST COLLOQUIUM ON THE LAW OF OUTER SPACE 5 (1959); *Space Communications—A Current Report:* Address by _____, Sacramento Section of the American Rocket Society in Sacramento, Oct. 26, 1961; *Space Radio —A World System of Communications:* Address by _____, Chicago Section of the American Rocket Society Presidential Banquet in Chicago, Sept. 25, 1961; *Space Communications—Framing the Windows:* Paper by _____, Before the

AGARD Eleventh General Assembly in Oslo, July 27, 1961; *Outline of Program for Astronautical Communications:* Paper by ——, Before the Symposium on Space Research in Buenos Aires, Nov. 28-Dec. 3, 1960; *Preparation for the 1963 Extraordinary Astronautical Radio Conference:* Paper by ——, Before the 12th Annual Meeting of the Deutsche Gesellschaft für Raketentechnik und Raumfahrt in Heidelberg May 25, 1960; *Space Communications—A Decade of Progress:* Paper by ——, Before the American Rocket Society Semi-Annual Meeting in Los Angeles, May 9-12, 1960; ——, *Space Communications—A First Approximation of Legal Problems:* Submitted to the American Bar Association Committee on Space (on request), July 8, 1961; ——, *Testimony and Statement, Hearings Before the House Committee on Science and Astronautics,* 87th Cong., 1st Sess. May 10, 1961; ——, *Space Spectrum Problems,* Unpublished Paper, Mar. 27, 1961; ——, *Space Law: The Need for International Agreement on Astronautical Radio Allocations,* Unpublished Paper, May 1, 1959; ——, *Space Communications and Astronautical Radio Activities and Proposals of the American Rocket Society and the International Astronautical Federation,* Statement Before the Federal Communications Commission, upon reopening of Hearings regarding Docket No. 11997, July, 1959.

Liability for personal and property damages in space activities

In this chapter the problems of liability for damage to real and personal property, as well as injury to third persons, are discussed. In a detailed survey of the extant and potential domestic law applicable in such cases the importance of the established doctrines of nuisance, absolute liability, negligence, and sovereign immunity are evaluated in light of the past experience of courts. Problems of evidence, its procurement and production in cases involving space activities, are also discussed. The Federal Tort Claims Act is evaluated in a space context, and the questions of compulsory insurance and recovery of vehicles are dealt with. On the international level, the questions posed by the claims of individual aliens as well as governmental claims are evaluated in detail. In view of the international problems of applicable law, determination of the proper forum for legal action, and other considerations, the need for a treaty clearly emerges. The problems of international vehicle and astronaut recovery are then discussed in the concluding portions of this chapter, along with some recent Soviet and United States proposals relating to space legal questions.

THE DOMESTIC ASPECTS OF THE PROBLEM: LAW IN THE UNITED STATES

It is entirely reasonable to assume that within the foreseeable future rocket vehicles will be used commercially as carriers between points on earth as well as in space. Before investing his capital and talent in this new endeavor, the industrialist will demand to know the risks he will have to run. Government agencies involved in such activities will also look for clarifications of the scope of governmental liability.

When a vehicle weighing thousands of pounds carrying great quantities of the most volatile fuels known to man leaves the earth, it depends entirely for its guidance on an intricate system of thousands of precisely designed and engineered parts, both in the missile itself and on the ground. The slightest miscalculation in the design, manufacture, or function of any single part, could result in disaster.

Today, in spite of the extraordinary technological advances which have been made, a launched rocket vehicle occasionally descends to earth far from the spot chosen as its destination. Not only may the place of recovery prove to be miscalculated, but also there is a possibility of misfiring and failure of safety equipment to operate satisfactorily. Inevitably, the ever-increasing range attainable by rocket vehicles will enhance the probability of such mishaps, since the greater distance will magnify the result of any error or defect in the vehicle's guidance system.

In addition to possible denial of the product of their endeavors, industry and government must consider other financial risks entailed in entering the field of space development. To perfect a particular space project requires experimentation and testing which in turn create hazards. The dangers to individual and property rights, therefore, cannot be minimized. The potential harm is demonstrated by the inability even of manned aircraft, after many years of experience and experimentation, completely to curtail the incidence of air mishaps. It is unrealistic, therefore, to assume the missile/space industry is equipped to bring about perfection during its infancy.

There are several aspects to the problem. Foremost, industry must exercise every safeguard at its command to protect human life and property. With the potential harm so great, society must insist upon no less than the exercise of the utmost care by those participating in space research and development. If this be done, then we can hope to keep at a minimum the incidence of damage caused by space exploration.

A second factor requiring examination is on what basis, if any, will the innocent and injured citizenry be compensated. Familiar legal principles tell us there usually is no liability without fault. The mere causing of a mishap does not necessarily carry with it the responsibility to make restitution to those injured thereby. An unavoidable accident may not be actionable. To recover damages the injured party may have to establish that the purported wrongdoer violated a duty imposed by society which directly resulted in the loss the injured victim suffered. The burden will be on the party claiming injury. If these principles be held applicable to damages caused by errant missiles or crashed satellites, the injured party in many instances will be left without adequate legal remedy.

Inability to marshal proof and the high costs of litigation will induce many to forego their legal rights. Even in instances where proof can be had and costs met, the great distances involved between the points of missile discharge and contact will dissuade resort to legal forums. Our traditional legal concepts are simply not equipped to cope with this problem presented by the space age.

Of course, the doctrine that ultrahazardous activity gives rise to absolute liability might be resorted to by some jurisdictions to take care of cases where damage is caused by the vagrant rocket. Ultrahazardous activity is defined as an act or conduct, not of common usage, which necessarily involves a risk of serious harm to the person or property of others which cannot be eliminated by the exercise of utmost care. This description perhaps aptly fits the launching of missiles at the present time, since the complexity of the rocket propulsion and guidance systems and the myriad possibilities of malfunctions present such a risk. If the absolute liability principle be held applicable, however, will industry be able to underwrite the tremendous costs that might very well be involved?

The excessive jury verdicts so prevalent in our large cities today could easily bankrupt a single corporation held liable for some misguided rocket. This prospect might discourage capital from entering the field at all or encourage undercapitalization, which would reduce the risk to the company but be unfair to the innocent victim.

The common law as developed in this country provides analogies which may prove helpful in the process of adapting the existing rules to the new events. In addition, statutory law is playing an ever-increasing role in the regulation of aeronautic and space activities.

8–1 The doctrine of nuisance

A type of case which appears to be close to the situation of the misguided rocket presents itself: the liability of a person in discharging fireworks. Is not the rocket vehicle a gigantic skyrocket? Most instances of damage or injury caused by fireworks have been decided on the grounds of nuisance.[1] When nuisance was not applicable, the decisions were based on negligence,[2] but it would be incorrect to think that negligent acts cannot themselves constitute an actionable nuisance. Such an action can be based on negligent acts,[3] abnormal and inappropriate activities,[4] or merely

[1] E.g., Cleveland v. Ferrando, 114 Ohio St. 207, 150 N.E. 747 (1926); Doughty v. Atlantic City Business League, 80 Atl. 473 (N.J. Ct. Err. & App. 1911); Jenne v. Sutton, 43 N.J.L. 257, 39 Am. Rep. 578 (1881).

[2] E.g., Shannon v. Dow, 133 Me. 235, 175 Atl. 766 (1934); Crowley v. Rochester Fireworks Co., 183 N.Y. 353, 76 N.E. 470 (Ct. App. 1906).

[3] McFarlane v. City of Niagara Falls, 247 N.Y. 340, 160 N.E. 391 (Ct. App. 1928); Downes v. Silva, 57 R.I. 343, 190 Atl. 42 (1937).

[4] McAndrews v. Collerd, 42 N.J.L. 189, 36 Am. Rep. 508 (1880); Landau v. City of New York, 180 N.Y. 48, 72 N.E. 631 (Ct. App. 1904).

an invasion of a public or private right caused by an unreasonable use of one's property.[5] As Professor William Prosser has said: "Nuisance, in short, is not a separate tort in itself, subject to rules of its own. Nuisances are types of damages—the invasion of two quite unrelated kinds of interests [i.e., public and private rights], by conduct which is tortious because it falls into the usual categories of tort liability."[6]

It is doubtful, however, that the doctrine of nuisance could apply to the launching of a rocket in one place and its accidental destruction of property many thousands of miles away. Nuisance usually covers damage to others caused by the use of one's own property.[7] Following our analogy between missiles and fireworks we see that, when nuisance has been applied to the use of fireworks, the damage caused has always been in the immediate area in which the fireworks were ignited.[8] This has also been true of the other kinds of acts which have been held to be nuisances: operation of a disorderly house,[9] use of explosives,[10] storage of gasoline,[11] and operation of mills and factories.[12]

The liability of aircraft owners for damage caused by crashing airplanes seems to offer a better analogy with the potential liability arising from errant rockets. In the case of aircraft the doctrine of nuisance has but a limited application. Most instances of nuisance caused by aviation have concerned the operation of airports [13] and low-flying aircraft,[14] where the activities had been unreasonable and caused substantial interference with the rights of others. The application of the nuisance doctrine to rocket operations because of unreasonable conditions existing at the launching and landing sites may be presaged by the cases involving airports. It does not appear likely that there will be any difficulty caused by low-flying rockets.

[5] Vaughn v. Missouri Power and Light Co., 89 S.W. 2d 699 (Mo. App. 1935). See Smith, *Reasonable Use of One's Own Property as a Justification for Damage To a Neighbor*, 17 Colum. L. Rev. 383, 388-90 (1917).

[6] Prosser, Handbook of the Law of Torts, §70, at 395 (2d ed. 1955).

[7] Maier v. Publicker Commercial Alcohol Co., 62 F. Supp. 161, 165 (E.D. Pa. 1954), *aff'd*, 154 F.2d 1020 (3d Cir. 1946).

[8] Cleveland v. Ferrando, 114 Ohio St. 207, 150 N.E. 747 (1926); Doughty v. Atlantic City Business League, 80 Atl. 473 (1911); Jenne v. Sutton, 43 N.J.L. 257, 39 Am. Rep. 578 (1881).

[9] Martin v. State, 62 G. App. 902, 10 S.E. 2d 254 (1940); State v. Berman, 120 N.J.L. 381, 199 Atl. 776 (1938).

[10] The Ingrid, 195 Fed. 596 (S.D.N.Y. 1912), *aff'd*, 216 Fed. 72 (2d Cir. 1914), *cert. denied*, 238 U.S. 615 (1914).

[11] Phillips v. Allingham, 38 N.M. 361, 33 P.2d 910 (1934).

[12] Krocker v. Westmoreland Planing Mill Co., 274 Pa. 143, 117 Atl. 669 (1922).

[13] Thrasher v. City of Atlanta, 178 Ga. 514, 173 S.E. 817 (1934); Swetland v. Curtiss Airports Corp., 41 F.2d 929 (N.D. Ohio 1930), *modified* 55 F.2d 201 (6th Cir. 1932).

[14] United States v. Causby, 328 U.S. 256 (1945); Swetland v. Curtiss Airports Corp., *supra* note 13.

8-2 The doctrine of absolute liability

Another basis of liability which seems almost certain to be applied in the case of damage caused by a vagrant rocket is the doctrine of strict or absolute liability arising from activities of an abnormal or ultrahazardous nature. The Restatement of Torts defines an ultrahazardous activity as an act or course of conduct which "necessarily involves a risk of serious harm to the person, land or chattels of others which cannot be eliminated by the exercise of utmost care" and which "is not a matter of common usage." [15] This description aptly fits the launching of rockets and will continue to do so for some time. The complexity of the rocket's propulsion and guidance systems and the myriad possibilities of malfunctions will present just such a risk; and for many years to come rocket launching will be an act "not a matter of common usage."

At an early point in the development of the law there was little or no concern with the fault or culpability of the defendant in a tort action. The rule then was quite objective: he who injured another had to make restitution; the fact that the defendant had not intended to harm his victim did not relieve him of the liability for his actions.[16] While it may be said that at no time was a man held to act at his peril,[17] liability was imposed regardless of any intent to injure or damage another.[18] This strict rule gave way over the years to a sentiment in the law that a person ought not to answer for damages which were not his fault. By the end of the 19th century the "no liability without fault" doctrine had achieved a dominant position; [19] however, the same century had witnessed the first return to the principles of strict liability which have since found a wider application in certain fields of human activity.[20] With the growth of the machine age which produced more numerous instances of serious property damage and personal injury, it was felt necessary to extend the doctrine of absolute liability in order to place the loss on those who, though free from negligence or tortious intent, had control over the instrumentality causing the harm and who, in most cases, were better able to foresee

---

[15] RESTATEMENT, TORTS §520 (1938).

[16] See discussion of history of liability without fault in PROSSER, op. cit. supra note 6, at 14-16, 315.

[17] Winfield, *The Myth of Absolute Liability*, 42 L.Q. REV. 37, 38 (1926).

[18] Lambert v. Bessey, T. Raym. 421, 83 Eng. Rep. 220 (K.B. 1680).

[19] RESTATEMENT, TORTS §520 (1930).

[20] In Fletcher v. Rylands, [1866] L.R. 1 Ex. 265; *aff'd* [1868] L.R. 3 H.L. 330, a new doctrine was introduced, that the occupier of land who brings and keeps upon it anything likely to do damage if it escapes is bound at his peril to prevent such escape even if no negligence could be imputed to him. See the doctrine as formulated in SALMOND, TORTS 553 (12th ed. 1957) and PROSSER, SELECTED TOPICS IN THE LAW OF TORTS 170 (1953). And see for the interpretation of the doctrine of Rylands v. Fletcher as related to ultrahazardous activities, Stallybrass, *Dangerous Things and the Non-natural User of Land*, 3 CAMBRIDGE L.J. 376, 387 (1929).

the possibility of financial loss and protect through insurance techniques against it. In recent years it has been advocated that the law of torts be used as a tool in a process of "social engineering" to discourage anti-social activities and to induce members of society to take steps to prevent injuries or to foresee and insure against the financial loss they cause.[21]

It is interesting to note that the revival of the doctrine of liability without fault has coincided with the growth of aviation. This is not to say that aviation has had any special role in this revival, but it does mean that aviation law is permeated with the concepts of "social engineering." The history of liability for damage to property caused by crashing aircraft may well indicate the course which the law will take in regard to missile and spacecraft accidents. In the early days of aviation, aircraft and balloon flights were held to be ultrahazardous activities.[22] In his treatise on air law Hotchkiss stated:

> It has been generally recognized that where an aircraft descends on a person or property on the ground beneath, or where objects thrown from the aircraft cause damage, the owner or operator of the aircraft should be held to the strictest accountability.[23]

Many states and nations passed laws making the owner of aircraft absolutely liable for any damage or injury caused by the crash of his aircraft. Thus section 5 of the Uniform Aeronautics Act [24] reads:

> The owner of every aircraft which is operated over the lands or waters of this state is absolutely liable for injuries to persons or property on the land or water beneath, caused by the ascent, descent or flight of the aircraft or the dropping or falling of any object therefrom, whether such owner was negligent or not, unless the injury is caused in whole or in part by the negligence of the person injured or the owner or bailee of the property injured.

This statute was adopted in the period from 1920 to 1930 by twenty-one states and territories in the United States.[25] States which did not adopt the Uniform Aeronautics Act have also imposed absolute liability in cases of ground damage.[26] In spite of the fact that New York did not impose

---

[21] Pound, *Theory of Social Interests,* 4 PUB. AM. SOC. SOCIETY 15 (1920). See also discussion in Bohlen, *Fifty Years of Torts,* 50 HARV. L. REV. 725 (1937); Isaacs, *Fault and Liability,* 31 HARV. L. REV. 954 (1918).

[22] Guille v. Swan, 19 Johns, R. 381, 10 Am. Dec. 234 (N.Y. Sup. Ct. 1822).

[23] HOTCHKISS, THE LAW OF AVIATION 35 (2d ed. 1938).

[24] Uniform Aeronautics Act, §5. Applying this act as adopted in South Carolina, the Fourth Circuit explained, by quoting from its prior decision in D'Anna v. United States, 181 F.2d 335, 337 (4th Cir. 1950), that "at common law the hazardous nature of the enterprise subjected the operator of the plane to a rule of absolute liability to one upon the ground who was injured." United States v. Praylou, 208 F.2d 291, 293 (4th Cir. 1953).

[25] Arizona, Delaware, Hawaii, Idaho, Indiana, Maryland, Michigan, Minnesota, Missouri, Montana, Nevada, New Jersey, North Carolina, Rhode Island, South Dakota, Tennessee, Utah, Vermont, and Wisconsin.

[26] Connecticut imposed strict liability by statute. Conn. Laws 1911, ch. 86, §11, repealed by Conn. Laws 1925, ch. 249 and Conn. Laws 1927, ch. 324. Massachusetts

strict liability by statute, a court decision held, in *Rochester G. & E. v. Dunlap*,[27] that "such chance as there may be that a properly equipped and well-handled aeroplane may still crash upon and injure private property, shall be borne by him who takes the machine aloft," and that the defendant cannot escape liability by showing that he was free from negligence. It is to be noted that in this decision it is implicit that the court did not view the airplane as an ultrahazardous instrument but rather ruled on the basis of the philosophy of "social engineering" referred to above.

As technological developments made air accidents less a product of a dangerous instrumentality than a result of human negligence, the tide turned against the imposition of strict liability in these cases.[28] Of the original twenty-one states and territories adopting the Uniform Aeronautics Act, today only six maintain the strict liability imposed by Section 5.[29] Some of the states which have abandoned strict liability have made negligence the only test.[30] Others have modified section 5 by making proof of land damage by a crashing aircraft a *prima facie* case of negligence.[31] Still others have repealed the section in its entirety and treat such a situation in the same way as they treat all tortious acts.[32] Today, most cases of liability from crashes are judged only under the general law and rules of negligence pertinent and applicable to the case,[33] and, with the exception of the six states which still enforce section 5 of the Uniform Aeronautics Act, aviation is no longer held to be an ultrahazardous activity.[34]

From this brief discussion it can be seen that the operator of a rocket range or service in the years to come can expect that his activities will be viewed by the courts as being ultrahazardous and that, at least until such operations become commonplace, he can expect to be held liable for dam-

---

similarly imposed strict liability, Acts and Resolves 1919 ch. 306, Acts and Resolves 1922, ch. 535, Acts and Resolves 1925, ch. 189 created a rebuttable presumption of negligence.

[27] 148 Misc. 849, 852, 266 N.Y. Supp. 469, 473 (Monroe County Ct. 1933).

[28] It is to be noted, however, that the return to the general rules of negligence in aviation cases does not have a counterpart in all foreign jurisdictions, many of which still apply the doctrine of absolute liability to such cases. See *infra* §8–9.

[29] Wolff, *Liability of Aircraft Owners and Operators for Ground Injury,* INSURANCE L. J. 629 (1957). The states retaining §5 are Delaware, Minnesota, New Jersey, North Dakota, South Carolina, and Tennessee.

[30] ARIZ. REV. STAT. ANN. §2–208 (1956); IDAHO CODE §21–205 (1948).

[31] ANN. CODE OF MD. art. 1A §9 (1957).

[32] MICH. COMP. LAWS ch. 259 (1948).

[33] Parker v. James E. Granger Inc., 4 Cal. 2d 668, 52 P.2d 226 (1935); *cert. denied,* 298 U.S. 644 (1935).

[34] Wilson v. Colonial Air Transport, 278 Mass. 420, 180 N.E. 212 (1932). *Cf.* 83 A.L.R. 329 (1933). The rules controlling the operation and management of aircraft are analogous to those which relate to the operation of vehicles, particularly motor vehicles, on land. But see Williams et al. v. United States, 218 Fed. 473 (5th Cir. 1955), where the Court indicates that it did not have sufficient knowledge to hold that *jet* aircraft may not normally explode in the absence of negligence.

age caused by an errant rocket although he is free from negligence.[35] As technology advances and rockets become less of a novelty, it is probable that the rule will be changed and that, as in the case of aircraft, liability will be based solely on fault.

It is to be observed that liability for such mishaps may not be limited to the owner or operator of the rocket, but that the manufacturer as well may be held to strict liability. Such a rule is advocated by Prof. Fleming James, Jr.[36] Taking a view similar to that expressed by Dean Roscoe Pound,[37] James maintains that the manufacturer should be held to strict liability because thereby he will be induced to be more astute to discover imperfections in his product, thus advancing the art and lessening the individual and social burden of the losses arising from such accidents. As had been expressed by Justice Cardozo in *Mac Pherson v. Buick Motor Co.*,[38] where a duty was found to exist running from the manufacturer through the user to the person injured even when there was no privity of contract, James states that "all limitations imposed by the doctrine of privity should go. Liability should extend to anyone who is hurt by a foreseeable use of the product." [39]

If strict liability is to be imposed on the operator of the rocket, it is to be anticipated that the manufacturer and supplier will be held similarly accountable.

8–3   *Liability based on negligence—problems of evidence*

Despite the fact that most recent writings on space law advocate the imposition of absolute liability,[40] other possibilities should not be neglected.[41] The claim that the operator of a space vehicle should be free of

[35] Prosser, speaking of nuclear liability, explained that "the first case involving damage from the escape of radiation from the use of atomic energy has yet to reach the courts" and has also predicted that, when it does, no court will refuse to apply to it "the principles of strict liability found in the cases which follow Rylands v. Fletcher." PROSSER, HANDBOOK OF THE LAW OF TORTS 336 (1959).

[36] James, *General Products—Should Manufacturers Be Liable Without Negligence,* 24 TENN. L. REV. 923 (1957). And see a discussion of the problem in the context of nuclear liability in Harvard Study, INTERNATIONAL PROBLEMS OF FINANCIAL PROTECTION AGAINST NUCLEAR RISK 52-56 (1959).

[37] Pound, *op. cit. supra* note 21.

[38] 217 N.Y. 382, 111 N.E. 1050 (Ct. App. 1916).

[39] James, *op. cit. supra* note 36, at 925. The principle has been extended to aviation cases. Manufacturers of aircraft have been held liable to their ultimate purchasers. E.g., Northwest Airlines, Inc. v. Glenn L. Martin Co., 224 F.2d 120 (6th Cir. 1955); Smith v. Piper Aircraft Corp., 18 F.R.D. 169 (M.D. Pa. 1955).

[40] E.g., JESSUP & TAUBENFIELD, CONTROLS FOR OUTER-SPACE 243 (1959); Beresford, *Liability for Ground Damage Caused by Spacecraft,* 19 FED. BAR J. 244, 246 (1959); Schachter, Comments 52 PROC. AM. SOC. INT'L L. 245, 247 (1958); Weinmann & H. C. MacDougall, *The Law of Space,* FOREIGN SERVICE J. April 1958, p. 22.

[41] It is to be noted that most of the writings calling for absolute liability have asked also for the limitation of liability and/or for compulsory insurance, as a counterpart to the aggravated system of liability. See for an instructive study of the situation in air law DRION, LIMITATION OF LIABILITIES IN INTERNATIONAL AIR LAW (1954).

any legal liability receives but little support in current discussions.[42] As a result, the alternative will be the application of the general rules of negligence as the basis of space liability. It is clear that anyone who launches a rocket has a duty to use care that his act will not injure others. If resulting damage can be shown to be a direct result of a failure on the launcher's part to exercise the care required of him, he will be held liable. No liability will ensue, however, if all that is claimed is the use of the airspace and the outer space above one's own property which does not cause an unreasonable interference with the complete enjoyment of the surface. Modern decisions setting aside the *ad coelum* doctrine give the individual no right in the airspace beyond what he can reasonably use.[43]

One seeming difficulty in the area of negligence is the determination of the standard of conduct to be observed. However, as Professor Prosser points out,[44] it is erroneous to speak of varying degrees of care. All that is required of anyone is that he act as a reasonable man. The standard of reasonable conduct requires that the care exercised be proportionate to the apparent risk. The care to be shown in keeping a stallion will be greater than that required in keeping a mare,[45] but the standard is the same in each case. Therefore, the operator of a rocket service or range will be required to show that degree of care which a reasonable man would exercise in similar circumstances. That the amount of care required of him will be greater than that required of the operator of an airline is obvious. Rockets present a greater apparent risk of damage than airplanes do.

One of the greatest problems presented by the prospect of property damage and personal injury caused by a negligently constructed or operated rocket is the difficulty of proof. In the case of an aircraft accident it is extremely difficult to obtain facts on which to base a claim of negligence. The complexity of the mechanisms involved, the impossibility in many cases of obtaining the reports of investigatory bodies, and the inadequacies of state and federal discovery techniques will all militate against the plaintiff claiming negligent damage by rockets. When the defendant is the Federal Government as will probably be the case in the next few years, these difficulties will become much more severe.

---

[42] This claim was raised, without support, by a speaker before the International Astronautical Federation in Amsterdam, 1958. It has been advocated on the ground that a satellite's flight is analogous to that of a meteor in not being subject to human control. Levitt, *Space Age Question: Who Owns a Fallen Satellite*, Army-Navy-Air Force Register, July 19, 1958 p. 10; Levitt, *Here's Tough Legal Point for Missilemen*, Army-Navy-Air Force Register, July 26, 1958, p. 10. And see other grounds for the same claim in CHAUMONT, LE DROIT DE L'ESPACE 83 (1960).

[43] E.g., United States v. Causby, 328 U.S. 256, 261 (1956); Swetland v. Curtiss Airport Corp., 55 F.2d 201 (6th Cir. 1932). And see Simeone, *Private Rights and Space Activity*, 6 ST. LOUIS U.L.J. 50 (1960).

[44] PROSSER, *op. cit. supra* note 6, at 147.

[45] Meredith v. Reed, 26 Ind. 334 (1866).

When a United States rocket lands on someone's property, the military can be expected to block off the area immediately, to set up the strictest security measures, and to be less than willing to make available to the complaining party a report on the accident. Moreover, the private citizen will find it impossible to get experts to testify on matters relating to military operations. The case of *Reynolds v. United States* [46] is much in point here. In this case a military plane testing secret equipment crashed, killing three civilian engineers who were aboard. In a suit by their next of kin the Secretary of the Air Force and the Attorney General filed a formal claim of privilege, refusing to introduce any of the reports or transcribed testimony pertaining to the accident on the basis that security procedures required such action. The District Court requested all such records in order to determine whether or not their use would jeopardize security matters. When the Air Force refused, the court held that the reluctance of the government to furnish any evidence on the question of freedom from negligence established that negligence was involved and that the claim of one plaintiff was valid. But this decision was reversed by the Supreme Court. [47]

When it is impossible to obtain evidence which is in the possession of the defendant concerning an instrumentality which is in his control, the doctrine of *res ipsa loquitur* may provide a solution. This doctrine states, in essence, that when damage has been caused by some object and it can be shown that the defendant had exclusive control over the object, and that the occurrence was such as would not normally occur if the responsible person used proper care, then it is permissible in such a situation for the jury to infer negligence. [48] It is basically a "but for" rule. If the damage could not have occurred *but for* the negligence of the defendant, the jury is permitted to weigh that possibility along with the other facts in the case.

The courts have not been uniform in determining when *res ipsa loquitur* can be applied in the case of airplane accidents. In the case of *McDonald Aviation Co. v. Queen Charlotte Air, Ltd.* [49] the court said that "the doctrine of *res ipsa loquitur* may apply to airplane accidents just as it does in other negligence cases." In a case where passengers boarded a plane and disappeared, the court held that the doctrine applied, reasoning that planes do not normally disappear in the absence of negligence. [50] In another case a federal court states that *res ipsa loquitur* could apply to establish an inference of negligence where an auxiliary fuel tank fell from

[46] 10 F.R.D. 468 (1950).
[47] 345 U.S. 1 (1953).
[48] PROSSER, *op. cit. supra* note 6, at 199f.
[49] 1950 U.S. Av. 432 (British Colombia, Can., Sup. Ct. 1950).
[50] Haasman v. Pacific Alaska Air Express, 100 F. Supp. 1 (D.C. Alaska 1951).

a diving Navy plane and crashed on private property.[51] Similarly it was held in another action, for damage to property sustained when a Navy plane crashed on it, that where the evidence shows that the day of the crash was clear and ideal for flying, the doctrine *res ipsa loquitur* may apply.[52]

However, in *William v. United States*,[53] a case involving an Air Force *B-47* that exploded in the air and showered flaming gasoline on private property, the Court of Appeals held that the doctrine could not apply. The court felt that while *res ipsa loquitur* was applicable to cases involving conventional aircraft, it could not be applied to jet aircraft because the court did not have sufficient knowledge to hold that jet aircraft may not normally explode in the absence of negligence. If the courts are unwilling to hold that the doctrine applies in cases where jets explode, there is even less likelihood that the doctrine would apply in cases of similar accidents involving rockets. The rule of *res ipsa loquitur* is a rule of human experience. While it may be inapplicable at one time for sufficient reason, it may become applicable later when experience in the area is so uniform and well established that it is not necessary to prove specific acts of negligence.[54]

In connection with the *Williams* case, the language of a court in an earlier case is enlightening. The court in *Parcell v. United States* said that the reasons for not applying *res ipsa loquitur* must be substantial:

> Mere possibilities [are] insufficient to overcome the inference supplied by the doctrine of *res ipsa loquitur*. The concept of such a doctrine would be of little value to a plaintiff if the defendant could defeat his case by introducing evidence to the effect that the accident *might* have happened in this way or that.[55]

It can be seen that in the *Williams* case the court may have usurped the function of the jury in holding that the rule could not apply. The court was technically within its rights in finding that jet explosions are not events which usually do not occur in the absence of negligence. Yet, in view of the millions of flight hours which have been logged by jet aircraft the world over, this finding may appear unrealistic. While the court's decision could not be contested on appeal, if the court was wrong it erroneously

---

[51] Dianna v. United States, 181 F.2d 335 (4th Cir. 1950). In this case a state statute made the owner of the aircraft *prima facie* liable for any damage done. The fact that the court applied that statute to the federal government indicates that, under the Federal Tort Claims Act, state law may greatly affect the liability of the government for damages caused by errant missiles.

[52] Norden v. United States, 187 F. Supp. 594 (D.R.I. 1960).

[53] 218 F.2d 473 (5th Cir. 1955).

[54] Note, *Torts—Res Ipsa Loquitur—Mid Air Explosion of Aircraft*, 33 N.C.L. REV. 670 (1955).

[55] 104 F. Supp. 110-15 (S.D. W. Va. 1952).

withheld from the jury an issue which the latter should have been allowed to consider. The court may thus have treated *res ipsa loquitur* as if it were a presumption, the application of which is a question of law to be determined by the judge. Under the majority—and best—view it is not a presumption at all.[56] The facts which give rise to a *res ipsa loquitur* situation are to be found by the jury as all other facts are found. The effect of the doctrine is not substantive, it does not determine the liability or lack of liability of the defendant; *res ipsa loquitur* is a procedural device which allows the question of negligence to go to the jury when facts are introduced which indicate that the doctrine applies.[57] Whether or not negligence can be inferred from a given set of facts is clearly a question for the jury. Thus in the *Parcell* case,[58] involving two jet aircraft which disappeared into a cloud-bank only to fall to earth moments later, the jury was properly allowed to determine whether negligence could be inferred from these facts. Similarly, in the *Williams* case [59] the jury should have been allowed to determine whether an inference of negligence could be drawn from those facts.

It may be that in the event of rocket damage the *Williams* case will be followed, with the courts holding that mishaps in the guidance of rockets are of such an uncertain causation that there could be no reasonable inference of negligence drawn from the facts that the vehicle was (or should have been!) in the control of the defendant and that it crashed injuring the plaintiff. It was seen in the discussion of the doctrine of absolute liability that, while legal principles do not change, their application does vary with circumstances. While at one time an activity may be so uncertain and obsure that the doctrine of *res ipsa loquitur* cannot apply, it being just as probable that a causation other than negligence was present, at another time the probability of negligence can become so strong that the doctrine will be applied. Thus some courts now have accepted the argument that the hazards of flying are so reduced that planes do not crash unless there is negligence.[60] A similar development will probably take place in the case of rocket damage. In passing, it should be noted that if rocket flights are so uncertain and prone to accidents with causation other than the negligence of the manufacturer, owner, or operator, they should be treated as an ultrahazardous activity with absolute liability being imposed. As the safety factor in such flights increases, as they become less an ultrahazardous activity, the doctrine of strict liability should

56 PROSSER, *op. cit. supra* note 6, at 211-14.

57 *Ibid.* See also McCORMICK, HANDBOOK OF THE LAW AT EVIDENCE 643-44 (1954) where a similar result is reached although the term "permissive presumption" is applied to *res ipsa loquitur.*

58 *Op. cit. supra* note 54.

59 Williams v. United States, 218 F.2d 473 (5th Cir. 1955).

60 United States v. Kesinger, 190 F.2d 529 (10th Cir. 1950). Note, 6 W. RES. L. REV. 420 (1955).

cease to apply, and its place should be taken by the procedural doctrine of *res ipsa loquitur.*

Before passing from our consideration of this doctrine, mention should be made of the possibility that when atomic reactors are to be used in propelling rockets, as in the Nuclear Rocket Program, the doctrine of *res ipsa loquitur* will be applied to radiation damage caused by contamination at the site of the accident.[61] Here we would have a case of damage whose cause would be extremely difficult to prove since radiation tests will, in all probability, be included in the accident reports to which the plaintiff would be denied access. All of the problems connected with the application of *res ipsa loquitur* in the case of damage caused by the vehicle's impact will also be present in determining the doctrine's application to radiation injury.[62]

8–4   Problems of sovereign immunity and the application of the Federal Tort Claims Act

Even if we are certain as to the basis of liability for rocket damage and can prove facts sufficient to entitle us to a judgment, we may still not be able to recover damages, because the defendant is immune from suit. This does not mean that the defendant has not committed a tort, but that against him the tort is not actionable.[63] There are a few well-settled cases in which a private individual has been held to have such immunity: charitable organizations, infants in certain situations, and insane persons. Presuming that a private operator of a rocket site or system will not be numbered among any of these classes, his actions will not be immune unless a statute makes him so. It may well be that society will place such a high value on these operations that to encourage the development of this art a certain degree of immunity may be extended to those who would enter the field. Obviously, a statute granting immunity in the state where the rocket is launched will have no effect in another state, perhaps thousands of miles away, in which it thunders to earth; such immunity, if it is to be effective, will have to be granted by the Federal Government or be provided by international treaty. The constitutional questions presented by such a statute or treaty are important and fascinating, but space does not permit their discussion here.

---

[61] See the British decision in Walsh v. Holst & Co., Ltd., [1958] 3 All. E.R. 33 (C.A.) applying the maxim *res ipsa loquitur.* And see Hutton, *Res Ipsa Loquitur and Actionable Radiation Injury,* 25 TENN. L. REV. 327 (1958).

[62] Hardy, *Nuclear Liability: the General Principles of Law and Future Proposals,* 36 BRIT. YB. INT'L L. 223 (1960); Hutton, *Evidentiary Problems in Proving Radiation Injury,* 46 GEO. L.J. 52 (1957) Becker & Huard, *Tort Liability and the Atomic Energy Industry,* 44 GEO. L.J. 58 (1955).

[63] PROSSER, *op. cit. supra* note 6, at 770-74.

In all probability the first tort cases concerning rocket damage will find the Federal Government as the defendant. Here the problem of immunity will be much more complex. Traditionally the sovereignty has been held to be immune from suit under the ancient and imperious maxim *rex non potest peccare*,[64] the king can do no wrong. Under this rule the Government of the United States was able to avoid liability for its tortious acts for more than 150 years in cases in which it did not consent to be sued.[65] Were this still the law, the burden of much of this chapter would be rendered academic. However, this is no longer the law. In certain cases and circumstances the Federal Government by statute has given its consent to be sued for tort. In 1946 Congress passed and the President signed into law the Federal Tort Claims Act (F.T.C.A.) [66] The act reads:

> The United States shall be liable, respecting the provisions of this title relating to tort claims, in the same manner and to the same extent as a private individual under like circumstances, but shall not be liable for interest prior to judgment or for punitive damages. . . .[67]

It would appear that this section is clear and unambiguous and that the problem of governmental tort liability is solved. This is far from true. The history of strict liability under the F.T.C.A. will illustrate this fact.[68]

The first of this line of cases was *Boyce v. United States* [69] involving a situation in which a state statute imposed strict liability for damages caused by blasting and other uses of explosives. The court held that the strict liability arising from the statute applied to the Federal Government under the Tort Claims Act unless the activity was exempt under the Act's discretionary clause (to be discussed *infra*). The next step was made in the case of *Parcell v. United States*.[70] There, the court held that the phrase "negligent or wrongful act or omission" as used in section 1346 of F.T.C.A.[71] was broad enough to cover acts giving rise to strict liability. The court indicated that:

> To say that a tort giving rise to absolute liability is not a "wrongful act" would be a technical refinement of language incompatible with that liberal

---

[64] Vates v. Alexander, 2 Rolle 292, 304, 81 Eng. Rep. 808, 815 (K.B. 1676).

[65] Osborn v. United States Bank, 22 U.S. (9 Wheat.) 738 (1824).

[66] 28 U.S.C. §2674 (1958).

[67] *Ibid.*

[68] See Note, 70 HARV. L. REV. 829 (1957); Note, 45 KY. L.J. 518 (1957); Peck, *Absolute Liability and the Federal Tort Claims Act,* 9 STAN. L. REV. 433 (1957).

[69] 93 F. Supp. 866 (S.D. Iowa 1950).

[70] 104 F. Supp. 110 (S.D. W. Va. 1952).

[71] 28 U.S.C. §1346(b) (1958): "The district courts . . . shall have exclusive jurisdiction of civil actions on claims against the United States for money damages . . . for injury or loss of property, or personal injury or death caused by the negligent or wrongful act or omission . . . if a private person would be liable to the claimant in accordance with the law of the place where the act or omission occurred."

interpretation of the sovereign's waiver of immunity which the highest court in the land has admonished us to employ.[72]

Another court in *United States v. Gaidys* [73] held that claims for property damage and personal injuries sustained when a military airplane crashed were within the kinds and classes of claims for tort wrongs which Congress intended should be judically determined under the Federal Tort Claims Act.

This orderly development of judicial doctrine was startlingly interrupted in 1953 when the Supreme Court decided the case of *Dalehite v. United States.*[74] This case, which grew out of the Texas City explosions, involved some 300 claims against the government, totaling in excess of $200,000,000. The case turned on the discretionary clause; however, there was a dictum to the effect that Congress did not intend to make the United States liable under the F.T.C.A. for torts giving rise to strict liability. While it may be said that the *Dalehite* case confirmed the adage that "hard cases make bad law," the case was a turning point in the history of strict liability under the F.T.C.A.

Soon thereafter the dictum in the *Dalehite* case was used as the basis of a decision in a case where a child was injured by a military blasting cap found near an army base. The case was *United States v. Inmon,*[75] and the court, citing the *Dalehite* decision, refused to apply the doctrine of strict liability under the Tort Claims Act.

At this point, the courts began to reconsider the problem presented by the F.T.C.A. in the area of strict liability as exemplified by the conflicting decisions in the *Parcell, Dalehite,* and *Inmon* cases. After the Court of Appeals for the Fifth Circuit had decided the *Inmon* case, the issue was also discussed in the *Dahlstrom* case. In the first instance the United States District Court, although citing the *Dalehite* decision, found that "there is persuasive authority to the effect that where the law of the state where the accident occurred makes the injurious flight of aircraft a trespass and therefore imposes liability even in the absence of negligence, then that flight is 'wrongful' within the meaning of the Tort Claims Act." [76] The court, however, allowed the discretionary function exception and dismissed the claim accordingly. On appeal, the Court of Appeals for the Eighth Circuit held that the lower court had erred in its conclusion that the plaintiff's claim was based upon the performance of a discretionary function. Although this could have enabled the court to apply directly the

---

[72] 104 F. Supp. 110, 116 (S.D. W. Va. 1952). *Cf.* United States v. Aetna Casualty and Surety Co., 338 U.S. 366 (1949); United States v. Yellow Cab Co., 340 U.S. 543 (1950).

[73] 194 F.2d 762 (10th Cir. 1952).

[74] 346 U.S. 15 (1953).

[75] 205 F.2d 681 (5th Cir. 1953).

[76] Dahlstrom v. United States, 129 F. Supp. 772, 774 (D. Minn. 1955).

F.T.C.A. to cover the absolute liability imposed by the law of the place where the accident occurred,[77] the court concluded instead that "the District Court should make specific finding whether or not the pilots of C.A.A. were guilty of negligence proximately causing injury to plaintiff and award damage if they were and deny it if they were not." [78] Thus, the court affirmed anew the dictum in the *Dalehite* case that the F.T.C.A. requires "some brand of misfeasance or nonfeasance upon which to fasten liability." An important case interrupting this chain was decided two years before the *Porter* case. In the case of *Praylou v. United States*,[79] the Court of Appeals held that where a state imposes strict liability for damage under section 5 of the Uniform Aeronautics Act [80] the United States is liable under the F.T.C.A. To hold otherwise, the court maintained, would negate the effective meaning of the section of the Tort Claims Act (28 U.S.C.A. 1346) which states that the United States can be sued in the District Courts ". . . under circumstances where the United States, if a private person, would be liable to the claimant in accordance with the law of the place where the act or omission occurred." In spite of this conflict with its dictum in the *Dalehite* case, the Supreme Court, in 1954, denied a writ of *certiorari*.[81]

Therefore, the situation as it stands today is that the Supreme Court has yet to meet the issue head on. There is the dictum of 1953 and the denial of *certiorari* in 1954. Neither can be said to be a precedent, and it is difficult to say which of the two the Court will follow when the question is again presented. Yet, if it is true that the extent of the government's liability under the F.T.C.A. is "still undetermined," [82] it is almost certain that the government will hold liable when its act is plausibly characterized as a "wrongful" trespass "not involving discretion." [83]

At the level of the Courts of Appeal and the District Courts, while doubt still persists, the tendency is in favor of the interpretation that the F.T.C.A. does not cover the acts causing absolute liability except if negligence on the part of the defendant could be adequately proven.[84] It is

---

[77] MINN. STAT. ANN., §260.012 Subd. 4 (1957).

[78] Dahlstrom v. United States, 228 F.2d 819, 824 (8th Cir. 1956).

[79] 208 F.2d 291 (4th Cir. 1953), *cert. denied* 347 U.S. 934 (1954). Porter v. United States, 128 F. Supp. 590, *aff'd*, 228 F.2d 389 (1955).

[80] Uniform Aeronautics Act §5, *supra* in §8–2 of this chapter.

[81] 347 U.S. 934 (1954).

[82] See Indian Towing Co. v. United States, 350 U.S. 61 (1955), rejecting the governmental function criterion.

[83] See Hatahley v. United States, 351 U.S. 173, 181 (1956).

[84] See, in addition to the authorities cited above, United States v. Ure, 225 F.2d 709 (9th Cir. 1955); Harris v. United States, 205 F.2d 765 (10th Cir. 1953); Woodbury v. United States, 192 F. Supp. 924 (D. Ore. 1961); Barroll v. United States, 135 F. Supp. 441 (D. Md. 1955); Bulloch v. United States, 133 F. Supp. 885 (D. Utah 1955). The last case has explicitly affirmed the idea that, if absolute liability is imposed under state law against individuals, the government will be held liable *where negligence is established*.

the author's view, however, that the reasoning of the *Parcell* case is superior to that of the *Dalehite* dictum and the *Porter* case, for it seems strange that Congress, in making a broad waiver of immunity, would have intended to maintain immunity in the case of acts causing absolute liability. If such is the case, then "negligent" and "wrongful act," as used in 28 U.S.C.A. 1346(a), mean the same thing. Such a view would be contrary to the tenets of statutory interpretation.

Another difficulty attending any attempt to predict federal liability for damage caused by a misguided rocket is the fact that the Federal Tort Claims Act creates an exception in the case of discretionary acts. The relevant portion, which is found in 28 U.S.C.A. 2680(a), reads:

Sec. 2680 Exceptions.

The provisions of this chapter and section 134(b) of this title shall not apply to:

a. Any claim based upon an act or omission of an employee of the Government, exercising due care, in the execution of a statute or regulation, whether or not such statute or regulation be valid, or based upon the exercise or performance or the failure to exercise or perform a discretionary function or duty on the part of a federal agency or an employee of the Government, whether or not the discretion involved be abused.

The hearings on the Federal Tort Claims Bill [85] clearly indicated the limited scope which Congress intended this exception to have. It was stated in the report of the House Judiciary Committee:

This is a highly important exception, designed . . . to preclude application of the Act to a claim based upon an alleged abuse of discretionary authority by a regulatory or licensing agency—for example, the Federal Trade Commission . . . or others. It is neither desirable nor intended that . . . the propriety of a discretionary administrative act should be tested through the medium of a damage suit for tort.[86]

In view of the clarity of the language used in the statute and this statement in the committee report, it seems strange that the courts have had such difficulty in finding sensible decisions for cases arising under the F.T.C.A.[87] In too many cases the line between discretionary and nondiscretionary actions has been drawn far from the point of high-level policy decision implied by the committee report. Courts have held the following to be discretionary acts excepted from the F.T.C.A.: spraying herbicide,[88] uprooting a dead tree,[89] failure to rebuild a navigational aid.[90]

[85] *Hearings on H.R. 5373 and H.R. 6463 Before the House Committee on the Judiciary,* 77th Cong. 2d Sess. (1946).

[86] *Ibid.*

[87] E.g., Dalehite v. United States, 346 U.S. 15 (1953); Coates v. United States, 181 F.2d 816 (8th Cir. 1950).

[88] Harris v. United States, 106 F. Supp. 298 (E.D. Okla. 1951).

[89] Toledo v. United States, 95 F. Supp. 838 (D.P.R. 1951).

[90] Kline v. United States, 113 F. Supp. 298 (S.D. Tex. 1953).

In the *Dalehite* case [91] the Supreme Court held the handling of fertilizer to be a discretionary act. The Court went so far as to state:

> [D]iscretionary function or duty . . . includes more than the initiation of programs and activities. It also includes determinations by executives or administrators in establishing plans, specifications, or schedules of operation. Where there is room for policy judgment and decisions there is discretion.[92]

In view of the Court's earlier admonition to use a broad construction of the Act,[93] this narrow language is surprising indeed.

Obviously, if the discretionary clause is to be so narrowly construed there could never be any recovery for damage done by an errant space vehicle. Such a construction is not reasonable; it turns the Act into nothing more than a federal motor vehicle accident law.[94] Some courts have long recognized that even if the inception of a project is discretionary, this does not mean that every subsequent step taken in furtherance of the project is also discretionary. While an act may be discretionary at the outset, it must be performed with due care and not negligently.[95] If there is negligence there can be recovery.[96] In the light of these decisions, the true meaning of the discretionary clause of the F.T.C.A. becomes clear.[97]

Fortunately, as a result of a recent Supreme Court decision, the discretionary clause is now being properly interpreted. In the case of *Rayonier, Inc. v. United States* [98] a claim for losses resulting from the negligence of government employees in allowing a forest fire to be started on government land, and in failing to act with due care in putting out the fire, was sustained. The District Court had dismissed the claim on the

[91] Dalehite v. United States, 346 U.S. 15 (1953).

[92] *Id.* at 35-36 (Footnote omitted).

[93] In United States v. Yellow Cab Co., 340 U.S. 543, 550 (1951), the Supreme Court states:

> Recognizing such a clearly defined breadth of purpose of the bill as a whole, and the general trend toward increasing the scope of waiver by the United States of its sovereign immunity from suit, it is inconsistent to whittle it down by refinements.

See also United States v. Aetna Casualty and Surety Co., 338 U.S. 366 (1949).

[94] Gelhorn and Lauer, *Federal Liability for Personal and Property Damage,* 29 N.Y.U.L. Rev. 1325, 1326 (1954).

[95] Somerset Seafood Co. v. United States, 193 F.2d 631 (4th Cir. 1951) (negligence in marking a wreck); Bevilacqua v. United States, 122 F. Supp. 493 (W.D. Penn. 1954) (failure of lockman to set out lantern at night); Pennsylvania R.R. v. United States, 124 F. Supp. 52 (D.N.J. 1954) (negligence of Coast Guard noncommissioned officer in supervising explosives).

[96] Worley v. United States, 119 F. Supp. 719 (D. Ore. 1952).

[97] Old King Coal Co. v. United States, 88 F. Supp. 124 (S.D. Iowa 1949) is the type of case where it was intended under the F.T.C.A. that the government retain its immunity. In that case the Secretary of the Interior took over operations of the company's coal mines and then decided not to operate the plaintiff's mine. As this was truly a discretionary function, there was no recovery. Another instance is Schmidt v. United States, 198 F.2d 32 (7th Cir. 1952).

[98] 352 U.S. 315 (1957).

basis of the *Dalehite* decision.[99] The Court of Appeals affirmed the ruling.[100] But the Supreme Court, with two members dissenting, reversed the lower courts, stating in clear terms that:

> ... an injured party cannot be deprived of his rights under the Act by resort to an alleged distinction, imported from the laws of municipal corporations, between the Government's negligence when it acts in a "proprietary" capacity and its negligence when it acts in a "uniquely governmental" capacity.[101]

The court also pointed out that while the heavy claims resulting from such a decision might bankrupt a municipality, they could scarcely bankrupt the United States. Thus a municipality may be exempt from liability under common law doctrines while the United States would not be under the F.T.C.A.[102] Accordingly, it is now reasonable to expect that the person injured by an errant rocket will not be denied the chance of attempting to prove the government guilty of negligence.

Another point which has caused confusion under the F.T.C.A. is the language of section 2674. There it is said that the government shall be liable "... to the same extent as a private individual *under like circumstances* ..." [103] (Emphasis added.) The argument was frequently advanced by the government that if the activity was not one which a private citizen conducted or could conduct there were no "like circumstances" and, hence, no liability.[104] However, in the case of *Indian Towing Company v. United States* [105] the Supreme Court pointed out that the Federal Tort Claims Act cannot be construed to mean that the United States had consented to be sued only when it is engaged in a type of activity that private persons perform; further, that "like circumstances" does not mean the *same* circumstances. What is meant is that the test to be applied is whether a private citizen would be liable if he were conducting the activities involved. Four of the members of the Court dissented on the ground that private persons do not perform the act upon which liability was based (maintenance of a lighthouse).[106] Even so, it would appear that rocket launching and operation will be viewed as an activity for which the government could incur liability.

The potential difficulties surrounding the application of the F.T.C.A. in this field resulted in a suggestion by some writers for its amendment so as to render the United States Government expressly liable for "any

---

[99] 346 U.S. 15 (1953).

[100] 225 F.2d 642 (9th Cir. 1955).

[101] 352 U.S. 315, 319 (1957).

[102] *Id.* at 320.

[103] 28 U.S.C. §2674 (1958).

[104] E.g., National Mfg. Co. v. United States, 210 F.2d 263 (8th Cir. 1954).

[105] 350 U.S. 61 (1955).

[106] The majority view in the *Indian Towing* case was followed in the *Rayonier* case, 352 U.S. 315 (1957).

harm caused by aircraft or spacecraft," [107] but this suggestion has not led to any positive result to date. It should be noted, however, that the F.T.C.A. is not the only applicable statute in case of damage caused by a space vehicle. Apart from the Foreign Claims Act which will be discussed later,[108] claims may be settled under the Military Claims Act [109] and the National Aeronautics and Space Act.[110] The Military Claims Act authorizes the secretaries of the various services to consider and settle claims not in excess of $5,000 arising from damage caused by non-combat military activities. Meritorious claims in excess of $5,000 arising under the Military Claims Act may be certified to Congress for settlement by the secretary of the military department concerned. Similarly, the Space Act authorizes the National Aeronautics and Space Administration (NASA) to "consider, ascertain, adjust, determine, settle, and pay, on behalf of the United States . . . any claim . . . resulting from the conduct of the Administration's functions." [111]

As in the Military Claims Act, the maximum payment authorized under the Space Act is $5,000. Also in both cases, settlements are not limited to claims arising within the United States. Nor is there any discretionary function exemption or requirement of negligence in either act. As a result, the difficulties which may arise in the application of the F.T.C.A. will not have counterparts in the application of these two acts. On the other hand, the provisions of both acts are far from satisfactory as they are limited to relatively trifling claims and stand short of covering the meritorious larger claims in excess of $5,000.

8–5   Problems of compulsory insurance

Limitation of liability and/or compulsory insurance have often been recommended to counteract the hardships of absolute liability.[112] The potential claimants for indemnities in a future space incident, like the victims of an air crash, are unknown until the damage is already inflicted; yet they cannot themselves take insurance in advance. In such a case, insurance should necessarily be made by the operator,[113] be it the Federal

---

107 See, e.g., Simeone, *Private Rights and Space Activity*, 6 St. Louis U.L.J. 50 (1960).

108 See §8–6 *infra*.

109 57 Stat. 372 (1943) as amended, 10 U.S.C. §2733 (1958)

110 72 Stat. 426, 431 (1958); 42 U.S.C. §2473 (1958).

111 *Ibid*. §203 (13)(a).

112 *Supra*, note 41.

113 A model might be the provisions for indemnification, limitation of liability, and compulsory insurance which apply to atomic energy licenses, 71 Stat. 576 (1957), 72 Stat. 525 (1958), 72 Stat. 837 (1958), 42 U.S.C. §2210 (1958); de Rode-Verschoor, in *The Responsibility of the States for the Damage caused by Space Bodies*, Symp. 460, proposed the establishment of an international guarantee fund for paying the damage caused by satellites and that each state "interested in astronautics" deposit a sum of money in the fund.

Government or a private corporation. Another suggestion has been offered, however, with respect to air crashes and might still be advocated for space accidents, that is, to impose a general insurance to spread the risk, at a trifling cost per unit, over the property on the earth's surface.[114] This proposal amounts in fact to the imposition of a tax for the benefit of the potential claimants in future crashes. It has not been taken seriously in the field of air law and one may not expect a better chance for it in the field of space law.

One working solution would be a system of compulsory insurance operating essentially on the successful pattern of workmen's compensation laws. An administrative board, e.g., one set up under United Nations auspices, would process and assess claims. Under such a system, industry benefits by being able to assign a fixed cost to this item and by obtaining protection against excessive verdicts. The claimant enjoys the advantage of a prompt settlement and the right to compensation without having to prove fault, a fair exchange for the uncertain possibility of a higher jury award.

8–6 Problems of recovery of space vehicles

Several complex problems arise in connection with attempts to recover errant rockets or crashed satellites. Does the finder of such property have any claim to it? Is he entitled to a reward for its recovery? Can he retain it until he receives compensation for the damage it has inflicted? May the government enter upon his land to look for it?

A brief review of the general law applicable to lost property should be helpful in obtaining an understanding of some of these problems. In general, "lost" property may be defined as property as to which the owner has involuntarily parted with possession and the location of which is unknown to him. "Abandoned" property, on the other hand, is property as to which the owner has parted with possession voluntarily. Abandonment occurs when the owner, with the specific intent of desertion and relinquishment, casts away or leaves behind his property. If the owner of lost property gives up all efforts to recover it, then a case of "constructive abandonment" has arisen. Thus it is evident that abandonment is a question of intent.[115]

These distinctions in the various types of "lost" property are important because they determine to a large extent the rights of the finders. Abandoned property is generally regarded as belonging to the first finder. The discoverer of lost property, on the other hand, though it be discovered on

---

[114] De la Pradelle, Preface to Stanesco, LA RESPONSIBILITÉ DANS LA NAVIGATION AÉRIENNE (1951); Knauth, *Aviation and Admiralty*, 6 AIR L. REV. 226, 237 (1937).

[115] Brown, *The Law of Personal Property* §§6, 157 (2d ed. 1955); 1 C.J.S. Abandonment §2(b) (7) (1936).

his own land, has no rights of ownership in the lost article as against the true owner. If the finder knows or has reasonable means of discovering the owner, but appropriates the goods to his own use, he is guilty of larceny.

Applying these general legal principles to the case of errant missiles or spacecraft, it can be seen that such vehicles must be considered legally "lost" property of the United States inasmuch as there is an involuntary separation of owner and property. It is true that by releasing the vehicle the government voluntarily parted with it in a very liberal sense. Such a separation process, however, may be regarded as having been effected only to enable the vehicle to arrive at its planned destination and not as a "release" on an uncharted course in such a manner as to remove it from the classification of "lost" property. It cannot be regarded as legally "abandoned," since the intent to abandon is lacking.[116] The elaborate preparations and planning which go into the launching of a rocket vehicle and the technically intricate instruments used to guide it negate any implication that abandonment might be intended. Clearly, unforeseen circumstances or accident, rather than intent, determine the errant rocket's erroneous destination. In certain cases, notification in the form of a statement on the vehicle that it is the property of the United States Government, together with instructions for reporting to the proper authorities, further augment the claim that retention of ownership is intended. The strongest argument against any assertion by a finder of such property that he acquires any rights thereto is the fact that Congress has specifically provided various means by which government property can be abandoned [117] and that, while missiles and similar devices may be "abandoned" in the physical sense, there can be no abandonment which transfers title to another person unless the statutory methods of abandonment are complied with.

In short, under applicable law the finder of one of these devices acquires no rights therein. Consequently, an appropriation to his own use would constitute larceny. One who converts government property to his own use may be subjected to a fine of $10,000 and/or imprisonment for ten years.[118] Incidentally, it should be pointed out that though reluctance to approach such an awesome-appearing weapon as a guided rocket might

---

[116] In the case of many earth satellites there is no predictable destination; on the contrary, it is often not expected that any portion of the satellite will be recovered. Even so, the intent is certainly not to abandon the satellite if it can possibly be recovered.

[117] E.g., 66 Stat. 593 (1952), 40 U.S.C. §483h (1958); 63 Stat. 398 (1949), 40 U.S.C. §512 (1958).

[118] 62 Stat. 725 (1948), 18 U.S.C. §641 (1958). In addition, existing laws make it a crime for an unauthorized person to photograph or sketch certain government equipment. The definitions under this statute are sufficiently broad to include guided missiles and similar devices. 62 Stat. 737 (1948), 18 U.S.C. §795 (1958), and Executive Order No. 10104, 15 Fed. Reg. 597 (1950).

not deter a finder from harmful tampering, notification on the rocket of the existence of legal penalties might accomplish this result.

Granting, then, that the United States does not lose title to an errant vehicle by virtue of an unforeseen landing on non-government property,[119] we must now consider the method by which the government could recover its property.

May government agents enter upon the private land in question, or must resort be made to the courts? As a consequence of the action of frictional forces of the atmosphere, it is probable that portions of crashed rockets which land on the soil will be fused metallic lumps, scarcely distinguishable in many instances from meteorites. Consequently, where the landowner asserts that a meteorite has landed on his soil and that it belongs to him,[120] may the government enter upon his land to examine the object and assure that it is in fact a meteorite and not a portion of a rocket?

While the laws on the right of the owners of a lost object to enter upon the property of another to effect its recovery are not wholly clear, the view adopted in the majority of court decisions and the *Restatement of Torts* is to the effect that, while the entrance legally constitutes a trespass, it is privileged if carried out in a reasonable manner, at least in cases where an article is present through no fault of the owner.[121] The same rule is generally applied where the property on another's land is not "lost" because of the fact that the owner knows its location. Thus, for example, where the government has been able to track a vehicle and know its location, it could be recovered by entry into the land under the general law so long as the landing thereon was not previously planned.[122]

Naturally, the government should compensate the landowner for any damage done by the object, as well as for any damage caused by the recovery thereof.[123] Such compensation probably could be made under the Federal Tort Claims Act, as already discussed, or in some instances under the Military Claims Act. Thus far, we have painted a relatively simple picture. Let us now deal with some of the more complex factors involved.

In order to provide adequate defense measures against vehicles

---

[119] Nor would a landing on state-owned property alter the results, with the possible exception that the additional problem of whether the state or the individual finder was entitled to any offered reward might arise.

[120] An aerolite embedded in the soil belongs to the property owner and not to the finder. Goodard v. Winchell, 86 Iowa 71, 52 N.W. 1124 (1892); accord, Oregon Iron Co. v. Hughes, 47 Ore. 313, 81 Pac. 572 (1905) (meteorite landing on a person's property belongs to him).

[121] RESTATEMENT, TORTS §198 & §200.

[122] While demand of the landowner for return of the article is sometimes said to be required prior to entry, this is not essential if the circumstances would make such a demand unreasonable. PROSSER, HANDBOOK OF THE LAW OF TORTS 143-50 (2d ed. 1955).

[123] Under existing law it might be liable only for the latter item if not negligent. HARPER & JAMES, THE LAW OF TORTS §1.17 (1956).

launched by unfriendly foreign nations, and in order to protect life and property, it would seem desirable for Congress to institute measures designed to insure knowledge, examination, and recovery of all such objects. Besides the need to render these objects harmless as expediently as possible, it is essential that the United States be in a position to examine such objects for the purpose of obtaining knowledge of any technological developments incorporated therein. Further, if rockets from a friendly foreign nation accidentally land on United States soil, sound foreign policy dictates their immediate acquisition by the government for appropriate disposition.

The author has discussed with members of Congress a measure which would overcome many of these problems. The proposed law would prohibit the unauthorized possession, acquisition, or receipt of any errant rocket or similar device except as might be required in the interests of the United States as prescribed in equitable regulations.[124] In addition, the bill would place a duty upon any person having information as to the existence or whereabouts of such a device to report the same to the Department of Defense or to any military or naval installation. Authority would be provided to offer appropriate rewards for such information. Moreover, the proposed bill would permit the recovery and disposition of missiles, rockets, earth satellites, and meteorites by such persons and in such manner as the Secretary of Defense might prescribe by regulation. Authorized persons would be permitted to enter upon public or private land where such objects are located in order to effect recovery or possession thereof. The United States would hold the landowner harmless from any claim based upon his compliance with the provisions of the law and would, in addition, entitle the landowner to compensation for any damage done to his property.

The authorization to enter upon private property is not unique in Congressional legislation. The Atomic Energy Act of 1946 granted the Atomic Energy Commission permission to enter upon private property with or without the owner's consent for purposes of investigation and inspections

[124] Precedent for making unlawful the unauthorized possession or acquisition by private individuals of devices essential to the nation's security may be found in the Atomic Energy Act of 1954, 68 Stat. 921 (1954), as amended, 42 U.S.C. §2011, §2077 (1958), in which similar provisions were enacted with regard to atomic weapons and atomic source materials. However, it is possible that little difficulty would be experienced in the subject field even in the absence of the proposed legislation, since it may be assumed that the average citizen for his own protection as well as in the public interest will cooperate in such situations. In addition, retention of any foreign missile might be prohibited in certain situations by virtue of 62 Stat. 745 (1948), 18 U.S.C. §957 (1958), which makes possession or control of any property in aid of a foreign government a crime if such property is designed or intended for use in violating any rights, obligations or laws of the United States. Nevertheless, the field with which this proposed legislation deals is of far too vital a nature to depend on conjecture and speculation as to the voluntary cooperativeness of the people.

in connection with the discovery of source materials.[125] This legislation was justified on the basis of the "common defense and security"[126] and the protection of public health and safety.[127] Further, the Act of September 30, 1950,[128] as amended, provided that in any major disaster federal agencies are authorized, when directed by the President, to render assistance and to perform on public or private lands protective and other activities essential for the preservation of life and property. The power necessary in this connection stems from the very essence of sovereignty—a nation's right to maintain its existence and to carry on its governmental functions. At the same time, the proposed legislation would impose a duty similar to that found in existing state and municipal statutes requiring finders of lost property to notify or turn it over to the police officials for return to the legal owner. An analogy for the authority to offer rewards for information on these devices is to be found in the Atomic Weapons Reward Act of 1955, which authorized payments up to $500,000 for information concerning atomic weapons unlawfully possessed or introduced into the United States.[129]

INTERNATIONAL
LIABILITY FOR SPACE ACTIVITIES

The question of payment for damage done in foreign states by errant rockets presents problems similar in some respects to those already discussed in the law of the United States. One should distinguish, however, between two types of claims—the claim of an individual alien and the claim of a foreign government.

8–7 The claim of an individual alien

As a sovereign nation the United States is not responsible to any individual nor is it subject to suit in the courts of any foreign country, except as it accepts such responsibility or permits itself to come within the jurisdiction of any such court. Obviously, from the standpoint of shouldering its responsibilities to fellow member states of the community of nations, the United States can be expected to make just compensation for any damage done by crashing errant vehicles.[130]

In 1942 Congress enacted a measure for the purpose of promoting and

[125] 60 Stat. 762 (1946).
[126] 60 Stat. 756 (1946).
[127] *Ibid.*
[128] 64 Stat. 1110 (1950), 42 U.S.C. §1855(b) (1958).
[129] 69 Stat. 366 (1955), 50 U.S.C. §§47a–47b (1958).
[130] Compare Korovin, *International Status of Cosmic Space*, Symp. 1062, 1067.

maintaining friendly relations by the prompt settlement of meritorious claims for damages, personal injuries, or death occurring in a foreign country to an inhabitant of that foreign country and caused by acts or omissions of military personnel or civilian employees of our military forces or otherwise incident to the noncombat activities of such military forces. This law, familiarly known as the Foreign Claims Act, permits the Secretary of a military department to settle and pay any claim for not more than $15,000 for damage caused by noncombat activities of the armed forces under his jurisdiction. Claims in excess of $15,000 may be certified to the Congress for settlement.[131] Under the terms of the Foreign Claims Act certain claims arising from errant United States missiles could be expeditiously settled. On the other hand, the purview of the law does not encompass all the foreseeable problems of damage caused by errant rockets. In those cases not covered, the affected nation will have to rely on treaties with this country which set up means for presenting such claims or, in the alternative, will present its claims through established diplomatic channels.

In the past there have been numerous instances where claims have been presented to the State Department in this manner. In such instances, the State Department can, upon determination that there is merit to the claim, request Congress to grant the money requested. Such a procedure has been followed many times in instances involving damage caused by American ships.[132] Similarly, when an aircraft of our Marine Corps crashed in the Dominican Republic, killing an inhabitant of that country, Congress, upon the recommendation of the State Department, appropriated funds for the family of the deceased in spite of the fact that an investigation disclosed the accident was in no way attributable to any fault on the part of this country.[133] The same procedure was followed in payment for injuries sustained by a Canadian citizen when a water-filled dummy bomb dropped from a Navy plane.[134] Still another procedure could also be cited. In the past this country has, by agreement with other nations, established joint commissions authorized to hear and decide claims by citizens of one nation against another nation.[135] Such procedure should be appropriate in cases involving errant space vehicles.

It seems likely that, because of the defense of sovereign immunity, aliens will have little opportunity to recover their losses through domestic

[131] 57 Stat. 66 (1943), 10 U.S.C. §§2734, 2735 (1958).

[132] 5 HACKWORTH, DIGEST OF INTERNATIONAL LAW 476 (1943).

[133] Id. at 477.

[134] Id. at 478.

[135] 2 HACKWORTH, DIGEST OF INTERNATIONAL LAW 344 (1941) discusses the work of the claims commission set up by the United States and the U.K. which dealt with the claims arising from damage to trees in the State of Washington caused by fumes coming down from Canada. The exchange of diplomatic notes between this country and Mexico for damages caused by Mexican bullets crossing the border into the United States is discussed in the same volume at 282.

judicial means. Such individuals may, however, be paid *ex gratia* [136] with no admission of legal fault, or they may persuade their own governments to handle their claims on the international level.

8–8 The claim of a foreign government

Along with private claims of the victims of a space vehicle accident, there also can be claims initiated or espoused by a foreign government as a result of damage caused to it or to its individual citizens. The crash of a space vehicle may cause enormous damage to the territory of a foreign state or to public properties in it. It may also constitute an affront to its sovereignty. In such cases the foreign government may be expected to raise the issue of the responsibility of the nation from which the vehicle was first launched. The claim in this case will be made by the foreign government in its own behalf to recover indemnities for the monetary loss and/or the moral damage it has suffered. On the other hand, a government as the *parens patriae* of its citizens may espouse the claim of any of them against a foreign government since individual citizens cannot pursue their claims in international courts except in limited cases. Only states may be parties in cases before the International Court of Justice (I.C.J.),[137] but according to the orthodox theory upheld in the *Mavromatis* [138] and the *Nottebohm* [139] cases a state may ensure respect for international law in the person of its own individual citizens by bringing their claims before the World Court.

Since the early writings on space law, emphasis has been put on the necessity of submitting disputes between governments over claims arising from space exploration to the I.C.J.[140] The jurisdiction of this court is limited, however, by the provisions of its statute and by the reservations in the declarations of acceptance of its jurisdiction. Assuming that these instruments will not preclude the court from ruling in an indemnification case for damage caused by the crash of a space vehicle, the remaining problem will be, what substantive rules could it apply to such a case?

8–9 Determination of the applicable rules: liability in actual practice and in the general principles of law

We have elsewhere advocated the idea that space travel and space relations in general would be better regulated by new rules, and that natural

---

[136] Staff of the House Select Committee on Astronautics and Space Exploration, SURVEY OF SPACE LAW, H. Doc. No. 89, 86th Cong. 1st Sess. 25 (1959).

[137] STAT. INT'L CT. JUST. art. 34.

[138] P.C.I.J. ser. A, No. 2 at 12 (1924).

[139] [1955] I.C.J. Rep. 4.

[140] E.g., Schachter, *Who Owns the Universe?*, in ACROSS THE SPACE FRONTIER 118, 127 (Ryan ed. 1953). And see Report of the *Ad Hoc* Committee on the Peaceful Uses of Outer Space, U.N. Doc. A/414 (1959).

law is the correct basis for unrestricted activities in space.[141] Yet, when the legal problem is reduced to the responsibility of the launching state toward those injured through the operation of its space program, the existing norms may prove helpful in allowing a just remedy. An investigation of these existing rules is thus imperative, and as the World Court will, in the absence of international conventions, apply international custom and the general principles of law recognized by civilized nations, the inquiry will be limited to the potential basis of space liability under these two sources of law.

Apart from the few cases in which state responsibility was founded on the mere occurrence of damage and the bond of causality,[142] the general rule of international law applied today is still what Oppenheim formulated half a century ago in the following words:

> An act of State injurious to another State is nevertheless not an international delinquency if committed neither wilfully and maliciously nor with culpable negligence.[143]

In the *Corfu Channel* case,[144] the International Court discussed in detail the basis of state responsibility in order to decide whether Albania was answerable to the damage sustained by the United Kingdom as a result of the explosion of mines destroying its ships in Albanian waters. The court found that Albania, having exclusive control over its territory should have known of the mine-laying and should have taken necessary steps to warn shipping. As Albania had neglected to do so, the court reached the conclusion that "these grave omissions involve the international responsibility of Albania." [145] In so holding, the court was still in the limits of the traditional rule, as an act of omission is not less a fault than an act of commission leading to the same result. In his dissent, Judge Azevedo noted that "the notion of *culpa* is always changing and undergoing a slow process of evolution; moving away from the classical elements of imprudence and negligence, it tends to draw nearer to the system of objective liability." [146] Admitting that the stage has not been reached where absolute liability becomes the rule, the same judge found that the tendency to establish presumptions that would simply shift the burden of proof to the defendant must be accepted in international law.

The arbitral award in the *Trail Smelter* arbitration [147] was much closer

---

[141] See Appendix V-B, Item 63. See also Chapter 2, *supra*.

[142] See SOHN & BAXTER, CONVENTION ON THE INTERNATIONAL RESPONSIBILITY OF STATES FOR INJURIES TO ALIENS, DRAFT No. 12 WITH EXPLANATORY NOTES 70 (1961).

[143] OPPENHEIM, 1 INTERNATIONAL LAW 343 (New York: Longmans, Green & Co., Lauterpacht ed., 8th ed. 1955; Courtesy of David McKay Company, Inc.).

[144] [1949] I.C.J. Rep. 4.

[145] *Ibid.* at 23.

[146] *Ibid.* at 85.

[147] (United States v. Canada), U.N. Rep. Int'l Arb. Awards 1905 (1938); 33 AM. J. INT'L L. 182 (1939).

to the notion of absolute liability. In this award Canada was held liable for the damage done to crops over the American border by an installation in British Columbia. The only basis of liability that was found on the part of Canada was its knowledge of the potential cause of harm and its inaction towards it.

Moreover, the Franco-Mexican Mixed Claims Commission had ruled at an earlier date that when a damage occurs to aliens because of an incompetent officer the international responsibility of a state will have a purely objective character, and that it will rest upon "a conception of guarantee where the subjective notion of fault plays no part." [148]

A more recent and more relevant precedent, thought non-judicial, is the payment by the United States to the Government of Japan *ex gratia*, without recognition of liability of the sum of two million dollars in compensation for injuries or damage sustained as a result of nuclear tests in the Marshall Islands in 1954.[149]

This small number of cases can hardly establish a rule of law according to which a state would be liable if its injurious act is committed neither maliciously nor with negligence. Yet, there is a growing concern in modern writings about situations in which considerations of justice and fair play require the establishment of a new rule. Two types of situations were particularly noticed in this respect.[150]

The first would be the violation of the territory of a state, causing damage in it, made by another state which did not intend the violation nor the resulting harm and which took all possible precautions against the causing of injury. The second instance would be the conduct of ultra-hazardous activities with resultant harm to aliens. Clearly both situations find their typical application in the context of space exploration—a fact which makes this field a potential area for a radical development in the rules of state responsibility, to bring it closer to the strict standards of absolute liability. The weight of precedent is still against such a solution, however, insofar as customary law is concerned,[151] and were it the only source of the rules applied by the court, the determination of fault in the conduct of the defendant state would normally be required in this field as in other instances of state responsibility.

Another source of the applicable rules before the World Court is what is termed in Article 38(1)(c) of its statute, "the general principles of law

---

[148] Caire (France v. Mexico), Jurisprudence de la Commission franco-mexicaine 207; [1929-30] Ann. Dig. 146 (No. 91).

[149] U.S. Note to the Japanese Government, 32 DEP'T OF STATE BULL. 90 (1955).

[150] SOHN & BAXTER, *op. cit. supra* note 142, at 143.

[151] An application of absolute liability already exists in conventional law: Convention on Damage Caused by Foreign Aircraft to Third Parties on the Surface, Oct. 7, 1952, I.C.A.O. Doc. 7364, 52 AM. J. INT'L L. 593 (1958). See Latchford, *The Bearing of International Air Navigation Conventions on the Use of Outer Space*, 53 AM. J. INT'L L. 405 (1959), and generally SEARA VÁZQUEZ, INTRODUCCIÓN AL DERECHO INTERNACIONAL CÓSMICO 69-90 (Mexico 1961).

recognized by civilized nations." If this source is to provide the court with workable rules, there should not be any requirement of unanimity among domestic legal systems. It may prove adequate that the majority of the legal systems in force indicate the existence of a general principle which is applied in one way or another in most domestic systems and which shocks the fundamentals of none of them. In this respect the role of the court should not be to import private law institutions "lock, stock, and barrel," but rather as Lord McNair stated in his separate opinion in the *International Status of South West Africa Advisory Opinion:*

> [T]he true view of the duty of international tribunals in this matter is to regard any features or terminology which are reminiscent of the rules and institutions of private law as an indication of policy and principles rather than as directly importing these rules and institutions.[152]

It is, then, in this light that the law of different nations should be carefully examined to find out what *policy and principles* could be concluded from the specific rules which their courts will apply when confronted with the same problem.[153] As yet no instance of space liability has been brought before domestic courts, and so the study must be directed to the field of liability for damage caused through ultrahazardous activities in general, with particular emphasis on liability in private air law.

Enough has been said above concerning the applicable rules in the courts of the United States. The law in the United Kingdom is not much different. *Rylands v. Fletcher,* which established the rule that actual negligence need not be proved in connection with damages due to ultrahazardous activities, is followed within the limits of its application,[154] and absolute liability is furthermore imposed by special legislations for damage caused by a plane [155] or by ionizing radiations.[156]

In France, the simple language of the Civil Code [157] enacted in 1804 has been reinterpreted through the judiciary to make the "guardian of the thing" liable for damage caused by it unless he proves that the accident was due to either a general *force majeure,* an act of the plaintiff himself, or an unforeseeable and irresistible act of a third party.[158] Along with this

---

[152] [1950] I.C.J. Rep. 128, 148.

[153] See generally Minasjan, Istochniki Sovremennogo Mezhdunarodnogo Prava (Sources of Contemporary International Law) (USSR 1960).

[154] *Supra* note 20.

[155] The Air Navigation Act, 1920, 10 & 11 Geo. 5, c. 80, §9. The Air Navigation Act, 1936, 26 Geo. 5 & 1 Edw. 8, c. 44 makes certain amendments and provides for the limitation of liability.

[156] The Nuclear Installations Act, 1959, 7 & 8 Eliz. II, c. 46, §4(1); and see Hardy, *Nuclear Liability: The General Principles of Law and Further Proposals,* 36 Brit. Yb. Int'l L. 223 (1960).

[157] Art. 1384 of the *Code Civil* states that whoever has the custody of a chattel is liable for any damage caused by that chattel.

[158] See generally 2 H. & L. Mazeaud & Tunc, Responsabilité Civile 340-46 (5th ed. 1958).

general judicial trend, the French legislators have made provision in several cases to ensure the compensation of losses caused by hazardous instrumentalities without requiring proof of fault or negligence on the part of the defendant. Most relevant among such cases is the law of May 31, 1924 imposing absolute liability in air navigation.

In Germany, while the Civil Code has based liability on fault, special legislations have imposed strict liability for damage caused by railways, cars, aeroplanes, and nuclear reactors.[159]

The Soviet legal system, like the American, has seen a retreat from the standard of absolute liability in aviation cases for damage inflicted upon third persons. The 1935 Air Code provided for liability for damage to third persons and property in all cases "where the defendant does not prove that the damage was the result of the intent or gross negligence of the victim." [160] The 1961 Air Code, however, makes no provision for liability to third parties.[161] Therefore, the governing law is that found in § 90 of the Fundamentals of Civil Legislation of the USSR and the Union Republics (1961), which provides that the defendant will be held liable unless he proves that "the injury was the result of *force majeure* or the intent of the person injured."

The influence of the legal systems cited above on large areas of the world is not unknown. One could thus trace the imposition of strict standards of liability for damage caused in the course of dangerous activities in common law countries as well as in civil law countries and in the countries influenced by Soviet law. Insofar as liability in aircraft cases is concerned, it is much harder to find a country where the ordinary rules of tort are applied in this field, than to find out where absolute liability is the rule.[162]

This review demonstrates that the general tendency of the world's domestic legal systems favors the imposition of stricter standards in liability when the damage is caused by an ultrahazardous instrumentality. Such a policy could, in the judgment of this writer, be embodied in a rule emerging from the source of law applied by the World Court under the name of "general principles of law recognized by civilized nations." [163] Such a rule could thus be claimed to be a part of the existing law and

[159] See Harvard Study, INTERNATIONAL PROBLEMS OF FINANCIAL PROTECTION AGAINST NUCLEAR RISK 24 (1959); Hardy, *supra* note 156, at 235-36.

[160] §78, FLEISHITS, OBYAZATEL'STVA IZ PRICHNENIYA VREDA I IZ NEOSNOVATEL'NOGO OBOGASHCHENIYA 149-50 (USSR 1951).

[161] The one exception is §68 which provides a rule of comparative negligence for collision of two or more aircraft.

[162] Eubank, *Land Damage Liability in Aircraft Cases,* 57 DICK. L. REV. 188 (1953). The following countries are enumerated as imposing strict liability: Austria, Belgium, Czechoslovakia, Denmark, Eire, Finland, France, Germany, Great Britain, Hungary, Italy, Norway, Sweden, Switzerland, USSR, Yugoslavia, Algeria, Chile, El Salvador, and Venezuela. This enumeration is not exhaustive, as a great number of other countries also follow the rule of strict liability in air accidents.

[163] Accord, Hardy, *op. cit. supra* note 156, at 237.

not merely a possibility for the future development of the law of state responsibility.

There should not be any doubt at the present time that this rule could be applied by the court in behalf of a victim of a space vehicle accident. Space exploration is a typical example of an activity which involves an unusual risk of harm to the public although the activity is undertaken for the general welfare.

8–10   The need for a treaty

Even though a rule of absolute liability could be advocated on the basis of such arguments as those provided above, all are agreed [164] that the question would be better settled by an international treaty on legal and financial liability for injuries resulting from space vehicle accidents. In this regard, the United States' position, as recently declared in the Legal Subcommittee of the United Nations Committee on the Peaceful Uses of Outer Space (UNCOPUOS), is to the effect that two basic principles should be contained in the proposed treaty.[165] One is that the liability of a launching state or launching organization should be absolute without requiring proof of negligence; the other principle is that liability should prevail whether injury or damage occurred on land, on the sea, or in the air. While this proposal has not yet resulted in any actual agreement, it is hoped that future discussions will eventually lead to the formal adoption of such principles in the international legal system.

More specifically, the United States proposal offered at Geneva requests the U.N. Secretary-General to constitute a small advisory panel of legal experts drawn from various geographic areas and that the panel so formed prepare a draft international agreement. The viewpoint of the United States is that such an agreement should provide for the launching state or international organization to be internationally liable for damage caused; proof of fault by a claimant should not be required; the care exercised by the launching party should be a mitigating factor; local remedies need not be exhausted before a claim may be placed against the offending state or organization; claims should be presented within a reasonable time of the loss, damage, or injury; and finally, the I.C.J. should have agreed jurisdiction to adjudicate disputes relating to the agreement in the absence of an accord between states on some other means of settlement. The draft agreement, when completed, would then be forwarded to the Legal Subcommittee of UNCOPUOS for further appropriate action.[166]

---

[164] E.g., Herczeg, *The Exploration of Outer Space and the Safety of States,* 5th Colloq. (Haley ed., Washington, D.C., 1963).

[165] N.Y. Times, May 29, 1962, p. 1, col. 4.

[166] See Appendix I-F(5).

8–11 Recovery of the space vehicle from foreign territories

The problem of recovering a United States rocket or similar device which accidentally crashes in another country will necessarily depend, in the absence of an international agreement, on the laws of that country.[167] A generally recognized rule of international law holds that the airspace over any nation belongs to that nation and that an unauthorized entry therein is prohibited. Thus, certain nations might hold that the accidental entry of a missile or spacecraft constituted a forfeiture of all title thereto. In cases involving aircraft, however, international law recognizes their right to enter sovereign airspace as a result of crisis or accident.[168] It can be argued that the accidental entry of an errant space vehicle is also an excusable act, but as a practical matter the success of recovery will depend in large part on the attitude of the entered nation towards the United States. It will be recalled that a few years ago, when an American plane was forced down in Hungary, that nation refused to return the plane and demanded large payments of money from this country before return of the fliers.[169] On the other hand, military planes that have in the past accidentally crashed in Mexico and Canada have been returned without any problem.

On liability for the damage caused by a fallen vehicle, I. M. Levitt reasons that the flight of a space vehicle is like that of a meteor, in that no human controls can be exerted upon it. This of course assumes an unmanned and motorless craft. Since the vehicle is not subject to human control, its fall is equivalent to an act of God, and on this basis the launching nation should be free from liability for re-entry damage. Continuing with this analogy between fallen craft and fallen meteor, Levitt concludes that the craft is the property of the state into which it falls.[170]

[167] Accord, Beresford, *Liability for Ground Damage Caused by Spacecraft*, 19 Fed. B.J. 242, 253 (1959). There was considerable discussion of the problem of return among Soviet writers leading up to the Soviet proposals to the Legal Subcommittee of UNCOPUOS (see Appendix I-F(3), e.g., Osnitskaya, *Mezhdunarodno-Pravovye Voprosi Osvoenija Kosmicheskogo Prostranstva* (International Law Problems of the Conquest of Cosmic Space), 1959 Sovetskij Ezhegodnik Mezhdunarodnogo Prava (Soviet Yearbook of International Law) 51, 62.

[168] See generally, Lissitzyn, *Treatment of Aerial Intruders in Recent Practice and International Law*, 47 Am. J. Int'l L. 559 (1953). An interesting situation arises when a pilot bails out of an airplane. Obviously the resulting situation could appear to be an abandonment of the craft, for the pilot has the specific intent to desert the property. If he is an agent of the government, his acts are the acts of the government, and it might then be reasoned that the owner of the property (viz., the government) had the intent to abandon it. However, there was no intent to relinquish the title to the aircraft but merely to desert the plane temporarily in the face of obvious danger. No case has ever held that a plane whose pilot has bailed out becomes abandoned. The drastic results of such a holding are obvious. See Korovin, Remarks, Symp. 1072, 1074-75.

[169] N.Y. Times, July 16, 1954, p. 4, col. 4.

[170] Levitt, *Legal Aspects of a Fallen Satellite*, in 2 parts, Army, Navy and Air Force Register, July 19 and 26, 1958.

The question of the ownership of the space vehicle may also arise while it is still in space—to determine, for instance, whether shooting it down by another state is a violation of the property rights of the launching state.[171] Obviously, the first problem in this situation is to decide what is the applicable law and in particular whether the notions of lost and abandoned property would apply to the vehicle when it is out of the jurisdictional domain of any legal system. G. A. Osnitskaya agrees with the author that space vehicles should be regarded as lost property and therefore be subject to return.[172] Although many solutions could be suggested for such a situation,[173] it is necessary to develop an agreed-upon rule to be inserted in the proposed treaty on space law. Such a rule should take in consideration the tests applied in domestic systems to differentiate between what is *res nullius* and what is not.

At the Geneva meetings of the UNCOPUOS Legal Subcommittee, held in May and June of 1962, both the United States and USSR submitted proposals concerning the rescue and return of astronauts and vehicles downed in a foreign state. The USSR proposal outlined the duties and responsibilities of the host states of fallen vehicles. In article 5 it states, "The assistance to be furnished when necessary by one Contracting State to another Contracting State shall in no way differ from the assistance which could be furnished to its own astronauts." Articles 6 and 7 detail the responsibility to return without delay any astronaut, spaceship, satellite, or capsule discovered down by a Contracting State. Article 8 then requires that any "expenses incurred by a State in fulfilling the obligations provided for in articles 6 and 7 of this Agreement shall be reimbursed by the launching State." The United States proposal agrees in all respects with the duties and obligations here discussed. The primary difference in the two proposals is couched in the reservations in article 7 of the Soviet proposal:

> Foreign spaceships, satellites, and capsules found by a Contracting State on its territory or salvaged on the high seas shall be returned without delay to the launching State if they have identification marks showing their national origin and if the launching State has officially announced the launching of the devices found.
>
> Space vehicles aboard which devices have been discovered for the collection of intelligence information in the territory of another State shall not be returned. [Appendix I-F(3)]

[171] Compare this with the situation of a state on whose territory a space vehicle is about to fall. In such a situation the state will be entitled to take necessary measures to protect itself from injury, including the destruction of the vehicle under the doctrine of self-defense. McDougal, *Artificial Satellite—A Modest Proposal*, 51 AM. J. INT'L L. 74 (1957).

[172] Osnitskaya, *Doktrina Mezhdunarodnogo Prava i Osvoenie Kosmosa* (International Law Theory and the Conquest of the Cosmos) in KOSMOS I MEZHDUNARODNOE PRAVO (The Cosmos and International Law) 88, 110 (Korovin ed. USSR 1962).

[173] See e.g., Danier and Saporta, *Les Satellites Artificiels*, 18 REV. GEN. DE L'AIR, 297, 300-01 (1955).

Nowhere in the Soviet proposal on astronaut and vehicle recovery is there any mention of liability for damages caused by falling vehicles. Neither was this topic mentioned in another Soviet proposal offered at the Geneva meetings, which is a suggested "Declaration of the Basic Principles governing the Activities of States pertaining to the Exploration and Use of Outer Space" (A/AC. 105/C.2/L.I). To be sure, a liability provision was incorporated in a revised version of the same declaration, which was submitted in April 1963 to the Legal Subcommittee.[174] However, it would appear that in the latter case the Soviets had in mind liability for more than just the damages that might be incurred as a result of space vehicle accidents, because the declaration itself referred to a wide range of space activities that were considered—at least from the Soviet standpoint—to be harmful if not downright criminal in nature.

GENOCIDAL CRIMES AND TORTS

8–12   *The experiments of which we have knowledge*

The Soviet Declaration of Basic Principles, as presented at Geneva, contained one provision which appeared to be aimed at certain United States space experiments:

> Cooperation and mutual assistance in the conquest of outer space shall be a duty incumbent upon all States; the implementation of any measures that might in any way hinder the exploration or use of outer space for peaceful purposes by other countries shall be permitted only after prior discussion of and agreement upon such measures between the countries concerned.

Although the above provision is couched in very general terms, other statements of Soviet spokesmen leave little doubt as to the type of space activity that it was referring to. Three obvious examples are the United States projects known as Argus, Westford, and Starfish, all of which had already aroused more than their share of international controversy, even though the last of the three had only been announced (not yet conducted) at the time of the Geneva sessions.

It will be recalled that Argus was the series of high-altitude nuclear detonations over the South Atlantic in the summer of 1958, designed to create an artificial belt of trapped radiation comparable to the recently discovered Van Allen belts. Westford, conducted in October 1961, featured the release of about 75 pounds of copper dipoles, tiny "needles" that were supposed to disperse into a narrow band around the earth at about 2,000 miles altitude for a study of new methods of long-range radio communications. This experiment was unsuccessful, because the needles

[174] *United Nations Committee Receives New Soviet Space Use Proposal,* Aviation Week & Space Technology, April 22, 1963, p. 29.

failed to disperse. A second try in 1963 was successful. The Starfish experiment, finally, conducted on July 9, 1962, was another high-altitude nuclear blast, which created an artificial radiation belt extending to within 200 miles of the earth at some points, and elsewhere blending with the Van Allen belts of natural radiation.

All three projects have been roundly condemned by Soviet spokesmen— and by an appreciable number of scientists and publicists in other countries too—as contrary to the concept of peaceful exploration and use of outer space. The more extreme critics have portrayed them as virtual crimes against mankind. To be sure, the immediate danger of radioactive fallout from Argus and Starfish was acknowledged to be far less than that associated with atmospheric testing, but some of the radiation would still seep down into the atmosphere, just as also happened with the natural Van Allen radiation. Moreover, the radioactive contamination of near-terrestrial space was decried as a direct hazard to astronauts, and also, by the inheritance of genetic damage, to their descendants in generations yet unborn. (In practice, the Argus radiation had been dissipated long before the first manned space flight occurred, but it appeared that some of the radiation injected into space from Starfish might persist for as much as ten years.[175]) Apart from the danger to human beings, there was the alleged danger of interference with other types of space experimentation, and in fact the Starfish radiation effects did adversely affect the instrumentation on board one or more previously launched scientific satellites.

A further peril was seen in these experiments by the noted British radio astronomer, Sir Bernard Lovell, who feared that man-made space radiation might somehow upset the "balance of nature" in the vicinity of the earth—with effects that no one could clearly foretell, but that might prove ultimately disastrous. Referring to the initial announcement of the proposed Starfish experiment. Lovell stated:

> Nevertheless, the earth is so minute on the cosmic scale and its environment is controlled by the delicate balance of such great natural forces that one must view with dismay a potential interference with these processes before they are investigated by the delicate tools of the true scientist.
> The Americans may have data which will remove these doubts and which will convince the international scientific community that the effects will be temporary. If so, they should produce the information before they make this sledge-hammer blow at the radiation environment of the earth.[176]

Though repeatedly attacked in the same breath with Argus and Starfish, Westford was really a somewhat different matter. It could not very easily be construed as a threat to human health or to the "balance of nature," but there were many who feared that it would, if successful,

[175] Washington Post, April 7, 1963, p. 1.
[176] Quoted in Lear, *The Facts About the 1962 Space Bomb*, Saturday Review, April 6, 1963, p. 46.

interfere with radio astronomical observations and possibly with other categories of scientific research. Thus, before the experiment was conducted, it was the subject of a protest by the International Astronomical Union, a member society of the International Council of Scientific Unions (ICSU); [177] and the subsequent failure of the test did little if anything to mollify the critics of United States policy.

Since no nation has power to exert its authority by an exercise of sovereignty over the areas in free space, the contamination of large areas of space in the immediate vicinity of earth may well constitute a tortious act on the part of any state engaging in such activity. The liabilities proceeding from damages caused by such acts would create wholly new legal problems of jurisdiction, applicable standards and law.

It remains an open question, however, whether these United States space experiments really did pose any serious danger of the dire consequences so freely predicted. As yet it certainly has not been established that they represented any kind of international crimes or torts. And it is possible that much of the criticism—at least of that criticism which was scientifically rather than politically motivated—was due to a failure on the part of the United States government to take the international scientific community sufficiently into its confidence. Argus, for example, remained an official secret until six months after it was conducted, and even then the news was forced into the open by *The New York Times* rather than willingly divulged. While both Westford and Starfish were preceded by public announcements of what was going to be done, it can reasonably be argued that the scientific issues involved did not have as full, free, and early a discussion as they should have received.

Dr. S. Fred Singer, the noted physicist and space scientist who took leave from the University of Maryland to head the Satellite Division of the U.S. Weather Bureau, is one of those who have stressed the need for complete and early discussion before a wide scientific audience, of all unclassified aspects of proposed military-scientific space experiments.[178] Singer considers the criticism of Argus, Westford, and Starfish to have been largely unfounded, but he also accepts the view that "no government has the right to change the environment in any significant way without prior international study and agreement." The trouble, he admits, is in deciding just what changes are "significant." However, as he sagaciously suggests,

> . . . the objections raised so forcefully by our British colleagues were partly provoked by the very real feeling of frustration of being "out" of important quasi-scientific, quasi-military experiments. Having been both "out" and "in," I know quite well how this feeling of frustration can develop, particularly

---

[177] Lear, *op. cit. supra* note 176, at 46.
[178] *Singer Urges Early Space Project Data,* Aviation Week & Space Technology, April 22, 1963, at 27.

when a scientist from the outside believes that an important aspect of a problem has been completely overlooked (as indeed, can and does happen). Contrasted with this is a smugness which sometimes develops among some "in" scientists, based on the feeling that people on the outside could not possibly know all of the details of the problem, and therefore, cannot really contribute. There is a lesson to be learned in this which should be valuable for the future.[179]

C. Wilfred Jenks, the noted British international lawyer, agrees in principle with Singer. "Any State," Jenks argues, "proposing to sponsor or permit an experiment, test, or development scheme which may prejudice the natural environment of another State should notify in advance the nature and anticipated and possible consequences of the proposed experiment, test or development scheme." [180]

As a corollary to his notification principle, Jenks advances the thesis that any State so notified should have a "recognized right to seek fuller information" about the experiment, and to make representations to the testing state if the other nation believes the experiment might alter its natural environment in a way it considered unwelcome. Such representations should be settled by negotiations, Jenks continues, and if these are unproductive, then an impartial enquiry on an international basis should be undertaken during the proceedings of which the proposed test would be held in abeyance.

Should the enquiry find that the protesting nation had grounds for its concern, "an international authority should be entitled to restrain by an injunction procedure ... experiments, tests, or development schemes calculated to modify the natural environment of another State." He concludes, "Within limits which remain to be defined, responsibility for loss or damage arising from changes in the natural environment of a State resulting from experiments or tests made by another State rests with the State making, sponsoring, or permitting such experiments or tests...." [181]

A possible solution was proposed by ICSU, on the eve of the Westford experiment, when it asked "all governments planning to launch space experiments which could possibly affect other scientific research adversely to make available to ICSU in timely fashion ... the facts and analyses needed ... for making wise and proper decisions concerning the proposed experiments." [182] The USSR Declaration of Basic Principles went even farther, in stating flatly that prior agreement should be obtained from the other "countries concerned." There is no indication that the United States is yet prepared to give either the Soviet Union or ICSU a veto power

[179] Letter from S. Fred Singer to The Science Editor, Saturday Review, April 15, 1963.

[180] Jenks, The Laws of Nature and International Law, NETHERLANDS INTERNATIONAL LAW REVIEW, Summer 1959 at 165-67.

[181] Id. at 167-68.

[182] Lear, op. cit. supra note 176, at 46.

over its space experiments, and there is probably good reason to doubt that the USSR itself would unconditionally accept any such arrangements. It is worth noting, however, that when the United States announced in the spring of 1963 that it would soon attempt a repetition of the Westford experiment, a special effort was made through the National Academy of Sciences and the International Astronomical Union to inform both foreign and domestic scientists of the technical details of the operation.[183] This still was not enough to allay all criticism, but at least the United States government was showing a keen awareness of the issues at stake.

8–13 *Potentially harmful space activities*

Nuclear experimentation and the scattering of copper dipoles are not, of course, the only kinds of space projects that might be construed as harmful to other nations or to mankind in general. Still another example which is, as yet, purely hypothetical but has been the subject of considerable speculation is the accidental (or, conceivably, intentional) misuse of large-scale weather modification. The weather satellites launched to date or currently in prospect are designed simply to gather data on the weather; despite some popular impressions to the contrary, such vehicles could not be used to *change* the weather, but only to help men *learn how* to change it. However, whenever the state of the art of meteorology does reach the point where large-scale modification is possible, it is quite conceivable that space instrumentalities may be used, along with other devices, to accomplish that objective.

Weather modification by man-made techniques has already been achieved, at least on a limited and local scale.[184] The results of "cloud-seeding" experiments, which have been carried out quite extensively in recent years, are still somewhat debatable, but meteorologists have been very successful indeed in such efforts as the dispersal of local fogs by heating the air or sprinkling with chemicals. We have also succeeded—unintentionally—in creating such local weather modifications as urban smog, a natural by-product of our automotive and industrial society. Hence it is not at all unreasonable to suppose that more far-reaching weather modification will ultimately become feasible, and that, in order to control weather processes close to their source, the "seeding" or other acts of human intervention may sometimes be carried out at the very top of the atmosphere or in near space.

Even the limited weather modification accomplished so far has raised some awkward legal and quasi-legal questions. For example, farmers have complained that cloud-seeding experiments, arranged by fruit growers for

---

[183] N.Y. Times, May 7, 1963.

[184] The following discussion is largely based on Cohen, *Should We Change the Weather?* Science Digest, November 1962, at 70-82.

the prevention of hailstorms, also kept their crops from receiving needed rain. The charge may or may not have been well founded. On the other hand, any increase in the technical scope or geographic extent of artificial weather modification is bound to produce a comparable increase in the number of complaints. Indeed, the balance of forces in the atmosphere is so complex that it is perfectly possible for desirable changes in the weather or climate of one area to set off undesirable effects somewhere else. And if one nation, by modifying the weather over a portion of its territory, should cause (or merely be accused of causing) undesirable weather conditions over the territory of another nation, an international controversy would be sure to develop. The same thing might occur, of course, in the eventuality already discussed in the preceding section—i.e., if some scientific experiment in space should have unintended harmful effects on planetary climate. At the very least, therefore, it will be necessary to make a thorough study in advance, of all possible ramifications of large-scale weather-modification experiments. Or, to express it differently, before we set out to control the weather by drawing on all the advances of space technology, we must first learn to control our own human carelessness in the handling of natural forces and resources.

One more example of potentially undesirable space activities is the use of space as a medium for "piratical" broadcasting activities.[185] In the radio broadcasting field, "piracy" has been an all-too-familiar phenomenon, involving both the use of shipboard stations lying just outside coastal waters to evade national and international broadcasting regulations; and the transmission, from stations legitimately established in one country, of programs actually intended for another country in which the stations are not licensed to operate. In terrestrial broadcasting, special measures must be taken in order to carry either radio or television programs very far across national boundaries. In space broadcasting, on the other hand, the range of transmissions would be almost unlimited, and so, too, would be the opportunities for "piratical" broadcasting activity.

The immediate danger of this kind of space piracy is not very great. So far, the broadcasting uses of space satellites—e.g., *Telstar*—have been limited to the relaying of programs from one country to another for retransmission through regular broadcasting channels. However, since the space medium is in some respects ideally suited for "piratical" broadcasting, there is need to establish a system of regulation that can prevent abuses before they actually occur. Otherwise the practice might endanger the development of many different space techniques, by usurping portions of the frequency spectrum on which all space activity is critically dependent. In certain circumstances, such unwarranted interference with either space or terrestrial radio communications might even produce, or

[185] Persin, *Will Space Be Open To Piracy?* TELECOMMUNICATIONS JOURNAL, Geneva, Vol. 30, No. 4, April 1963.

aggravate, national and international conditions of disaster. And certainly it would create still another source of discord among the nations of the earth, which have no trouble even now in finding things to quarrel about.

Additional References

Andrew G. Haley, *Space Exploration—The Problems of Today, Tomorrow and in the Future*, in Second Colloquium on the Law of Outer Space 44 (1960); ____, *The Law of Space and Outer Space*, 33 So. Cal. L. Rev. 370 (1960) reprinted in part, 10 L. Rev. Digest 77 (1960); ____, *Space Age Presents Immediate Legal Problems*, in First Colloquium on the Law of Outer Space 5 (1959); ——, *Space Vehicle Torts*, 36 Detroit L.J. 294 (1959), reprinted in 1959 Ins. L.J. 437; ____, *Current International Situation and the Legal Involvements with Respect to Long-Range Missiles and Earth-Circling Objects*, 1958 Vistas in Astronautics 310; *Current Congressional Legislation Affecting Aerospace Business:* Paper by ____, Before a Joint Meeting of the Institute of the Aerospace Sciences and the American Rocket Society in Los Angeles, June 14, 1961. (Revised Sept. 1, 1961); *Space Communications and Cooperation with Iron Curtain Countries:* Address by ____, Ft. Wayne Section of the American Rocket Society in Ft. Wayne, April 26, 1961; *Progress Made in the Use of Radio for Protection of Life and Property in Outer Space:* Paper by ____, Before the American Rocket Society Annual Meeting in Washington, D.C., Dec. 5-8, 1960; *Summation of Questions Involved in the Technical and Legal Regulations of Space Exploration:* Lecture by ____, Seminar Course on Space Science and Technology of the Instituto Nacional de Técnica Aeronáu-tica "Esteban Terradas" in Madrid, March 29, 1960; *Law of Outer Space—Practical Legal Rules for Human Conduct:* Paper by ____, Submitted to the Institute on World Organization in Washington, D.C., Oct. 23, 1958; *The Law of Outer Space—Scientific and Financial Considerations:* Address by ____, French Member Society of the International Astronautical Federation in Paris, June 9, 1958; *Legal and Economic Aspects of Astronautics:* Address by ____, Dansk Interplanetarisk Selskab in Copenhagen, March 14, 1958; *Some Future Problems for the Space Technicians:* Paper by ____, Before the American Rocket Society Space Flight Symposium in New York, Dec. 1, 1954; ____, *The Law of Outer Space: Programs and Progress*, Unpublished paper, Dec. 1959.

Space medical jurisprudence

The development of forensic medicine in space has been a seriously neglected topic in space literature. However, unless we pause now long enough to insure that law, sociology, medical jurisprudence, and regulation precede man into space in this advanced period of our civilization, we cannot be certain that man's conquest of space will result in blessings and not in scourges. After a brief history of the development of forensic medicine, and a discussion of the biological hazards facing man in flight through space, the exobiological problems are discussed in detail. The need for decontamination of space artifacts and for international regulation in this area is emphasized, and efforts made by the IAF and other organizations are briefly described. The "industrial" aspects of space medicine and related considerations of liability are also discussed. Finally, this chapter touches upon a few of the problems concerned with criminal investigation and responsibility under space-flight conditions.

9–1   A brief history

What is the meaning and scope of "forensic medicine," or legal medicine? The classical answer has been given by the great Scotsman, medical doctor, and philosopher, Sir Sidney Smith. He states that "forensic medicine may be defined as that body of medical and paramedical scientific knowledge which may be of service in the administration of the law." In discussing its history it is obviously impossible to indicate any particular date when forensic medicine emerged as a recognizable, separate scientific discipline. "Medicine probably has a history as ancient as man himself, for in his search for food, substances must have been tried which had medicinal qualities, and by process of trial and error he would certainly obtain a knowledge of those substances which could be used to assuage pain and combat disease and of others which were capable of causing death. Such knowledge, no doubt, was handed down from generation to generation, and as certain individuals became specially interested in matters of health and disease, the medicine man was evolved. His knowledge of drugs, blended with a knowledge of simple surgical procedures and reinforced by magic and witchcraft, made him a powerful and influential member of society." [1]

"Similarly," Sir Sidney continues, "the law may be said to be as old as society, for when men began to live in groups it must soon have become obvious that no member could be allowed to do just what he wished, but that the actions of all must conform to certain rules if the group was to survive. Sanctions had to be applied to curb the antisocial propensities of the few, and thus the law was born." [2]

Unexpectedly enough, forensic medicine had an important and formal position in civilization 1,000 years before the advent of formal legal codification by Hammurabi. The first medical legal expert was Imhotep, the Grand Vizier, chief justice and physician to the Egyptian Pharaoh Zoser of the third dynasty (c. 2980 B.C.). Imhotep is said to have acquired a great reputation for his wisdom and learning, to the extent that he became first a demigod and later, under the Ptolemies, the Egyptian god of medicine. By the Greeks Imhotep was called Imouthes, and by them he was identified with Asklepios, the god of healing. Although certain Egyptologists have regarded Imhotep as legendary, and have doubted that he lived as an actual man in the reign of Zoser, recent discoveries have converted into certainty what was before a probability. There can no longer be the slightest doubt that Imhotep is a historical personage, and that in common with other Egyptian nobles he held civil as well as religious offices.[3] Under the Ptolemaic dynasties he was invested with all the attributes of deity and was regarded as the son of the Memphite god Ptah, whose name is substituted for that of his earthly father, Kanufer. Imhotep had shrines as well as temples of his own in various parts of Egypt and of Nubia. It was believed that miraculous cures could be effected by his divine intervention, and his temples were thronged with sufferers, many of whom have left records of their gratitude. Statues and figurines of Imhotep as god of medicine have been found in considerable numbers, and these attest his widespread popularity. The evidence afforded by Egyptian and Greek texts supports the view that Imhotep's

---

[1] From Smith, *The History and Development of Legal Medicine*, in Gradwohl, Editor, LEGAL MEDICINE 1 (St. Louis, 1954, The C. V. Mosby Company).

[2] *Id.* at 1.

[3] Seth, *Imhotep, der Asklepios der Aegypter*, 2 UNTERSUCHUNGEN ZUR GESCHICHTE UND ALTERTUMSKUNDE AEGYPTENS, Heft 4 (Germany 1902).

reputation was respected in very early times and that he became at least a demigod not long after his death. His prestige increased with the lapse of centuries, and his temples in Greek times were the centers of medical teaching.[4]

From these early beginnings the story of forensic medicine constantly unfolds. As Sir Sidney points out, "In Babylon the Hammurabi Code was inscribed on stone about 2000 B.C. and is possibly the oldest written Code of Law. It was compiled from a mass of existing Sumerian Law and deals not only with crime and criminal law but also to a considerable extent with the practice of medicine. Severe penalties were inflicted for quackery, and malpractice by a surgeon might result in a fine, the loss of the hands, or the life of the unskilled operator. Sanctions of this kind would appear to us to have made medicine a somewhat hazardous profession and likely to deter would-be entrants. . . . The earliest record of a murder trial has been found in Sumeria, on a clay tablet dating back to about 1850 B.C." [5]

Largely because of the scientific outlook and methods of Hippocrates, forensic medicine developed rationally in the Greek complex. As Sir Sidney points out, not only was there a great advance in the practice of medicine in ancient Greece, "but there was also a remarkable development in the field of jurisprudence. The Greek Legal Code, especially as regards criminal procedure, was very full and elaborate. Although there is no clear evidence that medical knowledge was officially made use of in establishing proof in courts of law, Hippocrates and others discussed many medicolegal questions, such as the relative fatality of wounds in different parts of the body, the possibility of superfetation, the average duration of pregnancy, the viability of children born before full term, malingering, and other matters which almost inevitably must have been repeatedly at issue in the courts. In view of the high standing enjoyed by the physicians of ancient Greece, it is hard to believe that their opinions were disregarded by a legal system which was equally anxious to maintain its place of high esteem. It is interesting to note that the ancient Hippocratic Oath included an undertaking not to administer poison or to advise on the use of poisons, or to contribute to the procuring of abortion. Indeed, it is no exaggeration to say that the whole ethical outlook of the medical profession throughout the ages has been determined largely by the ethical teachings of Hippocrates more than two thousand years ago." [6]

The medical sciences flourished during the Roman Empire, and medical legislation followed the Greek pattern. Sir Sidney points out that "Galen, Celsus, and others, both Greek and Roman, continued the objective ra-

---

[4] Hurry, IMHOTEP, THE VISIER AND PHYSICIAN OF KING ZOSER (2d ed. 1928) (USSR).

[5] Smith, *op. cit. supra,* note 1 at 3.

[6] *Id.* at 4-5.

tional methods of the Greek physicians, and, if there is no reason to believe that the law made greater systematic use of the medical knowledge available, at all events the stage was coming nearer when objective factual medical findings could be of a standard admissible even under the strictest codes of evidence and procedure. Certain notable cases of medical evidence have frequently been quoted. For example, the body of Julius Caesar, assassinated in 44 B.C., was examined by a physician who pronounced the opinion that of all the twenty-three wounds sustained, only one, penetrating the chest, was of a fatal nature." [7]

In China, during the Middle Ages, the treatise "Instructions to Coroners" was compiled by panels of doctors. This was a codification of numerous earlier writings which incorporated new knowledge evolved during the passage of time.

Two centuries later, Paul Zacchia, physician to the Pope,". . . published his monumental, *Quaestiones Medico-Legales*, in three large volumes." Sir Sidney said that "of these, the first is of greatest interest, as it contains Zacchia's exposition of the existing state of knowledge and belief over the entire field of forensic medicine. In the second volume a great variety of hypothetical questions are raised and discussed, while the third volume contains the authoritative decisions of the Roman Rota on problems of all sorts." [8]

The modern developments in the field of forensic medicine, which were started in the Germanic States in the latter part of the 17th century and have continued on down through the decades, are sufficiently well known so that they do not require detailed commentary here. Indeed, the only purpose for taking this brief look into the past was to point out that medical jurisprudence had concerned humanity for a millennium before the advent of legal codes. It is strange indeed that the modern scientist has devoted so much of his time to purely technical efforts and has so "savagely" neglected the realm of social sciences!

Paraphrasing the famous words of the first beneficiary of the caesarean operation, it may be said that all space medical jurisprudence is divided into three parts, namely (item 1) public regulation of matters pertaining to health, contamination, quarantine, and so on; (item 2) the discovery of crimes and the adduction of proof establishing the facts; and (item 3) establishment of facts concerning personal injuries caused by negligence and tortious actions. The third covers matters which will become of increasing public importance as more human beings are involved in outer space adventures.

[7] *Id.* at 5.
[8] *Id.* at 8-9.

9–2 The organism man

Effective exploration of outer space by human beings must await the development of propulsion systems generating millions of pounds of thrust, with exhaust velocities in the order of one-third to one-half the speed of light. Such power plants appear to be quite feasible and are being developed. The limiting factors are entirely human, or more appropriately stated, are entirely anthropocentric. This is because the limiting factors center around the ability of the human being to withstand physically the stress of acceleration and deceleration to and from the luminar cruising speed. As a long-range prospect, mankind has every reason to believe that the problem of physical stress will be conquered. But what of the immediate problems of the conquest of outer space?

Much knowledge has been gained from the flights of American and Russian manned space vehicles; however, if humans are to travel extensively in space our knowledge must be expanded many times over by longer flights.

Still unknown is the effect of *long periods* of weightlessness. It will be recalled that Russian cosmonaut Gherman Titov was reported to have suffered nausea during his 25-hour flight in *Vostok II*.[9] Later Russian flights have placed men in orbit for periods in excess of three days, but full details as to the effects of weightlessness have not yet been released. Emotional and psychological problems are also bound to occur during extended trips to the planets and long tours of duty on space stations and the moon. Other problems include nutrition, sanitation, and the hazards of long existence in an artificial environment.

The problem that is least understood is radiation in space, yet it is here that man may well find the greatest stumbling block to human space travel. Space medicine has established that the brain and the lens of the eye are more highly radiosensitive than most other parts of the body, particularly at reduced levels of air pressure.[10] As a result, higher stand-

[9] N.Y. Times, Oct. 5, 1961, p. 8, col. 3.

[10] Schaefer, *Further Evaluation of Tissue Depth Doses in Proton Radiation Fields in Space*, Naval Aviation Medical Center, Pensacola, Fla., May 24, 1960; Schmidt, *Izmenenye Pronitsaemosti Gemato-entsefalicheskogo i Gemato-oftal'micheskogo Bar'erov pri Ponizhenij Atmosfernogo Davleniya*, 126 DOKLADY AKADEMII NAUK SSSR 696-98 (USSR 1959). Abstracts of many good Russian articles on space medicine are given every month in the section on cosmonautics, long-range development, and biological problems of the Referativny j Zhurnal, volume on Astronomiya, Geodesiya, which is published by the Institute of Scientific Information of the Soviet Academy of Sciences. Many of the best Soviet articles on space medicine are listed in the Library of Congress' *Abstracts of Current Literature;* prepared under the direction of Dr. Arnold J. Jacobius and published in the journal, Aerospace Medicine. Also useful is the Library's Monthly Index of Russian Accessions. English translations of readily available material are listed in the Consolidated Translation Survey, issued monthly by the Central In-

ards of radiation protection are required than one would otherwise deem to be reasonably necessary. In an article published in 1961, the Soviet scientist A. A. Gyrudzhain discusses the problem of avoiding foods which become contaminated by absorbing radioactivity in space.[11] These and innumerable specialized radiation problems must be studied in detail to avoid possible liability for improper protection of the space crew. Similarly, means of avoiding radiation must be employed, such as using polar exit and re-entry zones, increasing velocities to shorten exposure to planetary radiation belts, timing flights to avoid predictable periods to peak intensity due to solar disturbances, and following corridors of least radioactive resistance (if in fact such corridors exist) in extended flights through galactic space.

Another problem of radioactivity in space flight, and perhaps the gravest one in terms of establishing preventive measures, is the increase in radiation resulting from higher velocities of flight. This problem is also more serious in terms of liability because of the larger numbers of persons who will be carried in spaceships designed for travel at the higher velocities. Although this problem will become truly important only in interstellar flight, its gravity requires that it be considered in formulating rules of medical jurisprudence for outer space.

This problem has been widely discussed, but it seems to be more seriously considered by the Communists than by non-Communist scholars. Dr. Hubertus Strughold regards the problem as purely academic because he considers that flights beyond our solar system will not be possible for at least another century.[12] Some of the leading Communist scientists, however, relying on projected breakthroughs in scientific knowledge, regard the problem as worthy of earnest consideration.

The many dangers of interstellar travel were discussed recently in detail by Prof. S. M. Rytov of the Soviet Union, who stated:

For the relativistic rocket [specifically, a rocket traveling at 86.6% of the speed of light] interstellar hydrogen would present a stream of protons with energy exceeding one billion electron volts, i.e., a stream of cosmic rays with an intensity of the order of 10 billion particles per square centimeter per second. Let us recall that for the nonrelativistic [i.e., stationary] observer the intensity of the primary cosmic rays is not more than 2 particles per square meter per second. Accordingly, even assuming that the heating [from collision with interstellar dust and gas particles] or other destruction of the

telligence Agency. Translations of useful current newspaper materials are available in a publication issued regularly by the Joint Publications Research Service entitled Soviet-Bloc Research in Geophysics, Astronomy, and Space.
[11] Gyrudzhain, *Nekotorye Vaprosy Obespecheniya Uslovij Zhiznedatel'nosti pri Kosmicheskom Polete (Pitanie, Vodoobespechenie, Regeneratsiya Vozdukha, Assensizatsiya)*. (Some problems of Maintaining Life Support Conditions During Space Flight ...), 51 USPEKHI SOVREMENNOJ BIOLOGII (USSR 1961).
[12] Strughold, *Space Medicine*, in 32 AEROSPACE MEDICINE 595-615 (1961).

interstellar vehicle could somehow be averted, we are still faced with a colossal cosmic radiation more than [50] billion times the average "norm." This tremendous amount of radiation could kill every living thing almost instantly.[13]

In a symposium in the summer of 1961 on the problems of "relativistic" flight, Dr. A. Dmitriev of the Soviet Union proposed that at speeds up to 90% of the speed of light an electric and magnetic field projected in advance of the spaceship would divert the cosmic rays (and in addition would convert neutral interstellar dust into ionized energy rays and divert this energy in the same way as it would the cosmic rays). Dr. R. Perel'man and Dr. K. Stanyukovich in this same symposium stated that the energy needed to maintain such a magnetic shield would be much less than that needed to power the rocket and intimated that energy could be recovered during the process to lower still further the net energy expenditure. With respect to the time factor, which compounds the dangers of exposure to the environment of outer space, Dr. Dmitriev pointed out that the higher the velocity the greater would be the time dilation, so that a ten-light-year trip at an average velocity of 99.5% of the speed of light would take only one year.[14]

The above discussion of the radiation effects at very high velocities and possible means of protection against these effects indicates not so much the feasibility of interstellar flight as the extreme gravity of the danger and consequently the high degree of care which must be required of all who participate in the planning, design, and execution of such flight. Indeed, one problem that is common to all phases of space-flight development but is most acute in interstellar flight is the difficulty of obtaining advance knowledge of the dangers which might be encountered. Advanced telemetry techniques with radiotelescopic dishes of several thousand feet in diameter installed on the moon may enable unmanned research to reduce the risks involved in interstellar flight. Nevertheless, interstellar flight is a prime example of a space activity which is likely to give rise to liability more on the basis of faulty planning than on the basis of faulty construction.

9–3 The problem of contamination

Dr. Hubertus Strughold, the first man to hold the post of Professor of Space Medicine at the U.S. Air Force School of Aviation Medicine and a peerless authority on both air and space medicine, delivered an address in mid-1962 before a symposium on the problems of life in space, sponsored by the American Bar Association. Dr. Strughold pointed out that

[13] Rytov, *Chto Uvidet i s Chem Stolknetsya Astronavt, Letyashchij s Okolosvetovoj Skorost'yu*, Priroda, April 1960, pp. 64, 70 (USSR).

[14] Dmitriev, Chudakov, Smilga, Karev, Perel'man, and Stanyukovich, *Pomechtayem, Posporim o Polete k Dalekim Miram*, Znanie Sila, July 1960, p. 30 (USSR).

the most important news man may some day receive from space would be that "there is life out there—for instance on Mars." He observed that "verification of the *exolife* theory would be *the* news of the millennium and would open a new era for mankind." However, he warned that contamination is one of the greatest problems space medicine must face, and he recommended that serious and exacting attention be given this problem. "Thorough sterilization of the vehicles and even of the instrumentation must be guaranteed." [15]

As exemplified by the remarks of Dr. Strughold, the greatest emphasis so far among the advocates of sterilization and decontamination has been directed toward safeguarding the unparalleled opportunity for controlled scientific investigation which the advent of interplanetary communication has provided. Some of the research possibilities most highly valued by the world's scientists, including those from both the United States and the Soviet Union,[16] concern the origin of life and the origin of the universe. The inquiry into the origin of life, for example, could be facilitated by analysis of the dust on the surface of the moon. Because the moon cannot support a biology of its own—at least not one like that of the earth, i.e., containing deoxyribonucleic acid—the discovery of material of organic origin would lend support to the disputed panspermia hypothesis of Arrhenius, according to which life on the earth originated from spores of living organisms transported through space.[17] (The panspermia theory has been known since the times of Anaxagoras and Democritus.)

To prevent distortion of biological conditions on the moon by the introduction of living terrestrial organisms, sterilization of moon probes is necessary. Indeed, even if the rocket and payload are aseptic, the dead bacteria may serve as templates for "pre-life" processes. It is possible that some "pre-life" processes, i.e., the development of complex molecules, may be occurring on the moon, and these may be similar to or different from varieties which have evolved on earth. If there are such processes and "foreign" molecules are introduced, these may under lunar conditions act as templates and provide new foci for "pre-life" growth, thereby distorting the pattern all over the moon. To prevent this, measures must be taken not only to sterilize the terrestrial objects but to protect against impacts which could result in the dissemination of bacteria-size particles over large areas of the moon. "The March, 1959, report of the Committee on Contamination of Extraterrestrial Exploration (CETEX), sponsored by the

[15] *The Role of Medicine in the Space Age*, address by Hubertus Strughold at the Annual Meeting of the American Bar Association, Symposium on Contemporary Developments in Science, Life and Law of Space, San Francisco, Aug. 5, 1962.

[16] Report on the Moscow International Symposium on the Origin of Life on the Earth, Sponsored by the International Union of Biochemistry, Aug. 19-28, 1957, IICSU REVIEW 40 (1959).

[17] Phillips and Hoffman, *Sterilization of Interplanetary Vehicles*, 132 SCIENCE 991 (1960).

Committee on Space Research (COSPAR), contended, however, that lack of air would not facilitate dissemination of such particles but would 'prevent their dissemination by depriving the particles of a transport." [18] In addition, lunar probes, whether designed for mere impact or instrumented to function after hard landings, should be restricted to a limited area in order to localize the effects of terrestrial templates and to provide better control for research on nonimpact areas.

The problem on Mars and Venus is even more critical than on the moon, because on these planets, and particularly on Mars, there is a significant possibility that life forms do exist.[19] Whereas contamination by organic chemical pollution of the surface or by radioactivity, particularly from fusion explosions, is the principal problem in lunar research, the prevention of contamination by live biological organisms is more urgent in the case of planetary exploration.[20] Failure to exercise great caution might destroy or irreversibly change any existing life before it could be studied. Because of the perilous balance maintained by competing forms of life, one new terrestrial microorganism might cause a biological catastrophe.

Despite the limited terms of reference of most recent studies, the problem of interplanetary contamination extends beyond the preservation of ideal research conditions to the preservation or at least controlled exploitation of the solar system's planetary resources and, in fact, to the protection of other life systems for their own sake as creations of God. History shows how great waste and misery have followed from the thoughtless exploitation of newly found resources. With the growth of the human race seemingly by geometrical progression and an equally rapid increase in our advanced technical abilities, we may some day have both the need and the capability to utilize our planetary neighbors to optimum advantage. Planning for such eventualities, even though extremely provisional, cannot start too soon, and it may properly begin by the establishment of an international code of space medicine.

The possibilities in the field of conservation—and controlled exploitation—of interplanetary natural resources are indicated by Dr. Carl Sagan's report in an issue of *Science*,[21] the journal of the American Association for the Advancement of Science, in which he introduces the concept of "microbiological planetary engineering." Although this general subject had been much discussed before, Dr. Sagan's report was the first public statement by a scientist of great repute. According to Dr. Sagan, the in-

[18] Note 33, *Infra.*

[19] Davies and Comuntzis, *The Sterilization of Space Vehicles to Prevent Extraterrestrial Biological Contamination,* Tenth International Astronautical Congress, London 1959, External Publication 698 (1959); Davis and Fulton, Aeromedical Reviews No. 2-60 (1959).

[20] Statement by Dr. Wolf Vishniac of the National Academy of Sciences/National Research Council, NASA Technical Note D-771, at 30-31.

[21] Sagan, *The Planet Venus,* 133 SCIENCE 849, 857 (1961).

troduction of blue-green algae (primarily of the Nostocacae family) into the upper atmosphere of Venus and the inhalation of carbon dioxide and exhalation of oxygen by many generations of these microorganisms would be sufficient to reduce the high carbon-dioxide content of the atmosphere of Venus. This would reduce the "greenhouse effect" of the air on Venus and lower the temperature perhaps by hundreds of degrees. The decomposition of the carbohydrates of the algae into carbon and water would then produce a climate similar to that on earth.

Very recently well-known scientists have revived study of the theoretical possibilities—first advanced by Professor Fritz Zwicky ten years ago— of diverting the outer planets to orbits nearer the sun in order to gain vast areas of territory suitable for human occupation. Despite the seeming fantasy of such "interplanetary engineering," the realization of space travel itself is little less fantastic. Whether feats such as these that now appear incredible are destined to materialize in the chronicle of the Space Age is, of course, something only the enigmatic future can disclose. Should something of the sort achieve reality at a remote future date, however, there is no doubt that many of the bio-medical-jurisprudential problems posed will differ radically from those confronting us today. On the other hand, the basic issues remain the same regardless of whether any possible life systems on other celestial bodies prove subject to change by biological contamination, by chemical contamination, or by altering of the background radiation. This background continuum, for instance, probably could be seriously dislocated by nuclear (particularly fusion) explosions. Such dislocation may prove fatal to unadapted organisms. Then there is the question of the effects on conceivable other life systems produced by an increase or decrease in their environmental gravity, a manipulation considered by some scientists to be theoretically feasible. Ultimately, of course, all these matters might assume challengingly fresh aspects, in the event that it should become possible to reallocate choice orbiting space among the various planets by artificial planetary migration.

Dr. Joshua Lederberg, a member of the Space Science Board of the U.S. National Academy of Sciences, in his article *Exobiology—Experimental Approaches to Life Beyond the Earth* [22] considers some of the broader problems involved in interplanetary contamination. Referring to the immediate problems of biological contamination of our celestial neighbors, Dr. Lederberg suggests that we should

... deplore a heedless intrusion on other life systems. It would be rash to predict too narrowly the ways in which undisturbed planetary surfaces, their

[22] PROCEEDINGS OF THE IST INTERNATIONAL SPACE SCIENCE SYMPOSIUM (1960), excerpts reprinted in STAFF OF SENATE COMMITTEE ON AERONAUTICAL AND SPACE SCIENCES 86TH CONG., 2D SESS., SPACE RESEARCH IN THE LIFE SCIENCES: AN INVENTORY OF RELATED PROGRAMS, RESOURCES, AND FACILITIES 263 (Comm. Print 1960) [hereinafter cited as Life Sciences].

indigenous organisms, their molecular resources may ultimately serve human needs. If we have cause to prejudice these values, we surely would not wish to do so by inadvertence.

Lederberg then poses the question whether we can "afford to rely on any uncertain suppositions [as to the lack of need for meticulous sterilization] when the stakes are so high, and when we have practical means at hand for conservative protection." [23]

The lack of effective international negotiations to provide the needed rules to govern man's new extraterrestrial dimension of activity is perhaps most acute and, at the same time, least appreciated in this field of interplanetary sanitation, that is, the application of preventive medicine to avoid possible interplanetary bacteriological contamination. Several specialists have stated that, because effective sterilization of interplanetary probes requires changes in all stages of the design and construction of our space vehicles and payloads, the delay and expense involved would be prohibitive. Accordingly, these people consider that it is already too late to adopt an international code of regulations to prevent interplanetary contamination. This, however, is a defeatist and amoral attitude, which dangerously overlooks some of the principal factors involved.

Foremost among the writers supporting the necessity of sterilization is probably Dr. Lederberg, who points out that the introduction of exobiotic life to a planet may under certain conditions result in the explosive growth of the implant with far-reaching consequences of planet-wide scope. "With a generation time of 30 minutes, and easy dissemination by winds and currents, common bacteria could occupy a nutrient medium the size of the Earth in a few days or weeks, being limited only by the exhaustion of favorable nutrients." [24]

The danger to man himself derives in part from the fact that he has evolved his specific defenses against terrestrial bacteria and might be therefore less capable of coping with exobiotic organisms. Although Dr. Lederberg believes that the possibility of introducing here a new exobiotic disease imperiling human health or indeed human existence is highly doubtful, the danger may exist. It is only prudent to initiate precautions to cope with such a danger, regardless of what statistical probabilities can suggest as to its likely magnitude. The obvious course is the establishment of international legal norms to control our interplanetary communications.

Of lesser importance, but nevertheless of more immediate concern, is the danger of the unintentional spread of disease and other ecological disturbances through the artificial dissemination of terrestrial life to other celestial bodies. Terrestrial objects have already impacted on the moon

[23] *Id.* at 267.
[24] *Id.* at 266.

and within the present decade will probably reach our two neighboring planets. Failure to apply preventive space medicine in the form of standardized and effectively controlled sanitation measures may cause incalculable damage.

9–4 Preventive measures

The foregoing discussion has pointed out the need for an international space-medicine code covering the sterilization of interplanetary vehicles. In formulating such a code one must strongly emphasize the necessity of thorough coordination with the technicians and scientists who must eventually comply with the code provisions. A few points which should be considered in drafting such a code, however, may and should be set forth now.

Immediate consideration should be given to the following recommendations:

1. Provide for maintenance of prelaunch sterilization or else for in-flight sterilization of rocket exteriors, unless and until it is proven that life on the rocket exteriors cannot survive the ultraviolet radiation in space.

2. Provide for internal sterilization (for example, by the construction of parts tolerant to sterilization by heat or radiation or else containing internal disinfectants) to avoid contamination from break-up of the rocket or payload on impact.

3. Provide for sterilization not only of flights designed for impact on celestial bodies, but of all flights destined to approach the vicinity of these bodies.

4. Maintain sterile conditions within a high probability figure, perhaps one chance in a million (of putting one living microorganism on a celestial body).[25] The argument that sterilization is useless because one living organism is as dangerous as 1,000 or even 1,000,000,000, if it multiplies, does not overcome the desirability of practically eliminating the chance that this one organism will ever be able to reach another planet.

5. Limit areas of landing to localize effects of possible contamination by either live organisms or macromolecular templates.

6. Prohibit explosion of nuclear devices whether to provide seismic data on the interior and age of celestial bodies or for any other reason until after tests have been completed which would be endangered by nuclear fallout. Thereafter a maximum limit of fallout must be imposed according to the established needs of the environment. Control of atomic-wastes disposal should be maintained with equal rigidity.

[25] The one in a million figure was advanced in the paper by Davies and Comuntzis at the 1959 Congress of the International Astronautical Federation and was discussed by Dr. Charles Phillips at the June 29, 1960, NASA Technical Note D-771, at 32-33.

7. Prohibit chemical contamination either by markers or by soft-landings which would so disturb prevailing conditions on the celestial body as to prevent recognition of elements of earthly origin.

8. Provide that all matter to be returned to the earth from outer space pass inspection at an international quarantine space station. The space station shall be supplied with automatic processing and telemetering facilities to report back the results of research not approved for earth laboratories. Due to possibly dangerous mutations in outer space, provisions should perhaps be made to test even normally harmless terrestrial organisms during return flights.

Supplementary provisions would include the following:

1. Refrain from any possible major interference with life systems on other celestial bodies unless the scientific need has been clearly established and international approval has been obtained. The lower life forms may be regarded as subservient to the use of man, but nevertheless they should never be needlessly injured.

2. Establish rigid controls as to the minimum amount of research that is required to ascertain the lack of danger of contamination, before any possibly contaminating actions are permitted. This is particularly important if any higher forms of life may be involved, and it applies to radioactive as well as to chemical and biological contamination.

Recent research by Dr. John Lilly, Director of the Communications Research Institute on the Virgin Islands, on the brain complexity and learning speed of the common porpoise and dolphin indicates that forms which we would not ordinarily associate with the highest stage of life may be sufficiently advanced to warrant the application of sets of rules different from those we would apply to the lowest and even the intermediate forms of animals.[26] Sentient beings with powers equal to those of man may not conform openly to the behavior patterns we expect of man; they may also be of small physical size or in some other not easily identifiable form.

3. Apply the principles of metalaw to any forms of life which in any way give rise to suspicion that they may be of an order similar to man. This principle is condensed in the formula, "Do unto others as they would have done unto them." Any other treatment may result in their accidental destruction.

4. If forms of life capable of intelligent communication are discovered, the spaceship from earth should not land until an invitation has been issued based on full and mutual knowledge of the risks involved.

[26] See generally Lilly, Man and Dolphin (1961). Others most active in this area of research are Galler of the Office of Naval Intelligence, Washington, D.C. and Scheville, Ass't Curator of Vertebrates at Harvard who is conducting research at the Woods Hole Oceanographic Institute. The legal problems are discussed in Bauza Araujo, Derecho Astronautico 179-80 (Uruguay 1961); Seara Vasquez, Introducción al Derecho Internacional Cosmico 145-46 (Mexico 1961).

5. Establish the principle of jurisprudence that man has a positive duty to use his environment to best advantage whether on earth or in outer space, and not merely a negative duty to prevent misuse. This principle is appreciated by Communist jurists probably more than by those trained in the Common Law of the United States.

6. Establish administrative procedures to facilitate the implementation of the above principle. The benefits of space experiments should become the immediate property of all mankind. Advantages to man may accrue from research in weightless therapy, genetic mutation, hypothermia of the body or freezing to facilitate surgery, and the use of radiation to eliminate cancer; from experiments in adapting man to foreign environments by cyborgnetics (the creation of cyborgs by the replacement of man's vital organs with mechanical apparatus); and from any of a vast array of possible research programs, many as yet undreamed of. The results of this research as well as its initiation and progress should be registered in an international clearing house for immediate dissemination to other scientists. Among the most important research projects may be studies directed to the adaptation of foreign life forms to terrestrial conditions, in order to develop improved agricultural products capable of utilizing the vast deserts of our planet. The possible effect on the world food output may be graphically indicated by the fact that 85% of the land area of China is incapable of cultivation for present terrestrial agricultural crops.

7. Establish an international board of arbitration to select the particular organisms deemed suitable to be introduced on earth, with minimum chance of untoward effects for any country. For instance, the introduction of an organism which would be beneficial to northern Canada might have catastrophic effects if it spread to Mexico. The introduction of new problems of bio-politics and even of biological warfare could be eliminated or alleviated by setting up international controls before any countries have vested interests in the importation and use of new life forms.

8. Provide for international control of "planetary engineering," including that affecting our own planet. Experience in solving problems of conflicting interests in the control of weather, fallout, and ocean resources may provide precedents for the major problems which may some day arise from planetary engineering.

9–5 Efforts at international action

The history of international action to develop and implement an international code to prevent interplanetary contamination is closely interwoven with the history of the International Astronautical Federation (IAF). In its VIIth International Congress held in Rome in September 1956, the IAF provided the forum for the first international presentation of the problem of interplanetary contamination and the first proposals for meeting this problem.[27]

After the advent of space flight in 1957, the IAF served to coordinate international work on the scientific and technical aspects of interplanetary contamination. For example, in London in September 1959, the Xth Congress of the International Astronautical Federation sponsored a paper by R. W. Davies and M. G. Comuntzis, entitled *The Sterilization of Space Vehicles to Prevent Extraterrestrial Biological Contamination.*[28] This paper was distributed throughout the world and has been of help to virtually all subsequent writers on the subject.

In 1959 the IAF established as a subsidiary body the International Institute of Space Law, which is divided into eleven functionally oriented working groups. Each of these groups focuses on a specific aspect of the general field of space law and holds an annual meeting at which papers on the particular subject matter of the group are discussed under the supervision of the chairman. Working Group 5, chaired by the distinguished Manfred Lachs of Poland, was entrusted with (among other things) the following inquiry: "What should be the nature and scope of regulations governing the prevention of contamination of earth and celestial bodies?" American representatives on Working Group 5 have included John Hogan of the Rand Corporation and John A. Johnson, General Counsel of the National Aeronautics and Space Administration.

Because of its nongovernmental nature and the support it has had from both non-Communist and Communist individuals and governments, the IAF is exceptionally well qualified to serve as an organ to facilitate international agreement on and implementation of a code of space medicine covering some if not all of the points suggested above for immediate consideration. Besides the IAF, there are various other organizations which have sought to further international action on the sterilization of space vehicles. The most important of these at present are the United Nations Committee on the Peaceful Uses of Outer Space (UNCOPUOS), which is composed of official government representatives, and the Committee on Space Research (COSPAR) of the International Council of Scientific Unions, which may be classified as semiofficial and technically experienced. To date, however, neither of these two organizations has achieved any success in facilitating agreement between the Communists and non-Communists.

The present U.N. committee was preceded by an *ad hoc* Committee on the Peaceful Uses of Outer Space established on December 13, 1958. This committee was boycotted by the Eastern European governments but succeeded, nevertheless, in the publication on July 14, 1959, of a Com-

---

[27] See Appendix V-B, Item 164. Some of the concepts contained in these proposals are discussed in Chapter 12 §12-5, *infra*.

[28] *Supra* note 20.

mittee Report.[29] In accordance with the mandate of the committee expressed in General Assembly Resolution 1348 (XIII), Paragraph 1(d), the report considered the problem of interplanetary contamination and announced that

> ... the Committee took notice of the apprehensions that have been expressed that activities in outer space might bring to those regions, by inadvertence, living or other matter from the earth capable of interfering with orderly scientific research. It was agreed that further study should be encouraged under appropriate auspices to specify the types of risks, the gravity of dangers, and the technical possibilities, as well as the cost, of preventive measures. Such a study should also cover safeguards against similar contamination as well as protection against other hazards to health and safety that might be created by the carrying out of programmes to explore outer space.[30]

To the above announcement (which was the result of work by the Technical Committee of the Whole) the Legal Committee, after discussion on June 11, 1959, added the following: "This study could be undertaken with a view to the possible formulation of appropriate international standards." [31]

Unfortunately, this concern of the committee for the formulation of international standards was weakly stated and was seriously undermined by the committee's designation of the contamination problem as a legal problem not requiring priority treatment.[32] The outstanding weakness of the entire report, of course, was the lack of Eastern European participation.

The third international organization which has sought to further international action on the sterilization of space vehicles was the Committee on Contamination by Extraterrestrial Exploration (CETEX), established as an *ad hoc* committee of the International Council of Scientific Unions in March 1958, and raised to the status of a regular committee in October of the same year. Before abdicating its jurisdiction to the Council on Space Research (COSPAR) in March 1959, CETEX [33] held two meetings,

[29] U.N. Doc. A/4141, Symp. 1246.

[30] U.N. Doc. A/4141, Part III (III)29, Symp. 1270.

[31] U.N. Doc. A/AC. 98/C.2/SR.5, at 9-10.

[32] U.N. Doc. A/4141, Part II (II, III); Symp. 1268, 1270.

[33] The formation of CETEX resulted from a proposal of the U.S. National Academy of Sciences, suggested by the Technical Panel for Earth Satellite Programs of the U.S. National Committee of the IGY, which in June 1958, became the Academy's Space Science Board. The Bureau of ICSU (at its 19th Meeting held on March 3-5, 1958) unanimously approved the proposal of the U.S. National Academy of Sciences. This proposal is published in 1 ICSU REVIEW, 88-89 (1959). The ICSU Bureau at this meeting appointed an *ad hoc* Committee on Contamination by Extraterrestrial Exploration (CETEX) to represent the seven international unions interested in the problem and to prepare a report for presentation to all members of ICSU prior to the 19th Meeting of the ICSU Executive Board and the VIIth General Assembly of ICSU in Washington in the week of Sept. 29 to Oct. 6, 1958. The report of CETEX (issued

the first one in May 1958,[34] and the second in March 1959.[35] At the first meeting, a report was prepared which warned of the danger of contaminating extraterrestrial bodies and urged that a code of conduct regarding the dangers of contamination be drafted as soon as possible.[36] The report pointed out, however, that CETEX was unable to propose a specific code of conduct embodying a reasonable compromise between the desire to start lunar and planetary exploration at the earliest possible moment and the need to safeguard future research.

The second report, issued at the March 1959 meeting, was almost a verbatim copy of the first report. It observed that CETEX was able only to state general principles and that the detailed function of coordinating a sequence of experiments so as to provide maximum research benefit and prevent one experiment from spoiling another properly belonged to the newly founded COSPAR. The value of the CETEX report suffered from its limited scope of reference, in that it was concerned merely with the danger to optimum research conditions in outer space and ignored the wider implications of interplanetary contamination emphasized by the IAF. Just as in the case of the *ad hoc* U.N. committee, the report did not reflect participation of the East European countries, although a Soviet citizen was invited to serve on CETEX as a representative of the International Union of Pure and Applied Chemistry. The successor of CETEX in the field of interplanetary contamination, COSPAR, has had Soviet participation in its work, but like the successor of the *ad hoc* U.N. committee it has encountered nothing but failure in its efforts to gain cooperation from the East European countries in regulating the sterilization of space vehicles.

The report issued by CETEX is nevertheless of value in its statement of principles. The general principle was adopted that

> . . . in view of the great uncertainties which face space research, all operations which are not capable of conveying meaningful scientific data are to be discouraged even if they do not appear to carry with them a known source of contamination. Risks with the unexpected must be taken, as otherwise no

---

at its first meeting in The Hague on May 12-13, 1958) was approved by the ICSU Executive Committee on Oct. 2, 1958, and the President of ICSU stated that CETEX would meet again under the auspices of COSPAR (which was given formal approval the same day) to formulate a code of conduct for lunar and planetary observation. At its second and last meeting on March 11-14, 1959, CETEX in substance reissued its earlier report and in effect terminated its existence. The original proposals of CETEX were again reissued in condensed form in Resolution No. 13 of COSPAR at its January, 1960, International Space Science Symposium.

34 ICSU Quarterly Bull., Jan.-March 1954, pp. 3-4.

35 1 ICSU REVIEW 63, 88-90 (1959).

36 1 ICSU REVIEW 100-103 (1959); *Contamination by Extraterrestrial Exploration*, 183 NATURE 925 (1959).

space exploration is possible, but such risks must be justified by the scientific content of the experiment.[37]

The CETEX report added that "it is of the greatest importance that space vehicles should not land either accidentally or deliberately on Mars (and possibly also Venus) unless all precautions have been taken to exclude living organisms from them. Otherwise, the most challenging of all planetary studies, that of extraterrestrial life, may be put in jeopardy."[38] However, CETEX adopted the vague principle that Mars and Venus need to remain uncontaminated only until study by manned spaceships becomes possible. CETEX also suggested that moon probes should be sterilized "so that the difficult techniques of sterilization may be worked out in practice,"[39] and it adopted a position on some disputed technical theories, such as the panspermia hypothesis of Arrhenius and the danger of dissemination of particles by a hard impact on the moon's surface.

Despite almost unanimous agreement on the value of sterilization and decontamination of space vehicles, little has been achieved toward international regulation in this area, especially at the official level in the U.N. committee and at the semiofficial level in COSPAR. The difficulty involved in reaching international agreement is in large measure a politico-legal problem; and the rationale pro and con applies to the United States just as much as to the Soviet Union.

The most forceful argument yet voiced in the United States against sterilization of space vehicles and space payloads was published in the April 1959 issue of the *Proceedings of the National Academy of Sciences*,[40] in the form of a revised version of a paper delivered by Dr. Philip H. Abelson at the December 1958 meeting of the American Association for the Advancement of Science. Dr. Abelson, who is a consultant to NASA from the Geophysical Laboratory of the Carnegie Institution of Washington, stated flatly that the introduction of a whole new set of restraints for sterility would cost $10,000,000 and would set back the progress of the American space program by a full year. Similar considerations are no doubt voiced by scientists in the Soviet Union and by the Soviet military strategists, who, though unofficially, have great influence over the technical measures to be adopted by Soviet space scientists.

The literature pro and con has become rather voluminous and the scope of this chapter does not allow even a summary of the arguments. A very useful discussion of the problems involved is contained in the proceedings of a Meeting on Problems and Techniques Associated with the Decon-

[37] 1 ICSU REVIEW 101 (1959).
[38] *Ibid.*
[39] *Ibid.*
[40] 47 PROCEEDINGS OF THE NATIONAL ACADEMY OF SCIENCES 575-81 (1959).

tamination and Sterilization of Spacecraft, held on June 29, 1960, in Washington, D.C., by the National Aeronautics and Space Administration. These proceedings were edited by Jack Posner of the Office of Life Sciences Programs, NASA, and published in NASA Technical Note D-771, January 1961. The discussion covers the sterilization of spacecraft and the sterilization of animals, and it briefly deals with the more remote problem of preventing contamination by returning space vehicles. The sum of the discussion is to the effect that sterilization is feasible, but that sterilization at minimum cost entails planning for sterilization requirements at the beginning of the rocket and component-part design stage. Although effective sterilization may be burdensome at present, the design of vehicles and parts to facilitate sterilization even during last minute corrections and repairs on the pad would remove many of the objections now posed by the rocket technicians.

The urgency of the need for international agreement on sterilization requirements derives from the extensive preparatory work necessary before the actual sterilization. Dr. Charles R. Phillips, Chief of the Physical Defense Division of the U.S. Army Chemical Corps Biological Laboratories, wrote that "once the decision has been made to perform the final sterilization with ethylene oxide at the last possible moment before launching the probe, one can proceed backward and design a probe suited to the ethylene oxide treatment, just as one designs the probe to withstand the forces of acceleration or vibration to which it will be exposed during launching." [41] In answer to the question whether sterilization can be accomplished without additional crippling restrictions to the space exploration program, Dr. Phillips emphasized that this question can be answered affirmatively, but "only if attention is given to the sterilization requirements in all stages of design and construction." [42]

It may be argued, of course, that if the Soviets do not sterilize their rockets, there is no reason for the United States to do so. We must therefore consider the approach the United States should take if the Soviet Union refuses to cooperate in an international program of space-flight sterilization, and if available sanctions prove to be ineffective. However, we should remember in this connection that both the USSR and the United States have announced that their initial moon probes were sterilized.[43] And even if the Soviets do not adequately sterilize all their probes, we must exercise caution. As Dr. Charles Phillips pointed out by analogy, during the NASA meeting on June 29, 1960, "even though some

[41] Phillips and Hoffman, *Sterilization of Interplanetary Vehicles*, 132 SCIENCE 991, 994 (1960).

[42] *Id.* at 995.

[43] N.Y. Times, Sept. 14, 1959, p. 1, col. 8; Phillips and Hoffman, *op. cit., supra,* note 17, at 991.

careless motorist is seen throwing away a lighted cigarette, we still do not take down our signs cautioning against doing this." [44]

American concern for the problem of interplanetary contamination was indicated by an article by Heather David, at the time of the February 1961 Soviet Venus probe launching, which began with the statement:

> Officials of National Aeronautics and Space Administration last week expressed fear that the planet Venus would be seriously contaminated with earth microorganisms if the Soviet probe has not been sterilized. If it has not, landing of the vehicle could render the planet virtually useless for further study in the search for extraterrestrial life.[45]

The NASA Office of Information and Educational Programs has prepared a series of four twenty-minute educational films to explain the NASA viewpoint on interplanetary sterilization. The first film, entitled *Exobiology—Life on Other Planets*, was prepared under the direction of Dr. Joshua Lederberg in January 1961. The last of the series, which was prepared under the direction of Dr. Charles Phillips, is entirely on the problem of decontamination.

It is important to realize that pure physical power, as demonstrated by success in space exploration, is not the sole criterion of America's foreign policy. It is the express "intent of Congress that the United States should assume leadership in international cooperative arrangements to insure the peaceful uses of outer space." [46] Basic to this policy is the understanding that the pursuit of science is a major source of our nation's prestige and stature and in fact one of the most positive elements of our foreign policy. Both Christian teachings of morality and the dictates of political expediency thus demand that, in formulating an international code of space medicine, the decisive criteria should be the pursuit of science and the protection of human life.

The problem of interplanetary sanitation, then, seems to be less one of technical difficulties than one of national purpose and planning in the countries concerned. As Dr. Joshua Lederberg has stated, in a paper on exobiology, "the human species has a vital stake in the orderly, careful, and well-reasoned extension of the cosmic frontier; it will be a crucial

[44] Proceedings of Meeting on Problems and Techniques Associated with the Decontamination and Sterilization of Spacecraft, June 29, 1960, Washington, D.C., NASA Technical Note D-771, at 8 (1961).

[45] David, *Experts Fear Venus Contamination*, Missiles and Rockets, Feb. 20, 1961, p. 30.

[46] From a speech by U.S. Senator Howard W. Cannon in Washington, D.C., at the Nov. 8, 1959, Meeting of the American Rocket Society. In his address, Senator Cannon stated that there is a serious lack of "cooperative study by scientists, lawyers, and those concerned with foreign affairs of the implications of international science from the standpoint of national policy," and that "U.S. foreign relations with respect to science must take on a more positive and active character than has obtained heretofore."

measure of the maturity of our national consciences and their concern for posterity, how we react to the adventuresome and perplexing challenges of space flight." [47]

9-6 *Personal injury and crime*

The "public" aspects of space medical jurisprudence are, by all odds, initially the most worthy of detailed regulatory and legislative consideration. At the outset, medical jurisprudence must give first priority not to other fascinating subjects of legal speculation, but to the prevention of "industrial" wrongs and hazards through the constructive use of regulations and the sobering use of sanctions against negligence.

The industrial nature of space medicine is indicated, first, by the medical consultative role in the design and engineering phase of the space vehicle. Secondly, this industrial nature is manifested in the actual medical problems faced in connection with space flight, which poses many of the same industrial hazards (though often in a somewhat different form) that are found in large factories, such as the hazards of toxic fuels, air pollution, heat generation, noise, vibration, explosion, radiation, and faulty instrumentation control.[48]

The difference between the space and the nonspace aspects of industrial medicine consists in the type of risk and, perhaps even more so, in the gravity of the dangers and in the difficulty of applying preventive and corrective measures. The importance of these factors from the legal standpoint derives primarily from the fact that they are the chief variables determining the extent of the duty of care and the liability of those who are responsible for injury, whether caused by factory work or by space flight. (See Chapter 8, *supra*.)

One of the most widely discussed problems of space flights is that of injury from radiation. This radiation may come from the power source of the rocket motor or of the radio equipment within the vehicle, from the sun, or from other energy sources in outer space.

The power source of the rocket may give rise to liability through injury not only to the crew of the vehicle but also to third parties on the ground. This problem has been a subject of discussion for many years. As far back as 1932, the Czechoslovak lawyer Vladimir Mandl, in his treatise, *Weltraum Recht, Ein Problem der Raumfahrt*, wrote a detailed ten-page analysis of liability resulting from space flight and advocated absolute liability for injury caused by rocket propellants, mentioning specifically electron or ion propulsion. Liability for injury caused by rockets with atomic propulsion has also been a subject of widespread discus-

---

[47] Lederberg, *Exobiology—Experimental Approaches to Life Beyond the Earth*, Life Sciences 263, 266.
[48] Strughold, *supra* note 12, at 596.

sion and was considered by the Soviets in 1956 as an important problem of space law.[49]

Writers in both Communist and non-Communist countries advocate state responsibility for injuries caused to third parties by rockets. Dr. Jacek Machowski, Counsellor of the Polish delegation to the United Nations, thus states, "The acceptance of liability for injuries or damages caused by an unmanned [and even more so, by a manned] space vehicle is the logical consequence of adoption of the right of its ownership by the launching State." [50] Eastern European writers do not explicitly advocate absolute liability for the injury but state their acceptance of liability, nevertheless, in absolute terms.[51] Opinion is divided on this point among the Western writers, and one author considers that the deliberations of the United Nations *ad hoc* Committee on the Peaceful Uses of Outer Space on July 11, 1959, reveal "the prevalence of the view that liability for damage caused by spacecraft should be based on fault." [52] (This problem is more fully discussed in Chapter 8, *supra.*)

The potential role of space medical jurisprudence in cases of injury from nuclear power plants of space vehicles is best seen in practice in the Mars Bluff Case, described in April 1961, at a meeting of the Aerospace Medical Association in Chicago. This case arose out of the inadvertent release of a nuclear weapon on March 11, 1958, from a *B-47* aircraft flying near a small South Carolina town and the detonation of a high-explosive component of the bomb. Some of the interesting aspects of the case were the allegations of alleged exposure to ionizing radiation, apprehension regarding the presence of radioactive material, and hearing loss due to blast effects. The expert assistance given the U.S. Attorney in preparing background material on the medical and public health connotations of the case, the development of questions, and the conduct of the trial itself typify the problems that almost any medical service officer may come in contact with as the result of radiation injury to third parties caused by space vehicles.[53]

The other source of liability caused by the rocket's power plant is

[49] Shternfel'd, Iskusstvennye Sputniki Zemli 176 (USSR 1956). The passage discussed does not appear in the 1958 edition.

[50] Machowski, *The Legal Status of Unmanned Space Vehicles,* 2d Colloq. 111, 117 (Vienna: Springer-Verlag, 1960), Symp. 1204, 1212.

[51] Korovin, *International Status of Outer Space,* International Affairs (Moscow), Jan. 1959, pp. 53, 58, Symp. 1062, 1070; see generally Csabafi, *A kozmikus terseg jogi problemai* (Legal Problems of Cosmic Space), Egyetemi apok, March 12, 1961; Imre, *A legiter es kozmikus ter seg jogi helyzete* (Legal Status of Airspace and Cosmic Space) (mimeo, 1960); Szadecky-Kordoss, *A vil'a gurkutatas nehany jogi vonatkozasu kerdeserol* (On Certain Legal Aspects of Space Research) Borsodi Szemle, Nov. 1959 (Hungary).

[52] Beresford, *Liability for Ground Damage Caused by Spacecraft,* 19 Fed. B.J. 242, 252 (1959), Symp. 540, 550.

[53] Bedwell et al., The Mars' Bluff Case—A Medicolegal Case History in a Nuclear Weapons Incident (1961).

injury to the crew. An analogy to this situation may be found in an incident at the Idaho Falls National Reactor Testing Station in January 1961, involving the first three deaths to be caused by a reactor of the Atomic Energy Commission.[54] The most interesting aspect of this case is the difficulty encountered in establishing the sequence of events—specifically whether the men were killed by heat, steam, or radiation—because of the presence of radioactivity. This illustrates what will be one of the principal features of space medical jurisprudence, namely, the difficulty or even impossibility of securing exact proof of causation. In outer space, even with the best telemetry and medical astro-instrumentation, proof of negligence will frequently be impossible to obtain.

Without proof of negligence, recovery by the injured or by his survivors, at least in the United States (on any other than a contractual basis), is extremely limited at best. The prevailing law in the United States admits the liability of the government (with certain exceptions under the Tort Claims Act[55]) and of the private component-parts manufacturer only for negligence.[56] The recognition of absolute liability would remove the difficulty of obtaining proof, but such liability would adversely affect private investment in space exploration, and as yet the National Aeronautics and Space Act recognizes absolute liability for injury related to space flight only to the extent of $5,000.[57]

Other than those already mentioned, sources of radiation injury related to space flight are external to the vehicle. Liability for injury to the crew from this external radiation would stem from improper or inadequate protective measures. It is the function of astrophysics to determine the radiation to be expected under various conditions of flight, of space technology to determine the technological measures which will maintain radiation levels within given limits, and of space medicine to determine human tolerances for given periods of time. Error in any three of these functions conceivably may give rise to liability.

Finally, with respect to the criminal aspects of space medical jurisprudence, in all probability new methods of detecting and proving criminal offenses involving human beings will have to emerge, through further scientific investigation and refinement of methods. The coroner system and even the existing medical examiner system will have to be replaced by the development of new techniques in the field of legal medicine and legal pathology. Specialists will be required to diagnose the effect of trauma upon pre-existing disease, and the effect of disease following trauma. In this new dimension, the effect of trauma with disease as a

54 Newsweek, Jan. 16, 1961, p. 74.
55 See Ch. 8, §8–4.
56 See Ch. 8, §8–3.
57 See Ch. 8, §8–4.

contributing cause will certainly lead to most interesting problems. The theory and technique of narcoanalysis will stand study.

In the vast field of forensic psychiatry, myriad new factors will need investigation leading toward the discovery of causes and the development of cures, and the impact upon criminal capacity and criminal intent will require complete re-evaluation. The medical legal interpretation of phenomena we now call intoxication will have to be completely reassessed in the light of responsibility for crimes and other types of wrong-doing. And this thought may even be extended to the field of toxicology. Similarly, the effects of high and low temperatures and radiation in outer space will undoubtedly require thoughtful appraisal of such conditions on the responsibility and capacity of the human being in his relationships with other human beings.

Additional References

Andrew G. Haley, *Medical Jurisprudence in Outer Space*, 3 ARCHIVES OF ENVIRONMENTAL HEALTH (publication of the American Medical Association) 315 (1961); _____, *Space Exploration—The Problems of Today, Tomorrow and in the Future*, in SECOND COLLOQUIUM ON THE LAW OF OUTER SPACE 44 (1960); _____, *Law of Outer Space—Practical Legal Rules for Human Conduct*, 16 FED. COM. B.J. 163 (1959); *Space Communications and Exobiological Problems:* Address by _____, Arizona Broadcasters Association in Tucson, May 19, 1961; *Medical Jurisprudence in Outer Space:* Paper by _____, Before the Medical Society of the State of New York Convention in Rochester, May 9, 1961.

10

Intergovernmental organizations in space activities

A significant organizational contribution of the twentieth century is the creation of permanent international intergovernmental organizations. Development of effective international regulation of space activities will probably be based on existing intergovernmental organizations, or at least affected by our experience with them. In this chapter, the origin, structure, and functions of those organizations which would most likely be adapted as regulatory institutions for space are described, including primarily those which are part of the United Nations Organization. These include two of the principal organs—the General Assembly and the Economic and Social Council. Four of the specialized agencies affiliated with the United Nations are discussed—the United Nations Educational, Scientific, and Cultural Organization (UNESCO), the International Civil Aviation Organization (ICAO), the International Telecommunication Union (ITU), and the World Meteorological Organization (WMO). The activities of the United Nations Committee on the Peaceful Uses of Outer Space are reviewed as the most extensive U.N. attempt to date to contribute to the international coordination of space activities. Other organizations, also engaged in international space activities, are analyzed—the International Council of Scientific Unions (ICSU) with its Committee on Space Research (COSPAR), the United States National Aeronautics and Space Administration (NASA), and finally, the all-important National Aeronautics and Space Council.

UNITED NATIONS PRINCIPAL ORGANS

10-1 General Assembly

An international organization, in its most elemental form, is only one step removed from an international conference. It merely represents the decision of several governments to deal with a mutual problem together rather than separately. None of these organizations can enact legislation, levy taxes, raise armies, or enforce laws. While an international organization can make decisions about the structure and functioning of its secretariat and can assess member governments for annual dues, any member government that has serious objections to these arrangements can always, as a last resort, withdraw. "Likewise, each [organization] can draft and *approve* treaties and conventions on particular subjects, if the member states want to do so, but these are *binding* only upon those governments which subsequently take their own constitutional steps or accept them. In our [the United States] case, this means approval by the United States Senate." [1]

The purposes of the United Nations Organization, as expressed in Article I of its Charter, are:

1. To maintain international peace and security, and to that end: to take effective collective measures for the prevention and removal of threats to the peace, and for the suppression of acts of aggression or other breaches of the peace, and to bring about by peaceful means, and in conformity with the principles of justice and international law, adjustment or settlement of international disputes or situations which might lead to a breach of the peace;

2. To develop friendly relations among nations based on respect for the principle of equal rights and self-determination of peoples, and to take other appropriate measures to strengthen universal peace;

3. To achieve international cooperation in solving international problems of an economic, social, cultural, or humanitarian character, and in promoting and encouraging respect for human rights and for fundamental freedoms for all without distinction as to race, sex, language, or religion; and

4. To be a center for harmonizing the actions of nations in the attainment of these common ends.

The supreme organ of the United Nations is the General Assembly,[2] composed of all the member nations. Each member nation has one vote, although it can send as many as five representatives to the Assembly. The General Assembly would thus be the parallel organ to a parliament in a national government, although without the latter's law-making power. The General Assembly may consider any questions related to the maintenance of international peace and security and the promotion of international justice and well-being, except matters under consideration by the Security Council or matters which are exclusively the internal affairs of member nations. In practice, if Security Council action is blocked by the use of a veto by a major nation, the Assembly may then take up the question. The tendency has also been for the area defined as exclusively

---

[1] Wilcox, *Importance of the U.N. Specialized Agencies to the United Nations*, 34 Dep't of State Bull. 480, 482 (1956).

[2] The following discussion is based on Coyle, The United Nations and How it Works 143-45 (3rd printing rev.) (New York: New American Library, 1958).

"internal affairs of member nations" to become more and more circum-scribed. The end products of the Assembly's deliberations are not laws carrying binding force in and of themselves, but resolutions carrying moral weight resulting from their assumed representation of the consen-sus of the nations. The Assembly decides "important" questions, includ-ing those on organizational matters such as the election of members to the U.N. itself or to subsidiary bodies, by a two-thirds vote.

The General Assembly elects a President and Vice-Presidents for each session. The President of the Assembly is able to exercise considerable in-fluence on the course of its deliberations through his control over various parliamentary coordinating procedures. The Assembly has an extensive committee structure. (See chart of the U.N.) The seven main commit-tees, composed of a representative from each member nation, discuss items on the agenda in their particular areas of specialization, and recom-mend action by the Assembly. There are also procedural or "housekeep-ing" committees on credentials and other details. Subsidiary bodies and *ad hoc* committees are set up to deal with particular problems such as disarmament and the peaceful uses of atomic energy. The Assembly adopts the general budget for the whole U.N. organization and assesses the members for their shares based on their ability to pay. The Assembly cannot force a member to pay (which would be a governmental act), but it can deny a member its Assembly vote for non-payment. All subsidiary bodies and specialized agencies of the U.N. report directly or indirectly to the General Assembly, which can discuss any of their activities and recommend appropriate action.

10–2   Economic and Social Council

The Dumbarton Oaks Proposals, which foreshadowed the United Na-tions Charter, contained certain provisions relating to economic and social matters. When the United Nations Charter was drawn up at San Fran-cisco, these proposals were greatly expanded.[3] More functions were speci-fied and more agencies suggested. The preamble of the Charter states that one of the aims of the United Nations is "to employ international machin-ery for the promotion of the economic and social advancement of all peoples." No power, however, was given to any U.N. organ to make laws or regulations binding upon a member without its consent; the majority rule was to apply to resolutions within an organ, but not to ratifications by states themselves of treaty law embodying such resolutions. Thus, while no international instrumentality had ever gone so far in recognizing the obligation of states to advance the welfare of individual human beings, legislative measures to that end were to be taken by states, not by the United Nations itself. The United Nations, for its part, collects and dis-

[3] Eagleton, *The United Nations: Aims and Structure*, 55 YALE L. J. 974-994 (1946).

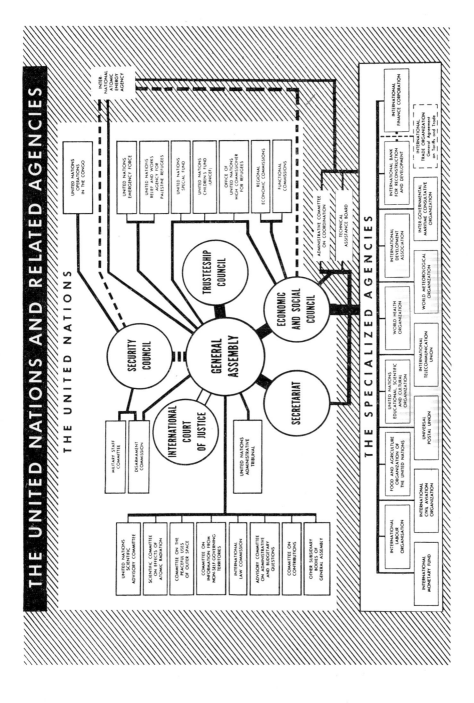

tributes information, makes studies, and negotiates with and makes recommendations to the member states.[4]

The chief agency through which the promotion of "economic and social advancement of all peoples" is accomplished is the Economic and Social Council, treated in chapter 10 of the Charter. This Council consists of the representatives of 18 states, chosen by the General Assembly, but has much freedom of action. It studies problems in the wide field assigned to it: "International economic, social, cultural, educational, health, and related matters." It makes reports and recommendations to the General Assembly, to members, and to specialized agencies operating within the United Nations. It may also draft conventions (which must be submitted to the General Assembly), summon international conferences (in accordance with rules prescribed by the United Nations), and create such subordinate agencies as it deems necessary.

The United Nations does not seek, as did the Covenant of the League of Nations, to bring all international activities into one system.[5] Rather, it encourages the development of "specialized agencies," each independently constructed upon a separate treaty basis, working expertly in its own particular field [6] and cooperating with the United Nations pursuant to an agreement defining the relationship. (See chart of the U.N.) It is the function of the Economic and Social Council to negotiate these agreements.[7] This is done by a special committee with representatives of each specialized agency, whose work is then reviewed by the Council and presented to the General Assembly. Such agreements are in fact *negotiated* agreements and not a unilateral expression of the United Nations concept of what the relationship ought to be; essentially the agreements are for cooperation as partners.

In general the provisions of these agreements fall into three categories. One is made up of articles providing for *reciprocal* arrangements, such as nonvoting representation at each other's meetings, reciprocal proposals

[4] *Id.* at 994-95.

[5] *Id.* at 983.

[6] Article 57 of the Charter of the United Nations provides:

1. The various specialized agencies, established by intergovernmental agreement and having wide international responsibilities, as defined in their basic instruments, in economic, social, cultural, educational, health, and related fields shall be brought into relationship with the United Nations in accordance with the provisions of Article 63.

2. Such agencies thus brought into relationship with the United Nations are hereinafter referred to as specialized agencies.

[7] Article 63 of the Charter of the United Nations provides:

1. The Economic and Social Council may enter into agreements with any of the [specialized agencies], defining the terms on which the agency concerned shall be brought into relationship with the United Nations. Such agreements shall be subject to approval by the General Assembly.

2. It may coordinate the activities of the specialized agencies through consultation with and recommendations to such agencies and through recommendations to the General Assembly and to the Members of the United Nations.

of agenda items, exchange of information and documents, and the furnishing of information requested by the International Court in exchange for the right of the agency in turn to call on the Court for advisory opinions. The second category includes articles which obligate the specialized agencies to take *unilateral* actions, such as transmitting annual reports to the United Nations, consulting with the United Nations in preparation of the agencies' budgets, and considering recommendations made to them by the General Assembly and the Council. The third category contains provisions relating to administrative and financial cooperation.

The Economic and Social Council works in partnership with these intergovernmental organizations, attempting to coordinate their work and prevent duplication, and periodically reporting to the General Assembly on the success of these efforts. Thus the specialized agencies are primarily technical organizations, the General Assembly primarily political, and the Economic and Social Council the coordinator and connecting link between the two.

A United States Assistant Secretary of State for International Organization Affairs, speaking on the subject of the specialized agencies, observed:

> In fact, relatively few people realize the importance of the Specialized Agencies. They lack the glamour and the drama of the General Assembly or the Security Council. While the political debates in New York make headlines, the specialized agencies are engaged in the relatively humdrum job of solving fundamental problems in economic, technical, and social fields.[8]

However, the potentially fruitful activities of these agencies over the long run, as compared to direct national confrontations in the General Assembly, are well stated in the following comments by David Cushman Coyle:

> The U.N. was organized to deal with the quarrels between nations that might lead to war. At the same time, the U.N. and its many working agencies have been helping the member nations in the agelong fight against human misery, injustice, and oppression. . . . People who work together against the hostile forces of nature often become friends. . . .
>
> The material works of the U.N. agencies—helping to build dams, to kill mosquitoes, to teach people to read—and its spiritual works, such as framing the Declaration of Human Rights, may be fully as important for peace as the great conferences and the search for a way to control the atom.
>
> World-wide struggles against the hostile forces of nature are easily understood by millions of people who feel baffled by the harder problems of quarreling human nature. These material works of the U.N. therefore serve as a background for the U.N. efforts to hold the conflicts of human nature below the explosion point.[9]

[8] Wilcox, *op. cit. supra* note 1, at 480.
[9] Coyle, *op. cit. supra* note 2, at ix-x.

While for the most part the specialized agencies are organized in a similar fashion, each is an independent, international legal entity, with its own legislative and executive body and secretariat and its own primary functions. In addition to working closely with the United Nations, the specialized agencies also cooperate closely with each other. The heads of the several organizations meet at regular intervals in the Administrative Coordination Committee under the chairmanship of the Secretary-General of the United Nations, to discuss common problems, plan joint programs, and strive to eliminate overlapping functions.[10]

With this information as background, we can now take a closer look at the workings of those specialized agencies whose functions and interests are most relevant to astronautics—a field in which such international technical organizations are destined to play an increasingly vital role.

SPECIALIZED AGENCIES
AFFILIATED WITH THE UNITED NATIONS

10–3   United Nations Educational, Scientific, and Cultural Organization

A considerable portion of the task of coordinating the work of the specialized agencies is performed by the United Nations Educational, Scientific, and Cultural Organization, commonly referred to as UNESCO. The history of the organization dates back to a meeting of the Conference of Allied Ministers of Education which was held in 1942 and was concerned primarily with cultural and educational rehabilitation. In 1944, at a later meeting sponsored by the conference, proposals were made for a United Nations agency for cultural and educational reconstruction. These proposals formed the basis of a draft constitution presented to the Allied Ministers of Education meeting in April 1945. As a result, the United Nations Conference on Educational and Cultural Organization, held in London in November of 1945, drew up and adopted the UNESCO Constitution, which entered into force on November 4, 1946.

Membership in the United Nations carries with it the right to membership in UNESCO. In addition, states not members of the United Nations may be admitted to membership in UNESCO following the approval of their applications by the Economic and Social Council, the recommendation of the Executive Board, and a two-thirds majority vote of the General Assembly.

Member nations of UNESCO are authorized by the UNESCO Constitution to make arrangements to associate their national educational, scientific, and cultural organizations with UNESCO. For this purpose

10 Wilcox, *op. cit. supra* note 1, at 481.

a national commission is generally established in each country. In the United States, for example, the United States National Commission for UNESCO comprises 100 members appointed by the Secretary of State from among national organizations, representatives of federal, state, and local governments, and certain citizens at large. These members assist the United States Government in carrying out its responsibilities as a member of UNESCO.

The central objective of UNESCO is to contribute to peace and security by promoting collaboration among nations in educational, scientific, and cultural fields. It seeks to encourage the exchange of knowledge and the furtherance of scientific research through the international interchange of information, students, scholars, and teachers, and the holding of conferences and seminars of teachers, scholars, and experts throughout the world. The organization is thus often referred to as a "catalyst" for the assembly of scientific data and a forum for its dissemination. One of the principal activities sponsored by UNESCO is the Council for European Cooperation in Nuclear Research, in which eleven European countries have pooled their research facilities to explore peaceful uses of atomic energy. Through its regional scientific information offices in Egypt, Uruguay, India, and Indonesia, UNESCO provides technical assistance in all fields of science to numerous nations. Finally, UNESCO stimulates the exchange of ideas and knowledge in technical and scientific fields through its monthly illustrated magazine, the *UNESCO Courier*, plus other specialized publications.[11]

UNESCO is not especially interested in space research, as such, but it is very much interested in peaceful cooperation among nations in scientific and technical matters. It was thus among the very first international organizations that showed an interest in supporting international scientific endeavors such as the IGY, which in turn played a major role in space exploration. At the general conference of UNESCO held in November-December 1958, moreover, a resolution was passed specifically authorizing UNESCO participation in programs related to space research. In line with this policy, UNESCO has given important support to the activities of other agencies in space affairs, and in particular to the work of the International Astronautical Federation (IAF) and the Committee on Space Research (COSPAR) of the International Council of Scientific Unions (ICSU).[12] Its contribution will therefore be discussed mainly in connection with those two organizations.

[11] See generally Coyle, *op. cit. supra* note 2, at 30-40.
[12] SCHWARTZ, INTERNATIONAL ORGANIZATIONS AND SPACE COOPERATION 90-92 (Philadelphia: Rittenhouse Press, Inc., 1962).

10–4 *International Civil Aviation Organization*

Another specialized agency of particular relevance to astronautics is the International Civil Aviation Organization. In the rapid development of international military air transportation during World War II, the allied governments foresaw the possibility of problems in postwar international civil aviation. The International Commission for Air Navigation (CINA), established under the Paris Convention of 1919, had set up a number of technical standards for civil air transportation and arranged for exchange of aviation information among member states. CINA, however, although it represented 33 states by 1939, was never able to deal with international aviation on a world-wide basis. Membership consisted mostly of European nations. The United States, Germany, and the countries of Latin America were not participants.[13]

Consequently, through the initiative of the United States, 54 nations convened in Chicago to draw up the Convention on International Civil Aviation, which was concluded on December 7, 1944. The ICAO was established under this Convention.[14] Its purposes are briefly:

(a) to assist international civil aviation by encouraging use of safety measures, uniform regulations for operation, and similar procedures at borders;

(b) to promote the use of new technical methods and equipment;

(c) to participate in United Nations Technical Assistance Programs to help underdeveloped nations extend their internal transportation systems.

The ICAO includes an assembly, in which each member state is represented, and a council elected by the assembly. The assembly, which elects its own officers and determines its own rules of procedure, has the function of taking appropriate action upon the reports of the council. The council, or executive body, complies with the directives of the assembly, maintains liaison with member states and with other international bodies, and is generally responsible for carrying out the work of the organization. In session about eight months of the year, the council is assisted by subsidiary working groups such as the Air Navigation Commission and the Air Transport and Legal Committees.[15]

The Air Navigation Committee directs the technical work of the organization, which is divided into roughly ten special categories: aerodromes, air routes, and ground aids; meteorology; rules of the air and air-traffic control; communications; aeronautical maps and charts; search and res-

---

[13] Aspects of United States Participation in International Civil Aviation, Dep't of State Pub. No. 3209, at 1 (1948).

[14] International Civil Aviation Conference, Chicago, 1944, Final Act and Related Documents, Dep't of State Conference Ser. No. 64 (1945).

[15] *Op. cit. supra* note 13.

cue; personnel licensing; accident investigation; operating practices; and airworthiness.[16]

As part of its technical work, the ICAO issues annual reports on traffic trends, cargo and mail statistics, safety matters, and meteorology, and conducts international conferences, examples of which were the North Atlantic Ocean Stations Agreement Conference of 1954 (relating to the maintenance of ships in the water areas over which commercial aircraft fly) and the Conference on Air Navigation Services Arrangements in Iceland, Greenland, and the Faroes. In addition, ICAO Technical Assistance Programs station experts throughout the world to give technical assistance, to supervise training, and to distribute funds for the improvement of civil aviation.

A permanent Legal Committee was created by the First Assembly of ICAO in May 1947, and the organization thereby took over the work of unifying and codifying private international air law which formerly had been handled by the *Comité International Technique d'Experts Juridiques Aériens* (CITEJA), established at Paris in 1926. In addition to handling private air law matters, the Legal Committee is charged with advising the organization on all matters of public law.[17]

The Preamble to the Chicago Convention recognizes that through abuse, international civil aviation "can become a threat to the general security." Since the United Nations is designed to preserve the peace, it follows that the United Nations must consider the status of international aviation whenever it presents a case threatening to the general security.[18] Therefore it is not surprising that the ICAO, with its international headquarters in Montreal, Canada, works closely with the United Nations as a specialized agency. In addition, ICAO cooperates with a number of other specialized agencies including: (1) the ILO, which concerns itself with such pertinent matters as employment problems in civil aviation; (2) the WHO, which deals with problems of quarantine, sanitary regulations, and so on; (3) the ITU, which is involved in the extensive communications aspects of civil aviation; (4) the WMO, dealing with weather conditions; and (5) the UPU, which is concerned with airmail transportation, charges, services, and facilities.

As one of the first postwar intergovernmental organizations to begin operation, ICAO has made a major contribution to international air transportation by standardizing in large part the techniques of air navigation.[19] It has also been suggested that ICAO or an agency connected with it be assigned a part in the task of formulating a space code and regulating

[16] *Ibid.*

[17] *Ibid.*

[18] Cooper, *Air Transport and World Organization*, 55 Yale L. J. 1911, 1210-11 (1946).

[19] *Op. cit. supra* note 13.

space traffic,[20] although other authors have argued that ICAO is not suited to this task. The latter have reasoned, for example, that ICAO was created expressly to deal with problems of conventional aviation and that it must not extend its sphere of activity to the regulation of space flight without international agreement.[21]

Meanwhile, ICAO has on various occasions expressed an interest in space activities, without having undertaken any major studies or projects of its own related to outer space. In 1959 the ICAO Council brought to the attention of the assembly the suggestion that ICAO study the legal status of outer space and the regulation of spacecraft, with special reference to the relationship between space traffic and civil air traffic. At that time the ICAO decided not to attempt an independent study. On the other hand, it can be expected at the very least that there will be a requirement for careful coordination between the ICAO and agencies concerned with space navigation. As the Secretary-General of ICAO stated in his 1959 report, "Cooperation will be required at the international level in order to insure the safety of air navigation during the time of launching or of re-entry of spacecraft." Still other problems of space flight in which ICAO would seem to have a direct interest include radio frequency assignment, identification of space vehicles, and space vehicle accidents.[22]

10–5 International Telecommunication Union

Of special interest in the field of astronautical communication is the specialized agency known as the International Telecommunication Union. The term *telecommunication* was first officially adopted in 1932 in the Annex to the Madrid International Telecommunication Convention [23] and is defined as "any telegraph or telephone communication of signs, signals, writings, images, and sounds of any nature, by wire, radio, or other systems or processes of electric or visual (semaphore) signalling." [24]

The international regulation of telecommunications began, however, long before the term was officially adopted. It began in 1865, twenty years

[20] Aaronson, *The Legal Control of Space*, The Listener, Dec. 19, 1957, p. 1018; Meyer, Remarks, Proceedings of the American Society of International Law Fiftieth Annual Meeting, Washington, D.C., April 25-28, 1956, 96; Pépin, *Introduction to Space Law*, 4 N.Y.L.F. 258 (1958).

[21] Colclaser, Remarks, Proceedings of the American Society of International Law, Fiftieth Annual Meeting, Washington, D.C., April 25-28, 1956, 99-102; Cooper, *The Russian Satellite—Legal and Political Problems*, 24 J. Air L. & Com. 379 (1957); Keating, *Space Law and the Fourth Dimension of Our Age*, 1st Colloq. 83, 89; Smirnoff, *The Need for a New System of Norms for Space Law and the Danger of Conflict with the Terms of the Chicago Convention*, 1st Colloq. 105.

[22] Schwartz, *op. cit. supra* note 12, at 93-94.

[23] Dec. 9, 1932, 151 L.N.T.S. 5, 49 Stat. 2391, T.S. No. 867.

[24] DeWolf, *Telecommunications in the New World*, 55 Yale L. J. 1281 (1946).

after the invention of the electric telegraph, with the establishment of the International Telegraph Union. At the time of its creation, there was no corresponding international political organization anywhere in the world. But while international political organization developed, and the technology of communications matured, international technical organization for telecommunication questions remained relatively stagnant. The International Telegraph Union was primarily an organization of continental European nations concerned with wire telegraphy when it was established. The emergence of radio subsequently made it truly global in function, but no fundamental administrative changes were made from 1865 until 1947.[25] One writer in 1946 criticized this fact and pointed out that the Union was merely a consultative group having no bodies which could effectively dispose of problems that arose between conferences. He therefore recognized the need for a close tie with the United Nations.[26]

The 1947 (Atlantic City) Telecommunication Convention replaced the 1932 Convention between the contracting parties and created the International Telecommunication Union in its present form so as to insure more adequate service to the world.[27] An agreement of relationship with the United Nations under which the ITU was recognized as a specialized agency of the United Nations entered into force on January 1, 1949. Provision is made in Chapter IV of the General Regulations annexed to the ITU Convention for nonvoting participation by representatives of other international organizations and recognized private operating agencies in meetings of various bodies of the Union. Scientific organizations may, moreover, present petitions and resolutions to an ITU Conference with the consent of the official head of the delegation of the country concerned.

The mission of the ITU is threefold:

(1) to maintain and extend international cooperation for the improvement and rational use of telecommunications;

(2) to promote the development and most efficient operation of technical facilities by establishing standards and operating rules designed to improve telecommunication services, increase their usefulness, and, as far as possible, make them generally available;

(3) to harmonize the actions of individual nations in the attainment of these common ends.

Briefly stated, the ITU engages in four general courses of action to accomplish its mission. It:

(1) allocates radio frequencies and registers radio frequency assignments;

25 *Id.* at 1281-82.
26 *Id.* at 1284.
27 Oct. 2, 1947, 63 Stat. 1309, T.I.A.S. No. 1901.

(2) seeks to establish the lowest rates possible that are consistent with efficient service and with the necessity for keeping the independent financial administration of telecommunications on a sound basis;

(3) promotes measures to insure safety of life through the cooperation of telecommunications;

(4) makes studies and recommendations and collects and publishes information for the benefit of its members.

Structurally the International Telecommunication Union is composed of two organizations known as the Administrative Radio Conference and the Administrative Telegraph and Telephone Conference. The Radio Conference, which has responsibility for space communications, has two subordinate bodies: the International Radio Consultative Committee (CCIR), set up in 1932 to study and make recommendations on technical radio questions and operating procedures, and the International Frequency Registration Board, set up in 1947 to record and insure international recognition of assigned frequencies. The CCIR is organized into fourteen individual study groups, of which Study Group IV has been entrusted with study of the problems of space communications.

The ITU organizational structure also includes a General Secretariat, whose duties are to collect and publish data, both national and international, regarding telecommunications throughout the world. It seeks to disseminate information that will assist members and associate members in the development of more efficient technical methods, and especially in the best possible use of radio frequencies so as to diminish interference; and it publishes a journal of general information and documentation concerning telecommunications.

The ITU as a whole meets about once a decade. The CCIR meets in Plenary Assembly at intervals of about three years to consider specific recommendations submitted by any of its study groups and forward those recommendations which it adopts to the Administrative Radio Conference for deliberation and possible action. Proposals for action, originating either with the CCIR directly (possible only since 1959) or with individual countries, if adopted by the Conference, are then referred back to the individual countries for ratification in multilateral treaty form.

The duties of the 11-member International Frequency Registration Board (IFRB) are set forth in Article 6 of the ITU Convention:

(a) to effect an orderly recording of frequency assignments made by the different countries so as to establish, in accordance with the procedure provided for in the Radio Regulations, the date, purpose, and technical characteristics of each of these assignments, with a view to insuring formal international recognition thereof;

(b) to furnish advice to members and associate members with a view to the operation of the maximum practicable number of radio channels in those portions of the spectrum where harmful interference may occur.

The IFRB has published technical standards which are not only helpful for informative purposes but also useful in providing a common basis for engineering evaluation of proposed radio frequency operations. The Board also publishes frequencies used by all nations, thus enabling one country to use a frequency free from interference by any other nation.[28]

The ITU is, without question, the appropriate organization for regulation of the use of radio in space. Indeed, its activities in this field to date—involving both the actual allocation of radio frequencies for space use and technical studies of space telecommunication problems and requirements—form a major part of the subject matter of Chapter 7, *supra*, which deals with space communications regulation. The ITU has also entered into collaboration for the study of space telecommunications with the International Astronautical Federation, as discussed in Chapter 11, *infra*, and with still other international organizations such as COSPAR.[29]

10–6 World Meteorological Organization

Several of the specialized agencies of today have ancient origins. One of the oldest is the World Meteorological Organization, whose roots go back to 1853 when ship owners throughout the world exchanged meteorological observations over the oceans. In 1878 a committee composed of directors of meteorological bureaus of France, Germany, Great Britain, Italy, and the Netherlands drafted the statutes of the International Meteorological Organization; and in 1879 a Congress of Meteorological Representatives of States, meeting in Rome, adopted those statutes. The organization continued in existence until 1951, when its successor, the World Meteorological Organization, commenced activity. The new organization, whose purposes are to coordinate, standardize, and improve the meteorological services rendered throughout the world, includes most of the nations of the world. Any state or territory which administers a meteorological service of its own may join the organization. By an agreement with the United Nations in December 1951, WMO was recognized as a specialized agency with the functions of implementing international cooperation in meteorology.

The WMO acts as a clearing house for information exchange, makes recommendations and promotes all forms of technical cooperation among its members. As a general rule, its recommendations and any resulting agreements are carried out not by the WMO itself but by the weather services of the member nations. It has, however, provided technical assistance to the newly emerging countries in the form of expert missions, fel-

[28] E.g., International Telecommunications Bureau, Bern, *Liste des fréquences pour les stations fixes en service* (1934-present).

[29] In addition to the relevant sections of this book, see SCHWARTZ, *op. cit. supra* note 12, at 76-81.

lowships, training seminars, and the like, in close collaboration with other specialized agencies.

One of the principal scientific activities of the WMO in recent years was its extensive participation in the International Geophysical Year (IGY), for which it set up an IGY working group and operated an IGY Meteorological Data Center. It has also collaborated effectively with other organizations interested in the application of meteorology to aeronautics, maritime shipping, and various phases of industry. It has worked with the ICAO, the ITU, the International Ice Patrol, and the International Union of Geodesy and Geophysics, to mention only a few.[30]

The participation of WMO in the IGY naturally had a direct bearing on space research and exploration. In addition, the Executive Committee of WMO decided early in 1958 that the organization should accept responsibility for meteorological questions related to artificial satellites, insofar as they call for action or study by a specialized agency of the United Nations. Subsequently the Third Congress of WMO formally laid down the policy that the organization would encourage the development and use of artificial satellites as a means of providing meteorological data and would collaborate as required with the United Nations and other organizations (in particular COSPAR) in artificial satellite programs which were of interest to meteorologists or on which the advice of meteorologists would be useful. In accordance with this policy, the Executive Committee established a panel of experts to review continuously possible meteorological uses of satellites and make suggestions as to how WMO could best assist such activities.

The U.N. General Assembly, as part of its Resolution 1721 of December 20, 1961, took note of the progress opened up in the field of meteorology by advances in space technology. The same resolution called upon the WMO to continue to make expert studies and recommendations for the advancement of meteorological science and the improvement of weather forecasting techniques. The WMO has actively complied with the Assembly's request; and it has also taken a leading role in coordinating the related efforts of other organizations.[31]

[30] See, e.g., Joint ICAO/WMO Meteorological Telecommunications Meeting for Europe, Geneva, 1958, Final Report (1958); WMO Commission for Aeronautical Meteorology, abridged Final Report (1954-present); SCHWARTZ, op. cit. supra note 12, at 82-83.

[31] SCHWARTZ, op. cit. supra note 12, at 83-87.

UNITED NATIONS COMMITTEE
ON THE PEACEFUL USES OF OUTER SPACE

10–7   The ad hoc Committee, 1958-1959

The most important action taken so far by the United Nations relative to space activities was the establishment by the General Assembly of an *ad hoc* Committee on the Peaceful Uses of Outer Space on December 13, 1958. The resolution establishing this committee recognized the common interest of mankind in the exploration of outer space; stressed the desire of the Assembly that space activities be used for peaceful purposes; urged the nations "to avoid the extension of present national rivalries into this new field"; commended the pattern of scientific cooperation evidenced by the International Geophysical Year; and drew attention to the section of the U.N. Charter which provides that "the Organization is based on the principle of the sovereign equality of all its Members." The general assumption underlying the establishment of the *ad hoc* Committee was that extensive information about the problem involved in the peaceful uses of outer space was required before specific programs could be recommended.[32]

The *ad hoc* Committee was requested to provide information on the following topics:

1. Programs of international cooperation in the peaceful uses of outer space which could appropriately be undertaken under United Nations auspices to the benefit of nations regardless of the state of their economic and scientific development.

2. Present organization, activities, and resources of the U.N., its specialized agencies, and other international bodies relating to the peaceful uses of outer space; and future organizational requirements to facilitate international cooperation in this field within the framework of the United Nations.

3. The nature of the legal problems which may arise in outer space activities.[33]

Unfortunately, the Committee did not get off to an auspicious start. After having been appointed to the Committee, the Soviet Union, Czechoslovakia, and Poland decided not to participate in its work. The Soviet delegate charged that its membership had "a one-sided character" which

---

[32] U.N. Doc. C. 1/L. 220/Rev. 1 (1958); the discussion which follows is based upon Galloway, *The United Nations Ad Hoc Committee on the Peaceful Uses of Outer Space: Accomplishments and Implications for Legal Problems,* Symp. 613, 614. See generally Zhukov, *OON:problema Mirnogo Ispol'zovanija Kosmicheskogo Prostranstva* (The UNO and the Problem of the Peaceful Use of Cosmic Space), 1960 Sovetskij Ezhegodnik Mezhdunarodnogo Prava (Soviet Yearbook of International Law) 177.

[33] U.N. Doc. C. 1/L. 220/Rev. 1 (1958).

was "not consistent with an objective consideration of this important problem." He suggested further that the Committee could not perform any useful function without Soviet participation, and that consequently nothing would be accomplished.[34] By the time the Committee actually began its work in May 1959, the United Arab Republic and India had also decided not to participate. The remaining thirteen nations, however, determined to perform the task assigned to the Committee in spite of these developments.

The Committee elected Dr. Koto Matsudaira (Japan) as chairman, Dr. Mario Amadeo (Argentina) as vice-chairman, and Joseph Nisot (Belgium) as rapporteur. Two subcommittees were established: a technical subcommittee with Dr. D. C. Rose (Canada) as chairman, and a legal subcommittee with Prof. Antonio Ambrosini (Italy) as chairman. These subcommittees held a total of twenty-five meetings in which working papers were discussed, and their deliberations served in large part as the basis for the final report, which was unanimously adopted on June 25, 1959.[35]

The response of the *ad hoc* Committee to the question of particular programs which might fruitfully be undertaken was based primarily on the work of the technical subcommittee.[36] On this point the report of the *ad hoc* Committee observed that international cooperation in the conduct of space activities could well be achieved in such specific areas as the use of radio frequencies, central registration of orbital elements to identify space vehicles, termination of radio transmissions which are no longer needed, destruction or recovery of spent satellites, return of equipment to launching nations, and prevention of contamination of celestial bodies. The Committee emphasized that immediate action was required in the allocation of radio frequencies for space vehicles and suggested that such action be taken at the forthcoming 1959 ITU Administrative Radio Conference.

It was also pointed out in the report that international cooperation in space endeavors could be furthered by joint programs emphasizing simultaneous launchings of sounding rockets; international use of launching ranges; contributions from the scientists of many nations in the instrumentation of satellites; international systems for tracking, telemetering, and

[34] Zhukov has discussed the Soviet objections to the Committee membership at length. Zhukov, *Mezhdunarodnoe Sotrudnichestvo v Mirnom Ispol'zovanii Kosmosa* (International Cooperation in the Peaceful Use of the Cosmos), in Kosmos i Mezhdunarodnoe Pravo (The Cosmos and International Law) 114, 140-43 (Korovin ed. USSR 1962).

[35] U.N. Doc. A/4141 (1959).

[36] The discussion that follows is based upon Galloway, *Peaceful Uses of Outer Space and the Military Role, Hearings on H.R. 1010 (Superseded by H.R. 11737 [1963 NASA Authorization] Before the Subcommittee on Manned Space Flight of the House Committee on Science and Astronautics),* 87th Cong., 2d Sess., pt. 2, at 1051, 1058 (1962).

data processing and interpretation; educational activities of the type in which UNESCO has had wide experience; and the use of world data centers for space information. The Committee likewise called for international cooperation in the strengthening of *national* scientific capabilities for space research. And it felt that established intergovernmental agencies should play a role in the development of space activities in the areas mentioned so that they might become increasingly subject to international agreements. It even mentioned the possibility of an international team to launch satellites and space probes sponsored by the United Nations or the International Council of Scientific Unions (ICSU).

In response to the second question posed, that of existing and proposed organizational structure to support international cooperation in space activities for peaceful purposes, the Committee observed that the major scientific fields concerned with experimentation in outer space were already organized in a number of nongovernmental unions designed to promote and coordinate research, exchange information, and publish reports. The fields so organized included astronomy, geodesy and geophysics, chemistry, radio, physics, biology, mechanics, physiology, and biochemistry. The organizations representing the preceding fields were all members of ICSU—which is partially supported by UNESCO. The already extensive accomplishments of international cooperation in space activities in the International Geophysical Year through ICSU's Special Committee for the IGY (CSAGI) were noted, as was the fact that ICSU had established a post-IGY organ, the Committee on Space Research (COSPAR), to continue such international cooperation. However, the Committee also observed that three nongovernmental scientific organizations which it considered to be significant for the development of international space activities were not affiliated with ICSU, and thus were not integrated through ICSU into the U.N. framework. These were the organizations in the fields of medicine, engineering, and astronautics.

With respect to intergovernmental organizations, the Committee noted that in pursuit of the United Nations goal of promoting the harmonious solution of international economic and social problems, including those of a scientific nature, numerous subsidiary entities had been established under the U.N. General Assembly—i.e., the specialized agencies coordinated through the Economic and Social Council. The Committee observed that the specialized agencies then having a substantial interest in space activities were UNESCO, WMO, ITU, and ICAO; and that the following did not then have space programs but were likely to develop related projects in the future: the International Atomic Energy Agency (IAEA), World Health Organization (WHO), and Intergovernmental Maritime Consultative Organization (IMCO).

The Committee's general conclusions with respect to the existing organizational structure emphasized that space programs were often integral parts of broader programs that also included many other activities. Outer space had simply been added as a new environment into which present and projected human activities were being extended. Thus an organization such as the WMO, for example, could not make hard and fast distinctions between its space-related and non-space interests. By the same token, the *ad hoc* Committee did not feel that the time had come to establish a new autonomous intergovernmental agency within the U.N. framework for the direction of space programs. Neither did the Committee feel that it would be practicable to delegate the over-all task to any one of the existing specialized organizations. The continuance of present procedures was favored, by and large, together with the suggestion that information on space activities be incorporated in the reports of the various specialized organizations to the United Nations.

The report of the legal subcommittee became the primary basis for the Committee's response to the third question posed for it: namely, that of identifying the legal problems which may arise in carrying out programs of space exploration. The Committee came to a consensus that since it seemed impossible to define all the space legal problems that might arise, it would proceed to identify and classify certain problems on a priority basis, and to distinguish between those which seemed amenable to early resolution and those whose solution appeared more remote. The Committee recommended the following general principles: (1) The United Nations Charter and the Statute of the International Court of Justice are not confined to the earth, and their provisions can be extended to include activities in outer space. (2) Extensive study of the principles and procedures which apply to the sea and to airspace is necessary in order to determine their relevance to space regulation. (3) It is neither practicable nor desirable at the present time to create a comprehensive code of space law. The Committee held that "the rule of law is neither dependent upon, nor assured by, comprehensive codification and . . . premature codification might prejudice subsequent efforts to develop the law based on a more complete understanding of the practical problems involved." At the same time, however, it recognized that it is necessary for the law to keep pace with the situation it regulates.

The Committee listed six priority problems as being amenable to early resolution:

1. Whether the satellite programs of the International Geophysical Year, in which satellite vehicles were launched which traveled over other nations, had in fact established that outer space is freely available for exploration and use by all in accordance with existing or future international law or agreements.

2. What type of injury and kind of conduct should establish liability for injury or damage caused by space vehicles, and who will determine liability and ensure payment for damages. In this connection the Com-

mittee recommended studies of a proposed agreement providing for compulsory jurisdiction of the International Court of Justice, and of the experience of the ICAO with the "Convention on Damage Caused by Foreign Aircraft to Third Parties on the Surface."

3. Allocation of radio frequencies to space vehicles.

4. Prevention of interference between space vehicles and aircraft.

5. Identification and registration of space vehicles and the coordination of launchings.

6. Problems resulting from the re-entry, descent, and landing of space vehicles in other nations than those from which they were launched. In this last connection, the Committee recommended consideration of the possibility that the rules of international law which now apply to aircraft landing in distress be applied to space vehicles.

Other problems ranked lower in order of priority were:

1. Official definitions of airspace and outer space, which were deemed premature at the time. The Committee noted that the problems to which it had given highest priority did not depend for their solution on establishing this boundary. Two possible approaches were suggested—establishing the boundary as a range rather than a line, or using the type of space activity rather than its location as the basis for legal control.

2. Exploration of celestial bodies. Although this problem was not considered pressing at the moment, the Committee suggested "the sovereignty should not be claimed by a nation over celestial bodies; that such areas should be used solely for mankind's benefit; and that an international administration might handle such matters."

3. Interference of space vehicles with each other. The Committee believed that there was not much present danger of such interference, but noted that it was a future possibility and suggested that the rules now applying to air traffic might be related to space traffic.

Although completed in June 1959, the report of the *ad hoc* Committee on the Peaceful Uses of Outer Space remained in limbo for a number of months, since the nations which originally chose to boycott the Committee's deliberations decided to ignore its resulting report. However, continued efforts on the part of delegations who strongly believed in the Committee's work eventually led to positive action. In December 1959, the General Assembly First Committee met to discuss the report and to consider the creation of a permanent outer space committee. The United States and Soviet delegations reached agreement on a membership formula and a draft resolution, to which ten other nations adhered, thus making it possible to establish a permanent committee.

10–8   *The permanent committee (since 1959)*

The General Assembly adopted Resolution 1472 on December 12, 1959, creating the United Nations Committee on the Peaceful Uses of Outer Space (UNCOPUOS). The instructions given to the Committee were similar to those previously given to the *ad hoc* Committee. It was assigned to consider the following means of international cooperation in space activities: continuation of the IGY program on a permanent basis; U.N. assistance for research; exchange and dissemination of information; encouragement of national research programs; study of legal problems arising from space exploration; and the arrangement of an international scientific conference.

After having agreed initially to the creation of UNCOPUOS and to the membership arrangements, the Soviet Union once again raised objections. These concerned membership, the distribution of committee offices, and the voting procedures, with the Soviets insisting that decisions be made by unanimous rather than majority vote. The United States and other nations refused to accede to these demands, particularly since the rules of the General Assembly specify decisions by majority or two-thirds vote. The delay in the Committee's work resulting from this second rupture in negotiations proved to be four times as long as the one resulting from the first. The United Nations Committee on the Peaceful Uses of Outer Space did not meet from the time it was established in December 1959 until late November 1961, shortly before the terms of its members were due to expire. (During this period of inactivity, however, the United States and other nations continued to press for the Committee to meet and to start work.)

Toward the end of November 1961, the second stalemate began to dissolve. All members of UNCOPUOS, including the Soviet Union, attended a meeting of the Committee held on November 27, 1961. Moreover, informal discussions among the American, Soviet, and other delegations led to agreement on a draft resolution originally proposed by the United States on "International Cooperation in the Peaceful Uses of Outer Space." The substance of this solution was passed unanimously by the General Assembly on December 20, 1961, as Resolution 1721.[37] (See Appendix I-F(1).)

In this resolution, the General Assembly recognized "the common interest of mankind in furthering the peaceful uses of outer space and the urgent need to strengthen international cooperation in this important field," and suggested that "the exploration and use of outer space should

[37] See generally *Outer Space Cooperation and the United Nations*, Address by Richard N. Gardner, Deputy Assistant Secretary of State for International Organization Affairs, Before the Section on International and Comparative Law of the American Bar Association, San Francisco, Cal., Aug. 4, 1962.

be only for the betterment of mankind and to the benefit of States irrespective of the stage of their economic or scientific development." The following principles were commended to states for their guidance in the exploration and use of outer space:

(a) International law, including the Charter of the United Nations, applies to outer space and celestial bodies;

(b) Outer space and celestial bodies are free for exploration and use by all States in conformity with international law and are not subject to national appropriation.

The Assembly called upon "States launching objects into orbit or beyond to furnish information promptly to the Committee on the Peaceful Uses of Outer Space, through the Secretary-General, for the registration of launchings," and requested the Secretary-General "to maintain a public registry of the information furnished." The Committee was requested "to maintain close contact with governmental and nongovernmental organizations concerned with outer space matters," and "to provide for the exchange of such information relating to outer space activities as Governments may supply on a voluntary basis, supplementing but not duplicating existing technical and scientific exchanges."

The resolution emphasized two special areas—weather and communications—by devoting entire sections to each. The Assembly recommended the development of measures "to advance the state of atmospheric science and technology so as to provide greater knowledge of basic physical forces affecting climate and the possibility of large-scale weather modification," and "to develop existing weather forecasting capabilities and to help Member States make effective use of such capabilities through regional meteorological centers." WMO, UNESCO, COSPAR (ICSU), and other specialized agencies and nongovernmental organizations were requested to report to the Economic and Social Council on appropriate organizational arrangements to achieve these ends.

In the area of space communications, the Assembly recommended that "communication by means of satellites should be available to the nations of the world as soon as practicable on a global and non-discriminatory basis." In order to achieve this end, the Assembly invited the U.N. Special Fund and the Expanded Program of Technical Assistance, in consultation with the ITU, to consider requests from member nations "for technical and other assistance for the survey of their communication needs and for the development of their domestic communication facilities so that they may make effective use of space communication," and it again requested the ITU, UNESCO, COSPAR (ICSU), and other specialized agencies and nongovernmental organizations to report to the Economic and Social Council on appropriate organizational arrangements. In the areas of both weather and communications, the Assembly requested

UNCOPUOS to review the reports submitted to the Economic and Social Council and to submit its comments and recommendations to both the Council and the Assembly.

One significant feature of the resolution was the wording which suggested that a number of U.N. organizational units should consider problems concerned with the peaceful uses of outer space. For the preceding three years, there had been a tendency among various other U.N. bodies to wait upon action by the *ad hoc* Committee and its successor, the permanent committee. Now, however, the resolution implied that space problems might be included among the responsibilities of the ITU, WMO, the Economic and Social Council, and the Secretary-General.

The resolution produced as an almost immediate result the registration of space vehicles in sustained orbit or space transit by both the United States and the Soviet Union, in accordance with the Assembly request. Then, too, in the cooperative atmosphere which was evidenced by the unanimous passage of the resolution and which continued for some time thereafter, UNCOPUOS was able to hold eight meetings in New York in late March 1962. The problem of unanimous versus majority voting, upon which much Soviet opposition to the Committee had been based, was resolved by an agreement to conduct its business without voting: the chairman simply stated the consensus of views which had been expressed. Using this approach, at the conclusion of this series of meetings, the chairman reported that two subcommittees were being created to continue the Committee's work: a Scientific and Technical Subcommittee and a Legal Subcommittee. The consensus of views as to the Committee's function was that it should promote international cooperation in space activities by coordinating (but not duplicating) the programs of the relevant U.N. specialized agencies and nongovernmental organizations. Furthermore, observers from UNESCO, WMO, ITU, and COSPAR were invited to participate in the Committee's work.

At the March meetings the Soviet Union and the United States both put forward the initial proposals which became the basis for their more detailed proposals at the June meeting of the Legal Subcommittee in Geneva. (See below.) Other Committee members also suggested items for study by the Legal Subcommittee, many of which were similar to the proposals of the Soviet Union and the United States. The proposals of the Indian and Canadian representatives are set out in Appendices I-F(6) and I-F(7). However, non-overlapping proposals were made by Canada and France to give priority to the establishment of a boundary between airspace and outer space; by France and Poland to require taking of measures to prevent contamination; and by India, Japan, and Hungary to prohibit the use of outer space for "military" purposes.[38]

---

[38] American Bar Association, Section of International and Comparative Law, Committee on the Law of Outer Space, 1962 Report, pp. 6-8.

Both subcommittees of UNCOPUOS met during June 1962 in Geneva. The Scientific and Technical Subcommittee invited UNESCO, WMO, WHO, IAEA, ITU, and COSPAR to participate in its work as observers. However, it was pointed out at Geneva that while ITU represented the telecommunications specialists, WMO the meteorologists, IAEA the nuclear scientists, and WHO the health experts, no organization had been asked to participate as a representative of the space engineers and technicians who were actually working to make the world's space programs a reality.[39] The appropriate organization, of course, would be the International Astronautical Federation (IAF). Meanwhile, the organizational gap noted in the 1959 report of the *ad hoc* Committee remained in effect.

In its Geneva sessions, the Scientific and Technical Subcommittee directed its efforts particularly to developing practical suggestions for programs of international cooperation in space activities to implement Assembly Resolutions 1472 and 1721. The recommendations fell under three main headings: exchange of information, encouragement of international programs, and international equatorial sounding-rocket launching facilities.

Exchange of information. The subcommittee particularly recommended that COSPAR, UNESCO, and other appropriate bodies, make available to all member nations information on establishing small-scale satellite tracking and sounding-rocket launching facilities which would be within the means of most nations; and that COSPAR make available to member nations the services and facilities of the World Data Centers for Rockets and Satellites and the Spacewarn communications network.

Encouragement of international programs. The subcommittee noted with approval the establishment of ICSU of programs of international scientific cooperation including the International Year of the Quiet Sun (IQSY), the World Magnetic Survey (WMS), and synoptic rocket and polar cap experiments. The subcommittee also noted with approval the actions of the ITU in seeking international coordination of space communications; the WMO proposals for an international meteorological satellite system; and the UNESCO programs for education of scientists and technicians from all member nations in space sciences and technology, both through fellowships at leading observatories and institutions and through international exchange of personnel. In all these instances, it called upon the U.N. and member nations to cooperate.

International equatorial sounding-rocket launching facilities. Noting the usefulness of sounding rockets in the experimental study of a large region of the atmosphere, and the existence of major gaps in the world coverage of sounding-rocket launching sites—especially in the equatorial region and the Southern Hemisphere—the subcommittee proposed that such a facility be established on the geomagnetic equator as soon as possible,

[39] U.N. Doc. A/AC. 105/C. 1/SR. 2, at 6 (1962).

under United Nations sponsorship. This would achieve a partial closing of the existing gaps and at the same time would be an important step in direct participation in space activities by the U.N. itself. A list of suggested basic principles for the creation and operation of international sounding-rocket launching facilities was included with the recommendation.[40]

Reflecting the closer relationship of space legal problems to international politics than space scientific problems, and the existing lack of consensus in the international political community, the Legal Subcommittee, unlike the Scientific and Technical Subcommittee, was unable to come to a consensus on anything other than the usual minimal conclusion that "the meetings offered the possibility for a most useful exchange of views." The Legal Subcommittee invited UNESCO, WMO, WHO, ITU, and COSPAR to participate in its work as observers. In addition, the Soviet Union submitted two major proposals for consideration by the subcommittee, both of which had been foreshadowed at the March meetings of UNCOPUOS.

The first of the Soviet proposals, a "Declaration of the Basic Principles Governing the Activities of States Pertaining to the Exploration and Use of Outer Space," included the following significant points:

> Outer space and celestial bodies are free for exploration and use by all States; no State may claim sovereignty over outer space and celestial bodies.
>
> . . . the use of outer space for propagating war, national or racial hatred or enmity between nations shall be prohibited.
>
> . . . Cooperation and mutual assistance in the conquest of outer space shall be a duty incumbent upon all States; the implementation of measures that might in any [way] hinder the exploration or use of outer space for peaceful purposes by other countries shall be permitted only after prior discussion of and agreement upon such measures between the countries concerned.
>
> . . . All activities of any kind pertaining to the exploration and use of outer space shall be carried out solely and exclusively by States; the sovereign rights of States to the object they launch into outer space shall be retained by them.
>
> . . . The use of artificial satellites for the collection of intelligence information in the territory of foreign States is incompatible with the objectives of mankind in its conquest of outer space.[41]

Thus the Soviet Union took a position favoring minimal participation in space activities by international intergovernmental organizations.

The second Soviet proposal was an "International Agreement on the

---

[40] U.N. Doc. A/AC. 105/C. 1/L. 2/Rev. 2 (1962). See generally Gardner, *supra* note 37.

[41] U.N. Doc. A/AC. 105/C. 2/L.2 (1962). See also Appendix I-F(2).

Rescue of Astronauts and Spaceships Making Emergency Landings," which has already been discussed in Chapter 8, *supra*. However, the Soviet delegation summarized the basic Soviet position as being that the subcommittee's work should consist above all in preparing, on the basis of the General Assembly resolutions, a declaration on use of the outer space. The United States took the position that any attempt to codify space law at that time was unrealistic; that the committee should not attempt to draft a treaty but should prepare resolutions for submission to the General Assembly; and that the drafting of a treaty should first be undertaken by experts appointed by the Secretary-General (who might, however, be provided with guidelines by the committee). The United States submitted two proposals addressed to specific problems: "Assistance to and Return of Space Vehicles" and "Liability for Space Vehicle Accidents." The latter proposal was based on the principle of the absolute liability of those launching space vehicles, under the assumption that to require proof of negligence would generally be tantamount to denying the possibility of compensation. The former proposal embodied the principle that all possible aid should be afforded space vehicles in distress.[42] (These proposals have also been discussed in Chapter 7.)

In reviewing the work of the Legal Subcommittee, the General Counsel of the United States National Aeronautics and Space Administration, John A. Johnson, observed that the Soviet delegates knew on the basis of prior consultation that neither of their proposals was acceptable to the United States. He suggested that the points quoted above from the proposed declaration of basic principles "appeared to be designed primarily to provide a basis for propaganda against certain U.S. activities. These points ... obviously involved questions of a primarily political rather than legal nature." The most objectionable feature to the United States of the second Soviet proposal, on assistance to and return of space vehicles, was that it would allow a state to decide unilaterally to keep a satellite by asserting that the satellite's launching had not been properly registered or that it was designed for the collection of intelligence data. Mr. Johnson also pointed out that, following the Soviet action, "the United States introduced two proposals ... on which it had not reached prior agreement with the USSR," but that the Soviet Union refused to consider any efforts directed toward reaching an agreement on the question of liability "in the absence of agreement to proceed simultaneously with its Declaration of Basic Principles and draft international agreement concerning assistance and return." [43]

Subsequent events simply seem to confirm that in a world divided by contending ideologies, the difficulties attending the adoption of some form of an agreement that would guarantee the rule of law in outer space

[42] U.N. Doc. A/AC. 105/C. 2/L.2-3. See also Appendices I-F(4) and I-F(5).
[43] John A. Johnson, Comment on work of Legal Subcommittee.

are virtually insurmountable. This thesis was driven home during the months of April and May, 1963, when the Legal Subcommittee of the United Nations Committee on the Peaceful Uses of Outer Space met to continue their efforts to draft a declaration of basic principles which would govern the activities of states in the exploration and use of outer space.

As has been adverted to in a resolution passed on December 14, 1962, the General Assembly of the United Nations urged the Committee on the Peaceful Uses of Outer Space to pursue its work on these basic legal principles. The Committee turned over the task of drafting these principles to its Legal Subcommittee. Composed now of twenty-eight members and reflecting the entire spectrum of contending world views—neutralist, Western-oriented, and Soviet-bloc—the subcommittee had, in the words of one member, "a clear and far-reaching mandate from the General Assembly...." [44] Its task, in a sense, was to elaborate on and breathe life into the first principle of the General Assembly's now famous resolution, No. 1721, which stated that "international law, including the Charter of the United Nations, applies to outer space and celestial bodies." [45]

It was a foregone conclusion among most members of the subcommittee that any declaration they might adopt would perforce be a simple statement of principles rather than a detailed and rigid set of rules. Other representatives, particularly Miss Gutteridge of the United Kingdom, differed, maintaining that some, although by no means all, of the principles should be set forth in detail. In any event, all the members agreed that a simple draft declaration would suffice for the present, for most of the points at issue.[46]

The draft declaration of basic principles that loomed largest during the debates of the subcommittee was that offered by the Soviet delegation. It was a slightly revised version of the draft declaration submitted by the Soviets at Geneva the previous year. A few of the revisions, adopted from suggestions proposed by the United Arab Republic and the United Kingdom, were all for the better as far as most members were concerned. Two of the Soviet points, however, would deadlock the subcommittee and put an end to its useful work for the present.

Since the Soviet draft declaration touched nearly all the points that the members of the subcommittee felt needed to be considered in a final declaration, it might be useful to cite it in a somewhat shortened form. Its eleven points were: (1) space exploration shall be carried out for the benefit of the whole of mankind; (2) all states are free to explore outer space, and national sovereignty cannot be acquired over any part of it;

[44] *Provisional Summary Record of the Legal Subcommittee of the Committee on the Peaceful Uses of Outer Space,* April 22, 1963, at 3. Hereinafter cited as *Legal Subcommittee Record.*

[45] *Id.* at 3-4.

[46] *Id.* at 3, 9; *Legal Subcommittee Record,* May 2, 1963, *passim.*

(3) all states have equal rights in outer space; (4) all space activities will be carried out in accordance with the generally recognized principles of international law and the principles of the United Nations; (5) outer space shall not be used for the purposes of war propaganda; (6) states may cooperate and assist themselves mutually in the conquest of outer space; (7) all activities in outer space shall be carried out solely by states; (8) objects launched into outer space are the property of the state launching them; (9) artificial satellites shall not be used for the collection of intelligence data in the territory of a foreign state; (10) all states shall assist spaceships and crews in distress and permit emergency landings on their territory; (11) a state causing personal or property damage to another state as a result of space activities will bear the responsibility for such damage.[47]

A conspicuous omission from the Soviet draft, as far as a good many states were concerned, was a declaration to the effect that activities in space would be restricted to peaceful purposes. What might be surprising at first was that neither the United States' draft declaration nor the draft declaration of the United Kingdom contained such a clause either. Indeed, on this score, both the United States and the USSR were as one in their insistence that such a clause was out of place in a declaration of basic principles. They maintained, rather, that this was a question for the Eighteen Nation Committee on Disarmament. It was thus that the two principal space powers, the United States and the Soviet Union, as members of the Committee on the Peaceful Uses of Outer Space, refused to go on record as favoring the exclusive use of outer space for peaceful purposes. It was a point which a good many neutrals could not quite fathom.[48]

The United Arab Republic had in fact led the way in urging that such a principle be adopted by inserting the principle as the first point of its own draft declaration.[49] The Japanese delegate, Mr. Matsui, took up the UAR theme by stressing, "The basic theme of the law of outer space must be that outer space must be used for peaceful purposes only. . . ." [50] Mr. Chakravarty, the Indian delegate, agreed. Although conceding that the question of the peaceful uses of outer space was indeed connected with disarmament, Chakravarty made the point that "a declaration to the effect that outer space should be kept free from military use would constitute a significant step in the development of the rule of law in outer space." [51] He went on:

[47] U.N. Committee on the Peaceful Uses of Outer Space, USSR: *Draft Declaration of the Basic Principles Concerning the Activities of States in New Exploration and Use of Outer Space*, April 16, 1963.
[48] *Legal Subcommittee Record*, May 1, 1963, at 13.
[49] *Legal Subcommittee Record, op. cit. supra* note 44, at 4.
[50] *Legal Subcommittee Record*, April 26, 1963, at 11.
[51] *Id.* at 8.

To the extent that it excluded outer space from the area of conflict, such a declaration might facilitate the achievement of an agreement on general and complete disarmament and would make it possible to concentrate efforts on international cooperation for the peaceful uses of outer space.[52]

The neutrals, however, were probably not prepared to fight for this point to the bitter end. Moreover, it seemed apparent that if a draft declaration had any likelihood of being adopted, some form of compromise would have been reached on the issue. Miss Gutteridge pointed the way when she declared on May 1 that the United Kingdom would not oppose the inclusion of the principle "as a statement of an objective to be achieved. . . ." [53]

Both the Soviet Union's and the United States' drafts failed to include a statement to the effect that states planning experiments in outer space should consult with other states before undertaking them, that was sufficiently explicit to please the neutrals. Actually, this demand was aimed directly at the United States and in particular, its 1962 high-altitude nuclear experiment which had partially disrupted the Van Allen belts.[54] The Soviet proposal did make reference to the need for consultation before conducting certain types of space activities, but apparently its language did not go far enough. The United States yielded on the point, declaring that it considered it desirable to reach some international agreement on the mode of consultation preceding such experiments.[55]

On more than one point included in the Soviet draft declaration there was unanimity among the members of the subcommittee. There was complete agreement on the first four principles, as well as on principles No. 6 and No. 8. Some confusion reigned in the beginning over what the points on liability and assistance in the Soviet draft meant. The United Kingdom, for example, felt that the point concerning liability was apt to be misconstrued and asked that that particular point be drawn up in detail. In addition, the Japanese felt that with regard to emergency landings on foreign territory, the launching states should notify the non-launching states before such a landing is made. In any event, all were agreed on the basic principles contained in these points, and before the subcommittee broke up there was a growing *rapprochement* on these questions.[56]

Another point which caused a great deal of difficulty but appeared to be resolved toward the end was that confining space activities to states only. Apparently, the Soviets decided to propose the principle just after the American Congress had acted to allow a private corporation to launch

[52] *Ibid.*

[53] *Legal Subcommittee Record, op. cit. supra* note 48, at 13.

[54] *Legal Subcommittee Record, op. cit. supra* note 44, at 5; *Legal Subcommittee Record, op. cit. supra* note 50, at 7, 11.

[55] *Legal Subcommittee Record,* May 6, 1963, at 5.

[56] *Legal Subcommittee Record, op. cit. supra* note 44, at 3; *Legal Subcommittee Record, op. cit. supra* note 50, at 9, 12; *Legal Subcommittee Record,* May 2, 1963, *Passim; Legal Subcommittee Record, op. cit. supra* note 55, at 5; *Legal Subcommittee Record,* May 7, 1963, at 3, 5, 6.

Telstar. The Soviet delegate, Mr. Fedorenko, maintained that the principle was included in the Soviet draft "in order to ensure that no irresponsible acts were perpetrated by individuals or companies. . . ." Allowing private corporations to take part in space activities "could lead to private capitalist competition and other undesirable phenomena from the point of view of international cooperation." [57] More than one member of the subcommittee answered the Soviet delegate by pointing out that the presence of private shipping firms did not in the least hinder international cooperation on the high seas. Delegates from the West, however, did not stop merely with this argument. The Soviet proposal, in their view, was an attempt to extend the Soviet system of state monopoly into the realm of outer space. ("The proposals put before the subcommittee," said the French delegate, "should not be concerned with matters—such as the establishment of a state monopoly—which [are] directly related to the political, social, and economic systems of states concerned.") The United States yielded all it could on the issue by declaring that it would agree to the inclusion of a statement that states would be responsible for the space activities of national organizations. To most members, this appeared sufficient to satisfy the Soviet demand, although the USSR itself did not say so.[58]

It was the questions of propaganda and the use of satellites to collect intelligence data that finally deadlocked the subcommittee. The Soviet delegate maintained that the prohibition against the use of satellites to collect intelligence was simply "a confirmation and extension of an accepted principle of international law." [59] The Canadian Government replied that ships on the high seas were every day collecting intelligence data and that international law had never prohibited such practices.[60] What did not come out in the debate, however, was probably a strong suspicion in the West that the Soviets would never comply with the principle, even if it were adopted. What was probably also looming in the back of the Western delegates' minds was the difficulty of proving whether or not a satellite was actually used for spying. Under the circumstances, the United States probably felt that an agreement on this point would tie its hands, while, at the same time, the Soviets presumably would still act in whatever manner they chose.

As to the use of communication satellites for the purpose of disseminating propaganda, the West was of the opinion that this was something which should be handled at the disarmament table. The Canadians

[57] *Legal Subcommittee Record,* April 19, 1963, at 7; *Legal Subcommittee Record, op. cit. supra* note 50, at 4.

[58] *Legal Subcommittee Record, op. cit. supra* note 50, at 9, 11, 14; *Legal Subcommittee Record, op. cit. supra* note 48, at 11-12; *Legal Subcommittee Record, op. cit. supra* note 55, at 5.

[59] *Legal Subcommittee Record, op. cit. supra* note 50, at 5.

[60] *Legal Subcommittee Record, op. cit. supra* note 50, at 5; *Legal Subcommittee Record, op. cit. supra* note 48, at 12.

pointed out that such propaganda was still being transmitted by radio and that all efforts to ban these broadcasts had proved futile in the past.[61] Argentina suggested that the Soviets were merely raising insoluble political questions and that the whole idea should be dropped by the subcommittee.[62] The Polish delegate, Mr. Wyzner, answered with some force, however, that as early as 1926 the International Broadcasting Union recommended that broadcasts inimical to the spirit of international goodwill should be banned. He also reminded his fellow delegates that the General Assembly itself had condemned all forms of propaganda in a 1947 resolution.[63] But Mr. Mendez of Argentina was quick to reply that since such a resolution had already been adopted, there seemed no point in raising the question again.[64] Brazil, however, was not satisfied. The recent success of *Telstar* made it necessary that some control be exercised over the content of global telecommunications. With a recent article in *Foreign Affairs* to back him up, the Brazilian delegate told his fellow delegates that communication satellites would soon possess a potential audience of 1000 million people. This communications network might soon become, he concluded, "a new instrument for intensifying political and ideological antagonism between states and spreading distorted information." [65]

The West stuck by its guns. What was and what was not propaganda was a matter of opinion. The term would be too difficult to define. So its argument went. In the end, on this point—as on the point of satellite observations—there was no meeting of the minds, and the subcommittee broke up with no agreement in sight.[66] As the Mexican delegate, Mr. Cuevas Cancino, pointed out with some truth during the subcommittee debates, ". . . the problems confronting the subcommittee [are] no longer new but [appear] to be a repetition, on a large scale, of the old and complex problems arising from the enmity between states." [67]

OTHER ORGANIZATIONS

10–9   International Council of Scientific Unions and Committee on Space Research

Much of science knows no national boundaries. Thus international cooperation among scientists, and international professional organizations

---

[61] *Legal Subcommittee Record, op. cit. supra* note 50, at 4.
[62] *Legal Subcommittee Record, op. cit. supra* note 48, at 10.
[63] U.N. Committee on the Peaceful Uses of Outer Space, *Statement by Mr. E. Wyzner,* April 19, 1963.
[64] *Legal Subcommittee Record, op. cit. supra* note 48, at 10.
[65] *Id.* at 6-7.
[66] *Legal Subcommittee Record,* May 7, 1963, at 5-6.
[67] *Legal Subcommittee Record, op. cit. supra* note 44, at 6.

in the various scientific fields, have been long and well established. There are thirteen major scientific fields organized in nongovernmental unions designed to promote and coordinate research, exchange information, and publish reports. These organizations include:

International Astronomical Union (IAU)
International Geographical Union (IGU)
International Scientific Radio Union (URSI)
International Union of Biochemistry (IUB)
International Union of Biological Sciences (IUBS)
International Union of Crystallography (IUCr)
International Union of Geodesy and Geophysics (IUGG)
International Union of the History of Science (IUHS)
International Union of Mathematics (IUM)
International Union of Physiological Sciences (IUPS)
International Union of Pure and Applied Chemistry (IUPAC)
International Union of Pure and Applied Physics (IUPAP)
International Union of Theoretical and Applied Mechanics (IUTAM) [68]

Most of the world's scientists are also joined together, through membership in these separate international unions, in one great international professional organization—the International Council of Scientific Unions (ICSU), which aims to advance science generally and to coordinate voluntary international activities which involve many of the sciences. The General Assembly of ICSU is composed of representatives from the national scientific institutions of many of the nations of the world, as well as from the thirteen international scientific unions. ICSU also maintains relations with national governments through its affiliation with UNESCO, from which it receives an annual grant of about $200,000.[69]

The complex structure of ICSU makes the question of whether it is a governmental or nongovernmental organization rather ambiguous. In some countries, most of the scientists who constitute its ultimate membership (through various component organizations) are not employed by the national government but by private institutions such as universities; while in other countries, most scientists would be classified as employed by the national government since universities and academies are government agencies. (Being employed by a state university in the United States would not fall under the category of "government-employed" as the term is used here, since the meaning implied is the possibility of being subject to policy control by the national government.) However, since ICSU itself has such extensive ties to governments *per se*, it is probably more appropriate to classify it as a governmental than as a nongovernmental organization.

ICSU has been especially active in programs of scientific research in

[68] Galloway, *supra* note 32, at 616.
[69] *Id.* at 617.

space. As early as 1950, scientists began to consider the possibility of setting aside a period of time during which all scientists could coordinate observations of the sun, the earth, and outer space. In 1951, ICSU created the Comité Spécial de l'Année Géophysique Internationale (CSAGI) to arrange such a world-wide cooperative effort. The International Geophysical Year (IGY) was scheduled to extend from July 1, 1957 to December 31, 1958.[70]

CSAGI invited individual countries to set up national committees to organize and support research during the IGY. In the United States, this was done by the National Academy of Sciences—National Research Council, a quasi-official agency representing the United States scientific community. This institution is privately organized and administered but is obligated under its charter to perform research for government agencies when so requested. It was the U.S. National Committee for the IGY which, after deciding in 1954 that it would be technically feasible to launch a scientific satellite into orbit during the IGY, obtained the necessary government sponsorship and support for the project, which was administered through the National Science Foundation.[71]

The IGY itself was, of course, a remarkable occurrence in all respects, including the pattern of international scientific cooperation which was enlarged considerably from its already sizable dimensions. As a result of the success of the IGY, both in its substantive achievements and in the degree of cooperation attained, three special bodies were established as subsidiaries of ICSU to carry on permanent programs of international scientific cooperation in particular areas—the Special Committee on Antarctic Research (SCAR), the Special Committee on Ocean Research (SCOR), and the Committee on Space Research (COSPAR).[72]

COSPAR was formally organized at a meeting in Amsterdam on November 13, 1959. The membership is comprised of those national scientific institutions and international scientific unions which are members of ICSU, which are actively engaged in space research, and which wish to participate. The Executive Council is composed of representatives of the adhering scientific unions, plus a seven-member Bureau which includes a president, two vice-presidents, and four other members elected from lists furnished by the vice-presidents. The United States National Academy of Sciences and the Academy of Sciences of the USSR, representing the two countries which have placed satellites in orbit, each designate one vice-

[70] Galloway, *supra* note 36, at 1051.
[71] *Ibid.*
[72] Statement by Maurice Roy, President of COSPAR, Before the Fourth Meeting of the Scientific and Technical Subcommittee of the UNCOPUOS, May 31, 1962, p. 1, U.N. Doc. No. PUOS/62/Misc. 9 GE. 62-7724. See generally Sztucki, *Security of Nations and Cosmic Space*, Symp. 1164, 1201-1203; Vereshchetin, *Mezhdunarodnye Organizatsii v Oblasti Issledovaniya Kosmicheskogo Prostranstva* (International Scientific Organizations in the Field of the Study of Cosmic Space), in KOSMOS I MEZHDUNARODNOE PRAVO 153, 161-170 (Korovin ed. USSR 1962).

president. Elections of the other Bureau members have tended to produce a balanced representation of nations identified with both major blocs.[73]

COSPAR, as well as ICSU itself, has close ties with the United Nations. Under an agreement between COSPAR (ICSU) and UNESCO, UNESCO stimulates space research by promoting both world and regional arrangements and by supporting COSPAR (financially and otherwise) in its work. UNESCO itself considers only those individual requests for support for space research which COSPAR cannot handle and/or which require intergovernmental agreement. In addition to its link with UNESCO (through the UNESCO Department of Natural Sciences), COSPAR has consultative status both with the United Nations Committee on the Peaceful Uses of Outer Space and with the International Telecommunication Union (through the ITU Administrative Radio Conference).[74]

COSPAR, like ICSU, concerns itself only with fundamental scientific research and thus is not interested in what it considers to be simply technological or engineering problems, such as rocket construction, propulsion, guidance, and control.[75] Although this general policy of ICSU and COSPAR has some justification and advantages in certain situations, it has also produced the organizational gap noted in the 1959 report of the United Nations *ad hoc* Committee on the Peaceful Uses of Outer Space —namely, that three international nongovernmental organizations which are of significance in the development and coordination of space exploration were not integrated into the general organizational structure of international space activities through the ICSU-COSPAR-UNESCO affiliation since they had not been admitted to ICSU. The organizations so noted were:

Council for International Organizations of Medical Sciences (CIOMS)
Union of International Engineering Organizations (UATI)
International Astronautical Federation (IAF)

At the outset COSPAR established three continuing working groups concerned with (1) Tracking and Transmission of Scientific Information, (2) Scientific Experiments, and (3) Data and Publications. The first of these was later renamed the Working Group on Tracking and Telemetry, while the second became the Working Group for the International Year of the Quiet Sun (IQSY), reflecting the deep interest and involvement of COSPAR in programs to be carried out during the quiet sun year (1964-65). In April 1961, a Working Group 4 on International Reference Atmosphere was also created. In addition, COSPAR contributes to the development of space science by holding yearly assemblies which combine both business sessions and the presentation of scientific papers; gen-

[73] Roy, *supra* note 72, at 2. See also Appendix III-D where the Charter of COSPAR is set out.
[74] Galloway, *World Security and the Peaceful Uses of Outer Space*, Symp. 684, 687.
[75] Roy, *supra* note 72, at 1.

eral international symposia on space research, which are open to scientists from all countries including those not represented in COSPAR; and more specialized symposia dealing with particular areas of space research.

By its very existence, COSPAR serves as a forum for the discussion of experimental ideas and the presentation of new projects and proposals. Typically, it served as the medium of transmission for the United States' proposal to launch individual space experiments or complete payloads of mutual interest prepared by scientists of other nations. It publishes an information bulletin which is designed to serve as an authoritative medium for news of interest to space scientists, and it has prepared and published tables of atmospheric density, pressure, temperature, composition, etc., for altitudes from 30 kilometers to the theoretical upper limit. These tables are under constant review and revision by Work Group 4. Furthermore, COSPAR took over responsibility for the world rocket and satellite data centers that were originally established in connection with the IGY, to collect rocket/satellite data and make it readily available to scientists of all nations.

One of the most important activities of COSPAR is the operation of the Spacewarn network for rapid transmission of satellite information to institutions and scientists throughout the world. The main types of information transmitted are launching announcements of satellites and space probes, orbital elements for predictions, ephemerides for individual stations, and approximate tracking observations. For this purpose COSPAR has developed a system of uniform codes to be used in the communication of space data. It likewise prepares world lists of optical and radio satellite tracking stations, including the fullest possible information on the location and equipment of the stations and the precision of their instrumentation; and it has made studies and recommendations with a view to securing a more scientifically rational distribution of tracking stations.

Another significant activity of COSPAR is its sponsorship of the International Rocket Intervals, which feature rocket firings coordinated on a world-wide basis for purposes of upper-atmosphere research. And it has shown a continuing interest in the matter of radio frequency allocation for space research. In this respect COSPAR has worked closely in a consultative capacity with the ITU. Within the ICSU framework, it helped to form the Inter-Union Committee on Frequency Allocations, which has made important studies and recommendations relating to this critical problem.

It has also been pointed out, in Chapter 9, *supra,* that COSPAR took over the work of the ICSU Committee on Contamination by Extra-Terrestrial Exploration (CETEX). Indeed COSPAR, as an organization devoted to the study, discussion, and coordination of space science activities, is concerned either directly or indirectly with virtually all the major issues of space exploration that are surveyed in this book.[76] As this is a book on law, it must be pointed out that it is extremely unfortunate that most of the work done by COSPAR is strictly *ultra vires* and lacking in legal authorization—because such activities are forbidden by the basic statutes of ICSU.

10–10   United States National Aeronautics and Space Administration

Although it is not by origin an international organization, it seems appropriate in this survey of governmental organizations involved in international space activities to include one of the largest such entities, the United States National Aeronautics and Space Administration (NASA), since NASA has developed substantial international programs. The genesis of the establishment of NASA was, of course, the Russian launching of the first artificial earth satellite, together with the growing realization on the part of the United States that its space program was being hindered by lack of coordination among the various agencies involved in the program and by a scale of priorities which did not take sufficient account of the impact of non-military scientific achievements on the U.S. position in the world.

The opinions of scientists and engineers involved in the space program through universities, industrial firms, the Department of Defense, and the IGY, were quite influential in the decision-making process which led to creation of the new space agency. The Rocket and Satellite Research Panel, chaired by James A. Van Allen, issued the report *A National Mission to Explore Outer Space* in late November 1957 recommending that a national space agency be created. An independent study published at approximately the same time by the American Rocket Society made the same recommendation. Opposition to the idea had been expressed by a number of prominent military and civilian representatives from the Department of Defense, but the preponderant opinion favored a national space agency oriented primarily toward the civilian space program, with provision made for coordination with defense programs. As one commentator has perceptively noted: ". . . this was not a problem of civilian control inasmuch as both the Department of Defense and the proposed new space agency would be directed by civilian officials. The problem was essentially one of achieving emphasis and priority for projects which transcended the missions of the Armed Forces. . . ." This same commentator concluded that the reasons for deciding on a civilian space agency could be summarized as follows:

> 1. National security requires an outstanding space program which will insure pre-eminent U.S. leadership in a broad field encompassing many beneficial civilian applications which are not military in nature.

[76] Roy, *supra* note 72, at 2-4; SCHWARTZ, *op. cit. supra* note 12, at 36-55.

2. Space technology has become a factor in the position of the United States in the world, and being connected with the conduct of foreign policy is often more related to the mission of the Department of State than that of the Department of Defense.

3. The space program should be funded on a long-term basis and not depend upon shorter term military appropriations or have to compete for funds within the Department of Defense.

4. The national space effort could not develop its own essential priorities if it were under the administration of one military service or subject to dispersal among the three services.

5. The Department of Defense must prove it has a military requirement for new projects and would be unlikely to undertake space programs which are primarily scientific, commercial, and cultural in nature.[77]

The first concrete step toward the establishment of NASA was the action of President Eisenhower in creating a Scientific Advisory Committee, headed by M.I.T. President James R. Killian, in November 1957, to propose national objectives and requirements in space. This body also sought to recommend a basic organizational framework which would effectively integrate science and technology into the space program in particular and national policy-making in general, so as to secure the maximum results from research efforts.[78] The significance of space activities to the nation was described by the Committee in its report published in late March 1958 entitled "Introduction to Outer Space." The report cited four primary considerations justifying a large space program: (1) man's urge to explore the unknown, (2) new opportunities for scientific research made possible by space technology, (3) the effect of scientific and technological accomplishment on national prestige, (4) the necessity to be prepared for defense if space is used militarily. The report stressed the value of peaceful applications of space science and technology, such as world-wide communications systems and improved weather prediction, and noted that research always has "a remarkable way of paying off." This report formed the basis of the message which President Eisenhower sent to the Congress on April 2, 1958 recommending the establishment of a civilian space agency, the National Aeronautics and Space Administration.[79]

Except for the initial opposition by some members of the Department of Defense, the Eisenhower proposal achieved a remarkable affirmative consensus. It did not become an issue either between the executive and legislative branches of the Government or between the political parties. The National Aeronautics and Space Act (also known simply as the "Space Act") establishing NASA, passed both houses of Congress without

[77] Galloway, supra note 36, at 1053.
[78] Emme, Historical Origins of NASA (Revised), p. 2 (mimeo. 1962).
[79] Galloway, supra note 36, at 1052.

a dissenting vote, and was signed by President Eisenhower on July 29, 1958.[80] The Act declared that "it is the policy of the United States that activities in space should be devoted to peaceful purposes for the benefit of all mankind." [81] Activities in space primarily associated with military operations in the defense of the United States were reserved to the Department of Defense. Recognizing that a number of other federal agencies had interests in space activities besides NASA and the Defense Department, the Act also established the National Aeronautics and Space Council to achieve the maximum possible interdepartmental coordination.[82]

Almost immediately NASA assumed control of, and responsibility for, many of the already far-flung United States space activities. However, the agency's interests and activities were not destined to be purely national in scope, for the National Aeronautics and Space Act provided that space activities of the United States should be conducted so as to contribute materially to "cooperation by the United States with other nations and groups of nations. . . ." [83] The implementation of this policy was also provided for in the Act:

> The Administration [NASA], under the foreign policy guidance of the President, may engage in a program of international cooperation in work done pursuant to this Act, and in the peaceful application of the results thereof, pursuant to agreements made by the President with the advice and consent of the Senate.[84]

In signing the Act, President Eisenhower stated that he interpreted this provision "merely as recognizing that international treaties may be made in this field, and as not precluding, in appropriate cases, less formal arrangements for cooperation. To construe the section otherwise would raise substantial constitutional questions." [85] The relation of the space program to international relations was also recognized by including the Secretary of State in the Space Council established by the Act.[86]

Based upon the national policy declarations in the Space Act, NASA established an Office of International Programs to work with the Department of State in establishing arrangements for international cooperation, and by 1962 these had already been extended to more than fifty nations.[87] NASA also cooperates with the United Nations and with the Committee

[80] *Id.* at 1053. For the full text of the National Aeronautics and Space Act, see Appendix II-A.
[81] Emme, *op. cit. supra* note 78, at 3.
[82] Galloway, *supra* note 36, at 1054.
[83] Galloway, *supra* note 74, at 688.
[84] *Ibid.*
[85] Galloway, *supra* note 36, at 1054-55.
[86] *Id.* at 1054.
[87] *Id.* at 1055.

on Space Research (COSPAR) of the ICSU, working through the U.S. National Academy of Sciences.[88] NASA international programs that are already well-established include: (1) the world-wide network of tracking and telemetry stations required for the acquisition of data from satellites and space probes; (2) the launching for other nations of individual experiments or complete scientific payloads in artificial earth satellites; (3) joint programs with scientists and engineers of other nations cooperating in space research; (4) exchange of scientific and technical information, including the making available of data from United States space activities to scientists throughout the world for evaluation; (5) training programs and exchanges with foreign scientists.[89] A dramatic example of the truly international spirit of the United States space program was the offer made to the Soviet Union in December 1959 of the use of the special tracking facilities designed for the Project Mercury man-in-space program. The NASA Administrator suggested that "data could be acquired and transmitted in its raw state to the Academy of Sciences in Moscow," and noted that "a precedent for this sort of thing has been established in the IGY operation when the United States supplied to the Soviet scientists, as of July 1959, some 46 tape recordings of *Sputnik I, II,* and *III.*" [90]

While NASA's contributions to international space cooperation have been on the whole extremely heartening, its administration of the United States space program has been something less than satisfactory in the area of patent law, as a result of the patent provisions in the 1958 Space Act which created NASA. Since the experience of NASA in this matter has an important bearing both on the problems involved in the establishment of an international treaty on patent law and more generally on the future course of the national space effort, the subject deserves careful consideration in this volume. The issues at stake concern not only the government itself but even more directly the industries involved in the space program including thousands of companies and hundreds of thousands of employees. The government has brought private enterprise into a partnership in this program to a far greater extent than in any previous program: in the case of atomic energy, by contrast, it is still a dominating overlord.

This partnership is hailed as particularly encouraging by the proponents of free enterprise. If it fails, our political as well as our economic institutions will be seriously jeopardized. Moreover, for the partnership to work requires substantially more than the mere declaration by the government of its announced policy to have private enterprise participate in its space endeavors. Private enterprise must have a voice in whether it is going to participate and on what terms.

Notwithstanding their desire to perform a service to the country, and

[88] Galloway, *supra* note 74, at 688.
[89] *Id.* at 688-89.
[90] *Id.* at 688.

the promise of adequate remuneration for the efforts expended, some corporations have flatly refused to enter the program and others have done so only reluctantly. The principal reason for industry's reluctance is Section 305 of the National Aeronautics and Space Act of 1958, which deals with property rights in inventions made under federal space contracts. The first clause reads in essence: "Whenever any invention is made in the performance of any work under any contract of the [National Aeronautics and Space] Administration such invention shall be the exclusive property of the United States, and if such invention is patentable a patent therefor shall be issued to the United States . . . unless the Administrator waives all or any part of the rights of the United States to such invention in conformity with the provisions of subsection (f)." It further provides that no patent may be issued to any person if the invention involved appears to the Commissioner of Patents to have "significant utility" for the space program, unless the applicant swears under oath that he developed his invention without aid from the space agency. Even then, the applicant may be overridden by the NASA administrator and be compelled to find any remedy due him through complicated appeal procedures.[91]

It is not clear from the legislative history how this provision crept into the statute. During the hearings on the Space Act of 1958, the subject was rarely mentioned. The first proposed draft omitted entirely any comment on patent rights. President Eisenhower's message was similarly silent on this point. Since a comparable provision appears in the Atomic Energy Act, some commentators theorize that the House and Senate Committees automatically assumed it appropriate to incorporate this provision in the Space Act. If so, however, Congress overlooked government's almost exclusive role in the atomic power field. Moreover, the drafters failed to consider the regulations governing property interests in contracts let by the Defense Department. In this respect, the Department of Defense is not governed by statute but by regulation. The Department of Defense acquires no patent rights on contracts calling exclusively for delivery of supplies. On research and development contracts, the Department requires only an irrevocable, royalty-free, non-exclusive license to make or have made any invention arising thereunder.[92]

For some inexplicable reason, Congress patterned the patent section of the Space Act after the corresponding provision in the Atomic Energy Act instead of fashioning the provision along the lines of the Department of Defense regulations. Despite the drafters' thoughts to the contrary, NASA deals with products more like those of the Defense Department

[91] See generally Maltby, *The National Aeronautics and Space Act of 1958, Patent Provisions,* 27 GEO. WASH. L. REV. (1958).

[92] REPORT OF THE SUBCOMMITTEE ON PATENTS AND SCIENTIFIC INVENTIONS TO THE HOUSE COMMITTEE ON SCIENCE AND ASTRONAUTICS, 86TH CONG., 2D SESS., PROPOSED REVISIONS TO THE PATENT SECTION, NATIONAL AERONAUTICS AND SPACE ACT 1958 25 (Comm. Print 1960).

than of the Atomic Energy Commission. Indeed, Congress has recognized this by determining that in general procurement regulations, NASA is to follow the procedures of the Department of Defense.

In many instances, NASA will procure its needs through Department of Defense personnel where both agencies contract with the same private contractor. NASA, in order to carry out the spirit of Section 305, then requires the special Section 305 clause to be incorporated in the contract covering the NASA purchase. This leads to a highly anomalous result where two agencies of the government contract for the identical commodity from the same contractor—with respect to one, the contractor retains his property rights, and with respect to the other, he may lose his rights.

The inequality of treatment between the Department of Defense and NASA is simply one instance demonstrating the statute's inadequacy. It suffers from other infirmities. For instance, Section 305 is not restricted to research and development projects but embraces any work performed at the insistence of the administrator. For example, if a particular fine, patentable, welding torch were developed, to fulfill an over-all NASA contract, under the statute the administrator could insist upon ownership rights in the torch.

Contractors contemplating bidding for space work must consider with particular attention the statutory definition that the term "made," when used in relation to any invention, means the conception or first actual reduction to practice of such invention. Since "made" encompasses not only conception but also reduction to practice, a contractor who has in fact secured a patent may still be deprived of proprietary interests if the patent is first reduced to practice under a NASA contract.

The reasoning of those who resist amendment of the NASA patent provisions is predicated on the theory: "if the government pays for the invention, it should own that which it purchased." There is no dispute that the government is entitled to all the benefits that may be derived from spending its citizens' hard-earned tax dollars. This, however, is achieved by the government's reserving a royalty-free, irrevocable license on all patents attributed to work performed with the aid of government funds.

In certain isolated cases, perhaps more is required. For instance, if through space exploration a cancer cure can be discovered, then it would be unconscionable to deny to the public the benefit of such a discovery.

That adequate protection of the government's interest is afforded by a royalty-free irrevocable license is indicated by the government's refusal to protect the patents which it now owns. *It does not sue infringers.* Exclusive licenses cannot be had from the government, for if the government did grant such licenses, it would expose itself to severe criticism. More important, it would be seriously impinging upon areas heretofore deemed within the exclusive preserve of private enterprise.

NASA has a very liberal policy regarding waiver of patent rights. This policy is designed to encourage prompt public and industrial benefit from the byproducts of its space research and development activity. The waivers may be voided after five years if the recipients do not show that the inventions have been developed to the point of practical application or were made available for license by others. At the same time, the government does retain a license for governmental use of the inventions.[93]

In 1960 the House of Representatives, mindful that defense and space postures are at stake, extensively amended Section 305, deleting the principal offending portions. Unfortunately, the Senate did not act on the House bill. As a consequence, industry remains plagued by these burdensome provisions.

When the domestic problems involved in patent law are as complex and unattended as those of the United States, no rational observer can hope for the immediate development of treaties to control international abuses of patent rights. Yet, in an industry so demanding of genius and invention, men ought to be most concerned with and interested in the rights of inventors. The greatest problem in the formulation of any treaty on patents will obviously be enforcement. Identification of infractions and the speedy prosecution of claims are essential to a working system to protect patent rights. Today, however, there is neither an agency nor a forum within which we can hope to handle these problems. Like so many of the various space legal problems, patents present a case *sui generis,* requiring a structure which will have to be built from the ground up.

10-11   National Aeronautics and Space Council—Senate Committee on Aeronautical and Space Sciences—House Committee on Science and Astronautics

The world community of non-Communist nations is indeed fortunate in that the ultimate responsibility for the American space effort reposes, for legislative action, in the committees of the United States Congress; and for executive action, in the National Aeronautics and Space Council. No better informed or enlightened official *detente* could be created from the best fabric of United States expertise.

The National Aeronautics and Space Council is in the Executive Office of the President and was established by the National Aeronautics and Space Act of 1958. It has the responsibility for advising and assisting the President with respect to policies and performance throughout the entire aeronautics and space field. This includes the space activities of the Department of Defense, the National Aeronautics and Space Administration, the Atomic Energy Commission, the State Department, etc. As outlined in the law, the Council's functions include the following:

[93] NASA News Release No. 63-128, June 11, 1963.

1. survey all significant aeronautical and space activities, including the policies, plans, programs, and accomplishments of all departments and agencies of the United States engaged in such activities;

2. develop a comprehensive program of aeronautical and space activities to be conducted by departments and agencies of the United States;

3. designate and fix responsibility for the direction of major aeronautical and space activities;

4. provide for effective cooperation among all departments and agencies of the United States engaged in aeronautical and space activities, and specify, in any case in which primary responsibility for any category of aeronautical and space activities has been assigned to any department or agency, which of those activities may be carried on concurrently by other departments or agencies; and

5. resolve differences arising among departments and agencies of the United States with respect to aeronautical and space activities under this Act, including differences as to whether a particular project is an aeronautical and space activity.

The members of the Council are the Vice President (Chairman), the Secretary of State, the Secretary of Defense, the Administrator of NASA, and the Chairman of the AEC. The Executive Secretary of the Council is the statutory officer in charge of the staff.

Long before President Eisenhower's famous proclamation of July 29, 1955, authorizing the earth-orbiting satellite in connection with the International Geophysical Year, Lyndon B. Johnson was profoundly interested in all aspects of rocketry and space exploration. As one facet of his distinguished career, history must record that Vice President Johnson is the father of astronautics legislation in the United States. Assisting Vice President Johnson as Executive Secretary of the National Aeronautics and Space Council is Dr. Edward C. Welsh whose outstanding competence is founded upon profound knowledge of economics and finance, which he has reduced to practice in teaching, industry, and organization. These qualifications now culminate in a felicitous and enlightened as well as a most penetrating administration on the highest echelon in the United States space effort.

Secretary of State, Dean Rusk, during the past decade has shown intense interest in the United States space effort as exemplified by one small example in his attendance at the American Rocket Society Space Law and Sociology Conference in New York, in March 1959. Robert S. McNamara, Secretary of Defense, was ultimately responsible for inaugurating space activities in the Ford Motor Company.

The Chairman of the Senate Committee on Aeronautical and Space Sciences, Clinton P. Anderson, is a veteran legislator and administrator whose interest in the space sciences parallels the experience of the many highly qualified senators for members of his committee, including such

well informed persons as Warren G. Magnuson, Stuart Symington, Thomas
J. Dodd, Howard W. Cannon, Bourke B. Hickenlooper, and Kenneth B.
Keating.

The Chairman of the House Committee on Science and Astronautics,
George P. Miller, on April 24, 1962, was the recipient of the Testimonial
Award of the American Rocket Society Committee on Space Law and
Sociology; and the citation reads:

> Distinguished Chairman of the Committee on Science and Astronautics of
> the United States House of Representatives, conservator of the nation's natural
> resources, soldier and statesman. Chairman Miller is a true pioneer of the
> Space Age. He is a Founding Member of the Science and Astronautics Com-
> mittee, and his intensive interest in aeronautics dates back to the dark days
> of the Second World War when his leadership in the field was first asserted—
> leadership which has encouraged and inspired the scientific and technological
> communities of the United States and of the nations of the world. For his
> superb leadership, his indomitable industry, and his enlightened statesman-
> ship in the cause of astronautics, this Testimonial to George Paul Miller is
> inscribed and signed on the Twenty-fourth day of April, 1962, on the occa-
> sion of the Space Law and Sociology Conference at the Carnegie Endowment
> for International Peace Building, New York.

The House committee is highly competent and includes such outstanding
experts as Olin E. Teague, Joseph E. Karth, Ken Hechler, John W. Davis,
Carl Albert, Joseph W. Martin, Jr., James G. Fulton, and J. Edgar Cheno-
weth.

The Counsel for the Senate committee consists of Everard H. Smith,
Jr., William J. Deachman, Dr. Glen P. Wilson, and Richard R. Wolfe.
The Counsel for the House committee consists of Charles F. Ducander,
Philip B. Yeager, and Frank R. Hammill, Jr.

Undoubtedly the most informative and reliable source material on the
United States space effort is contained in the Annual Report of the
President to the Congress. This Report is prepared by the National Aeronautics and Space Council under the direction of Dr. Welsh and the
highly qualified staff of the Council with the direct and scrupulous oversight of the President, the Vice President, and the members of the Council.
There is no other publication which parallels the Report to the Congress.

The well-established format includes a brief and accurate summary
of the United States Aeronautics and Space activities for the preceding
year. This is followed by the Vice President's special summary report to
the President on the accomplishments of the Council. In rapid succession
and in amazingly accurate detail are outlined the activities and achievements of the National Aeronautics and Space Administration, Department
of Defense, Atomic Energy Commission, Department of State, National
Science Foundation, Department of Commerce, Space Science Board,
Smithsonian Astrophysical Observatory, Federal Aviation Agency, Federal Communications Commission and the United States Information

Agency. The Committee reports and Staff reports of the House and Senate "Space Committees" afford a living panorama of the day to day United States space projects—and of the failures and successes achieved by the nation's astronautics community.

Only by diligent study of the reports of the National Aeronautics and Space Council and the House and Senate committee reports may the interested person achieve a true perspective of the current posture of the space effort. Other sources of information such as periodicals and specialized commentaries are quite valuable and have their place in any research program. But the reports to and from Congress are the most informative and authentic.

Additional References

Andrew G. Haley, ROCKETRY AND SPACE EXPLORATION: THE INTERNATIONAL STORY (1958); ____, *Space Communications and Cooperation With Iron Curtain Countries: Part I,* Signal, Nov. 1961, p. 39; ____, *Space Communications and Cooperation With Iron Curtain Countries: Part II,* Signal, Dec. 1961, p. 12 ____, *Rule of Law in Outer Space: Letter to the Editor,* New York Times, Feb. 18, 1961, p. 18; ____, *International Scene—Preliminary Report on the Actions of the Geneva Meeting With Respect to Astronautical Radio,* Astronautics, Nov. 1959, p. 20; ____, *International Astronautical Federation and Space Communications: Remarks before the Delegates to the Administrative Radio Conference of the International Telecommunication Union, Geneva, Switzerland, Oct. 1959,* Reprinted in TELECOMMUNICATIONS JOURNAL, Nov. 1959; ____, *Space Age Presents Immediate Legal Problems,* in FIRST COLLOQUIUM ON THE LAW OF OUTER SPACE 5 (1959); ____, *International Cooperation in Astronautics,* Foreign Service Journal, April 1958, p. 1; ____, *Seventh IAF Congress Stresses Cooperation,* 27 JET PROPULSION 60 (1957); ____, *International Cooperation in Rocketry and Astronautics,* 25 JET PROPULSION 627 (1955); *Space Law: Recent Practical Achievements:* Paper by ____, Before the American Rocket Society 13th Annual Meeting in New York, Nov. 17-21, 1958; *Scientific and Social Developments of Outer Space:* Lecture by ____, National Capital Section of the American Rocket Society and Army Corps of Engineers' Course on "Science and Rocketry" in Ft. Belvoir, Va., Nov. 8, 1958; *Some Immediate Jurisdictional Problems:* Address by ____, Military Librarians Groups, Special Libraries Association in Ft. McNair, Washington, D.C., Oct. 15, 1958; *The Sociological Implications of Astronautics:* Address by ____, Canadian Astronautical Society in Montreal, April 18, 1958; *Space Flight as World Economic Solution:* Address by ____, Member Society of the International Astronautical Federation in Dublin, Feb. 23, 1958; *Current International Situations and the Legal Involvements With Respect to Long-Range Missiles and Earth-Circling Objects:* Paper by ____, Before the Astronautics Symposium in San Diego, Feb. 18-20, 1957.

11

Nongovernmental
organizations

The role of nongovernmental organizations in the coordination of international space activities has grown increasingly important over the last decade. This chapter examines principally the history of the International Astronautical Federation (IAF), which is composed of scientists and technicians from all over the world. Founded in 1950, it has contributed to international cooperation by sponsoring annual astronautical congresses, by holding colloquia on space legal problems, and by the creation of two affiliates to coordinate legal and scientific research—the International Institute of Space Law and the International Academy of Astronautics. Cooperation of the IAF with other organs including UNESCO, ICSU, ITU, and national astronautical groups is traced. The role of other outstanding organizations in encouraging and furthering the international coordination of astronautical activities is also evaluated. The American Bar Association, the American Institute of Aeronautics and Astronautics (successor of the American Rocket Society and the Institute of Aerospace Sciences), and the International Astronautical Federation are treated here as examples of the many nongovernmental organizations that are working toward the sound development of an international astronautical program.

DIRECT INTERNATIONAL
COORDINATION OF SPACE ACTIVITIES
THROUGH THE INTERNATIONAL ASTRONAUTICAL FEDERATION

11-1 Background of its founding

Cooperation in any aspect of astronautics did not exist prior to the twentieth century, and substantial developments did not occur until the 1930s. Rockets were weapons, and the military guarded their rocket secrets; difficulties of travel and of communications further retarded the dissemination of data on rockets. Nevertheless, during the first three decades of the twentieth century the great rocket pioneers earnestly undertook theoretical formulations of rocket and astronautical projects. Hermann Oberth [1] of Rumania and Germany, Konstantin Tsiolkovsky [2] of Russia, Hermann Noordung [3] of Austria, Walter Hohmann [4] of Germany, Robert Esnault-Pelterie [5] of France, Robert H. Goddard [6] of the United States, and many other eminent engineers, scientists, and industrial experimenters, published basic studies that led to the great mass of literature and the extensive experimentation which burst forth about 1930, and which underlie our present-day rocket knowledge.[7]

One of the splendid international pronouncements of the pre-1930 era was the statement contained in a letter by Oberth to Goddard in 1922. With respect to space flight, he said, "... 1 think that only by common work of the scholars of all nations can be solved this great problem." And in fact many of the early pioneers did exchange letters and on a few occasions visit one another. An exception was Tsiolkovsky (1857-1935), who remained in seclusion in Russia where he wrote a number of works on space flight.[8] Because he understood only Russian he was unacquainted with the West, and the Western pioneers did not understand Russian so they were not acquainted with Tsiolkovsky. Also Goddard himself, who was both theorizing and working tirelessly on the actual rocket hardware, and who had by 1929 fired the world's first successful continuously-firing liquid-propellant rocket, was extremely prudent about disseminating information. It is now interesting to read the old publications of the American Rocket Society (ARS) [9] in which writers indicate in the 1930s that it was easier to obtain an interchange of information from the German rocketeers than from Dr. Goddard. Goddard had more to offer than he had to receive by way of an interchange of information in the particular field in which he worked: he knew the theory and was conquering the hardware. If he had lived beyond World War II, it is certain Goddard would have been in the forefront of those advocating space flight.

[1] OBERTH, WEGE ZUR RAUMSCHIFFAHRT (Germany 1929).

[2] TSIOLKOVSKY, SOBRANIE SOCHINENIE (Collected Works) (USSR 1951-59).

[3] NOORDUNG, DAS PROBLEM DER BEFAHRUNG DES WELTRAUMS (Germany 1929).

[4] HOHMANN, DIE ERREICHBARKEIT DER HIMMELSKÖRPER; UNTERSUCHUNGEN ÜBER DAS RAUMFAHRTPROBLEM (Germany 1925).

[5] ESNAULT-PELTERIE, L'ASTRONAUTIQUE (France 1930).

[6] GODDARD, A METHOD OF REACHING EXTREME ALTITUDES (1919).

[7] Letter from R. H. Goddard to G. E. Pendray, Bull. of the American Interplanetary Soc., June-July 1931, p. 9.

[8] Op. cit. supra note 2.

[9] For some years the American Rocket Society was known as the American Interplanetary Society, but for the sake of simplicity only the later name and initials will be used.

The first common forum for astronauts in all nations was established in Germany in 1927—The Society for Space Travel (VfR).[10] The Russians may dispute this statement, as announcement was made in 1926 of a "World Center for All Inventors and Scientists" which was somehow integrated with reaction research societies in Moscow and Leningrad.[11] No evidence is available, however, that this was more than a paper project, and short-lived at that. In any event, the German society grew very rapidly. Five hundred members from Germany, Austria, Russia, and France *joined the first year.*[12] Similar societies also sprang up in other countries. In those days, membership in such societies did not improve one's professional standing, and much effort of the societies was devoted to proving to the public that astronautics was a science which could be pursued by sane men.

While the societies were engaged with this and more theoretical pursuits, the Austrian Max Valier startled his fellow members of the VfR, including Oberth, by a spectacular use of an improvised rocket automobile powered by powder charges. He also arranged a rocket mail delivery. Unfortunately, Valier was killed in a rocket automobile demonstration.[13] Under these circumstances it was difficult to establish the respectability of the rocket worker. But courageous people carried on. In 1931 G. Edward Pendray of the ARS went to Berlin and spent some time discussing rocket engine problems with Oberth, Johannes Winkler, and others.[14] Later ARS rocket motors showed the influence of "Raketenflugplatz," the testing ground of the VfR. This visit was none too soon. The German Army confiscated both plans and personnel from Raketenflugplatz by degrees and set up another larger installation near Kummersdorf. The start of German Army experimentation was in accord with the provisions of the Versailles Treaty, which—with rather great lack of foresight—had not included rockets on the list of weapons forbidden to the vanquished Germany. However, it had an adverse effect on the hapless German Society, which by 1932 began to fade.

Meanwhile, the American Rocket Society (ARS) was growing. In 1930 the first bulletin of the society appeared, containing an article on the *Universal Background of Interplanetary Flight.* For many years this early ARS publication carried a column on *News from Abroad* suggesting strong interest in international astronautical affairs. France's great pioneer astronaut, Robert Esnault-Pelterie, presented to the society an autographed copy of his historic *L'Astronautique,* and in January 1931 arrived in New

[10] LEY, ROCKETS, MISSILES AND SPACE TRAVEL 116-17 (1958).

[11] *Id.* at 117.

[12] *Id.* at 118.

[13] Bull. of the American Interplanetary Soc., June 1930, p. 3.

[14] Bull. of the American Interplanetary Soc., May 1931, p. 5.

York. Two thousand people turned out at an ARS meeting to hear him speak.[15]

The world was then in the throes of the great depression, and rocketry was proceeding on a very small scale. In 1932 the Russian-Polish space-flight enthusiast, A. Sternfel'd, went to France where he saw A. Ananoff, a leader in French astronautical circles. Ananoff, himself an ex-Russian, had for a long time attempted to maintain some sort of liaison with Russian astronautical scientists and was responsible, through his books, for providing the West with knowledge of Russian writings.[16]

In 1933 Philip Cleator founded the British Interplanetary Society (BIS) which was to become an influential force in astronautics.[17] A year later he traveled to Germany to find that the VfR "was no more." He wrote that the Raketenflugplatz "appeared derelict": the Army had really taken over German rocketry.[18]

Patrons of the arts and sciences also made earnest efforts to stimulate world-wide activity in astronautics through awards and prizes. Their efforts can be regarded as another major step toward international cooperation in astronautics. The first serious gesture of this sort was the establishment in 1929 by Robert Esnault-Pelterie and a banker, André Hirsch, of the "REP-Hirsch-Prize." This prize was for the author or experimenter who had done the most to further the idea of space travel in a given year and was administered by the Société Astronomique de France. It was actually awarded between 1929 and 1936, with the exception of three years when it was considered that no worthwhile contribution had been made. Hermann Oberth received a double award in 1929 for his *Road to Space Travel*. In 1930 and 1933, Pierre Montague received the prizes for papers on gaseous mixtures usable in the propulsion of rockets. In 1933 A. Sternfel'd received an additional prize for a paper, *Invitation to Cosmonautics*, and in 1934 Louis Damblac received a "Prize of Encouragement" for a paper on ground tests. Alfred Africano and the American Rocket Society were honored with the prize in 1936 for design of a high-altitude rocket.[19]

International cooperation of a friendly, competitive sort could be detected elsewhere, too, in the 1930s, if one looked hard enough. Gerhard Zucker, owner of a mail-rocket franchise from the German Post Office, went to Scotland for a friendly mail-shooting contest between the two countries.[20] Mail rockets were enjoying a vogue at the time, one which

---

[15] At the last minute Esnault-Pelterie was detained by illness and his paper was read by G. Edward Pendray.

[16] ANANOFF, L'ASTRONAUTIQUE (France 1950).

[17] GARTMANN, THE MEN BEHIND THE SPACE ROCKETS, 162-65 (1956).

[18] See generally LEY, *op. cit. supra* note 10, at 160-62.

[19] LEY, *op. cit. supra* note 10, at 123 n8; *The History of the REP-Hirsch Award*, Astronautics, June 1936, p. 6.

[20] Astronautics, Jan. 1938, p. 6.

did not subside completely until some ten years later. By 1937 the French, under the initiative of Robert Lancement, felt that the time had arrived when it would be appropriate to make an astronautical exhibit. The place and occasion: Paris, during the 1937 International Exhibition.[21] At the Paris exhibition astronautical material from America was shown, as well as from Austria, France, Germany, Great Britain, and Russia. The Cleveland Rocket Society sent a half-scale model of a research rocket.

In 1938 Group-Captain Frank Whittle of the Royal Air Force successfully flew a turbojet-powered aircraft.[22] As the turbojet, like the rocket, was a reaction engine, it created immediate interest in engineering circles. For the first time in history there was a prospect of an extremely fast reaction-powered aircraft. During these same years, however, the international political situation was getting tense. A civil war was in progress in Spain, and Hitler was expanding his control in Europe. America was showing signs of rearmament. World War II was about to break out.

The exigencies of warfare necessarily foreclosed cooperation between private individuals in areas essential to national defense. In fact this situation has really persisted from about 1934 to the present time. Within the framework of the establishments of friendly governments, on the other hand, there has been very free exchange of information between individuals, and this without doubt has added immensely to the prospects for space flight.

11–2 Early organizational development

After years of private studies and the establishment of national rocket societies, it was only natural that the rocket technicians of the world should associate formally in an international organization.[23] All who were interested in space travel realized that interplanetary flight would cost huge sums, and many, such as Germany's Dr. Gunter Loeser, held that "this huge task cannot be performed by a single country." The first formal act leading to the creation of the International Astronautical Federation (IAF) was taken by the newly-formed Society for Space Research (Gesellschaft für Weltraumforschung or GfW) in Germany on June 22, 1949. On that date the society adopted a resolution, signed by Drs. H. Gartmann and H. H. Koelle on behalf of the Board of Directors, which stated:

> The rocket is not only a weapon, but also an instrument of peaceful research. The Society for Space Research therefore considers one of its most important

[21] See Ananoff, *op. cit. supra* note 16, at 150.

[22] N.Y. Times, July 30, 1939, §10, p. 4, col. 3.

[23] The history of the IAF is discussed in Vereshchetin, *Mezhdunarodnye Nauchnye Organizatsii v Oblasti Issledovaniya Kosmicheskogo Prostranstva* (International Scientific Organizations in the Field of the Study of Cosmic Space), in KOSMOS: MEZHDUNARODNOE PRAVO 153-161 (Korovin ed. USSR 1962).

tasks to be the emphasis of the peaceful possibilities of space travel. . . . The Society for Space Research, accordingly, recommends an international meeting . . . to explore the possibilities of forming an international association for astronautics.[24]

A. Ananoff of France made elaborate preparations for the proposed meeting, and he had the close cooperation of H. Gartmann of Germany and A. V. Cleaver of the BIS. Although the later contributions of Gartmann and Cleaver to the world organization were immense, it must be recorded that Ananoff organized the First International Astronautical Congress almost single-handedly.

The Congress convened in Paris on September 30, 1950, with representatives of France, Germany, Austria, Great Britain, Denmark, Spain, and Argentina present. The United States did not participate. A. Ananoff was elected president of the Congress, and H. Mineur was named honorary president. Madame Gabrielle Camille Flammarion and Madame de Vendeuvre were named vice-presidents. Britain's Cleaver held the chair for the important October 2 session, at which time the general nature of the federation was agreed upon. The First Congress specifically recognized the need for a world-wide organization to promote the achievement of space flight as a peaceful project. The organization was to be inaugurated at the next congress. Before that time the various societies would send in proposals for a constitution, voting procedure, membership, and so on, which would be studied by the BIS and coordinated by it and by a temporary international body headed by Dr. Eugen Sänger of Austria. No technical sessions were held.[25] Nevertheless, the First Congress was a significant step in the history of rocketry; science had crossed national boundaries. Some of the most interested persons, such as Oberth, were prevented from attending because of visa trouble, but glowing reports of the Congress were brought back to them. The mission of the proposed new organization was clear: to convert the rocket from an engine of war to a peaceful vehicle of interplanetary exploration.

During the year following the First Congress, the international activities of the societies which later were to become the IAF were conducted by a Provisional Committee for International Cooperation, of which the chairman was Dr. Sänger. On the operational level, the international leaders during this first year were A. V. Cleaver and Dr. Guenter Loeser, who had been delegates respectively of the British and German astronautical societies at the First Congress.[26]

Cooperation was sought during this first year with astronautical societies in the two countries most advanced in astronautics. The American

[24] Shepherd, *The International Astronautical Federation*, 1 SPACEFLIGHT 159 (London, B.I.S. 1957).

[25] *Ibid.*

[26] Carter, *The Artificial Satellite*, PROCEEDINGS OF THE SECOND INTERNATIONAL CONGRESS ON ASTRONAUTICS (1952).

Rocket Society rapidly became one of the International Astronautical Federation's most active supporters. In response to invitations to attend the next astronautical congress, the Russians, however, sent only brief replies of regret. Although informal correspondence was maintained with individual Soviet scientists during succeeding years, the Russians did not join the IAF until after the USSR announced its satellite program in 1955.

The Second International Astronautical Congress was held in London at Caxton Hall, from September 3 to September 8, 1951. The original societies were in attendance, and the United States was also represented by the ARS, the Reaction Research Society, the Pacific Rocket Society, and the Detroit Rocket Society.[27] The Second Congress witnessed the juridical establishment of the International Astronautical Federation on September 4, 1951, and determined the direction of the IAF's future international development. A secretariat was authorized in Switzerland. Sänger was elected president. Loeser of GfW and Haley of ARS were elected vice-presidents, and Joseph A. Stemmer of Switzerland was named secretary.

Final details as to the Constitution of the IAF were to be cleared up before the next Congress by vice-presidents Loeser and Haley. The BIS had already done much to prepare a tentative draft, and during the Second Congress the all-important question of voting was studied. With the two previously-existing German astronautical societies now merged, it was feared that if the principle of representation of societies were adopted the United States would dominate the voting. Thus, the provision adopted earlier at Paris for one vote per nation was firmly established as the final voting arrangement.

The Second Congress featured considerable technical exchange.[28] A popular technical symposium was held in which delegates discussed the over-all aspects of interplanetary flight. Some of the scientists proposed the foundation of an International Institute of Astronautics, but this move was postponed indefinitely. The primary scientific interest of the Second Congress was in artificial satellite vehicles. The exchange of knowledge at London was the first organized attempt to promote world cooperation among rocket and astronautics workers. As such, it was a significant milestone in the history of science.

During the IAF's second year of existence (1951-52), its international activities were conducted by Haley, as chairman of an International Relations Committee, and by Dr. Loeser, as director of European operations.

The Third International Astronautical Congress convened in Stuttgart

[27] The statements in the rest of this chapter are based upon unpublished materials in files of the IAF and upon the direct participation of the author, except as noted otherwise. Also see L&K Rep. 124 §§781–84, 787–88, and 111, 48, 50, 64, 65, 75.

[28] The individual technical papers will not be discussed in this chapter. They have been summarized in 25 JET PROPULSION 384 (1953) (Zurich Congress); 21 JET PROPULSION 192 (1951) (London Congress).

on September 1, 1952. Sänger was re-elected president, and Haley was re-elected vice-president. Shepherd of the BIS was elected vice-president, and Stemmer was re-elected secretary.

The Constitution of the IAF which had been finally drafted during the previous year by the Loeser-Haley committee was adopted. The principle of one vote per nation, regardless of the size of the country or the number of its rocket or astronautical societies, which had been strongly advocated by the ARS delegation among others at the London Congress, received formal approval. It was decided that the ARS would be the voting member from the United States. The IAF Constitution stated the fundamental purpose of the organization in Article I as follows: "The IAF shall exist to promote and stimulate the achievement of space flight as a peaceful project."

The Congress then turned to technical matters. Prof. Oberth presented a paper which might well keynote all congresses. Discussing "Private Research in Astronautics," he outlined the many problems which should be investigated with the aid of astronautical societies (as distinct from large-scale, government-subsidized classified research) and which thereafter would form the basis of world cooperation. On this fundamental theme the Third Congress ended.

The International Relations Committee was disbanded by Haley at the Third Congress, when Dr. Loeser was unofficially appointed honorary vice-president of the IAF for international relations.

The Fourth International Astronautical Congress convened in Zurich in the Technical University on August 2, 1953. Societies from ten nations were represented, and three new members were admitted: the Philadelphia Astronautical Society, the South African Interplanetary Society, and the Yugoslavian Astronautical Society. Japan and Israel sent observers. The great shock was that France was not represented. New societies in Spain and Egypt were reported in formative stages. Frederick C. Durant III was elected president, and Haley was re-elected vice-president. Dr. Friedrich Hecht was elected as second vice-president, and Stemmer retained his position as secretary.

An important matter considered at the Fourth Congress was the establishment of an official publication. The need for such a publication was evident, since meetings were held only once a year, and even the annual meetings were often hard to attend for members located in distant lands. Recognizing the need for a year-round means of international dissemination of information, the Congress appointed Hecht, Sänger, G. P. Casiraghi, Shepherd, and Ordway as a committee to set up a quarterly publication, *Astronautica Acta*.

It was evident throughout the Fourth Congress that the IAF was becoming a potent factor in international scientific cooperation. Through the efforts of the Federation, for example, the United States Air Force gave permission for the Swiss Prof. Jakob Eugster to fly 400-gram packages of nuclear track plates on high-altitude constant-level balloons launched by Air Force experimenters.

The Fifth International Astronautical Congress met at Innsbruck, Austria, starting August 2, 1954. The Austrian Society was host. The opening session was held in the Great Hall of the University of Innsbruck. Durant was re-elected president, Teofilo Tabanera of Argentina and E. Buch Andersen of Denmark were elected vice-presidents, and Stemmer was re-elected secretary. The ARS took a strong stand at this Congress against continuation in office, contending that offices should be rotated among delegates of all societies, large and small. Otherwise, a clique would dominate the Federation, resulting in ultimate disintegration.

The American Astronautical Society, the Spanish Astronautical Society, the Egyptian Astronautical Society, the Japanese Astronautical Society, and the Brazilian Interplanetary Society were admitted to membership. France sent a large delegation for the first time since 1952, but the French did not seek formal accreditation. Russia again failed to send observers. The Croatian Society for Natural Sciences, Astronautical Section, sent an observer.

With increased membership and other encouraging signs of further international cooperation, the delegates approved publication of *Astronautica Acta* by Springer-Verlag, the great Austrian publishing firm; editorial functions, however, remained with the IAF. The news section was dropped from *Astronautica Acta,* and instead a special news bulletin was set up for publication by the provisional secretariat in Zurich. An international astronautical research institute was again considered, but no action was taken. Research teams, abstracting activities, and the creation of IAF panels on such special subjects as nuclear propulsion, flight mechanics, history of astronautics, and the like, were planned. A system of annual reports by these panels was proposed.

Shortly after the Fourth Congress in 1953, Haley had agreed to re-establish the International Relations Committee, and when he retired from the vice-presidency of the IAF at the Fifth Congress in 1954, the plenary assembly asked him to continue as president of an IAF Committee for International Relations. This represented the first official organizational provision for the pursuit of the IAF's international goals.

In 1955, major developments were in the air, so Haley proceeded to Paris with Frank Malina to finalize the association between the IAF and UNESCO (see Section 11-6, *infra*) and to help organize a French astronautics society. After the conference with UNESCO officials in Paris, a meeting was held with General Paul J. Bergeron, Chairman of the Committee for Scientific Research for the National Defense (France), and other French astronautical leaders.[29] At this conference General Bergeron gave assurances that a French astronautical society would be formed and that its membership would consist of the most capable scientists, engineers, and industrialists of France. On the same day came the United States' announcement of its satellite project, as well as UNESCO agreement to cooperate with the IAF and its space-flight program.

The Sixth International Astronautical Congress convened at Copenhagen on August 1, 1955. All the officers were re-elected, but the ARS again nominated Shepherd of the BIS for president, repeating the view that the officers should rotate and that continuation in office is undesirable. Upon the advice of Professor Friedrich Hecht, the Editorial and Advisory Boards of *Astronautica Acta* were strengthened by the addition of new members. The Constitution was amended to permit the adherence of corresponding members—educational and other institutions, which could not qualify as "societies"—but careful limitations were placed upon such adherence, the main safeguard being that any institution applying from a particular nation must have the approval of the voting member society of such nation. A Committee on International Affairs was again constituted: Haley (ARS), chairman; Shepherd (BIS), Sänger (GfW), Ake Hjerstrand (Sweden), and Tabanera (Argentina).

Of particular interest at this Congress was the attendance in person of a two-man delegation from the Yugoslavia society—M. Ajvaz and K. Sivcev. During the course of the second day of plenary session, K. Ogorodnikov and Leonid I. Sedov, Russian academicians, also appeared. The Russians necessarily attended as observers because no rocket society from Russia had applied for membership.

The Seventh International Astronautical Congress held in Rome, Italy, September 17-22, 1956, was remarkable in many ways. The organization of the Congress itself was outstanding, including excellent conference facilities, efficient use of simultaneous translation (into four languages), and a beneficial camaraderie in the secretariat. Over 450 experts in the natural and social sciences attended the meetings; approximately fifty papers were presented.[30] The chief failure of this Congress was imperfect screen-

---

[29] Present at the meeting were: General Bergeron, Chairman of the Committee for Scientific Research for the National Defense; Chief Engineer Wanner of the Aeronautical, Technical and Industrial Department of the Defense Ministry; Professor Vassy of the National Meteorological Department; Delval, Technical Director of SNCASO; Pillorget, Director of the Technical Association for the Study of Rocketry; Turcq, President of the Turcq Corporation; Corbeau, Principal Engineer of the Armament Section for Research and Development of the Defense Ministry; Moureau, Director of the Municipal Laboratory; Wattendorf, Director of the AGARD Secretariat; Malina, former Director of Jet Propulsion Laboratory; S. F. Singer of the University of Maryland; and Haley, host of the meeting.

[30] The authors included, among others: R. M. L. Baker (USA), G. Baumann (Germany), P. F. Bedinger (USA), H. Bednarczyk (Austria), B. Bergquist (Sweden), A. Boni (Italy), R. W. Buchheim (USA), A. A. Cocca (Argentina), R. M. Corelli (Italy), G. A. Crocco (Italy), J. De Nike (USA), E. De Zubay (USA), M. Dubin

ing of the papers read to the delegates. While most papers were of extraordinary merit, the rest were weak and not worthy of presentation. The fault, however, may not be attributed to the management of the Congress—undertaken by G. Arturo Grocco, Antonio Eula, and Glauco Partel, who had no real control over the papers submitted by societies of the twenty-one participating nations. Well-deserved criticism may be directed at the societies themselves.

The most felicitous occasion of the Congress was the special audience with Pope Pius XII, who showed a far-reaching knowledge of the history and activities of IAF and other leading rocket and interplanetary societies. In reviewing the history and contributions of the IAF, the Pope noted particularly the leading role played by the Federation in bringing about the proposed launching of the artificial earth satellite. He pointed out that God did not intend to limit man's knowledge to the earth alone. Rather, He offers to the human mind the whole creation so that man may see through it and "thus may understand always more profoundly the infinite grandeur of his Creator." But the Pope added:

> Without delving into details, I might say, Gentlemen, that plans of such a range entail intellectual and moral aspects which cannot be ignored; they require a certain conception of the world, its meaning, its end. . . . The most advanced explorations into space will serve only to bring a new reason for disunion if they are not effected along with a deeper moral intention and a more conscious attitude of devotion in the higher interests of mankind.

In conclusion, he blessed the delegates, their families, and associates.

Administratively, the most important achievement of the Congress was the unanimous adoption of amendments to the IAF Constitution. In brief, these amendments increased the authorized number of vice-presidents of the Federation from three to five and established new procedures for nominating and electing IAF officers. Article 25 was amended to require that officers shall be members of the voting societies; that no officer other than the secretary may succeed himself except by unanimous vote, and then for one year only; that officers shall be nominated by a committee elected by the Council in plenary session, and consisting of five members of the Council; that no member society shall succeed itself on the nominating committee; that officers shall be elected by secret ballot during the course of the plenary session; that nominations and elections shall be

---

(USA), R. Engel (Egypt), K. Ehricke (USA), N. E. Felt (USA), R. Foster (USA), S. J. Gerathewohl (USA), H. Grosch (USA), A. G. Haley (USA), H. E. Hinteregger (USA), H. J. Kaeppeler (Germany), J. J. King (USA), W. B. Klemperer (USA), J. Kooy (Netherlands), H. Krause (Germany), B. Langenecker (Austria), T. Nonweiler (England), W. Peschka (Austria), N. V. Petersen (USA), J. Pressman (USA), A. C. Robotti (Italy), F. Romano (Italy), D. Romick (USA), H. Ruppe (Germany), E. Sanger (Germany), D. G. Simons (USA), S. F. Singer (USA), K. R. Stehling (USA), H. Strughold (USA), M. Vertregt (Netherlands), and K. Zarankiewicz (Poland).

held at each plenary meeting of the IAF Council but not more frequently than once a year; and that the officers shall hold office until their successors are duly elected and qualify.

As officers for the succeeding year the Congress chose L. R. Shepherd as president and Frederick C. Durant III, Teófilo Tabanera, Paul J. Bergeron, L. Sedov, and Julio Marial, as vice-presidents. Three new national societies were elected to membership; namely, Committee on Astronautics, Academy of Sciences (USSR), Polskie Towarzystwo Astronautyczne (Poland), and Société Française d'Astronautique (France), making a total of twenty-one voting members.

Throughout 1956 there were many other instances of cooperation and interest in astronautics by international organizations and their members. In January, for example, C. Wilfred Jenks of the International Labour Office published one of the truly great papers on the subject of space law. In December, the National Congress of Electronics, Telecommunications and Broadcasting, convening in Mexico City, considered space travel problems.

11-3 More recent organizational development

The Eighth International Astronautical Congress in Barcelona, October, 1957, was highlighted by the news of the launching of *Sputnik I*. The great achievement of the USSR was acclaimed throughout the Congress. Only brief information about *Sputnik I* was contained in the Barcelona papers, and Spanish censorship prevented distribution of newspapers from other countries.

The Congress may be characterized as having placed emphasis on the organizational and business aspects of the Federation. Stemmer, secretary of the Federation, immediately raised questions concerning the legality and propriety of actions taken during the preceding congresses—a matter of real and legitimate concern to him because of his duty to conform the actions of the Federation to appropriate Swiss law. The British delegation, under the leadership of Dr. L. R. Shepherd and L. J. Carter, formally moved for the creation of a committee to correct thoroughly and revise the constitution of the Federation. The basic British proposal was enlarged somewhat by the action of the delegates in authorizing the committee to consider entirely new additions to the constitution. The committee appointed by President Shepherd consisted of Haley, Chairman (USA); Fritz Gerlach (Germany); Alla Massevitch (USSR); Georges Delval (France); L. J. Carter (England); and J. A. Stemmer (Switzerland).

Haley was elected president of the IAF for the ensuing year. Vice-presidents elected were A. Hjertstrand, Sweden; J. M. J. Kooy, Holland;

Leonid I. Sedov, USSR; L. R. Shepherd, Great Britain; Teófilo M. Tabanera, Argentina; and K. Zarankiewicz, Poland. This was the first time a representative of the social sciences (an international lawyer) was elected president. There was a consensus among the delegates to take advantage of the long organizational experience of a person with such a background, and they were also impressed by the fact that the legal problems presented by the advent of space flight had become climacteric, as space technology had far outstripped the formulation of legal rules, and the gap had widened to the point that the peace of the world was threatened.

The assembled delegates were pleased to hear from Dr. W. Schwabl of Springer-Verlag, the publisher of *Astronautica Acta*, that his company would print the papers delivered at the Barcelona Congress. By unanimous agreement, Dr. Friedrich Hecht was again named chairman of the *Astronautica Acta* Committee.

One of the most extensive educational efforts undertaken on behalf of the IAF was the lecture tour of the United States by Dr. Welf Heinrich Prince of Hanover and Haley in late 1957. The two presented addresses on space law in thirty educational and scientific institutions in seventeen states. This was followed by a European tour in 1958, when lectures were given at the Universities of Paris, Stockholm, Copenhagen, Berlin, Munich, Stuttgart, Madrid, Lisbon, Belgrade, Prague, Warsaw, Moscow, Leningrad, and so on; and before numerous learned societies and other technical institutes and groups.

The Ninth International Astronautical Congress held at Amsterdam, August 25-30, 1958, attracted the largest attendance in IAF history and produced more than seventy technical papers by scientists and engineers from fourteen countries. The Ninth Congress has been characterized as one which possessed "an atmosphere less charged with tension than that prevailing at [the previous] year's Congress in Barcelona, but a more realistic approach to practical problems." At Barcelona in 1957, the world had been thrilled by the successful launching of Russia's *Sputnik I*. Information then available was scanty; speculation and misinformation were widespread. But at the Amsterdam Congress a year later great bodies of data were available, and the over-all spirit was one of cooperation. The central theme of the Congress was Propulsion and Propellant Systems. A vast collection of technical data on the subject was read during the six-day Congress.

An important step taken at Amsterdam was the unanimous approval by the delegates of a four-point program to pave the way for international cooperation in future astronautical projects. Drawn up by the International Affairs Committee, the program called for:

(1) Collection and dissemination from one focal point of information on plans and progress of space-flight research activities of all nations.

(2) Establishment of international research fellowships in astronautical subjects.

(3) Setting up an international competition for selection of research experiments for satellite vehicles.

(4) Holding an international conference on the subject of peaceful applications of rockets and satellite vehicles.

A Committee on the Revision of the Constitution was established at the Ninth Congress to consider the proposal that the Federation be divided into three distinct divisions—space sciences, space technology, and social sciences relating to space problems. The committee had to receive, evaluate, and coordinate the views and proposals of all member nations on this fundamental matter—a prodigious undertaking when it is recalled that there were thirty member societies in the IAF representing citizens of twenty-five nations.

The Tenth International Astronautical Congress was held at Church House, Westminster, London, in September, 1959, and was organized by the British Interplanetary Society. Coming on the heels of the special British Commonwealth Spaceflight Symposium, the Tenth Congress attracted an outstanding group of scholars and scientists. There was a record attendance of more than 650 experts, from some forty-five nations. In a significant action, Leonid I. Sedov, Chairman of the Commission for Astronautics of the Soviet Academy of Sciences, was unanimously elected president of the Federation.

Of equal importance with the election of the first Russian to head the IAF was the action taken by the Congress to establish an International Academy of Astronautics. (See Section 11-4, *infra.*)

The Tenth Congress elected as vice-presidents of the IAF Col. John P. Stapp, ARS president, who led the United States delegation to the Congress; A. Hjerstrand of Sweden; L. R. Shepherd, chairman of the BIS Council; Eugen Sänger of Germany; and General P. J. Bergeron of the French Astronautical Society. Haley, the outgoing president, was unanimously elected to the newly created post of General Counsel and was cited in a special resolution for his work on behalf of the IAF and astronautics. Stemmer of Switzerland was re-elected as secretary.

Admitted as voting members of the IAF during the Congress were the Belgian Astronautical Society, the Commission on Astronautics of the Czech Academy of Sciences, and the Indian Astronautical Society. In addition, two Canadian societies were admitted as members, with each permitted to cast the Canadian vote on an alternating basis from year to year. The Aero-Space Medical Association of the United States, the Astronautical Society of Rome, and two Portuguese astronautical societies were admitted as non-voting members, while an Iranian delegation was given observer status.

A major step was taken toward the establishment of a *permanent* IAF secretariat with the formation of a four-member committee, headed by L. J. Carter, BIS secretary, to deal with the problem. The committee had as its goal the study of locations for the permanent home of the Federation. Paris was eventually selected, because its central location made it most convenient for all the members of the Federation. The Tenth Congress also saw the formation of a committee to draw up plans for lecture tours by eminent astronautical scientists, to be co-sponsored by UNESCO and the IAF, and steps toward the establishment of an International Institute of Space Law within the framework of the IAF.

The Eleventh International Astronautical Congress was held in Stockholm, Sweden, in August 1960 with the Swedish Interplanetary Society as host. Every year the size and enthusiasm of the IAF membership has grown and the Stockholm Congress was evidence of such growth. The main meeting of the Congress consisted of double and triple technical sessions. In conjunction with the main meeting, two special symposia considered problems in the fields of space medicine and small sounding rockets, and there were two colloquia that dealt with space law and astrodynamics.

More than 200 technical papers were read at the various sessions. Outstanding among the contributions made were the lecture on the United States' space-rocket program by Dr. Wernher von Braun, the paper on trajectories above the denser portions of the earth's atmosphere presented by Marcel Nicolet of Belgium, and a report on the progress made in electrical propulsion systems delivered by Ernst Stuhlinger.

The symposia and colloquia evoked a great deal of interest at the Congress. The Space Medicine Symposium ran two days and included more than fifteen papers. The Small Sounding Rocket Symposium, which was organized by Nicolai Herlofson and Ake Hjerstrand of Sweden, also ran for two days, with about twelve papers presented. The one-day Space Law Colloquium planned by Kurt Gronfors of Sweden, as well as the Astrodynamics Colloquium organized by Samuel Herrick and Erik Tengstron, was an outstanding success. The Iranian Astronautical Society was admitted to full voting membership, as was the German Astronautical Society which is composed of scientists from the eastern part of Germany. A new French society, the AERA, was also admitted to non-voting membership.

The Twelfth International Astronautical Congress was held from October 1 to 7, 1961, in Washington, D.C. The Sociedad Mexicana Interplanetaria, the Cyprus Astronautical Society, and the Rumanian Academy of Sciences were unanimously voted into IAF membership. The Gropo

Portuguesa Astronautica was designated the voting member from Portugal. Organizational developments of special significance included the adoption of a new constitution, the revision of the program planning procedures for the annual congresses, and the establishment of a permanent secretariat.

The original constitution of the IAF had been rather "rough" as a result of the usual difficulties of a new organization which was just getting started. At the Ninth Congress, in 1958, then-President Haley had been asked to revise the constitution, and at the Tenth Congress he had been asked now as General Counsel to have a complete new constitution ready for consideration at a meeting of the IAF Presidium to be held in the spring of 1960. This meeting was duly called by President Sedov and was held in Heidelberg during May 1960. The so-called Haley draft of April 1960 was wholly unacceptable to the USSR member society. The members of the Presidium then proceeded to frame the "Revised Draft of Heidelberg Meeting, May 26, 1960." The main changes included: (1) the creation of a Bureau; (2) requirement that the Bureau should always include an officer from the USSR and from the United States; (3) requirement that no actions might be taken without the affirmative consent of the voting societies from the USSR and the United States; and (4) rather extensive changes in nomenclature. This Heidelberg Constitution was presented to the Eleventh Congress (1960), at which time considerable controversy resulted. President Sedov appointed Messrs. Vladimir Kopal, Sedov, E. Brun, Shepherd, W. H. Pickering, and Haley as a committee to produce the final draft.[31] The entire committee met in March 1961 in Paris, where differences of opinion were resolved and unanimous agreement was obtained on the final form for the new constitution. Copies of the draft produced were sent to all member societies, and no adverse comment was received. At the Twelfth Congress, after adoption of a proposal from the floor that delegates be allowed to appoint alternates to attend meetings, the new constitution was unanimously adopted. The constitution of the IAF in its present form appears in Appendix III-A.

The increasing difficulties in preparing for the annual meetings, the technical content of which is the IAF's primary *raison d'être,* received special attention at the Twelfth Congress. A Program Committee was appointed, consisting of Hjerstrand (Sweden); N. Bonef (Bulgaria); S. Herrick (USA); J. Perès, chairman (France); Sedov (USSR); and M.

---

[31] This committee consisted of representatives of six member societies who were nominated and elected by the member societies, and one of whom was designated as Chairman by the President. The committee was charged with the following mandate: "Each member society is required to submit to the President its recommendations for the correction and revision of the Constitution. Each such recommendation shall be considered and finally disposed of by the committee, and brief reasons shall be given for every such action. The committee shall meet *in persona* at a fixed date, and it shall submit to the President a corrected and revised Constitution with brief statements of reasons for each such correction and revision."

Summerfield (USA).[32] It was determined to give each Program Committee two years to prepare for its assigned Congress. A major change in procedure was made to the effect that papers offered for a particular Congress need not be nominated or approved by the host society or by the member society in the country of origin. Rather, the decision on acceptance will rest completely with the Program Committee. It was noted that the success of such a system, because of the great number of papers to be processed, depended on having well-established office procedures, i.e., a permanent secretariat.

The particular problem of establishing a permanent secretariat in order to support expanding activities had been given attention over several preceding years by the Committee on Permanent Headquarters. At the Twelfth Congress, Chairman L. J. Carter reported that the committee had successfully completed its assigned task. An arrangement was negotiated with the Academy of Astronautics, which already had a full-time secretariat in Paris provided through the French Astronautical Society, to provide secretariat services for the Federation for a period of two years. It was resolved that the secretary of the Academy of Astronautics should be designated the Acting Executive Secretary of the Federation, with duties including the organization of the business sessions of the IAF Bureau and liaison with governmental, United Nations, and international nongovernmental organizations. It was also proposed that the International Institute of Space Law might become part of the permanent headquarters establishment. Haley, as chairman of the International Affairs Committee, noted that the IAF had developed a "very fine relationship" with UNESCO through Mr. Kovde. The Congress proceeded to adopt a resolution of appreciation for the cooperation of UNESCO, which was presented to the UNESCO General Assembly by the IAF permanent delegate to UNESCO, Frank J. Malina.[33]

[32] The committee was assigned as its principal tasks:

(a) Define far ahead of time the relative emphasis to be given to various subjects according to current and future importance, and decide on the number of sessions to be given to each such subject.

(b) Name on its own authority a series of technical committees in the different fields, who will accept the responsibility for building up the sessions in their fields. These technical committees shall be international in character, and the persons honored by such membership should be those whose very names would draw good papers in their field.

[33] The resolution read as follows:

The General Assembly notes with greatest satisfaction the financial assistance extended by UNESCO in 1961 to the IAF for travel grants to young scientists to attend the XII Congress in Washington, D.C., and for holding a Study Group for an international symposium on "Man in Space" which is being organized jointly by the IAF, UNESCO, and the International Academy of Astronautics in Paris, at the end of November 1961. The General Assembly expresses the desire to continue and expand cooperation between the IAF and UNESCO in very way possible to further the peaceful exploration of outer space.

The choice of the officers who will guide the activities of the Federation during the time between the annual plenary conferences is always a crucial decision. At the Twelfth Congress, Chairman Martin Summerfield of the Nominating Committee outlined the considerations underlying the committee's choices for officers of the Federation:

(1) The United States and USSR had already been honored amply in the past with the presidency.

(2) Consideration should be given to other countries developing strong programs in astronautics.

(3) One officer should be from the host country for the following year—in this case, Bulgaria.

(4) The United States and USSR should each have at least one voting officer on the Bureau.

(5) Consideration must be given to geographical distribution.

(6) Above all, the personalities of the nominees should bring prestige to the IAF.

The following individuals were nominated and were unanimously elected: President—Perès (France); Vice-presidents—Shepherd (U.K.), William H. Pickering (USA), Nikola Boneff (Bulgaria), and Tabanera (Argentina); General Counsel—Haley (USA). According to the new constitution, the voting members of the Bureau include the President, Vice-Presidents, General Counsel, and the Past President. The USSR thus voluntarily relinquished its claim to one of the vice-presidencies, as Professor Sedov would continue to have a vote on the Bureau in his capacity of Past President. Finally, Stemmer was unanimously voted Honorary Secretary.

The Thirteenth Congress of the IAF, held at Varna, Bulgaria, in September 1962, was notable as the first to take place in an Eastern European country. Delegations from the Eastern European nations were considerably larger than in the past, and the proceedings were more genuinely multilingual, with English experiencing a relative decline from its usual position of pre-eminence. In general, however, the "language barrier" was successfully overcome—and the international flavor was enjoyed by all. Interestingly, the large Soviet delegation included Cosmonaut Gherman Titov, who addressed a special session on the first day of the gathering.

The Thirteenth Congress was notable also because for the first time the technical program was organized by the IAF International Program Committee, established at the Washington Congress a year earlier. The impact of the International Program Committee could be seen both in the fact that United States papers did not dominate the program, as had been the case in previous years, and in the quality of the papers, which was exceptionally high in the opinion of all delegates.

The plenary sessions at Varna dealt largely with routine matters. New member societies elected in 1962 included the Hungarian Astronautical Society and the Institute of Aerospace Sciences, the latter being admitted as a non-voting member from the United States. The Congress chose Prof. Edmond A. Brun of France to serve as president for the coming year. Vice-presidents chosen were Sedov (USSR), Boneff (Bulgaria), Prof. Martin Summerfield (USA), and Prof. Michal Lunc (Poland). Dr. Leslie R. Shepherd (Great Britain), who had succeeded to the office of president on the death of Prof. J. Perès, continued on the IAF Bureau as immediate past president, as did General Counsel Haley.

11-4 Creation of the International Academy of Astronautics

At the Tenth Congress in London in 1959, initial action was taken to establish the International Academy of Astronautics, to be made up of individuals who had distinguished themselves in one of the fields of astronautics or some branch of science fundamental to the exploration of space. On May 13, 1960, the creation of the Academy was announced. Its stated objectives were to provide world technical leadership for the peaceful conquest of space and to serve as a clearing house for astronautical information. The composition of the Academy includes many of the world's leading scientists in three broad areas—the basic sciences, engineering, and the life sciences, the latter including medicine, law, and other fields dealing with life in space. (The Statutes of the Academy are set out in Appendix III-B.)

The principal functions assigned to the Academy were (1) to provide advice to the President of the IAF when requested, (2) to hold scientific meetings and make scientific studies and reports, (3) to publish *Astronautica Acta* as an international technical journal devoted to astronautics, (4) to award medals and prizes intended to further progress in the field, and (5) to carry out such other tasks as may be deemed desirable for promoting the advancement of astronautics. The Academy received generous donations of funds, headquarters space, and other assistance. The Daniel and Florence Guggenheim Foundation of New York approved a grant of a total of $75,000 for its work, and headquarters office space in Paris was furnished free of charge for three years through the efforts of General Paul Bergeron.

The Academy was formally organized in Stockholm during the Eleventh Congress of the IAF in August 1960. The first meeting of the Academy took place during the Congress on August 16, 1960. Dr. Theodore von Kármán, Chairman of the Founding Committee, was designated as Director of the Academy. Professor J. Perès and Dr. Frank J. Malina were designated as Deputy Directors. The Academy was organized in three sections: (1) Basic Sciences, (2) Engineering Sciences, and (3) Life

Sciences. The chairmen selected were Professor A. Ehmert, R. Pesek, and M. Florkin, respectively. The Academy established several working committees to carry on special projects. These included Finances, Publications, Academy Award and Fellowship, and Lunar International Laboratory Committees. The Academy also became active in various allied endeavors. A committee was appointed to function as part of a joint commission of the Academy and the International Institute of Space Law to consider technical aspects of space law. Investigations were begun on the feasibility of cooperating with UNESCO in holding a symposium on the scientific and technical problems of "Man in Space."

The future program of the Academy was described in some detail by Dr. von Kármán at the first meeting. With regard to the publication of *Astronautica Acta*, he noted that its editorial management had been reorganized under his direction early in 1960 and that a number of the initial members of the Academy were serving either in an editorial capacity or on the Editorial Advisory Board. He emphasized that the journal was

> ... intended to serve the rapidly growing community of scientists and engineers who are devoting themselves to any of the many aspects of astronautics as a publication having a widely international character. Furthermore, it is planned to cooperate closely with the publishers of several national journals. It is the intention of the editors of the *Acta* to supplement rather than compete with other journals in this field. Special attention will be given to articles of the type that will serve as valued cornerstones of the edifice of astronautical literature. It is also planned to publish periodically survey papers in the selected fields of the fundamental, engineering, and life sciences bearing on astronautics.

Consideration was also being given, he said, to the possibility of adding special sections for short reports submitted by Academy members, for letters dealing with matters published in the journal, and for Academy news.

Von Kármán went on to state, in connection with scientific meetings, that no change was

> ... contemplated as far as the Congress of the Federation is concerned. It is proposed, however, that smaller scientific meetings of the symposium type held in conjunction with the Congress be the responsibility of the Academy, at least as far as the technical programmes of these meetings are concerned. Meetings initiated by the Academy, whether held in conjunction with the Congress or at other times and places would, of course, be the responsibility of the Academy.

In addition, von Kármán mentioned the interest of the Academy in the preparation of a multilingual handbook of terms used in space research. As he pointed out, the IAF had for some time been giving attention to the problem of the definition in various languages of terms used in the field of space exploration, and in fact it had requested financial assistance from UNESCO for completion of the work. Then, with regard to the establishment of an Academy award and fellowships, he stated:

> During my discussion with the Daniel and Florence Guggenheim Foundation I mentioned that the Academy may wish to establish a medal or award of the highest international significance in the field of astronautics, possibly to be named after a leader or family which has made contributions of outstanding importance to the development of this field. The Academy may also wish to establish a postgraduate fellowship programme and to direct its efforts toward finding funds for such a programme.

Von Kármán recommended that the Academy set up a committee expressly to study the question of an award and fellowships, and it proceeded to do so.

At its November-December 1960 session, the UNESCO General Conference approved the granting of a sum of $9,600 for the IAF for 1961-62. The IAF allocated a portion of this money to the International Academy of Astronautics to enable a small study group to decide on the desirability and feasibility of holding a symposium in 1962 on "Man in Space."

However, the first symposium held by the Academy took place in June 1961 at Louveciennes, France, with an attendance of about one hundred.

Other plans of cooperation with UNESCO contemplated the establishment of an international astronautical laboratory on the moon. The Academy instructed its Lunar International Laboratory Committee, formed in August 1960, to report in succeeding years on the technical problems related to the construction of a manned research laboratory on the moon and the kinds of research which would initially be carried out by such a laboratory. It was hoped that a study group would meet in 1964, under UNESCO sponsorship, to review the work of the committee and make recommendations to the Academy on the future work of the committee and to UNESCO on the steps that might be taken to bring about the creation of the proposed international laboratory.

The potential of the Academy for expanding its contribution to international cooperation in space activities is illustrated by these additional proposals for the future:

1. The creation of a commission composed of approximately nine competent scientists from throughout the world for the purpose of formulating a highly inclusive program—to be followed through by a number of working groups whose membership need not come from the Academy—to process and adapt the scientific knowledge and inventions gained in the astronautic effort into applications of immediate benefit to mankind. For example, the "Man in Space" program has resulted in the development of strains of algae to be used for food and for scavenging in a space vehicle, which may well have applications with respect to the fixation of nitrogen in the soil—or other very down-to-earth and direct benefits to agriculture. Similarly, in connection with the astronautic effort

tremendous work has been done in the field of solid state physics and thermo-electricity. Developments resulting from such work might provide power for refrigeration in inaccessible torrid areas or for radio transmission and reception in distant Arctic regions.

2. The creation of a commission on the codification of the law of outer space. Such an activity by a nongovernmental agency was advocated during the debates of the Legal Committee of the *ad hoc* Committee on the Peaceful Uses of Outer Space, as well as in the final report of the committee itself. A similar recommendation has been made by the American Bar Association. A commission established for this purpose would, of course, require the elaboration of many working groups.

3. The creation of a special commission to encourage and coordinate astronautical research and development within nations and groups of people who lack the resources to provide facilities and hardware for complete systems of their own. Here again, many working groups would be organized to examine and report upon the multitude of opportunities that certainly exist.

11–5 Creation of the International Institute of Space Law

The natural scientists have been the first to recognize the essential proposition that public order and justice must accompany man into space. An independent framework for consideration of law and equity had to be set up among the nations of the earth. It was to work toward this goal on a nongovernmental basis that the IAF founded the International Institute of Space Law.[34]

As early as the Third Congress held in Stuttgart in September 1952, the IAF showed the beginnings of its concern with the development of an over-all legal framework for international astronautics. Several leading members of the present International Institute of Space Law participated in the activities of that Congress, including Hans Achtnich, Fritz Gerlach, and two of the great pioneers of space law, Dr. Welf Heinrich Prince of Hanover and Dr. Alex Meyer. Dr. Meyer, Director of the Institute of Air Law of the University of Cologne, delivered a paper entitled *Legal Problems of Flight into Outer Space* in which he opposed the application of the law of war to outer space and supported the January 1952 proposal of the Director of the General Legal Division of the United Nations, Oscar Schachter, to the effect that the various states should start work on a declaration of abstention from the use of outer space for military purposes.

[34] The organization and work of the Institute has been treated in detail by two Soviet jurists. Cheprov and Vereshchetin, *Obsuzhdenie Pravovykh Voprosov Issledovanija Kosmosa v Mezhdunarodnoj Astronavticheskoj Federatsii* (Discussion of Legal Problems of the Investigation of the Cosmos, in the International Astronautical Federation), SOVETSKOE GOSUDARSTVO I PRAVO, April 1962, at 126. See also Crane, *The International Institute of Space Law*, IV SPACEFLIGHT 3 at 89 (1962).

The comprehensive study of space law problems by an official body of the IAF was proposed by Haley in 1954, but it remained for some time in the discussion stage. However, important groundwork for such study was laid at the Seventh Congress in Rome in 1956 with the presentation and discussion of two basic papers on space law, one by Haley, entitled *Space Law and Metalaw—A Synoptic View*, and one by Dr. Aldo Armando Cocca of Argentina, entitled *A Method of Studying Various Legal Problems in Connection with the Attempt to Conquer Interplanetary Space*.

The first formal action to establish an IAF organ to study space legal problems was taken at the Eighth Congress in Barcelona, in October 1957, within a matter of hours after *Sputnik I* inaugurated the Space Age. In an address to the delegates, Haley requested that

> ... at a plenary session of the Congress the President of the International Astronautical Federation be authorized to appoint a committee of seven persons, consisting of four physicists and three lawyers, who will draft a definition of "airspace" and recommend a rule delimiting airspace jurisdiction, such definition and rule to be supported by a statement of Findings of Fact and Conclusions of Law. The resolution should be transmitted to the attention of the Secretary-General of the United Nations and to the Secretary-General of the International Civil Aviation Organization (ICAO) with the statement that the committee will cooperate with the appropriate officials of said organizations.

In response to this request, the IAF in plenary session unanimously established a special or *ad hoc* Committee, which was directed specifically "to define the regions of jurisdiction of air law, and of space law." As finally constituted, this committee consisted of Dr. L. R. Shepherd of Great Britain, Dr. A. F. Spilhaus and Professor John Cobb Cooper of the United States, Drs. Leonid Sedov and Alla Massevitch of the USSR, Dr. Alex Meyer of Germany, Dr. Jacob Ackeret of Switzerland, and Haley, who served as *ex officio* member in his capacity as president of the IAF.

During the ensuing year Haley arranged several meetings of members of the committee under the able chairmanship of Professor Cooper and traveled widely throughout the world to ascertain the consensus of opinion of the world's jurists on the jurisdiction of space law. In the spring of 1958 Haley corresponded with more than one hundred of these jurists specifically to obtain their advice on the utility of the "von Kármán line" concept as presented at the Barcelona Congress. (For a full discussion of this line, see Chapter 4, *supra*.)

The following year, 1958, witnessed the first comprehensive international study and analysis of space legal problems at the First Colloquium on the Law of Outer Space, held at The Hague on August 29.[35] At this

---

[35] 1st Colloq. See generally Smirnoff, Review of the *First Colloquium on the Law of Outer Space*, 1961 Arhiv za Pravnei Drustvene Navke 443 (Yugoslavia).

colloquium, an integral part of the Ninth IAF Congress, legislators, jurists, lawyers, and other participants from a score of nations, discussed questions concerning allocation of space radio frequencies; avoidance of interference between space vehicles and aircraft; questions of freedom of outer space for exploration and use; liability for injury or damage caused by space vehicles; questions concerning re-entry and landing of space vehicles; and questions concerning the determination of sovereignty in outer space, including specifically the jurisdictional point where outer space begins. The discussions of The Hague Colloquium were of great value to the Legal Subcommittee of the U.N. *ad hoc* Committee on the Peaceful Uses of Outer Space during its deliberations in 1959, and in fact they anticipated the main points in the subcommittee's final report.

At the same Hague Colloquium, Haley reported on the success of the IAF's *ad hoc* Committee and advocated the formation of a Permanent Legal Committee to draft proposals for an international agreement on space legal problems. A resolution was introduced by Dr. E. Pépin and was unanimously approved by the participants in the Colloquium calling for the establishment by the IAF of such a Permanent Committee, which would be "open to lawyers of the various societies or groups affiliated to the Federation," and whose members would be "entrusted with the study of all the problems of the law of space to be included in the [proposed international] Convention. . . ." The resolution contained a provision that it should be communicated to the Secretary-General of the United Nations, with the express assurance that the IAF desired to cooperate with any initiative that might be undertaken by the United Nations in the field of astronautics. The same day, the plenary session of the IAF Congress formally established a Permanent Legal Committee, confirmed Haley as its chairman, and also re-elected him to the office of IAF President.

During the year 1958-59 the Permanent Legal Committee expanded to include well over one hundred members, many of them among the world's leading jurists. Accordingly, at the Tenth IAF Congress in London in 1959, the Permanent Legal Committee was replaced by a new, more ambitious organization, known as the International Institute of Space Law. The birth of the Institute took place formally on August 31, 1959, when the plenary session of the Tenth Congress unanimously approved the following resolution:

> Resolved that the presently constituted Permanent Legal Committee of the International Astronautical Federation be replaced by an International Institute of Space Law and that an *ad hoc* organizing committee consisting of five persons and a secretary, be authorized to draft by-laws for the organization and government of the proposed institute, which will be in accordance with the constitution of the IAF, and subject to the approval of the Council of the IAF at a future meeting.
>
> That the General Counsel of the IAF is authorized to establish immediately such working groups as are necessary to consider the legal problems of space,

which are today considered perhaps capable of resolution, for example, space radio allocation frequencies, now being considered by the International Telecommunication Union in Geneva, Switzerland.

An organizing committee for the Institute of Space Law was set up consisting of Christopher Shawcross, Q.C., as chairman, Haley as executive secretary, and Prof. Cooper, M. Homburg, Dr. Gerlach, and Dr. Michel Smirnoff.

The Second Colloquium on the Law of Outer Space was held at historic Lincoln's Inn in London on September 4, 1959, in conjunction with the Tenth Congress. Chairmen of this colloquium were Shawcross and Prof. Cooper. Co-chairmen included U.S. Representative Victor L. Anfuso; Luis de Gonzaga Bevilacqua (Brazil); Fritz Gerlach (Germany); D. Goedhuis (Netherlands); Robert Homburg (France); Manfred Lachs (Poland); Alex Meyer (Germany); E. Pépin (France); H. Safavi (Iran); Michel Smirnoff (Yugoslavia); and F. W. von Rauchhaupt (Germany). Over thirty papers were presented by eminent lawyers and sociologists from more than a score of nations.

The truly happy marriage of the social and natural sciences was strikingly exemplified in Moscow on September 14, 1959, when Haley, a social scientist and retiring IAF President, heard his successor, Leonid I. Sedov, a natural scientist, disclaim any Russian pretension of sovereignty over the moon as a result of the successful *Lunik II* moon shot. The natural scientist bespoke the juridical philosophy of his colleague.

During the winter of 1959-60, Haley, now as General Counsel of the IAF and as executive secretary of the *ad hoc* Organizing Committee of the International Institute of Space Law, canvassed the members of the old Permanent Legal Committee to determine what ten legal subjects would be most suitable for study by small working groups of the Institute. He also prepared a draft of statutes for the Institute. In March 1960, at the Paris meeting of the *ad hoc* Organizing Committee, the proposed statutes and a tentative proposal for the subject matter of the working groups were approved with minor changes. The current statutes of the Institute are set out in Appendix III-C.

In April 1960, the working groups were constituted and their chairmen appointed. The services of these working groups were offered to the United Nations Committee on the Peaceful Uses of Outer Space (UNCO-PUOS), which had been formed in December 1959, and Dr. Franco Fiorio of Italy, and Haley were designated as representatives at the deliberations of the U.N. Committee.

At the Eleventh IAF Congress held in August 1960 in Stockholm, the constitution of the International Institute of Space Law was approved at the plenary session of the IAF, and the *ad hoc* Organizing Committee, pursuant to Article V, Section 6, of the constitution, elected an Executive Committee, which in turn elected Michel Smirnoff of Yugoslavia to be chairman of the International Institute of Space Law and Haley to be secretary. The Executive Committee also created the office of Director of Research, to which it unanimously elected Professor John Cobb Cooper. His role in this capacity was to coordinate the working groups and to preside at the sessions devoted to working group reports at the annual colloquiums.

As a result of the elections held in August 1960 and in March 1961, the Executive Committee had eight members: Antonio Ambrosini of Italy, John Cobb Cooper and Haley of the United States, Fritz Gerlach of Germany, Robert Homburg and Eugène Pépin of France, Vladimir Kopal of Czechoslovakia, and Michel Smirnoff of Yugoslavia.

At the plenary session of the membership of the International Institute of Space Law in Washington, D.C., on October 4, 1961, the Executive Committee was replaced by a Board of Directors, and the offices of President and Secretary were established. The following members of the old Executive Committee were elected to the new Board of Directors: Ambrosini, director of the Legal Subcommittee of UNCOPUOS; Cooper and Haley, who were elected, respectively, as president and secretary of the International Institute of Space Law; Kopal, a member of the Czechoslovakian Academy of Sciences; and Smirnoff, who was designated as retiring president of the International Institute of Space Law. The seven legal scholars who completed the Institute's first Board of Directors were Luis de Gonzaga Bevilacqua of Brazil, Cyril Horsford of the United Kingdom, Fumio Ikeda of Japan, Alex Meyer of Germany, Antonio Francoz Rigalt of Mexico, P. K. Roy of India and the International Civil Aviation Organization, and Hassan Safavi of Iran.

At the Fourth Colloquium on the Law of Outer Space held October 3 and 4, 1961, five sessions were devoted to the delivery of papers on the legal problems of space activities and to the presentation of reports by Working Groups I, III, VI, VII, VIII, and IX. The presentation by Working Group I included a discussion by Antonio Ambrosini, Haley, John A. Johnson (General Counsel of the National Aeronautics and Space Administration), and Meyer. Also at this Fourth Colloquium, the first Andrew G. Haley Awards were presented to John Cobb Cooper, who became First Laureate of the Gold Medal of the Institute for the greatest contributions toward formulation of the rule of law in outer space; and awards carrying monetary honorariums, to Michel Smirnoff for the most distinguished contributions toward the definition of jurisdiction and sovereignty relating to natural objects in outer space, and to Vladimir Kopal for the most distinguished contribution to the codification of space law and for his major contribution as chairman of the committee which drafted the revised constitution of the IAF.

Through 1961, Soviet jurists declined invitations to participate in the colloquiums and to join in the activities of the International Institute of

Space Law. Following the statement by two Soviet scholars, however, that "without active participation by and equal rights for jurists from the Socialist and neutral countries, the activities of the Institute cannot be fruitful," [36] the Soviets did finally participate in the Fifth Colloquium on the Law of Outer Space, which was convened in Varna on September 25, 1962. At Varna the report of John Cobb Cooper, president of the International Institute of Space Law, was presented. The report covered intergovernmental space law developments since the Twelfth IAF Congress and the progress of nongovernmental national and international organizations. There was also a survey of the work of the Institute itself, with recommendations for future actions. During the Colloquium, presentations were made by representatives of more than thirty different countries. In all, six sessions were devoted to the delivery of papers and reports of the Institute's Working Groups III, VII, IX, and X. Chairmen of the sessions were Michel Smirnoff (Yugoslavia), Marko G. Markoff (Bulgaria), William Hyman (USA), Andrew Haley (USA), Ernst Fasan (Austria), and Alex Meyer (Germany).

Perhaps most significant was the fact, already mentioned, that for the first time there was Soviet participation in the work of the Institute. The Soviet Union sent its "first team" of jurists to the Fifth Colloquium on the Law of Outer Space of the International Institute of Space Law. Members of the team were: E. A. Korovin, chairman of the Commission on the Legal Problems of Interplanteary Space, USSR Academy of Sciences; G. P. Zhukov, academic secretary; and G. A. Osnitskaya, legal counsel for the USSR Ministry of Foreign Affairs. These famous jurists participated actively in the Colloquium and made many valuable contributions in the discussions. The recent formation of the Commission on Legal Problems of Interplanetary Space of the Academy of Sciences of the USSR, under the chairmanship of Professor E. A. Korovin, has marked the start of a period of greatly increased activity in the Soviet Union with respect to space law. Two important books have recently been published —*The Cosmos and International Law,* a collection of essays edited by Korovin, and *Toward Cosmic Law* by F. N. Kovalev and I. I. Cheprov. While the views expressed in these books are sharply at variance with those of the great majority of non-Communist scholars, the mere fact of their expression serves a vital purpose in a world where a misjudgment of the intentions of a great power could lead to catastrophe. There were also several outstanding articles by a number of Soviet authors, which explained and discussed the work of the various international organizations in the field of astronautics.

The 1962 Andrew G. Haley Awards of the Institute, selected by Professor Cooper, Dr. P. K. Roy of ICAO (India), and Dr. Smirnoff, were made to Professor Meyer, Professor Manfred Lachs of Poland, and Pro-

[36] Cheprov and Vereshchetin, *supra* note 34, at 127.

fessor Antonio Ambrosini of Italy. The Gold Medal was presented to Professor Meyer at the Annual Meeting of the German Rocket Society held in Coblenz the week prior to the Varna meeting. Professor Meyer was cited for his contributions in the field of space jurisdiction and sovereignty and his pioneer educational work. An award and honorarium were presented to Dr. Antonio Ambrosini by Dr. Georgiev for his work as the chairman of the first U.N. Legal Subcommittee on the Peaceful Uses of Outer Space. An award and honorarium to Professor Lachs, who succeeded Professor Ambrosini as chairman of the subcommittee, were presented by the president of the IAF, Dr. L. R. Shepherd, and the new president of the Institute, Dr. Georgiev, at the closing banquet. Professor Lachs was cited for his outstanding contributions to the formulation of the rule of law in outer space.

IAF EFFORTS TO ACHIEVE INTERNATIONAL COORDINATION OF SPACE ACTIVITIES THROUGH INTERGOVERNMENTAL ORGANIZATIONS

11–6   The IAF and the United Nations Educational, Scientific, and Cultural Organization

One of the principal activities of the IAF in pursuit of its basic aims has been to seek effective cooperation with other international organizations. The original purpose of this cooperation was not only to advance the cause of international astronautics as such, but to secure international recognition of the IAF and, if possible, financial support so that it could work more effectively. Lack of funds had become so serious by 1953 that several of the European officials of the IAF were seriously questioning whether the organization could continue to exist.

At first it was planned to join UNESCO only after the IAF had obtained the status of a member in the International Council of Scientific Unions (ICSU). This plan was abandoned in January 1953, after it was learned that only societies which had been in existence for six years were eligible for membership in ICSU and that the General Secretary of ICSU also had some doubt that the IAF would meet other eligibility requirements.

Haley, who was chairman of the IAF Finance Committee as well as vice-president of the IAF, offered to take immediate steps to follow up the exploratory talks he had conducted in 1952 on IAF association with UNESCO. He made a thorough investigation of the legal and other requirements for a successful application to UNESCO and learned that the IAF must first exhaust the possibilities of joining the International Union of Engineer Associations, the International Medical Association, and any other related associations already existing under the sponsorship of

UNESCO. Haley, accordingly, conducted a campaign to join the International Union of Engineer Associations and presented recommendations from many of the world's leading scientists and engineers, but he was met with many of the same arguments advanced by ICSU.

At the Fourth IAF Congress in 1953 Haley delivered a report to the plenary session on the results of his investigation, concluding that further efforts should be made to obtain membership in international societies eligible for financial aid from UNESCO and that after these efforts had been exhausted the IAF should apply directly to UNESCO for membership as a nongovernmental organization on a consultative basis. The delegates requested that he stay on as vice-president of the IAF in order better to continue these efforts.

At the Fifth Congress in 1954 Haley reported that he had traveled to Paris and conferred with UNESCO officials, who agreed to send Dr. Pierre Auger, Director of Natural Sciences of UNESCO, to observe the conference. Haley reported that international acceptance of the IAF was maturing slowly but surely, and that the following year strong representations to UNESCO would be in order.

During the following year, Haley prepared a proposal to present to UNESCO on the planning, organization, and execution of a program relating to space flight and astronautics in general. He also proceeded again to Paris to consummate the UNESCO association. He conferred with V. Hercik, who was then in charge of international organizations for UNESCO, and with N. B. Cacciapuoti, associate director of the Department of Natural Sciences of UNESCO. Both officials showed extreme interest in the purposes of the IAF, as set forth in its constitution; they both said that UNESCO would be most happy to have a well-thought-out space-flight program presented to it, and that such a program might even be expedited on an emergency basis. They concluded that with such a program authorized the IAF could then qualify as a consultative nongovernmental adjunct of UNESCO.

Throughout the initial troublesome period and in the ultimately successful outcome, major assistance was given by Frank J. Malina, pioneer American rocket expert and formerly a high official of UNESCO. Indeed, without his help the entire effort might well have failed. For several years now, Dr. Malina has been the IAF official observer to UNESCO.

On Friday morning, July 24, 1955, the very day on which the United States announced its plans to launch an artificial earth satellite, the UNESCO officials agreed to cooperate with the IAF and its space-flight program. Later that same year, at the plenary session of the Sixth Congress in Copenhagen, a report was made on this mission, and the Committee on International Affairs was again constituted. The committee met and decided to submit recommendations to UNESCO within three months.

At the Seventh Congress of the IAF in Rome, in 1956, Haley presented a program by which the IAF proposed to act as a consultative nongovernmental organization to UNESCO, for the planning, organization, and execution of activities relating to space flight and astronautics in general. He was elected official IAF representative to the Ninth Session of the General Conference of UNESCO, which met at New Delhi in November 1956, and he personally presented the IAF application for consultative status.

The IAF was officially accorded observer status at the New Delhi Session, but unfortunately this vote was rescinded the day following the enactment. A policy question concerning the admission of *all* international nongovernmental organizations to UNESCO was raised, and it was decided to rescind the previous vote admitting the IAF and other groups to consultative arrangements. Some UNESCO officials belatedly decided that too many organizations were being admitted to consultative status and felt that further investigation should be made to determine whether the objectives of the organizations were in accord with those of UNESCO. This result was a source of extreme disappointment after the long trip from Washington to New Delhi.

The IAF was not the only group singled out for further investigation. Even many of those groups which had previously been accorded status were placed under examination. Meanwhile, the IAF request for admission to consultative status was simply deferred. However, the Director General of UNESCO, in a note of January 17, 1957, in which he reviewed the status of the IAF application and related matters, emphasized that "under the existing directives" he was

> . . . authorized to maintain unofficial working relations with the International Affairs Committee [of the IAF]. These relations provide an opportunity for your organization to develop with the Secretariat of UNESCO an exchange of information and documentation on questions of common interest.

Members of the International Affairs Committee of the IAF thereafter arranged for general meetings at Paris in April 1957, when UNESCO Secretariat officials could attend. The chairman felt that it would be useful for the IAF members to meet with UNESCO officials and endeavor to work out definite areas in which all appropriate groups could cooperate. It was important also to renew personal negotiations with UNESCO officials looking toward the admission of the IAF to consultative status.

Specific ways and means of collaborating with UNESCO from an administrative standpoint were discussed at length during the April 1957 meetings. It was pointed out that any committees or working groups constituted by the IAF should have terms of reference corresponding to UNESCO. In this connection, it was observed that the Department of Social Sciences of UNESCO had complete jurisdiction over law, economics, and certain activities in the field of medicine, and that the Department of Natural Sciences, generally speaking, had jurisdiction over other scientific areas. Careful consideration was given to the need to avoid overlapping with the activities of any other scientific unions. One long-range proposal that came out of these discussions was that the IAF undertake to prepare studies concerning peaceful uses of rocket vehicles and the social and legal implications of astronautics. It was proposed that the studies consist of reports of outstanding authorities which might be published with the assistance of UNESCO.

After detailed and wholly satisfactory discussion, it was also decided that certain steps could be taken immediately. These included: (1) the attendance of representatives of UNESCO at meetings of the IAF—as had formerly occurred in Rome when Dr. Cacciapuoti attended the Seventh Congress on behalf of UNESCO; (2) the invitation, by UNESCO, of IAF experts to attend UNESCO meetings; (3) constant exchange of information between the IAF and UNESCO with respect to proposals of cooperation in the fields of the natural and social sciences relating to astronautics; (4) IAF participation in the world-touring exhibitions organized by UNESCO, by providing astronautical features; [37] (5) dissemination of astronautical information, magazines, books, etc., throughout the world through the facilities of UNESCO; (6) the creation of a committee by the IAF to outline programs of collaboration with UNESCO which could be considered by appropriate officials of the latter organization.

In July 1957, the IAF was advised that the Executive Board of UNESCO had postponed until 1958 action on all applicants for admission to nongovernmental consultative status. The IAF application was therefore brought up to date for consideration the following year and, finally, at the Tenth Session of the General Conference of UNESCO in November 1958, the IAF was granted consultative status. The Program Committee of UNESCO at the same time approved the recommendation of the UNESCO Natural Sciences Working Party that the Director General be given official jurisdiction over matters concerning the "exploration of extraterrestrial space." Thus the formal IAF liaison with UNESCO was conveniently achieved in time to make possible advising UNESCO on its new official responsibilities.

At the Tenth IAF Congress in 1959 a special committee was formed, headed by ARS board member Martin Summerfield, to work with UNESCO in establishing a series of traveling lectureships by prominent astronautical scientists. The lectureships were designed to be sponsored jointly by UNESCO and the IAF. Frank J. Malina handled these negotia-

[37] In this connection, UNESCO's representative stated that UNESCO desired a model of the IGY earth-circling satellite launching vehicle. It had been unable to obtain such a model, but one of the IAF members attending the meeting duplicated a model of the vehicle and presented it to UNESCO.

tions to a successful conclusion. Still another example of cooperation between the two organizations was the UNESCO grant of slightly under $10,000 to the IAF for 1961-62, which has already been noted in connection with the work of the International Academy of Astronautics. This grant served, in part, to assist the Academy in its preparations for a "Man In Space" symposium. It was likewise intended to support the Academy in the preparation of a multilingual dictionary of space terms (which has also been mentioned earlier), the general dissemination of the results of space research, and the making of travel grants to enable young scientists to attend mechanical meetings of the IAF.[38]

11-7   The IAF and the International Council of Scientific Unions

The need to obtain recognition from world scientific organizations was given considerable attention from the very beginning. Without such recognition, the professional standing of the IAF was seriously impaired. In 1951, therefore, Vice-President Haley started work on the problem of obtaining membership in the International Council of Scientific Unions (ICSU).

At the Fourth Congress of the IAF in 1953, Haley advised the delegates that negotiations with ICSU were at a standstill because (1) an applicant for membership must be in *de jure* existence for six years and (2) the General Secretary of ICSU had expressed strong doubts that the IAF would be eligible for membership in any event. A. V. Hill, General Secretary of ICSU, had said in a letter of January 21, 1953: "It is not for me to decide whether the International Astronautical Federation is qualified for membership in the International Council of Scientific Unions, but I have a strong impression the Executive Board will decide otherwise." As already noted in connection with the discussion of IAF-UNESCO relationships, Haley then advised that the IAF should immediately take steps to become a consultative nongovernmental organization to UNESCO, and major attention was devoted by the IAF over the next few years to the development of this affiliation.

Until 1957, no further progress was made in establishing an affiliation with ICSU. In 1957, however, as soon as the IAF was able to meet the requirement of six years' legal existence, Haley initiated correspondence with Dr. L. V. Berkner, then president of ICSU. This correspondence led to a meeting in April 1958 between Haley, as president of the IAF, and the ICSU Bureau. As a result of this meeting the Bureau unanimously approved the establishment of an *ad hoc* committee consisting of Professor H. S. W. Massey (U.K.) as Convenor, Professor P. Swings (Belgium) and Professor F. L. Whipple (USA) representing ICSU, and

[38] SCHWARTZ, INTERNATIONAL ORGANIZATIONS AND SPACE COOPERATION 91 (Philadelphia: Rittenhouse Press, Inc., 1962).

Professor Theodore von Kármán (USA) as Co-convenor, Professor L. I. Sedov (USSR) and Professor E. Vassy (France) representing the IAF. The stated objective of the committee was to examine the possibilities of making contact between ICSU and the IAF within the terms of Article 2(d) of the ICSU Constitution. It was also proposed that Haley consider with his organization the possibility of sponsoring a scientific union or, alternatively, the reorganization of the IAF.

In August 1958 the committee met in Moscow under the chairmanship of Prof. Massey and unanimously stated:

(1) The Committee recommends to ICSU that the IAF be considered for recognition as an international organization rendering valuable services to the science and technology of astronautics, subject to the Executive Board of the IAF satisfying the President of ICSU that its constitution and by-laws are in accordance with internationally recognized standards for such organizations.

(2) In attempting to define astronautics the Committee considers that it includes the following: design, construction, operation, guidance, navigation and tracking of extraterrestrial vehicles, space medicine, and biology.

Dr. Berkner advised Haley that the recognition requested was unprecedented, and that approval probably would be denied by the Executive Board of ICSU on the ground that the IAF would first have to reorganize to set up a division concerned solely with the appropriate natural sciences. Berkner stated that in the meantime, and for at least one year, the scientific astronautical activity could be pursued by the International Committee on Space Research. (At the first organizational meeting for the latter committee—which subsequently became known as COSPAR—in March 1958, it had been agreed that it would be composed exclusively of ICSU members.)

This very development had been anticipated at the Ninth Congress of the IAF in Amsterdam (August 1958), in a meeting of the above-mentioned ICSU/IAF exploratory committee under the chairmanship of Dr. von Kármán, which recommended that the IAF form three divisions: (1) a Division of Space Sciences, concerned with the broad spectrum of physical, mathematical, astrophysical, and other sciences related to the study of space, (2) a Division for Space Technology, and (3) a Division of Social Sciences Related to Space Problems. The committee felt that the Division of Space Sciences would be qualified as one of the participating groups of the proposed Space Science Commission of ICSU. However, it was decided at Amsterdam that sufficient consideration could not be given by the Council of the IAF to the proposed IAF reorganization because of lack of time and because of the announced determination of some member societies that no current action would be acceptable and that reorganization should be studied during the interim before the Tenth Congress of the IAF in September 1959.

In accordance with the regular procedures of ICSU, the report of the ICSU/IAF exploratory committee was considered at the meeting in Washington of the ICSU Executive Board on October 1, 1958, prior to General Assembly consideration on October 6. Haley, as IAF President, was afforded full observer privileges at the board and assembly sessions and was able to present the position of the IAF. The official action of the ICSU Executive Board followed the course predicted by Dr. Berkner. Nevertheless, the IAF was afforded significant recognition at the Eighth General Assembly of ICSU by the unanimous adoption of a resolution reading:

> The General Assembly is aware of the useful activities of the International Astronautical Federation (IAF) in furthering the science and technology of astronautics. The General Assembly welcomes the interest shown by the International Astronautical Federation (IAF) in furthering the International Council of Scientific Unions and looks forward to the possibility of arranging in the future a more formal affiliation in matters of common concern.

This resolution was reported to the plenary session by an assembly committee of ICSU consisting of Professor K. F. Ogorodnikov, Academy of Sciences USSR, Moscow; Professor John T. Wilson, Geophysical Laboratory, University of Toronto, Canada; and Dr. Allan Shapley, United States National Bureau of Standards.

The following year, bodies were established within the IAF which resembled the first and last of the three divisions recommended by the ICSU/IAF committee, namely, the International Academy of Astronautics and the International Institute of Space Law. The matter of formal affiliation, however, is still pending.

11-8   The IAF and the International Telecommunication Union

Another aspect of international coordination on which the IAF has placed considerable emphasis has been the allocation of the radio spectrum for tracking, guidance, and information recovery, for radio astronomy, and for the commercial uses of space communications. This branch of space law was considered by the U.N. *ad hoc* Committee on the Peaceful Uses of Outer Space as a "matter of life and death" for space exploration.

The only official international body authorized to make studies on the fundamental problems involved in international radio (and space) communications is the International Radio Consultative Committee (CCIR) of the International Telecommunication Union (ITU). The CCIR adopts recommendations of its component groups for submission to the Administrative Radio Conferences which meet at intervals of about three years to draft and submit to ITU member governments international treaty provisions on radio communications.

In view of the importance of telecommunications in the astronautics program, Chairman Haley of the IAF's Committee on International Affairs submitted a proposal to the ITU on April 16, 1956, concerning procedures to effect allocations for space radio. The IAF urged that working arrangements be set up between the IAF and the ITU "looking toward the optimum plan for allocation of frequencies in the radio spectrum for ... communications in outer space." The IAF proposal contained a five-point plan along the following lines: (1) the International Radio Consultative Committee (CCIR) of the ITU should study the *requirements* of astronautical radio use; (2) the International Frequency Registration Board (IFRB) of the ITU should study the frequencies available to meet these requirements; (3) the IAF should send representatives to the sessions of the CCIR and the IFRB; (4) the ITU should send representatives to IAF meetings, including the forthcoming Seventh Congress to be held at Rome in September 1956; and (5) after completion of these steps the ITU should initiate formal action to effect radio allocations for use in space. However, the ITU responded negatively to the IAF proposal. On June 11, 1956, the Secretary-General of the ITU informed the IAF that the Union felt the matters raised by the IAF should be referred to the individual member nations.

Thereafter the IAF renewed its proposals, both in presentations to the ITU itself and in proposals to the constituent organizations of the ITU. The first of the latter category to which a formal proposal was made was the CCIR. Haley, as a representative of the IAF, traveled to Warsaw to attend the CCIR conference in that city during August and September 1956, and on September 3 submitted an IAF proposal that the CCIR establish a new study group for extraterrestrial communications. In this proposal, the IAF reviewed progress up to that time in earth-orbital satellite programs and in the development of cislunar circumlunar space vehicles, and discussed the importance of radio communications and guidance in such space-flight activities. The IAF document concluded with the statement that the CCIR was the only international body authorized to study communications and guidance in extraterrestrial projects, and it urged that a study of requirements for astronautical radio frequencies be completed and a report rendered in time for presentation to the ITU International Radio Conference of 1959 in Geneva. The CCIR responded officially to the IAF proposal by suggesting that the IAF apply for consultative membership in the CCIR. The CCIR Director, Professor Van Der Pol, suggested further to the IAF that it choose from among the list of then-existing CCIR Study Groups the ones in which it would desire to participate. The hope was expressed that "collaboration with [the IAF] would give excellent results." The CCIR did not agree to undertake studies at that time, however.

Pursuant to the advice of the CCIR Director, the IAF on May 10, 1957, made appropriate application for association with the ITU to the then Secretary-General of the ITU, Marco Aurelio Andrada. The IAF pointed out its interest in participating in all conferences related to the study of radio requirements and the allocation of frequencies for activities in space.

The ITU Administrative Council, at its May 1957 session, voted to grant the IAF full nongovernmental consultative status. This action testified to the effectiveness of the liaison work at the preceding Warsaw Conference. The Administrative Council of ITU agreed to include the IAF on the list of nongovernmental international organizations to be notified of the next Administrative Radio Conference scheduled to meet in July, 1959, and it was agreed also that the two organizations could exchange representatives at international meetings without having to share in the cost of such meetings. As a result of this protocol, the president of the IAF invited the Secretary-General of the ITU to send a representative to the Eighth Congress of the IAF in Barcelona.

A letter was sent by the IAF to the CCIR in August 1957, stating that the IAF was seeking "intelligent studies of the technical aspects of radio communication under operating conditions in space flight." The CCIR responded by noting that the IAF was admitted to participate as an international organization in the work of ITU.

In December 1957, the IAF renewed its proposal that the CCIR set up a Space Communications Study Group. At the same time, it supplied the CCIR with copies of the American Rocket Society's *Appearance and Comments* in the inquiry by the Federal Communications Commission into radio allocations between 25 and 890 megacycles.

In April 1958, the IAF advised the CCIR of its intention and desire to participate in two of the then-existing study groups of the CCIR most closely connected with the subject of radio communications in space. Thereafter, the IAF was formerly advised by the CCIR that it would be allowed to participate in CCIR Study Groups VI (Ionospheric Propagation) and XI (Television).

A meeting of Study Group XI of the CCIR was scheduled to be held in Moscow in May and June 1958. The IAF was advised of this meeting, and it sent a representative in order to draw attention to the need to study specific space requirements for consideration by the forthcoming ITU Administrative Radio Conference in 1959. Study Group XI is chiefly concerned with various aspects of television systems, television standards, and requirements for the transmission of television over long distances. The IAF decision to participate in this study group was influenced by the statements of President Eisenhower, members of the USSR Academy of Sciences, and numerous other scientists throughout the world proposing the use of satellites as passive and active television relay stations and as television originating bases for the dissemination of scientific data to earth from outer space. Since a specific topic on the agenda for the study group meeting concerned television transmission over extremely long distances, the IAF submitted some draft study questions that were directly related to astronautical requirements.[39]

At the twelve-day meeting of Study Group XI it was decided that the questions, problems, and study proposals which were submitted by the IAF to the plenary session could better be acted upon by Study Groups V (Tropospheric Progagation) and VI (Ionospheric Progagation). The Director of the CCIR then proposed—and at the next meeting of the CCIR it was formally agreed—that in view of the rapidly growing importance of astronautical communications the following questions should be studied: (1) what frequencies are specially suitable for penetration of the layers of the earth's atmosphere; (2) what are the influences on these frequencies of the hour of the day, the season, the geographical location, and solar activity; (3) what deviations in propagation direction can be expected as a result of the penetration of the ionosphere; (4) what, if any, will be the differences in propagation between in-going and out-going signals relative to the earth; (5) what special phenomena are to be expected that do not occur in transmission between two points on earth; and (6) what is the possible influence of the troposphere on wave propagation to and from extraterrestrial objects.

Study Group VI of the CCIR met at Geneva in July and August 1958, and at this meeting the IAF submitted a lengthy proposal for consideration. The IAF proposal was twofold. First, a study of technical requirement was outlined which included the subjects just listed. Second, a thorough review of the then-known frequency allocation needs of astronautical radio services was made. Each portion of the radio spectrum was analyzed both as to the need for its use in astronautical radio and as to the effects of any re-allocation on existing users.

In addition to the foregoing, the United States Preparatory Committee,

---

[39] These study questions dealt with the following subjects:

1. What practicable measures can be taken to provide for the transmission of television signals in connection with activities in astronautics?
2. How can the various uses of such transmission of television signals be categorized?
3. What are the requirements as to definition, frame rate, field rate, and other parameters for signals for the various categories of use?
4. How can standardization be effected which will promote the best international usage of such signals and the most efficient and useful employment of communications, telemetry, and guidance by means of such signals?
5. For the transmission of television signals over extremely long distances between earth and positions and objects in space:
   A. What are the characteristics of the signal, circuitry, and propagation paths that must be considered? What are their recommended values? And what tolerances must be imposed in order to ensure satisfactory transmission?
   B. How do these characteristics and their values and tolerances differ as between the requirements for the transmission of monochrome signals and color signals?
   C. What methods of measurement and what test signals can be recommended for checking these characteristics?

International Radio Conference—which was helping to lay the groundwork for the Ninth Plenary Assembly of the CCIR to be held at Los Angeles in April 1959—circulated a proposal that took note of the fact that "radio emissions of the first earth satellite have already yielded valuable information about the ionosphere, as well as about problems of space travel" and, accordingly, recommended that "clear channels be set aside for the use of satellite and space ship emissions." These observations and recommendations were timely, as they were available for consideration by CCIR Study Group VI in its Geneva meeting during August 1958, at which the IAF had an official observer.

Following the Geneva meeting of the CCIR study group, the IAF commenced its preparation for two major international radio conferences scheduled for 1959. These were the Ninth Plenary Assembly of the CCIR at Los Angeles in April and the Administrative Radio Conference at Geneva from August to December. As background for the CCIR Plenary Assembly in Los Angeles, the IAF supplied to the more than 950 delegates copies of the ARS comments prepared in anticipation of the Geneva Conference, as well as copies of the direct testimony of a score of technical experts given under ARS auspices to the Federal Communications Commission in connection with the Commission's over-all frequency allocation hearings.

The Plenary Assembly of the CCIR proceeded to reorganize study groups by merging Study Group IV (Ground-Wave Propagation) into Study Group V (Tropospheric Propagation), so that the new Study Group V would deal with propagation, including the effects of the earth and troposphere. At the same time, a new Study Group IV (Space Systems) was formed "to study systems of telecommunications with and between locations in space." On July 14, 1959, in response to the request of the IAF, the CCIR formally included the IAF as a participant in this new study group on space communications.

The results of the 1959 Geneva Conference have already been discussed in Chapter 7. As pointed out there, the first international radio allocations specifically for space purposes were made at Geneva, but these allocations were by no means adequate for the present and future requirements of space projects. On the other hand, the needs of astronautics were to be considered again at the Extraordinary Administrative Radio Conference called for 1963. In the meantime, the IAF and its member societies have been working closely with the ITU and CCIR, with a view to obtaining more adequate treatment of space telecommunication problems at the forthcoming conference.

SOME OTHER NONGOVERNMENTAL ORGANIZATIONS IN THE INTERNATIONAL COORDINATION OF SPACE ACTIVITIES

11-9   *American Bar Association*

Another example of the ways in which both international and national nongovernmental organizations can contribute to international coordination of space activities is the work of the American Bar Association (ABA). Through the activities of its many sections, such as the Administrative Law Section and the International and Comparative Law Section, this professional organization attempts to encourage the development of bodies of law which achieve order in human relationships in such a way as to permit and stimulate the attainment of the maximum potentials of human civilization. This goal may be pursued by ordering the basic principles which have developed in a field of law; by drafting new legislation and suggesting revisions of existing statutes; by seeking uniform procedures, etc.; and by generally serving as an enlightened and constructive critic of contemporary public and private policy.

Major efforts of the American Bar Association to stimulate the development of international law for outer space date from early 1957. At that time, the author suggested to President David F. Maxwell of the ABA that a committee on space law be set up in the Section of International and Comparative Law. The proposal pointed out that the "tremendous implications" of recent progress in rockets and guided missiles, of the International Geophysical Year satellite program, and of the prospects for manned space flight had so far "escaped the attention of a group of scientists who are most concerned, namely, the legal profession." [40] Maxwell replied that the proposal "sounded a responsive chord" in his own thinking: "The effect of the amazing technological developments in recent years upon international law has been a source of great concern...." [41] However, as the ABA President was not empowered to direct the work of the sections, decision on the proposal rested with the section concerned. Unfortunately, administrative problems, including the usual difficulties of coordination accompanying an annual change of officers, prevented immediate action on the proposal. [42]

The launching of *Sputnik I* on October 4, 1957, had a stimulating effect since it made the need for development of law for outer space seem much

[40] Letter From Andrew G. Haley to the Honorable David F. Maxwell, President, American Bar Association, May 24, 1957.
[41] Letter From Maxwell to Haley, May 28, 1957.
[42] Letter From Victor C. Folson, Chairman, Section of International and Comparative Law, ABA, to Haley, June 7, 1957; Letter From Haley to Homer G. Angelo, Chairman, Section of International and Comparative Law, ABA, Sept. 10, 1957; Letter From Angelo to Haley, Sept. 13, 1957.

more immediate than before. As Homer G. Angelo, new chairman of the Section of International and Comparative Law, noted shortly thereafter: "Obviously recent events have demonstrated the timeliness and urgency of the establishment of such a committee with the Association." [43] The organization of the committee thus moved swiftly: by December 1957, a Committee on the Law of Outer Space was officially established within the Section of International and Comparative Law, with David F. Maxwell, then immediate past president of the ABA, as chairman, the author as vice-chairman, and Frank Simpson III, as secretary.[44] Members appointed to the committee were: Loftus E. Becker, Legal Advisor, Department of State; Ralph E. Becker; John Cobb Cooper, Professor of Air Law, McGill University (Canada) and Legal Advisor, International Air Transport Association; Arnold W. Knauth, Chairman, Air Law Committee, American Branch of the International Law Association; Albert C. Lazure, General Counsel, Ordnance Department, United States Army; Edward H. Levi, Dean, University of Chicago Law School; Leon Lipson, Professor of Law, Yale University; Myres S. McDougal, Professor of International Law, Yale University; John Ritchie III, Dean, Northwestern University Law School; Robert E. Sullivan, Dean, Law School, Montana State University; and Rear Admiral Chester C. Ward, Judge Advocate General, United States Navy.[45]

The first meeting of the committee was held in February 1958 and was devoted to an initial probing of the problems involved in space law. Although the chairman had stated as the main concern of the committee that the scientists were outstripping the lawyers and that the ABA should take some action immediately, the great diversity of views resulting from the ensuing discussion made it apparent that the problems were even more complex than most of the individual members had previously imagined. Hence the committee determined that, in spite of its urgency, the matter demanded further consideration, and it resolved that the ABA not adopt any position on the law of outer space until adequate study could be made. Meanwhile, a subcommittee was established to identify and state the problems and to prepare a bibliography.[46]

At the meeting of the Committee on the Law of Outer Space held in August 1958, in conjunction with the annual ABA Convention, a resolution was adopted stating that the committee should:

(1) Recommend to appropriate agencies of the Association, in particular the American Bar Foundation, an analytical survey of the literature on the law of space, reporting and classifying the issues of fact and law that have been

[43] Letter From Angelo to Haley, Oct. 21, 1957.
[44] Letter From Angelo to Haley, Dec. 23, 1957.
[45] Letter From Maxwell to Haley, Jan. 20, 1958; Minutes of Meeting, Committee on the Law of Outer Space, Feb. 21, 1958.
[46] Minutes of Meeting, Committee on the Law of Outer Space, Feb. 21, 1958.

raised and the positions that have been taken; (2) Undertake to rank the issues, developed in that survey, in order of priority for desirable special study and further recommendation.[47]

The committee also discussed and expanded a draft annual report prepared by John Cobb Cooper and Frank Simpson III, for submission to the Section of International and Comparative Law. The report included: (1) a review of previous space technological developments and a projection of future developments, to provide the factual basis for legal analysis; (2) an analysis of the National Aeronautics and Space Act of 1958 as the charter for United States space activities; (3) a review of existing rules of law affecting use of outer space, and of the situations for which there were no rules; and (4) an inventory of present space problems having legal implications.[48]

The committee determined that a literature survey of sufficient depth to fill the need would require financing, and it therefore set about to obtain the funding of this research. In October 1958, the Board of Directors of the American Bar Foundation, the research affiliate of the American Bar Association, approved the research project, and it was publicly announced in the *American Bar News*.[49] Since the committee's analysis had revealed that the responsibility of the National Aeronautics and Space Administration (NASA) extended to research on the legal and social ramifications of space activities as well as the basic technical research to make such activities possible, the Bar Foundation submitted an application to NASA for a grant to support research on the law of outer space. The application stated that a review and analysis of "all available space law literature" was contemplated, and it emphasized that the results of the survey would be made available not only to the ABA Committee on Space Law but also to the appropriate Congressional Committees, to NASA, and other government agencies, and to the United Nations and the International Civil Aviation Organization.[50]

The application was accepted and a grant was made by NASA; work on the project was begun in early 1959. Professors Leon S. Lipson of the Yale Law School and Nicholas de B. Katzenbach of the University of Chicago Law School were engaged as project reporters by the Bar Foundation. The Committee on the Law of Outer Space was also engaged in an advisory capacity by the Bar Foundation. The committee was aware of the precedent set in connection with the Atomic Energy Act, when Congress sought the aid of the ABA in drafting the legislation which es-

[47] Minutes of Meeting, Committee on the Law of Outer Space, Aug. 24, 1958, p. 4.
[48] *Ibid.*
[49] American Bar News, Nov. 15, 1958.
[50] Letter From Ross L. Malone, President, American Bar Foundation, to Dr. Thomas Keith Glennan, Administrator, National Aeronautics and Space Administration, Nov. 17, 1958.

tablished basic United States policy on atomic energy, and it desired to be prepared as early as possible for providing similar assistance in the case of outer space.[51]

The determination of the committee to come to grips with the issues involved was indicated at its spring 1959 meeting, when it was frankly decided "that the final report should be as complete as possible." The Committee felt that there should be no attempt to "dodge the several controversial problems inherent in the outer space field," but rather that controversial matters should be met "head on," even if this meant that in the end a minority as well as a majority report might have to be submitted.[52]

The 1959 annual report of the Committee on the Law of Outer Space was based on a preliminary draft prepared by the survey project reporters Lipson and Katzenbach. The body of the report consisted of three major parts, of which the first was a general background survey. It contained a comparative analysis of the atomic energy control problem; a review of United Nations actions relating to outer space, particularly the work of the *ad hoc* Committee on the Peaceful Uses of Outer Space; a review of existing international agreements on air space and the status of outer space; an analysis of the problem of the boundary between air space and outer space; a discussion of analogies from the law of the sea and other special areas, and an assessment of the need for an international agreement on a law for outer space. Next came an inventory of selected legal problems of outer space, including (a) radio spectrum management, (b) conservation of space, (c) radio and television relay satellites, (d) weather forecasting and control, (e) safety standards and possible damage to subjacent states, aircraft, and vessels, (f) repossession of space projectiles and repatriation of personnel, (g) occupation of space and other bodies, and (h) coordination of space programs. The third section of the report was a discussion of the potential structure and functions of an international space agency.[53]

In addition, the report proposed that the committee recommend to the House of Delegates of the ABA a number of resolutions which upheld the principle of free and peaceful use of outer space by all nations, even while recognizing that "the freedom of space must be regarded as compatible with the rights of security and self-defense. . . ." The proposed resolutions called for prompt international action on the allocation of space radio frequencies, space vehicle registration, retrieval and return of landed space vehicles, liability for injury or damage caused by such vehicles, and so forth; and they included a statement that the disposition of all these problems should "be pursued independently of the question

---

[51] Letter From Frank Simpson III, Secretary, Committee on the Law of Outer Space, to Maxwell, April 20, 1959.

[52] Minutes of Meeting, Committee on the Law of Outer Space, May 20, 1959.

[53] Report of the Committee on Law of Outer Space, July 8, 1959.

of the establishment of boundaries marking the outer limit of air space
or the inner limit of outer space." The resolutions also included one
recommendation stating:

> That an attempt at comprehensive codification of space law would be
> premature at present but that the list and relative priority of specific urgent
> problems of space law should be kept under regular review by appropriate
> international bodies.[54]

In its conclusion the committee report offered these general observations:

> This memorandum has attempted a provisional appraisal of the more urgent
> of the legal problems that will arise from national and international space
> activities. It has not attempted to resolve those problems, and has rejected as
> analytically unsound and impractical an approach that essays a single com-
> prehensive solution. We believe that both the spirit and the letter of the
> United Nations Charter oblige all members to cooperate in seeking solution
> to particular problems and to avoid, insofar as is consistent with consider-
> ations of self-defense, unilateral solutions that, even though they may not
> violate international law, create friction and impair friendly relations. We
> have, therefore, rejected lines of reasoning that on the one hand suggest that
> national programs should be subject to no international control short of the
> use of space for military aggression, and on the other hand suggest that
> almost nothing can be done in space with prior agreement.
>
> . . . To the extent that formal legal agreement can be achieved, difficulties
> and friction may be obviated; but even an unsuccessful attempt to reach such
> agreement on a well-defined set of practical, impending problems may be
> helpful in the making of national decisions, by influencing states with space
> capability to conduct their space activity in ways that avoid major disagree-
> ments and reduce international tension.
>
> . . . We [the United States] are one of the two powers with experience in
> launching objects into outer space. Not only is the law of outer space of
> special interest to us; but also we have a special responsibility to use every
> conceivable means to insure that the applicable law will serve the needs of
> the whole international community and the cause of peace and human dig-
> nity. Through its representatives in the United Nations, and in the public
> utterances of the President, the Government has welcomed the opportunity
> afforded by the Age of Space to continue and deepen the channels of inter-
> national cooperation. We have seen too the magnificent cooperative efforts of
> scientists the world over during the IGY to make science the servant of all
> mankind; and it is in a similar spirit, and with similar objectives, that lawyers
> should approach the legal problems now upon us.
>
> Through clarifying and proposing legal arrangements within the modest
> scope of those set forth in this memorandum, lawyers can contribute most
> to fostering, in common with our public officials, a climate in which more
> durable institutional machinery and more comprehensive codes can be
> launched when this appears practical and necessary. . . . The prospective
> conquest of space is too grave and portentous an undertaking to be made
> the vehicle for selfish national aggrandizement or to be used for propa-
> gandistic or other political advantage. Posterity deserves something better.[55]

[54] *Id.* at 1.
[55] *Id.* at 19-20.

Four members of the committee—Becker, Beresford, Haley, and Huard —suggested certain changes in the language of the report, affecting both the proposed resolutions and the conclusion. Most significant, perhaps, was their suggested modification of the resolution which held the "comprehensive codification of space law" to be "premature." This resolution they wished to rephrase in the following terms:

> That an attempt at comprehensive codification of space law might be premature at present, but that it would be timely for private and public international bodies to begin intensive study of a basic framework for space law and simultaneously to attack specific urgent problems on a previously selected priority basis.[56]

Meanwhile, work continued on the survey of the literature and problems of the law of outer space. The survey was finally published in October 1960 as *The Law of Outer Space: Report to the National Aeronautics and Space Administration* (often referred to as the Lipson-Katzenbach Report, after the project reporters). This report immediately took its place as the basic work on the law of outer space and contributed significantly to further development of thinking in this crucial problem area. Indeed, the production of this report was undoubtedly the most significant contribution made by the ABA Committee on the Law of Outer Space in its early years.

Having accomplished a basic survey of the law of outer space as a precondition for further development in this field, the committee then turned its attention to some specific problems which called for immediate amelioration. The 1961 report of the committee, for which Spencer M. Beresford, Special Counsel of the House Committee on Science and Astronautics, and Haley were project reporters, covered the problems of government indemnification of space contractors and space telecommunications regulation. In both areas, the technological considerations underlying the problems were analyzed, and the development of such law as had come into existence up to that time was reviewed. Similarly, the various goals which might be considered in formulating public policy were catalogued, and proposals reconciling all these goals and factors were formulated.

With regard to the specific problem of indemnification of space contractors, the report observed:

> Government contractors entering into research and development, supply or construction contracts with the government are concerned with the risk which they are taking of incurring public liability which could reduce them to bankruptcy should some unforeseen accident occur. The implications to the space program of reluctance of qualified contractors to enter into "high-liability" contracts with the Federal Government are clear. A solution to the

[56] Ralph E. Becker, Spencer Beresford, Andrew G. Haley, and Leo A. Huard, Critique of the Report and Recommendations of the Committee on Outer Space, p. 1 [1959].

space contractor's liability problem is required now in the interest of further space activity and defense planning.[57]

Accordingly, the committee recommended that the ABA adopt a resolution calling for "appropriate legislation" to deal with the problem. Such legislation "should protect persons concerned who may become liable, including private contractors and sub-contractors engaged in supply and construction contracts, as well as research and development contracts." However, the proposed solution stated that indemnification (and also liability) "should be limited to a high level of damages, such as $500,000,000 for each incident," and that as a condition of indemnification contractors should be required to "maintain the maximum amount of financial protection, including insurance, available on reasonable terms." Administrative settlement was proposed for minor claims, Congressional action for the "payment of meritorious claims above a stated amount." Finally, the resolution urged that due consideration "be given to seeking appropriate international agreements" on the settlement of claims for personal injury and property damage resulting from "unusually hazardous risks" in government-sponsored space activities.[58]

The committee also noted in its 1961 report that *The Law of Outer Space* (i.e., the Lipson-Katzenbach Report) had been incorporated in the *Legal Problems of Outer Space,* issued by the Senate Committee on Aeronautical and Space Sciences in March 1961. Indeed, it was pointed out that "many of the other articles" included in the latter compilation were "reprintings of published articles and addresses by members of this Committee." [59]

In its 1962 report, the committee noted that the most important development in space law in the preceding year had been without question the revived functioning of the United Nations Committee on the Peaceful Uses of Outer Space. The ABA Committee on the Law of Outer Space supported the activities of the U.N. Committee by participating in the briefing session of the United States space law delegation to the March 1962 UNCOPUOS meetings. Also during 1962, the committee initiated action to bring the Lipson-Katzenbach Report up to date and to carry it further by including an over-all analysis of the document, and recommendations based thereon. The committee likewise sponsored a public symposium in San Francisco during August 1962, in conjunction with the annual ABA meeting. The symposium was entitled "Contemporary Developments in Science, Life and Law in Space" and included a discussion by a five-man panel consisting of representatives chosen from the fields of natural science, law, and medicine.[60]

[57] Report of the Section of International and Comparative Law, ABA, Aug. 6, 1961.
[58] *Id.* at 13-15.
[59] *Id.* at 21.
[60] American Bar Association, Section of International and Comparative Law, Committee on the Law of Outer Space, 1962 Report, pp. 1, 10-11.

In reviewing the activities of the Committee on the Law of Outer Space from 1958 to 1962, Chairman Maxwell expressed the belief that it had already "made a substantial contribution to the literature on the subject." He was confident that NASA and the Department of State had found *The Law of Outer Space* "of considerable value in negotiating with the USSR and other nations through the United Nations organizations." And he pointed out that on numerous occasions the committee had been "called in, in an advisory capacity, by Congressional committees and the State Department with respect to the delineation of principles upon which the peaceful uses of outer space for the benefit of all mankind can be assured." He went on to say:

> Since 1958 we have conducted a number of panel discussions in connection with the meeting of the American Bar Association in various cities, all of which have been exceedingly well attended and widely reported. These too, by reason of the quality of the speakers procured and the depth of their experience and knowledge in the space law field, have represented important contributions to the evolution of the law for outer space.[61]

The efforts of the author, leading to the original formation and staffing of this committee, have had on the whole very gratifying results. The ABA Committee has contributed immeasurably to increased awareness among the lawyers of the world of the many problems which are intricately woven into the development of law for the space age.

11–10   American Rocket Society (American Institute of Aeronautics and Astronautics)

The activities of the American Rocket Society—a national professional organization of individuals, groups, and corporations involved in astronautics—further illustrate the role of nongovernmental organizations in the international coordination of space activities.

An early major effort of the ARS was its attempt to persuade the United States National Science Foundation (NSF) to undertake a space exploration program, since only governmental agencies would have sufficient resources to support such a venture.[62] A Space Flight Committee was set up by the ARS in 1951 to have charge of this effort, with Haley as chairman.

The first report of the Space Flight Committee, issued in 1952, called for an orbital unmanned satellite project and observed that "at this stage of man's knowledge the Committee believes that a study program of all

[61] Letter From Maxwell to the Honorable James E. Webb, Administrator, National Aeronautics and Space Administration, Feb. 27, 1962.
[62] The statements in this section are based upon files of the ARS and the direct participation of the author, except as noted otherwise.

phases of space flight, supported by the government, possibly by the National Science Foundation, would provide a sound basis for a vehicle construction program in the least possible time." The committee frankly stated its view "that exploratory space flight as a speculative venture into the unknown should be regarded as the ultimate objective of a reasonable effort on the part of the United States and mankind as a whole."

In 1953 the chairman of the Space Flight Committee invited Alan T. Waterman, Director of the NSF, to attend a plenary meeting of the committee, and thereafter a confidential report was issued in which the committee proposed that the "National Science Foundation study the utility of an unmanned satellite vehicle to science, commerce and industry, and national defense." The report stated that such a study "should precede any considerations of feasibility and cost," which could be fully investigated "if the utility study showed a definite need for a satellite vehicle. . . ." Various examples of possible research uses were given, including satellite-based astronomical observations, biological and chemical research under non-gravity conditions, electronic research using a more perfect vacuum of unlimited size in free space, cosmic-ray and nuclear research, and so forth. President Eisenhower's "open skies" proposal at Geneva was anticipated by the suggestion that a satellite be used for "large-scale accurate reference mapping and surveying" and "accurate mapping of areas not otherwise accessible to us."

In 1954 the ARS submitted to the National Science Foundation a proposal "On the Utility of an Artificial Unmanned Earth Satellite." This report was written by Milton W. Rosen, who succeeded Haley as chairman of the ARS Space Flight Committee. The report was backed up by a series of excellent studies on the utility of an artificial unmanned earth satellite.

Then, on Friday, July 29, 1955, the White House announcement of the United States satellite project was released from Washington. Interestingly enough, the Space Flight Committee of the ARS had anticipated the details and even much of the language of the official statement. There were naturally some changes, but the substance of the first, second, and third reports of the Space Flight Committee in many respects paralleled the American announcement, and it was particularly gratifying that a major government proposed to go forward with a satellite project in connection with the program of the International Geophysical Year.

With the advent of actual space flight in 1957 and after, the ARS, like other organizations, expanded its concern to include not only the physical technology and resources necessary for the realization of space exploration but also the legal and social coordination required in order to obtain maximum benefits from such activities. This expansion of concern was demonstrated by the establishment of an ARS Space Law and Sociology Committee, with Haley as chairman, and by the highly successful conference which the committee held on March 20, 1959, in New York City. The conference had three striking and surprising results. First, an officially designated subcommittee of the House Committee on Science and Astronautics attended in a body. The subcommittee was composed of Representatives Victor L. Anfuso, chairman; Leonard G. Wolf; Walter H. Moeller; Ken Hechler; David S. King; Gordon L. McDonough; and Spencer M. Beresford, counsel. Second, diplomatic personnel from Eastern European nations attended the meeting, including V. A. Kuznetsov, counselor, and V. I. Oberemko, first secretary, of the Permanent Mission of the USSR to the United Nations. In conjunction with the meeting, Jacek Machowski of Poland delivered a paper entitled *Problems of Space Law* at the 13th Session of the U.N. General Assembly. Third, university professors, jurists, and sociologists from throughout America attended the meeting, which constituted, in reality, the first major conference on the social sciences relating to astronautics. The effort was duplicated to a lesser degree later in the year by the holding of another meeting of the Space Law and Sociology Committee at San Diego on June 9, 1959. The papers read and the facts developed at these two conferences undoubtedly were most helpful to the members of the U.N. Legal Committee, whose report, dated June 12, 1959, re-expressed in somewhat attenuated form the views covered in these sessions as well as in some of the meetings of the IAF described previously.

The Space Law and Sociology Committee, under Chairman Haley, held another conference in New York in April 1962. This conference was the first at which U.S. Government, Congressional, and U.N. officials were joined in their presentations by outstanding student contributions. Attending the meeting were Professor John Cobb Cooper, Representative James E. Fulton, John A. Johnson of NASA, David F. Maxwell, Colonel Martin Menter, Paul Dembling, Mrs. Eilene Galloway, Representative John W. Davis, William S. Strauss, and representatives of the student bodies of the Duke, Harvard, and Virginia Law Schools.

Needless to say, this brief discussion does not do justice to the contributions of the ARS to astronautics in general, and to the development of a space legal structure in particular. Some of its most valuable work has been done through the IAF, where it has served as the United States voting member; and still other ARS contributions have been cited elsewhere in this volume in connection with specific space law problems. In late 1962, the ARS agreed to a merger with the Institute of the Aerospace Sciences, resulting in the creation of the American Institute of Aeronautics and Astronautics in 1963. This new organization, however, can be expected to show the same concern for the social and legal aspects of space flight as did the ARS in recent years; and it has automatically inherited the ARS position as voting member of the IAF. Haley was appointed chairman of the Legal Technical Committee of the AIAA, and was succeeded on June 20, 1963 as chairman by Professor Howard J. Taubenfeld of Southern Methodist University.

11–11 International Aeronautical Federation

The Fédération Aéronautique Internationale (FAI) was born in the early years of the present century, roughly coinciding with the birth of the Air Age. To be more precise, it was formed in Paris on October 14, 1905, when the first statutes and by-laws were signed by aero club representatives of eight nations. The founding countries were Belgium, France, Germany, Great Britain, Italy, Spain, Switzerland, and the United States.[63]

The establishment of the FAI thus came shortly after the successful achievement of powered heavier-than-air flight; and it reflected a belief that the science and practice of aeronautics called for international control and guidance, including a high degree of voluntary cooperation among nations. Its best known function has been to serve as an impartial arbiter of all categories of aeronautical records. In July 1962, for example, both the United States and the USSR had reason to correspond with the FAI in an official capacity. The two countries were submitting information on two new world's records, the United States for altitude and the USSR for speed of a manned vehicle. On July 1, 1962, to be exact, Major Robert M. White of the United States had become the first man to exceed fifty miles in altitude in a winged vehicle when he climbed to 314,750 feet (59.6 miles). As for the Soviet accomplishment, *Tass*, the Russian news service, reported that on July 7, Lt. Col. Georgy Mosolov achieved an average speed of approximately 1,660 miles per hour in a two-way flight over a 15 to 25 kilometer course at an airdrome near Moscow.[64]

Today, when FAI membership stands at more than five times the original, the Air Age has evolved into the Missile and Space Age. Nevertheless, the spirit of the founding fathers of the FAI can and must be adapted for international control and guidance in this new age of man's history, so that humanity can continue to look skyward with hope and not despair. Fortunately, the FAI has already sought to meet this challenge. It has established an Astronautics Documentation Subcommittee, and in response to claims made by the USSR and the United States it has given official recognition to a number of space flight records. Those set

[63] The following countries are now represented in FAI: Argentina, Australia, Austria, Belgium, Brazil, Bulgaria, Canada, Chile, Colombia, Cuba, Czechoslovakia, Denmark, Dominican Republic, Ecuador, Egypt, France, Finland, Germany, Great Britain, Greece, Guatemala, Netherlands, Hungary, Iceland, India, Ireland, Israel, Italy, Japan, Korea, Luxembourg, Mexico, Monaco, New Zealand, Norway, Peru, Poland, Portugal, Romania, Spain, Sweden, Switzerland, Turkey, Union of South Africa, United States, Uruguay, USSR, Venezuela, and Yugoslavia.

[64] *X-15, Soviet Fighter Claims New Records,* Aviation Week & Space Technology, July 23, 1962, p. 25.

by Yuri Gagarin in the first manned orbital flight of April 12, 1961, and by Alan Shepard in his suborbital Project Mercury experiment of not quite one month later both obtained FAI recognition on the same day, July 18, 1961.[65]

The work of the FAI is another example of valuable service performed by a nongovernmental international organization. By acting as a central information bureau and certifying point for international flight records, it provides the basis for one more cooperative effort at international agreement on matters both "aeronautique" and "astronautique."

11–12   Institute of International Law

The Institute of International Law, which was founded in 1873, established a committee on the international law of outer space under the chairmanship of C. Wilfred Jenks in 1959. The committee, composed of members from both the Soviet and Western nations, has reached substantial accord on many topics and will present a report to the Institute late in 1963.[66]

[65] AERONAUTICAL AND ASTRONAUTICAL EVENTS of 1961 32, 34 (Comm. Print of House Committee on Science and Astronautics, 1962).

[66] Institut de droit international, 2ème Commission *Le droit international des espaces célestes,* Rapport provisoire présenté par C. Wilfred Jenks et Rapport definitif et projet de Résolution présentés par C. Wilfred Jenks, 1963, to be reprinted in *Annuaire de l'Institut de droit international,* Vol. 50.

Additional References

Andrew G. Haley, ROCKETRY AND SPACE EXPLORATION: THE INTERNATIONAL STORY (1958): ———, *The International Academy of Astronautics of the International Astronautical Federation,* Signal, Feb. 1961, p. 39; ———, *Commercial Aspects of Our National Space Law,* The Commercial and Financial Chronicle, Jan. 5, 1961, p. 1; ———, *The International Academy of Astronautics,* 3 SPACEFLIGHT 119 (1961); ———, *International Cooperation in Rocketry and Astronautics,* 7 HANDBUCH DER ASTRONAUTIK, 197 (1961); ———, *International Astronautical Federation Aims and Constitution,* The Aeroplane and Astronautics, Aug. 28, 1959; ———, *International Cooperation in Astronautics,* Foreign Service Journal, April 1958, p. 1; ———, *International Scene—Subjects of a Long Journal,* Astronautics, Jan. 1958, p. 70; ———, *Law of Outer Space—A Problem for International Agreement,* 7 AM. U.L. REV. 70 (1958); ———, *Law Must Precede Man Into Space,* Missiles & Rockets, Nov. 1957, p. 67; ———, *The International Astronautical Federation,* 43 FED. B.J. 470 (1957); ———, *Seventh IAF Congress Stresses Cooperation,* 27 JET PROPULSION 60 (1957); ———, *International Cooperation in Rocketry and Astronautics During 1956,* 26 JET PROPULSION 1 (1956); ———, *International Cooperation in Rocketry and Astronautics,* 25 JET PROPULSION 627 (1955); *Current Congressional Legislation Affecting Aerospace Business:* Paper by ———, Before a Joint Meeting of The Institute of the Aerospace Sciences and The American Rocket Society in Los Angeles, June 14,

1961 (Revised Sept. 1, 1961); *Space Communications and Cooperation With Iron Curtain Countries:* Address by ____, Ft. Wayne Section of the American Rocket Society in Ft. Wayne, April 26, 1961; *Space Law and Astronautics— Preparing for the Next Thirty Years:* Paper by ____, Before the AGARD Combustion and Propulsion Panel Technical Meeting on "Advanced Propulsion Techniques" in Pasadena, Aug. 24, 1960; *The International Astronautical Federation and Space Communications:* Paper by ____, Before the Second Colloquium on the Law of Outer Space in London, Sept. 4, 1959; *Accomplishments of the International Astronautical Federation and Some Proposed Objectives:* Address by ____, Before the International Astronautical Federation Xth Annual Congress in London, Aug. 31, 1959; *Some Practical Suggestions for World Cooperation Through the International Astronautical Federation:* Address by ____, Conference of the Space Law & Sociology Commitee of the American Rocket Society in New York, March 20, 1959; *International Cooperation in the Field of Astronautics:* Paper by ____, Before the Second Annual Meeting of the American Astronautical Society in New York, Dec. 1, 1955.

12

Metalaw

The indefinite projection of a system of anthropocentric law beyond the planet Earth would be the most calamitous act man could perform in his dealings with the cosmos. To extend our existing systems of law, with their imperfections and ideological limitations, their inherent conflicts and inconsistencies, under the guise of an "international law" which is to apply to "outer space and celestial bodies," would be to spread our terrestrial conflicts and intolerances wide and far through a universe that potentially offers tremendous vistas of a new age for man—an age of peace, cooperation, and advancement in medicine, science, and philosophy. The propositions set forth in this chapter are original with the author but are neither newly-stated nor sounded in a vacuum. In 1955 the concept of metalaw was first introduced to a public audience, and since that time commentaries, expansions, and renunciations of the concept have been printed in many languages by scholars of international repute. This chapter presents some basic thoughts on a space legal order and some reasons for the consideration of metalaw. After simply stating the central precept of metalaw, it sets forth some preliminary rules that may be derived from that precept, and discusses various problems that require further study.

THE POSSIBILITY OF
OTHER WORLDS WITH INTELLIGENT LIFE

12–1 Some general considerations

SAPIENT LIFE ON EARTH AND THE DESTINY OF CELLULAR EVOLUTION OR DEGENERATION

The views expressed in preceding chapters on such topics as (1) the rules of space flight, (2) regulation of space communications, (3) space quarantine and inspection, (4) landing and takeoff regulations, and (5)

space immigration, among others, have had to do primarily with regulations of men to govern men. In its ultimate form, however, the regulatory scheme for outer space must take account of the possible existence of other sapient forms. The possibility that such forms exist and that sooner or later man may establish contact with them provides the central theme of this discussion. Indeed the problem of a "rule of law" governing relations between sapient beings different in kind may first be encountered by man himself on earth.

In metalaw we deal with all frames of existence—with sapient beings different in kind. We must do unto others as they would have done unto them. To treat others as we would desire to be treated might well mean their destruction. We must treat them as they desire to be treated. This is the simply expressed but vastly significant premise of metalaw.

During the long centuries of human civilization no law-giver has framed the Golden Rule in the language of the rule of metalaw. This is probably due to some inherent necessity in our civilization to relate all law to oneself. Anthropocentric law is a law for one frame of existence. The Golden Rule has no application other than to humans in the field of metalaw.

It is quite obvious that speculation on metalaw beyond the application of principles of pure justice which flow from man's nature is quite purposeless and, indeed, intellectually unnecessary, if two conclusions are posited: (1) the human evolutionary process has been concluded and there is no further prospect of changing the nature of man; and (2) in the universe there exist no other sapient creatures.

It may be said that no *direct* proof exists that man is evolving toward a new and higher plane of existence, or that sapient creatures exist elsewhere in the universe. Until now it is assumed that no positive identification of either process has been demonstrated.

Metalaw would become an urgent science indeed if man should evolve cellular life in the test tube, because such an achievement might well lead to the alteration of present evolutionary processes or to the beginning of new evolutionary processes of prime importance. In this area we already find that metalaw has a most vital place in any juridical system because man now has the power to change many aspects of the reproduction and functioning of *Homo sapiens.*[1]

Scientists and philosophers have envisioned man as uncompleted.[2] One

---

[1] The author was led to the formulation of the Rule of Metalaw, "We must do unto others as they would have done unto them," following a discussion in Brussels in September 1956, with Dr. Frank J. Malina, founder and wartime director of Jet Propulsion Laboratory at the California Institute of Technology, who had remembered a conversation with Dr. Merle A. Tuve, Director of the Department of Terrestrial Magnetism of the Carnegie Institution, during which they considered an alternate formulation of the anthropocentric Golden Rule. For basic writings on metalaw, see the end of this chapter.

[2] Haldane, SCIENCE AND LIFE, London, 1928.

may disregard these views, but sometimes stark truths are found even in *a priori* rationalization, and one must always bear in mind that the basic mission of science is prediction.[3] In man's ascent (if one should accept this hypothesis) from the primordial hydrogen atom through a series of associated atoms, thence into the molecular, thence into megamolecules, thence into cellular life, and through an amazing and myriad series of steps to the numenon, the monad, the "thing-in-itself," and on to become the psychosocial individual known as *Homo sapiens*, one finds only "on-wardness" and "upwardness" and there is no positive evidence to indicate that the evolutionary process has stopped or that *Homo sapiens* (or his successor) may emerge as a creature having such transcendental quali-ties as to require another and even a different classification on the ladder of life. Indeed, a new order of sapient creatures may evolve on earth having origin in entirely different atomic combinations and surpass man in all sentient and intellectual capabilities.

In examining the nature of creation at our plateau of knowledge, it may be assumed that every "change" in creation is simply a product of the hydrogen atom (eventually combining with some other element) and that the center of the universe resides in each of us as truly as it does in the Milky Way or in the Constellation Andromeda.

From the foregoing it may also be logically assumed that in the process which has been so briefly and "roughly" described, some sort of "cyclic" behavior is inherent, which may result in a degeneration back to the dissociated hydrogen atom and termination in a simple form of matter, and thus the ending of all cellular life, of all molecular construction, of all association of atoms—indeed, a return to the electron itself and thence into energy.

This viewpoint, while completely logical, is no more demonstrable than a viewpoint which would assert that the strange additive of the psycho-social which has appeared in the most recent hours of creation may well survive any cycle of an evolutionary process. If the ultimate destiny of the material world is the completion of a cycle ending in the elimination of cellular life, and if this means at the same time that the psychosocial life would also disappear, then indeed there is no necessity, in any event in the human frame of reference, to consider the problems of metalaw. This *ultima ratio* will not be considered further.

SAPIENT LIFE ON OTHER WORLDS

Capable and reliable scientists tell us that the possibility of the exist-ence of life in some form on other planets in the universe has a very high mathematical probability.

Elaborating on the mathematical probabilities of extraterrestrial life in

---

[3] A. I. Oparin, THE ORIGIN OF LIFE (New York: Dover Publications, 1953).

Of Stars and Men, Dr. Harlow Shapley, emeritus director of the Harvard College Observatory, has pointed out:

> . . . our sampling of space shows that at least a billion galaxies are within four billion light years. If they are on the average only one-tenth as rich in stars as our own galaxy, there must be $10^9 \times 10^{10} = 10^{19}$ stars now within our present sampling. A reach to only ten times our present probe would run the number of stars to something like 10^{22}. And that extension of reach is not asking too much of the future. Between 1915 and 1930 we increased the length of our celestial surveying rod by nearly a million times and therefore increased the explorable volume by the cube of that number.[4]

Using a conservative estimate of the proportion of stars likely to come equipped with planetary systems, but bearing in mind both "the climatic and physical extremes" known to be capable of supporting life and "the possibility of organic origins and evolutions based on other chemical operations," Shapley then concludes that:

> . . . we should contemplate at least 10^{14} planetary situations for life at our level of sentiency. In other words, we surmise that at least one star out of every million supports some kind of high-level protoplasmic operation on one or more of its planets. Many, but not necessarily all, of these 10^{14} planets probably have the plant-animal interdependence in which we ourselves participate.[5]

In a recent article discussing the possibility of extraterrestrial life, Dr. Shapley is quoted as saying further that the imagination "boggles at the possibilities of self-heating giant planets that do not depend, as we do, on the inefficient process of getting warmth through radiation from a hot source, the Sun, millions of miles away." At some size between that of Jupiter and the dwarf red stars, he states, the surface temperature must be right for a permanent crust to form and for water molecules to appear in a liquid state—not steaming hot, not frozen cold. Then, Dr. Shapley believes, "something momentous can and undoubtedly does occur. Slowly but inevitably, with lightning playing on the primitive atmospheric gases, natural chemical reactions produce amino and nucleic acids—the forerunners of proteins, of biological cells, and of organisms. . . ." And he calculates further: "Among the billions of planetary systems in the Milky Way galaxy . . . and the multitrillion planets in the billions of other galaxies, there must be innumerable instances where the planets are much bigger than Jupiter and therefore must have richer internal sources of heat." [6]

In this last discussion, Dr. Shapley is considering only the possibilities of life on a particular type of planet—or on tiny, dark stars, which amount to approximately the same thing. Such bodies have not actually been dis-

---

[4] Harlow Shapley, OF STARS AND MEN 80 (Boston: The Beacon Press, 1958).

[5] *Id.* at 84.

[6] Shapley, *Life on Tiny, Dark Stars,* Science News Letter, July 21, 1962.

covered, for our present observing equipment is not equal to the task, but Shapley feels there is good reason to believe that they do exist in large numbers. He summarizes his views as to possibilities in *all* realms by stating that biochemistry and microbiology, with the assistance of geophysics, astronomy, and other disciplines, have gone so far in bridging the gap between the inanimate and the living that we can no longer doubt that wherever the physics, chemistry, and climates are right on the surface of a celestial body, life will emerge and persist. He stated in connection, however, that he is not necessarily "suggesting . . . that *Homo* is repeated," for "there are millions of variations on the animal theme." [7]

There are other leading scientists who have exhaustively examined this question. To cite just one more example in a work sponsored by the Atomic Energy Commission [8] Professor Melvin Calvin concludes from his own studies and those of other eminent scholars that there are (conservatively) 100 million "habitable planets to be found in the universe"— that is, planets "which are the correct size," will have the proper atmosphere containing carbon, hydrogen, nitrogen, and oxygen, and could therefore support "cellular life as we know it on earth." He states further that we may expect to find, if not cellular life, then perhaps "precellular life" on many of these habitable planets; just as logically, we might also encounter what he chooses to call "posthuman life." [9] Calvin's calculations are limited to those planets which will offer conditions within the range compatible with cellular life based on carbon, as we know it on Earth. They do not make allowance for "systems, which conceivably we can imagine, based on other elements, such as silicon, or nitrogen, or perhaps even antimatter." But he quickly adds, "Such worlds and such systems may very well exist." [10]

Not everyone, of course, is so optimistic as Shapley about the number of planetary systems bearing life on our level of sentience. Only recently, S. von Hoerner, in an article in *Science*, arrived at a very pessimistic estimate of the number of extraterrestrial civilizations in the sky. Moreover, von Hoerner, along with J. R. Pierce and E. Purcell, are very doubtful as to the ultimate prospects for interstellar space flight. By way of countering these views, a colleague of Shapley's at Harvard University, Professor Carl Sagan, has presented the case for relativistic interstellar space flight. It is Sagan's contention that technically advanced extraterrestrial civilizations are not only abundant, but also within man's ultimate reach through the medium of relativistic interstellar spaceflight.[11]

A mere dozen years ago the question of whether or not technically

7 *Ibid.*
8 Melvin Calvin, *The Path of Carbon in Photosynthesis.*
9 *Ibid.*
10 *Ibid.*
11 Carl Sagan, Direct Contact Among Galactic Civilizations by Relativistic Interstellar Spaceflight, at 3-4.

advanced civilizations existed beyond Earth was not even slightly trac-
table to serious scientific investigation. But with the advent of stellar statistics the question has become the legitimate occupation of more than one
serious student. Thus, Professor Sagan, by using a statistical method devised by F. D. Drake, was able to come to the conclusion that "life is a
pervasive constituent of the universe." [12] The actual computation was a
rather complicated affair, taking into account the rate of star formation
in the universe, the frequency of favorably situated planets, the probability of the existence of technical civilizations, and the lifetimes of such
civilizations. As Sagan admits, our knowledge of such things is, to say the
least, rather tenuous; but he was able, nevertheless, to say with some
assurance that 0.001 percent of the stars in the sky have a planet upon
which is harbored an advanced civilization. This brings the total of extant advanced technical civilizations in our galaxy to about 106. The
nearest such civilization, Sagan estimates, is several hundred light years
away.[13]

How does one communicate at such a distance? Sagan proposes that the
most feasible means is by relativistic interstellar space flight. Electromagnetic communication, while a simpler undertaking than relativistic space
flight, presents some difficulties which could become quite serious over
great distances. For example, a simple query and response by radio emission between Earth and the nearest technical civilization would require
something like a thousand years. An extended conversation might require
something like 100 thousand years. Moreover, there is the question of
what signal frequency to choose. There is no necessarily obvious choice,
since we must assume that the thought processes and habit patterns of
other civilizations differ from ours. But even if radio contact were successfully made, it would still not permit the exchange of artifacts and
biological specimens. In other words, Sagan maintains, there is no substitute for direct contact.[14]

But how does one make direct contact? According to Sagan the nearest
extant advanced technical civilization is several hundred light years away.
Since nothing can travel faster than the speed of light, the time required
for just one leg of an interstellar journey in search of life would easily
exceed the lifetime allotted to man (or so it would appear). Does one,
then, pack into a spaceship a colony of men and women, so that it might
reproduce and give way to another colony, which in turn would give way
to another, and in this manner keep the ship staffed over its centuries-long
journey? The difficulties attendant to such an undertaking are all too
evident, not the least being the task of launching a ship capable of ac-
commodating so many people over so long a period of time. But Sagan

[12] *Ibid.*
[13] *Id.* at 4-10, 22.
[14] *Id.* at 10-11.

sees no need for such an undertaking. "If relativistic velocities can be achieved," he points out, "time dilation will permit very long journeys within a human lifetime." [15]

What Sagan is saying essentially is that time moves slower for someone who is traveling at a uniform rate at a speed close to the speed of light than for someone who is earth-bound. His argument is based on the concept of time dilation, which has been drawn from Einstein's theory of relativity. Actually, the concept of time dilation has not been entirely free of controversy; an English physicist, Herbert Dingle, has been particularly vocal in denouncing it. Given all this, Sagan still appears to be on solid ground, especially since the discovery of the Mössbauer effect. Named after a young German physicist, Rudolf L. Mössbauer, this discovery opened the way for making a nuclear clock which keeps incredibly accurate time. Such a clock, it was found, actually ticked slower when placed on a rapidly rotating disk than when it was stationary. (One more experimental proof of time dilation is the observed fact that muons produced by cosmic radiation have longer lifetimes than muons produced on Earth by accelerators.) It appears, then, that time does actually move differently for a stationary observer than for a moving observer. Of course, while time will dilate for the space traveler, it will not for an earth-bound observer; and the generator which sends the first man in the direction of the nearest advanced technical civilization will never live to see his return. He will be greeted, perhaps, by his great-grandchildren, who quite possibly will be older than himself.

Sagan disposes of one more remaining difficulty, this one involving the spaceship itself. The problem here is devising a spaceship that can attain a speed close to the speed of light. Even if mass (i.e., in this case, fuel) can undergo a complete conversion into energy, which is not possible under ordinary circumstances, extreme mass ratios would be required if all the fuel were to be launched with the ship. Sagan estimates that even with complete mass-energy conversion, for a ship to reach a velocity of $0.999c$, the liftoff weight would have to be approximately 2000 times the payload. In actuality it would have to be even greater than this, for complete conversion of the fuel into energy is not possible unless at least half the fuel were composed of antimatter. (Matter and antimatter annihilate themselves, giving off pure energy.) But as Sagan explains, "the containment of antimatter—to say nothing of its production in the quantities required—is clearly a very serious problem." There is one more difficulty attendant to launching an interstellar spacecraft which carries all its fuel: the gamma ray exhaust would be lethal for the inhabitants of the launch planet if the drive were turned on near the planet. Obviously, for the present at least, such an idea has to be abandoned.[16]

[15] *Id.* at 11.
[16] *Id.* at 12-13.

Sagan points to a suggestion by R. W. Bussard for a way out. Bussard suggested that an interstellar space flight could be accomplished by a ramjet that used interstellar materials for fuel. Such a ramjet would require rather moderate liftoff velocities. Once out in space it would capture and ionize whatever materials there were in the medium it was traveling in. The ions would then be deflected and captured by a magnetic field and funneled into the ship's reactor.[17]

It is not merely astronomers and physicists, such as Shapley and Sagan, that have speculated on the existence of extraterrestrial life; biologists and biochemists are also having their go at the game. Stanley L. Miller, a biochemist from the University of California, San Diego, is among them. Miller's speculations are based less on statistical probability than those of Shapley, for example. His studies represent an effort to bring the most recent ideas on how life originated on earth to bear upon speculations concerning the existence of extraterrestrial life. The verdict is, according to Miller, that life does exist outside the Earth.[18]

During the course of a lecture delivered before the Air Force's School of Aerospace Medicine, Miller examined four different hypotheses dealing with how life first originated on Earth: (1) by a supernatural event, (2) from outer space, (3) from inorganic matter, and (4) in the Earth's oceans under favorable conditions. Miller dismisses the first hypothesis since it is not subject to scientific verification. He dwells a little longer on the second. This hypothesis has taken two essentially different forms. One is that life traveled to the Earth from another planet as a spore on a small piece of cosmic dust. Miller believes it very doubtful that this could have ever happened. For one thing, he does not feel that an organic spore could have survived ultraviolet and cosmic ray bombardment over such enormous distances. The second form of the hypothesis is that life, like matter, always existed. There was, therefore, no origin, for life was always here, always a part of the universe. As Miller points out, however, recent studies show that matter did not always exist; then, life, which is made up of matter, could not have always existed either. The belief that life arose from inorganic matter is also held to be improbable by Miller. Living matter, he contends, is just too complex to have been formed by some happy combination of previously inorganic matter. It is the fourth hypothesis, that life arose in the oceans under favorable conditions, that Miller upholds.[19]

What were these favorable conditions? Twenty years ago it was proposed by the great Russian biologist, Oparin, that life probably had its beginnings when there were large enough quantities of organic com-

[17] Id. at 13-16.
[18] Stanley L. Miller, *Extraterrestrial Life*, in USAF Aerospace Medical Division, LECTURES IN AEROSPACE MEDICINE (Brooks Air Force Base, Texas, 1962), 277-98.
[19] Id. at 279-81.

pounds in the Earth's oceans which could combine and form more and more complex structures, until, finally, after a series of such combinations, these compounds took the form that we could describe as living.[20]

There is one crucial condition to Oparin's scheme. The Earth's atmosphere must have been different at the time life was created than it is now. It had to be a reducing atmosphere, containing methane, ammonia, water, and hydrogen, instead of an oxidizing atmosphere, as it is now, containing carbon dioxide, nitrogen, oxygen, and water. Actually, as Miller points out, there is an excellent possibility that this was so. When one looks around in other parts of the universe, there is approximately 1000 times as much hydrogen as oxygen. Moreover, there are heavy concentrations of ammonia and methane. It is reasonable to believe, however, that the Earth's atmosphere at one time possessed a preponderance of hydrogen. But because of a fortuitous combination of circumstances the Earth's atmosphere was able to undergo an evolutionary process which resulted ultimately in the formation of life.[21]

The two principal factors contributing to this evolutionary process were the presence of a sufficiently weak gravitational field, which permitted hydrogen (and helium) to escape, and a sufficiently strong energy source, which, when enough hydrogen was gone, initiated a process of photochemical dissociation among the other elements in the atmosphere. When one looks at planets such as Jupiter and Saturn, whose atmospheres contain considerable concentrations of hydrogen and helium, one can see why life never arose there. Both these planets, when compared to the Earth, are extremely massive and very cold. Thus, their atmospheres are probably about the same size as when the planets were created and they probably contain the same approximate proportion of ingredients.[22]

To recapitulate and elaborate further, the Earth at one time possessed an atmosphere composed largely of hydrogen. But because of its comparatively weak gravitational field and because of its exposure to strong energy sources (ultraviolet rays, lightning, and corona discharges from pointed objects), its atmosphere went through a process of reduction. It was during this reduction process that life was first formed. As more and more hydrogen and helium escaped, the methane and the ammonia in the atmosphere were photochemically dissociated. This resulted in oxidation and the formation of a large quantity of organic compounds. These compounds accumulated in the oceans, were polymerized to more complex structures (polypeptides and polynucleotides) and finally formed enzymes and self-duplicating polynucleotides, which in turn gave birth to life as we know it.[23]

[20] *Id.* at 281.
[21] *Id.* at 281-83.
[22] *Id.* at 283.
[23] *Id.* at 281-83.

All of these steps, of course, have not been tested in the laboratory, and are not likely to be. Miller, however, was able to test some of the earlier steps by exposing to electric discharges roughly the same elements in the Earth's original atmosphere. While proof is not yet conclusive, Miller still feels strongly that it was conditions such as these that gave rise to life on Earth, and that similar conditions are likely to prevail or to have prevailed on other planets.[24] But even if such conditions did prevail elsewhere, Miller admits that it does not necessarily follow that life would be created. However, the possibilities are strong that it will. "In fact," he points out, "given geological time scales and the variety of conditions that would be present on a planet, it seems likely that life *would* arise rather than it would not." [25]

Miller takes a short look at conditions on other planets in our solar system to determine whether they could support life. Mercury, the planet closest to the sun, has no atmosphere and is much too hot to contain life. Venus has an atmosphere, but it contains mostly carbon dioxide. Moreover, the temperature on the surface of Venus is estimated to be about 300°C. Mars is perhaps the best place to look for life in our solar system. At its equator its temperature gets as high as 25°C. There is some water on the planet. The planet changes colors seasonally. All these are favorable signs. Another sign—and perhaps the strongest unearthed so far—was discovered by William Sinton, who examined the planet's reflection spectrum in the infrared. He found that there was an absorption in the region of 3.43 microns. This corresponds to the carbon-hydrogen stretching frequency of most organic compounds. This means that there is a definite possibility that there are carbon-hydrogen bonds somewhere on Mars. If such bonds do exist, then organic compounds exist. And where there are organic compounds there is life. There is, however, one catch to all of this. There are a number of inorganic compounds that also have absorptions in the 3.43 microns regions. And Miller gives fair warning that Sinton may have been observing events due to inorganic compounds.[26]

The National Aeronautics and Space Administration is doing perhaps more than any other organization, federal or otherwise, in preparing for an eventual encounter, planned or otherwise, with extraterrestrial life. The agency already has a well organized research program directed toward the identification of life outside the Earth's confines. This program, for lack of a better name, can be termed, bioastronautics, and can be broken down into four principal areas: (1) environmental biology, (2) physiological and behavioral sciences, (3) bioengineering, and (4) exobiology. These four areas were discussed at a November 1962 conference on the science and technology of space exploration. Among the principal

[24] *Id.* at 285-90.
[25] *Id.* at 290.
[26] *Id.* at 290-91.

participants were Dr. George B. Smith, Jr., Chief of the Environmental Physiology Branch of NASA's Spacecraft Center; Dr. Siegfried J. Gerathe-wohl, Chief of the Biotechnology Division of NASA's Ames Research Center; Dr. Bo E. Gernandt, staff scientist in the Environmental Biology Division of the Ames Research Center; Mr. Richard S. Johnston of the Crew Systems Division of NASA's Manned Space Center; and Dr. Richard S. Young, a member of the Exobiology Division of the Ames Research Center.[27]

"Space is a hostile, uninhabitable environment for man," points out George B. Smith, Jr. "It is necessary for man to take his environment with him into space."[28] But such an environment must be one which will not only guarantee the astronaut's survival, it must also permit the astronaut to take active participation in many phases of the journey. This means that a variety of environmental factors which will be imposed upon an astronaut, have to be intensively investigated. What effects will such factors as noise, vibration, sustained acceleration, impact, and sustained weightlessness have on a human space traveler? It is known, for example, that the tolerance of a human being to vibrations of up to 20 cycles a second is rather low. But such advanced boosters as *Titan* and *Saturn* are expected to have vibration frequencies of 2,000 cycles a second. This, therefore, is definitely a problem with which NASA will have to reckon.[29]

The same goes for exposure to prolonged periods of weightlessness and sustained accelerations. In the case of weightlessness, however, there are some hopeful signs. Neither the Russian cosmonauts nor the American astronauts experienced, as far as is known, any serious ill effects due to weightlessness during or after their orbital flights. Nevertheless, it has been proposed that an artificial gravitational field be produced inside the spaceship by having the craft go through a constant spin or rotation. It is suspected, however, that the rotation of the craft might itself tend to produce some ill effects for the astronaut. As for acceleration stress, numerous studies have shown that people in good health can sustain the stress of both negative and positive acceleration. This has been true, however, only when the acceleration was in the main direction of motion. Moreover, it has to be proven that man will be able to perform tasks well during periods of extreme acceleration stress.[30]

Such stresses are only the beginning. Also to be reckoned with are the physiological patterns of the basic deprivation states. Thirst, hunger, fatigue, deprivation of sleep—all will have to be studied in order to formulate an objective description of man's response patterns of such stresses

[27] NASA, PROCEEDINGS OF THE NASA-UNIVERSITY CONFERENCE ON THE SCIENCE AND TECHNOLOGY OF SPACE EXPLORATION (NASA SP-11), Vol. I, pp. 391-429.

[28] George B. Smith, Jr., *Environmental Biology, Id.*, p. 395.

[29] *Id.* at 395-96.

[30] *Id.* at 96; Siegfried J. Gerathewohl and Bo E Gernandt, *Physiological and Behavioral Sciences, in* NASA-UNIVERSITY CONFERENCE, pp. 400-01.

and their relief. Then, too, there are the psychological factors. How will man react to periods of extremely long confinement in a small compartment? What will the personal relationships among the members of a crew be like during such confinement? How will such confinement affect the crew's performance? The questions are endless, and scarcely any of them were of very much importance in the Mercury program, where the main emphasis was on maintaining the astronaut's ability to perform his flight tasks under conditions of weightlessness and high acceleration.[31]

Neither has NASA up to now had to contend with the effects of radiation on a space traveler—all the Project Mercury flights not having gone out far enough to be exposed to ambient space radiation. But with Project Apollo and other more advanced systems, NASA will have to deal with the problem of shielding its astronauts from radiation from the sun, the stars, the Van Allen belts, and, perhaps, from nuclear reactor power systems.[32]

Now to turn to bioengineering. As defined by Richard S. Johnston, this area deals "with the application of engineering principles to provide life-support and crew systems to meet the physiological requirements of aerospace flight." [33] This field was ushered in during World War II when the military air arm had to contend with aircraft capable of flying 20,000 feet or more. The development of breathing-oxygen apparatus was one of its major contributions during that period. But today the bioengineer's problems are much more challenging and complex. Along with maintaining adequate breathing oxygen, the bioengineer must construct an atmosphere in the spacecraft that will keep the astronaut's body functioning as nearly normal as possible. This means maintaining a satisfactory atmospheric pressure and controlling the metabolic products of carbon dioxide, water, and heat. Moreover, he must provide for collecting, storing, and disposing of human body wastes.[34]

The environmental system developed for Mercury was essentially a closed system. Dictating such a system was the requirement to conserve oxygen and thereby reduce the weight and volume required by an open aircraft environmental system. Mercury's environmental system consisted of the now all-too-familiar space suit, which the astronaut had to wear at all times. The Apollo environmental system will be somewhat different. As Johnston describes it, "It is basically a closed system which provides a normal 'shirt-sleeve' cabin environment with provisions for pressure suit operation during critical flight periods...." The system for a space station will be even more different. From considerations of weight and space, oxygen to be used by the astronauts will no doubt be regenerated from

[31] Gerathewohl and Gernandt, op. cit., pp. 401-04, 408-09.
[32] Smith, op. cit., p. 397; Gerathewohl and Gernandt, op. cit., p. 405.
[33] Richard S. Johnston, Bioengineering, in NASA-UNIVERSITY CONFERENCE, p. 415.
[34] Id. at 415-16.

carbon dioxide. Drinking water will be extracted from sweat and urine.[35] A recent proposal by NASA for the design study of a so-called Psychophysiological Information Acquisition, Processing and Control System (PIAPACS), gives an indication of the problems and considerations involved in ultimately building a suitable environmental system: [36]

> The function of the proposed PIAPACS is to sense, correlate, predict, and display the critical psychophysiological parameters and to sense and control the environmental parameters (e.g., atmosphere, temperature, pressure) which determine the well-being of man during any mission. . . . Parameters to be considered are those defining the dynamic state of the man and those defining the environment external to but not independent of the man and of the machine.

The space agency's exobiology program can be broken down into roughly three different phases: (1) laboratory studies on how life began in primitive environments, (2) the detection and study of extraterrestrial life, (3) the simulation of primitive and extraterrestrial environments. The first group of studies are essentially on the same order as those conducted by Miller. Ultraviolet light, electrical discharge, heat, or other suitable energy sources are applied to various mixtures of gases, including such ingredients as ammonia, methane, carbon dioxide, and hydrogen. (Oxygen is purposely excluded from these mixtures.) The object is to determine what, if any, organic compounds will be formed. The results have been heartening. No matter what form of energy has been used and no matter what the different gas combinations may have been, organic molecules that are biologically important have always taken form. This has been particularly true of the amino acid building blocks of proteins.[37]

But success has not stopped merely with the formation of amino acids. Whenever amino acids have taken form in sufficient quantities, heat has been applied to them also, and invariably these compounds polymerize, forming protein-like molecules. There is also evidence, based on unpublished data, that even more significant molecules have taken shape— among them, components of the life-giving molecule, DNA.[38]

As for the detection and study of extraterrestrial life, much of it is centered around Mars, since it is the one planet in our solar system that holds any promise of supporting some form of life. The question of whether or not Mars does support life will probably be settled during the next few years. There are several approaches open to NASA for making such a determination. Life-detection instruments could be flown to within a few

[35] Id. at 417-22.
[36] NASA Flight Research Center Statement of Work, PR-3175, "Design Study of a Psychophysiological Information Acquisition, Processing and Control System (PIAPACS)," dated 4 March 1963.
[37] Richard S. Young, Exobiology, in NASA-UNIVERSITY CONFERENCE, pp. 423-24.
[38] Id. at 425.

thousand miles of the planet. Or else, such instruments could be landed on the planet itself. But most satisfactory of all, men could be landed on the surface of Mars. For the most part, however, the first two methods are the ones getting NASA's immediate attention.[39]

It is possible to devise life-detection devices such as those under development by NASA only because certain molecules are found in living systems and only in living systems. These instruments, therefore, will be devised to identify such molecules or their components. Hence, they are underpinned by one assumption: that life on Mars will have the same characteristics as life on Earth. This is to say that these instruments will be capable of detecting a form of life which has its basis in carbon chemistry. Should Mars contain a form of life which is, in its chemistry, alien to life on Earth, then such life will not be detected—short of landing a man on the surface of the planet. There are a variety of life-detection techniques that NASA can put to use, and is indeed working on a number of them: (1) turbidity and pH, (2) microchemical and microbiological, (3) metabolic C^{14}, (4) optical rotation, (5) "J" band formation, (6) optical-particle detection, (7) mass spectrometry. Almost any one of these techniques can be used with equally good—or bad—results, depending on the nature of life—if any—on the planet.[40]

NASA's third area of interest in exobiology consists of simulating extraterrestrial and primitive environmental conditions. The importance of these studies cannot be over-emphasized, for upon them will depend a great deal of the success or failure of a scientific life-detection space expedition. The main consideration is to keep the extraterrestrial environment and its inhabitants as intact as possible. Consider a space vehicle, for example, which has made a successful landing on another planet. Everything is in excellent working order, and signals are being transmitted to Earth with precision and regularity. The trouble is, however, that the signals do not reflect the true conditions on the planet, for the vehicle was contaminated with organic compounds from Earth. As Young himself stated the case, "... we must be certain the life we detect is not from Earth, carried along by the vehicle itself." But even more important is what Earth organisms might do to extraterrestrial organisms. Should an Earth organism be able to flourish on, say, Mars, then the biology of that planet will never be the same. "In other words," Young notes, "an irreversible process may have begun which will mask or perhaps destroy the existing ecology through biological interaction and competition." Thus, NASA is taking precautions to avoid such an eventuality, and has several studies underway to determine the best means of doing it.[41]

How important is this considerable expenditure of time, energy, and

[39] *Id.* at 424.
[40] *Id.* at 425-27.
[41] *Id.* at 427-28.

wealth upon extraterrestrial matters? According to a report of a study conducted under the auspices of the Space Board of the National Academy of Sciences, it is a very important business indeed. The exploration of space, in the words of this report, "will prove to be one of man's truly great adventures." [42]

Of all the opportunities that space exploration holds out for man, the opportunity to encounter extraterrestrial life, according to the report, is the most exciting: [43]

> The scientific question at stake in exobiology is . . . the most exciting, challenging, and profound issue, not only of this century but of the whole naturalistic movement that has characterized the history of western thought for three hundred years. What is at stake is the chance to gain a new perspective on man's place in nature, a new level of discussion on the meaning and nature of life.

If life were discovered on Mars, for example, it would have an immediate impact on our notion of the uniqueness of life. "Arising twice in a single planetary system," the report states, "it must surely occur abundantly elsewhere in the staggering number of comparable planetary systems." [44]

Actually, space biology or exobiology got a late start at NASA. Most of the agency's programs grew out of the International Geophysical Year program; but space biology did not play a significant role in the IGY effort. And, as a consequence, NASA's space biology effort has now been redoubled. The main effort has been to get man into space. This, the report says, is confusing ends with means: ". . . we believe there may be some danger in encouraging accelerated efforts to get man into space without NASA having clearly in view what he is to do there." The Space Science Board thus urges NASA to support studies on the origin of terrestrial life and then to energetically pursue "the search for extraterrestrial life . . . as an important step toward a unified view of cosmobiology." [45]

Encouraged that NASA is doing all it should in developing life detection devices, the Space Science Board also had several recommendations on how NASA should proceed to identify extraterrestrial life. The primary target will, of course, be Mars, and life identification could be accomplished in several different ways—all of which the report urges upon the space agency: (1) laser techniques, (2) carbon dioxide assimilation, (3) enzyme activity, (4) motion detectors. But the Space Science Board does not stop with Mars. It proposes that a serious attempt be made to identify extraterrestrial life elsewhere. As a first step it urges the systematic collection and examination of interplanetary materials for carbonaceous

---

[42] Space Science Board, NAS, *A Review of Space Research* (Washington: National Academy of Sciences, 1962), p. 9-1.

[43] *Id.* at 9-2, 9-3.

[44] *Id.* at 9-3.

[45] *Id.* at 9-4 through 9-6.

compounds. The Board made a host of other recommendations, with the principal emphasis being placed on the development of more sophisticated space systems.[46]

That this whole effort is still in its infancy and thus inadequate for the challenges ahead is readily admitted even by NASA. In the words of Orr E. Reynolds, Director of NASA's BioScience Program,[47]

> Almost everything which now can be said about the effects of extraterrestrial environments and about life on the moon or the planets lies in the realm of pure speculation. There is one prediction, however, that can be made with certainty by reason of historical precedent: the presentation of an opportunity to investigate a wholly new area, such as is offered by space exploration, is certain to produce a burst of scientific interests as soon as the path is charted by a few pioneers. It seems to me that over the next few decades a progressively larger proportion of biological interests will turn to space. We may well expect that the discoveries made here will revolutionize some of our concepts in biology.

A most useful tool was added to NASA's kit of knowledge and implementation by the activation early in 1963 of the Biotechnology and Human Research office in the Advanced Research and Technology activity of NASA. Dr. R. H. Bisplinghoff, Director of the Office of Advanced Research and Technology has under him a highly skillful and active group of scientists. Biotechnology and Human Research is headed by Dr. E. B. Konecci whose indefatigable efforts are already yielding commendable results.

Dr. Konecci is responsible for directing research and technology leading to development of future life-support systems, advanced systems to protect man in the space environment, determination of how man can be best utilized in space-flight missions, and the research required to assure man's performance capabilities in space.

It is believed that this brief review of the knowledge being acquired and the efforts being made concerning the survival of terrestrial life and the recognition of other forms of cosmic life in the area of the natural sciences, afford a reasonable and even urgent basis for parallel efforts within the scope of the social sciences and, consequently, for the thoughtful consideration of metalaw.

12–2 The precept simply stated

The concept of metalaw has been examined by philosophers, ethicists, and jurists in its essence and without the conscious knowledge of the definitive label "metalaw." In his memorable speech at the Georgia Insti-

[46] *Id.* at 9-6 through 9-11; 9-15 through 9-19.

[47] Orr E. Reynolds, "Space BioSciences," *AIBS Bulletin,* Vol. XII (October 1962), p. 51.

tute of Technology (adverted to in an earlier chapter), Earl Warren, Chief Justice of the United States,[48] points out that we know there must be a law of space if men are to fly to the moon and the planets. He states that "change is a law of life" and that "new powers entrusted to man, require . . . new decisions by the courts, new interpretations by theoretical philosophers and ethicists."

The Chief Justice states,

> It would be equally foolhardy and likewise impossible to declare a moratorium on emerging jurisprudence, as it struggles to meet the challenges of our time, which are so different from those of even our immediate ancestors, and even of our youth.

He explains that "what is conceived to be just when human beings are engaged in one sort of activity may become unjust when they are engaged in another." He adds,

> Moreover, legal problems arising in a new society may differ totally from those of a simpler society. When hunters became nomads; when nomads became shepherds; when shepherds settled down to agriculture; when farmers invented cities; when cities began to serve as bases for states and nations; new problems arose of which the earlier generations were unaware.

With regard to the substantive problem, the Chief Justice declares,

> How much better the world would be if we would develop a kind of Maser for the Rule of Law—if the elemental principles of law and justice could be broken down and reflected and re-reflected, striking sparks from all who want freedom under law, and if the mixture could produce a beam of coherent legal light of immense power capable of revealing the Rule of Law in its full glory to any and every part of the earth.

The Chief Justice asserts the clearest justification for pursuing the rule of law to govern the whole concept of space activity in these words,

> The simple fact is that law has not kept abreast of science. It is not that science is running away and endangering civilization. The real danger lies in the lack of a lawful world, and the absence of a world ordered under law which will negate the pressures to use scientific knowledge for destructive rather than for peaceful purposes.
>
> In all countries and from the beginning of literature, it is traditional to express our ideas about education, the pursuit of knowledge and progress towards ideals by analogy to the sun and to the mysteries of light.

Ambassador Manfred Lachs, Chairman of the United Nations Legal Subcommittee on the Peaceful Uses of Outer Space, touched upon the basic aspects of metalaw in his article, *Outer Space and Coexistence*.[49]

[48] Address by Earl Warren, Chief Justice of the United States, at Georgia Institute of Technology, Atlanta, Georgia, February 12, 1963.

[49] *Polish Perspectives*, March 1963, Vol. VI, No. 3.

Ambassador Lachs reviewed the development of the "first quinquennium of what can fairly be called the age of space." His work is a plea for coexistence in all dimensions. He states that law must follow in the wake of the *Sputniks* and astronauts as it once moved with man in his exploration of our globe, crossed new continents, oceans, and seas.

Ambassador Lachs emphasized the necessity for a rule of law governing all creation.

> A recent report by a group of prominent American scientists rightly points out that Oparin's theory has led to "questioning the uniqueness and centrality of man in the universe in an even profounder way than the Copernican and Darwinian insight forced upon us."

In an earlier context the fundamental principles of two basic theories of law were discussed, and it was shown that for many reasons, a system of law to organize and regulate man's activities in the universe should be based on immutable, undeniable, universally accepted principles. A survey of past maxims and interpretations of anthropocentric law pointed clearly to the elementary rule that man should do unto others as he would have them do unto him. This is the "basic tenet," the "golden rule," the primary principle of a system of laws created by man for man. We must ask ourselves now if this is a sufficient basis for the law which is to regulate the universe. We must examine its ramifications and possible limitations, along with the possibility of other worlds, other natures, and other legal systems, and the reasonableness of concerning ourselves with such questions at this time. Arriving at the conclusion that the "golden rule" is not sufficient to meet possible needs, we are left with the requirement to state an alternative approach to the problem of a legal structure. It is out of these considerations that the concept of metalaw has grown, and, in the context of the cosmos, this jurisprudential system provides a working basis for the universal development of a cosmic law of the space age.

The thinkers and the great works of history have variously defined the naked essence of anthropocentric law in one simple concept: Aristotle, "We should behave to friends as we would wish friends to behave to us"; the Babylonian Talmud, "What is hateful to thyself do not unto thy neighbor"; Epictetus, "Therefore if anyone would take these two words to heart and use them for his own guidance, he will be almost without sin. These two words are bear and forbear"; the New Testament, "Therefore all things whatsoever ye would that men should do to you, do ye even so to them: for this is the law and the prophets"; Seneca, "You must expect to be treated by others as you yourself have treated them"; Ahikar, "According as I do to you so also to me"; Abdullah Ansari, "Treat others as thou wouldst be treated, dispense not to others what thou likest not for thyself"; Bidpai, "Men are used as they use others"; Mohammed, "Do good unto others as God has done unto thee"; Sadi, "Accept for thyself what thou wouldst accept for others"; Confucius, "What I do not wish others to do unto me, that also I wish not to do unto them"; Mahabharata, "This is the sum of all true righteousness; deal with others as thou wouldst thyself be dealt by. Do nought to others which if done to thee, would cause thee pain"; Sutra-Kritanga, "A man should treat all living creatures as he himself would be treated"; Rabbi Hillel, "Whatsoever is hateful unto thee, do it not unto thy neighbor. This is the whole of the Torah, the rest is but commentary." Thus it will be seen that all of the precepts of the great law-givers, even that of the heterodox Hindu religion of Jainism, are, in each case, starkly anthropocentric.

Speaking specifically with respect to space law, Dr. Welf Heinrich Prince of Hanover, in obvious philosophical concern over the essential conflicts of law, states that our legal concepts must be as absolutely just as the concept of Kant's categorical imperative—a law that is unconditional and absolute, and whose validity does not depend on any ulterior motive or end. Kant states as one formulation: "Act only on such a maxim as you can will that it should become a universal law." Again Kant says, "So act as to treat humanity, whether in your own person or in another, always as an end, and never as only a means." [50]

Today, man has about as clear a vision of the space law that will prevail one or two centuries from now as Hammurabi in the twenty-second century B.C. might have had of our private and public international law of the present day. This is not said by way of minimizing the vision and prescience of that ancient, wise lawmaker. Quite to the contrary, a proper appreciation of the legal framework constructed by Hammurabi and other great lawmakers—a framework which basically has withstood the erosion of four score generations—should encourage us to face the formulation of a space legal structure.

In the bleak beginnings of human civilization, Hammurabi and Moses, and others, provided a needed and fundamental service in laying down a set of ground rules for *Homo sapiens*, a creature who has changed very little, if at all, during the eighty generations that have lived since his emergence. Expanding upon the wisdom of the past, even in the realm of space law, we are fairly competent to devise and promulgate rules and regulations to govern man as man, even if at this time we can only dimly envision the legal parameters, in the same way as Hammurabi might have dimly envisioned ours.

It has been insisted by certain writers of positivistic orientation that any discussion of a law of space must be posited on the premise that "only one law is applicable to all questions connected with space flight" and that "this law is based upon exact legal science." The attempt is thus made to enshrine the positivistic concepts of existing national and international

[50] Hanover, *Sovereignty in Space*, 4th Colloq. (Norman, Oklahoma: University of Oklahoma Research Institute, 1963).

law which have been the scourge of civilization. These concepts would clearly prevent the projecting into outer space of free and enlightened groups of human beings spiritually conditioned on the one hand to carve out new habitations from new land on new planets and, on the other hand, to proceed on their quest under rules of law requiring respect for the *whole integrity* of other sapient beings.

When we apply laws to man as man, wherever man may be, we can always preserve order by means of tried and true human sanctions—that is, we can always use force in shaping and controlling human conduct. The use of humanly organized force against other human beings, either as individuals or as integrated societies, no matter how small or how large such societies may be, has colored all our thinking. We have thus seen eminent publicists advocate the projection of modern international law, which cannot be readily separated from traditional concepts of enforcement, as the basis for space law. This approach was explicitly reflected in the December 1961 resolution of the United Nations.

The author believes, however, that no concepts of human law, civil or criminal, which in any manner whatsoever are framed for the purpose of being enforced—except, perhaps, on other human beings—should be projected for the government of intelligent beings who dwell elsewhere in the cosmos. The only exception to this principle lies in the possibility that we may find another world and another intelligent race identical with ours, (1) but even this would not necessarily justify such an exception. In shaping the basic concepts of a law for space, man must construct the law for the eventuality that other intelligent beings will not be identical with him in kind or nature. (2) If it should happen that they are identical, man will simply profit by this bonus of simplicity and share in their sorrow.

To pursue the thought further, man must be prepared to deal with intelligent beings who are by nature different in kind and who live in environments which are different in kind. Although these propositions open great areas of juridical speculation, it is sufficient at this time to establish the simple proposition that we must forego any thought of enforcing our legal concepts on other intelligent beings in the manner we have on the American Indians, i.e., on the theory that they could not withstand our force. Quite apart from all considerations of altruism, we must bear in mind the hapless possibility that the situation might be reversed, and we may turn out to be the savages who are decimated and enslaved.

It follows, therefore, that in the realm of space law the principle of enforcement is *malum in se*. In establishing spatial relationships of any kind, no force of any kind may be used. As the dealings would be with intelligent beings who are different in kind, the use of force by one such being or the other would be destructive to the one or the other.

If such life is discovered, and no prior thought has been afforded these questions, man may be faced then with the terrible alternative of either proceeding with no rule or guide, or simply extending existing rules, which we have seen to be a woefully inadequate provision.

In examining our own world we find that the fact that man has lived on a confined surface has resulted in the concentration of contacts and an intensification of his social and political development. His psychosocial relationships commenced to form at the moment of his emergence as *Homo sapiens,* and day by day during the course of civilization this confined surface has inexorably brought men closer and closer together until the very geography of man's confinement has caused him to create artifacts which enable him to meet, and merge, and enhance his psychosocial nature on every part of the globe.

By the same process, it may reasonably be assumed that psychosocial creatures will evolve on other planets, conditioned by the nature of their chemical elements, the forces of gravity, and the myriad variations which characterize their own confinement, and that they will in turn develop into highly specialized sapient beings. On each of the multitude of possibly inhabited spheres, as psychosocial creatures reach a certain degree of maturity, it must be expected that the emergent race will give expression, just as on earth, to the eternal yearnings to explore the mother universe. Thus it may also be assumed that the regimes of metalaw are always emerging—and that *Homo sapiens* is only now breaking through his chrysalis.

In any event, if even the possibility exists that there may be other intelligent forms of life, man cannot in arrogant disregard for such forms proceed into space without a guiding standard of conduct, or principle of behavior—a basic rule by which man and other forms of life can abide so as to insure peaceful and harmonious existence of both in the universe. It has been stated elsewhere in this book that new demands are being constantly made upon international organizations of all kinds for greater efforts toward the attainment of international peace and a world rule of law. The science of astronautics is in the process of providing expanding services to mankind, and the lawyers must insure that political organization and the development of legal structures keep pace. Yet we must realize that this new environment necessitates a new orientation. The framework of existing terrestrial law will not suffice in space: analogies, carryovers, carrybacks, and extensions will never fulfill the need.

To metalaw we can project only one principle of human law, namely, the stark concept of absolute equity. The natural law of man, as we know it, is anthropocentric in kind, and while such law must govern in space among human beings, it nevertheless is the law of human nature alone. With the concept of absolute equity, we shall be prepared to face the possibility of an indefinite number of natures and, therefore, of an indefinite number of frameworks of natural laws.

12–3 The jurisdiction of metalaw

The scope and application of metalaw has been under active consideration since 1955 but lawyers were understandably slow to consider in
detail jurisdictional questions. It is a remarkable fact that scientists and
philosophers so frequently take the initiative in urging the jurists to examine legal problems which are inexorably emerging from scientific achievements. Recently the Journal of the British Interplanetary Society published
a communication from Mr. Alan Wright,[51] who states that although considerable attention has now been given in astronautical circles to the
human aspects of space law, very few authorities even mention the legal
and social implications of encountering alien intelligence during our cosmic explorations. Two main reasons are probably responsible for this
neglect, Mr. Wright continues, firstly, extreme scepticism prevailed among
astronomers for many years on the subject of extraterrestrial life, particularly in its highest forms; and secondly, even assuming intelligent beings
would be encountered, to devise methods of establishing relations with
such beings beforehand, without some knowledge as to their form, outlook, and cultural level, would, to say the least, be extremely difficult.
But now, opinion is changing regarding the former question, and recent
space probe successes make it imperative that space lawyers prepare
themselves for possible surprises with the latter.

"After a rather hysterical period following the discovery of the Martian
'canals,'" Mr. Wright states, "astronomers in general reverted to the opposite extreme—the solar system was regarded an almost impossible fluke,
and other planets as uninviting deserts. Both these views have changed
drastically in recent years. Planetary systems are now seen as a natural
evolutionary step in the life of most normal stars and Mars, Venus, the
Moon, and even Jupiter have lately been cited as possible abodes of life
(if only bacteria in Jupiter's case) by well-known authorities such as
Academician G. Tikhov, Professor Salisbury, V. A. Firsoff, and many
others. Besides this, there is evidence that microscopic life forms are
reaching the Earth in meteorites, and NASA has plans for investigating
the possibility of living organisms existing in interplanetary space itself!"

"After all," Mr. Wright contends, "living creatures have amazing adapta-
bility here on Earth, they flourish in the most extreme conditions of
pressure and temperature, from the highest mountains to the greatest
depths of the sea. If it is accepted that simple life forms from Earth could
survive on other worlds then it seems logical to assume that similar,
indigenous forms would have developed to more advanced creatures
suitably adapted to their environment." Mr. Wright concludes by stating,

[51] Journal of The British Interplanetary Society, Volume 18, Numbers 11-12, December 1962, London.

"Whether inside or outside the solar system, I believe it is only a matter of time before alien intelligence is met with in space, at which time space lawyers should have already a few basic principles on which to try to build a mutually beneficial relationship. At all costs, we must avoid a repeat of what happened to the native civilization of Mexico and Peru in the sixteenth century."

The great American pioneer in the law of aeronautics and astronautics, Professor John Cobb Cooper, responded to Mr. Wright, in a letter to Mr. G. V. E. Thompson, Editor of the Journal of the BIS, by initially defending the jurists, stating, "The purpose of this letter is to suggest that members of the legal profession have not been entirely unaware of this problem. May I refer you to the well-known article by Mr. A. G. Haley entitled 'Space Law and Metalaw—A Synoptic View' published in the Harvard Law Record for November 1, 1956 and translated into German and published in 1957 in *Zeitschrift für Luftrecht*, page 59. Mr. Haley's article is mentioned by Professor Dr. Alex Meyer, director of the Institute of Air Law and Space Law at the University of Cologne, in his article on legal problems of outer space appearing in 28 *Journal of Air Law and Commerce*, page 339. May I also refer you to the paper entitled 'The Legal Status of Celestial Bodies' by Dr. Michel Smirnoff at page 385 of the same issue of the *Journal of Air Law and Commerce*. Dr. Smirnoff of Yugoslavia is a past president of the International Institute of Space Law." Dr. Smirnoff says in part:

> With the successes of space flights and especially with the landing of a Russian spaceship on the Moon it became clear that the landing of manned space vehicles on the Moon and other planets is only a question of time and financial resources. This fact showed clearly that the problem of the legal status of celestial bodies becomes one of the most important problems of Space Law. There are many reasons why this problem grew up to such an important issue. In a paper read before the Washington Colloquium on the Law of Outer Space we spoke of this aspect of Space Law as being one of the most important reasons to create a friendly atmosphere among the peoples on Earth. As a matter of fact this problem is closely connected with the possibility of finding some living beings on planets. This could lead to two kinds of situations. In one variant we could find on the planets living beings of every low grade of civilization or without civilization, and our role would be to unite and to play the role of guide to such beings. In the other variant we could find there living beings whose civilization could be on a very high level. This means that these beings could be much stronger than we are. In this case mankind must be united to defend itself from these living beings from other planets, or at least to be able to represent the united community of Earth.

"May I add on my own account," Professor Cooper continues, "that I have had occasion to give a great deal of thought to various phases of the problem of the rule of law in outer space. It is obvious that we must first have some understanding as to what we mean by the term *law*. If it is a rule depending on the consent of the governed, then how is such consent to be arrived at so far as intelligent beings are concerned who may be discovered on celestial bodies. If law is considered as a rule imposed by an authority which has the power to enforce sanction, then what authority shall we look to as the basis for an enforceable rule applicable at the same time to the inhabitants of celestial bodies and of the Earth? These are only two of the basic legal, political, and perhaps religious problems involved in possible future relationship between intelligent beings on other planets and the race of man inhabiting this tiny speck in the universe which we call Earth.

"Mr. Wright, in his letter referred to above, says that 'at all costs, we must avoid a repeat of what happened to the native civilizations of Mexico and Peru in the sixteenth century.' While agreeing in substance with Mr. Wright, I would at the same time point out that the greatest humanist living in that era, Francisco de Vitoria, did not approve the position taken by the powerful king of his native Spain as evidenced in the classical lecture on 'De Indis et de Ivre Belli Relectiones.' It was there that the courageous jurist stated to his students at the University of Salamanca about 1532 that, 'the Aborigines undoubtedly had true dominion in both public and private matters, just like Christians, and that neither their princes nor private persons could be despoiled of their property on the ground of their not being true owners.'

"Not withstanding the foregoing comments, I wish to say that I concur fully in the wish expressed by Mr. Wright that the BIS will not fail to consider 'the legal and social implications of encountering alien intelligence during our cosmic explorations.' While I do not personally expect to live to see the day, I am reasonably convinced that the time will come when the problem becomes immediate and practical." [52]

Even granting that it is impossible at this time to formulate detailed applications of metalaw, it may be desirable to make certain assumptions in advance as to the nature of the extraterrestrial beings with whom space exploration may bring us in contact. The minimum assumption is that they are composed of the same elementary substances that are now known to us. The next assumption is that they are large aggregates of atoms capable of sensation, locomotion, and thought. From consideration of biophysics and the theory of logical machines, it may be possible to arrive at a statement of the minimum size and weight of such extraterrestrial beings. From considerations of the dynamics of bodies and structural analysis, it may also be possible to arrive at a statement of their maximum size and weight. In this way, we may be able to bracket between lower and upper limits the probable size of extraterrestrial beings.

[52] Letter, dated February 14, 1963, from Professor John Cobb Cooper, Princeton, New Jersey, to Mr. G. V. E. Thompson, Editor, Journal of The British Interplanetary Society, London (vol. 19, no. 3, May-June 1963).

Flights into interplanetary and interstellar space will have an appreciable effect on possible extraterrestrial beings only if they intercept a certain minimum amount of energy, for there is a minimum condition which just barely allows the radiated energy to be noticed above the background noise. Thus, the particles radiated from a space vehicle have to be noticeable against a background of cosmic rays in order to represent an "interference" on our part. Similarly, thermal radiation must be noticeable against the thermal background of the prevailing temperature, and radio waves must be noticeable against the background radio noise.

Considering the probable limits of size and weight of extraterrestrial beings regarded as receivers of physical radiation, and the signal-noise problems outlined above, it should be possible to calculate for each mode of energy transfer the limits of free space, that is, the closest distance of approach outside of which no possible effect can be exerted upon the hypothetical being. In other words, it should be possible to estimate the size of the sphere surrounding each individual that may be called his zone of sensitivity.

The size of the zone will depend on various factors, including the size of the transmitter, i.e., the space ship, and what energy it radiates and in what form. In any event, for this question in metalaw, the rule should be that space outside an individual's zone of sensitivity is free space to which the traditional freedom of the seas may apply.

It should be possible, also, to list the manifestations of man and his artifacts on which we are not ignorant and, having listed them, to make some estimate of their possible effects on other creatures. For example, one might briefly consider the effects on other creatures of the following phenomena associated with man's flight in space:

(1) Communications systems
    (a) electromagnetic waves
    (b) light signalling (photons), lasers, masers
    (c) pressure waves, in an atmosphere

(2) Propulsion
    (a) infrared rays, from heat
    (b) radiation from a nuclear process
    (c) pressure waves, in an atmosphere

(3) Man's physical and mental properties
    (a) parapsychological or telepathic impacts
    (b) body offenses and germ dissemination
    (c) impact of human ideas and customs

Even at this time we may postulate another profoundly necessary rule of space exploration, namely, that in any instance where there is reason to believe life exists on a planet, no terrestrial space ship may land without having satisfactorily ascertained that the landing and contact will injure neither the explorer nor the explored, and until the ship has been invited to land by the explored. "But!" the impatient one may say, "this is like a requirement that man must make intelligible communication with an amoeba!" The answer is, nevertheless, that the regulation must be adhered to without exception, or we will project into space the bleak and devastating geocentric crimes of mankind. The regulation is so necessary that it would be better to deprive mankind of the opportunity to explore the cosmos, or indeed to leave the planet Earth.

In connection with this basic problem of unlawful interference in metalaw, Professor Martin Summerfield has developed a series of comments that are worth quoting at length:

> However one point is fundamental in the philosophical approach to metalaw, that is, there has to be the possibility of an interaction between the two societies that can be sensed by at least one of them. To start the discussion of this point, a hypothetical penetration is made by some extraterrestrial society, into the proper domain of human society on earth. Two important questions have to be decided. One is, what is the proper domain in space that belongs to human society on earth? A spherical domain just barely containing the earth's atmosphere, that is, about 100 miles out? A domain containing the earth's principal satellite, that is, about 250,000 miles out? The second question is, what constitutes an unlawful penetration, assuming that advance permission for the penetration has not been requested or given? If the mass of the projectile or vehicle is less than a detectable minimum, it would be illogical to protest the penetration. If the mass can be detected, but its penetration does no detectable harm, would there be a legal basis for protest? Suppose the mass is not the significant criterion, but the energy. A high speed atomic particle from outer space would not be detected by its mass but perhaps by its impact on a gene in plant or animal, and even in small numbers, such penetrations might constitute an unlawful interference. If the penetration is by radio waves or more generally, by electromagnetic frequency as well as energy flux, the ability to detect becomes even more difficult because of the wide variety of physical possibilities. Recapitulating, to define an unlawful penetration or interference in metalaw, it will be necessary to define the proper domain that belongs to each society, and in particular, to human society on earth, and it will be necessary to define for every conceivable physical means of penetration an interference level of such penetrations. It is obvious that each physical means of penetration will have a multitude of possible effects. To use Zwicky's idea for approaching a problem of this kind, a morphological box must be laid out to bring forth all possible penetrations and their effects, and agreement will have to be achieved on each of them. It seems premature to try to put numbers on any of these matters, the dimensions of the terrestrial domain in space, the masses or energy levels of unlawful penetrations, etc., but when the time comes, the metalawyer will be surrounded by scientists in every field.[53]

The willingness of Professor Summerfield, and other men of his scientific stature, to examine and discuss these problems indicates the serious-

[53] Dr. Martin Summerfield, Professor of Jet Propulsion, Princeton University, letter to A. G. Haley, Feb. 23, 1959.

ness with which they are approached by responsible and farsighted members of the different disciplines inexorably associated with the development of the age of space.

12–4 Concluding observations

In the not distant future, lawyers, scientists, and sociologists will undertake studies of a substantive statement of metalaw, and as a by-product of these studies our own anthropocentric law undoubtedly will be improved. However, the philosophical and jurisprudential "gilding of the lily" which will inevitably begin with any extensive discussions of the ideas set out here must be tempered by one overriding consideration: the eventual structure of metalaw must not be allowed to reorient itself on anthropocentric or geocentric bases. The function of discussing a legal system such as the author projects in metalaw is precisely to *discourage* the narrow and fruitless intellectual exercises that would proceed from the mere extension of our own systems of law. In *Le droit de l'espace*, Charles Chaumont points out lucidly:

> One might well, for convenience, state that space is at the service of mankind, but this does not lead to the conclusion that space belongs to mankind. The era in which the first reaction after discovery and exploration was appropriation, is passed; and the right of property has lost its former prestige. Moreover, the real disproportion between the scale of humanity and the scale of the universe and of the worlds which only God's vision can comprehend, would render presumptious and ridiculous the appropriation of the universe by mankind (even if this appropriation is limited to the solar system).[54]

Another question which grows out of our anthropocentric orientation is, What of the problem of evil? We know that there are many sunlike stars, some older and some younger than our sun. We may find inferior beings, and these we may keep from harming us by purely protective means. From superior beings we may expect wise tolerance of ourselves, because such tolerance would flow from their lack of fear. The problem of evil may, of course, arise in acute form if we encounter other races that are comparable to use both in their level of technical achievement and in their moral qualities (or lack thereof). But we have no right, in any case, to assume beforehand that other intelligent species are "fallen" like ourselves, in the theological sense of that term. And we must bend our efforts, first and foremost, to make sure that our human law is unconditioned and absolute in our control of the relationships of our own kind

[54] CHAUMONT, LE DROIT DE L'ESPACE 57-58 (translation) (Paris: Les Presses Universitaires de France, 1960).

with all others. We must not set out to conquer—if we do, we may find ourselves not the triumphant perpetrators of oppression, but the prisoners of the just.

Another human objection is contained in the familiar query, Why spend time on such theoretical and speculative endeavors, when so much remains to be done here on earth? This matter has been dealt with at some length at another point, as well as in the writings of numerous other authors. Arthur C. Clarke, for example, proceeds to answer the question by pointing out the many advantages of space exploration.[55] These are, briefly, that the physical resources of our planet are limited; that the increasing pressure of population may force us to other worlds; that only through space flight can mankind find a permanent outlet for its aggressive and pioneering instincts; and that the advent of space travel will produce an expansion of scientific knowledge unparalleled in history. Clarke observes further that even if there were not a single good scientific reason for going to other planets, man would still want to go there. Moreover, one of the most important, and profoundly human, reasons for exploring space is precisely the intrinsic desire of mankind to make contact with other intelligent beings.

And yet we must never lose sight of the urgent need for our legal structure to keep pace with our technical progress in the penetration of space, both during the present early stages when an anthropocentric formulation of space law can still suffice and in the more distant future when only a formulation in terms of metalaw will be acceptable.[56]

[55] Clarke, The Exploration of Space 193-94 (1951).
[56] See also, Cooper, Legal Problems of Upper Space. Address delivered before XIth Annual Meeting, American Rocket Society, New York, Nov. 27, 1956.

Additional References

1955

Nov. 14-18   *Basic Concepts of Space Law*, 25th Anniversary Meeting of ARS at Chicago. Introduction to and first chapter of book on space law, pp. 3-5, p. 59. Same paper (Nov. 1955) p. 3, brings out relation of existing international law with space law; discussed also in June 7, 1955 speech to Rotary Club at Charlotte, N.C.

June 7   *Jurisdiction Beyond the Earth*, p. 7 (Charlotte, N.C. Rotary Club); "... faced with the need for some sort of international commission to administer the planets far out in space and to protect the rights of beings who may be living there." Advocates U.N. action now, since no nation had yet made claim on space.

1956

Sept. 19   VIIth IAF Congress, *Space Law and Metalaw—A Synoptic View*, 25 page mimeographed version. Most of paper on metalaw; Har-

VARD LAW R. Nov. 8, 1956, *Zeitschrift für Luftrecht,* #31957 p. 13, PROCEEDINGS VIITH IAF CONG. p. 14, first defines metalaw in terms of "indefinite number of frameworks of natural laws," p. 4 mimeo, p. 3 of PROCEEDINGS. Also defines metalaw rule, p. 3. PROCEEDINGS.

Nov. 27   *The Present Day Developments in Space Law and the Beginning of Metalaw,* Canadian Oil Journal, pp. 14-15. First time goes into detail on radiation danger and states: "Hence, for this question in metalaw, the rule should be that space outside an individual's zone of sensitivity is free space to which the traditional freedom of the seas may apply." p. 15. Also p. 66 mimeo #378-56.

Dec. 3-8   *Space Law and Metalaw—Fundamental Juridical Considerations.* Paris, p. 5, defines metalaw, and discusses it in detail, quoting from Nov. 27, 1956 speech (paragraph next above) pp. 40-46.

1957

Feb. 7   HARV. LAW R. pp. 1 & 4, Metalaw.

Apr. 3-7   *Space Law and Metalaw—Jurisdiction Defined* does not mention metalaw except in the title. German article. Sept. 19, 1956 above.

Oct. 8-12   *Space Law—The Development of Jurisdictional Concepts,* discusses metalaw in detail, pp. 23-28:
             I am deeply disturbed that the concept of metalaw has not generally been understood, even by some great scientists, as witness the complete lack of understanding voiced by . . . Ambrosini in his comments at the Rome Congress.
             First introduces complications of multi-dimensional creatures, p. 28. Also *Zeitschrift für Luftrecht* #21957.

November   Missiles & Rockets, p. 70; repeats largely the Oct. 6-12, 1957 article (see above).

November   University tour, UNIV. OF ST. LOUIS LAW J., p. 9-10, condensation of metalaw principles.

1958

March   *The Law of Outer Space—Scientific and Anthropocentric Considerations,* Astronautik, Vol. 1, #2, 1958, mimeo, p. 809, outlines a metalaw and also that law applies irrespective of governments and natural law follows man into space, so that man must not harm other beings.

Feb. 28   Loccum Spiritual Foundations article covers same as March 1958 Astronautik article (next paragraph above) on metalaw.

May 8   Testimony before Select Committee on Astronautics and Space Exploration, House of Representatives, on HR 11, 881, p. 1441, discusses metalaw briefly.

1959

July 15   *Sociological Transition—Space Law and Metalaw;* expanded coverage of metalaw theories; also says world authority would provide safeguards against harm to others and to selves; discusses problem of evil, p. 15, and repeats phrase that it is better to destroy mankind than to violate metalaw.

1961

May 9   *Medical Jurisprudence in Outer Space,* published by the American Medical Association in ARCHIVES OF ENVIRONMENTAL MEDICINE, September 1961, covers metalaw as part of space medicine code, and quotes earlier works.

APPENDIX

II. **United States Laws**

    A. National Aeronautics and Space Act, As Amended

    B. Communications Satellite Act of 1962

III. **International Organizations**

    A. Constitution and Member List of the International Astronautical Federation

    B. Statutes and Structure of the International Academy of Astronautics

    C. Statutes of the International Institute of Space Law

    D. Charter of COSPAR

    E. CCIR Study Groups

IV. **Miscellaneous**

    A. Definitions of "Atmosphere" and "Air"

    B. Abbreviations and Acronyms

V. **Bibliography**

    A. Bibliographies of Space Legal Literature

    B. Selected and Partial Bibliography of the Works of the Author

I. INTERNATIONAL CONVENTIONS, AGREEMENTS, RESOLUTIONS, AND PROPOSALS

I-A. THE ANTARCTIC TREATY *

The Governments of Argentina, Belgium, Chile, the French Republic, Japan, New Zealand, Norway, the Union of South Africa, the Union of Soviet Socialist Republics, the United Kingdom of Great Britain and Northern Ireland, and the United States of America,

Recognizing that it is in the interest of all mankind that Antarctica shall continue forever to be used exclusively for peaceful purposes and shall not become the scene or object of international discord;

Acknowledging the substantial contributions to scientific knowledge resulting from international cooperation in scientific investigation in Antarctica;

Convinced that the establishment of a firm foundation for the continuation and development of such cooperation on the basis of freedom of scientific investigation in Antarctica as applied during the International Geophysical Year accords with the interests of science and the progress of all mankind;

Convinced also that a treaty ensuring the use of Antarctica for peaceful purposes only and the continuance of international harmony in Antarctica will further the purposes and principles embodied in the Charter of the United Nations;

Have agreed as follows:

* The reader's attention is especially called to another treaty which is pertinent to outer space: "The Radio Regulations, with Appendixes and an Additional Protocol," signed at Geneva, Dec. 21, 1959. This treaty concerns international allocation of radio channels, their regulation and use, a subject of significance to space law. This technical document is not included in this work because of its length. See U.S. Senate, Executive I, 86th Cong., 2d Sess. June 9, 1960. 571 pp.

ARTICLE I

1. Antarctica shall be used for peaceful purposes only. There shall be prohibited, *inter alia*, any measures of a military nature, such as the establishment of military bases and fortifications, the carrying out of military maneuvers, as well as the testing of any type of weapons.

2. The present Treaty shall not prevent the use of military personnel or equipment for scientific research or for any other peaceful purpose.

ARTICLE II

Freedom of scientific investigation in Antarctica and cooperation toward that end, as applied during the International Geophysical Year, shall continue, subject to the provisions of the present Treaty.

ARTICLE III

1. In order to promote international cooperation in scientific investigation in Antarctica, as provided for in Article II of the present Treaty, the Contracting Parties agree that, to the greatest extent feasible and practicable:

(a) information regarding plans for scientific programs in Antarctica shall be exchanged to permit maximum economy and efficiency of operations;

(b) scientific personnel shall be exchanged in Antarctica between expeditions and stations;

(c) scientific observations and results from Antarctica shall be exchanged and made freely available.

2. In implementing this Article, every encouragement shall be given to the establishment of cooperative working relations with those Specialized Agencies of the United Nations and other international organizations having a scientific or technical interest in Antarctica.

ARTICLE IV

1. Nothing contained in the present Treaty shall be interpreted as:

(a) a renunciation by any Contracting Party of previously asserted rights of or claims to territorial sovereignty in Antarctica;

(b) a renunciation or diminution by any Contracting Party of any basis of claim to territorial sovereignty in Antarctica which it may have whether as a result of its activities or those of its nationals in Antarctica, or otherwise;

(c) prejudicing the position of any Contracting Party as regards its recognition or non-recognition of any other State's right of or claim or basis of claim to territorial sovereignty in Antarctica.

2. No acts or activities taking place while the present Treaty is in force shall constitute a basis for asserting, supporting or denying a claim to territorial

sovereignty in Antarctica or create any rights of sovereignty in Antarctica. No new claim, or enlargement of an existing claim, to territorial sovereignty in Antarctica shall be asserted while the present Treaty is in force.

ARTICLE V

1. Any nuclear explosions in Antarctica and the disposal there of radioactive waste material shall be prohibited.

2. In the event of the conclusion of international agreements concerning the use of nuclear energy, including nuclear explosions and the disposal of radioactive waste material, to which all of the Contracting Parties whose representatives are entitled to participate in the meetings provided for under Article IX are parties, the rules established under such agreements shall apply in Antarctica.

ARTICLE VI

The provisions of the present Treaty shall apply to the area south of 60° South Latitude, including all ice shelves, but nothing in the present Treaty shall prejudice or in any way affect the rights, or the exercise of the rights, of any State under international law with regard to the high seas within that area.

ARTICLE VII

1. In order to promote the objectives and ensure the observance of the provisions of the present Treaty, each Contracting Party whose representatives are entitled to participate in the meetings referred to in Article IX of the Treaty shall have the right to designate observers to carry out any inspection provided for by the present Article. Observers shall be nationals of the Contracting Parties which designate them. The names of observers shall be communicated to every other Contracting Party having the right to designate observers, and like notice shall be given of the termination of their appointment.

2. Each observer designated in accordance with the provisions of paragraph 1 of this Article shall have complete freedom of access at any time to any or all areas of Antarctica.

3. All areas of Antarctica, including all stations, installations and equipment within those areas, and all ships and aircraft at points of discharging or embarking cargoes or personnel in Antarctica, shall be open at all times to inspection by any observers designated in accordance with paragraph 1 of this Article.

4. Aerial observation may be carried out at any time over any or all areas of Antarctica by any of the Contracting Parties having the right to designate observers.

5. Each Contracting Party shall, at the time when the present Treaty enters into force for it, inform the other Contracting Parties, and thereafter shall give them notice in advance, of—

(a) all expeditions to and within Antarctica, on the part of its ships or nationals, and all expeditions to Antarctica organized in or proceeding from its territory;

(b) all stations in Antarctica occupied by its nationals; and

(c) any military personnel or equipment intended to be introduced by it into Antartica subject to the conditions prescribed in paragraph 2 of Article I of the present Treaty.

ARTICLE VIII

1. In order to facilitate the exercise of their functions under the present Treaty, and without prejudice to the respective positions of the Contracting Parties relating to jurisdiction over all other persons in Antarctica, observers designated under paragraph 1(b) of Article III of the Treaty, and members of the staffs accompanying any such persons, shall be subject only to the jurisdiction of the Contracting Party of which they are nationals in respect of all acts or omissions occurring while they are in Antarctica for the purpose of exercising their functions.

2. Without prejudice to the provisions of paragraph 1 of this Article, and pending the adoption of measures in pursuance of subparagraph 1(e) of Article IX, the Contracting Parties concerned in any case of dispute with regard to the exercise of jurisdiction in Antarctica shall immediately consult together with a view to reaching a mutually acceptable solution.

ARTICLE IX

1. Representatives of the Contracting Parties named in the preamble to the present Treaty shall meet at the City of Canberra within two months after the date of entry into force of the Treaty, and thereafter at suitable intervals and places, for the purpose of exchanging information, consulting together on matters of common interest pertaining to Antarctica, and formulating and considering, and recommending to their Governments, measures in furtherance of the principles and objectives of the Treaty, including measures regarding:

(a) use of Antarctica for peaceful purposes only;

(b) facilitation of scientific research in Antarctica;

(c) facilitation of international scientific cooperation in Antarctica;

(d) facilitation of the exercise of the rights of inspection provided for in Article VII of the Treaty;

(e) questions relating to the exercise of jurisdiction in Antarctica;

(f) preservation and conservation of living resources in Antarctica.

2. Each Contracting Party which has become a party to the present Treaty by accession under Article XIII shall be entitled to appoint representatives to participate in the meetings referred to in paragraph 1 of the present Article, during such time as that Contracting Party demonstrates its interest in Antarctica by conducting substantial scientific research activity there, such as the establishment of a scientific station or the despatch of a scientific expedition.

3. Reports from the observers referred to in Article VII of the present Treaty shall be transmitted to the representatives of the Contracting Parties participating in the meetings referred to in paragraph 1 of the present Article.

4. The measures referred to in paragraph 1 of this Article shall become effective when approved by all the Contracting Parties whose representatives were entitled to participate in the meetings held to consider those measures.

5. Any or all of the rights established in the present Treaty may be exercised as from the date of entry into force of the Treaty whether or not any measures facilitating the exercise of such rights have been proposed, considered or approved as provided in this Article.

ARTICLE X

Each of the Contracting Parties undertakes to exert appropriate efforts, consistent with the Charter of the United Nations, to the end that no one engages in any activity in Antarctica contrary to the principles or purposes of the present Treaty.

ARTICLE XI

1. If any dispute arises between two or more of the Contracting Parties concerning the interpretation or application of the present Treaty, those Contracting Parties shall consult among themselves with a view to having the dispute resolved by negotiation, inquiry, mediation, conciliation, arbitration, judicial settlement or other peaceful means of their own choice.

2. Any dispute of this character not so resolved shall, with the consent, in each case, of all parties to the dispute, be referred to the International Court of Justice for settlement; but failure to reach agreement on reference to the International Court shall not absolve parties to the dispute from the responsibility of continuing to seek to resolve it by any of the various peaceful means referred to in paragraph 1 of this Article.

ARTICLE XII

1. (a) The present Treaty may be modified or amended at any time by unanimous agreement of the Contracting Parties whose representatives are entitled to participate in the meetings provided for under Article IX. Any such modification or amendment shall enter into force when the depository Government has received notice from all such Contracting Parties that they have ratified it.

(b) Such modification or amendment shall thereafter enter into force as to any other Contracting Party when notice of ratification is received within a period of two years from the date of entry into force of the modification or amendment in accordance with the provisions if subparagraph 1(a) of this Article shall be deemed to have withdrawn from the present Treaty on the date of the expiration of such period.

2. (a) If after the expiration of thirty years from the date of entry into force of the present Treaty, any of the Contracting Parties whose representatives are entitled to participate in the meetings provided for under Article IX so requests by a communication addressed to the depositary Government, a

Conference of all the Contracting Parties shall be held as soon as practicable to review the operation of the Treaty.

(b) Any modification or amendment to the present Treaty which is approved at such a conference by a majority of the Contracting Parties there represented, including a majority of those whose representatives are entitled to participate in the meetings provided for under Article IX, shall be communicated by the depositary Government to all the Contracting Parties immediately after the termination of the Conference and shall enter into force in accordance with the provisions of paragraph 1 of the present Article.

(c) If any such modification or amendment has not entered into force in accordance with the provisions of subparagraph 1(a) of this Article within a period of two years after the date of its communication to all the Contracting Parties, any Contracting Party may at any time after the expiration of that period give notice to the depositary Government of its withdrawal from the present Treaty; and such withdrawal shall take effect two years after the receipt of the notice by the depositary Government.

ARTICLE XIII

1. The present Treaty shall be subject to ratification by the signatory States. It shall be open for accession by any State which is a Member of the United Nations, or by any other State which may be invited to accede to the Treaty with the consent of all the Contracting Parties whose representatives are entitled to participate in the meetings provided for under Article IX of the Treaty.

2. Ratification of or accession to the present Treaty shall be effected by each State in accordance with its constitutional processes.

3. Instruments of ratification and instruments of accession shall be deposited with the Government of the United States of America, hereby designated as the depositary Government.

4. The depositary Government shall inform all signatory and acceding States of the date of each deposit of an instrument of ratification or accession, and the date of entry into force of the Treaty and of any modification or amendment thereto.

5. Upon the deposit of instruments of ratification by all the signatory States, the present Treaty shall enter into force for those States and for States which have deposited instruments of accession. Thereafter the Treaty shall enter into force for any acceding State upon the deposit of its instrument of accession.

6. The present Treaty shall be registered by the depositary Government pursuant to Article 102 of the Charter of the United Nations.

ARTICLE XIV

The present Treaty, done in the English, French, Russian and Spanish language, each version being equally authentic, shall be deposited in the archives of the Government of the United States of America, which shall transmit duly certified copies thereof to the Governments of the signatory and acceding States.

List of Nations which have ratified the Antarctic Treaty:

Nations	*Dates of Ratification*
United States	August 18, 1960
Belgium	July 26, 1960
France	September 16, 1960
Japan	August 4, 1960
New Zealand	November 1, 1960
Norway	August 24, 1960
Union of South Africa	June 21, 1960
U.S.S.R.	November 2, 1960
United Kingdom	May 31, 1960

I-B. ITU RADIO FREQUENCY ALLOCATIONS (Geneva, December 1959)

Frequency for space use	ITU regulation page	Status	Parent band	Primary use	Secondary use [9]	Region
10 003-10 005 kc/s	50	Footnote 215; and Rec. 31	9995-10 005 kc/s	Standard Frequency	Service for space research	Worldwide [1]
19 990-20 010 kc/s	53	Footnote 221; and Rec. 31	19 990-20 010 kc/s	Standard Frequency	Space and Earth-space services for research purposes	Worldwide [1]
39 986-40 002 Mc/s	56	Footnote 235	29.7-41 Mc/s	Fixed, mobile	Space,[2] Earth-space [2]	Worldwide [6]
136-137 Mc/s	65	Allocation Table	136-137 Mc/s	Space,[2] fixed, and mobile, Earth-space [2][3]		Worldwide
183.1-184.1 Mc/s	70	Footnote 294	174-216 Mc/s	Fixed, mobile broadcasting	Space,[2] Earth-space [2]	Worldwide [8]
400-401 Mc/s	72	Allocation Table	400-401 Mc/s	Meteorological aids, space, Earth-space [2]	RAS [4]	Worldwide [5]
1427-1429 Mc/s	80	Allocation Table	1427-1429 Mc/s	Space,[2] fixed and mobile except aeronautical mobile, Earth-space [2]		Worldwide
1700-1710 Mc/s	82	Allocation Table	1700-1710 Mc/s	Fixed, region 1	Space,[2] mobile, Earth-space [2]	Region 1 [6]
			1700-1710 Mc/s	Fixed, and mobile in regions 2 and 3	Space,[2] Earth-space [2]	Region 2, 3

2290-2300 Mc/s	82	Allocation Table	2290-2300 Mc/s	Fixed, region 1	Space,[2] mobile, Earth-space [2]	Region 1 [6]
				Fixed, and mobile, regions 2 and 3	Space,[2] Earth-space [2]	Regions 2, 3
5250-5255 Mc/s	89	Allocation Table	5250-5255 Mc/s	Radiolocation	Space,[2] Earth-space [2]	Worldwide
8400-8500 Mc/s	91	Allocation Table	8400-8500 Mc/s	Fixed, and mobile	Space,[2] Earth-space [2]	Worldwide [7]
15.15-15.25 Gc/s	95	Allocation Table	15.15-15.25 Gc/s	Space,[2] Earth-space [2]	Fixed, and mobile	Worldwide [7]
31.5-31.8 Gc/s	97	Allocation Table	31.5-31.8 Gc/s	Space,[2] Earth-space [2]	Fixed, and mobile	Worldwide

1. It is recommended that administrations take all practicable measures to safeguard the standard frequency bands from harmful interference.

2. For research purposes.

3. Aeronautical mobile (OR) service will be the primary service for as long as it continues to operate in this band. On discontinuation of this service, the space and earth-space services will be the primary services.

4. In the United Kingdom, the band 400-410 Mc/s is allocated to radiolocation service on a secondary basis.

5. In Greece, Yugoslavia, Albania, Bulgaria, Hungary, Poland, Rumania, Czechoslovakia, USSR, and Sweden, the band 400-401 Mc/s is also allocated to fixed and mobile services.

6. Bands are allocated on a secondary basis to the space and the earth-space services, subject to causing no harmful interference with the other services to which these bands are allocated.

7. In Australia and the United Kingdom, the band 8250-8500 Mc/s is allocated to the radiolocation service; the band 8400-8500 Mc/s is also allocated on a secondary basis, to the space and earth-space services for research purposes.

8. Allocation to space and earth-space services, for research purposes subject to causing no harmful interference.

9. Stations of a secondary service shall not cause harmful interference to stations of primary services and cannot claim protection from harmful interference of a primary service. They can claim protection from the same service (Radio Regulations No. 139, Geneva, 1959).

I-C. IAF PROPOSED ALLOCATIONS (1959)

Frequency Band Mc/s	IAF Proposal Allocation to Services (World-wide)
21.01	Astronautical Mobile (Ionospheric propagation)
37.00	Astronautical Mobile (Ionospheric propagation)
107.0-108.0	Astronautical Mobile Astronautical Radiolocation (Tracking)
148.0-150.8	Astronautical Radionavigation (Command)
320-328.6	Astronautical Mobile (Telemetry and Television)
450-455	Astronautical Mobile Astronautical Radiolocation (Tracking)
890-942 *	Astronautical Mobile
4, 380-4, 400	Astronautical Mobile
10,000 to 10,100	Astronautical Mobile Astronautical Radiolocation
17,500-20,000	Astronautical Mobile Astronautical Radiolocation
36,000-38,000	Astronautical Mobile Astronautical Radiolocation

I-D. KENNEDY-KHRUSHCHEV LETTER EXCHANGE, March 1962
(Extracts)

Kennedy Letter to Khrushchev, March 7, 1962

On February 22 last I wrote you that I was instructing appropriate officers of this Government to prepare concrete proposals for immediate projects of common action in the exploration of space. I now present such proposals to you.

The exploration of space is a broad and varied activity and the possibilities for cooperation are many. In suggesting the possible first steps which are set out below, I do not intend to limit our mutual consideration of desirable cooperative activities. On the contrary, I will welcome your concrete suggestions along these or other lines.

1. Perhaps we could render no greater service to mankind through our space programs than by the joint establishment of an early operational weather satel-

* The frequency 915 Mc/s is designated for industrial, scientific and medical purposes. Emissions must be confined within the limits of + 25 Mc/s of that frequency. Radiocommunication services operating within those limits must accept any harmful interference that may be experienced from the operation of industrial, scientific, and medical equipment.

lite system. Such a system would be designed to provide global weather data for prompt use by any nation. To initiate this service, I propose that the United States and the Soviet Union each launch a satellite to photograph cloud covers and provide other agreed meteorological services for all nations. The two satellites would be placed in near-polar orbits in planes approximately perpendicular to each other, thus providing regular coverage of all areas. This immensely valuable data would then be disseminated through normal international meteorological channels and would make a significant contribution to the research and service programs now under study by the World Meteorological Organization in response to Resolution 1721 (XVI) adopted by the United Nations General Assembly on December 20, 1961.

❈   ❈   ❈   ❈   ❈

I believe it is both appropriate and desirable that we take full cognizance of the scientific and other contributions which other states the world over might be able to make in such programs. As agreements are reached between us on any parts of these or similar programs, I propose that we report them to the United Nations Committee on the Peaceful Uses of Outer Space. The committee offers a variety of additional opportunities for joint cooperative efforts within the framework of its mandate as set forth in General Assembly Resolutions 1472 (XIV) and 1721 (XVI).

I am designating technical representatives who will be prepared to meet and discuss with your representatives our ideas and yours in a spirit of practical cooperation. In order to accomplish this at an early date, I suggest that the representatives of our two countries who will be coming to New York to take part in the United Nations Outer Space Committee meet privately to discuss the proposals set forth in this letter.

Khrushchev Letter to Kennedy, March 20, 1962

Acquainting myself attentively with your message of March 7 of this year, I note with satisfaction that my appeal to you of February 21 with a proposal that both countries should pool their efforts to explore outer space, has been met with the necessary understanding of the U.S. Government.

Advancing this proposal, we proceeded from the premise that all the peoples, all mankind, are interested in solving the problem of exploration and peaceful uses of outer space, and that the huge dimensions of this problem, as well as the difficulties which are to be overcome, imperatively demand an extensive pooling of scientific, technical and material opportunities and resources by states.

❈   ❈   ❈   ❈   ❈

It seems to me, Mr. President, that in general it is now being recognized increasingly that practical steps are needed in the noble cause of developing international cooperation in space research for peaceful purposes. Your message shows that your trend of mind actually does not differ from our idea of practical measures in the field of this cooperation. What should we start from?

I should like to point out in this connection several problems of exploration and peaceful uses of outer space, for whose solution, in our view, the pooling of efforts by states is required. Some of them, envisaged in the recent decisions of the United Nations General Assembly, adopted on the initiative of our two countries, are mentioned in your message.

* * * * *

2. It is difficult to overestimate the benefit which could be brought to mankind by organizing a world weather observation service with the aid of artificial earth satellites. Precise and timely weather forecasts will be another important step along the way to man's conquering of nature, will help him still more successfully cope with natural calamities and open up new prospects for improving the well-being of mankind. Let us cooperate in this field, too.

* * * * *

Mr. President, I have stated only several of the questions, the solution of which, in our point of view, has become ripe already now and demands cooperation between our countries. In the future international cooperation in space exploration, if we can now lay a firm basis for it, will doubtlessly spread to ever new and new fields of space research. We hope that the scientists of the Union of Soviet Socialist Republics and the United States of America will be able, hand in hand with the scientists of other countries, to take up the elaboration and implementation of many projects for space exploration.

The Soviet representatives in the United Nations Space Committee will be instructed to meet with U.S. representatives to discuss the concrete questions of cooperation in the exploration and peaceful use of outer space, that are of interest to our two countries.

* * * * *

I-E.   A/AC.105/C.1/L.2/Rev.2
                                                                                         Annex III

Annex III

Joint communique on the USSR-United States talks, issued on 3 June 1962

Following the exchange of views between N. S. Khrushchev, Chairman of the Council of Ministers of the Union of Soviet Socialist Republics and John F. Kennedy, President of the United States of America regarding cooperation in the exploration and use of space for peaceful purposes, representatives of the USSR and USA, headed by Academician Blagonravov and Dr. Hugh Dryden, have discussed in some detail the possibilities of cooperation in meteorology, a world magnetic survey, and satellite telecommunications, and forwarded recommendations to their governments.

Plans were discussed for the gradual increase in the exchange of data from weather satellites during the next few years, looking toward eventual coordinated launchings of meteorological satellites with rapid dissemination of data to other states in accord with the general recommendations of the World Meteorological Organization (WMO).

Arrangements were discussed for a joint effort to map the magnetic field of the earth in conjunction with the International Year of the Quiet Sun which has been planned by the International Union of Geodesy and Geophysics (IUGG). Such cooperation would probably involve the coordinated launching of a satellite by each country in conjunction with ground observations by many other countries.

International cooperation in the field of communications by means of satellites was considered and will be discussed further at later meetings, taking into consideration the need to realize the goal of all countries to improve international and their own internal communications. Future discussions may include other subjects for cooperation mentioned in the correspondence between Chairman Khrushchev and President Kennedy.

I-F. SIGNIFICANT RECENT UNITED NATIONS DOCUMENTS

I-F(1). Resolutions Adopted by the General Assembly

[on the report of the First Committee (A/5026)]

1721 (XVI). *International cooperation in the peaceful uses of outer space*

A/RES/1721 (XVI)

A

The General Assembly,

Recognizing the common interest of mankind in furthering the peaceful uses of outer space and the urgent need to strengthen international cooperation in this important field,

Believing that the exploration and use of outer space should be only for the betterment of mankind and to the benefit of States irrespective of the stage of their economic or scientific development,

1. *Commends* to States for their guidance in the exploration and use of outer space the following principles:

(*a*) International law, including the Charter of the United Nations, applies to outer space and celestial bodies;

(*b*) Outer space and celestial bodies are free for exploration and use by all States in conformity with international law and are not subject to national appropriation;

2. *Invites* the Committee on the Peaceful Uses of Outer Space to study and report on the legal problems which may arise from the exploration and use of outer space.

B

The General Assembly,

Believing that the United Nations should provide a focal point for international cooperation in the peaceful exploration and use of outer space,

1. *Calls upon* States launching objects into orbit or beyond to furnish information promptly to the Committee on the Peaceful Uses of Outer Space, through the Secretary-General, for the registration of launchings:

2. *Requests* the Secretary-General to maintain a public registry of the information furnished in accordance with paragraph 1 above;

3. *Requests* the Committee on the Peaceful Uses of Outer Space, in cooperation with the Secretary-General and making full use of the functions and resources of the Secretariat:

(*a*) To maintain close contact with governmental and nongovernmental organizations concerned with outer space matters;

(*b*) To provide for the exchange of such information relating to outer space activities as Governments may supply on a voluntary basis, supplementing but not duplicating existing technical and scientific exchanges;

(*c*) To assist in the study of measures for the promotion of international cooperation in outer space activities;

4. *Further requests* the Committee on the Peaceful Uses of Outer Space to report to the General Assembly on the arrangements undertaken for the performance of those functions and on such developments relating to the peaceful uses of outer space as it considers significant.

C

The General Assembly,

Noting with gratification the marked progress for meteorological science and technology opened up by the advances in outer space,

Convinced of the world-wide benefits to be derived from international cooperation in weather research and analysis,

1. *Recommends* to all Member States and to the World Meteorological Organization and other appropriate specialized agencies the early and comprehensive study, in the light of developments in outer space, of measures:

(*a*) To advance the state of atmospheric science and technology so as to provide greater knowledge of basic physical forces affecting climate and the possibility of large-scale weather modifications;

(*b*) To develop existing weather forecasting capabilities and to help Member States make effective use of such capabilities through regional meteorological centres;

2. *Requests* the World Meteorological Organization, consulting as appropriate with the United Nations Educational, Scientific and Cultural Organization and other specialized agencies and governmental and nongovernmental organizations, such as the International Council of Scientific Unions, to submit

a report to its member Governments and to the Economic and Social Council at its thirty-fourth session regarding appropriate organizational and financial arrangements to achieve those ends, with a view to their further consideration by the General Assembly at its seventeenth session;

3. *Requests* the Committee on the Peaceful Uses of Outer Space, as it deems appropriate, to review that report and submit its comments and recommendations to the Economic and Social Council and to the General Assembly.

D

The General Assembly,

Believing that communication by means of satellites should be available to the nations of the world as soon as practicable on a global and non-discriminatory basis,

Convinced of the need to prepare the way for the establishment of effective operational satellite communication,

1. *Notes with satisfaction* that the International Telecommunication Union plans to call a special conference in 1963 to make allocations of radio frequency bands for outer space activities;

2. *Recommends* that the International Telecommunication Union consider at that conference those aspects of space communication in which international cooperation will be required;

3. *Notes* the potential importance of communication satellites for use by the United Nations and its principal organs and specialized agencies for both operational and informational requirements;

4. *Invites* the Special Fund and the Expanded Programme of Technical Assistance, in consultation with the International Telecommunication Union, to give sympathetic consideration to requests from Member States for technical and other assistance for the survey of their communication needs and for the development of their domestic communication facilities so that they may make effective use of space communication;

5. *Requests* the International Telecommunication Union, consulting as appropriate with Member States, the United Nations Educational, Scientific and Cultural Organization and other specialized agencies and governmental and nongovernmental organizations, such as the Committee on Space Research of the International Council of Scientific Unions, to submit a report on the implementation of those proposals to the Economic and Social Council at its thirty-fourth session and to the General Assembly at its seventeenth session;

6. *Requests* the Committee on the Peaceful Uses of Outer Space, as it deems appropriate, to review that report and submit its comments and recommendations to the Economic and Social Council and to the General Assembly.

E

The General Assembly,

Recalling its resolution 1472 (XIV) of 12 December 1959,

Noting that the terms of office of the members of the Committee on the Peaceful Uses of Outer Space expire at the end of 1961,

Noting the report of the Committee on the Peaceful Uses of Outer Space,*

1. *Decides* to continue the membership of the Committee on the Peaceful Uses of Outer Space as set forth in General Assembly resolution 1472 (XIV) and to add Chad, Mongolia, Morocco, and Sierra Leone to its membership in recognition of the increased membership of the United Nations since the Committee was established;

2. *Requests* the Committee to meet not later than 31 March 1962 to carry out its mandate as contained in General Assembly resolution 1472 (XIV), to review the activities provided for in the present resolution and to make such reports as it may consider appropriate.

10th Plenary Meeting
20 December 1961

I-F(2).† USSR Proposal: Declaration of the Basic Principles Governing the Activities of States Pertaining to the Exploration and Use of Outer Space

(A/AC.105/C.2/L.1)

The Governments of the States whose representatives have signed this Declaration,

Inspired by the great prospects opening up before mankind as a result of penetration into outer space,

Recognizing that the peoples of all the countries of the world are interested in the conquest of outer space,

Desiring to promote broad international cooperation in the exploration and use of outer space for peaceful purposes,

Taking into consideration resolution 1721 (XVI) of the United Nations General Assembly approved unanimously by all the States Members of the United Nations,

Solemnly declare that in the exploration and use of outer space they will be guided by the following principles:

1. The exploration and use of outer space shall be carried out for the benefit and in the interests of the whole of mankind.

2. Outer space and celestial bodies are free for exploration and use by all States; no State may claim sovereignty over outer space and celestial bodies.

3. All States have equal rights to explore and use outer space.

4. The activities of States pertaining to the conquest of outer space shall be carried out in accordance with the principles of the United Nations Charter and with other generally recognized principles of international law in the in-

---

* A/4987.

† Appendices I-F(2) through I-F(7) are proposals submitted to the Legal Subcommittee of UNCOPUOS during the May-June 1962 meetings in Geneva.

terests of developing friendly relations among nations and of maintaining international peace and security.

5. Scientific and technological advances shall be applied to outer space in the interests of a better understanding among nations and the promotion of broad international cooperation among States; the use of outer space for propagating war, national or racial hatred or enmity between nations shall be prohibited.

6. Cooperation and mutual assistance in the conquest of outer space shall be a duty incumbent upon all States; the implementation of any measures that might in any way hinder the exploration or use of outer space for peaceful purposes by other countries shall be permitted only after prior discussion of and agreement upon such measures between the countries concerned.

7. All activities of any kind pertaining to the exploration and use of outer space shall be carried out solely and exclusively by States; the sovereign rights of States to the objects they launch into outer space shall be retained by them.

8. The use of artificial satellites for the collection of intelligence information in the territory of foreign States is incompatible with the objectives of mankind in its conquest of outer space.

9. States shall regard all astronauts as envoys of mankind in outer space and shall render all possible assistance to spaceships and their crews which may make emergency landing on the territory of a foreign State or on the high seas; spaceships, satellites and capsules found beyond the limits of the launching State shall be returned to that State.

The Governments of the States signatories to this Declaration call upon all the States of the world to accede to it.

I-F(3). USSR Proposal: International Agreement on the Rescue of Astronauts and Spaceships Making Emergency Landings

(A/AC.105/C.2/L.2)

The Governments of . . .

Recognizing the common interest of mankind in furthering the peaceful uses of outer space,

Wishing to do their utmost to assist the crews of spaceships which may meet with an accident,

Have decided to conclude this Agreement and for this purpose have appointed their representatives who, having exchanged their full powers, found in good and due form, have agreed on the following provisions:

Article 1

Each Contracting State shall render assistance to the crews of spaceships which have met with an accident and shall take steps to rescue astronauts making an emergency landing; to this end it shall employ every means at its disposal, including electronic and optical equipment, means of communication, and rescue facilities of different kinds.

Article 2

A Contracting State which discovers that the crew of a spaceship of another Contracting State has met with an accident shall do its utmost to notify the launching State without delay.

Article 3

In the event of astronauts of a Contracting State making an emergency landing on the territory of another Contracting State, the latter shall immediately inform the launching State of the occurrence and shall take all possible steps to rescue the astronauts making the emergency landing and to render them the necessary assistance.

Article 4

If the astronauts are presumed to have made an emergency descent on the high seas, a joint search for them shall be made, if necessary, by those Contracting States to which the launching State may make application.

Article 5

The assistance to be furnished when necessary by one Contracting State to another Contracting State shall in no way differ from the assistance which could be furnished to its own astronauts.

Article 6

Each Contracting State shall do its utmost to facilitate the early return to their own country of any astronauts of another Contracting State who may make an emergency landing on its territory or who may be rescued on the high seas.

Article 7

Foreign spaceships, satellites and capsules found by a Contracting State on its territory or salvaged on the high seas shall be returned without delay to the launching State if they have identification marks showing their national origin and if the launching State has officially announced the launching of the devices found.

Space vehicles aboard which devices have been discovered for the collection of intelligence information in the territory of another State shall not be returned.

Article 8

The expenses incurred by a State in fulfilling the obligations provided for in articles 6 and 7 of this Agreement shall be reimbursed by the launching State.

Article 9

This Agreement shall be open for accession to all the States of the world.

I-F(4). United States Proposal: Assistance to and Return of Space Vehicles and Personnel

(A/AC.105/C.2/L.3)

The General Assembly,

Recognizing that the personnel of space vehicles may from time to time be the subject of accident or experience conditions of distress,

Recognizing that there may occur landings of space vehicles, and their personnel in the case of manned vehicles, by reason of accident, distress, or mistake, or otherwise than as planned,

Believing that in such circumstances the action of States should be governed by humanitarian concern and with a due regard for scientific needs,

Commends to States for their guidance the following principles:

1. All possible assistance shall be rendered to the personnel of space vehicles who may be the subject of accident or experience conditions of distress or who may land by reason of accident, distress, or mistake, or otherwise than as planned;

2. Space vehicles, and their personnel in the case of manned vehicles, that land by reason of accident, distress or mistake, or otherwise than as planned, shall be safely and promptly returned to the State or States or international organization responsible for launching;

3. Any expense incurred in providing assistance to or return of space vehicles and their personnel shall be borne by the State or States or international organization responsible for launching.

I-F(5). United States Proposal: Liability for Space Vehicle Accidents

(A/AC.105/C.2/L.4)

The Legal Subcommittee of the United Nations Committee on the Peaceful Uses of Outer Space,

Recognizing that there may occur personal injury, loss of life, or property damage as a result of space vehicle accidents,

Recognizing that States and international organizations responsible for the launching of space vehicles should be liable internationally for such injury, loss, or damage,

Believing that there should be agreed rules and procedures applicable to such cases,

1. *Requests* the Secretary-General to constitute a small advisory panel of legal experts drawn from various geographic areas;

2. *Requests* the advisory panel thus constituted to prepare a draft of an international agreement dealing with the liability of States and international organizations for injury, loss, or damage caused by space vehicles;

3. *Commends* to the advisory panel for its guidance the following principles:

(a) States or international organizations responsible for the launching of space vehicles should be liable internationally for personal injury, loss of life, or property damage caused thereby, whether such injury, loss, or damage occurs on land, on the sea, or in the air;

(b) A claim based on personal injury, loss of life, or property damage caused by a space vehicle should not require proof of fault on the part of the State or States or international organization responsible for launching the space vehicle in question, although the degree of care which ought reasonably to have been exercised by the person or entity on whose behalf claim is made might properly be taken into account;

(c) A claim may be presented internationally to the State or States or international organization responsible for the launching of a space vehicle causing injury, loss, or damage without regard to the prior exhaustion of any local remedies that may be available;

(d) The presentation of a claim should be made within a reasonable time after the occurrence of injury, loss, or damage;

(e) The International Court of Justice should have jurisdiction to adjudicate any dispute relating to the interpretation or application of the international agreement on liability in the absence of agreement between the States concerned upon another means of settlement.

4. *Requests* the advisory panel to transmit the draft international agreement to the Legal Subcommittee at an early date.

I-F(6). Indian Proposal: Suggested Draft-Conclusions

(A/AC.105/C.2/L.5 and Corr. 1)

1. The Subcommittee will give further consideration at its subsequent sessions to the principles that should govern the activities of States in the exploration and use of outer space, taking into account proposals already made; and in this connexion members of the Subcommittee are requested to submit any additional proposals at least one month before the next session of the Subcommittee.

2. The Subcommittee endorses the principle that States shall render all possible assistance to astronauts who have met with accident or have made emergency landings and shall return space vehicles and personnel to the launching State.

3. The Subcommittee endorses the principle that States shall be liable internationally for personal injury, loss of life or property damage caused by space vehicles which they have launched.

4. The Subcommittee decides to set up a working party of the Subcommittee to go into the question of what further measures should be adopted to implement the principles stated in paragraphs 2 and 3.

5. The Subcommittee decides to include in its report a provisional list of additional subjects which may be taken up by the Subcommittee at its subsequent sessions.

I-F(7). Canadian Proposal: Suggested Draft-Conclusions

(A/AC.105/C.2/SR.13)

1. No statement has been made in the Committee or in our consultations with other delegates which would suggest opposition to the idea of requesting a working group to prepare a draft international agreement dealing with liability for space vehicle accidents. Indeed the Committee has entirely endorsed action along these lines.

2. The Committee also agreed that the subject of the question of general principles be regarded as an important matter but that a more detailed consideration of this subject may be left until a later meeting.

3. The one subject on which there has not been agreement is the subject as to how best the question of assistance and return should be handled. The difference in approach regarding this question raises in turn the important issue as to whether this difference in approach should be of such a wide-spread character as to prevent useful progress being made in regard to a separate question, namely the question of liability for space vehicle accidents.

I-F(8). Fourth Meeting of the Scientific and Technical Subcommittee of the United Nations Committee on the Peaceful Uses of Outer Space

Statement made by Mr. Maurice Roy, President of COSPAR (May 31, 1962)

Mr. Chairman,

May I first thank you for this invitation to make a statement concerning the International Committee on Space Research (COSPAR), which is, I am proud to say, already generously represented in this Subcommittee whose members, I notice, include:

Mr. Blagonravov, the USSR Vice President of COSPAR.
Dr. Porter, the U.S. Vice President.
Mr. Rose, the delegate for Canada.
Mr. Sarabahai, the delegate for India.
Mr. Hatanaka, the delegate for Japan.
Mr. Robins, the delegate for the United Kingdom.

and, last but by no means least, yourself, Mr. Chairman, the delegate for Australia.

By way of background, it may be useful if I say a word about COSPAR's origin and organization.

COSPAR is a special committee set up by the International Council of Scientific Unions (ICSU) following the International Geophysical Year, which was in itself a remarkable demonstration of world-wide international scientific cooperation and which was also the occasion of the first satellite launching.

COSPAR is thus similar to the Special Committees on Antarctic and Oceanic Research (SCAR and SCOR) which were also established as a result of the International Geophysical Year.

COSPAR came into being officially in November 1959 when its charter was approved by ICSU. It has therefore existed officially for only two and a half years. COSPAR's purpose under its charter is to promote, at the international level, the advancement of scientific research of all kinds involving the use of rockets or rocket-propelled vehicles. Its activities are concerned only with fundamental space research and normally do not cover such problems as rocket construction and propulsion guidance and control.

COSPAR's objective of the maximum development of space research programmes can be achieved only by the international community of scientists working through ICSU and its adhering national academies and international unions.

By the terms of its charter COSPAR is an a-political body and is as a matter of principle precluded from recommending to any nation any course of action in regard to another, or from engaging in any activities which are the exclusive concern of governmental authorities or intergovernmental agencies.

COSPAR consists of:

one representative designated by each national scientific institution adhering to ICSU, which is actively concerned with space research and wishes to be represented in COSPAR

one representative of each of the international scientific unions represented in ICSU which wishes to take part in COSPAR's work.

This membership is designed to ensure both broad scientific representation and the widest possible representation of nationalities among the representatives of the Unions. COSPAR's activities are directed and guided by a Bureau and an Executive Council.

The Bureau consists of the President, two Vice Presidents, one designated by the Soviet Union and the other by the United States—the two countries which have placed artificial satellites into orbit—and four elected members.

The Executive Council consists of the members of the Bureau plus the representatives of the adhering unions. The membership of the general assembly is composed of the representatives of the adhering national scientific institutions as well as the members of the Executive Council.

The COSPAR Secretariat is at The Hague (Netherlands). The Executive Secretary is Mr. Bealieu.

I should point out that COSPAR's activities are governed by the rules which the ICSU charter lays down for committees set up by ICSU. They are also limited by the strictly scientific nature of COSPAR's functions.

I may add, without any false modesty—since I was elected only a month ago and the credit belongs to my predecessor that COSPAR has been able to transact its business in a most satisfactory manner, all decisions and recommendations having been adopted unanimously after objective discussion.

To give you some idea of the work COSPAR has undertaken and planned, I shall, with your permission, list a number of specific examples of the activities undertaken;

(1) Each year COSPAR holds a general assembly at which the representatives of the adhering national scientific bodies present very well docu-

mented papers on space research activities in their fields during the past year and programmes and plans for future scientific work. These reports are available to anyone on application to the COSPAR secretariat at The Hague. Similar papers are presented by the adhering scientific unions and by other interested organizations, such as UNESCO and ITU, with which COSPAR has relations. Subjects of general interest to space research are discussed at these meetings, generally on the basis of reports or proposals by *ad hoc* COSPAR working groups, of which there are now four. Resolutions are put forward and adopted whenever it is considered necessary or desirable to do so.

(2) COSPAR also organizes an annual international symposium on space research which is open to scientists of all countries, including those not represented in COSPAR. The first was held at Nice in 1960, the second at Florence in 1961 and the third in Washington a month ago. At the Washington symposium 114 papers were presented by scientists from over 30 countries.

These scientific gatherings cover all the disciplines in which research is conducted by means of space vehicles—geodesy, scientific meteorology, upper atmosphere physics and chemistry radiations or particles trapped by magnetic fields, solar physics, earth-sun relationships, the interplanetary medium, the moon and planets, galactic astronomy, the study of the existence of life outside the terrestrial atmosphere, space research technologies and instrumentation, etc.

COSPAR makes great efforts to ensure the speedy publication of papers presented at its meetings and the important works published have become fundamental documents in the scientific literature of the disciplines concerned.

(3) Specialized symposia dealing with limited areas are also organized in addition to the general symposia, usually in relation to the work of one or two unions; for example a symposium on space biology and the prevention of the biological contamination of extraterrestrial bodies organized jointly by COSPAR and the International Union of Biochemistry was held last August in Moscow.

(4) COSPAR stimulates and encourages the conclusion of bilateral or multilateral arrangements for international cooperation in carrying out space experiments. The satellite launching recently carried out jointly by Great Britain and the United States is an example.

(5) Projects associating a number of scientific disciplines in studies of important events relevant to solar influences on the earth, such as those of July 1959, are also undertaken. Reports on such studies were presented in 1960 to the IUGG Assembly at Helsinki and to the COSPAR Assembly in Florence in 1961.

(6) COSPAR has prepared and published tables known as the "international research atmosphere" tables (density, pressure, temperature, composition, etc.), for altitudes from 30 kilometres to the theoretical upper limit.

(7) COSPAR has organized world experimental periods using sounding rockets and other synoptic programmes of experiments using rockets.

(8) It is concerned with the establishment of scientific space research programmes to be carried out during the quiet sun year and in relation with the WMO—and is making preparatory organizational arrangements.

(9) It is also engaged in the preparatory organization of space research projects on polar cap phenomena.

(10) COSPAR is revising a manual on the use of world data centres for space research rockets and satellites. This implies international agreement for the exchange of scientific information in this field.

(11) COSPAR prepares a world list of optical and radio satellite tracking stations, including the fullest possible information on the location and equipment of stations and the precision of their equipment.

(12) Work is in progress on the preparation of an international code approved by all the members of COSPAR for the transmission of satellite tracking and observation data.

(13) Studies are in progress with a view to securing a scientifically rational distribution of tracking stations. Consideration is being given to possible recommendations on this subject to the national scientific bodies concerned.

(14) On consultation COSPAR makes recommendations to ITU concerning the allocation of frequencies for space research. It participates in IUCAF (Inter-Union Committee on the Allocation of Frequencies for space research and radio astronomy) and is continuing to provide it with financial assistance.

(15) COSPAR sponsors SPACEWARN, an international communications system used for the transmission of information regarding the launching of space vehicles containing scientific instruments, and information concerning orbital data and other characteristics of value to satellite observers and interested scientists.

(16) COSPAR edits and publishes an information bulletin containing scientific news of current interest to scientists engaged in space research.

Having provided a fairly complete picture of the various activities undertaken by COSPAR during the last two and a half years, I should like to say a few words regarding the activities planned for the immediate future. They are:

(1) Revision and improvement of the international reference atmosphere, based on a critical analysis of new data;

(2) The improvement and expansion of the COSPAR Bulletin, to make it an increasingly useful tool for space research scientists;

(3) International studies on astronomical constants and ephemerides in cooperation with IAU;

(4) Preparation of a technical manual for the construction and use of low-cost simplified tracking and telemetry stations, which could be used by scientists in countries with limited space research resources; the manual is being prepared in cooperation with UNESCO;

(5) The scientific, objective and quantitative examination of proposed space

experiments with potential undesirable effects on other scientific studies or activities.

This action is being taken in response to resolution No. 10/1961 of the ICSU General Assembly. The text of the resolution is:

The General Assembly,

considering that certain experiments conducted by means of space vehicles and contributing in an important way to the advancement of science, may also affect present or future scientific activities in other fields, *invites* the Committee on Space Research to examine any proposed experiments or other space activities that may have potentially undesirable effects on scientific activities and observations, to arrange for careful, objective, quantitative studies and to make available to Scientific and National Members, adhering to the International Council of Scientific Unions, and to Governments, the facts and analyses needed by them for making wise and proper decisions concerning the proposed experiments; and, *appeals* to all Governments planning to launch space experiments which could possibly affect other scientific research adversely to make available to ICSU in timely fashion the information and data about the proposed experiments necessary to make the desired studies.

On 9 May, at its Washington Assembly COSPAR adopted the following decision:

In order to carry out the responsibility for careful, objective, quantitative studies of space experiments with potentially undesirable effects on scientific activities and observations, which COSPAR has accepted in response to ICSU resolution 10 (1961), the Executive Council decides to establish a Consultative Group on Potentially Harmful Effects of Space Experiments to consist of not more than six broadly competent scientists having among them specialized knowledge of Astronomy, Radiation Physics, Atmospheric Physics and Chemistry, Communications, Meteorite Penetration and Microbiology, to be named by the President of COSPAR.

It is expected that this Consultative Group will act as a focal point in ICSU for consideration of all questions regarding potentially harmful effects of space experiments on scientific activities and observations, and that in this capacity it would: (1) examine in a preliminary way all questions relating to possibly harmful effects of proposed space experiments, including but not restricted to questions referred to it by any of the ICSU Unions; (2) determine whether or not any serious possibility of harmful effects would indeed result from the proposed experiment; (3) in consultation with appropriate Unions, appoint and arrange for convening an *ad hoc* Working Group or Groups to study any expected effects which are considered to be potentially harmful, such Working Group or Groups to include competent scientists in the appropriate specialized disciplines; (4) receive and consider conclusions or recommendations of these *ad hoc* Working Groups in a timely manner; and (5) prepare final recommendations to the COSPAR Executive Council for its further action. Positive or negative recommendations or studies considered appropriate by the Council for dissemination would then be made available to all COSPAR adherents, the ICSU Bureau, the appropriate Unions of ICSU, and to appropriate bodies of the United Nations or its specialized agencies.

The Consultative Group is in the process of formation.

May I in conclusion, as the new President of COSPAR, give you my assurance that COSPAR is determined to develop and as far as possible, strengthen and accelerate the activities it has already undertaken with satisfactory results, as well as the activities it proposes to undertake.

In particular, I should draw to your attention the resolution adopted by COSPAR at its Washington Assembly on 9 May in which it renewed its offer to the United Nations of assistance or cooperation in the scientific field, within the framework of its charter and its relationship with ICSU, to which I referred at the beginning of my statement.

I-G. PRELIMINARY VIEWS OF THE UNITED STATES FOR FRE-QUENCY ALLOCATIONS FOR SPACE RADIOCOMMUNICATION (Extracts)

September 7, 1961

[It is important to understand that the discussion following is not an international conference proposal of the United States but only a paper prepared for discussion at international level. It will be noted that the paper is similar in many respects to an earlier version dated May 17, 1961, attached to the Commission's Second Notice of Inquiry in Docket No. 13522, In the Matter of an Inquiry into the Allocation of Frequency Bands for Space Communications adopted on that date.

For information, the date of September 7, 1961, which appears above, is the date on which the Telecommunications Coordinating Committee (TCC) recommended adoption of the paper by the Department of State for purposes of consultation abroad. The TCC is an interagency governmental committee which advises the Department of State on matters of international telecommunication policy.

October 30, 1961]

1 *Introduction.* Studies of the world trend in telecommunication requirements and the known plans for expansion of existing telecommunication facilities throughout the world have repeatedly indicated that beginning about 1965 the loading of these facilities will approach saturation in many areas. This is particularly true of such facilities as submarine cables and high-frequency radio circuits. With regard to cables, economic factors will govern the number of cables which will be installed and the location of the terminals which they will serve. The matter of congestion in the high frequency spectrum has concerned Members of the International Telecommunication Union (ITU) for many years. There is no foreseeable reduction in the use of high frequencies for global communication. On the other hand, expansion of service in the high frequency bands will become increasingly impracticable. Accordingly, it becomes necessary to seek alternative means to satisfy growing telecommunication needs of the peoples of the world, including those of new or developing countries. These alternative means are needed for growth. Global communication via earth-satellite relays promises to afford such an alternative which will be required beginning about 1965. It is the purpose of this paper to set forth in broad outline certain initial conclusions with regard to frequency allocations for this promising new telecommunication development, and other space radiocommunication needs.

1.1   Since the first demonstration of the practicability of transmitting intelligence from one part of the earth to another by the use of radio waves relayed by artificial satellites, the U.S.A. has been studying the technical parameters which appear to be relevant to eventual frequency allocations for all categories of space radiocommunication, in the context of Recommendation No. 36 of the Ordinary Administrative Radio Conference (OARC), Geneva, 1959.

1.2   The uses of space radiocommunications may be grouped as follows:

   a. Aeronautical Mobile.
   b. Broadcasting.
   c. Meteorological.
   d. Navigation.
   e. Space Research—guidance, control and associated communications, including tracking and telemetering.
   f. Communication relay (both active and passive).

1.3   While radio astronomy is not classified by the ITU as a space service, nevertheless, because of its scientific importance, the matter of radio astronomy allocations is under study.

1.4   An operating world-wide communication satellite space service is probably one of the first areas in which a practical use may be made of satellites, involving high-capacity, reliable information exchange between points on the earth's surface, including ships, aircraft and aerospacecraft. Relay may be effected by several means—e.g., low or intermediate altitude satellites in random or controlled orbit, high altitude satellites in synchronous orbit, natural or manmade passive reflectors, etc. International standardization of frequency allocations is a prerequisite to the introduction of world-wide operational communication satellite systems.

1.5   Certain relevant radio wave propagation data were made known at the Plenary Assembly of the CCIR at Los Angeles in 1959. Subsequently, the 1959 OARC at Geneva established certain allocations for space research. These allocations, however, were not intended to accommodate the larger bands of frequencies required by satellite communication systems equipped for high-capacity, multi-channel transmission.

2   *Aeronautical mobile.*   The advances in the field of air transportation in recent years point to the approaching need to accommodate communications for aircraft and aerospacecraft operating at extremely high speeds and altitudes. Present indications are that the speeds and altitudes of aeronautical operations will increase on an evolutionary basis to speeds many times in excess of that of sound and altitudes beyond 160 kilometers. Further, these operations are unique in that the aircraft or aerospacecraft must operate in the earth's atmosphere during the departure and re-entry phase of the flight and in space or near space during the middle portion of the flight.

2.1   Such flights, when operating in the atmosphere and traveling at high speeds, are expected to require frequency bands much higher than those aviation bands presently allocated due to ion shielding created by thermal friction. For example, present indications are that 5 Gc/s frequencies are the lowest usable order of the spectrum which will satisfy radio communication with vehicles traveling in the atmosphere at 17 times the speed of sound. Until substantially more research and development has been accomplished in this field, however, it is not possible to set forth the entire space radiocommunication needs for the aeronautical mobile services.

2.2   On the other hand, during the earlier stages of aeronautical evolution toward space operations, space radiocommunication techniques will be required. That is to say, aircraft operating at speeds of 2-7 times the speed of sound and at altitudes beyond 80-100 thousand feet will probably require a constant communication link with ground stations. Flights of this nature can be controlled by a computer and automatic data communications throughout the entire flight. Since constant radiocommunications of this type would be incompatible with the present aviation system of common user frequency deployment, additional spectrum space is required. Accordingly, the U.S. proposes to provide for aeronautical mobile (R) service operation in the band 1540-1660 Mc/s on a shared basis with radionavigation for this mode of aeronautical communications.

3   *Broadcasting.* "Broadcasting" as the term is used in the Radio Regulations means transmissions intended for direct reception by the general public. It is probable that communication satellites will be used to relay aural and television broadcast programs. However, the likelihood that the general public will be receiving such transmissions directly from satellites in the near future seems remote. Special receiving stations on the earth's surface may be established to relay programs over conventional communications systems to the broadcasting stations which already serve the general public. The relaying of broadcast programs by means of satellites would not be an operation in the broadcasting service.

4   *Meteorological.* A "universal" meteorological satellite has been the subject of international study in the World Meteorological Organization (WMO). The United States has participated in this planning and is anticipating the ultimate use of meteorological satellites on an operational basis.

4.1   Two types of satellites are under consideration for the operational meteorological satellite system—polar or quasi-polar orbiting satellites and the so-called synchronous orbiting satellites. Three types of transmissions are planned with each of these systems:

a.   From Command Data Acquisition station (CDA) to the satellite(s) during periods when the satellite is within line-of-sight of the CDA station.
b.   From the satellite to the CDA station on command during the time the satellite is within line-of-sight of the CDA station.
c.   Continuous transmission from the satellite.

4.2   Several frequency channels with various bandwidths will be needed to meet these requirements, as follows:

4.2.1   The command frequency requirements can be met in the manner proposed in paragraph 8 below.

4.2.2   Two channels of 90 kc/s bandwidth each will be required for digital and slowed down video transmission from the satellite to the ground. It is proposed to satisfy this requirement in the band 137-138 Mc/s. These transmitters will have up to a possible maximum of 50 watts power output and may operate continuously or on command.

4.2.3   Four channels of 5 Mc/s bandwidth each (includes guard band) will be required for broad-band video transmission from the satellite to the ground. Power output of these transmitters will be up to a possible maximum of 50 watts, and initially will operate only on command and in the vicinity of the CDA stations. The bands 1660-1670 and 1690-1700 Mc/s are proposed for the satisfaction of this requirement.

4.2.4   A 100 Mc/s band is required for satellite weather radar. It is proposed that this requirement for suitable precipitation detection, be met in the radiolocation band 9.8-10.0 Gc/s in the manner indicated in paragraph 8.

4.2.5   A channel of approximately 100 Mc/s bandwidth is required to transmit a large volume of high resolution picture data from the satellite to the CDA station on each orbital pass. It is proposed that this requirement be met in the band 7.2-7.65 Gc/s in the manner indicated in paragraph 8.

4.2.6   One channel of 100 Mc/s bandwidth is required for cloud detection radar. These pulsed radars will have power output as high as 100 KW peak power and operate throughout the orbit. It is proposed that this requirement be met in the band 33.4-36.0 Gc/s.

5   *Navigation.* At such time as there is available an operational space satellite navigational aid of widespread interest to aviation and shipping, appropriate frequency allocation provision for such a navigational system may be derived from bands available to the radionavigation service. The roles of the International Civil Aviation Organization (ICAO) and the Inter-governmental Maritime Consultative Organization (IMCO) with respect to such aids are recognized in this regard.

6   *Space Research.* The experience of the U.S.A., to date, with the "space research" bands allocated at the 1959 OARC at Geneva, together with present planning estimates, indicate these should be augmented. There have been more than 50 earth satellites launched, all with transmitters on board. There has never been any report of interference to other services from the space service although the space vehicles have experienced interference from these other services. Consequently, the U.S.A. suggests more protection to the space bands as well as some deletions and augmentations. Command frequencies are mentioned for the first time, and these can be accommodated on an area basis, but should be noted in the table.

7   *Communication satellites.* The establishment of frequency allocation for communication satellites requires evaluation of various types of information. The principal factors to be considered can be grouped under the following main headings:

a.   Radio wave propagation characteristics.
b.   State of the art.
c.   Amount of spectrum space required.
d.   Feasibility of sharing.
e.   Selection of bands.

7.1   The conclusions which can be drawn after evaluation of these five factors are not in all respects mutually consistent. For example, analysis of some of the parameters involved will lead to a conclusion that the allocation for communication satellites should be established in one part of the spectrum, while analysis of other parameters will indicate a need for a quite different part of the spectrum. The following paragraphs sum up presently available information on each of the factors which appear to be relevant.

7.2 *Radio wave propagation characteristics.* Radio wave propagation data now available indicate there are several "windows" in different parts of the radio spectrum through which radio signals may be transmitted from the surface of the earth to points outside the earth's atmosphere, and vice versa. The most significant of these "windows" from the standpoint of the present state of development of the radio art and the limitations presently imposed by space technology, appears to lie roughly between 100 Mc/s and 20 Gc/s. Within the general range of frequencies between about 100 Mc/s and 20 Gc/s there are varying degrees of attenuation affecting radio signals transmitted from the earth's surface to a satellite in space, or vice versa. The choice of frequency bands within the broad area represented by the "window" between about 100 Mc/s and 20 Gc/s must necessarily take into account considerations other than the absorption and attenuation factors. . . . Consideration of bandwidth and state of the art indicate the desirability of employing bands above 4 Gc/s. Satellite-to-satellite relaying can be performed above 20 Gc/s without interference to or from earthbound radio services.

7.3 *State of the art.* Provision of spectrum space by the ITU for communication satellites, when effected, should serve to guide Administrations for some years to come. It therefore appears necessary to take into account both the present state of the radio art and the anticipated developments for the next several years. From available information it would appear that the present state of the art lends itself to the inauguration of the communication satellite space service only in those frequency bands below about 10 Gc/s. This is because the available receiver input power, with practical systems which can be built at the present time, will not overcome the various absorption and attenuation factors sufficiently to provide continuous, reliable communication, under practical operating conditions, at frequencies much above 10 Gc/s. . . . Satellite powers of the order of only a few watts are presently available. The intensive research and development programs now under way will, however, lead to various improvements in the state of the art, including much greater satellite transmitter power and supporting energy sources therefor, and it may be expected that frequencies up to about 16 Gc/s may become usable for practical satellite systems.

7.4 *Amount of spectrum space required.* An appreciation of the amount of spectrum space required for allocation to communication satellite systems of the future requires taking into account the present and foreseeable capacities of other communication systems and the anticipated growth and demand for service, at least until about 1970. The existing systems include transoceanic cables, conventional microwave radio relay systems, tropospheric scatter systems, ionospheric scatter systems, land line circuits and high-frequency fixed radio circuits.

7.4.1 The requirements of the peoples of the world to communicate are not susceptible to exact mathematical prediction. It has been well established over the years, however, that given a new communication facility, the requirements to use it are seldom lacking. If a large number of new international communication facilities of any type could be made available at once, there is little doubt that they would soon be in regular use.

7.4.2 An important consideration is that the financial costs involved in building and launching communication satellites are such that a large number of communication channels will have to be provided if the satellites are to prove economically feasible.

7.4.3 Compared with conventional communication techniques, a relatively small number of communication satellite channels can presently be derived from a given amount of spectrum space. This is due to modulation techniques presently employed which are chosen because of the relatively low orders of power presently realizable in satellite transmitters. As advances in the state of the art are made it can be expected that the number of actual communication satellite channels that can be derived from a given amount of spectrum space will progressively increase. Nevertheless, the efficiency (ratio of intelligence bandwidth to radio frequency bandwidth), at the present time, is of the order of 10-15%. This consideration is influential in estimates of the amount of spectrum space to be allocated initially for communication satellites. Moreover, the expected increase in channel efficiency should serve to offset future growth requirements as communication satellite uses expand and the demands placed on them increase. A further consideration is that the available channels in a given satellite must, in effect, be divided among the various (earth) satellite terminal stations in simultaneous communication with that satellite.

7.5 *Feasibility of sharing.* On the basis of information currently available, there is little doubt that it is feasible for a communication satellite space service to share frequency bands with fixed and mobile services to which these bands are now allocated, provided reasonable engineering care is exercised by each of the sharing services. Because of the low transmitting power capability of satellites expected to be used during the next several years, it appears necessary to employ wideband modulation techniques on board the satellites to improve the signal-to-noise ratios to a usable level at the earth receiving terminal, even when using high gain antennas and parametric or maser amplifier techniques. As a result, the satellites' signals at the earth's surface will not be detectable by receivers in the fixed and mobile services. Satellite-to-earth signals can thus be discounted as potential interference sources for several years to come, despite probable improvements in both microwave and satellite techniques, within reasonable limits. Conversely, the likelihood of harmful interference to the reception on board satellites which might be caused by terrestrial fixed and mobile stations, other than tropospheric scatter stations, also appears to be negligible. The problem remaining then becomes one of preventing mutual interference between the receiving and transmitting earth terminals of the space system and stations of the services with which sharing is desired. Factors to be considered in preventing this interference are: geographical separation, minimum permissible antenna elevation angles for earth terminals, transmitter powers, antenna gain and directivity, receiver bandwidth, antenna orientation, local terrain, and receiver noise. However, mobile requirements are foreseen which dictate the need for minimal allocation provisions on an exclusive basis.

7.5.1 Sharing criteria applicable to the above problem are currently under study in U.S. CCIR Study Group IV. Based on information currently under development for introduction into that Study Group, it appears that 75 miles separation between earth stations will provide adequate protection from mutual interference. This assumes that earth station antennas will not be depressed below 7½° and a mean power of 1 KW into the earth station antenna. This also assumes a smooth earth condition, and that the antennas are separated in azimuth by at least 10°. The separation criteria, of course, will vary with powers and topography.

7.6 *Selection of bands.* The U.S.A. estimates that a total of about 3000 Mc/s of spectrum space should be allocated at this time to meet foreseeable requirements until about 1970. Between 3700 and 8400 Mc/s, the existing fixed and mobile space should be designated in the Table of Frequency allocations as follows:

3.7-4.2   Gc/s   COMMUNICATION SATELLITE SPACE (Space stations)
                     FIXED
                     MOBILE

5.925-6.425 Gc/s   COMMUNICATION SATELLITE SPACE (Earth stations)
                     FIXED
                     MOBILE

6.425-7.2   Gc/s   COMMUNICATION SATELLITE SPACE (Earth and Space stations)
                     FIXED
                     MOBILE

7.2-7.65   Gc/s   COMMUNICATION SATELLITE SPACE (Space stations)
                     FIXED
                     METEOROLOGICAL SATELLITE SPACE (100 Mc/s)
                     MOBILE

7.65-7.7   Gc/s   COMMUNICATION SATELLITE SPACE (Space stations)

7.7-7.9   Gc/s   COMMUNICATION SATELLITE SPACE (Earth and space stations)
                     FIXED
                     MOBILE

7.9-8.35   Gc/s   COMMUNICATION SATELLITE SPACE (Earth stations)
                     FIXED
                     MOBILE

8.35-8.4   Gc/s   COMMUNICATION SATELLITE SPACE (Earth stations)

This arrangement of bands provides:

a. A total of 1000 Mc/s for satellite-to-earth transmissions of which 50 Mc/s (7.65-7.7 Gc/s) is conclusively for that purpose and the remaining 950 Mc/s shared with the fixed and mobile services.

b. A total of 1000 Mc/s for earth-to-satellite transmissions of which 50 Mc/s (8.35-8.4 Gc/s) is exclusively for that purpose, and the remaining 950 Mc/s shared with the fixed and mobile services.

c. Two bands, shared with fixed and mobile services, not designated at this time, either for earth stations only or satellite stations only. These two bands (6.425-7.2 and 7.7-7.9 Gc/s) are so placed as to permit later adjustment as needed dependent upon the nature and magnitude of requirements and advancements in the state of the radio art.

d. A total of 2975 Mc/s for the communication satellite space service.

8 *Conclusions.* The U.S.A. has concluded that, in order to:

a. Accommodate aerospacecraft,
b. Accommodate meteorological satellites,
c. Augment the Space and Earth-Space (space research) bands contained in the Geneva Radio Regulations, and
d. Provide frequency allocations in the immediate future for the reliable exchange, via communication satellite relay, of high-capacity information between points on the earth's surface, including ships, aircraft and aerospacecraft,

the Table of Frequency Allocations should be amended as follows:

Band (Mc/s)	Allocation	Footnotes
136-137	SPACE RESEARCH	
137-138	METEOROLOGICAL SATELLITE SPACE SPACE RESEARCH SPACE (TRACKING)	
138-144	FIXED MOBILE *Radiolocation* *	The frequencies 144.0 and 148.0 Mc/s, with a maximum bandwidth of 20 kc/s, may be used for satellite command purposes subject to agreement between administrations concerned and those whose services, operating in accordance with the Table, may be affected. 287 **
144-148	AMATEUR	
148-174	FIXED MOBILE	
400-401	METEOROLOGICAL AIDS SPACE RESEARCH	
406-420	FIXED MOBILE except aeronautical mobile	The frequencies 420.0 and 450.0 Mc/s, with a maximum bandwidth of 25 Kc/s, may be used for satellite command purposes subject to agreement between administrations concerned and those whose services, operating in accordance with the Table, may be affected. 317 ** 318 **
420-450	RADIOLOCATION Amateur	
450-470	FIXED MOBILE	
1427-1525	FIXED MOBILE	

* Permitted service.
** Footnote as contained in Geneva Radio Regulations.

Band (Mc/s)	Allocation	Footnotes
1525-1540	SPACE	In the band 1525-1535 Mc/s, telemetry only; In the band 1535-1540 Mc/s, command only.
1540-1660	AERONAUTICAL MOBILE (R) AERONAUTICAL RADIONAVIGATION	The use of the band 1540-1660 Mc/s by the aeronautical mobile (R) service is limited to radiocommunications along civil routes for flights utilizing space radiocommunication techniques and which may be operating in the space environment. In the band 1600-1660 Mc/s the aeronautical radionavigation service will be protected from harmful interference from the aeronautical mobile (R) service for an unspecified period of time. 341 ***
1660-1670	METEOROLOGICAL SATELLITE SPACE Radio Astronomy	The radio astronomy service is authorized to use the band 1664.4-1668.4 Mc/s. The radio astronomy service shall be protected from harmful interference from services operating in other bands only to the extent that those services are protected from each other.
1670-1690	METEOROLOGICAL AIDS (Radiosonde)	
1690-1700	METEOROLOGICAL SATELLITE SPACE	
1700-1710	SPACE RESEARCH	
1710-2290	FIXED MOBILE	The band 2110-2120 Mc/s may be used for command of spacecraft engaged in deep space research, subject to agreement between administrations concerned and those whose services, operating in accordance with the Table, may be affected.
2290-2300	SPACE RESEARCH	For deep space research only.

*** Footnote as contained in Geneva Radio Regulations, but with the limits of the appropriate band changed to read: 1540-1660 Mc/s.

Band (Gc/s)	Allocation	Footnotes
3.7-4.2	COMMUNICATION SATELLITE SPACE FIXED MOBILE	For transmission only by communication satellite stations whose field strength at the earth's surface is below that which will cause harmful interference to stations in the fixed and mobile services.
5.925-6.425	COMMUNICATION SATELLITE SPACE FIXED MOBILE	For transmission only by earth stations, subject to agreement between administrations affected.
6.425-7.2	COMMUNICATION SATELLITE SPACE FIXED MOBILE	Transmission by earth stations in this band is subject to agreement between administrations affected. When used for communication satellite stations, the field strength at the earth's surface shall be below that which will cause harmful interference to stations in the fixed and mobile services. The band 7.12-7.13 Gc/s may be used for command of spacecraft subject to agreement between administrations affected.
7.2-7.65	COMMUNICATION SATELLITE SPACE FIXED METEOROLOGICAL SATELLITE SPACE MOBILE	For transmission only by communication satellite and meteorological satellite stations whose field strength at the earth's surface is below that which will cause harmful intereference to stations in the fixed and mobile services. Meteorological satellite stations share 100 Mc/s of this band.
7.65-7.7	COMMUNICATION SATELLITE SPACE	For transmission only by communication satellite stations.
7.7-7.9	COMMUNICATION SATELLITE SPACE FIXED MOBILE	Transmission by earth stations in this band is subject to agreement between the administrations affected. When used for communication satellite stations, the field strength at the earth's surface shall be below that which will cause harmful interference to stations in the fixed and mobile services.
7.9-8.35	COMMUNICATION SATELLITE SPACE FIXED MOBILE	For transmission only by earth stations and subject to agreement between administrations affected.
8.35-8.4	COMMUNICATION SATELLITE SPACE	For transmission only by earth stations.

Band (Gc/s)	Allocation	Footnotes
8.4-8.5	SPACE RESEARCH	
9.8-10.0	RADIOLOCATION	The band 9.9-10.0 Gc/s may be used for satellite weather radar for precipitation detection.
15.15-15.25	SPACE RESEARCH	
31.5-31.8	SPACE RESEARCH	
33.4-36.0	RADIOLOCATION	Satellite weather radars for cloud detection share 100 Mc/s of this band.

9 . . . .

10   These preliminary views of the U.S.A. are put forth at this time for informal discussion in the hope that such discussions, together with additional experience and subsequent developments in the state of the art, will lead to firm conclusions which can become the basis of action in whatever administrative radio conference takes up the question referred to in Recommendation No. 36 of the 1959 OARC, Geneva.

I-H. PROPOSED PROGRAM FOR PREPARATION FOR THE ITU 1963 CONFERENCE

A. *Limitations and characteristics of space radio uses*

1. What frequencies, general types of modulation, band widths, power level and other operational factors have been involved in space programmes of the USA and USSR to date?
    (*a*) Vehicle type
    (*b*) Spacecraft

2. What is the present extent of knowledge as to the following factors affecting frequency selection?

    (*a*) Space and weight limitations on transmitting equipment in the vehicle
    (*b*) Power source limitations
    (*c*) Antenna arrays
        (*i*) Space based
        (*ii*) Earth based
    (*d*) Area in which used
        (*i*) transmissions through the earth's atmosphere and ionosphere, especially attenuation of radio transmissions from space vehicles
        (*ii*) transmissions not passing through the earth's atmosphere and ionosphere

(*e*) Time phasing and frequency sharing: periods when various portions of the spectrum will be used
(*f*) Cosmic and solar noise background
(*g*) Data bandwidth
(*h*) Receiver noise figure limitations

3. What are the limitations and the characteristic parameters required for space radio systems in the foreseeable future?

(*a*) Frequencies
(*b*) Nature of communications
    (*i*) Telephone
    (*ii*) Telegraph
(*a*) Facsimile
(*b*) Photo transmissions
    (*iii*) Television
    (*iv*) Data transfer
    (*v*) Other
(*c*) Interference
(*d*) Ranges
(*e*) Costs
(*f*) Efficiency
(*g*) Effects of atmosphere and ionosphere
(*h*) Equipment characteristics
    (*i*) Antennas—physical size and beamwidth
    (*ii*) Power sources—capacity, efficiency, size
    (*iii*) Transmitters—power output, efficiency, frequency, bandwidth
    (*iv*) Receivers—sensitivity, noise factor, size
    (*v*) Modulation subsystems
    (*vi*) Others
(*i*) Ground receiving and transmitting equipment
(*j*) Classes of satellites proposed for relay communications
    (*i*) Low attitude passive
    (*ii*) Low attitude active
    (*iii*) 24 hour orbit passive
    (*iv*) 24 hour orbit active
    (*v*) planets, artificial minor planets, etc., as satellites
(*k*) Sensitivity

B. *Foreseeable uses of radio in astronautics and frequencies required therefor*

4. What are the nature and extent of the problems of radio transmission from Earth to positions in space such as Mars, Venus and Moon? And from Earth to a satellite, and thereafter to a position in space such as Mars, Venus and Moon?

(*a*) Doppler shifts due to the relative motion of the earth and of the planets
(*b*) Faraday rotation, tropospheric and ionospheric absorptions, bending and diffusion

(c) Tracking and stabilization of antennas on planets

(d) Axial rotation of planets

(e) Communications systems on planets—effects of lack of ionosphere around planets on beyond line of sight transmissions

(f) Others

5. To what extent is extraterrestrial noise a factor in space communications?

(a) Galactic noise

(b) Radio stars

(c) Solar radiation
   (i) constant
   (ii) sudden ionospheric disturbances (I.D.)

(d) Planetary radiation

(e) Other factors

6. With particular reference to interplanetary telemetering by means of telecommunications, what is the extent of present knowledge and what are the foreseeable requirements of

(a) Equipment
   (i) frequency requirements
   (ii) power supply
   (iii) antenna characteristics
   (iv) type of modulation

(b) Uses of telemetry

7. With reference to the allocations for space radio purposes adopted at the 1959 Radio Conference in Geneva, what additional spectrum space should be proposed for space radio uses in the following bands?

(a) Research

(b) Commercial and military

(c) Sharing 2500 kc/s to 25 Mc/s
           25 Mc/s to 8700 Mc/s
           890 Mc/s to 8700 Mc/s
           8700 Mc/s to 35 000 Mc/s
           above 35 000 Mc/s

8. What are the foreseeable frequency allocation requirements of the several uses of radio in astronautics?

(a) Tracking

(b) Command

(c) Guidance

(d) Telemetry

(e) Communications

(f) Navigation

(g) Research

(h) Reentry; the plasma effect; achievement of control on occasion of reentry

(i) Others

9. What bandwidths will be required for the foreseeable future?

10. What provisions should be made for identification and silencing?

11. What provisions should be made for guard bands?

12. Information rates.

C. *Comparative efficiency of the several types of emission proposed for communications in space*

13. Utilizing a single basis of comparison what are the relative efficiencies of the several communications systems available for transmissions from space vehicles:
    (a) AM
    (b) FM
    (c) FM/FM
    (d) Orthogonal matched filter communications system
    (e) PCM (pulse code modulation)
    (f) Other systems
        (i) Time multiplying pulse code
        (ii) Pulse duration modulation

D. *Interplanetary navigation*

14. In what manner and to what extent could a system using natural electromagnetic radiation in the space environment be used for navigational purposes?

15. In what manner and to what extent could a system using Doppler radar and ranging or some similar form of electromagnetic radiation be used for navigational purposes in the space environment?

16. What frequencies, bandwidth and emission will be required for the operation of a navigation system such as that described in paragraphs 14 and 15 above?

E. *Navigation on Earth using signals from high altitude satellites*

17. Can celestial navigation and electronics be combined to produce a system having the universality of a celestial system and the all-weather capability of electronics, with essential freedom from the limitations encountered by present systems?

18. What would be the equipment requirements?
    (a) Antenna size and characteristics
    (b) What frequencies would be most suitable
    (c) What power sources would be needed

19. What method of determining distance would be used?
    (a) Measurement of the Doppler shift
    (b) Angle measurement

20. How many satellites would be required for navigation system?

21. What degree of accuracy could be achieved?

22. What installations on earth would be required?

23. What will be the frequency requirements?

F. *What other major categories of data should be developed in connection with the study of the adequacy of present provisions for space radio needs?*

24. What provisions should be made for Search and Rescue?

   (*a*) Transmission region
      (*i*) Satellite to earth search
      (*ii*) Earth to satellite search
      (*iii*) Satellite to satellite search
      (*iv*) Distress frequency for use in space
   (*b*) Use of normal "distress frequency" protection and allocation of a higher frequency
   (*c*) Use of interrogation frequency (command) normal and higher frequencies
   (*d*) Use of rebroadcast frequency

25. What provisions should be made for mission problems and requirements?

26. What are the particular problems affecting the use of the radio spectrum in space regions only, e.g., Mars to Venus, or from deep space probe to a communication satellite, and what provisions therefor should be made in the International Telecommunication Convention?

   (*a*) Use of low frequencies for non-earth reception
   (*b*) Allocation of frequencies for guidance and navigation (Loran, etc.)
   (*c*) Planetary atmospheres and ionospheres.

I-J.

Unclassified

DEPARTMENT OF STATE
Telecommunications Division

TD Serial No. 908
International Radio
Consultative Committee (CCIR)
Doc. No. 26
June 10, 1960

UNITED STATES AND INTERNATIONAL ACTION IN CCIR AND ITU ON SPACE TELECOMMUNICATIONS

1. *CCIR VIIIth Plenary Assembly, Warsaw, 1956*

   In the CCIR the need to study the requirements of space telecommunications received first attention when Mr. Andrew G. Haley, President of the American

Rocket Society and of the International Astronautical Federation, visited the Assembly at Warsaw and distributed a paper pointing to the need for study in this new field.

2. *CCIR Study Group XI (Television) Meeting, Moscow, May 1958*

Mr. Haley attended this meeting representing the International Astronautical Federation and called attention to the progress being made in space research and drew attention to the need to study specific requirements for space telecommunication service for consideration by the forthcoming ITU Administrative Radio Conference. It was noted by the experts at Moscow that the questions posed should be referred to CCIR Study Groups V and VI to meet later in 1958.

3. *Initial Study of the Questions by United States Committees for CCIR Study Group VI*

On the basis of Mr. Haley's representations, the United States Committee for Study Group VI drafted a proposed new question for study: "Protection of Frequencies used by Artificial Earth Satellites or Other Space Vehicles for Communication and Positional Observation," dated February 24, 1958. This new question was approved by the United States CCIR Executive Committee in Document No. 166 of March 4, 1958 and forwarded to the Director of the CCIR on March 14, 1958.

4. *CCIR Study Group V and VI Meetings, Geneva, August 1958*

The United States proposed new question appeared as Document VI/18 of the Study Group VI meeting. The International Astronautical Federation, represented by Mr. Haley, submitted a document proposing studies of the questions which appeared as Document VI/87 of Study Group VI and V/44 of Study Group V. The action of the meetings is reported in the following excerpts from the Report of the United States Delegation to Study Group VI (TD Serial No. 892, December 1, 1958):

B. *Selection and Presentation of Material for the International Radio Conference*
After some discussion in the Study Group, it seemed that there were two principal items of sufficient importance to require submission, through the Director of the C.C.I.R., to the International Radio Conference to be held next year in Geneva.
The first of these concerns the *"Protection of Frequencies Used for Radio Astronomical Measurements"* and is before the C.C.I.R. at present as Warsaw Recommendation No. 173. This recommendation has been very slightly modified, and thereby strengthened, in Document VI/92.
The other item has to do with the *"Protection of Frequences Used by Artificial Earth Satellites or Other Space Vehicles for Communication and Positional Observation."* The particular text is contained in the amended version of Annex (b) to Document VI/93, which was in turn based on a United States preparatory contribution contained in Document VI/18. As a result of representations made with the support of Document VI/87 (which is also Document V/44) by Mr. A. G. Haley, President of the International Astronautical Federation, an international organization now accredited to the I.T.U., it was decided that the question should be put directly to administrations at this time with the hope that responses might be received in time for consideration at the IXth Plenary Assembly at Los Angeles. This was accomplished in accordance with para. 2 of Article 7 of the International Telecommunications Convention (Buenos Aires 1952) by obtaining signatures of authorized representatives of 14 different administrations (12 signatures are the minimum necessary). The matter was handled by the Secretariat in such a way

that the 12 signatures covered a separate question from Study Group V having the same title and contained in Document V/41-Rev.

The questions adopted for study were published and circulated as Questions 168 and 169 in Addendum 3 to Volume I of the documents of the VIIIth Plenary Assembly of the CCIR, Warsaw, 1956.

5. *Action by United States Committees for CCIR Study Groups V and VI on Questions 168 (V) and 169 (VI)*

The United States Committees prepared a proposed Recommendation to respond to these questions which was approved by the United States CCIR Executive Committee in Document No. 210 of December 8, 1958. This proposed Recommendation was forwarded to the Director of the CCIR and published as Document No. 75 of the IXth CCIR Plenary Assembly, Los Angeles, April 1959.

6. *United States Committee for CCIR Study Group VIII*

This Committee drafted a proposed new question entitled "Monitoring at Fixed Monitoring Stations of Radio Transmissions from Space Vehicles," which was approved by the Executive Committee in Document No. 211 of December 8, 1958. This was forwarded to the Director of the CCIR and appeared as Document No. 417 of the IXth Assembly.

7. *CCIR IXth Plenary Assembly, Los Angeles, April 1959*

The results of the consideration of the subject by the Assembly are produced in CCIR printed Volumes I, II and III of the Assembly. They are:

(a) Recommendation 259 (Volume I, page 172): "Selection of Frequencies Used in Telecommunication With and Between Artificial Earth Satellites and Other Space Vehicles."

(b) Report No. 115 (Volume III, page 114): "Factors Affecting the Selection of Frequencies for Telecommunication With and Between Space Vehicles."

(c) The establishment of a new Study Group No. IV on Space Systems "To Study Technical Questions Regarding Systems of Telecommunication With and Between Locations in Space." Chairman, Prof. I. Ranzi (Italy); Vice Chairman, Dr. W. Klein (Switzerland). (Volume III, page 91).

(d) Question 188 (Volume II, page 137): "Monitoring at Fixed Monitoring Stations of Radio Transmissions from Space Vehicles." This question is assigned for study to CCIR Study Group VIII on Monitoring.

8. *United States Preparatory Committee for the ITU Administrative Radio Conference*

Concurrently with the actions on the subject in the CCIR, the United States Preparatory Committee for the Radio Conference considered the frequency needs for the new service of space telecommunications and included proposals for frequency allocation to the service.

9. *ITU Administrative Radio Conference, Geneva, August-December 1959*

The Conference made provision for frequencies to be used for research in connection with space telecommunications. The details of the allocations are contained in the new Radio Regulations. The Conference recognized that research and developments in this service were moving rapidly and the full needs of the service were not yet known and adopted Recommendation No. 35: "Relating to the Convening of an Extraordinary Administrative Radio Conference to Allocate Frequency Bands for Space Radiocommunication Purposes." The sense of the Recommendation is that consideration should be given to convening an Extraordinary Administrative Radio Conference, in principle during the latter part of 1963, to consider the matter of allocations for this service. Administrations are called on to inform the appropriate organs of the Union of the frequencies used and the technical progress achieved in the use of radio communication for space research purposes. The Recommendation refers to the studies already undertaken by the CCIR and calls on the ITU Administrative Council to take into account the results of the work of the CCIR and the information provided by administrations in making the final determination of the need to convene this Conference.

10. *ITU Plenipotentiary Conference, October-December 1959, Geneva*

The action of this Conference in the field of space communications was the adoption of Resolution No. 34: "Telecommunication and the Peaceful Uses of Outer Space Vehicles," which instructs the Secretary-General to inform the United Nations and other international organizations concerned of the decisions of the Administrative Radio Conference, Geneva, 1959, and of the technical studies being undertaken by the International Radio Consultative Committee.

11. *United States Action to Carry Out Work for CCIR Study Group IV*

The Department of State took action, in the summer of 1959, to form a United States Preparatory Committee for CCIR Study Group IV. Dr. John Hagen, NASA, was named as Chairman of the Committee.

12. *United States Action to Comply with Requirements of Recommendation 35*

The Department of State, in March 1960, requested the Federal Communications Commission and the Interdepartmental Radio Advisory Committee to bear in mind the requests in Recommendation 35 and to furnish the Department in due course their views or other information to be submitted to the appropriate organs of the ITU. Any matters involving CCIR study would of course be referred to the appropriate United States CCIR groups. In this connection, it should be noted that the Federal Communications Commission has reopened its Docket No. 11866, released as of May 20, 1960, in the matter of Allocation of Frequencies in the Bands above 890 M/C and has, in Docket No. 13522, released May 20, 1960, initiated an Inquiry into the Allocation of Frequency Bands for Space Communications.

13. *Possible International Meeting of CCIR Study Group IV*

While no definite date has been determined for a meeting of Study Group IV, the CCIR Assembly decided that in principle each Study Group should meet in the interim between Assemblies, and it is therefore likely that a meeting will be scheduled in 1962 to prepare any proposed recommendations or to formulate new questions for adoption by the Xth Plenary Assembly at New Delhi in early 1963.

14. *Xth CCIR Plenary Assembly—New Delhi, January-February, 1963*

The Assembly will review and approve the results of the work of the Study Groups and will formulate its recommendations on the subject for the information of the 1963 spring session of the Administrative Council and for direct submission to the Extraordinary Administrative Radio Conference under Article 13(2)(2) of the new ITU Convention, Geneva, 1959.

15. *Extraordinary Administrative Radio Conference*

Since the Council will decide on the time of the Conference only during its spring 1963 session, it can be assumed that, to allow time for preparation, the earliest date to convene it would probably be in the autumn of 1963.

NOTE: The information in this document was assembled primarily for the use of the United States Committee for CCIR Study Group IV on Space Systems. Since the subject has wide interest at this time, however, the document has been published in this form for general distribution.

	Unclassified
DEPARTMENT OF STATE	TD Serial No. 908
Telecommunications Division	Addendum 1.
	June 20, 1960
	International Radio
	Consultative Committee
	Doc. No. 26

Add to numbered paragraph 7 . . .

(e) Two questions directed to U.R.S.I. (Volume II, pages 32 and 36) Resolution 40, Influence of the Troposphere on frequencies used for telecommunication with and between space vehicles, and Resolution 47, Effects of the Ionosphere on Radio Waves used for telecommunication with and between Space Vehicles Beyond the Lower Atmosphere.

Add to numbered paragraph 9 . . .

Also the conference adopted Resolution No. 7 which has become CCIR Question 208, assigned to Study Group IV (Addendum 1, April 1960, page 92a, Volume II): "Radio Emissions from Artificial Earth-Satellites and other Space Vehicles."

II. UNITED STATES LAWS

II-A. NATIONAL AERONAUTICS AND SPACE ACT, AS AMENDED

AN ACT

To provide for research into problems of flight within and outside the earth's atmosphere, and for other purposes.

Be it enacted by the Senate and House of Representatives of the United States of America in Congress assembled,

TITLE I—SHORT TITLE, DECLARATION OF POLICY, AND DEFINITIONS

SHORT TITLE

Sec. 101. This Act may be cited as the "National Aeronautics and Space Act of 1958."

(a) The Congress declares that it is the policy of the United States that activities in space should be devoted to peaceful purposes for the benefit of all mankind.

(b) The Congress declares that the general welfare and security of the United States require that adequate provision be made for aeronautical and space activities. The Congress further declares that such activities shall be the responsibility of, and shall be directed by, a civilian agency exercising control over aeronautical and space activities sponsored by the United States, except that activities peculiar to or primarily associated with the development of weapons systems, military operations, or the defense of the United States (including the research and development necessary to make effective provision for the defense of the United States) shall be the responsibility of, and shall be directed by, the Department of Defense; and that determination as to which such agency has responsibility for and direction of any such activity shall be made by the President in conformity with section 201(e).

(c) The aeronautical and space activities of the United States shall be conducted so as to contribute materially to one or more of the following objectives:

(1) The expansion of human knowledge of phenomena in the atmosphere and space;

(2) The improvement of the usefulness, performance, speed, safety, and efficiency of aeronautical and space vehicles;

(3) The development and operation of vehicles capable of carrying instruments, equipment, supplies, and living organisms through space;

(4) The establishment of long-range studies of the potential benefits to be gained from, the opportunities for, and the problems involved in the utilization of aeronautical and space activities for peaceful and scientific purposes;

(5) The preservation of the role of the United States as a leader in aeronautical and space science and technology and in the application thereof to the conduct of peaceful activities within and outside the atmosphere;

(6) The making available to agencies directly concerned with national defense of discoveries that have military value or significance, and the furnishing by such agencies, to the civilian agency established to direct and control nonmilitary aeronautical and space activities, of information as to discoveries which have value or significance to that agency;

(7) Cooperation by the United States with other nations and groups of nations in work done pursuant to this Act and in the peaceful application of the results thereof; and

(8) The most effective utilization of the scientific and engineering resources of the United States, with close cooperation among all interested agencies of the United States in order to avoid duplication of effort, facilities, and equipment.

(d) It is the purpose of this Act, to carry out and effectuate the policies declared in subsections (a), (b), and (c) of this section.

DEFINITIONS

Sec. 103. As used in this Act—

(1) the term "aeronautical and space activities" means (A) research into, and the solution of, problems of flight within and outside the earth's atmosphere, (B) the development, construction, testing, and operation for research purposes of aeronautical and space vehicles, and (C) such other activities as may be required for the exploration of space; and

(2) the term "aeronautical and space vehicles" means aircraft, missiles, satellites, and other space vehicles, manned and unmanned, together with related equipment, devices, components, and parts.

TITLE II—COORDINATION OF AERONAUTICAL AND SPACE ACTIVITIES

NATIONAL AERONAUTICS AND SPACE COUNCIL

Sec. 201. (a) There is established, in the Executive Office of the President, the National Aeronautics and Space Council (hereinafter called the "Council") which shall be composed of—

(1) the Vice President, who shall be Chairman of the Council;
(2) the Secretary of State;
(3) the Secretary of Defense;
(4) the Administrator of the National Aeronautics and Space Administration; and
(5) the Chairman of the Atomic Energy Commission.

(b) The President shall from time to time designate one of the members of the Council to preside over meetings of the Council during the absence, disability, or unavailability of the Chairman.

(c) Each member of the Council may designate another officer of his department or agency to serve on the Council as his alternate in his unavoidable absence.

(d) Each alternate member designated under subsection (c) of this section shall be designated to serve as such by and with the advice and consent of the Senate unless at the time of his designation he holds an office in the Federal Government to which he was appointed by and with the advice and consent of the Senate.

(e) It shall be the function of the Council to advise and assist the President, as he may request, with respect to the performance of functions in the aeronautics and space field, including the following functions—

(1) survey all significant aeronautical and space activities, including the policies, plans, programs, and accomplishments of all departments and agencies of the United States engaged in such activities;

(2) develop a comprehensive program of aeronautical and space activities to be conducted by departments and agencies of the United States;

(3) designate and fix responsibility for the direction of major aeronautical and space activities;

(4) provide for effective cooperation among all departments and agencies of the United States engaged in aeronautical and space activities, and specify, in any case in which primary responsibility for any category of aeronautical and space activities has been assigned to any department or agency, which of those activities may be carried on concurrently by other departments or agencies; and

(5) resolve differences arising among departments and agencies of the United States with respect to aeronautical and space activities under this Act, including differences as to whether a particular project is an aeronautical and space activity.

(f) The Council may employ a staff to be headed by a civilian executive secretary who shall be appointed by the President by and with the advice and consent of the Senate and shall receive compensation at the rate of $20,000 a year. The executive secretary, subject to the direction of the Council, is authorized to appoint and fix the compensation of such personnel, including not more than seven persons who may be appointed without regard to the civil service laws or the Classification Act of 1949 and compensated at the rate of not more than $19,000 a year, as may be necessary to perform such duties as may be prescribed by the Council in connection with the performance of its functions. Each appointment under this subsection shall be subject to the same security requirements as those established for personnel of the National Aeronautics and Space Administration appointed under section 203 (b) (2) of this Act. Other provisions of law or regulations relating to Government employment (except those relating to pay and retirement) shall apply to council employees reporting directly to the chairman to the extent that such provisions are applicable to employees in the office of the Vice President.

NATIONAL AERONAUTICS AND SPACE ADMINISTRATION

Sec. 202. (a) There is hereby established the National Aeronautics and Space Administration (hereinafter called the "Administration"). The Administration shall be headed by an Administrator, who shall be appointed from civilian life by the President by and with the advice and consent of the Senate, and shall receive compensation at the rate of $22,500 per annum. Under the supervision and direction of the President, the Administrator shall be responsible for the exercise of all powers and the discharge of all duties of the Administration, and shall have authority and control over all personnel and activities thereof.

(b) There shall be in the Administration a Deputy Administrator, who shall be appointed from civilian life by the President by and with the advice and consent of the Senate, shall receive compensation at the rate of $21,500 per annum, and shall perform such duties and exercise such powers as the Administrator may prescribe. The Deputy Administrator shall act for, and exercise the powers of, the Administrator during his absence or disability.

(c) The Administrator and the Deputy Administrator shall not engage in any other business, vocation, or employment while serving as such.

FUNCTIONS OF THE ADMINISTRATION

Sec. 203. (a) The Administration, in order to carry out the purpose of this Act, shall—

(1) plan, direct, and conduct aeronautical and space activities;

(2) arrange for participation by the scientific community in planning scientific measurements and observations to be made through use of aeronautical and space vehicles, and conduct or arrange for the conduct of such measurements and observations; and

(3) provide for the widest practicable and appropriate dissemination of information concerning its activities and the results thereof.

(b) In the performance of its functions the Administration is authorized—

(1) to make, promulgate, issue, rescind, and amend rules and regulations governing the manner of its operations and the exercise of the powers vested in it by law;

(2) to appoint and fix the compensation of such officers and employees as may be necessary to carry out such functions. Such officers and employees shall be appointed in accordance with the civil service laws and their compensation fixed in accordance with the Classification Act of 1949, except that (A) to the extent the Administrator deems such action necessary to the discharge of his responsibilities, he may appoint and fix the compensation (at not to exceed the highest rate of grade 18 of the General Schedule of the Classification Act of 1949, as amended, or, for a maximum of thirty positions, not to exceed $21,000 a year) of not more than four hundred and twenty-five (of which not to exceed three hundred and fifty-five may be filled prior to March 1, 1962 and not to exceed three hundred and ninety may be filled prior to July 1, 1962) of the scientific, engineering, and administrative personnel of the Administration without regard to such laws, and (B) to the extent the Administrator deems such action necessary to recruit specially qualified scientific and engineering talent, he may establish the entrance grade for scientific and engineering personnel without previous service in

the Federal Government at a level up to two grades higher than the grade provided for such personnel under the General Schedule established by the Classification Act of 1949, and fix their compensation accordingly;

(3) to acquire (by purchase, lease, condemnation, or otherwise), construct, improve, repair, operate, and maintain laboratories, research and testing sites and facilities, aeronautical and space vehicles, quarters and related accommodations for employees and dependents of employees of the Administration, and such other real and personal property (including patents), or any interest therein, as the Administration deems necessary within and outside the continental United States; to acquire by lease or otherwise, through the Administrator of General Services, buildings or parts of buildings in the District of Columbia for the use of the Administration for a period not to exceed ten years without regard to the Act of March 3, 1877 (40 U.S.C. 34); to lease to others such real and personal property; to sell and otherwise dispose of real and personal property (including patents and rights thereunder) in accordance with the provisions of the Federal Property and Administrative Services Act of 1949, as amended (40 U.S.C. 471 et seq.); and to provide by contract or otherwise for cafeterias and other necessary facilities for the welfare of employees of the Administration at its installations and purchase and maintain equipment therefor;

(4) to accept unconditional gifts or donations of services, money, or property, real, personal, or mixed, tangible or intangible;

(5) without regard to section 3648 of the Revised Statutes, as amended (31 U.S.C. 529), to enter into and perform such contracts, leases, cooperative agreements, or other transactions as may be necessary in the conduct of its work and on such terms as it may deem appropriate, with any agency or instrumentality of the United States, or with any State, Territory, or possession, or with any political subdivision thereof, or with any person, form, association, corporation, or educational institution. To the maximum extent practicable and consistent with the accomplishment of the purpose of this Act, such contracts, leases, agreements, and other transactions shall be allocated by the Administrator in a manner which will enable small-business concerns to participate equitably and proportionately in the conduct of the work of the Administration;

(6) to use, with their consent, the services, equipment, personnel, and facilities of Federal and other agencies with or without reimbursement, and on a similar basis to cooperate with other public and private agencies and instrumentalities in the use of services, equipment, and facilities. Each department and agency of the Federal Government shall cooperate fully with the Administration in making its services, equipment, personnel, and facilities available to the Administration, and any such department or agency is authorized, notwithstanding any other provision of law, to transfer to or to receive from the Administration, without reimbursement, aeronautical and space vehicles, and supplies and equipment other than administrative supplies or equipment;

(7) to appoint such advisory committees as may be appropriate for purposes of consultation and advice to the Administration in the performance of its functions;

(8) to establish within the Administration such offices and procedures as may be appropriate to provide for the greatest possible coordination of its activities under this Act with related scientific and other activities being carried on by other public and private agencies and organizations;

(9) to obtain services as authorized by section 15 of the Act of August 2, 1946 (5 U.S.C. 55a), at rates not to exceed $100 per diem for individuals;

(10) when determined by the Administrator to be necessary, and subject to such security investigations as he may determine to be appropriate, to employ aliens without regard to statutory provisions prohibiting payment of compensation to aliens;

(11) to employ retired commissioned officers of the armed forces of the United States and compensate them at the rate established for the positions occupied by them within the Administration, subject only to the limitations in pay set forth in Section 212 of the Act of June 30, 1932, as amended (5 U.S.C. 59a);

(12) with the approval of the President, to enter into cooperative agreements under which members of the Army, Navy, Air Force, and Marine Corps may be detailed by the appropriate Secretary for services in the performance of functions under this Act to the same extent as that to which they might be lawfully assigned in the Department of Defense; and

(13) (A) to consider, ascertain, adjust, determine, settle, and pay, on behalf of the United States, in full satisfaction thereof, any claim for $5,000 or less against the United States for bodily injury, death, or damage to or loss of real or personal property resulting from the conduct of the Administration's functions as specified in subsection (a) of this section, where such claim is presented to the Administration in writing within two years after the accident or incident out of which the claim arises; and

(B) if the Administration considers that a claim in excess of $5,000 is meritorious and would otherwise be covered by this paragraph, to report the facts and circumstances thereof to the Congress for its consideration.

(14) to reimburse, to the extent determined by the Administrator or his designee to be fair and reasonable, the owners and tenants of land and interests in land acquired on or after November 1, 1961, by the United States for use by the Administration by purchase, condemnation, or otherwise for expenses and losses and damages incurred by such owners and tenants as a direct result of moving themselves, their families, and their possessions because of said acquisition. Such reimbursement shall be in addition to, but not in duplication of, any payments that may otherwise be authorized by law to be made to such owners and tenants. The total of any such reimbursement to any owner or tenant shall in no event exceed 25 per centum of the fair value, as determined by the Administrator, of the parcel of land or interest in land to which the reimbursement is related. No payment under this paragraph shall be made unless application therefor, supported by an itemized statement of the expenses, losses, and damages incurred, is submitted to the Administrator within one year from (a) the date upon which the parcel of land or interest in land is to be vacated under agreement with the Government by the owner or tenant or pursuant to law, including but not limited to, an order of a court, or (b) the date upon which the parcel of land or interest

in the land involved is vacated, whichever first occurs. The Administrator may perform any and all acts and make such rules and regulations as he deems necessary and proper for the purpose of carrying out this paragraph. All functions performed under this paragraph shall be exempt from the operation of sections 1001-1011 of Title 5, except as to the requirements of section 1002 of Title 5. Funds available to the Administration for the acquisition of real property or interests therein shall also be available for carrying out this paragraph.

CIVILIAN-MILITARY LIAISON COMMITTEE

Sec. 204. (a) There shall be a Civilian-Military Liaison Committee consisting of—

(1) a Chairman, who shall be the head thereof and who shall be appointed by the President, shall serve at the pleasure of the President, and shall receive compensation (in the manner provided in subsection (d) at the rate of $20,000 per annum;

(2) one or more representatives from the Department of Defense, and one or more representatives from each of the Departments of the Army, Navy, and Air Force, to be assigned by the Secretary of Defense to serve on the Committee without additional compensation; and

(3) representatives from the Administration, to be assigned by the Administrator to serve on the Committee without additional compensation, equal in number to the number of representatives assigned to serve on the Committee under paragraph (2).

(b) The Administration and the Department of Defense, through the Liaison Committee, shall advise and consult with each other on all matters within their respective jurisdictions relating to aeronautical and space activities and shall keep each other fully and currently informed with respect to such activities.

(c) If the Secretary of Defense concludes that any request, action, proposed action, or failure to act on the part of the Administrator is adverse to the responsibilities of the Department of Defense, or the Administrator concludes that any request, action, proposed action, or failure to act on the part of the Department of Defense is adverse to the responsibilities of the Administration, and the Administrator and the Secretary of Defense are unable to reach an agreement with respect thereto, either the Administrator or the Secretary of Defense may refer the matter to the President for his decision (which shall be final) as provided in section 201(e).

(d) Notwithstanding the provisions of any other law, any active or retired officer of the Army, Navy, or Air Force may serve as Chairman of the Liaison Committee without prejudice to his active or retired status as such officer. The compensation received by any such officer for his service as Chairman of the Liaison Committee shall be equal to the amount (if any) by which the compensation fixed by subsection (a) (1) of this section for such Chairman exceeds his pay and allowances (including special and incentive pays) as an active officer, or his retired pay.

Sec. 205. The Administration, under the foreign policy guidance of the President, may engage in a program of international cooperation in work done pursuant to this Act, and in the peaceful application of the results thereof, pursuant to agreements made by the President with the advice and consent of the Senate.

REPORTS TO THE CONGRESS

Sec. 206. (a) The Administration shall submit to the President for transmittal to the Congress, semiannually and at such other times as it deems desirable, a report of its activities and accomplishments.

(b) The President shall transmit to the Congress in January of each year a report, which shall include (1) a comprehensive description of the programed activities and the accomplishments of all agencies of the United States in the field of aeronautics and space activities during the preceding calendar year, and (2) an evaluation of such activities and accomplishments in terms of the attainment of, or the failure to attain, the objectives described in section 102(c) of this Act.

(c) Any report made under this section shall contain such recommendations for additional legislation as the Administrator or the President may consider necessary or desirable for the attainment of the objectives described in section 102(c) of this Act.

(d) No information which has been classified for reasons of national security shall be included in any report made under this section, unless such information has been declassified by, or pursuant to authorization given by, the President.

TITLE III—MISCELLANEOUS

NATIONAL ADVISORY COMMITTEE FOR AERONAUTICS

Sec. 301. (a) The National Advisory Committee for Aeronautics, on the effective date of this section, shall cease to exist. On such date all functions, powers, duties, and obligations, and all real and personal property, personnel (other than members of the Committee), funds, and records of that organization, shall be transferred to the Administration.

(b) Section 2302 of title 10 of the United States Code is amended by striking out "or the Executive Secretary of the National Advisory Committee for Aeronautics." and inserting in lieu thereof "or the Administrator of the National Aeronautics and Space Administration."; and section 2303 of such title 10 is amended by striking out "The National Advisory Committee for Aeronautics." and inserting in lieu thereof "or National Aeronautics and Space Administration".

(d) The Unitary Wind Tunnel Plan Act of 1949 (50 U.S.C. 511-515) is amended (1) by striking out "The National Advisory Committee for Aeronautics (hereinafter referred to as the 'Committee')" and inserting in lieu thereof "The Administrator of the National Aeronautics and Space Administration (hereinafter referred to as the 'Administrator')"; (2) by striking out "Committee" or "Committee's" wherever they appear and inserting in lieu thereof

"Administrator" and "Administrator's", respectively; and (3) by striking out "its" wherever it appears and inserting in lieu thereof "his".

(e) This section shall take effect ninety days after the date of the enactment of this Act, or on any earlier date on which the Administrator shall determine, and announce by proclamation published in the Federal Register, that the Administration has been organized and is prepared to discharge the duties and exercise the powers conferred upon it by this Act.

TRANSFER OF RELATED FUNCTIONS

Sec. 302. (a) Subject to the provisions of this section, the President, for a period of four years after the date of enactment of this Act, may transfer to the Administration any functions (including powers, duties, activities, facilities, and parts of functions) of any other department or agency of the United States, or of any officer or organizational entity thereof, which relate primarily to the functions, powers, and duties of the Administration as prescribed by section 203 of this Act. In connection with any such transfer, the President may, under this section or other applicable authority, provide for appropriate transfers of records, property, civilian personnel, and funds.

(b) Whenever any such transfer is made before January 1, 1959, the President shall transmit to the Speaker of the House of Representatives and the President pro tempore of the Senate a full and complete report concerning the nature and effect of such transfer.

(c) After December 31, 1958, no transfer shall be made under this section until (1) a full and complete report concerning the nature and effect of such proposed transfer has been transmitted by the President to the Congress, and (2) the first period of sixty calendar days of regular session of the Congress following the date of receipt of such report by the Congress has expired without the adoption by the Congress of a concurrent resolution stating that the Congress does not favor such transfer.

ACCESS TO INFORMATION

Sec. 303. Information obtained or developed by the Administrator in the performance of his functions under this Act shall be made available for public inspection, except (A) information authorized or required by Federal statute to be withheld, and (B) information classified to protect the national security: Provided, That nothing in this Act shall authorize the withholding of information by the Administrator from the duly authorized committees of the Congress.

SECURITY

Sec. 304. (a) The Administrator shall establish such security requirements, restrictions, and safeguards as he deems necessary in the interest of the national security. The Administrator may arrange with the Civil Service Commission for the conduct of such security or other personnel investigations of the Administration's officers, employees, and consultants, and its contractors and sub-contractors and their officers and employees, actual or prospective, as he deems appropriate; and if any such investigation develops any data reflecting that the individual who is the subject thereof is of questionable loyalty the matter shall be referred to the Federal Bureau of Investigation for the conduct of a full field investigation, the results of which shall be furnished to the Administrator.

(b) The Atomic Energy Commission may authorize any of its employees, or employees of any contractor, prospective contractor, licensee, or prospective licensee of the Atomic Energy Commission or any other person authorized to have access to Restricted Data by the Atomic Energy Commission under subsection 145b. of the Atomic Energy Act of 1954 (42 U.S.C. 2165(b)), to permit any member, officer, or employee of the Council, or the Administrator, or any officer, employee, member of an advisory committee, contractor, subcontractor, or officer or employee of a contractor or subcontractor of the Administration, to have access to Restricted Data relating to aeronautical and space activities which is required in the performance of his duties and so certified by the Council or the Administrator, as the case may be, but only if (1) the Council or Administrator or designer thereof has determined, in accordance with the established personnel security procedures and standards of the Council or Administration, that permitting such individual to have access to such Restricted Data will not endanger the common defense and security, and (2) the Council or Administrator or designee thereof finds that the established personnel and other security procedures and standards of the Council or Administration are adequate and in reasonable conformity to the standards established by the Atomic Energy Commission under section 145 of the Atomic Energy Act of 1954 (42 U.S.C. 2165). Any individual granted access to such Restricted Data pursuant to this subsection may exchange such Data with any individual who (A) is an officer or employee of the Department of Defense, or any department or agency thereof, or a member of the armed forces, or a contractor or subcontractor of any such department, agency, or armed force, or an officer or employee of any such contractor or subcontractor, and (B) has been authorized to have access to Restricted Data under the provisions of section 143 of the Atomic Energy Act of 1954 (42 U.S.C. 2163).

(c) Chapter 37 of title 18 of the United States Code (entitled Espionage and Censorship) is amended by—

(1) adding at the end thereof the following new section:
"§799. Violation of regulations of National Aeronautics and Space Administration

"Whoever willfully shall violate, attempt to violate, or conspire to violate any regulation or order promulgated by the Administration for the protection or security of any laboratory, station, base or other facility, or similar vehicle, or part thereof, or other property or equipment in the custody of the Administration, or any real or personal property or equipment in the custody of the Administration, or any real or personal property or equipment in the custody of any contractor under any contract with the Administration or any subcontractor of any such contractor, shall be fined not more than $5,000, or imprisoned not more than one year, or both."

(2) adding at the end of the sectional analysis thereof the following new item:

"§799. Violation of regulations of National Aeronautics and Space Administration."

(d) Section 1114 of title 18 of the United States Code is amended by inserting immediately before "while engaged in the performance of his official duties" the following: "or any officer or employee of the National Aeronautics and Space Administration directed to guard and protect property of the United States under the administration and control of the National Aeronautics and Space Administration,".

(e) The Administrator may direct such of the officers and employees of the Administration as he deems necessary in the public interest to carry firearms while in the conduct of their official duties. The Administrator may also authorize such of those employees of the contractors and subcontractors of the Administration engaged in the protection of property owned by the United States and located at facilities owned by or contracted to the United States as he deems necessary in the public interest, to carry firearms while in the conduct of their official duties.

PROPERTY RIGHTS IN INVENTIONS

Sec. 305. (a) Whenever any invention is made in the performance of any work under any contract of the Administration, and the Administrator determines that—

(1) the person who made the invention was employed or assigned to perform research, development, or exploration work and the invention is related to the work he was employed or assigned to perform, or that it was within the scope of his employment duties, whether or not it was made during working hours, or with a contribution by the Government of the use of Government facilities, equipment, materials, allocated funds, information proprietary to the Government, or services of Government employees during working hours; or

(2) the person who made the invention was not employed or assigned to perform research, development, or exploration work, but the invention is nevertheless related to the contract, or to the work or duties he was employed or assigned to perform, and was made during working hours, or with a contribution from the Government of the sort referred to in clause (1),

such invention shall be the exclusive property of the United States, and if such invention is patentable a patent therefor shall be issued to the United States upon application made by the Administrator, unless the Administrator waives all or any part of the rights of the United States to such invention in conformity with the provisions of subsection (f) of this section.

(b) Each contract entered into by the Administrator with any party for the performance of any work shall contain effective provisions under which such party shall furnish promptly to the Administrator a written report containing full and complete technical information concerning any invention, discovery, improvement, or innovation which may be made in the performance of any such work.

(c) No patent may be issued to any applicant other than the Administrator for any invention which appears to the Commissioner of Patents to have significant utility in the conduct of aeronautical and space activities unless the applicant files with the Commissioner, with the application or within thirty days after request therefor by the Commissioner, a written statement executed under oath setting forth the full facts concerning the circumstances under which such invention was made and stating the relationship (if any) of such invention to the performance of any work under any contract of the Administration. Copies of each such statement and the application to which it relates shall be transmitted forthwith by the Commissioner to the Administrator.

(d) Upon any application as to which any such statement has been transmitted to the Administrator, the Commissioner may, if the invention is patentable, issue a patent to the applicant unless the Administrator, within ninety days after receipt of such application and statement, request that such patent be issued to him on behalf of the United States. If, within such time, the Administrator files such a request with the Commissioner, the Commissioner shall transmit notice thereof to the applicant, and shall issue such patent to the Administrator unless the applicant within thirty days after receipt of such notice request a hearing before a Board of Patent Interferences on the question whether the Administrator is entitled under this section to receive such patent. The Board may hear and determine, in accordance with rules and procedures established for interference cases, the question so presented, and its determination shall be subject to appeal by the applicant or by the Administrator to the Court of Customs and Patent Appeals in accordance with procedures governing appeals from decisions of the Board of Patent Interferences in other proceedings.

(e) Whenever any patent has been issued to any applicant in conformity with subsection (d), and the Administrator thereafter has reason to believe that the statement filed by the applicant in connection therewith contained any false representation of any material fact, the Administrator within five years after the date of issuance of such patent may file with the Commissioner a request for the transfer to the Administrator of title to such patent on the records of the Commissioner. Notice of any such request shall be transmitted by the Commissioner to the owner of record of such patent, and title to such patent shall be so transferred to the Administrator unless within thirty days after receipt of such notice such owner of record requests a hearing before a Board of Patent Interferences on the question whether any such false representation was contained in such statement. Such question shall be heard and determined, and determination thereof shall be subject to review, in the manner prescribed by subsection (d) for questions arising thereunder. No request made by the Administrator under this subsection for the transfer of title to any patent, and no prosecution for the violation of any criminal statute, shall be barred by any failure of the Administrator to make a request under subsection (d) for the issuance of such patent to him, or by any notice previously given by the Administrator stating that he had no objection to the issuance of such patent to the applicant therefor.

(f) Under such regulations in conformity with this subsection as the Administrator shall prescribe, he may waive all or any part of the rights of the United States under this section with respect to any invention or class of inventions made or which may be made by any person or class of persons in the performance of any work required by any contract of the Administration if the Administrator determines that the interests of the United States will be served thereby. Any such waiver may be made upon such terms and under such conditions as the Administrator shall determine to be required for the protection of the interests of the United States. Each such waiver made with respect to any invention shall be subject to the reservation by the Administrator of an irrevocable, nonexclusive, nontransferable, royalty-free license for the practice of such invention throughout the world by or on behalf of the United States or any foreign government pursuant to any treaty or agreement with the United States. Each proposal for any waiver under this subsection shall be referred to an Inventions and Contributions Board which shall be established by the Administrator within the Administration. Such Board shall accord to each interested party an opportunity for hearing, and shall transmit to the Administrator its findings of fact with respect to such proposal and its recommendations for action to be taken with respect thereto.

(g) The Administrator shall determine, and promulgate regulations specifying, the terms and conditions upon which licenses will be granted by the Administration for the practice by any person (other than an agency of the United States) of any invention for which the Administrator holds a patent on behalf of the United States.

(h) The Administrator is authorized to take all suitable and necessary steps to protect any invention or discovery to which he has title, and to require that contractors or persons who retain title to inventions or discoveries under this section protect the inventions or discoveries to which the Administration has or may acquire a license of use.

(i) The Administration shall be considered a defense agency of the United States for the purpose of chapter 17 of title 35 of the United States Code.

(j) As used in this section—

(1) the term "person" means any individual, partnership, corporation, association, institution, or other entity;

(2) the term "contract" means any actual or proposed contract, agreement, understanding, or other arrangement, and includes any assignment, substitution of parties, or subcontract executed or entered into thereunder; and

(3) the term "made", when used in relation to any invention, means the conception or first actual reduction to practice of such invention.

CONTRIBUTIONS AWARDS

Sec. 306. (a) Subject to the provisions of this section, the Administrator is authorized, upon his own initiative or upon application of any person, to make a monetary award, in such amount and upon such terms as he shall determine to be warranted, to any person (as defined by section 305) for any scientific or technical contribution to the Administration which is determined by the Administrator to have significant value in the conduct of aeronautical and space activities. Each application made for any such award shall be referred to the Inventions and Contributions Board established under section 305 of this Act. Such Board shall accord to each such applicant an opportunity for hearing upon such application, and shall transmit to the Administrator its recommendation as to the terms of the award, if any, to be made to such applicant for such contribution. In determining the terms and conditions of any award the Administrator shall take into account—

(1) the value of the contribution to the United States;

(2) the aggregate amount of any sums which have been expended by the applicant for the development of such contribution;

(3) the amount of any compensation (other than salary received for services rendered as an officer or employee of the Government) previously received by the applicant for or on account of the use of such contribution by the United States; and

(4) Such other factors as the Administrator shall determine to be material.

(b) If more than one applicant under subsection (a) claims an interest in the same contribution, the Administrator shall ascertain and determine the respective interests of such applicants and shall apportion any award to be made with respect to such contribution among such applicants in such proportions as he shall determine to be equitable. No award may be made under subsection (a) with respect to any contribution—

(1) unless the applicant surrenders, by such means as the Administrator shall determine to be effective, all claims which such applicant may have to receive any compensation (other than the award made under this section) for the use of such contribution or any element thereof at any time by or on behalf of the United States, or by or on behalf of any foreign government pursuant to any treaty or agreement with the United States, within the United States or at any other place.

(2) in any amount exceeding $100,000, unless the Administrator has transmitted to the appropriate committees of the Congress a full and complete report concerning the amount and terms of, and the basis for, such proposed award, and thirty calendar days of regular session of the Congress have expired after receipt of such report by such committees.

APPROPRIATIONS

Sec. 307. (a) There are hereby authorized to be appropriated such sums as may be necessary to carry out this Act, except that nothing in this Act shall authorize the appropriation of any amount for (1) the acquisition or condemnation of any real property, or (2) any other item of a capital nature (such as plant or facility acquisition, construction, or expansion) which exceeds $250,000. Sums appropriated pursuant to this subsection for the construction of facilities, or for research and development activities, shall remain available until expended.

(b) Any funds appropriated for the construction of facilities may be used for emergency repairs of existing facilities when such existing facilities are made inoperative by major breakdown, accident, or other circumstances and such repairs are deemed by the Administrator to be of greater urgency than the construction of new facilities.

Original Act Approved July 29, 1958.

II-B. COMMUNICATIONS SATELLITE ACT OF 1962

AN ACT

To provide for the establishment, ownership, operation, and regulation of a commercial communications satellite system, and for other purposes.

Be it enacted by the Senate and House of Representatives of the United States of America in Congress assembled,

TITLE I—SHORT TITLE, DECLARATION OF POLICY, AND DEFINITIONS

SHORT TITLE

Sec. 101. This Act may be cited as the "Communications Satellite Act of 1962."

DECLARATION OF POLICY AND PURPOSE

Sec. 102. (a) The Congress hereby declares that it is the policy of the United States to establish, in conjunction and in cooperation with other countries, as expeditiously as practicable a commercial communications satellite system, as part of an improved global communications network, which will be responsive to public needs and national objectives, which will serve the communication needs of the United States and other countries, and which will contribute to world peace and understanding.

(b) The new and expanded telecommunication services are to be made available as promptly as possible and are to be extended to provide global coverage at the earliest practicable date. In effectuating this program, care and attention will be directed toward providing such services to economically less developed countries and areas as well as those more highly developed, toward efficient and economical use of the electromagnetic frequency spectrum, and toward the reflection of the benefits of this new technology in both quality of services and charges for such services.

(c) In order to facilitate this development and to provide for the widest possible participation by private enterprise, United States participation in the global system shall be in the form of a private corporation, subject to appropriate governmental regulation. It is the intent of Congress that all authorized users shall have nondiscriminatory access to the system. That maximum competition be maintained in the provision of equipment and services utilized by the system; that the corporation created under this Act be so organized and operated as to maintain and strengthen competition in the provision of communications services to the public; and that the activities of the corporation created under this Act and of the persons or companies participating in the ownership of the corporation shall be consistent with the Federal antitrust laws.

(d) It is not the intent of Congress by this Act to preclude the use of the communications satellite system for domestic communications services where consistent with the provisions of this Act nor to preclude the creation of additional communications satellite systems, if required to meet unique governmental needs or if otherwise required in the national interest.

DEFINITIONS

Sec. 103. As used in this Act, and unless the context otherwise requires—

(1) The term "communications satellite system" refers to a system of communications satellites in space whose purpose is to relay telecommunication information between satellite terminal stations, together with such associated equipment and facilities for tracking, guidance, control, and command functions as are not part of the generalized launching, tracking, control, and command facilities for all space purposes;

(2) the term "satellite terminal station" refers to a complex of communication equipment located on the earth's surface, operationally connected with one or more terrestrial communication systems, and capable of transmitting telecommunications to or receiving telecommunications from a communications satellite system;

(3) the term "communications satellite" means an earth satellite which is intentionally used to relay telecommunication information;

(4) the term "associated equipment and facilities" refers to facilities other than satellite terminal stations and communications satellites, to be constructed and operated for the primary purpose of a communications satellite system, whether for administration and management, for research and development, or for direct support of space operations;

(5) the term "research and development" refers to the conception, design, and first creation of experimental or prototype operational devices for the operation of a communications satellite system, including the assembly of separate components into a working whole, as distinguished from the term "production," which relates to the construction of such devices to fixed specifications compatible with repetitive duplication for operational applications; and

(6) the term "telecommunication" means any transmission, emission or reception of signs, signals, writings, images, and sounds or intelligence of any nature by wire, radio, optical, or other electromagnetic systems;

(7) the term "communications common carrier" has the same meaning as the term "common carrier" has when used in the Communications Act of 1934, as amended, and in addition includes, but only for purposes of sections 303 and 304, any individual, partnership, association, joint-stock company, trust, corporation, or other entity which owns or controls, directly or indirectly, or is under direct or indirect common control with, any such carrier; and the term "authorized carrier", except as otherwise provided for purposes of section 304 by section 304 (b) (1), means a communications common carrier which has been authorized by the Federal Communications Commission under the Communications Act of 1934, as amended, to provide services by means of communications satellites;

(8) the term "corporation" means the corporation authorized by title III of this Act;

(9) the term "Administration" means the National Aeronautics and Space Administration; and

(10) the term "Commission" means the Federal Communications Commission.

TITLE II—FEDERAL COORDINATION, PLANNING, AND REGULATION

IMPLEMENTATION OF POLICY

Sec. 201. In order to achieve the objectives and to carry out the purposes of this Act—

(a) the President shall—

(1) aid in the planning and development and foster the execution of a national program for the establishment and operation, as expeditiously as possible, of a commercial communications satellite system;

(2) provide for continuous review of all phases of the development and operation of such a system, including the activities of a communications satellite corporation authorized under title III of this Act;

(3) coordinate the activities of governmental agencies with responsibilities in the field of telecommunication, so as to insure that there is full and effective compliance at all times with the policies set forth in this Act;

(4) exercise such supervision over relationships of the corporation with foreign governments or entities or with international bodies as may be appropriate to assure that such relationships shall be consistent with the national interest and foreign policy of the United States;

(5) insure that timely arrangements are made under which there can be foreign participation in the establishment and use of a communications satellite system;

(6) take all necessary steps to insure the availability and appropriate utilization of the communications satellite system for general governmental purposes except where a separate communications satellite system is required to meet unique governmental needs or if otherwise required in the national interest; and

(7) so exercise his authority as to help attain coordinated and efficient use of the electromagnetic spectrum and the technical compatibility of the system with existing communications facilities both in the United States and abroad.

(b) the National Aeronautics and Space Administration shall—

(1) advise the Commission on technical characteristics of the communications satellite system;

(2) cooperate with the corporation in research and development to the extent deemed appropriate by the Administration in the public interest;

(3) assist the corporation in the conduct of its research and development program by furnishing to the corporation, when requested, on a reimbursable basis, such satellite launching and associated services as the Administration deems necessary for the most expeditious and economical development of the communications satellite system;

(4) consult with the corporation with respect to the technical characteristics of the communications satellite system;

(5) furnish to the corporation, on request and on a reimbursable basis, satellite launching and associated services required for the establishment, operation, and maintenance of the communications satellite system approved by the Commission; and

(6) to the extent feasible, furnish other services, on a reimbursable basis, to the corporation in connection with the establishment and operation of the system.

(c) the Federal Communications Commission, in its administration of the provisions of the Communications Act of 1934, as amended, and as supplemented by this Act, shall—

(1) insure effective competition, including the use of competitive bidding where appropriate, in the procurement by the corporation and communications common carriers of apparatus, equipment and services required for the establishment and operation of the communications satellite system and satellite terminal stations; and the Commission shall consult with the Small Business Administration and solicit its recommendations on measures and procedures which will insure that small business concerns are given an equitable opportunity to share in the procurement program of the corporation for property and services, including but not limited to research, development, construction, maintenance, and repair;

(2) insure that all present and future authorized carriers shall have nondiscriminatory use of, and equitable access to, the communications satellite system and satellite terminal stations under just and reasonable charges, classifications, practices, regulations, and other terms and conditions and regulate the manner in which available facilities of the system and stations are allocated among such users thereof;

(3) in any case where the Secretary of State, after obtaining the advice of the Administration as to technical feasibility, has advised that commercial communication to a particular foreign point by means of the communications satellite system and satellite terminal stations should be established in the national interest, institute forthwith appropriate proceedings under section 214 (d) of the Communications Act of 1934, as amended, to require the establishment of such communication by the corporation and the appropriate common carrier or carriers;

(4) insure that facilities of the communications satellite system and satellite terminal stations are technically compatible and interconnected operationally with each other and with existing communications facilities;

(5) prescribe such accounting regulations and systems and engage in such ratemaking procedures as will insure that any economies made possible by a communications satellite system are appropriately reflected in rates for public communication services;

(6) approve technical characteristics of the operational communications satellite system to be employed by the corporation and of the satellite terminal stations; and

(7) grant appropriate authorizations for the construction and operation of each satellite terminal station, either to the corporation or to one or more

authorized carriers or to the corporation and one or more such carriers jointly, as will best serve the public interest, convenience, and necessity. In determining the public interest, convenience, and necessity the Commission shall authorize the construction and operation of such stations by communications common carriers or the corporation, without preference to either;

(8) authorize the corporation to issue any shares of capital stock, except the initial issue of capital stock referred to in section 304 (a), or to borrow any money, or to assume any obligation in respect of the securities of any other person, upon a finding that such issuance, borrowing, or assumption is compatible with the public interest, convenience, and necessity and is necessary or appropriate for or consistent with carrying out the purposes and objectives of this Act by the corporation;

(9) insure that no substantial additions are made by the corporation or carriers with respect to facilities of the system or satellite terminal stations unless such additions are required by the public interest, convenience, and necessity;

(10) require, in accordance with the procedural requirements of section 214 of the Communications Act of 1934, as amended, that additions be made by the corporation or carriers with respect to facilities of the system or satellite terminal stations where such additions would serve the public interest, convenience, and necessity; and

(11) make rules and regulations to carry out the provisions of this Act.

TITLE III—CREATION OF A COMMUNICATIONS SATELLITE CORPORATION

CREATION OF CORPORATION

Sec. 301. There is hereby authorized to be created a communications satellite corporation for profit which will not be an agency or establishment of the United States Government. The corporation shall be subject to the provisions of this Act and, to the extent consistent with this Act, to the District of Columbia Business Corporation Act. The right to repeal, alter, or amend this Act at any time is expressly reserved.

PROCESS OF ORGANIZATION

Sec. 302. The President of the United States shall appoint incorporators, by and with the advice and consent of the Senate, who shall serve as the initial board of directors until the first annual meeting of stockholders or until their successors are elected and qualified. Such incorporators shall arrange for an initial stock offering and take whatever other actions are necessary to establish the corporation, including the filing of articles of incorporation, as approved by the President.

DIRECTORS AND OFFICERS

Sec. 303. (a) The corporation shall have a board of directors consisting of individuals who are citizens of the United States, of whom one shall be elected annually by the board to serve as chairman. Three members of the board shall be appointed by the President of the United States, by and with the advice and consent of the Senate, effective the date on which the other members are elected, and for terms of three years or until their successors have been appointed and qualified, except that the first three members of the board so appointed shall continue in office for terms of one, two, and three years, respectively, and any member so appointed to fill a vacancy shall be appointed only for the unexpired term of the director whom he succeeds. Six members of the board shall be elected annually by those stockholders who are communications common carriers and six shall be elected annually by the other stockholders of the corporation. No stockholder who is a communications common carrier and no trustee for such a stockholder shall vote, either directly or indirectly, through the votes of subsidiaries or affiliated companies, nominees, or any persons subject to his direction or control, for more than three candidates for membership on the board. Subject to such limitation, the articles of incorporation to be filed by the incorporators designated under section 302 shall provide for cumulative voting under section 27(d) of the District of Columbia Business Corporation Act (D.C. Code, sec. 29-911(d)).

(b) The corporation shall have a president, and such other officers as may be named and appointed by the board, at rates of compensation fixed by the board, and serving at the pleasure of the board. No individual other than a citizen of the United States may be an officer of the corporation. No officer of the corporation shall receive any salary from any source other than the corporation during the period of his employment by the corporation.

FINANCING OF THE CORPORATION

Sec. 304. (a) The corporation is authorized to issue and have outstanding, in such amounts as it shall determine, shares of capital stock, without par value, which shall carry voting rights and be eligible for dividends. The shares of such stock initially offered shall be sold at a price not in excess of $100 for each share and in a manner to encourage the widest distribution to the American public. Subject to the provisions of subsections (b) and (d) of this section, shares of stock offered under this subsection may be issued to and held by any person.

(b) (1) For the purposes of this section the term "authorized carrier" shall mean a communications common carrier which is specifically authorized or which is a member of a class of carriers authorized by the Commission to own shares of stock in the corporation upon a finding that such ownership will be consistent with the public interest, convenience, and necessity.

(2) Only those communications common carriers which are authorized carriers shall own shares of stock in the corporation at any time, and no other communications common carrier shall own shares either directly or indirectly through subsidiaries or affiliated companies, nominees, or any persons subject to its direction or control. Fifty per centum of the shares of stock authorized for issuance at any time by the corporation shall be reserved for purchase by authorized carriers and such carriers shall in the aggregate be entitled to make purchases of the reserved shares in a total number not exceeding the total number of the nonreserved shares of any issue purchased by other persons. At no

time after the initial issue is completed shall the aggregate of the shares of voting stock of the corporation owned by authorized carriers directly or indirectly through subsidiaries or affiliated companies, nominees, or any persons subject to their direction or control exceed 50 per centum of such shares issued and outstanding.

(3) At no time shall any stockholder who is not an authorized carrier, or any syndicate or affiliated group of such stockholders, own more than 10 per centum of the shares of voting stock of the corporation issued and outstanding.

(c) The corporation is authorized to issue, in addition to the stock authorized by subsection (a) of this section, nonvoting securities, bonds, debentures, and other certificates of indebtedness as it may determine. Such nonvoting securities, bonds, debentures, or other certificates of indebtedness of the corporation as a communications common carrier may own shall be eligible for inclusion in the rate base of the carrier to the extent allowed by the Commission. The voting stock of the corporation shall not be eligible for inclusion in the rate base of the carrier.

(d) No more than an aggregate of 20 per centum of the shares of stock of the corporation authorized by subsection (a) of this section which are held by holders other than authorized carriers may be held by persons of the classes described in paragraphs (1), (2), (3), (4), and (5) of section 310(a) of the Communications Act of 1934, as amended (47 U.S.C. 310).

(e) The requirement of section 45(b) of the District of Columbia Business Corporation Act (D.C. Code, sec. 29-920(b) as to the percentage of stock which a stockholder must hold in order to have the rights of inspection and copying set forth in that subsection shall not be applicable in the case of holders of the stock of the corporation, and they may exercise such rights without regard to the percentage of stock they hold.

(f) Upon application to the Commission by any authorized carrier and after notice and hearing, the Commission may compel any other authorized carrier which owns shares of stock in the corporation to transfer to the applicant, for a fair and reasonable consideration, a number of such shares as the Commission determines will advance the public interest and the purposes of this Act. In its determination with respect to ownership of shares of stock in the corporation, the Commission, whenever consistent with the public interest, shall promote the widest possible distribution of stock among the authorized carriers.

PURPOSES AND POWERS OF THE CORPORATION

Sec. 305. (a) In order to achieve the objectives and to carry out the purposes of this Act, the corporation is authorized to—

(1) plan, initiate, construct, own, manage, and operate itself or in conjunction with foreign governments or business entities a commercial communications satellite system;

(2) furnish, for hire, channels of communication to United States communications common carriers and to other authorized entities, foreign and domestic; and

(3) own and operate satellite terminal stations when licensed by the Commission under section 201 (c) (7).

(b) Included in the activities authorized to the corporation for accomplishment of the purposes indicated in subsection (a) of this section, are, among others not specifically named—

(1) to conduct or contract for research and development related to its mission;

(2) to acquire the physical facilities, equipment and devices necessary to its operations, including communications satellites and associated equipment and facilities, whether by construction, purchase, or gift;

(3) to purchase satellite launching and related services from the United States Government;

(4) to contract with authorized users, including the United States Government, for the services of the communications satellite system; and

(5) to develop plans for the technical specifications of all elements of the communications satellite system.

(c) To carry out the foregoing purposes, the corporation shall have the usual powers conferred upon a stock corporation by the District of Columbia Business Corporation Act.

TITLE IV—MISCELLANEOUS

APPLICABILITY OF COMMUNICATIONS ACT OF 1934

Sec. 401. The corporation shall be deemed to be a common carrier within the meaning of section 3(h) of the Communications Act of 1934, as amended, and as such shall be fully subject to the provisions of title II and title III of that Act. The provision of satellite terminal station facilities by one communication common carrier to one or more other communications common carriers shall be deemed to be a common carrier activity fully subject to the Communications Act. Whenever the application of the provisions of this Act shall be inconsistent with the application of the provisions of the Communications Act, the provisions of this Act shall govern.

NOTICE OF FOREIGN BUSINESS NEGOTIATIONS

Sec. 402. Whenever the corporation shall enter into business negotiations with respect to facilities, operations, or services authorized by this Act with any international or foreign entity, it shall notify the Department of State of the negotiations, and the Department of State shall advise the corporation of relevant foreign policy considerations. Throughout such negotiations the corporation shall keep the Department of State informed with respect to such considerations. The corporation may request the Department of State to assist in the negotiations, and that Department shall render such assistance as may be appropriate.

SANCTIONS

Sec. 403. (a) If the corporation created pursuant to this Act shall engage in or adhere to any action, practices, or policies inconsistent with the policy and purposes declared in section 102 of this Act, or if the corporation or any other person shall violate any provision of this Act, or shall obstruct or interfere with any activities authorized by this Act, or shall refuse, fail, or neglect to discharge his duties and responsibilities under this Act, or shall threaten any such violation, obstruction, interference, refusal, failure, or neglect, the district court of the United States for any district in which such corporation or other person resides or may be found shall have jurisdiction, except as otherwise prohibited by law, upon petition of the Attorney General of the United States, to grant such equitable relief as may be necessary or appropriate to prevent or terminate such conduct or threat.

(b) Nothing contained in this section shall be construed as relieving any person of any punishment, liability, or sanction which may be imposed otherwise than under this Act.

(c) It shall be the duty of the corporation and all communications common carriers to comply, insofar as applicable, with all provisions of this Act and all rules and regulations promulgated thereunder.

REPORTS TO THE CONGRESS

Sec. 404. (a) The President shall transmit to the Congress in January of each year a report which shall include a comprehensive description of the activities and accomplishments during the preceding calendar year under the national program referred to in section 201(a)(1), together with an evaluation of such activities and accomplishments in terms of the attainment of the objectives of this Act and any recommendations for additional legislative or other action which the President may consider necessary or desirable for the attainment of such objectives.

(b) The corporation shall transmit to the President and the Congress, annually and at such other times as it deems desirable, a comprehensive and detailed report of its operations, activities, and accomplishments under this Act.

(c) The Commission shall transmit to the Congress, annually and at such other times as it deems desirable, (i) a report of its activities and actions on anticompetitive practices as they apply to the communications satellite programs; (ii) an evaluation of such activities and actions taken by it within the scope of its authority with a view to recommending such additional legislation which the Commission may consider necessary in the public interest; and (iii) an evaluation of the capital structure of the corporation so as to assure the Congress that such structure is consistent with the most efficient and economical operation of the corporation.

III. INTERNATIONAL ORGANIZATIONS

III-A. CONSTITUTION OF THE INTERNATIONAL ASTRONAUTICAL FEDERATION

Chapter I--Name and Purposes

Article 1—Name
The name of this association is the International Astronautical Federation. The Federation is an international non-governmental scientific non-profit organization.

Article 2—Purposes
The Federation exists for the following purposes:
(a) To foster the development of astronautics for peaceful purposes.
(b) To encourage the widespread dissemination of technical and other information concerning astronautics.
(c) To stimulate public interest in and support for the development of all aspects of astronautics through the various media of mass communication.
(d) To encourage participation in astronautical research or other relevant projects by international and national research institutions, universities, commercial firms and individual experts.
(e) To create and foster as activities of the Federation academies, institutes and commissions dedicated to continuing research in, and the fostering of, all aspects of the natural and social sciences relating to astronautics and the peaceful uses of outer space.
(f) To convoke and organize with support of its respective academies, institutes and commissions international astronautical congresses, symposia, colloquia and other scientific meetings.
(g) To cooperate and advise with appropriate international and national, governmental and non-governmental organizations and institutions on all aspects of the natural, engineering and social sciences related to astronautics and the peaceful uses of outer space.

Chapter II—Legal Domicile and Applicable Law

Article 3—
The legal domicile of the Federation is at Geneva, Switzerland. When reference to a particular body of law is appropriate, the reference shall be to Swiss law.

Chapter III—Membership

Article 4—Eligibility
The International Astronautical Federation is an association of those organizations and bodies, duly organized under the laws of their country of origin,

which share the purposes declared in Article 2 and were elected in accordance with Articles 9 and 10 of this Constitution.

Article 5—Classification of Membership
(a) There shall be the following classes of Members: Voting Members, Non-Voting Members and Institution Members.
(b) Any Member is entitled to participate in all activities of the Federation and receive its services.

Article 6—Voting Members
(a) One Member only from any one nation, elected as provided in Articles 9 and 10 of this Constitution, may be a Voting Member of the Federation.
(b) Each Voting Member shall be entitled to vote on all matters brought before the General Assembly.

Article 7—Non-Voting Members
(a) Besides one Voting Member there may be further organizations from the same nation elected as Non-Voting Members of the Federation.
(b) Each Non-Voting Member may attend the plenary meetings of the General Assembly and participate in its discussions, but may vote only with the approval of three fourths of the Voting Members present in the General Assembly on a specific issue.

Article 8—Institution Members
(a) Universities, scientific or technical institutes and other similar bodies, or their parts, may become Institution Members of the Federation.
(b) Each Institution Member may attend the plenary meetings of the General Assembly and participate upon the invitation of the General Assembly, expressed by the majority of the Voting Members present, in the discussions on a specific issue.

Article 9—Application
(a) An applicant for admission to the Federation shall submit to the Executive Secretary two certified copies of its statutes and in the case of application for Voting or Non-Voting Member status, proof that such applicant has twenty-five or more individual members in good standing.
(b) The Bureau shall determine the applicant's eligibility for a certain category of membership and will report its recommendation at the next plenary meeting of the General Assembly.

Article 10—Election of New Members
New Members of the Federation shall be elected by a majority vote of the Voting Members present at the General Assembly at its plenary meeting. The elected Members of the Federation shall retain their full autonomy.

Article 11—Required Internal Membership of Applicants and Members of the Federation
(a) No organization which has less than twenty-five individual members currently in good standing may become a Voting or Non-Voting Member of the Federation.

(b) Whenever the number of internal members of any applicant or Member of the Federation is at issue, such applicant or such Member must provide proof of its declared membership if required by the Bureau. In case of a negative result the Bureau may recommend to the General Assembly the temporary suspension of rights of such Member.

Article 12—Amendment of Statutes by Members
Whenever a Member amends its statutes it shall immediately submit two certified copies of its statutes as amended to the Executive Secretary of the Federation.

Article 13—Registration of Signatures
Each Member shall register the signature of its officers with the Executive Secretary of the Federation.

Article 14—Expulsion from Membership
Upon the recommendation of the Bureau the General Assembly shall decide by a majority vote of the Voting Members present at the General Assembly at its plenary meeting on the expulsion of any Member. The Bureau shall make such recommendation if the Member has not fulfilled its contributions for two or more years, or if otherwise has grossly failed to conform to the requirements of this Constitution.

Article 15—Withdrawal from Membership
All Members of the Federation shall have the right of withdrawal from the Federation. Any Member may do so by a letter submitted to the Executive Secretary in due time before the plenary meeting of the General Assembly, which will take note of it.

Article 16—Extinction of Membership and Its Succession
(a) In the case of dissolution or other kind of extinction of a Member, the General Assembly shall declare upon the recommendation of the Bureau the extinction of its membership in the Federation.
(b) Upon the recommendation of the Bureau the General Assembly shall confirm the successor in membership of an extinct Member if the conditions required in Article 9 exist.

Article 17—Changes in Status of Members
Upon the recommendation of the Bureau the General Assembly may decide by a majority vote of the Voting Members present at the General Assembly at its plenary meeting the appropriate change of the membership status of any Member.

Chapter IV—The General Assembly

Article 18—Composition
The supreme governing body of the Federation shall be the General Assembly. It shall be composed of delegates for each Voting Member. One delegate of each Non-Voting and Institution Member may attend the plenary meetings of the General Assembly.

Article 19—Powers and Functions

The General Assembly shall have the following powers and functions:

(a) To examine and approve the credentials of the delegates.

(b) To approve and modify the Agenda of its plenary meetings proposed and submitted by the Bureau.

(c) To elect the new Members of the Federation.

(d) To suspend temporarily the rights of Members as provided in Article 11, to expel Members as provided in Article 14, to take note of the withdrawal of Members as provided in Article 15, to declare the extinction of and succession to the membership as provided in Article 16, and to decide the changes in status of Members according to Article 17.

(e) To approve the annual and special reports, statements, accounts, estimates of the budget and the disbursement of funds by the Bureau.

(f) To appoint committees necessary for the performance of its functions.

(g) To elect the officers of the Federation.

(h) To create such academies, institutes, and commissions as are deemed necessary to carry out the work of the Federation and to approve their statutes.

(i) To adopt such by-laws and rules as it may deem necessary.

(j) To exercise such other powers and functions, which are not reserved by this Constitution to another organ of the Federation, as might be necessary or proper to carry out purposes of the Federation.

Article 20—Plenary Meetings

The General Assembly shall hold its plenary meetings annually or if recommended by the Bureau and with the consent of a majority of Voting Members less frequently. At each plenary meeting the General Assembly shall determine the place and time of its next plenary meeting.

Article 21—Quorum and Majority

(a) A voting quorum of the General Assembly shall always consist of the majority of all Voting Members of the Federation.

(b) Unless otherwise specified in this Constitution, a majority of the Voting Members present at the plenary meeting of the General Assembly will be required to pass any action of this organ.

(c) If Non-Voting Members will be asked according to Article 7 to vote on any specific issue a majority of the total number of the Voting and Non-Voting Members present at the plenary meeting of the General Assembly will be required to pass any action of this organ.

Article 22—Voting by Proxy

If no delegate of a Voting Member is present, the vote of any Voting Member of the General Assembly may be cast by a proxy signed by the President or other duly authorized officer of this Member.

Article 23—Voting by Mail

If necessary, whenever the Bureau so determines or the General Assembly in advance decides, voting may take place by mail. In this case a ballot shall be sent by the Executive Secretary to all Voting Members, and to Non-Voting Members if entitled to vote in accordance with Article 7. Such ballot must be accompanied by a full and clear statement in writing of the matters to be voted upon. The result of a mail vote as stated by the President of the Federation shall be reported to all Members as soon as possible after the voting takes place.

Chapter V—Officers

Article 24—Titles of Officers
(a) The Federation shall have Elective Officers and Appointive Officers.
(b) Elective Officers shall be the President and the four Vice-Presidents.
(c) Appointive Officers shall be the General Counsel, the Honorary Secretary, and the Executive Secretary.

Article 25—Eligibility, Election and Term of Elective Officers
(a) No person may be an elective officer of the Federation who is not a repre-sentative of a Voting Member of this Federation. In the election of officers due regard shall be specially paid to candidates of Members from those countries where astronautics has reached the high degree of development and to the necessity of equitable geographical distribution.
(b) The General Assembly shall elect the officers at its plenary meeting by a majority of the Voting Members present. The term of office shall be one year or, if the next plenary meeting of the General Assembly will be post-poned according to Article 20, until their successors are elected.

Article 26—Authority to Sign Documents
The officers shall have the exclusive authority to sign documents and letters on behalf of the Federation.

Article 27—The President
(a) The President shall be the chief executive officer of the Federation. He may succeed himself only once.
(b) The President shall represent the Federation in all public ceremonies or events, if the Federation will be invited or if it will have some interest in participating. When the President cannot participate on such occasions he shall authorize a Vice-President or the General Counsel or a representative of a Voting Member of the Federation to represent the Federation. The President shall approve all public statements issued on behalf of the Fed-eration.
(c) The President shall preside at the plenary meetings of the General As-sembly. When the President cannot preside, any Vice-President designated by him or, if none is designated, any Vice-President selected by the Gen-eral Assembly or any other member of the General Assembly elected for this function may preside. The President or his deputy in this function shall not act in the General Assembly as a delegate of any Member and shall vote in the General Assembly only in case of a tie.
(d) The President shall preside at all meetings of the Bureau and report about its conclusions and recommendations to the General Assembly.

Article 28—Vice-Presidents
The Vice-Presidents shall be responsible to the President and according to Article 27 of this Constitution shall deputize for him. In the event of resigna-

tion of the President before the end of his term the remaining members of the Bureau shall select one of the Vice-Presidents to serve as President until the next election.

Article 29—General Counsel
The General Counsel of the Federation shall be appointed by the Bureau and confirmed by the General Assembly and shall serve until he resigns or is replaced. He shall serve as an ex-officio voting member of the committees and other bodies, set up according to Article 19 (f) and (h) and shall furnish legal advice on all problems requiring such consideration. The General Counsel may represent the Federation when asked by the President and may undertake such special missions, in particular with respect to the establishment and maintenance of relations between the Federation and other international organizations and bodies, as the Bureau shall direct.

Article 30—Honorary Secretary
The Honorary Secretary shall be a resident of Switzerland. He shall accept all legal processes and certify all official documents, and shall discharge such statutory duties as may be required by Swiss law. He shall be appointed by the Bureau and shall serve until he resigns or is replaced.

Article 31—Executive Secretary
The Executive Secretary shall act as secretary to the Bureau and shall perform such duties as are assigned to him by the Bureau. He shall be appointed by the Bureau and shall serve until he resigns or is replaced.

Chapter VI—Bureau

Article 32—Composition
(a) The Bureau consists of the elective officers of the Federation, the General Counsel, and the last retired President of the Federation as voting members.
(b) The directors of academies and institutes of the Federation, and the chairmen of its commissions shall be non-voting members of the Bureau.
(c) If necessary, chairmen of committees or their representatives appointed according to Articles 19 (f) and 35 (j) may be invited, when the questions relating to their activities will be considered, to participate and report in the relevant meetings of the Bureau without the right to vote.

Article 33—Meetings and Quorum
(a) The Bureau shall meet at such times and places as are duly determined by a majority thereof. The meetings of the Bureau shall be convoked by the President.
(b) The presence at a meeting or written answers of four voting members of the Bureau shall constitute a quorum.

Article 34—Decisions
(a) Decisions of the Bureau on procedural questions shall be taken by a majority of its voting members present at the meeting.
(b) Decisions on other than procedural questions shall be taken with unanimity of all voting members of the Bureau present at the meeting.

(c) If necessary and if the President so decides, voting may take place by mail. In this case a ballot shall be sent to all voting members of the Bureau, accompanied by a full and clear statement in writing of the matters to be voted upon. The decision shall be taken under analogous conditions as set forth in paragraphs (a) and (b) of this Article. The result of a mail vote as stated by the President of the Federation shall be reported to all officers of the Bureau, and if necessary to other officers, as soon as possible after the voting takes place.

(d) In the event of a tie, the vote of the President shall be decisive.

Article 35—Duties

The Bureau shall

(a) receive applications for membership and determine the applicant's eligibility for a certain category of membership and report its recommendation at the next plenary meeting of the General Assembly.

(b) Admit applicants for membership before their election to the plenary meetings of the General Assembly as observers. The Bureau may also admit or invite as observers to the General Assembly non-member organizations and bodies which have a deep interest in the development of astronautics.

(c) Require a proof of declared internal membership whenever it is at issue and in case of a negative result recommend to the General Assembly a temporary suspension of rights of such Member.

(d) Recommend to the General Assembly for consideration the expulsion of any Member under the conditions set forth in Article 14 of this Constitution, the declaration on the extinction of membership under Article 16, the confirmation of succession in membership according to paragraph (b) of the same Article and the change in the status of Members according to Article 17 of this Constitution.

(e) Recommend and supervise the arrangements for the plenary meetings of the General Assembly and, with the help of appropriate institutions mentioned in Article 19 (h) of this Constitution, for congresses, symposia, colloquia and other meetings of the Federation and to take all necessary steps for this purpose.

(f) Prepare and submit an agenda of the matters to be considered at the plenary meetings of the General Assembly. All matters which are to be decided by the General Assembly shall be considered in advance by the Bureau.

(g) Supervise the preparation of the accounts and the disbursement of funds, recommend an annual budget and present all pertinent information in the form of an annual report to the General Assembly.

(h) Make recommendations to the General Assembly concerning annual contributions of each Member Society.

(i) Accept on behalf of the Federation private donations or contributions from national or international organizations, or from governments.

(j) Appoint interim committees to discharge tasks arising since the last plenary meeting of the General Assembly.

(k) Perform such additional duties as may be directed by the General Assembly.

Chapter VII—Dissolution

Article 36—Procedure
The Federation may be dissolved with the approval of two-thirds of all Voting and Non-Voting Members. Any assets remaining after the discharge of all obligations shall be offered and transferred to an international institution devoted to scientific research having objectives similar to purposes set forth in Article 2 of this Constitution. If this transfer to such an institution cannot be accomplished, then to any international institution devoted to scientific research as may be designated by the Bureau.

Article 37—Winding Up
The Bureau shall be responsible for the winding up of the affairs of the Federation.

Chapter VIII—Amendments

Article 38—Procedure
Amendments to this Constitution shall be made with the approval of two-thirds of the Voting Members. All amendments shall, unless otherwise provided therein, take effect immediately upon such approval.

Chapter IX—Official Languages

Article 39—
The English, French, German, and Russian languages shall be official languages of the Federation.

Member Societies of the International Astronautical Federation

Argentina	Asociacion Argentina Interplanetaria
Austria	Osterreichische Gesellschaft fur Weltraumforschung
Belgium	Association Belge des Ingenieurs et Techniciens de l'Aeronautique et de l'Astronautique
Brazil	Sociedade Interplanetaria Brasileira
Bulgaria	Bulgarian Astronautical Society
Canada	Astronautical Society of Canada
Canada	The Canadian Astronautical Society
China, Republic of	Astronautical Society of the Republic of China
Cyprus	Cyprus Astronautical Society
Czechoslovakia	Commission on Astronautics at the Czechoslovak Academy of Sciences
Denmark	Dansk Astronautisk Forening
Egypt	Egyptian Astronautical Society
France	Societe Francaise d'Astronautique
France	Association for Encouragement of Astronautical Research
Germany	German Astronautical Society
Germany	Deutsche Raketen-Gesellschaft e. V.

Germany	Deutsche Gesellschaft fur Raketentechnik und Raumfahrt
Germany	Deutsches Raketen und Raumfahrtmuseum e. V.
Great Britain	The British Interplanetary Society
Greece	Hellenic Astronautical Society
India	Indian Astronautical Society
Iran	Iranian Astronautical Society
Israel	The Israel Astronautical Society
Italy	Associazione Italiana Razzi
Italy	Associazione por le Scienze Astronautiche
Japan	Japan Astronautical Society
Japan	Japanese Rocket Society
Mexico	Socieda Mexicana Interplanetaria
Netherlands	Nederlandsche Vereniging voor Ruimtevaart
Norway	Norsk Astronautisk Forening
Poland	Polskie Towarzysto Astronautiyczne (Polish Astronautical Society)
Portugal	Grupo Portuguese Astronautica
Portugal	Centro de Estudos Astronauticos of Lisbon
Rumania	Rumanian Academy of Sciences
Russia	The Commission on Astronautics of the Academy of Sciences of the USSR
South Africa	The South African Interplanetary Society
Spain	Agrupacion Astronautica Espanola
Sweden	Svenska Interplanetariska Sallskapet (Swedish Interplanetary Society)
USA	Aerospace Medical Association
USA	American Astronautical Society, Inc.
USA	American Rocket Society, Inc.
USA	Institute of the Aerospace Sciences
Yugoslavia	Yugoslav Astronautical Society

III-B. STATUTES AND STRUCTURE OF THE INTERNATIONAL ACADEMY OF ASTRONAUTICS

Statutes

Article 1
The International Academy of Astronautics of the International Astronautical Federation is Hereby Established. It shall consist of individuals who have distinguished themselves in some branch of the following sciences, especially in aspects connected with astronautics:
(1) *Basic Sciences*
(2) *Engineering Sciences*
(3) *Life Sciences,* including medical and other sciences dealing with life and survival in space.

Article 2

The powers and functions of the Academy of Astronautics shall be as follows:

(a) To provide advice to the President of the Federation when requested.

(b) To hold scientific meetings and to make scientific studies and reports.

(c) To publish the *Astronautica Acta*.

(d) To award medals and prizes.

(e) To carry out such other tasks which may be deemed desirable for promoting the advancement of astronautics.

(f) To adopt, add to or amend the Statutes for the regulation of the internal affairs of the Academy, provided that the Academy shall not enact Statutes, or amendments thereto, which are inconsistent with the provisions of the Constitution of the Federation or its resolutions pertaining to the Academy.

Article 3

The Academy shall have the following three Sections with maximum number of members as hereby specified:

(1) *Basic Sciences Section:* 60 members and 120 corresponding members.

(2) *Engineering Sciences Section:* 60 members and 120 corresponding members.

(3) *Life Sciences Section:* 45 members and 90 corresponding members.

Both members and corresponding members shall be deemed to be Academicians; however only members have the power to vote.

Article 4

The initial membership of the Academy shall include the participants in the Founding Committee and additional members chosen by the Founding Committee, provided that the total number of members in each Section shall not exceed one-third of the maximum authorized membership. The initial members shall signify their acceptance of membership and their agreement to these Statutes by depositing with the Chairman of the Founding Committee a letter to that effect. Thereafter, additional Academicians shall be elected only by the Academy as hereinafter provided. All members and corresponding members are elected for life.

Article 5

(a) The first election for additional members shall be held in the month of December, following the approval of these Statutes by the Council of the Federation, and the second election shall be held one year later. Members at each such election shall be elected to each Section from a list of qualified persons, each of whom has been nominated by at least three members of the Academy or by any of the voting-member organizations of the Federation.

At the first election, vacancies can be filled up to a total of not more than two-thirds of the authorized membership in each of the three Sections of the Academy. At the second election, vacancies can be filled up to the total authorized membership in each Section. All elections shall be by letter signed by a member, and mailed to the Secretary before the 15th day of the month in which the election takes place. New members shall in each such election be declared elected in the order of decreasing votes obtained, provided:

(i) that each obtains half the votes cast in his Section and that at least one-third of the members of the Section have voted,

(ii) that each has signified his willingness to accept election, and

(iii) that the President, in case of a tie, may cast the deciding vote.

(b) Thereafter in December of each year an election shall be held to fill vacancies in each Section.

(c) The new members of a Section at such elections provided for in (b) above shall be elected by the members of the Section exclusively from among the corresponding members of the Section. New members shall be declared elected in the order of decreasing votes obtained and only the number required to fill existing vacancies, provided each of such elections shall be subject to the conditions set out at the end of sub-paragraph (a) above.

(d) The first election for corresponding members shall be held in the month of June following the second election of members as specified in sub-paragraph (a) above, and at such election not more than one-third of the authorized corresponding membership in each of the three Sections of the Academy shall be elected. The procedure for election shall be as specified in sub-paragraph (a) above for the election of members.

(e) The second election for corresponding members shall be held in December of the year following the first such election, at which such second election vacancies can be filled up to a total of not more than two-thirds of the authorized corresponding membership in each Section. The third such election shall be held in December of the following year, at which election vacancies can be filled up to the total authorized corresponding membership in each Section. Thereafter in December of each year an election shall be held to fill vacancies in the corresponding membership of each Section.

(f) The new corresponding members of each Section, as specified in sub-paragraph (e) above, shall be elected by the members of the Section from a list containing the names of all persons who obtained in each of the prior two elections held at least five votes. Such list shall also contain the names of those who have been nominated by not less than three members of the Academy or by any of the voting-member organizations of the Federation prior to June 1st of each year. The combined list shall be communicated to the members by the Secretary as soon as possible after being completed. The procedure for election shall be the same as that indicated for the election of members.

(g) The election of honorary members shall take place once every two years in December prior to the bi-annual meeting. They shall be chosen by a majority vote of the members of the Award and Fellowship Committee from nominations made by any member of the Academy, provided that such nomination shall be communicated to the members of the Committee by the Secretary at least thirty days before the election.

Article 6

(a) The Academy shall hold a regular meeting once every two years at the place and time of the plenary session of the Federation beginning with the first Federation meeting after the approval of these Statutes.

(b) Special meetings, either for business or scientific purposes, may be held at times and places designated by a majority of the Assembly of the Academy.

(c) These Statutes are subject to amendment only by the Academy upon the affirmative vote of two-thirds of the members present at a regular meeting, or special meeting called for that purpose, provided that notice of any proposed amendment has been communicated in writing to the members by the Secretary at least thirty days prior to such meeting.

Article 7

(a) The Governing Body of the Academy shall be known as the Board of Trustees, to consist of a President, two Vice-Presidents and eleven Trustees.

(b) The Board of Trustees shall meet during the plenary session of the Federation. Five members shall constitute a quorum.

(c) Special meetings may be convened at the call of the President (or in his absence or inability to act, by one of the Vice-Presidents) and two Trustees, or at the call of any four members of the Board of Trustees.

(d) Medals and prizes for distinguished achievements in astronautics may be awarded *by a majority vote of the Award and Fellowship Committee, the members of which Committee shall be appointed bi-annually by the President and confirmed by the Board of Trustees.*

(e) The Board of Trustees shall be charged with the publication of *Astronautica Acta* under such directions as the Academy may adopt.

(f) The Board of Trustees shall adopt the seal of the Academy and fix the place of its principal office.

(g) The Board of Trustees shall transact such other business as may come before it not inconsistent with the Constitution of the Federation or of the Statutes of the Academy (including the power to constitute committees, a majority of whose members shall be Academicians, to study and report on scientific matters connected with astronautics).

Article 8

(a) The Trustees of the Academy shall be elected as follows: four members from the *Basic Sciences Section*, four members from the *Engineering Sciences Section*, and three members from the *Life Sciences Section*.

(b) Each Trustee shall be elected for a term of two years by the members of his Section, except two Trustees from the *Basic Sciences Section*, two from the *Engineering Sciences Section*, and one from the *Life Sciences Section*, who, at the first election to be held after the approval of these Statutes, shall be elected for a term of one year.
Thereafter, all Trustees shall be elected for a term of two years. Voting by members of a Section shall be by letter except in the years when the Academy holds its bi-annual meeting. Candidates holding the highest number of votes in either case shall be declared elected.

(c) In case the position of any Trustee becomes vacant for any cause including the election of a Trustee as President or Vice-President, the vacancy may be filled for the unexpired term at a special election called by the Board of Trustees.

Article 9

(a) The Officers of the Academy shall be a President and two Vice-Presidents to be elected from among the members for a term of two years each by a majority vote of members present at the bi-annual meeting of the Academy, beginning with the first meeting after the approval of these Statutes.

(b) The President, or in his absence or inability to act a Vice-President, shall preside at all meetings of the Academy and of the Assembly. Such presiding Officer shall be authorized to make a casting vote in case of a tie vote at any such meeting. The President shall appoint all members of Academy Committees, except the Finance Committee. In making such appointments at least a majority shall be Academicians. During the interim between the meetings of the Academy, the President shall supervise or direct the general business, research and other work, and finances of the Academy pursuant to these Statutes and to any decisions of the Academy or the Assembly.

(c) The President shall designate a Vice-President, or Trustee, as chairman of each Section of the Academy, such Chairman in each case to be named from the membership of the Section concerned.

(d) The President shall publish an annual report on the activities of the Academy which will be made available to the Council of the Federation and to other interested bodies.

Article 10

(a) A Finance Committee, to consist of a Vice-President and two Trustees shall be named by the Board of Trustees immediately after each regular meeting of the Academy, beginning in the year 1963, to serve for two years, beginning immediately after the regular meeting at which the Committee is appointed and continuing through the next regular meeting of the Academy. This Committee shall examine and submit its recommendations to the Board of Trustees covering a budget estimate to be prepared by the President for each of the years intervening between regular meetings of the Academy. After receiving such recommendations, the final budget for each such year shall be adopted by the Board of Trustees.

(b) The Finance Committee shall also examine the accounts of the Academy and report thereon to the Board of Trustees before such accounts are finally approved.

(c) All monies designated for the use or support of the Academy and its work, whether appropriated by the Federation or received by the Federation through grants, gifts or other sources shall be deposited in a special account to be opened by the Federation which shall be subject to withdrawal only for the use of the Academy and by such persons as the President, for that purpose, may from time to time designate.

Article 11

(a) The Secretary of the Academy shall be named by the Board of Trustees and shall act as Secretary of the Board of Trustees, and all committees. Under the supervision of the President, he shall conduct the correspondence of the Academy and of the Assembly and shall be the custodian of their records.

(b) The Academy may open offices to further its purposes, at such place or places as may be determined by the Board of Trustees or the President in any country which is represented by a member society in the Federation.

Structure of the International Academy of Astronautics

Functions

The International Academy of Astronautics consists of some 140 elected individuals from the following countries: Argentina, Australia, Austria, Belgium, Bulgaria, Canada, Czechoslovakia, Denmark, France, German Federal Republic, India, Italy, Japan, Netherlands, Norway, Rumania, Sweden, Switzerland, United Kingdom, United States of America, Uruguay, and Yugoslavia. Individual scientists elected to the Academy from the USSR have not as yet accepted membership. However, Soviet scientists do participate in several activities of the Academy.

The task of members of the Academy, through their elected officers, committees, and secretariat, is to carry out those functions which will contribute to the achievement of the objective of the Academy.

Article I of the statutes of the Academy contains the following list of functions:

(a) To provide advice to the President of the International Astronautical Federation when requested.
(b) To hold scientific meetings and to make scientific studies and reports.
(c) To publish the *Astronautica Acta.*
(d) To award medals and prizes.
(e) To carry out such other tasks which may be deemed desirable for promoting the advancement of astronautics.

Although the statutes of the Academy do not prohibit the Academy from carrying out original theoretical and experimental research, the program of activities carried out since 1960 has not included such work. Emphasis has been given to the exchange of scientific information through symposia and publications, and to the work of the committees on special selected subjects. Nor does the Academy, in general, attempt to coordinate national programs and plans for astronautical research and development, since efforts in this direction are more appropriately carried out on an intergovernmental level.

The fact that the Academy commits no governments or other organizations can be of great value, especially at the international level, for studies can be initiated on problems whose importance will be felt only in the long-range future.

Another of the great advantages of international nongovernmental organizations, such as the Academy, is that the leading men in the basic, engineering, and life sciences in different countries are willing to contribute to the objective of the Academy without remuneration. In most cases they attend meetings at their own expense.

The round table offered by the Academy to the men of astronautics of all nations gives a unique opportunity for original and novel ideas to be put forth.

Since ideas come unannounced and know no national frontiers, the interest of all nations is positively served in this way.

Accomplishments

The Academy has been in existence for only three years—its first meeting was held in Stockholm in August 1960. During this period it was possible to carry out a clearly defined program with the yearly grant of $25,000 provided by the Daniel and Florence Guggenheim Foundation, and with supplementary assistance provided by UNESCO, the International Atomic Energy Agency, and the World Health Organization, for activities jointly organized by the Academy and the International Astronautical Federation.

The program of the Academy has followed three main lines: (1) establishment of committees to carry out specific tasks, (2) development of a publications program, and (3) organization of symposia and meetings on selected subjects.

1. *Committees*

The following committees have been established:

(a) *Award and Fellowship Committee*. The Committee has selected annually the recipient of the $1,000 Daniel and Florence Guggenheim International Astronautics Award. In 1961, the award was given to Sir Bernard Lovell of Manchester University for his contributions through the use of the Jodrell Bank radio-telescope. In 1962, Dr. J. A. Van Allen of the State University of Iowa received the award for his work on space physics. The Chairman of the Committee was the late Dr. Th. von Kármán (USA) and the Vice-Chairman is Prof. E. A. Brun (France).

(b) *Publications Committee*. The Committee advises the Director concerning the various publication activities of the Academy including: *Astronautica Acta,* the scientific journal of the Academy; the multilingual astronautical dictionary project; and the program of monograph books. The Committee has met several times and, in addition to reviewing the foregoing activities, has given consideration to the problems of standardization of astronautical terms and classification of astronautical literature. The Chairman of the Committee is Dr. Irene Sänger-Bredt (German Federal Republic) and the Vice-Chairman is Prof. A. Eula (Italy).

(c) *Lunar International Laboratory Committee*. The Committee was established in 1960 at Stockholm, with the objective of studying during the next years the fields of research which should be given priority in an initial program of a manned laboratory on the Moon and thereafter, the technical problems related to the construction of such an international laboratory. A meeting of the Committee was held in Washington, D.C., in October 1961, and a second meeting is scheduled for September 26, 1963 in Paris. Several reports on selected topics are being prepared for the Committee. It is doubtful that solid planning of a manned laboratory can be initiated for about another ten years; however, the Committee serves to keep before the world the concept of an international laboratory. The chairman of the Committee is Dr. F. J. Malina (USA) and the Vice-Chairman is Sir Bernard Lovell (U.K.)

(*d*) *Committee on the History of the Development of Rockets and Astronautics.* It was decided at the first regular meeting of the Academy in Washington, D.C., in 1961, that it would be appropriate for the Academy to stimulate the preparation of a comprehensive history of the work done in the fields of rockets and astronautics from earliest times in various countries. A Chairman for the Committee has now been appointed and it is planned to have the first meeting of the Committee in Paris on September 27, 1963. The Committee will work in consultation with the International Union for the History and Philosophy of Science and the International Academy for the History of Science. The Chairman of the Committee is Mr. C. Dollfus (France).

(*e*) *Space Relativity Committee.* At the first regular meeting of the Academy in Washington, D.C., in 1961, the Director was authorized to establish a Space Relativity Committee to study ways in which developments in astronautics might be used, under international auspices, to carry out experiments helpful in verifying the general theory of relativity. A Chairman of the Committee has been appointed and the first meeting of the Committee will be held in October 1963. The work of the Committee will be closely coordinated with any plans which COSPAR might have in this field. The Chairman of the Committee is Prof. H. Thirring (Austria) and the Vice-Chairman is Prof. N. Boneff (Bulgaria).

2. *Publications.*

(*a*) *Astronautica Acta.* The scientific journal of the Academy is *Astronautica Acta.* It is published bi-monthly by the publishing house of Springer-Verlag in Vienna. The journal contains scholarly articles in English, French, and German, which are often too long for publication in journals of national astronautical societies. Scientists in countries which do not have appropriate journals also submit articles. The journal is purchased mainly by public libraries and the libraries of national and private research centers.

(*b*) *Academy monographs.* An arrangement has recently been concluded between the Academy and Springer-Verlag for the publication of monographs dealing with advanced subjects in various branches of the astronautical sciences.

(*c*) *Multilingual Astronautical Dictionary.* The Academy is making good progress in the preparation of a seven-language astronautical dictionary. The basic English word list has been provided by NASA. The Publishing House of the Czechoslovak Academy of Sciences has made a contract with the Academy to publish the dictionary in English, French, Russian, Spanish, German, Italian, and Czech. The dictionary is to be published in 1964.

(*d*) *Other publications.* The papers presented at Academy symposia, and subsequent discussion among participants, are published in book form. The proceedings of the 1961 International Symposium on Space Flight and Re-entry Trajectories has been published; the proceedings of the 1962 International Symposium on the Basic Environmental Problems of Man in Space are to be published in the near future.

3. *Academy Symposia and Scientific Meetings*

(*a*) *International Symposium on Space Flight and Re-entry Trajectories.* The first symposium organized by the Academy was held at Louveciennes near

Paris in June 1961. The organizing committee, under the chairmanship of Prof. Paul A. Libby (USA), arranged for the presentation of sixteen papers by authors from Belgium, Czechoslovakia, France, German Federal Republic, Italy, Netherlands, New Zealand, the United Kingdom, and the United States of America. The proceedings of the symposium were edited by Prof. Libby and published by Springer-Verlag, Vienna, both in *Astronautica Acta* and in book form. The participants believed that the symposium was such a signal success that the Academy should attempt to arrange a second symposium on the same subject in 1964.

(*b*) *International Symposium on the Basic Environmental Problems of Man in Space.* The symposium was organized jointly by the Academy and the International Astronautical Federation, with the support and cooperation of UNESCO, the International Atomic Energy Agency and the World Health Organization, at UNESCO House, Paris, in October-November 1962. In November 1961, a meeting of a study group, under the chairmanship of Prof. H. Bjurstedt (Sweden), was called in Paris by the Academy and the Federation, with financial assistance from UNESCO, to make preparations for the symposium. At the symposium, thirty-one papers were presented by participants from Austria (1 paper), Czechoslovakia (1), France (2), German Federal Republic (3), Poland (1), Sweden (2), United Kingdom (4), USA (8), the USSR (8), and Yugoslavia (1).

This symposium was the first international meeting at which problem areas of ecophysiology, psychophysiology, and data acquisition, analysis, and control as they pertain to manned space flight were discussed. Without a doubt this meeting represented the greatest single achievement of the Academy during the first three years of its existence. For the first time the two countries, the USSR and the USA, which have sent astronauts into space discussed the complex problems of manned space flight with scientists from other countries in significant detail.

In recognition of the success of the symposium, the participants recommended that a second symposium be organized by the Academy and the Federation in 1964 or 1965. To this end, UNESCO has provided funds for a second study group to meet under the auspices of the Academy and the Federation, in Paris, in September 1963. Its task is to make recommendations for a second symposium.

There is no doubt that in the study of manned space flight, the Academy and the Federation are the only international nongovernmental organizations which are in a position to bring together scientists from all countries of the world who can help to overcome the extremely difficult problems of man's survival in the space environment.

(*c*) *Review Meeting on the Recently Acquired Knowledge of the Space Environment.* The Academy and the Federation are jointly organizing this meeting with the support and cooperation of UNESCO and the scientific cooperation of COSPAR. At the meeting papers will be presented reviewing the present state of knowledge in selected branches of space physics. The papers will be especially directed to informing those working in the applied and engineering sciences of our present knowledge in this field. The Chairman of the organizing committee for this meeting is Prof. A. Ehmert (German Federal

Republic) and he is assisted by committee members from Belgium, France, the United Kingdom, the USA and the USSR. The proceedings of the meeting will be published in book form by Springer-Verlag, Vienna.

The International Academy of Astronautics (of the International Astronautical Federation), 1963

Directors:
Dr. Theodore von Kármán (USA) (1960-May 1963)
Dr. F. J. Malina (USA) (June 1963-Oct. 1963)

Deputy Directors:
Dr. F. J. Malina (USA) (1960-June 1963) (now vacant)
Prof. Joseph Perès (France) (1960-Feb. 1962)
Prof. U. S. von Euler (Sweden) (May 1962-   )

General Counsel:
Mr. A. G. Haley (USA)

Executive Secretary:
Dr. W. F. Hilton (U.K.)

Trustees:

Prof. N. Boneff (Bulgaria)   Dr. J. M. J. Kooy (Netherlands)
Prof. E. A. Brun (France)   Dr. W. R. Lovelace II (USA)
Prof. A. Ehmert (German Fed. Rep.)   Sir Bernard Lovell (U.K.)
Prof. A. Eula (Italy)   Prof. A. Meyer (German Fed. Rep.)
Prof. M. Florkin (Belgium)   Prof. R. Pesek (Czechoslovakia)
Dr. J. Kaplan (USA)

Section Chairmen:
Section 1: Prof. A. Ehmert (German Fed. Rep.)
Section 2: Prof. R. Pesek (Czechoslovakia)
Section 3: Prof. M. Florkin (Belgium)

Committees:
Award and Fellowship Committee:
Chairman (vacant)
Vice-Chairman, Prof. E. A. Brun (France)
Publications Committee:
Chairman, Dr. Irene Sänger-Bredt (German Fed. Rep.)
Vice-Chairman, Prof. A. Eula (Italy)
Lunar International Laboratory (LIL) Committee:
Chairman, Dr. F. J. Malina (USA)
Vice-Chairman, Sir Bernard Lovell (U.K.)
Committee on the History of the Development of Rockets and Astronautics:
Chairman, C. Dollfus (France)
Space Relativity Committee:
Chairman, Prof. H. Thirring (Austria)
Vice-Chairman, Prof. N. Boneff (Bulgaria)

III-C. STATUTES OF THE INTERNATIONAL INSTITUTE OF SPACE LAW

ARTICLE I

Section 1. The name of this Institute shall be the International Institute of Space Law of The International Astronautical Federation.

ARTICLE II

Section 1. The purposes and objectives of the Institute shall be as follows:

   a. To provide advice to the President of the Federation when requested.
   b. To carry out such other tasks which may be considered desirable for fostering the social science aspects of astronautics, space travel and exploration.
   c. To publish proceedings and reports and a periodical journal.
   d. To make awards.
   e. To hold meetings and colloquia on juridical and sociological aspects of the social sciences and to make studies and reports.
   f. To adopt, add to, or amend the statutes for the regulation of the internal affairs of the Institute, provided that the Institute shall not enact statutes or amendments thereto which are inconsistent with the provisions of the Constitution of the Federation, or its resolutions pertaining to the Institute.

ARTICLE III

Section 1. The initial membership of the Institute shall include the members of the Permanent Legal Committee [which was organized pursuant to the resolution of the Amsterdam plenary meeting and is now superseded by this Institute] and additional members chosen by the *ad hoc* organizing committee. The initial members shall signify their acceptance of membership and their agreement to these Statutes within three months of the approval of these Statutes by depositing a signed letter of acceptance with the Secretary of the Board of Directors. Thereafter, additional members shall be elected by the Board of Directors of the Institute as hereinafter provided. All members are elected for life.
Section 2. Applicants for membership in the Institute except the initial members must be nominated by a Director, a Member Society, or by three members of the Institute. The application shall be on a form prescribed by the Board of Directors and election shall be by a majority vote of a quorum of the Board of Directors in attendance at a regular or special meeting of the Board of Directors, or by a majority of the Board of Directors if the vote is held by mail.

ARTICLE IV

Section 1. The annual meetings of the Institute shall be held each year at such time and place as a majority of a quorum of the Board of Directors may determine at a regular or special meeting, or by a majority of the Board if the vote is taken by mail.

Section 2. The President and Secretary of the Institute shall also serve, respectively, as President and Secretary of the Board of Directors.

Section 3. The President and Secretary of the Institute and the remaining members of the Board of Directors shall be elected at the annual meeting of the Institute, as provided in Article VI, Section 1.

Section 4. The Board of Directors may cast their votes by mail or other written means as to any action to be taken by the Board.

ARTICLE V

Section 1. The governing body of the Institute shall be the Board of Directors whose members shall be chosen as provided in Article VI of these statutes.

Section 2. The President of the Board of Directors, or in his absence or inability to act, the Secretary, shall preside at meetings of the Institute and of the Board of Directors. He shall supervise and direct the general business of the Institute pursuant to these Statutes.

Section 3. Seven or more elected members of the Board of Directors shall constitute a quorum.

Section 4. The Board of Directors shall cause minutes to be kept of their meetings and of all action taken by them. Such minutes shall be kept by the Secretary of the Institute and it shall be the privilege of any Member Society of the Federation in good standing to inspect the same at any reasonable time.

Section 5. The Board of Directors shall

a. Carry out the purposes and objectives of the Institute as set forth in Article II.

b. Implement the resolutions and directives adopted at the annual meetings of the Institute.

c. Create working groups and committees for all appropriate purposes and functions.

d. Elect members of the Institute to fill vacancies occurring in the membership of the Board of Directors.

e. Supervise the correspondence of the Institute and provide for the safekeeping of the archives thereof.

f. Appoint a clerk, designate his duties and supervise all his activities.

g. Arrange for meetings and colloquia.

h. Arrange for the publication of reports and establish a periodical journal.

i. Recommend concerning the awarding of medals and prizes.

j. Prepare budgets and supervise the auditing of accounts.

k. Accept donations and legacies, and funds from any private sources, and contributions from national and international nongovernmental and international agencies and from governments.

l. Prepare an annual report to be presented at the plenary meeting of the Council of the Federation.

Section 6. Until the first annual meeting of the Institute to be held in the calendar year following the approval of these Statutes the membership of the *ad hoc* organizing committee shall act as the Board of Directors of the Institute.

ARTICLE VI

Section 1. The Board of Directors of the Institute shall consist of the President, the Secretary, and ten other members of the Institute to be elected from among the members by a majority vote of members present at the annual meeting, or by the Board of Directors to fill vacancies.

Section 2. At all times the General Counsel of the Federation shall be an *ex officio* voting member of the Board of Directors of the Institute.

Section 3. Members of the Board of Directors shall serve until the end of the annual meeting following their election, and may be reelected subject to the provisions of Section 1 of this Article.

ARTICLE VII

Section 1. These Statutes may be amended at any meeting by a two-thirds vote of all directors.

III-D. CHARTER OF COSPAR

(Committee on Space Research International Council of Scientific Unions, November 1959)

I. PURPOSE AND OBJECTIVES

COSPAR shall be a Special Committee of the ICSU.

The purpose of COSPAR is to further, on an international scale, the progress of all kinds of scientific investigations which are carried out with the use of rockets or rocket-propelled vehicles. COSPAR shall be concerned with fundamental research. It will not normally concern itself with such technological problems as propulsion, construction of rockets, guidance and control.

These objectives shall be achieved through the maximum development of space research programs by the international community of scientists working through ICSU and its adhering national academies and unions. Any arrangements involving national territories should be made by bilateral or multilateral discussion between the nations concerned. As a non-political organization COSPAR shall not, as a matter of policy, recommend any specific assistance of one nation by another. It will, however, welcome information concerning such arrangements and provide a convenient assembly in which such arrangements may informally be proposed and discussed.

Recognizing the need for international regulation and discussion of certain aspects of satellite and space probe programs, COSPAR shall keep itself informed of United Nations or other international activities in this field, to assure that maximum advantage is accorded international space science research through such regulations and to make recommendations relative to matters of planning and regulation that may effect the optimum program of scientific research.

COSPAR shall report to ICSU those measures needed in the future to achieve the participation, in international programs of space research, of all countries of the world with those which are already actively engaged in research programs within the domain of COSPAR.

II. COMPOSITION

The composition of COSPAR shall be as follows:

(a) One representative designated by each national scientific institution adhering to ICSU which is actively engaged in space research and desires representation in COSPAR.

(b) One representative designated by each international scientific union federated in ICSU which desires to participate in COSPAR. In order that, in addition to broad scientific representation, there should also be as wide a distribution of nationality as possible among the union representatives, the advice or assistance of ICSU shall be provided to the unions, if desired.

The rights and duties of the national scientific institutions represented in COSPAR shall be—

1. To be informed about and to send representatives to all meetings of the full COSPAR or sponsored by COSPAR and to participate in all the discussions therein.

2. To establish scientific channels for obtaining data and carrying out space experiments and to participate in obtaining data and evaluating information resulting from such experiments.

3. To make available scientific results of space research which may be conducted as part of their participation in the work of COSPAR.

4. To contribute to the financial support of COSPAR to an extent recommended by the COSPAR Executive Council, affirmed by COSPAR and approved by ICSU.

5. To vote on all matters.

The rights and duties of the international scientific unions represented in COSPAR shall be—

1. To be informed about and to send representatives to all meetings of the full COSPAR and to participate in all discussions therein.

2. To maintain liaison with COSPAR and its Working Groups in any way they may deem appropriate in order to ensure integration of the results obtained by space experiments with those obtained by other methods of scientific research, to avoid duplication and to achieve an efficient division of tasks.

3. To participate in evaluating and disseminating information resulting from space experiments.

4. To vote on all matters which do not involve major items of income or expenditure of money by COSPAR, or considerable expenditure of money by the national scientific institutions.

III. OFFICERS

COSPAR shall elect from among its own members a President, two Vice-Presidents, and four other members to serve on an Executive Council, hereinafter described. The method of election shall be such as to ensure a representation consistent with the distribution of major effort in space research among the members of COSPAR.

IV. EXECUTIVE COUNCIL

The Executive Council shall be responsible for administering and conducting the affairs of COSPAR between meetings in accordance with the policies and directives given to it by COSPAR and shall be responsible for the formulation of plans and policies for consideration by the full COSPAR. The Executive Council shall consist of the President, the Vice-Presidents and the four other members specifically elected for this responsibility, and of all the representatives of the scientific unions which are members of COSPAR. Only the elected members may vote on matters involving major items of income or expenditure of money by COSPAR, or considerable expenditure of money by the national scientific institutions, but all members of the Executive Council shall have the right to be heard and to have their opinions recorded on all matters.

Any decisions of the Executive Council must be confirmed by a vote of two-thirds of the seven elected members. The seven elected members may meet or vote separately and when acting in this way, shall be known as the Bureau of the Executive Council. The Chairmen of Working Groups shall be invited to attend all meetings of the Executive Council as consultants. The President and Vice-Presidents of COSPAR shall also act as President and Vice-Presidents respectively of the Executive Council and its Bureau.

V. FINANCE COMMITTEE

In accordance with Rule 15 (a) (i) of ICSU Rules for Special Committees, there shall be a Finance Committee consisting of two members: representatives of national scientific institutions.

VI. CONDUCT OF BUSINESS

1. The ICSU Rules for Special Committees shall be adopted for the conduct of COSPAR business.

2. COSPAR shall establish its own By-Laws and Procedures within the framework of this Charter and the ICSU Rules for Special Committees.

3. COSPAR may establish scientific Working Groups from time to time for the examination of special problems.

4. The President of COSPAR shall keep the Secretary General of ICSU fully and promptly informed of all COSPAR activities.

5. After approval by COSPAR, the Bureau will submit to ICSU budget estimates for all of the activities of COSPAR, and recommendations for a scale of contributions which shall be required from the participating national scientific institutions.

BY-LAWS

1. These By-Laws shall go into effect automatically upon approval by ICSU of the COSPAR Charter.

2. Changes in and additions to these By-Laws may be made at any time as provided for in Section 6(iv) below.

3. Election of officers.

(i) All officers shall be elected from among the members of COSPAR.

(ii) The President shall be elected for a term of three years by the full membership from a slate of nominees submitted by the Executive Council or, if the Executive Council is unable to nominate, from the floor of COSPAR.

(iii) Two Vice-Presidents shall be elected for a term of three years by the full COSPAR, one from a slate of nominees submitted by the Academy of Sciences of the USA and one from a slate of nominees submitted by the Academy of Sciences of the USSR, at present the only two nations engaged in launching artificial earth satellites and cosmic space vehicles.

(iv) Four additional members of the Bureau shall be elected for a term of three years by COSPAR, two from a slate of nominees submitted by one of the Vice-Presidents, and two from a slate submitted by the other.

(v) If an office is vacated for any reason it shall be filled for the remainder of the original term by nomination and election as specified above.

(vi) All officers shall continue to serve until their successors have been duly elected and have accepted.

4. Duties of Officers: The duly elected President of COSPAR shall preside at all meetings of COSPAR plenum, the Executive Council and Bureau, and shall conduct the affairs of COSPAR between designated meetings. In case of the inability of the President to carry out his responsibilities, the two Vice-Presidents shall alternately, as principal Vice-President, assume the responsibilities of the office of President. Alternation of the office of principal Vice-President shall take place each three months, with the U.S. Vice-President holding office during the first and third quarters of each year, and the USSR Vice-President holding office during the second and fourth quarters.

It shall be the prime responsibility of the principal Vice-President upon assuming the presidential responsibility, to convene COSPAR at the first opportunity for the purpose of electing a new President. In case of the inability of the President and Vice-Presidents to discharge these responsibilities, the elected members of the Executive Council may take such steps as may be necessary to ensure the continued activity of COSPAR.

5. Liaison with United Nations: The Executive Council shall arrange for liaison with the United Nations organizations on the subject of regulations affecting space research to the extent and for the purposes set forth in the Charter.

6. Rules of Order:

(i) *Quorum.* A quorum of the COSPAR or any of its constituent bodies shall consist of fifty percent or more of the members of such body. Members of COSPAR may name alternate delegates who, in the absence of the principal delegates, shall have voting authority at COSPAR meetings and shall be counted in determining a quorum. Votes may only be cast by persons present at the meeting, with the exception noted in (v) below.

(ii) *Right to vote on various subjects.* Voting in the COSPAR or any of its constituent bodies shall conform to the provisions of applicable sections of the Charter.

(iii) *Majority vote.* Official actions by COSPAR, except as provided in (iv), may be taken by a simple majority vote of those present and voting for or against each action. Abstentions from the voting will not be considered in determining the majority action but may be entered in the record if so desired by the abstaining delegates.

(iv) *Changes in By-Laws and financial assessments.* Any change in the By-Laws shall require a two-thirds majority vote of the full COSPAR. Actions involving financial assessments on the national scientific institutions which are represented in COSPAR, shall require a two-thirds majority vote of the national institutions.

(v) *Voting in the Executive Council.* Resolutions of the Executive Council may be made by a simple majority vote cast in any manner agreed upon by the Executive Council, but must be confirmed as provided in section IV, of the Charter. Decisions of the Bureau of the Executive Council shall be made by a two-thirds vote. Any member of the Bureau unable to attend a meeting may delegate his voting power to his representative.

(vi) *Agenda.* An agenda appropriate to the nature of the business to be discussed shall be prepared under the direction of the President for each meeting of COSPAR, its Executive Council, or its Bureau and shall be mailed at least three weeks prior to the meeting. Amendments to the agenda for any meeting may be proposed by any representative present at a meeting and shall be adopted by a simple majority of those present and voting.

(vii) *Reports of Meetings.* The preliminary drafts of the reports of all meetings of COSPAR, all meetings of the Executive Council and of the Bureau, and all meetings of Working Groups shall be circulated promptly to all members of the respective groups for approval; such report shall be considered approved as written if specific objections or recommendations for amendment to these drafts are not received within one month of date of transmittal. Following approval, the reports of the meetings of COSPAR, its Executive Council, and Bureau, and of COSPAR Working Groups shall be distributed to all members of COSPAR.

7. Formal Communications: When it is prescribed that COSPAR resolutions or actions be transmitted to ICSU, UNESCO, UN or other bodies, such transmittals shall be in writing, incorporating the language of such resolutions or actions, and copies shall be distributed to the COSPAR Executive Council.

8. Scientific Working Groups: Scientific Working Groups may be established, modified, or discontinued at any time by the full COSPAR upon the recommendations of the Executive Council. Each Working Group shall consist of a Chairman, who will call meetings and preside over them, and several other members, none of whom need necessarily be representatives of scientific bodies maintaining membership in COSPAR. Each Working Group shall adopt such working rules and procedures as may seem appropriate for its work.

Any communications by the Working Groups requiring actions by individuals or groups outside COSPAR shall be subject to approval in advance, either specifically or in principle, by the COSPAR Executive Council.

The COSPAR will arrange to provide funds for reasonable secretarial expenses for the Working Groups and for travel expenses in accordance with ICSU regulations, of Chairmen, members and invited consultants. Each Working Group shall prepare, on request, a budget of such expenses, which will be subject to approval and audit as directed by the Bureau after consideration by the Finance Committee. Expenditures within the budget shall be approved by the Working Group Chairman.

III-E. CCIR STUDY GROUPS

STUDY GROUP I—Transmitters

Terms of reference:
1. To make specific studies and proposals in connection with radio transmitters and generally to summarize and co-ordinate proposals for the rational and economical use of the radio spectrum.
2. To study a number of problems concerning telegraphy and telephony from the transmission point of view.
3. To study spurious radiation from medical, scientific and industrial installations.

STUDY GROUP II—Receivers

Terms of reference:
1. Measurement of the characteristics of receivers and tabulation of typical values for the different classes of emission and the various services.
Investigation of improvement that might be made in receivers in order to solve problems encountered in radio communication.

STUDY GROUP III—Fixed Service Systems

Terms of reference:
1. To study questions relating to complete systems for the fixed and allied services and terminal equipment associated therewith (excluding radio-relay systems). Systems using the so-called ionospheric-scatter mode of propagation, even when working on frequencies above 30 Mc/s are included.
2. To study the practical application of communication theory.

STUDY GROUP IV—Space Systems

Terms of reference:
To study technical questions regarding systems of telecommunication with and between locations in space.

STUDY GROUP V—Propagation including the effects of the earth and Troposphere

Terms of reference:
To study the propagation of radio waves over the surface of the earth, taking into account changes in the electrical constants of the earth and irregularities of terrain, and including the effects of the troposphere.

STUDY GROUP VI—Ionospheric Propagation

Terms of reference:
To study all matters relating to the propagation of radio waves through the ionosphere insofar as they concern radio communication.

STUDY GROUP VII—Standard-frequencies and Time Signals

Terms of reference:
Organisation of a world-wide service of standard-frequency and time-signal transmissions. Improvement of measurement accuracy.

STUDY GROUP VIII—International Monitoring

Terms of reference:
To study problems relating to the equipment, operation and methods of measurement used by monitoring stations established for checking the characteristics of radio-frequency emissions. Examples of such measurements are: frequency, field-strength, bandwidth, etc.

STUDY GROUP IX—Radio-relay Systems

Terms of reference:
To study all aspects of radio-relay systems and equipment operating at frequencies above about 30 Mc/s, including systems using the so-called tropospheric-scatter mode of propagation.

STUDY GROUP X—Broadcasting

Terms of reference:
To study the technical aspects of transmission and reception in the sound broadcasting service (except for tropical broadcasting), including standards of sound recording and sound reproduction to facilitate the international exchange of programmes; to study also the technical aspects of video recording in liaison with Study Group XI.

STUDY GROUP XI—Television

Terms of reference:
Technical aspects of television.

STUDY GROUP XII—Tropical Broadcasting

Terms of reference:

To study standards required for good quality service in the tropical zone, and for tropical broadcasting systems; interference in the shared bands; power requirements for acceptable service; design of suitable aerials for short-distance tropical broadcasting; optimum conditions for the utilisation of frequency bands used for broadcasting in the tropical zone; other associated questions.

STUDY GROUP XIII—Mobile Services

Terms of reference:

To study technical questions regarding the aeronautical, maritime, land mobile and radio location and navigation services, and miscellaneous operating questions of concern to several services.

STUDY GROUP XIV—Vocabulary

Terms of reference:

To study, in collaboration with the other Study Groups and, if necessary with the C.C.I.T.T., the radio aspect of the following: vocabulary of terms and list of definitions, lists of letter and graphical symbols and other means of expression, systematic classification, measurement units, etc.

IV. MISCELLANEOUS

IV-A. DEFINITIONS OF "ATMOSPHERE" AND "AIR"

Atmosphere

The term "atmosphere" usually refers to the gaseous envelope covering the surface of the earth. The word is derived from the Greek words ἀτμός, smoke or vapor and σφαῖρα, globe or sphere. The early Greeks were probably the first to study the weather in a regular and systematic way and the wind was defined by Anaximander as a "flowing of the air." Hesiod, in his treatise "Works and Days," discussed the origin of wind, and many observations of physical properties of the air were made by Ctesibus, Hero of Alexandria, and others. The material nature of air is clearly recognized in Hero's "Pneumatica."

Anaximenes (c. 500 B.C.) regarded the air as the primordial substance from which all matter was condensed. During the time of Socrates meteorology was neglected, but Aristotle revived interest in the study of the atmosphere and wrote about the winds. He regarded the atmosphere as consisting of three regions; the lowest in which plants and animals exist he supposed to be immovable like the earth; the uppermost region adjoined the fiery heavens and moved with them; the division intermediate between the other two, he believed to be exceedingly cold. Meteors were considered by Aristotle to be exhalations from the earth, which became incandescent when they reached the hot upper layer.

Very little progress was made from this time until the early part of the 17th century, although it is said that during the 11th century the Arabs calculated the height of the atmosphere, from the duration of twilight, as 92 kilometers. In 1643, Torricelli, a student of Galileo, found that if a long glass tube sealed at one end was filled with mercury and the open end closed with the finger while the tube was inverted in a vessel containing mercury, the liquid sank only to a certain level. It thus became possible to measure the pressure of the atmosphere, and the space above the mercury is still referred to as a Torricellian vacuum. This apparatus was called a barometer (q.v.) by Boyle and soon came into general use. Pascal demonstrated the decrease of the pressure of the air with altitude by measuring the height of the mercury column of a barometer at different points up a tower in Paris. In 1650 von Guericke (q.v.) found that he could pump air and was responsible for the famous experiment with the Magdeburg hemispheres.

That air consists chiefly of two gases was first recognized by Scheele (1772), but Cavendish (1781) was responsible for a larger number of analyses of the air and found that 100 volumes contain 20-83 parts by volume of oxygen and 79-17 of nitrogen. Similar experiments were carried out by Priestley (who thought the composition variable) and Lavoisier, but it was not until 1846 that it was definitely established by Bunsen that the composition of the atmosphere is not absolutely constant.

The Composition of the Atmosphere. Air is a mixture of gases and is not a chemical compound. This is proved by the following: (1) The composition of air is not constant, and the quantities present of the different components do not bear any simple relation to their atomic weights. (2) The constituents can be separated by diffusion and by the fractional distillation of liquid air. (3) Air dissolves in water in accordance with the law of partial pressures and hence air expelled from water contains an increased proportion of oxygen.

Below a height of 20 km (12½ mi.), the constituents of the atmosphere, with the exception of water vapor, are well mixed by winds and by diffusion. Slight changes in composition do occur, however, at the surface of the earth and these depend on latitude and the presence of large quantities of vegetation or sea water. The permanent constituents of the air are generally present in the following proportions (according to Humphreys in the *Scientific Monthly,* 1927):

Substance *Total atmosphere*	*Volume % in dry air*
Dry air	100.00
Nitrogen	78.03
Oxygen	20.99
Argon	0.9323
Water vapor	
Carbon dioxide	0.03
Hydrogen	0.01
Neon	0.0018
Krypton	0.0001
Helium	0.0005
Ozone	0.00006
Xenon	0.000009

The following table by Hann shows the variation with latitude.

	Nitrogen	Oxygen	Argon	Water Vapor	Carbon Dioxide
Equator	75.99	20.44	0.92	2.63	0.02
Latitude 50 N.	77.32	20.80	0.94	0.92	0.02
Latitude 70 N.	77.87	20.94	0.94	0.22	0.03

The composition also varies with altitude, but not to any very appreciable extent at heights at which respiration is still possible. The amount of water vapor present in the air is usually about 1.2% by volume, but in very cold weather this quantity falls almost to zero. At other times it may be as high as 5%.

Height of the Atmosphere. The height to which the atmosphere extends cannot be definitely stated, although at an altitude of 50 mi. the air cannot exert any measurable pressure. Three methods are available for the estimation of the height: (1) observation of meteors, (2) measurement of the duration of twilight, (3) observation of auroral displays. The first method gives results ranging from 150 to 300 km, while the duration of twilight indicates a value of about 64 km at lat. 45 degrees. It is difficult to make reliable calculations from auroral displays, but it is claimed that these occur up to a height of 500 km. If density of the atmosphere remained uniform throughout with the same value as at the earth's surface, the air would form a layer only 8 km thick and this is sometimes called the "height of the homogeneous atmosphere." Half of the air is below a height of 5-8 km. At low levels temperature is usually considered to decrease 0.56 degrees C per 100 meters increase in altitude, but the rate is extremely variable. Abov 2 km the temperature is on an average below 0 degrees C and continues to fall up to 10 km (6 mi.) when it is about −55 degrees C. At 37 km the temperature is practically the same as at 10 km. The lower region of the atmosphere is known as the "troposphere" and extends up to 10 km, beyond which clouds are not generally found, except in tropical latitudes.

Absorption of Radiation by the Atmosphere. The blue color of the sky is due to the fact that the air is not perfectly transparent and its particles reflect and scatter light, that from the blue end of the spectrum being most widely scattered. This effect also obscures the light of the stars. Very little of the sun's thermal radiation is absorbed by the air, which derives most of its heat from the earth by conduction and convection. A layer of air one meter thick absorbs about 0.007% of the radiant heat passing through it. Of the radiation incident on the outer atmosphere about 37% is lost by reflection and scattering. The fraction of the radiant energy from the sun which reaches the earth is termed the coefficient of transparency of the atmosphere. The absorption is chiefly dependent on the amount of water vapor, carbon dioxide and solid impurities present and consequently is much greater in the neighborhood of towns. The following coefficients of transparency are given by Wild for one meter of air: Dry, dust-free air, 0.99718, Dry air containing dust, from a room, 0.99520, Dust-free air saturated with water vapor 0.99328. The ozone, which appears to be present at very high altitudes, is responsible for the removal of practically all the ultraviolet radiation of wavelength shorter than $\lambda = 2{,}885$A. U.

Since the temperature of the upper atmosphere is practically constant and no convection or condensation takes place there, it is important to consider what would be the effect of dust particles which might be forced into the stratosphere by volcanic eruption. After certain eruptions, e. g., Krakatoa 1883, Mont Pele and Santa Maria 1902, Katmai 1912, a reddish halo was observed round the sun owing to the dust ejected to very great altitudes, and it was possible to calculate the size of the particles. It has been estimated that a quantity of dust of volume less than 1/174 cu km distributed in the upper layers of the air, would reduce the intensity of solar radiation by 20%. It is possible to explain the occurrence of ice ages in this way.

Air

(1) The mixture of gases in the atmosphere. (2) The element that gives lift to aircraft, or offers resistance to objects that move through it. (3) (a) The region above and around the earth, including the atmosphere and the space beyond, subject to control by air or space vehicles, in contradistinction to land and sea. (b) That part of this region that includes the atmosphere up to its effective upper limits, but not outer space.

Atmosphere

The body of air which surrounds the earth (or any other celestial body), defined at its outer limits by the actual presence of air particles but in such few numbers that collisions between them are so rare as to make the force of gravity the only means of keeping them associated with air particles at lower altitude.

Gaynor, Frank, Aerospace Dictionary. Philosophical
Library, New York, 1960, pp. 10 and
25 respectively.

Composition of (Chem., etc.)

Dry atmospheric air contains the following gases in the proportions (by weight) indicated: nitrogen, 75.5; oxygen, 23.2; argon, 1.3; carbon dioxide, 0.05-.4; krypton, 0.029; xenon, 0.005; neon, 0.00086; helium, 0.000056.

Chambers' Technical Dictionary. Ed. by C. F. Tweny and
L. E. C. Hughes. W. & R. Chambers, Ltd.
London, 1954, p. 57.

Definition of Air Space *

by Robert Jastrow **

The definition of air space is a matter of fundamental interest in jurisprudence, but it also poses an interesting physical problem. The boundary to the air space of a nation may be defined with respect to possible regime of flight,

---

* First Colloquium, 82.
** U.S. Naval Research Laboratory, currently with National Aeronautics and Space Agency, Washington, D.C., U.S.A.

as suggested by Professor von Kármán. However, I believe that outer space must be defined as *the region traversed by vehicles which have been placed in orbit around the earth, or which have escaped from the gravitational attraction of the earth.*

The reference to orbiting vehicles, or satellites, immediately introduces the possibility of a physically sound definition for the limits of air space. I have in mind the fact that at low altitudes a satellite is quickly destroyed by atmospheric friction. In order to be considered an orbiting satellite, the vehicle must last for at least one circuit of the earth before destruction by friction. Therefore, I suggest that the boundary to the air space of a nation should be defined as *the altitude at which the density of the atmosphere is sufficiently low to permit the completion of one circuit by an orbiting vehicle, without destruction by atmospheric friction.*

Our calculations of satellite lifetimes indicate that this critical altitude is 100 *miles* for a satellite of a typical weight and dimensions, i.e., a weight of one ton and a cross sectional area of 30 square feet. The critical altitude of 100 miles will vary approximately 5 miles when allowance is made for the uncertainty of the density of the atmosphere at that altitude, and also for reasonable variations in satellite mass and cross sectional area, or more properly, the ratio of these last two quantities. This figure of 5 miles represents the degree of arbitrariness in the proposed definition.

IV-B. ABBREVIATIONS AND ACRONYMS

ABA	American Bar Association
ACC	U.N. Administrative Committee on Coordination
AEC	Atomic Energy Commission
AFCEA	Armed Forces Communications and Electronics Association
AGARD	Advisory Group for Aeronautical Research and Development
AIAA	American Institute of Aeronautics and Astronautics
ARDC	Air Research & Development Command
ARPA	Advanced Research Projects Agency
ARS	American Rocket Society
AT&T	American Telephone & Telegraph Company
BIS	British Interplanetary Society
CCIR	International Radio Consultative Committee (ITU)
CCITT	International Telegraph & Telephone Consultative Committee (ITU)
CETEX	Committee on Contamination by Extraterrestrial Exploration
CINA	International Commission for Air Navigation
CIT	California Institute of Technology
CITEJA	International Technical Committee of Aerial Legal Experts
CMIT	(CCIR/CCITT Joint Commission for Television Transmissions)
Colloq.	Colloquium on the Law of Outer Space, at the Annual Congresses of the International Astronautical Federation. 1st, 1958, The Hague; 2d, 1959, London; 3d, 1960, Stockholm; 4th, 1961, Washington, D.C.; 5th, 1962, Varna, Bulgaria.

COSPAR   Committee on Space Research (ICSU)
CSAGI   Special Committee for the International Geophysical Year (ICSU)
DCA   Defense Communications Agency
DOD   Department of Defense
ECOSOC   United Nations Economic and Social Council
EHF   Extremely High Frequency
ELDO   European Launching Development Organization
ESRO   European Space Research Organization
ETAP   U.N. Expanded Technical Assistance Program
FAA   Federal Aviation Agency
FAI   Fédération Aeronautique Internationale
FCC   Federal Communications Commission
FTCA   Federal Tort Claims Act
GALCIT   Guggenheim Aeronautical Laboratory at California Institute of Technology
IAA   International Academy of Astronautics
IAEA   International Atomic Energy Agency
IAF   International Astronautical Federation
IAU   International Astronomical Union
ICAO   International Civil Aviation Organization
ICSU   International Council of Scientific Unions
IDA   International Development Corporation
IFC   International Finance Corporation
IFRB   International Frequency Registration Board (ITU)
IGC   International Geophysical Cooperation 1959 (ICSU)
IGY   International Geophysical Year (ICSU)
IISL   International Institute of Space Law
ILO   International Labor Organization
IMCO   International Maritime Consultative Organization
IQSY   International Year of the Quiet Sun
IRAC   Interdepartment Radio Advisory Committee
IRE   Institute of Radio Engineers
ITU   International Telecommunication Union
JPL   Jet Propulsion Laboratories (CIT)
JTAC   Joint Technical Advisory Committee (IRE–Radio Television Manufacturers Association)
LIL   Lunar International Laboratory
MIT   Massachusetts Institute of Technology
NACA   National Advisory Committee for Aeronautics
NAS   National Academy of Sciences
NASA   National Aeronautics and Space Administration
NASAA   National Aeronautics and Space Administration Act
NASC   National Aeronautics and Space Council
NRAO   National Radio Astronomy Observatory
NRC   National Research Council
NRL   Naval Research Laboratory
NSF   National Science Foundation

OCDM	Office of Civil and Defense Mobilization
OEP	Office of Emergency Planning
PC/IRC	Preparatory Committee for International Radio Conference (IRAC)
SAA	Schweizerische Astronautische Arbeitsgemeinschaft (Swiss Astronautical Study Group)
SCAR	Special Committee on Antarctic
SCOR	Special Committee on Oceanic Research
SHF	Super High Frequency
SICL	Section of International and Comparative Law (ABA)
SNCASO	Société Nationale de Constructions Aeronautique de l'Ouest
SSFA	Select Subcommittee on Frequency Allocations (IRAC)
Symp.	Committee on Aeronautical and Space Sciences, U.S. Senate, Doc. 26, 1961, LEGAL PROBLEMS OF SPACE EXPLORATION—A SYMPOSIUM (1961).
SYNCOM	Hughes Aircraft Co. program to develop an active 24-hour synchronous communication satellite in cooperation with NASA
TIAS	Treaties and other International Acts Series (Department of State)
TCC	Telecommunications Coordinating Committee
UHF	Ultra High Frequency
Ultracom	Ultraviolet Communications System
UN	United Nations
UNCOPUOS	United Nations Committee on the Peaceful Uses of Outer Space
UNESCO	United Nations Educational, Scientific, and Cultural Organization
UPU	Universal Postal Union
URSI	International Scientific Radio Union
USAF	U.S. Air Force
USIA	United States Information Agency
USNC-IGY	U.S. National Committee for the International Geophysical Year
UV	Ultraviolet
VfR	Verein für Raumschiffahrt (Society for Space Travel)
VHF	Very High Frequency
VOA	Voice of America
WHO	World Health Organization
WMO	World Meteorological Organization

V. BIBLIOGRAPHY

V-A. BIBLIOGRAPHIES OF SPACE LEGAL LITERATURE

1. Association of the Bar of the City of New York, Checklist of Materials on Law and Outer Space, The Record of the Association of the Bar of the City of New York, Vol. 13, *6*, 396.
2. John C. Hogan, *A Selective Bibliography on the Legal and Political Aspects of Space,* The Rand Corporation, 1958, also published in SAINT LOUIS UNIVERSITY LAW JOURNAL, Vol. 5, *1*, 108-133 (Spring, 1958).
3. John C. Hogan, *Space Law Bibliography,* THE JOURNAL OF AIR LAW AND COMMERCE, Vol. 23, *3*, 317-325 (Summer, 1956).
4. Yevgeny A. Korovine, *Bibliography, International-Legal Questions on the Mastery of Cosmic Space* (June, 1960).
5. MARTIN MENTER, ASTRONAUTICAL LAW, at 73-84 (Industrial College of the Armed Forces, Washington, D.C., 1959).
6. Eugène Pépin, *Bibliographie, Les Problèmes Juridique de l'Espace,* LA REVUE FRANÇAISE DE DROIT AÉRIEN, *4*, 24-46 (Sirey, Paris, 1959).
7. Michel S. Smirnoff, *Jugoslovenska Bibliografija Vazduhoplovnog Prava* (Institut Za Medunarodnu Politiku I Privredu, Belgrade, 1959).
8. Michel S. Smirnoff, *Svetska Bibliografija Astronautickoq Prava* (Institut Za Medunarodnu Politiku I Privredu, Belgrade, 1962).
9. United Nations, *A Bibliography of the Law of Outer Space—Preliminary Edition* (United Nations Library, New York, N.Y., 1958).
10. United States Department of State, Social Science Research on Outer Space, A Selective Listing, at 9-15 (External Research Division, Bureau of Intelligence and Research, Washington, D.C., 1959).
11. United States House of Representatives, Bibliography of Space Law, Staff Report of the Select Committee on Astronautics and Space Exploration, at 38-60 (United States Government Printing Office, Washington, D.C., 1959).
12. University of Oklahoma, *Bibliography of the Space Law Collection* (Law Library, Norman, Oklahoma, 1959).
13. United States Department of the Air Force, *Space Law—The Legal Aspect, Special Bibliography No. 161* (Air University Library, 1958).

V-B. SELECTED AND PARTIAL BIBLIOGRAPHY OF THE WORKS OF THE AUTHOR

Books

1. Haley, Space Law and Government (1963).
2. ——, Rocketry and Space Exploration: the International Story (1958).

Articles

3. Haley, *Who Owns the Moon?*, This Week Magazine, Jan. 20, 1963, p. 8.
4. ——, *Space Communications—Some Legal and Sociological Challenges,* in Fifth Colloquium on the Law of Outer Space (1963).
5. ——, *Metalaw—The Science of Universal Jurisprudence: The Third Essay,* in Fourth Colloquium on the Law of Outer Space (1963).
6. ——, *A Synoptic View of Space Communications,* Signal, March, 1962, p. 15.
7. ——, *Space Law and Sociology,* Astronautics, Dec. 1961, p. 50.
8. ——, *Space Communications and Cooperation With Iron Curtain Countries: Part II,* Signal, Dec. 1961, p. 12.
9. ——, *Space Communications and Cooperation With Iron Curtain Countries: Part I,* Signal, Nov. 1961, p. 39.
10. ——, *Metalaw—The Science of Universal Jurisprudence: The Third Essay,* Harvard L. Record, Nov. 9, 1961, p. 9.
11. ——, *Congress' Performance and Dynamic Aerospace Business,* The Commercial and Financial Chronicle, Sept. 14, 1961, p. 1
12. ——, *Rule of Law in Outer Space: Letter to the Editor,* New York Times, Feb. 18, 1961, p. 18.
13. ——, *The International Academy of Astronautics of the International Astronautical Foundation,* Signal, Feb. 1961, p. 39.
14. ——, *Commercial Aspects of Our National Space Law,* The Commercial and Financial Chronical, Jan. 5, 1961, p. 1
15. ——, *Developments Leading to and the Need for the 1963 Extraordinary Administrative Radio Conference on Space Communications,* Telecommunications J. 1 (1961).
16. ——, *The International Academy of Astronautics,* 3 Spaceflight 119 (1961).
17. ——, *International Cooperation in Rocketry and Astronautics,* 7 Handbuch der Astronautik, 197 (1961).
18. ——, *Medical Jurisprudence in Outer Space,* 3 Archives of Environmental Health 315 (1961).
19. ——, *Rocket Inventions,* in Dictionary of American History 218 (1961).
20. ——, *Sovereignty in Space,* Review of Contemporary Law, Dec. 1960, p. 3.
21. ——, *Space Law and Sociology,* Astronautics, Nov. 1960, p. 46.
22. ——, *International Scene,* Astronautics, Aug. 1960, p. 30.

23. Haley, *International Scene—Chinese Astronautical Research: Part III*, Astronautics, July 1960, p. 18.

24. ——, *International Scene—Chinese Astronautical Research: Part II*, Astronautics, June 1960, p. 20.

25. ——, *International Scene*, Astronautics, March 1960, p. 18.

26. ——, *International Scene—Chinese Astronautical Research: Part I*, Astronautics, Feb. 1960, p. 20.

27. ——, *International Scene*, Astronautics, Jan. 1960, p. 16.

28. ——, A Basic Program for the 1963 Extraordinary Administrative Radio Conference on Space Communications. PROCEEDINGS OF THE IXTH INTERNATIONAL ASTRONAUTICAL CONGRESS, STOCKHOLM 1960.

29. ——, *Space Exploration—The Problems of Today, Tomorrow and in the Future*, in SECOND COLLOQUIUM ON THE LAW OF OUTER SPACE 44 (1960).

30. ——, *The Law of Space and Outer Space*, 33 So. CAL. L. REV. 370 (1960) reprinted in part, 10 L. REV. DIGEST 77 (1960).

31. ——, *Space Law and Sociology*, Astronautics, Nov. 1959, p. 48.

32. ——, *International Scene—Preliminary Report on the Actions of the Geneva Meeting With Respect to Astronautical Radio*, Astronautics, Nov. 1959, p. 20.

33. ——, *International Astronautical Federation and Space Communications: Remarks before the Delegates to the Administrative Radio Conference of the International Telecommunications Union, Geneva, Switzerland, Oct. 1959*, Reprinted in TELECOMMUNICATIONS JOURNAL, Nov. 1959.

34. ——, *Space Communications*, Morning Electron (Bulletin of the International Telecommunications Conference), Sept. 25, 1959.

35. ——, *International Scene*, Astronautics, Aug. 1959, p. 94.

36. ——, *International Astronautical Federation Aims and Constitution*, The Aeroplane and Astronautics, Aug. 28, 1959.

37. ——, *International Scene*, Astronautics, July 1959, p. 110.

38. ——, *The Importance of Astronautical Radio in the Space Age*, Signal, May 1959, p. 82.

39. ——, *International Scene—Radio Allocations for Astronautics: Part 2*, Astronautics, April 1959, p. 18.

40. ——, *International Scene—Radio Allocations for Astronautics: Part 1*, Astronautics, March 1959, p. 78.

41. ——, *International Scene*, Astronautics, Feb. 1959, p. 9.

42. ——, *Law of Outer Space—Practical Legal Rules for Human Conduct*, 16 FED. COM. B. J. 163 (1959).

43. ——, *Space Age Presents Immediate Legal Problems*, in FIRST COLLOQUIUM ON THE LAW OF OUTER SPACE 5 (1959).

44. ——, *Space Vehicle Torts*, 36 DETROIT L. J. 294 (1959), reprinted in 1959 INS. L. J. 437.

45. ——, *International Scene*, Astronautics, Dec. 1958, p. 3.

46. ——, *International Scene*, Astronautics, Nov. 1958, p. 64.

47. ——, *Space Flight: A Look Ahead*, Astronautics, Nov. 1958, p. 28.

48. ——, *International Scene*, Astronautics, Aug. 1958, p. 64.

49. ——, *International Scene*, Astronautics, June 1958, p. 70.

50. Haley, *International Scene*, Astronautics, May 1958, p. 78.

51. ——, *International Cooperation in Astronautics*, Foreign Service Journal, April 1958, p. 1.

52. ——, *The Commercial Implications of Missiles–Satellite–Space Age*, The Commercial and Financial Chronicle, Mar. 13, 1958, p. 1.

53. ——, *International Scene*, Astronautics, Feb. 1958, p. 70.

54. ——, *Can Russia Claim the Moon?*, The American Weekly, Jan. 19, 1958, p. 2.

55. ——, *International Scene–Subjects of a Long Journey*, Astronautics, Jan. 1958, p. 70.

56. ——, *Current International Situation and the Legal Involvements With Respect to Long-Range Missiles and Earth-Circling Objects*, 1958 Vistas in Astronautics 310

57. ——, *Forward* (to Special Issue on Space Travel), 7 Avia/Vliegwereld (The Netherlands) 468 (1958).

58. ——, *Law and the Space Age*, 5 St. Louis U. L. J. 1 (1958).

59. ——, *Law of Outer Space–A Problem for International Agreement*, 7 Am. U. L. Rev. 70 (1958).

60. ——, *The Law of Outer Space: Scientific and Anthropocentric Considerations*, 7 Avia/Vliegwereld 478 (1958).

61. ——, *The Law of Outer Space–Scientific and Anthropocentric Considerations*, 1 Astronautics 65 (1958).

62. ——, *The Law of Space–Scientific and Technical Considerations*, 4 N.Y. L. F. 262 (1958).

63. ——, *The Rule of Law in the Space Age*, 37 Foreign Policy Bull. 189 (1958).

64. ——, *Space and Metalaw: Jurisdiction Defined*, 16 J. of the British Interplanetary Society 472 (1958).

65. ——, *Law Must Precede Man Into Space*, Missiles & Rockets, Nov. 1957, p. 67.

66. ——, *Recent Developments in Space Law and Metalaw*, Harvard L. Record, Feb. 7, 1957, special supplement.

67. ——, *The International Astronautical Federation*, 43 Fed. B. J. 470 (1957).

68. ——, *Seventh IAF Congress Stresses Cooperation*, 27 Jet Propulsion 60 (1957).

69. ——, *Space Law and Metalaw–Jurisdiction Defined*, 24 J. Air L. & Com. 286 (1957).

70. ——, *Space Law and Metalaw–A Synoptic View*, Harvard L. Record, Nov. 8, 1956, p. 1.

71. ——, *The Present Day Developments in Space Law and the Beginnings of Metalaw*, Canadian Oil Journal, March, April, May 1957.

72. ——, *Basic Concepts of Space Law*, 26 Jet Propulsion 951 (1956).

73. ——, *International Cooperation in Rocketry and Astronautics During 1956*, 26 Jet Propulsion 1 (1956).

74. ——, *Space Law and Metalaw*, Proceedings of the VIIth International Astronautical Congress, Rome 1956 435.

75. Haley, *Space Law—Basic Concepts*, 24 TENN. L. REV. 643 (1956), reprinted in 6 L. REV. DIGEST 71 (1956).

76. ——, *Outposts in the Sky*, The American Weekly, Feb. 20, 1955, p. 10.

77. ——, *International Cooperation in Rocketry and Astronautics*, 25 JET PROPULSION 627 (1955).

78. —— & Rosen, *On the Utility of an Artificial Unmanned Earth Satellite*, 25 JET PROPULSION 1 (1955).

Papers and Addresses

79. *Communications Satellites—Simple Relay Stations of Profound World Importance:* Paper by Andrew G. Haley, Before the American Rocket Society Annual Meeting in Los Angeles, California, Nov. 13-18, 1962.

80. *Opportunities for Youth in the Space Age:* Address by ——, Eighth Annual Scholastic Banquet of the American Legion Seattle Post No. 1 in Seattle, May 9, 1962.

81. *The Law of the Age of Space—A Statement of Possible Position Papers:* Address by ——, Columbia Society of International Law in New York, Dec. 1, 1961.

82. *Legal Problems of Man's Adventure into Outer Space:* Address by ——, Stetson Law Day 1961 Seminar in St. Petersburg, Fla., Nov. 17, 1961.

83. *Space Communications—A Current Report:* Address by ——, Sacramento Section of the American Rocket Society in Sacramento, Oct. 26, 1961.

84. *Space Communications of the Next Generation:* Paper by ——, Before the Space Law & Sociology Section of the American Rocket Society Space Flight Report to the Nation in New York, Oct. 10, 1961.

85. *Metalaw—The Science of Universal Jurisprudence: The Third Essay:* Paper by ——, Before the Fourth Colloquium on the Law of Outer Space, International Institute of Space Law, XIIth International Astronautical Congress in Washington, D.C., Oct. 3, 1961.

86. *Space Radio—A World System of Communications:* Address by ——, Chicago Section of the American Rocket Society Presidential Banquet in Chicago, Sept. 25, 1961.

87. *Space Communications—Framing the Windows:* Paper by ——, Before the AGARD Eleventh General Assembly in Oslo, July 27, 1961.

88. *Current Congressional Legislation Affecting Aerospace Business:* Paper by ——, Before a Joint Meeting of The Institute of the Aerospace Sciences and The American Rocket Society in Los Angeles, June 14, 1961. (Revised Sept. 1, 1961.)

89. *Space Communications and Exobiological Problems:* Address by ——, Arizona Broadcasters Association in Tucson, May 19, 1961.

90. *Medical Jurisprudence in Outer Space:* Paper by ——, Before the Medical Society of the State of New York Convention in Rochester, May 9, 1961.

91. *Space Communications and Cooperation With Iron Curtain Countries:* Address by ——, Ft. Wayne Section of the American Rocket Society in Ft. Wayne, April 26, 1961.

92. *Progress Made in the Use of Radio for Protection of Life and Property*

in Outer Space: Paper by ——, Before the American Rocket Society Annual Meeting in Washington, D.C., Dec. 5-8, 1960.

93. *Outline of Program for Astronautical Communications:* Paper by ——, Before the Symposium on Space Research in Buenos Aires, Nov. 28-Dec. 3, 1960.

94. *Commercial Aspects of Space Law:* Address by ——, American Management Association Session on "Finding a Place for Your Company in Space-Age Technology" in New York, Oct. 6, 1960.

95. *Legal Problems of Space 1960-1970:* Paper by ——, Before the Conference on Space Technology in Los Angeles, Oct. 1, 1960, and in Norman, Okla., Oct. 4, 1960.

96. *Space Law and Astronautics—Preparing for the Next Thirty Years:* Paper by ——, Before the AGARD Combustion and Propulsion Panel Technical Meeting on "Advanced Propulsion Techniques" in Pasadena, Aug. 24, 1960.

97. *Survey of Legal Opinion on Extraterrestrial Jurisdiction:* Paper by ——, Before the Space Law Colloquium of the IXth Congress of the International Astronautical Federation in Stockholm, Aug. 16, 1960.

98. *A Basic Program for the 1963 Extraordinary Administrative Radio Conference on Space Communications:* Paper by ——, Before the IXth International Astronautical Congress in Stockholm, Aug. 16, 1960.

99. *Preparation for the 1963 Extraordinary Astronautical Radio Conference:* Paper by ——, Before the 12th Annual Meeting of the Deutsche Gesellschaft fur Raketentechnik und Raumfahrt in Heidelberg, May 25, 1960.

100. *Space Communications—A Decade of Progress:* Paper by ——, Before the American Rocket Society Semi-Annual Meeting in Los Angeles, May 9-12, 1960.

101. *Summation of Questions Involved in the Technical and Legal Regulations of Space Exploration:* Lecture by ——, Seminar Course on Space Science and Technology of the Instituto Nacional de Tecnica Aeronautica, "Esteban Terradas" in Madrid, March 29, 1960.

102. *The Law of Space and Outer Space:* Address by ——, Pacific Southwest Conference on International Law at the University of Southern California, March 5, 1960.

103. *The Moon—Its Stark Importance to Humanity:* Remarks of ——, United Fund of Terre Haute and Vigo County, Inc. Panel Discussion on "Our Stake in the Space Age" in Terre Haute, March 1, 1960.

104. *The Moon—Its Stark Importance to Humanity:* Remarks of ——, National Missile Space Conference Panel Discussion on "The Space Challenge—Philosophy" in Washington, D.C., Feb. 16, 1960.

105. *Outer Space and Humanity:* Address by ——, The National Conference of Christians and Jews in New Orleans, Nov. 19, 1959.

106. *Space Law—Retrospect and Promise:* Address by ——, Space Law & Sociology Committee of the American Rocket Society in Washington, D.C., Nov. 17, 1959.

107. *Space Communications:* Address by ——, Radio Administrative Conference of the International Telecommunications Union in Geneva, Sept. 22, 1959.

108. *The International Astronautical Federation and Space Communications:* Paper by ——, Before the Administrative Radio Conference of the International Telecommunication Union in Geneva, Sept. 18, 1959.

109. *Space Exploration—The Problems of Today, Tomorrow and in the Future:* Paper by ——, Before the Second Colloquium on the Law of Outer Space in London, Sept. 4, 1959.

110. *Accomplishments of the International Astronautical Federation and Some Proposed Objectives:* Address by ——, Before the International Astronautical Federation Xth Annual Congress in London, Aug. 31, 1959.

111. *Astronautics—The Advent of a New Age:* Paper by ——, Before the Asociacion Argentina Interplaneteria in Buenos Aires, July 17, 1959.

112. *Sociological Transition—Space Law and Metalaw:* Paper by ——, Before the First Interamerican Symposium on Astronautics in Sao Paulo, July 15, 1959.

113. *Law of Space—Space Sovereignty:* Address by ——, Before the Universities and Scientific Groups in Vienna, Warsaw, Moscow, Prague, Belgrade, Athens, Cairo, Johannesburg, Rome, Barcelona, Madrid, Lisbon, Amsterdam and Paris, May-June 1959.

114. *Law of Space—Space Sovereignty:* Address by ——, Space Age Forum of the Southwest in Dallas, April 14, 1959.

115. *Some Practical Suggestions for World Cooperation Through the International Astronautical Federation:* Address by ——, Conference of the Space Law & Sociology Committee of the American Rocket Society in New York, March 20, 1959.

116. *The Peaceful Uses of Outer Space:* Address by ——, Ninth Annual Conference of National Organizations in Washington, D.C., March 9, 1959.

117. *Whither the Space Age in the Next Decade:* Paper by ——, Submitted to the Select Committee on Astronautics and Space Exploration, Nov. 24, 1958.

118. *Space Law: Recent Practical Achievements:* Paper by ——, Before the American Rocket Society 13th Annual Meeting in New York, Nov. 17-21, 1958.

119. *Scientific and Social Developments of Outer Space:* Lectures by ——, National Capital Section of the American Rocket Society and Army Corps of Engineers' Course on "Science and Rocketry" in Ft. Belvoir, Va., Nov. 8, 1958.

120. *Law of Outer Space—Practical Legal Rules for Human Conduct:* Paper by ——, Submitted to the Institute on World Organization in Washington, D.C., Oct. 23, 1958.

121. *The Law of Outer Space:* Address by ——, Delta Theta Phi Law Fraternity in Washington, D.C., Oct. 17, 1958.

122. *Some Immediate Jurisdictional Problems:* Address by ——, Military Librarians Groups, Special Librarians Association in Ft. McNair, Oct. 15, 1958.

123. *Law of Outer Space—Yesterday's Problems:* Address by ——, the American Institute of Electrical Engineers in Washington, D.C., Oct. 14, 1958.

124. *Law of Outer Space—Radio Controls Urgently Needed:* Paper by ——,

Before the Symposium on "Outer Space" of the Committee on Aeronautics of the Federal Bar Association of New York, New Jersey, and Connecticut in New York, Oct. 9, 1958.

125. *Space Law—Some Current Problems and Solutions:* Address by ——, 40th Annual Meeting of the Canadian Bar Association in Toronto, Sept. 10, 1958.

126. *Law of Outer Space—An Immediate Problem:* Paper by ——, Before the Colloquium on the Law of Outer Space, IXth Annual International Astronautical Federation Congress in The Hague, Aug. 29, 1958.

127. *The Law of Outer Space—Scientific and Anthropocentric Consideration:* Address by ——, Rotary Club of New York in New York, June 12, 1958.

128. *Space and the World Economy:* Address by ——, Before the International Astronautical Federation in Lisbon, June 10, 1958.

129. *The Law of Outer Space—Scientific and Financial Considerations:* Address by ——, French Member Society of the International Astronautical Federation in Paris, June 9, 1958.

130. *The Business Potential of the Missiles—Rockets—Space Flight Technology:* Submitted to the "Business Forecasting" Panel of the First National Missile Industry Conference in Washington, D.C., June 6, 1958.

131. *The Law of Outer Space—Scientific and Anthropocentric Considerations:* Address by ——, The Commission on Astronautics of the Academy of Sciences, in Moscow, May 29, 1958 .

132. *The Law of Outer Space—Scientific and Economic Considerations:* Address by ——, Instituto Nacional de Tecnia-Aeronautica Esteban Terradas in Madrid, May 20, 1958.

133. *Economic and Legal Developments in Connection With the Age of Space:* Address by ——, University of Virginia Student Chapter of the American Rocket Society in Charlottesville, May 15, 1958.

134. *Astronautics in Europe:* Address by ——, Northeastern New York Section of The American Rocket Society in Schenectady, May 8, 1958.

135. *Law, Rockets and the Space Age:* Address by ——, New York Law Review Alumni Association in New York City, May 7, 1958.

136. *The Law of Outer Space—Scientific and Anthropocentric Considerations:* Address by ——, Milwaukee Bar Association in Milwaukee, May 6, 1958.

137. *Legal Problems of Outer Space Occupancy:* Address by ——, Forum of the International Society of Aviation Writers in United Nations, New York, April 23, 1958.

138. *The Sociological Implications of Astronautics:* Address by ——, Canadian Astronautical Society in Montreal, April 18, 1958.

139. *The Space Age and Economics:* Address by ——, Associazione Italiana Razzi in Rome, March 19, 1958.

140. *The World Economy in the Age of Space:* Address by ——, Astronauticko Drustvo in Belgrade, March 17, 1958.

141. *Legal and Economic Aspects of Astronautics:* Address by ——, Dansk Interplanetarisk Selskab in Copenhagen, March 14, 1958.

142. *The Law of Space and World Economy:* Address by ——, Svenska Interplanetariska Sallskapet in Stockholm, March 12, 1958.

143. *The Law of Outer Space—Scientific and Economic Considerations:* Address by ——, Polskie Towarzystwo Astronautyczne in Warsaw, March 7, 1958.

144. *The Law of Outer Space—Scientific and Economic Considerations:* Address by ——, Deutsche Gesellschaft fur Raketentechnik und Raumfahrt in Berlin, March 5, 1958.

145. *The Law of Outer Space—Scientific and Economic Considerations:* Address by ——, Nederlandse Vereniging voor Ruimtevaart and Koninklijke and Nederlandse Vereniging voor Luchtvaart at The Hague, March 4, 1958.

146. *The Law of the Space Age—Spiritual and Scientific Considerations:* Address by ——, Evangelical Academy in Loccum, Germany, Feb. 28, 1958.

147. *New Perceptions of Space Law and World Economics:* Address by ——, Deutsche Gesellschaft fur Raketentechnik und Raumfahrt in Stuttgart, Feb. 24, 1958.

148. *Space Flight as World Economic Solution:* Address by ——, Member Society of the International Astronautical Federation in Dublin, Feb. 23, 1958.

149. *The Commercial Implications of Missiles, Satellites, and Space Flight:* Address by ——, American Management Association in New York, Feb. 21, 1958.

150. *The Utility of Rocket Devices and Financial Facts:* Address by ——, The Rotary Club in Washington, D.C., Feb. 12, 1958.

151. *The Space Age and Financial Implications:* Address by ——, Chamber of Commerce in Chambersburg, Pa., Feb. 6, 1958.

152. *The Law of Space and Financial Implications:* Address by ——, Chamber of Commerce in Des Moines, Jan. 31, 1958.

153. *Financial Aspects of the Age of Space:* Address by ——, American Friends of Hebrew University in New York, Jan. 30, 1958.

154. *Space Law:* Address by ——, JAGD Reserves at the Pentagon, Jan. 14, 1958.

155. Testimony of ——, *Hearings Before the Select Committee on Astronautics and Space Administration,* H.R. 1181, 85 Cong., 2d Sess., at 1431 (1958).

156. *Space Law and Economics:* Address by ——, California Law School Club in Washington, D.C., Dec. 8, 1957.

157. *The Russian Satellite—Legal and Political Problems:* Address by ——, The American Rocket Society in New York, Dec. 4, 1957.

158. *Law and Economics of the Space Age:* Lecture by —— and Dr. Welf Heinrich Prince of Hanover, Princeton University, Physicians Scientific Society, Detroit Law School, University of Michigan Law School, University of Chicago Law School, Northwestern University Law School, University of Wisconsin Law School, University of Minnesota Law School, Civic Group of Butte, Mont., University of Montana, Gonzaga University Law School, Civic Group of Seattle, University of Washington Law School, University of California Law School, Salt Lake City Chamber of Commerce, University of Utah College of Law, Denver Chamber of Commerce, University of Colorado Law School, St. Louis University and Washington University Law Schools, Harvard University International

Law Club, Institute of Military Law, Chicago Section of the American Rocket Society, Twin Cities Section of the American Rocket Society, Spokane Bar Association, Pacific-Northwest Section of the American Rocket Society, Northern California Section of the American Rocket Society, Southern California Section of the American Rocket Society, Holloman and New Mexico and West Texas Sections of the American Rocket Society at Holloman Air Force Base, Central Colorado Section of the American Rocket Society, St. Louis Section of the American Rocket Society, New England Section of the American Rocket Society, National Capital Section of the American Rocket Society, Georgetown Law School, American University Law School, Catholic University Law School, Maryland University Law School, November 1957.

159. *Space Law—The Development of Jurisdictional Concepts:* Paper by ——, Before the VIIIth Annual Congress of the International Astronautical Federation in Barcelona, Oct. 6-12, 1957.

160. *Space Law and Metalaw—Jurisdiction Defined:* Paper by ——, Before the American Rocket Society in Washington, D.C., April 3-6, 1957.

161. *Current International Situations and the Legal Involvements With Respect to Long Range Missiles and Earth-Circling Objects:* Paper by ——, Before the Astronautics Symposium in San Diego, Feb. 18-20, 1957.

162. *Space Law and Metalaw—Fundamental Juridicial Considerations:* Paper by ——, Before the International Congress of Rockets and Guided Missiles for Continental Connections and Telecommunications in Paris, Dec. 3-8, 1956.

163. *The Present Day Developments in Space Law and the Beginnings of Metalaw:* Paper by ——, Before the American Rocket Society 11th Annual Meeting in New York, Nov. 26-29, 1956.

164. *Space Law and Metalaw—A Synoptic View:* Paper by ——, Before the VIIth Annual Congress of the International Astronautical Federation in Rome, Sept. 19, 1956.

165. *International Cooperation in the Field of Astronautics:* Paper by ——, Before the Second Annual Meeting of the American Astronautical Society in New York, Dec. 1, 1955.

166. *Basic Concepts of Space Law—The Unmanned Earth Satellite:* Paper by ——, Before the Twenty-Fifth Anniversary Meeting of the American Rocket Society in Chicago, Nov. 14-18, 1955.

167. *Some Contributions to Advances in Rocketry,* Maryland Section of the American Rocket Society in Baltimore, Nov. 5, 1955.

168. *Current Developments in Rocketry and Astronautics:* Address by ——, American Rocket Society in Los Angeles, Sept. 20, 1955.

169. *Jurisdiction Beyond the Earth:* Address by ——, Rotary Club of Charlotte in Charlotte, N.C., June 7, 1955.

170. *Immediate Prospects; in Rocketry and Astronautics:* Address by ——, National Capital Section of the American Rocket Society in Washington, D.C., April 14, 1955.

171. *Some Future Problems for the Space Technicians:* Paper by ——, Before the American Rocket Society Space Flight Symposium in New York, Dec. 1, 1954.

172. *How a Rocket Works:* Address by ——, Academy of Sciences of St. Louis, March 1, 1954.

Articles in Foreign Languages

173. Haley, *Communições na era espacial,* Astronáutica (Brazil), Maio-Junho, 1962, p. 2.
174. ——, *Les Communications spatiales de la prochaine génération,* Journal des Telecommunications, Février, 1962, p. 39.
175. ——, *Obzor Pravovykh Konseptsiy Otnositelino Yuridiktsii za Predelami Zemli,* in Problemy Kosmicheskogo Prava (Korovin ed., 1961).
176. ——, *La Fédération astronautique internationale (IAF) et les communications spatiales,* Journal des Telecommunications, Nov. 1959.
177. ——, *El derecho interplanetario soberania sobre el espacio extraterrestre,* Ingenieria Aeronautica y Astronautica (Spain), Mayo-Junio, 1959, p. 1.
178. ——, *Derecho interplanetario,* Ingeniera Aeronautica (Spain), Mayo-Junio 1958, p. 7.
179. ——, *Der Mensch stösst in den Himmelsraum,* New York Staats-Zeitung und Herold, May 1, 2, 3, 5, 6, 7, 8, 1958.
180. ——, *El derecho tiene que preparar el hombre en el espacio extraterrestre,* 1958 Revista Aeronautica 161.
181. ——, *Loi, de l'espace et metaloi,* Le Courrier Interplanetaire (Switzerland), Feb. 1957, Mar. 5, 1957, April 10, 1957.
182. ——, *Weltraumrecht und Recht ausserhalb der Erde (Space Law and Metalaw), Eine Ubersicht (A Synoptic View),* Zeitschrift fur Luftrecht 1957, Heft 2, S. 1.
183. ——, *Weltraumrecht und Recht ausserhalb der Erde, Abgrenzung der Rechtsgebiete,* Weltraumfahrt, 1957, Heft 2, S. 57; Heft 3, S. 69.
184. ——, *Droit de l'espace et metadroit (Limites de juridiction)* Revue Générale de l'Air, 1957, p. 1.

Miscellaneous

185. Haley, ed., Fifth Colloquium on the Law of Outer Space, Varna, Bulgaria, 1962 (1963).
186. —— & Schwartz, ed., Fourth Colloquium on the Law of Outer Space, Washington, D.C., 1961 (1963).
187. ——, *Space Communications—A First Approximation of Legal Problems,* Submitted to the American Bar Association Committee on Space (on request), July 8, 1961.
188. ——, *International Scene—Astronautical Activity in South America,* Unpublished Paper, June 1961.
189. ——, *Testimony and Statement, Hearings Before 'the House Committee on Science and Astronautics,* 87th Cong., 1st Sess., May 10, 1961.
190. ——, *Space Spectrum Problems,* Unpublished Paper, Mar. 27, 1961.
191. ——, *Japanese Activity in Rocketry,* Unpublished Paper, Mar. 1961.
192. ——, *International Scene—Argentina Symposium on Space Research,* Unpublished Paper, Jan. 1961.

193. Haley & Gronfors, ed., 3 PROCEEDINGS OF THE XITH INTERNATIONAL AS-TRONAUTICAL CONGRESS, STOCKHOLM 1960, THIRD COLLOQUIUM ON THE LAW OF OUTER SPACE (1961).

194. ——, *Ley del espacio—soberania espacial,* Spanish Translation of Lecture Delivered Before the Agrupacion Astronautica Espanola, Barcelona, Spain, June 1, 1959.

195. ——, *Space Law: The Need for International Agreement on Astronautical Radio Allocations,* Unpublished Paper, May 1, 1959.

196. ——, "Space Communications and Astronautical Radio Activities and Proposals of the American Rocket Society and the International Astronautical Federation, "Statement Before the Federal Communications Commission, upon reopening of Hearings regarding Docket No. 11997, July, 1959.

197. ——, Testimony and Statement, *Hearings Before the House Committee on Science and Astronautics,* 86th Cong., 1st Sess., No. 9 at 64 (1961).

198. —— & Hanover ed., SECOND COLLOQUIUM ON THE LAW OF OUTER SPACE, LONDON 1959 (1960).

199. —— & Hanover ed., FIRST COLLOQUIUM ON THE LAW OF OUTER SPACE, THE HAGUE 1958 (1959).

200. ——, *The International Astronautical Federation and International Cooperation in Astronautics:* Unpublished Paper, May 26, 1958.

201. ——, *The Law of Outer Space: Problems and Progress,* Unpublished Paper, Dec. 1959.

202. ——, *Das Recht des Weltraumzeitalters—Geistige und wissenschaftliche Grundlagen,* Vortrag vor der Evangelischen Akademie Loccum am 28 Februar 1958.

203. ——, *International Cooperation in Astronautics,* Unpublished Paper, Feb. 28, 1958.

204. ——, Testimony and Statement, Hearings on H.R. 11881 Before the Select Committee on Astronautics and Space Exploration, U.S. House of Representatives 85th Cong., 2nd Sess., 1431 (1958).

205. ——, Report of the International Affairs Committee submitted by Andrew G. Haley, Chairman, VIIIth Congress, International Astronautical Federation, Barcelona, Spain, Oct. 6-12, 1957.

206. ——, DIE ENTWICKLUNG DER RECHTSBEGRIFFE IN WELTRAUMRECHT, German Translation of a Paper Delivered Before the VIIIth Annual Congress of the International Astronautical Federation, Barcelona, Spain, Oct. 1957.

207. ——, Remarks: Following the September 19, 1956, Technical Session of the VIIth Annual Congress of the International Astronautical Federation, Rome, Italy, September 17-22, 1956. Published in the PROCEEDINGS OF THE VIITH INTERNATIONAL ASTRONAUTICAL CONGRESS, Rome, 1956, 907.

INDEX